CHARTIST STUDIES

CHARTIST STUDIES

Edited by

ASA BRIGGS

PROFESSOR OF HISTORY IN THE UNIVERSITY OF SUSSEX

MACMILLAN
London · Melbourne · Toronto

ST MARTINS PRESS
New York
1967

MACMILLAN AND COMPANY LIMITED
Little Essex Street London WC2
also Bombay Calcutta Madras Melbourne

THE MACMILLAN COMPANY OF CANADA LIMITED
70 Bond Street Toronto 2

ST MARTIN'S PRESS INC
175 Fifth Avenue New York NY 10010

05 3

PRINTED IN GREAT BRITAIN BY
LOWE AND BRYDONE (PRINTERS) LTD, LONDON

Preface

It is many years since a full narrative history of Chartism was attempted. In the meantime, much valuable research has been carried out by many scholars, most of them working on local materials. This volume sets out some of the results of recent research. It tries to avoid dependence on secondary sources, and to approach Chartist history afresh. In editing it I have tried not to edit the views of the individual contributors, but to pull together what they have written into something more than a mere collection of separate studies. Inevitably there is some overlapping, but it has been kept to a minimum. There is room for further research both on places and on people, and I regret that it was not possible to use the brilliant recent study, the biography of Harney by A. R. Schoyen — *The Chartist Challenge* — which came out after the writing of this book had been completed. On the basis of such monographs and of further local studies it should eventually be possible to produce a new narrative history of Chartism which will do justice to the complexity and to the excitement of the subject. I would like to express my thanks to Mr M. G. Hutt for reading the proofs of this volume.

ASA BRIGGS

April 1958

Contents

Acknowledgements

THE editor and authors wish to acknowledge the kind assistance which they have received from librarians in many private and public libraries. These include the British Museum, the National Library of Wales, the Reference Libraries at Manchester, Birmingham, Hull, Ipswich, Leeds, Leicester and Sheffield, and the Mitchell Library, Glasgow.

Dr. Fearn wishes to thank Professor G. P. Jones who supervised his M.A. thesis on Suffolk Chartism at Sheffield. Mr. R. B. Pugh, who has already told the story of Wiltshire Chartism in *The Wiltshire Magazine*, vol. LIV (1951), has reproduced by permission a few passages from his article. Mrs. MacAskill wishes to thank Mr. R. H. Holloway of Minster Lovell for allowing her to inspect the title deeds, and Mr. W. Le Hardy, M.C., F.S.A., for drawing her attention to J. E. Cussens's note on Herringsgate.

Miss Brown wishes to thank Mr. N. McCord for allowing her to read his doctoral thesis on the Anti-Corn Law League before publication. Mr. Mather is grateful to Sir Fergus Graham, Bt., K.B.E., M.P., for permission to use the Graham Papers, and to Sir Owen Morshead, K.C.B., formerly Librarian of Windsor Castle, for access to the correspondence of Queen Victoria in the Royal Archives, Windsor.

Abbreviations

B.M.	British Museum
B.T.	Board of Trade
B.R.L.	Birmingham Reference Library
C.P.L.	Cardiff Public Library
D.N.B.	Dictionary of National Biography
H.O.	Home Office
H.R.L.	Hull Reference Library
M.R.L.	Manchester Reference Library
N.L.W.	National Library of Wales
P.P.	Parliamentary Papers
R.C.	Royal Commission
S.C.	Select Committee
S.R.L.	Sheffield Reference Library
V.C.H.	Victoria County History

Chapter One

The Local Background of Chartism

Asa Briggs

I

When Hippolyte Taine visited England in 1859, he wisely decided to see as many places as possible outside London. 'One ought to try and see the local districts', he remarked, 'for it is not possible to understand the social fabric properly until one has studied three or four of its component threads in detail.'[1]

Twenty years earlier in the age of the Chartists, before the development of a railway system, the comment would have been even more apposite. Conditions of life in various parts of the country differed considerably, not only between city, market town and countryside, but between one city and another, between one rural region and a second. An earlier French visitor to England, Léon Faucher, was impressed by the sharp contrasts between London and the provinces, between the social and political structures of Manchester and Birmingham, between York with its ancient minster and Leeds with its modern factories.[2] Other travellers were more sensitive than most Englishmen to the immediate social contrasts within the same city. Engels painted a grim but powerful picture of the extremes of life in Manchester:[3] an American visitor was equally shocked by the gulf in London which separated 'the splendor and gorgeousness' of the Court End and 'the wretchedness, dirt and squalidness' of the rest. 'In the midst of the most extraordinary abundance, here are men, women, and children dying of starvation; and running alongside of the splendid chariot, with its gilded equipages, its silken linings, and its liveried footmen, are poor, forlorn, friendless, almost naked wretches, looking like the mere fragments of humanity.'[4]

[1] *Notes on England*, translated and edited by E. Hyams (1957), p. 127.
[2] *Études sur l'Angleterre* (2 vols., 1845).
[3] *The Condition of the Working Class in England* (new English translation by W. O. Henderson and W. H. Chaloner, 1958).
[4] H. Colman, *European Life and Manners* (1849) Vol. II, p. 380, Vol. I, p. 155.

A study of Chartism must begin with a proper appreciation of regional and local diversity. Some of the elements of diversity are measurable, and although adequate statistics do not always and did not exist, contemporaries were beginning to take an increasing interest in their measurement — rents, wages, prices, the incidence of unemployment, the degree of dependence on foreign markets. It is impossible to understand either the birth of Chartism or its fluctuating fortunes between the date of the publication of the Charter on 8 May 1838 and the withering away of the agitation in the 1850's without examining the movement of the relevant economic indices. Historians of Chartism have always recognised the importance of relating Chartism as a social and political force to the general economic history of the period, but recent refinements in the analysis of the changing structure and the cyclical fluctuations of the early nineteenth-century British economy make possible a deeper understanding both of the chronology and the geography of Chartism.[1]

Some of the elements of diversity, however, cannot be measured quantitatively. Variations in local class structure, in the content of local grievances, in the traditions of political leadership and mass agitation, and in the adaptability and persistence of the Chartists themselves and of their opponents, require detailed investigation. It is the purpose of the essays on local Chartism, collected in this volume, to set out some of the materials and conclusions of such an investigation. They do not cover the whole of the country — the key centres of London and Birmingham, the militant Chartist stronghold of Newcastle, and turbulent Nottingham, which once had nurtured the Luddites and elected Feargus O'Connor to Parliament in 1847, demand fuller study — but they are designed both to provide a sample, rural and industrial, Welsh and Scottish as well as English, and to add an extra and necessary dimension to the Chartist story. A new narrative history of Chartism, long overdue, cannot be written until these and other local histories have been adequately treated. Chartism was a snowball movement which gathered together local grievances and sought to give them common expression in a nation-wide agitation. Many of the internal conflicts which divided it had their origins in the differences of background

[1] See W. W. Rostow, *British Economy in the Nineteenth Century* (1948); A. D. Gayer, W. W. Rostow and A. J. Schwartz, *The Growth and Fluctuations of the British Economy*, 2 vols. (1953); R. C. O. Matthews, *A Study in Trade-Cycle History, Economic Fluctuations in Great Britain, 1833–42* (1954); C. N. Ward-Perkins, 'The Commercial Crisis of 1847' in *Oxford Economic Papers* (1953).

and outlook in what the Chartists called 'the localities'. The differences ante-dated both the publication of the Charter and the onset of the business depression which gave the new movement its greatest momentum. Some of them — like the differences between English and Scottish Chartism — had deep roots in pre-industrial history:[1] others were associated with the growth of machine industry.

The pull of early Chartism seems to have been strongest in two ✗ kinds of place — first, in old centres of decaying or contracting industry, like Trowbridge in Wiltshire or Carmarthen in Wales, and second, in the new or expanding single-industry towns like Stockport, described by Engels as 'one of the darkest and smokiest holes in the whole industrial area'.[2] Big cities, which served as regional capitals, had large numbers of Chartists, but were sometimes less militant than adjacent industrial areas. Manchester and Birmingham, for example, were less active in the middle years of Chartism than the textile and metal-working districts nearby: Leeds was quieter than Halifax. In the big cities, where political radicalism had established itself long before the drafting of the Charter, there were more attempts at political accommodation between Chartists and other reformers, although most of them were unsuccessful. Chartism was not strong — and in some cases it was almost non-existent — in completely agricultural villages, those of Kent or Dorset, for example, in old market towns like Ripon or Bedford, and in new industrial centres with a mixed economy, like St Helens.

Such differences in appeal cannot be attributed to the accident of the presence or absence of active Chartist personalities, however significant was the influence of personality in particular cases.[3] Nor can they be evaluated, however, within a framework of geographical determinism. It is dangerous to personify Manchester and Birmingham or to rely on broad generalisations about North and South or London and the provinces. Local differences need to be related to economic and social structure — to the composition of the labour force, the conditions of work, including relations between 'masters' and 'men', and the timing and extent of local unemployment. Other social factors, including the influence of

---

[1] See W. L. Mathieson, *The Awakening of Scotland* (1910); H. W. Meikle, *Scotland and the French Revolution* (1912).

[2] *Op. cit.*, p. 12.

[3] Opinions will always differ about the relative importance of personality. In two Wiltshire villages with similar social structures, however, the influence of a powerful local Chartist personality on one of them can be clearly recognized. See below, p. 217.

religion, may also be relevant. In many places Nonconformity figures prominently in the local Chartist story.

There were three main groups within the heterogeneous labour force which played a special part in the development of Chartism — a section of the superior craftsmen, including printers, cobblers, tailors, cabinetmakers, booksellers and small shopkeepers; factory operatives, concentrated in the textiles districts, and familiarly referred to in the current vulgar political economy of the times as 'hands'; and domestic outworkers, including not only handloom weavers but such producers as framework knitters and nailmakers. The economic interests and fortunes of these three groups were not always the same. W. T. Thornton, the economist, remarked in 1846 that 'the labouring population has . . . been spoken of as if it formed only one class, but it is really divided into several, among which the rates of remuneration are far from being uniform . . . so that, in order to represent with perfect fidelity the state of the labouring population, it would be necessary to describe each class separately'.[1] It was not only rates of remuneration which diverged, but the extent of social security, regularity of earnings, the climate of industrial relations, status in the local community, and prospects of future advancement, both for the individual and for members of the family.[2]

A main theme in Chartist history was the attempt to create a sense of class unity which would bind together these three groups.[3] The attempt was never completely successful, however, and differences not only between one Chartist 'locality' and another but within Chartist 'localities' can be explained in part by differences in the balance of the three groups.

Not all the superior craftsmen were drawn into Chartism. New-style craftsmen, like machine-builders, for example, were never prominent.[4] On the other hand, a minority of superior craftsmen, those described by William Lovett and the London Working Men's

[1] W. T. Thornton, *Over-Population and its Remedy* (1846), p. 10.
[2] For an interesting and valuable analysis, see E. J. Hobsbawm, 'The Labour Aristocracy in 19th Century Britain' in J. Saville (ed.), *Democracy and the Labour Movement* (1954).
[3] See below, pp. 294–7.
[4] In 1842 the 'Old Mechanics', the Journeymen Steam Engine and Machine Makers' Friendly Society, passed a vote of censure on one of their members for his 'impropriety of conduct during the late excitement' and went on to draft a rule that no member could claim benefit for being out of work due to 'any Political or Popular Movement'. Quoted by J. B. Jefferys, *The Story of the Engineers* (1945), p. 22.

Association as 'the *intelligent* and *influential* portion of the working classes in town and country',[1] were the leaven of the early Chartist movement, and many of them remained faithful to it until the end. Their belief in the Six Points of the Charter was not conditioned by the movements of the trade cycle, and many of them had been converted to belief in reform — if they needed to be converted — before the Charter was drafted. Although the most articulate of them often misunderstood those of their 'fellow workmen' who 'croaked over their grievances with maudlin brains' and were themselves misunderstood by those militant operatives who dismissed them as 'a middle-class set of agitators',[2] they sought to foster a 'union of sentiment' among the working classes, 'which is essential to the prosecution of any great object.' They refused to look to 'great men' or to 'idols' and endeavoured to create working-class 'discrimination and independent spirit in the management of their political affairs'. Scattered about the country, they were the pillars of the Working Men's Associations. They included men like Henry Lovewell, the Ipswich journeyman tailor who already possessed the franchise in 1837 and had been a foundation member of the Mechanics Institute.[3] Their very respectability, often associated with Nonconformity, which served as an asset to them in dealing with the 'middle classes', usually hindered them in dealing with 'fustian jackets, unshorn chins and blistered hands'.[4]

The factory operatives were concentrated in particular parts of the country — Lancashire, described by Engels as 'the mainspring of all the workers' movements',[5] the scene of the great industrial transformation of the late eighteenth and early nineteenth centuries, 'the cotton kingdom'; the West Riding of Yorkshire, where the woollen industry was in course of transformation, in what Faucher called 'a regime of transition' between old and new methods of production;[6] parts of Cumberland, Derbyshire, Wales and the West of England; and West Scotland. In 1839 there were

---

[1] For this and the following quotations in this paragraph, see *The Life and Struggles of William Lovett in his Pursuit of Bread, Knowledge, and Freedom* (1876), Ch. V.

[2] They were also described as 'tools o fthe Whig-Malthusians', and certainly some of them, in imbibing reform ideas, had imbibed other ideas too, from Malthus as well as from Owen. Francis Place was a firm believer in orthodox 'political economy'.

[3] See below, p. 157.

[4] *Northern Star*, 24 Feb. 1838; 16 May 1840. The phrase was repeated time and time again with slightly differing word order.

[5] *Op. cit.*, p. 50.   [6] *Op. cit.* (1856 edn), Vol. I, p. 398.

192 cotton mills in Scotland employing 31,000 workers.[1] All but 17 of these were located in Lanark and Renfrew. There was a further concentration within these counties as there was in Lancashire and the West Riding.

Work in factories entailed a new discipline and an enforced sub-ordination, but it also stimulated an enhanced sense of solidarity and a quest for social and political independence. In the words of Ernest Jones, who wrote vigorously and eloquently about the implications of steam power:

> Up in factory! Up in mill!
> Freedom's mighty phalanx swell . . .
> Fear ye not your masters' power;
> Men are strong when men unite . . .
> And flowers will grow in blooming-time,
> Where prison-doors their jarring cease:
> For liberty will banish crime —
> *Contentment* is the best *Police*.[2]

Both the myth of a pre-factory golden age and the dream of a new social order in the future influenced the thinking — and, equally important, the feeling — of the factory operatives, while both their means of action and their objectives shifted during the course of the 1830's and 40's. The pendulum swung between economic action through the trade unions and political action through Chartism. 'Good times' favoured the former: 'bad times' the latter. The rhythms of what the Leeds Socialist John Francis Bray called 'inordinate idleness and incessant toil'[3] influenced the timing and the intensity of all forms of organisation. At different times 'the equalisation of wages' through 'general union',[4] the Six Points of the Charter, the battle for the Ten Hours' working day, the slogan of 'a fair day's wages for a fair day's work', turn-outs and plug drawing,[5] the repeal of the corn laws,[6] and O'Connor's Land Plan[7] appealed to all or some groups of factory operatives. The Charter was thus one objective among several, and the extent to which it figured as the main objective depended not only on the

---

[1] L. J. Saunders, *Scottish Democracy, 1815-40* (1950), p. 102.
[2] 'The Factory Town', printed in *The Labourer*, Vol. I (1847), pp. 49ff.
[3] *A Voyage from Utopia* (1957 edn), p. 129.
[4] See G. D. H. Cole, *Attempts at General Union* (1953).
[5] See *inter alia* F. Peel, *The Risings of the Luddites, Chartists and Plug Drawers* (1888); G. Kitson Clark, 'Hunger and Politics in 1842' in the *Journal of Modern History* (1953).
[6] See below, pp. 349-50.   [7] See below, Ch. 10.

forcefulness and skill of Chartist leadership but on the state of the domestic and overseas market for textile goods. Some factory operatives remained faithful to Chartism through all its vicissitudes, but the crowds ebbed and flowed with the economic tides.

The absence of a factory system not only in London but in Birmingham is important in explaining local differences. In Birmingham the most important economic unit was not the factory, but the small workshop, and within the workshop small masters rather than industrial capitalists worked in close contact with skilled artisans. Economic development in Birmingham in the first half of the nineteenth century multiplied the number of producing units rather than added to the scale of existing enterprise. Labour-saving machinery, driven by steam power, was far less important than in Manchester. 'The operation of mechanism in this town', wrote a Birmingham man in 1836, 'is to effect that alone, which requires more *force* than the *arm* and the tools of the workman could yield, still leaving his skill and experience of head, hand and eye in full exercise; so that Birmingham has suffered infinitely less from the introduction of machinery than those towns where it is in marked degree, an actual substitute for human labour'.[1] Another feature of Birmingham society was marked social mobility which blurred sharp class distinctions. Small masters might fail in their enterprises and become journeymen again: journeymen had chances of rising when times were good. 'It is easy to see', Faucher said of the city, 'that the *bourgeoisie*, which in all urban centres is the basis of society, scarcely in Birmingham above the inferior groups in society'.[2] Engels and Cobden were agreed about the political consequences of this social system, and Engels quoted Faucher's phrase 'industrial democracy' and described the city as 'Radical rather than Chartist'.[3] In fact, as we shall see, Birmingham played an important part in the birth of the Chartist movement as an organised national force, although it had lost much of its importance by the time that Engels wrote.

The third labour group, which was generally recognised by contemporaries to be a key group in Chartist politics, consisted of

[1] W. Hawkes Smith, *Birmingham and its Vicinity as a Manufacturing and Commercial District* (1836), p. 16.
[2] *Op. cit.*, Vol. I, p. 495.
[3] *Op. cit.*, pp. 224–5. Cf. J. Morley, *The Life of Richard Cobden* (1881), Vol. II, pp. 198–9. For further comments on the differences between Manchester and Birmingham, see my article, 'The Background of the Parliamentary Reform Movement in Three English Cities' in the *Cambridge Historical Journal* (1952).

domestic outworkers. In the Black Country, adjacent to Birmingham, there were large numbers of nailmakers living near the starvation level. In Lancashire, the West Riding of Yorkshire, the
West Country, Wales and Scotland there were handloom weavers
fighting a grim losing battle against the machine. In the West Midlands there were framework knitters employed in an over-stocked
occupation where there was not enough work to go round. It was
because all other attempts at betterment broke down that most of
these outworkers turned towards Chartism. Many of them had had
the reputation in the 1820's of being a quiet, hard working, non-
political section of the population, and certainly their first reaction
to the privation and distress which followed the end of the Napoleonic Wars was to appeal to the local justices of the peace and to the
government for economic protection. The failure of this appeal
which ran counter to the interests of factory owners and the ideas
of the newly powerful political economists, led them direct into
politics along a road of despair. How little they could expect to get
from government was clearly brought out in the *Report of the Royal
Commission on Handloom Weavers*, appointed in 1838 'to report
whether any, and, if so, what measures could be devised for their
relief'. Nassau Senior, the economist, was the chief draftsman of
the Report, which has recently been described as an 'admirable
exercise in economic logic.[1] 'The power of the Czar of Russia', the
Commissioners concluded, 'could not raise the wages of men so
situate. He might indeed order a scale of prices to be paid them for
the work which they did, but in such cases the manufacturer would
soon cease to give out work, as it would be against his interest to do
it. The Czar of Russia, either by fixing on a high scale of wages, or
by a direct command, might put an end to the occupation altogether, and such would be a most merciful exercise of his unlimited
power; but the authority of the Government of a free country cannot thus control the subjects even for their own good; and all that
remains, therefore, is to enlighten the handloom weavers as to their
real situation, warn them to flee from the trade, and to beware of

[1] G. J. Stigler, *Five Lectures on Economic Problems* (1949), Ch. 3. It is interesting to compare the Report of this Royal Commission with the Report of a Select
Committee of the House of Commons, appointed in 1834 to consider handloom
weavers' petitions. The Royal Commission was hard where the Select Committee
was vague, and there is no better example of the differences between the two
procedures of investigation. For a brief discussion of the economic issues raised
see J. H. Clapham, *An Economic History of Modern Britain*, Vol. I (1939 edn)
pp. 551–6.

leading their children into it, as they would beware of the commission of the most atrocious of crimes'. Such advice, backed up as it was by economic as well as political authority, in considerable measure justifies Thomas Carlyle's emphasis on 'lack of due guidance' besides lack of food and shelter as the cause of the growth of the *isms* of his age. And long before the Commissioners reported nationally, handloom weavers had been told locally that their request for public help was 'absolute folly', 'founded in utter ignorance of the circumstances which regulate the wages of labour which it is impossible for Parliament to control'.[1] It is not surprising that after suffering severely even when times were 'good',[2] the weavers looked when times were bad not to the authority of a Czar of Russia but to the authority of local and national Chartist leaders. The leaders they preferred were those who knew how to use and were willing to use militant headstrong language, who painted bright pictures of the past — a past which had certainly provided handloom weavers not only with bigger wages but with an assured and recognised position in society — and who related the political demand for universal suffrage to the demand for food and shelter. The language of hunger was common to all those parts of the country where outworkers were concentrated. In Lancashire J. R. Stephens defined universal suffrage as the means to secure every working man's 'right' to a good coat on his back, a good roof over his head and a good dinner on his table.[3] In the West Riding Richard Oastler, who never committed himself to support of the Chartist political programme, attacked the factory system as a 'slaughterhouse system' and added that he did not 'think that the Government can claim on any ground the allegiance of the operatives when they see that capital and property are protected and their labour is left to chance'.[4] In the East Midlands, the editor of the *Leicester Chronicle* declared that, since the framework knitters could not hope to achieve genuine social independence, it was not surprising that they turned to a social Chartism, which offered the prospect of 'better wages, limited hours of labour, comfort, independence, happiness . . . all that the fond heart of suffering man

---

[1] *Manchester Times*, 16 Dec. 1837. See below, p. 32.
[2] Even when times were good and food was cheap, as in 1834, the Select Committee discovered 'sufferings scarcely to be credited or conceived'. (*Parliamentary Papers* (1834), Vol. X).
[3] See below, p. 34.
[4] Quoted, C. Driver, *Tory Radical* (1946), pp. 289–91.

pictures to him of joy and prosperity in his happiest moments'.[1] In Wiltshire, a Trowbridge Chartist put the matter even more plainly. He promised his audience 'plenty of roast beef, plum pudding and strong beer by working three hours a day'.[2]

There is a wide gap between language of this kind and the more sophisticated language of skilled artisans and craftsmen. It was the strength of O'Connor that he knew how to talk effectively to despairing domestic workers who were more interested during 1837 in the threat of the New Poor Law of 1834 than in political panaceas. The Poor Law Commissioners turned their attention in January 1837 to the industrial districts which hitherto they had left alone. They had met with some earlier resistance in the South — in Suffolk, for instance, and in small market towns like Bishop's Stortford and Saffron Walden — but in the north they were welcomed with what J. R. Stephens called 'the tocsin of revolt'. Oastler, the revered local leader, and O'Connor, who was beginning to fascinate angry audiences everywhere, both addressed a mass meeting in Huddersfield one week after the arrival of Alfred Power, the Assistant Poor Law Commissioner: it was Oastler who coined the phrase of the moment 'Damnation, eternal damnation to the fiend-begotten, coarser-food New Poor Law', the title he gave to the pamphlet version of his speech.[3] O'Connor was shrewd enough to encourage the proliferation of grievances rather than to canalise them. Later on he told Lovett in 1842, 'I don't lead; I am driven by the people. The people gave the lead to the agitation and we followed.'[4] The *Northern Star*, the first number of which appeared in Leeds on 18 November 1837, reported all local protest meetings with equal enthusiasm. It was not until the winter of 1837–8 that O'Connor turned decisively to the suffrage agitation,[5] and it was not until the

[1] *Leicester Chronicle*, 8 Apr. 1848. See below, p. 129. For an official account of the situation of the framework knitters, see *Report of the Commissioner appointed to inquire into the Condition of the Framework Knitters* (1845).

[2] H.O. 40/48, Dec. 1838. See below, p. 179.

[3] O'Connor, fresh from a tour of Scotland and the factory districts, arrived in Huddersfield on 14 Jan. 1837. See below, p. 254. There were riots in Huddersfield and other towns in the North of England later in the year. See C. Driver, *op. cit.*

[4] Quoted by Max Beer, *A History of British Socialism* (1940 edn), Vol. II, p. 129. Cf. Cooper's view of the role of a Chartist 'leader' see below, p. 143.

[5] O'Connor had lost his seat in Parliament in 1835 after quarrelling with O'Connell. The fact that he was not a 'working man' prevented him from playing a leading part in the L.W.M.A., but he visited Sheffield as early as December 1835. In 1837 he was associated with a body known as the Central National Association and was putting forward 'Five Cardinal Points of Radicalism'. For his role in 1837 and 1838, see below, pp. 25–6.

spring of 1838, on the eve of the drafting of the Charter, that the Anti-Poor Law movement was merged into the political agitation for parliamentary reform.[1]

Before examining in more detail the sequence of events which led to the extended nation-wide campaign, three features of the Anti-Poor Law movement need to be set in their place, and the relationship between Chartism and trade-unionism needs to be more fully considered.

The fact that the Poor Law Commissioners set out to put the 1834 Act into operation in the North of England just at the moment that business depression was leading to unemployment of factory operatives as well as starvation among the handloom weavers created the broadest possible front of local opposition. The Act had been intended not to solve the problems of an industrial society but to establish a free labour market in the pauperised agricultural counties. In the north a free labour market already existed. The principle of less eligibility, the cornerstone of the 1834 Act, had no relevance to conditions of involuntary mass industrial unemployment. The attempt to herd together inside the workhouses those people in receipt of poor relief was pointless as well as dangerous. 'It imposed a disgraceful stigma on the genuinely unemployed and their families, it was actuarially far more costly than out-relief, and finally it was tantamount to waging social war'.[2] The language of the opponents of the Act was as violent as any of the later language employed by the militant Chartists. The workhouses were universally known as 'Bastilles', orders were given by local leaders to destroy them, rioting was widespread, and memories of resistance influenced not only Chartist history but the later history of working-class movements in the nineteenth century. The attempt to apply the New Poor Law 'did more to sour the hearts of the labouring population than did the privations consequent on all the actual poverty of the land'.[3]

Before the Anti-Poor Law movement could merge into Chartism it had to shed many of its 'Tory' sympathisers, men who hated 'centralisation', looked to the restoration of an old form of society, deemed 'Whiggery' and 'the march of improvement' as the real curses of the country, and far from wanting further parliamentary

---

[1] See below, pp. 71–5.
[2] S. E. Finer, *The Life and Times of Sir Edwin Chadwick* (1952), p. 182.
[3] 'Alfred' (S. Kydd). *The History of the Factory Movement* (1857), Vol. II, p. 76.

reform intensely disliked the measure of 'middle-class' reform
which had been passed in 1832. In August 1837 the Whig whip E.
J. Stanley wrote to Edwin Chadwick, the most fervent and logical
advocate of the principles of 1834, that 'North of Trent the law is
as unpopular as it is possible with all classes — Justices and
Guardians for political purposes — overseers, now discontinued,
from interested motives.... The whole of the manufacturing
population vehemently against it, the agricultural population stub-
bornly against it'.[1] Before Chartism swallowed up the Anti-Poor
Law agitation, some of these critics had to be left by the wayside.
Oastler was one of the first to be left, Parson Bull of Bradford a
second. There were to be many flirtations between Tories and
Chartists in the future, but from the spring of 1838 onwards it was
abundantly clear that Chartism would depend on its own leaders
and not on alliances with people outside its ranks.[2]

There was a final complication. Although the 1834 Act was de-
tested by popular leaders in all parts of the country, its principles
were supported by many Radical members of Parliament, including Joseph Hume, Daniel O'Connell and some of the closest friends
of the London Working Men's Association. Some of the members
of the L.W.M.A. themselves believed in 'Malthusian principles'. It
was within a circle of men not basically unfriendly to the Act of
1834 that the Charter itself was being drafted. Bitterness between
O'Connell and O'Connor had an ideological twist to it, and differences between the L.W.M.A. and other working-class groups in
London included differences of approach as well as of background.
Before the Charter was published, some of the main conflicts within Chartism were clear for the world to see. Julian Harney, for example, one of the most interesting and articulate London Jacobins,
attacked the L.W.M.A. not only on the platform but in the correspondence columns of *The Times*.[3] Almost all the later divisions in
Chartism can be studied in microcosm in the London disputes of
1835, 1836 and 1837. Men like Harney were just as bitterly opposed
to the New Poor Law as the handloom weavers in the north, and
while missionaries of the L.W.M.A. were spreading their propaganda quietly and effectively in the provinces, links were being
forged between the enemies of the L.W.M.A. in the East End
of London and the leaders of discontent outside. The defeat of a

---

[1] Quoted, S. E. Finer, *op. cit.*, p. 135.
[2] See C. Driver, *op. cit.*, Ch. XXIX, *passim.*   [3] *The Times*, 13 Feb. 1838.

considerable number of Radical members of Parliament at the general election of July 1837 redirected Radical energies back into public agitation, but the Radicals were unable to direct provincial discontents because of their equivocal or even hostile attitude towards the views of some of the Chartists of the future. Just as those Tories, like Earl Stanhope, who dreamed of a national federation of Anti-Poor Law societies, pledged to repeal of the Act of 1834, could not take the lead in the years of increasing discontent, so those Radicals who believed in a substantial measure of parliamentary reform were doomed to play a restricted and limited part in popular agitation. Their ideas were written into the Charter, but ideas were not the most important elements in the political equation.

The business depression was more significant than any other factor in setting the tone of national agitation. In the years of relative prosperity, good harvests and expanding trade between 1832 and 1836 most working-class energies had been absorbed in trade-unionism. The Grand National Consolidated Trades Union was only one example of a number of attempts to form large unions designed not only to raise wages but, in a phrase of Bronterre O'Brien, to bring about 'an entire change in society — a change amounting to a complete subversion of the existing order of the world. The working classes aspire to be at the top instead of at the bottom of society — or rather that there should be no top or bottom at all'.[1] The architects of the new unions dreamed of a new kind of social organisation where Parliament would be replaced by a 'House of Trades', and they put forward ambitious claims for the Grand Council of the G.N.C.T.U. 'There are two Parliaments in London at present sitting', wrote J. E. Smith, the editor of the *Crisis* in 1834, 'and we have no hesitation in saying that the Trades Parliament is by far the most important, and will in the course of a year or two be the more influential.'[2] Although Robert Owen explicitly repudiated universal suffrage, James Morrison, the editor of the *Pioneer*, related this objective to trade-union growth and talked of an 'ascendant scale' by which universal suffrage would be realised. 'With us universal suffrage will begin in our lodges, extend to the general union, embrace the management of trade, and finally swallow up the political power.'[3]

The reasons for the failure of trade-unionism lay not so much in

---

[1] *Poor Man's Guardian*, 19 Oct. 1833.   [2] *Crisis*, 22 Feb. 1834.
[3] *Pioneer*, 31 May 1834.

the pricking of these giant bubbles — they fairly quickly pricked themselves — but in the resistance both of employers and local authorities to specific local trade-union claims. Before the prosperous years drew to a close, trade-unionism had been almost completely destroyed as a nation-wide force.[1] Owen himself, who had never agreed with the views of many of the unionists and had failed to understand the nature of the agitation he had helped to inspire, retreated without regret into sectarianism, to a renewed emphasis on 'the principles of the New Moral World in all their extent and purity'.[2] 'I am termed a visionary', he had told Ricardo years before, 'because my principles have originated in experiences too comprehensive for the limited locality in which people have hitherto been interested.'[3] The origins of Chartism as a national movement are to be discovered, as we have seen, in the 'localities'. Before another movement with large claims could be constructed, there first had to be a breaking down of utopian hopes as well as of vast organisations, for Chartism grew not only out of hunger and anger but out of disillusionment, disillusionment both with the Reform Bill of 1832, widely regarded as a 'sham', and with the ambitious trades-unionism of the 'good years'. When Henry Hetherington, the close friend and collaborator of William Lovett, visited Leeds in 1834 after the collapse of local trade-union efforts he drew the moral that nothing less than universal suffrage would break the workers' chains.[4] It was a moral which the *Poor Man's Guardian* preached on every available occasion, and it was a moral which the Chartists took up in 1838. By that time many grievances had accumulated in all parts of the country, and the snowball metaphor which Morrison first applied to trade-unionism was even more applicable to Chartism.[5]

There were links between trade-unionism and Chartism as well as differences of approach. Some local trade-union leaders, but by no means all, were Chartists a few years later. When the Dorchester labourers were sentenced to transportation, it was Lovett who was secretary of the national committee of protest set up in

[1] For the collapse see G. D. H. Cole, *op. cit.*, Ch. XVIII.
[2] Quoted, *ibid*, p. 154.
[3] Letter 3 to Ricardo. (N.L.W.)
[4] Quoted, Cole, *op. cit.*, p. 143. Some of the Leeds trade unionists were still talking of 'a big hammer, a universal strike . . . and then the chain will be broken from their necks and trampled under their feet'.
[5] 'Our little snowballs have all been rolled together and formed into a mighty avalanche. . . . The watchword now is "unity of action".' *Pioneer*, 22 Feb. 1834.

1834. The committee included many of the men who later drew up the Charter, and collected subscriptions from all the trades which contributed most to the L.W.M.A. — tailors, shoemakers, joiners, cordwainers and coachpainters. It summoned protest meetings in all parts of the country — in factory districts, country towns and large cities as well as the metropolis. Three years later when the 'new Tolpuddle martyrs', the leaders of the Glasgow cotton spinners, were sentenced in January 1838 to seven years' transportation there was a further outburst of working-class indignation. On this occasion, however, some of the differences which were to dog Chartism were again openly demonstrated. Daniel O'Connell was an outspoken critic of the trade unions, as were some of the other Radical members of Parliament, and when he successfully moved in the House of Commons for the setting up of a select committee to inquire into workingmen's combinations, O'Connor, Harney and the *Northern Star* launched a direct attack on the L.W.M.A. for supporting this manoeuvre. The ensuing quarrel between O'Connor and the L.W.M.A. exceeded in bitterness any that had arisen before, and in a sharp letter Lovett not only denied the charges but accused O'Connor of seeking to pose as 'the great I AM of politics'. 'You would have it believed, to our prejudice,' the letter concluded, 'that we have been neglectful of the interests of working men, because we choose another path from yours. But time will show, and circumstances soon determine, who are their real friends; whether they are "the leaders of the people" who make furious appeals to their passions, threatening with fire and sword, or those who seek to unite them upon principles of knowledge and temperance, and the management of their own affairs.'[1]

Within a few months of the writing of this letter the Charter had been published and the first steps were being taken to organise the election of delegates to the 'General Convention of the Industrious Classes'. It was clear from the start that there would be dramatic differences. The local materials out of which nation-wide Chartism was forged were many and various, and the founders of the movement were in disagreement about both tactics and social objectives.

II

It was O'Connor who did most to 'nationalise' discontents in 1838. By the end of the year he had succeeded in winning impressive

[1] Quoted, Lovett, *op. cit.*, pp. 159–62.

support both in the citadels of well-established local leaders, men like Oastler and Thomas Attwood of Birmingham, and in Lovett's London. These achievements were remarkable. During the early years of organised radicalism local leaders had usually proved irresistible and their citadels impregnable. Oastler was known as 'the Factory King': of Attwood, Disraeli asked, 'What was the Great King on the heights of Salamis, or in the Straits of Issus, what was Gengis Khan, what Tamerlane, compared with Mr Thomas Attwood of Birmingham?'[1] In the metropolis, although there were marked social and economic differences between the skilled artisans of Westminster, Charing Cross and Holborn on the one hand and the Spitalfields silk weavers and the east-end dockers on the other, the L.W.M.A., representative of the first group, was far stronger than the East London Democratic Association, which Harney, Allen Davenport and Charles Neesom founded in January 1837.[2] It was the L.W.M.A. which drafted the Charter and the Birmingham Political Union which drew up the equally popular National Petition, and it was these organisations which took the lead in sending out 'missionaries' to other parts of the country to mobilise opinion. O'Connor, however, reaped the harvest.

To appreciate the way in which he succeeded and the significance of his triumph, it is necessary to go back in time at least to the late 1820's, when the future leaders of the L.W.M.A. began to associate with each other and the Birmingham Political Union made its appearance on the political stage.

Lovett, Hetherington, John Cleave and James Watson, the leaders of the L.W.M.A., served their political apprenticeship in the London of Francis Place. They did not share Place's trust in 'political economy', looking to Owen and Thomas Hodgskin[3] rather than to Ricardo, but they learned much about tactics from the experienced Westminster tailor. They played a leading part in founding and organising three societies — the British Association

[1] *The Runnymede Letters*, reprinted in H. W. J. Edwards, *The Radical Tory* (1937), pp. 96–102.
[2] *Prospectus of the E.L.D.A.* in the Lovett Collection, B.R.L.
[3] Lovett probably heard Hodgskin lecture at the Mechanics Institute. For Hodgskin's views, see E. Halévy, *Thomas Hodgskin* (English translation by A. H. Taylor, 1956). Charles Knight, the publisher and populariser, warned the working classes against the dangers of his teachings. 'Such doctrines may begin in the lecture-room, and there look harmless as abstract propositions; but they end with maddening passion, the drunken frenzy, the unappeasable tumult — the plunder, the fire, and the blood.' Quoted *op. cit.*, p. 129.

for Promoting Co-operative Knowledge (1829),[1] the National Union of the Working Classes (1831), and the Association of Working Men to Procure a Cheap and Honest Press (1836). The second of these two societies was an outcome of the first, the link between them being the Metropolitan Trades Union (March 1831) which Lovett and his friends transformed from an attempt to create 'a general union' into a political organisation.[2] The L.W.M.A. was in a sense the outcome of the third, for the Association to Procure a Cheap and Honest Press was disbanded after the newspaper duty had been reduced from 4d. to 1d. in May 1836. 'We found, however,' Lovett wrote, 'that we had collected together a goodly number of active and influential working men, persons who had principally done the work of our late committee; and the question arose among us, whether we could form and maintain a union formed exclusively of this class and of such men.'[3] It is impossible to understand the contribution of the London artisan *élite* to Chartism without exploring in detail this continuous but intricate record of social and political commitment.

The National Union of the Working Classes is particularly important as a precursor of Chartism, as a link between the agitation of 1830–2 and the battle for the Charter, and as an element in the tangled network of political-economic action. It broke with non-political, communitarian Owenism:[4] it diverged from trade-union objectives.[5] It identified social injustice with political oppression, however, and sought in face of bitter opposition, including Radical opposition, to 'maintain the right of the toiling millions to some share in the government of the country they were enriching by their

[1] Lovett succeeded Watson as storekeeper to the First London Co-operative Association. He was secretary of the B.A.P.C.K.

[2] The B.A.P.C.K. was disbanded in April 1831 and the N.U.W.C. got its name at the end of May 1831. Its first rules were printed in *Poor Man's Guardian*, 27 May 1831.

[3] Lovett, *op. cit.*, p. 91.

[4] Some members of the B.A.P.C.K. were uninterested in 'political Owenism': some members of the N.U.W.C. supported Henry Hunt rather than Owen.

[5] Of the Metropolitan Trades Union Place wrote: 'its projectors in the first instance wished to form a trades' union for the purpose of raising wages and reducing the working day with a view to the ultimate object (of) the division of property among working people but the people they called to their assistance under the circumstances of the times, and the general agitation caused by the Reform Bills, at once converted it into a Political Union, leaving the proceedings of working men's trade unions as a secondary object, the main purpose being political, the trade portion as incidental, and the title of the society was changed'. (*Place Papers*, B. M. Add. MSS. 27,791, ff. 280–1). There were protests against this basic shift in emphasis and objectives. See, for example, a letter to the *Poor Man's Guardian*, 29 April 1831.

labours'.[1] It had its stronghold in the metropolis at the Rotunda in
Blackfriars Road, but it sent 'missionaries' to the provinces and
had branches there.[2] It was organised 'somewhat on the plan of the
Methodist Connexion' with class leaders and study groups.[3] It
planned a Convention of delegates from the working-class unions
of the kingdom, and it discussed such 'ulterior measures' as a
Grand National Holiday, a run on the banks and the use of force.
'If gold failed them,' it was stated in April 1833, 'steel must be
tried.'[4] Its newspaper, the *Poor Man's Guardian*, edited from
November 1832 onwards by James Bronterre O'Brien, was full of
ideas as well as of information, and although it ceased publication
in 1835 it remains an invaluable quarry for what have come to be
regarded as specifically Chartist arguments and proposals. Its
career was troubled by sharp differences of opinion and outlook
which anticipate the differences within Chartism, and although
there was a time lag between its demise in 1834 and the birth of
Chartism, many of the people who were active in it diverted their
energies into trade-union channels. There were echoes of old con-
troversies and suggestions of new ones in the ambitious trade-
unionism of 1833 and '34.[5]

Relations between the N.U.W.C. and the greatest provincial
organ of discontent, the Birmingham Political Union, were always
hostile. The Birmingham Union 'of the Lower and Middle Classes
of the People', founded in December 1829, was deliberately designed as an instrument of class collaboration. 'The interests of
masters and men', its founder Attwood always maintained, 'are in
fact one. If the masters flourish, the men are certain to flourish with
them; and if the masters suffer difficulties, their difficulties must

---

[1] Lovett, *op. cit.*, pp. 71–2.
[2] The *Poor Man's Guardian* records the existence of 32 local N.U.W.C. organisations in the provinces. Place claimed that it was strongest in the large manufacturing towns and in the South West, (Add. MSS., 27, 791, f. 333).
[3] Lovett, *op. cit.*, p. 68. For Methodist influences on working-class politics,
see R. B. Wearmouth, *Some Working-Class Movements of the Nineteenth Century*
(1948).
[4] *Poor Man's Guardian*, 30 March 1833.
[5] Some of the differences came to a head in May 1833 when a meeting called
by the N.U.W.C. in Coldbath fields was broken up by the police. There was a
quarrel after the event between Lovett and his friends and William Benbow, the
pioneer of the idea of a 'Grand National Holiday'. Benbow's ideas appeared in
both the unionist and the Chartist periods of agitation. The Chartists renamed
the Holiday 'The Sacred Month'. For Benbow's ideas, see the reprint of his 1832
pamphlet *Grand National Holiday, and Congress of the Productive Classes* with a
long commentary by A. J. C. Rüter in the *International Review for Social History*
(1936).

shortly affect the workmen in a threefold degree. The masters therefore ought to take their workmen by the hand and knock at the gates of government and demand the redress of their common grievances.'[1] Attwood's favourite project of currency reform — dismissed later on by O'Connor as 'rag botheration'[2] — was at the same time the chief objective of all his political activities and the theoretical foundation of class collaboration.[3] At heart a conservative,[4] as were many of the leaders of the B.P.U., Attwood was opportunist in his choice of means, and he succeeded between 1829 and 1832 in making the Union the strongest and most influential Radical organisation in the country. There was more than flattery in a remark of O'Connell that 'it was not Grey and Althorp who carried (the bill of 1832) but the brave and determined men of Birmingham'.[5]

When in October 1832, after the struggle was over, Hetherington arrived in Birmingham to spread the propaganda of the N.U.W.C., he was supported only by a small group of people who 'are tired of the Council (of the Union) and their leader'.[6] Dr Wade, the Warwick Radical parson, took the chair at Hetherington's meeting, however, and violently attacked Attwood and his 'flatterers and dependents'. Five reasons were advanced for separate and distinctive working-class action — conflict of interest between 'men of property' and 'the working man'; the need to represent not property but 'human beings'; the unsuitability of 'masters and capitalists' representing working men's interests in Parliament; the identification of 'those who move in a sphere above the working classes' with the aristocracy; and sufficiency of 'intelligence amongst the working classes to discuss all questions connected with their best interest, and a growing disposition to acquire further knowledge'.[7] All these

---

[1] *Report of the Proceedings of the Town's Meeting in Support of Parliamentary Reform*, 13 Dec. 1832 (B.R.L.).
[2] Quoted, F. F. Rosenblatt, *The Economic and Social Aspects of the Chartist Movement* (1916), p. 121.
[3] See my article 'Thomas Attwood and the Economic Background of the Birmingham Political Union' in the *Cambridge Historical Journal* (1948).
[4] 'What would be the dreadful misery every man would sustain,' Attwood once asked, 'if ever the complicated and wonderful machinery of English society were suffered to break up?' (*Report of the Proceedings*, 17 May 1830).
[5] *Report of the Proceedings*, 20 May 1833. At a dinner in 1836 a leader of the B.P.U. admitted that it was to O'Connell that 'they were indebted for the model of the Political Union. It was upon the example of the Catholic Association that the Union was established'. (*Birmingham Journal*, 11 June 1836).
[6] H.O. 52/20. Lee to Melbourne, 25 Oct. 1832.
[7] Place Papers, Add. MSS. 27, 796, f. 333: *Poor Man's Guardian* 10 Nov. 1832.

reasons, which were unpalatable to the leaders of the B.P.U., anticipate the propaganda of the L.W.M.A.

What made it possible for the revived B.P.U. and the L.W.M.A. to co-operate in 1838 was disillusionment with the Reform Bill of 1832, the impact of business depression, and a further shift in Attwood's views.

Disillusionment with the Act of 1832, which was expressed by the N.U.W.C. before the final passing of the measure, was expressed equally strongly in 1833 and 1834 by Attwood himself. 'ONCE MORE, *in your countless masses*, COME WITH ME', Attwood exclaimed in May 1833, 'HEARTS OF LIONS, but with the gentleness of lambs, meet me again at Newhall Hill.'[1] One of the speakers at a mass meeting in the same month attacked the government for its refusal to extend the suffrage still further and for 'the great hostility . . . shown to the interests of the working classes, which exceeded that exhibited by the Tories'.[2] A few months later the leaders of the B.P.U. joined with the local trade-union leaders to organise a parade in honour of Joseph Russell, an old ultra-Radical and free-thinking critic of Attwood, who had just been released after serving a sentence for libel. It was a friendly gesture which did much to heal old sores.[3] Attwood's criticism both of Whigs and Tories, his opposition to the New Poor Law, and his interest in suffrage extension, guaranteed his local popularity. Although the B.P.U. withered away in the period of relative prosperity,[4] Attwood had no doubts that it would revive if the economic climate worsened. On the eve of the depression, he prophesied a new political turn. 'Mr Cobbett used to say, "I defy you to agitate a fellow with a full stomach." Nothing is more true. Men do not generally act from abstract principles, but from deep and unrewarded wrongs, injuries and sufferings. The people of England never came forward to advocate the abstract principles of Major Cartwright . . . but

[1] Broadside of 9 May 1833 (B.R.L.).

[2] *Report of the Proceedings*, 20 May 1833. The meeting, which was addressed by O'Connell, was to protest against the government's Irish policy. Attwood said that 'he would never be content until . . . every honest man should have the free use of his right arm; that he should be independent of his master; and that instead of going to look for work from his master, his master should come to look to him for his work'.

[3] In 1832 Russell had been described by Attwood as a 'kind of ancient IAGO' (*The Substance of the Extraordinary Proceedings of the Birmingham Political Council*, 3 July 1832).

[4] There were demands for its revival by the 'Friends of Reform' in 1835. (*Birmingham Journal*, 28 Mar. 1835.) In September 1836 a Reform Association was set up (*ibid.*, 17 Sept. 1836).

when their employment and wages were gone ... the borough-mongers were very quickly cashiered. Now when the next opportunity comes, a further reform of Parliament will be a much quicker and easier operation.'[1]

Attwood's economic determinism provided the most realistic approach to Birmingham politics. In March 1837 Birmingham merchants, manufacturers and other inhabitants were drawing the 'serious and immediate attention of His Majesty's Government' to 'the general state of difficulty and embarrassment, threatening the most alarming consequences to all classes of the community'. The Government was duly warned that 'unless remedial measures be immediately applied, a large proportion of our population will shortly be thrown out of employment'.[2] A month later a 'deputation of the workmen assembled at the principal section houses of the B.P.U. of 1830' pressed for the revival of the Union. T. C. Salt, a small manufacturer and a vigorous advocate of suffrage extension, exclaimed that the sticks were now dry and that they only needed a match. R. K. Douglas, the editor of the *Birmingham Journal*, added that if a revived B.P.U. were to be effective a high proportion of the town's working-class population would have to join in from the start.[3] That there was a substantial measure of working-class support was quickly demonstrated. Workmen from a number of local factories sent representatives to a meeting at the Golden Eagle Tavern, an old Union rendezvous, and pledged full support. The Union was formally revived in May, published its first Address a few days later and celebrated its reappearance with a mass meeting on Newhall Hill on 19 June. Household suffrage, vote by ballot, triennial parliaments, payment of members and the abolition of the property qualification for members of parliament were all accepted, but in November the Union took the decisive step of supporting universal suffrage. The failure of the Government to put forward positive proposals to alleviate distress[4] and the

---

[1] *Ibid*, 12 Nov. 1836.

[2] *National Reformer*, 18 March 1837. In May a Working Men's Distress Committee presented a Memorial signed by 13,000 persons demanding 'an immediate and searching investigation' of the causes of trade depression. It referred to the manufacturers as 'our natural allies'. (*Birmingham Journal*, 20 May 1837). A joint committee of masters and men was set up later in May with Salt as secretary. (*Ibid*, 3 June.) Petitions continued to be sent to Parliament throughout the year.

[3] *Ibid.*, 22 Apr. 1837.

[4] A Birmingham deputation saw Melbourne on 2 Nov. 1837 and met with no success.

c

declaration of Lord John Russell against further parliamentary re
form stung Attwood to go much further than he ever had done be
fore. At a meeting of the Council of the Union on 19 December 'h
was greatly excited and put aside all his usual caution'. He attacke
the existing House of Commons — 'if the Queen's speech ha
been made by the Emperor of China, it could not have had les
reference to the wants of the British nation' — and he attacked th
parliamentary Radicals also as 'the bitterest enemies of the people'
They had supported the New Poor Law and they laughed when h
spoke of 'national distress' or of 'national disgrace'. A new nation-
wide movement of protest was necessary. 'The middle classes
could not be moved, they were choked with pride, jealousy and
servility[1]. . . . The masses of the people constituted the only hope
of the country. Into their hands the destiny of the country must be
committed . . . . They must bring 2,000,000 of men together to
stand by them and move legally at the word of command.'[2] By the
end of 1837 not only was there a large measure of local agreement
in Birmingham that the Union offered 'the only means of achieving
the great object they had in view — namely permanent employment and fair remuneration for it',[3] but the clarion call had been
sounded. 'More happiness and abundance to the labouring classes
than ever yet fell to the share of any people on earth could only fail
from the want of energy in the people.'[4] 'We have been long and
patiently silent. A period has at last arrived when silence is
shame . . . . That the Reform Bill may become what you hoped it
would be, a Great Charter of English liberty, depends on the
People alone. Let them speak and it is done! Before the majesty of
their united will, Whigs and Tories and all dark and deceitful
things will flee away as the shadow disappears before the rising
sun.'[5]

During the early months of 1838 the B.P.U. was a hive of activity. R. K. Douglas was drafting a National Petition in simple and
highly effective Biblical language. Salt was talking of collecting
millions of signatures in support of Chartist demands. P. H. Muntz
was working out plans for a Convention, 'a national meeting of

---

[1] An influential group of Birmingham merchants and manufacturers had protested against the revival of the B.P.U. (*Birmingham Gazette*, 22 May 1837).
[2] *Place Papers*, Add. MSS., 27, 819, f. 153.
[3] *Birmingham Journal*, 13 Jan. 1838.
[4] *Place Papers, loc. cit.*
[5] *Birmingham Journal*, 24 Dec. 1837.

elegates of the people'.[1] Attwood was thinking about a 'sacred eek'. Letters of encouragement were being sent to reformers in ther places, the first of which was near-by Coventry. For more istant pastures a missionary visit to Scotland was planned, 'a holy nd peaceful pilgrimage',[2] and after John Collins, a local shoe-aker, had prepared the way, an impressive Birmingham deputa-on reached Glasgow for a great public meeting on 21 May 1838.[3] t was at this meeting that Douglas's National Petition was dopted enthusiastically and that the leaders of the Birmingham eputation met Wade and Murphy of the L.W.M.A. On returning Birmingham 'the People's Charter' was the first item on the genda for the meeting of the Council of the Union on 5 June.[4]

The contact with the L.W.M.A. was a sign that all the protest novements were at last converging. As early as June 1837 the .W.M.A. had made friendly overtures to the revived B.P.U., but o action followed. After the B.P.U.'s clarion call had been ounded in December 1837 the L.W.M.A. was the first to re-pond.

The history of the launching by the L.W.M.A. of the People's Charter, which transformed the political situation in the spring and ummer of 1838, has often been told and need be only briefly des-ribed to complete the picture at this point.[5] In February 1837 the .W.M.A. made its first public appearance at a meeting held at the Crown and Anchor Tavern in the Strand. The meeting drew up he petition which included all the Six Points of the subsequent Charter.[6] A few months later in May and June 1837 two confer-nces took place between the leaders of the L.W.M.A. and a group of sympathetic Radical members of Parliament. At the second of hese conferences a committee of twelve was appointed — six epresentatives of the L.W.M.A., six M.P.s — to draft a parlia-nentary bill, incorporating annual parliaments, universal suffrage,

---

[1] *Ibid.*, 3 Feb. 1838.

[2] *Ibid.*, 24 Feb. 1838. The *Birmingham Advertiser* spoke contemptuously of this quixotic expedition'. Quoted, *Birmingham Journal*, 19 May 1838.

[3] For the choice of Scotland and the details of the meeting, see below, pp. 51–3. R. K. Douglas was a Scotsman, former editor of the *Dumfries Times.* Copies of the *Birmingham Journal* circulated in Scotland. (See S. Maccoby, *English Radicalism, 1832–1852* (1935), p. 167. For the influence of the B.P.U. in Wales, see below, pp. 222–3.

[4] *Place Papers*, Add. MSS., 27, 820, f. 129.

[5] M. Hovell, *The Chartist Movement* (1925) gives a good account. His discus-ion of the B.P.U. is far less satisfactory.

[6] It included universal female suffrage as well as male suffrage. This point was ater dropped.

equal electoral districts, payment of members and the abolition o
property qualifications. It was to be called the 'Outline of an Act o
Parliament to provide for the Representation of the People o
Great Britain in the Commons House of Parliament'. For variou
reasons the committee was not very energetic, and it was left t
Lovett—with help from J. A. Roebuck and Francis Place—to dra\
up the bill. It was printed and published on 8 May 1838 with a
eight page introduction by fifteen members of the L.W.M.A. –
before the Glasgow meeting — and it was known as 'the People'
Charter'.

There is evidence that the publication of the Charter influence
the tactics of Douglas in drafting his National Petition. On 5 Ma
1838 the *Birmingham Journal* hoped that 'only the great principle
of Radical Reform — Universal Suffrage and the Ballot' would b
included in the Petition. It preferred triennial to annual parlia
ments. Nevertheless, the final Petition demanded annual parlia
ments.[1] There is evidence on the other side also that the L.W.M.A
was being influenced by the upsurge of popular feeling. Th
leaders of the L.W.M.A. had begun by disparaging 'mere num
bers':[2] the B.P.U. revelled in them. Men like Attwood loved to tall
in terms of millions. As early as April 1838 Douglas dreamed of a
'petition signed by two million men, drawn, like a Cheshire cheese
of twenty feet diameter, in a cart of white horses to the House o
Commons'.[3] Some of the missionaries of the L.W.M.A. who were
successful in creating 150 working men's associations in the provinces[4] preferred the logic of numbers to the education of *élites*.
Henry Vincent, for example, 'the young Demosthenes of English
democracy' as Gammage · called him,[5] began his career as a
L.W.M.A. missionary, but he excelled in 'every capacity for exciting the multitude. To give stability to their wakened minds was a
very different matter . . . . Wherever he appeared his fervid declam-
ations awakened every sympathy of the heart . . . . His thrilling
tones, as he depicted the burning wrongs of the toiling classes,

[1] *Birmingham Journal*, 19 May 1838.
[2] There were 33 foundation members of the L.W.M.A. and still only 100 in
the summer of 1837.
[3] *Birmingham Journal*, 14 April 1838.
[4] *Place Papers*, Add. MSS., 27, 773, f. 99.
[5] R. G. Gammage, *The History of the Chartist Movement* (1854), p. 17. Vincent had joined the L.W.M.A. in November 1836 and was quickly elected to the
committee (Add. MSS., 37, 773, ff. 24–8). For his activities in the West, see below, pp. 206–7.

fanned their passions into a flame which no after prudence could allay.'[1]

The People's Charter was the work of Lovett, but when its virtues began to be extolled on the platform at mass meetings or at torchlight gatherings on the northern moors it was being used in a very different kind of way from what the L.W.M.A. had first intended. All the social grievances of a discontented Britain were poured into the political vessel. Along with Douglas's petition,[2] it became, in Carlyle's phrase, 'the cry of pent-up millions suffering under a diseased condition of society'.[3] Its basic strength lay in its power to unify discontented people in all parts of the country. 'In less than twelve months from the date of its publication', Lovett wrote, 'upwards of a million people had declared in its favour, and it was going on rapidly enlisting new converts and earnest supporters.'[4]

Against this background it is not difficult to see why and how O'Connor secured a commanding position in relation to the new united movement. To begin with, he was tactful and shrewd. He accepted the Charter as if it were his own, and, as 'the Apostle of the North',[5] carried it to Lancashire and the West Riding. He declared that the Great Northern Union, founded at Leeds on 5 June 1838,[6] was similar in purposes to the B.P.U., that Attwood was 'honest and straightforward in his principles' and that he (O'Connor) had 'great confidence in him'.[7] He used his position of strength in the north to make personal converts in other places, appearing on public platforms whenever and wherever he could, either with other prominent figures — Stephens, for example, or Collins — or with local Chartists. Gradually, however, by temperament as much as by design, he began to stress his own intense personal involvement in the new movement and his special claims to lead it:[8] he also took

---

[1] Gammage, loc. cit.

[2] Place was very disparaging about 'the artful, and to working men, catching style' of the petition (Add. MSS., 27, 820, f. 131): Rosenblatt, op. cit., p. 153 dismisses it as mild and 'spineless'. Both judgements are quite inadequate. Place's serious misunderstanding of Chartism has had a damaging effect on much subsequent writing of Chartist history.

[3] T. Carlyle, Chartism (1839).

[4] W. Lovett, op. cit., p. 171.

[5] Place Papers, Add. MSS., 27, 820, f. 135.

[6] See below, pp. 75-6. It completely superseded the Leeds Working Men's Association, founded in 1837.

[7] Northern Star, 28 July 1838. He was more cautious too in his relations with Lovett at this time.

[8] 'He would never accept place, pension, or employment from any Government

his cue from earlier Anti-Poor Law meetings and spoke more and more of physical force and resistance to the death. It was in Birmingham, indeed, at the great meeting of 6 August 1838, called together to select eight delegates for the proposed Chartist Convention, that he made what Lovett called his first intrusion 'at a Chartist meeting' of 'his physical force notions, or rather his Irish braggadocio about arming and fighting'. To the assembled crowds he declared that he had travelled over 2,000 miles during the previous six months, and that he had seen soldiers at work interfering with 'the meetings of the people'. 'He had told the soldiers', he went on, 'that if they were going to begin the work of carnage, to give him time to muster his battalions, and if 2,000,000 were not sufficient, 5,000,000 would stand up to do them justice'.[1] Such language, which made Lovett shiver, thrilled the crowds. And from that moment a sense of disillusionment (amid all the fervour) troubled some of the founders of the Chartist movement.

Most of the studies in this volume describe the exciting scenes which led up to the election of delegates for the 'General Convention of the Industrious Classes' which met in London, at the same time as Parliament met, in February 1839. They discuss the differences of opinion about tactics and purposes — particularly about the use of force — before the delegates assembled. The differences were more than accidental by-products of O'Connor's controversial personality, more than deliberate elements in his chosen designs. They must be related to the facts of geography and social structure described above. The Charter was a symbol of unity, but it concealed as much as it proclaimed — the diversity of local social pressures, the variety of local leaderships, the relative sense of urgency among different people and different groups.

Two local situations which are not described in the studies must be briefly mentioned in this introductory chapter — the situation in London and the situation in Birmingham.

Quietly and methodically Lovett and his friends arranged a meeting on 17 September 1838 in Palace Yard, Westminster to elect eight members to the Convention. The High Bailiff was in the chair, and it was estimated that 10,000 to 15,000 people were

---

save that which was erected by Universal Suffrage. He was the unpaid, undeviating, unpurchasable friend of liberty, and servant of the people.' (Speech at Carlisle reported in the *Northern Star*, 21 July 1838.)

[1] Quoted, Gammage, *op. cit.*, p. 51.

present. Among those excluded from the platform were the leaders of the East London Democratic Association and O'Connor himself. All the L.W.M.A. nominees were elected, and only O'Connor from the crowd and some of the delegates from the provinces, including Robert Lowery from Newcastle and R. J. Richardson from Manchester, talked ominously of physical force. Lovett's victory was a Pyrrhic one, however. The result of the meeting was that O'Connor and the *Northern Star* came out openly for the E.L.D.A., and that in the provinces there was more rather than less talk of force.[1] In London itself some of the members of the L.W.M.A. preferred consorting with O'Connor and his provincial allies to attacking them, and joint meetings in various parts of London began to be arranged and to be reported in the *Northern Star*. Finally, on 20 December 1838 at a public meeting held at the Hall of Science, Commercial Road, this time with the leaders both of the L.W.M.A. and the E.L.D.A. on the platform, O'Connor carried the day. When the Convention met, Lovett faced all his most powerful opponents flushed with their metropolitan and provincial victories.[2]

In Birmingham, the position of the B.P.U. was threatened almost from the time of the close of the triumphant meeting of 6 August. As news of 'physical force' speeches in the north arrived in the city, men like Douglas, Salt and Attwood himself began to be increasingly disturbed. In June 1838 Collins had reported to the Council of the B.P.U. a speech delivered by Stephens which he had heard at Saddleworth on the borders of Lancashire and West Riding. In it Stephens had remarked that the only question was 'when should they commence burning and destroying the Mills, and other Property'. Collins said that he had been driven to speak out against this advice at Saddleworth, feeling 'that he should be abandoning his duty if he did not reprobate such language'.[3] It was Stephens rather than O'Connor who first shocked the men of Birmingham —

---

[1] A meeting at Norwich on 5 November was particularly uninhibited in its language and arguments. Stephens thundered against the Poor Law so violently — 'men of Norwich, fight with your swords, fight with pistols, fight with daggers. Women, fight with your nails and your teeth, if nothing else will do' — that Place claimed that the the the *Northern Star* itself had to expurgate his speech. (Add. MSS., 27, 820, f. 295; see the *Northern Star*, 10 Nov. 1838). Harney spoke also — 'they would have the Charter or die in the attempt to obtain it' — and was elected a delegate to the Convention. Cleave, the L.W.M.A. candidate, was almost completely ignored.

[2] One of the most important victories was in Scotland where O'Connor was successful in having the Calton Hill resolutions — in favour of moral force — rescinded. See below, p. 256.

[3] *Place Papers*, Add. MSS., 27, 820, f. 141.

Collins, indeed, went out of his way to praise O'Connor in June, remarking that 'it was greatly to his credit that he had given up all other plans to go heart and hand with the men of Birmingham'. Annoyance with O'Connor himself mounted in September[1] and October, and on 13 November O'Connor daringly attended the weekly meeting of the B.P.U. to protest against complaints made by Salt and Douglas that he was preaching physical force. A week later he appeared again, and succeeded in splitting the ranks of the Birmingham Chartists. Muntz was hissed in his own stronghold and the meeting had to be adjourned. Although peace was patched up a week later, the unity of Birmingham Chartism had been shattered for all time. Working men began to meet independently in December to organise the collection of the National Rent. Collins was the chairman of the management committee, but its secretary was Edward Brown, a determined O'Connorite, who approved of Stephens's reliance on 'lead and steel'.[2] The more that Attwood warned his fellow-citizens of the machinations of 'imprudent and dangerous men,[3] the stronger they became. The well-known withdrawal of leading Birmingham delegates from the National Convention was in effect decided long before the Convention met. When a later attempt was made to unite middle-class and working-class leaders in Birmingham, it was Joseph Sturge, not Attwood, who was at the head of it, and it was repeal of the corn laws, not currency reform, which provided the economic ideology.[4]

In many other cities after the break-up of the Convention and the imprisonment of the Chartist leaders, old local agitations revived — as in Leeds[5] and Lancashire[6] — and the pattern of local politics returned to its pre-Chartist shape. It is impossible to generalise, however, for Chartism never completely disappeared in the 1840's even in its darkest hours. These studies give some idea both of the diversity of the pattern and the factors making for continued unity. Each study is complete in itself, and although the authors reveal certain differences of approach, the differences are never greater than those which existed in the local chronicles of Chartism itself.

[1] The *Birmingham Journal*, 8 Sept. 1838, reported 'rapturous applause' at a meeting addressed by O'Connor in Birmingham.
[2] *Ibid.*, 22 Dec. 1838.   [3] *Ibid.*, 19 Jan. 1839.
[4] See below, pp. 363–5.   [5] See below, p. 80.
[6] See below, p. 49.

Chapter Two

Chartism in Manchester

Donald Read

I

If, in the sixty years after 1789, England was to have a revolution on the French model, most Englishmen believed that it would begin in Manchester. 'How are you getting on in Manchester?' asked William IV apprehensively of John Dalton, the Manchester scientist, on his presentation at court. 'Well, I don't know, just middlin', I think,' was Dalton's guarded reply. Even staunch Mancunians could not claim that the social state of their town in the 1830's was better than 'middlin'. Outside observers were less restrained. Manchester, admitted a local guidebook in 1839, had 'obtained at a distance an unenviable notoriety on account of its rioting propensities'. Manchester was the centre, declared the historian Molesworth, of 'a lawless turbulence which embarrassed the Government, perplexed the legislature, and dismayed the inhabitants of more favoured parts of the kingdom'.[1]

But if outside observers were often alarmed by the aspect of Manchester, they were usually also fascinated by it. Manchester was the showpiece of the industrial revolution, a modern wonder of the world, 'an agglomeration' (in the words of Faucher) 'the most extraordinary, the most interesting, and in some respects the most monstrous, which the progress of society has presented.' What Art had been to the ancient world, exlaimed Disraeli, Science was to the modern, and the greatest triumphs of modern technological science were to be found in Manchester. 'Hast thou heard, with sound ears', asked Thomas Carlyle,

'the awakening of a Manchester, on Monday morning, at half-past five by the clock; the rushing off of its thousand mills, like the boom of an Atlantic tide, ten thousand times ten thousand spools and spindles

[1] See H. McLachlan, *Essays and Addresses* (1950), pp. 57–8; [B. Love], *Manchester as It Is* (1839), p. 26.

all set humming there — it is perhaps, if thou knew it well, sublime as a Niagara, or more so.'[1]

The blend of fear and fascination sprang from the fact that there was a human as well as a technological side to the industrial revolution, and that in the sphere of social readjustment Englishmen had proved themselves much less skilled than in the sphere of technical invention. Disraeli, who thought that Manchester was as great a human exploit as Athens, recognised that it was none the less an exploit founded on an insecure social basis, on a basis of mutual hostility between 'two nations', rich and poor, masters and men. Society in early industrial Manchester was centred almost exclusively on its cotton industry and reflected only the basic division within that industry. It lacked all the usual gentle gradations of status and of wealth: masters and men faced each other almost alone. At all times such social cleavage tended to social tension. But in the later 1830's this tension was much increased by the general prevalence of economic distress. This was the background of Manchester Chartism. Operatives went hungry, while their employers patently did not. Disparity of suffering gave the Chartist leaders their opportunity, and class conflict between cotton masters and cotton operatives became the basis of the Chartist movement in Lancashire.

The cotton operatives were of two main types, factory workers employed in the mills and handloom weavers working at home. In 1840 there were perhaps a quarter of a million cotton factory operatives in Lancashire (a majority of them women and children), and perhaps a hundred thousand handloom weavers. Many other workpeople also depended directly on the cotton trade for their livelihoods, especially those employed in machine making, in building, in coal mining and in transport. In all, it was estimated in 1835 that between two-thirds and three-quarters of the male population of Lancashire were 'engaged more or less directly in the production or sale of cotton fabric'.[2]

If the cotton operatives were many, the cotton masters were comparatively few. Many of them were as grim as the surroundings which they had helped to create, 'their souls bound up in gold . . .

[1] L. Faucher, *Manchester in 1844* (trans. J. P. Culverwell, 1844), p. 21; T. Carlyle, *op. cit.*, Ch. VIII; B. Disraeli, *Coningsby* (1844), Bk. IV, Ch. I.
[2] E. Baines, *History of the Cotton Manufacture in Great Britain* (1835), pp. 422–9; G. H. Wood, *History of Wages in the Cotton Trade during the past Hundred Years* (1910), p. 125.

as hardened as the bricks of their warehouses'.[1] Originally, there had been two main types of cotton master, the actual manufacturers and the cotton merchants; by the Chartist period, however, the functions of the two were tending to become combined.[2]

For both masters and men Manchester was the great metropolis. Its influence extended from Wigan in the west to Stalybridge in the east, from Preston and Blackburn in the north to Stockport in the south, an area with a population in 1841 of about one and a quarter millions. Its leadership was accepted not only in commerce but also in politics. Both masters and men tended to go to Manchester to express their opinions and to air their grievances. Among the operatives a working-class political tradition had grown up around the town, a tradition which by the Chartist period had already produced two great movements of popular opinion, the Radical movement of 1816–20 culminating in the Peterloo Massacre, and the campaign in support of the Reform Bill. The memory of these earlier campaigns, and especially of the tragedy of Peterloo, was very strong in Lancashire throughout the course of the Chartist movement. Manchester had taken the lead in both agitations: it was natural that it should take the lead in the Chartist agitation also.

The local Chartist agitation grew out of the almost unrelieved commercial depression which followed the collapse of the boom of 1836. Fifty thousand workers in the Manchester area alone were unemployed or on short time by June 1837.[3] The worst sufferers were the handloom weavers. Even in good times they were now only just able to make a living; the power loom, introduced increasingly during the 1820's and 30's, had disastrously undercut their prices. As a result, by the mid-30's large numbers of English handloom weavers seem to have given up their trade. But their places had been quickly taken by Irish immigrants who were flooding into the area. Over a hundred thousand Irish lived in Lancashire by 1841, some thirty-four thousand of them in Manchester.[4] Their attachment to the decaying handloom trade meant that the greater part of them existed in a state of chronic distress. 'Most of the cases of pauperism at Manchester, whether settled or casual, were of Irish weavers, and 70 per cent of the juvenile offenders

[1] [J. Easby], *Manchester and the Manchester People* (1843), p. 15.
[2] S. J. Chapman, *The Lancashire Cotton Industry* (1904), p. 114.
[3] *Manchester Times*, 17 June 1837.
[4] A. Redford, *Labour Migration in England (1760–1860)* (1926), pp. 112, 134.

were the children of Irish parents.'[1] Members of weavers' families, declared one petition at the end of 1837, had only 1½d. a day each to live on.[2]

This distress emphasised in terrible fashion the class cleavage within local society: it was not the cotton masters who had to live on 1½d. a day. A Manchester song of the period voiced the bitter feelings of the operatives:

> How little can the rich man know
> Of what the poor man feels,
> When Want, like some dark demon foe,
> Nearer and nearer steals!
>
> .   .   .   .
>
> *He* never saw his darlings lie
> Shivering, the flags their bed;
> *He* never heard that maddening cry
> 'Daddy, a bit of bread!'[3]

To the operatives the masters seemed not only well fed, but also callous. They would admit no attempts (other than sporadic charity) to alleviate distress. When, for example, in December 1837 the starving handloom weavers petitioned for a legislative minimum wage, the *Manchester Times* denounced their request as 'absolute folly'. It was 'a scheme', the paper declared, 'founded in utter ignorance of the circumstances which regulate the wages of labour, which it is . . . impossible for parliament to control.'[4]

The reason for this hard attitude was the attachment of the cotton masters to the principles of the new political economy. All the economic thinking of the Lancashire cotton men during the early nineteenth century was dominated by the principle of *laissez-faire*. Adam Smith and his successors, the cotton masters believed, had taught that to interfere with the free play of economic forces did always more harm than good. In this spirit therefore the petition of the distressed handloom weavers was brushed aside. Workmen must not try to interfere with economic processes, but must wait patiently until the course of economic events brought better things.[5]

---

[1] *Ibid.*, p. 112.
[2] *Manchester Times*, 16 Dec. 1837.
[3] Mrs Gaskell, *Mary Barton*, Ch. VI.
[4] *Manchester Times*, 16 Dec. 1837.
[5] For the local application of the principles of political economy, see the *Manchester Examiner*, 3 June 1848. 'A mill may be a text for expounding the great principles of Political Economy, and marking out what it is which constitutes Capital, to what extent the amount of Labour is limited by capital, and pointing

The attachment of the middle-class cotton masters of Lancashire to the principles of the new political economy thus only deepened still further the fundamental class division within local society. The handloom weavers had asked for work and wages: they were given instead a lesson in economics.

Such a widening of the class gulf was not, of course, an intended effect of the new *laissez-faire* economics. On the contrary an integral part of the new political economy was its theory of social union. The work of masters and men, the argument ran, was entirely complementary. They depended on each other and had everything in common: they ought always therefore to live and work together in amity. This argument leant heavily on wages fund theory and on the theory of beneficent self-interest. According to these theories even the most selfish employer was providing blessings for his workpeople. The more profits he made, the more was the fund augmented from which his workpeople derived their wages:

'The most wealthy millowner that ever rode in his carriage cannot eat and drink all his profits; and therefore, even though he be a selfish, grasping man, the increase of his wealth has a material tendency to promote the general wealth of the community.'[1]

Such a conclusion not unnaturally seemed selfish and specious to the operatives. The new political economy, they considered, was very convenient for cotton masters: masters might well be pleased with theories which justified their profit-making. But what, their workmen asked, had political economy to offer to operatives? — only limitless patience in times of adversity and unremitting work for their masters' profit in times of prosperity. We cannot wonder that the cotton operatives of Lancashire did not share their employers' enthusiasm for the new economic principles.

II

The failure of the middle-class cotton masters to offer any remedy other than patience for the distress which prevailed from 1837 to 1842 was the great opportunity for Chartism in Lancashire.

---

out what are the social errors which still infect men's minds on the great question of industrial freedom. . . . Counting-houses, warehouses, packing establishments, and shops, may afford indications of the laws which govern Production and Distribution.'
[1] *Manchester Examiner*, 8 July 1848.

The Chartist leaders seized their chance eagerly. From the start they addressed themselves first and foremost to the problem of economic distress.

> 'This question of universal suffrage', declared Rayner Stephens at the first great Lancashire Chartist meeting, 'is a knife-and-fork question, a bread and cheese question . . . . If any man ask what I mean by universal suffrage, I mean to say that every working man in the land has a right to a good coat on his back, a good hat on his head, a good roof for the shelter of his household, a good dinner upon his table, no more work than will keep him in health while at it, and as much wages as will keep him in the enjoyment of plenty, and all the blessings of life that reasonable men could desire.'[1]

It was language like this which won the working men of Lancashire to Chartism. Democratic representation in Parliament, they were assured, would make certain that they had always sufficient work and sufficient wages. 'In Lancashire', Cooke Taylor observed in 1842, 'the cry for the Charter means the list of wages for 1836.'[2]

The Chartist leaders went on to frame their own 'political economy' in opposition to that of the cotton masters. The idea of complementary roles, they asserted loudly, was only a selfish mockery: 'the truth was, the working men were all white slaves.'[3] And the idea that profit-making by the masters was of benefit to the whole community was mere selfish cant. In truth, the Chartist argument ran, the masters and their profits were virtually superfluous to the economic process. Labour not Capital was the all-important element in industry:

> 'The real strength and all the resources of a country ever have sprung, and ever must spring, from the *labour* of its people'. 'The people were those who had built our towns, who had made England what she is.'[4]

In this way the Chartist arguments exploited the opposition between masters and men in Lancashire:

> 'The labourer has a right to receive an adequate remuneration for his toil, before the landowner, whose soil he cultivates, or the master whose goods he manufactures, is entitled to receive rent or profit.'

---

[1] *Manchester Guardian*, 26 Sept. 1838.
[2] W. C. Taylor, *Tour in the Manufacturing Districts of Lancashire* (2nd edn, 1842), pp. 315–16.
[3] *Manchester Guardian*, 6 Dec.; *Manchester and Salford Advertiser*, 9 Dec. 1837.
[4] *Manchester and Salford Advertiser*, 15 Sept. 1838; 2 Jan. 1841.

These, the Chartist leaders asserted, were 'the rights of popular industry'.[1]

Emphasis on the essential opposition between masters and men was thus the fundamental device of the Lancashire Chartist leaders. They had tried the same approach with some success during the Trade Union, Anti-Poor Law, and Ten Hour agitations of the mid-30's, all of which merged into Chartism.

The cotton masters had opposed all three movements staunchly. Their *laissez-faire* principles would not allow interference in factory hours or permit trade-union combinations. As for the New Poor Law, it seemed to them eminently calculated to make the poor stand on their own feet, and therefore essentially in the spirit of *laissez-faire*. Such views made it easy for the working-class leaders to exploit the theme of class conflict. 'The hand-loom weavers, the poor of Great Britain and Ireland, and the factory children', declared Edward Nightingale early in 1838, 'were enslaved by their masters'. This condition of slavery would not be ended until a Ten Hours Act and a minimum wage for weavers had been secured, and the New Poor Law repealed.[2] The masters, asserted O'Connor at a trade-union meeting, fought 'the battle against labour'[3]: they were 'ready and willing', declared R. J. Richardson, 'to grasp at the hard earnings of the poor'.[4] The three movements were thus surrounded by an atmosphere of conflict between masters and men. And when in 1838 they merged into Chartism, they carried this atmosphere of conflict with them.

When the masters went on in 1838 to build up the Anti-Corn Law League most Chartists regarded it from the start as a great rival to their own movement. They refused to accept as sincere its professed motives and arguments. The masters maintained, for example, that free trade in corn would expand foreign markets and therefore increase both profits and wages. But this argument, the Chartist leaders replied, was only half sincere; the masters certainly expected higher profits from repeal of the corn laws, but they also expected not higher but lower wages:

'Why do the liberal manufacturers howl so lustily for a repeal of the corn laws? — Because with the reduced price of corn, they will be

---

[1] *Manchester and Salford Advertiser*, 19 Dec. 1840, quoting from a *Sun* correspondent.
[2] *Ibid.*, 5 May 1838.   [3] *Ibid.*, 23 Dec. 1837.
[4] *Ibid.*, 7 Oct. 1837.

enabled to reduce the wages of the working man, in order that they may compete with foreigners who live upon potatoes.'[1]

This was the real purpose, the Chartists asserted, of the 'hollow-hearted scheming of the millowners'.[2]

The Chartist opponents of the Anti-Corn Law League were divided into two groups, complete protectionists and qualified free traders. The protectionists were much the smaller group of the two. Their Chartism was essentially reactionary. They believed that the evils of which the operatives complained were due not to agricultural protection but to machinery:

'The corn laws were not the cause of the evils and sufferings of the labouring classes . . . . So long as the working classes had not the power of limiting the use of machinery, and controlling the grasping capitalist in his selfishness after wealth, cheap bread meant low wages, for machinery would multiply in proportion as trade increased, and by its competition with human labour, enable the capitalist to put all the profits of cheap food into his own purse.'

With this typical argument — more trade more machinery, more machinery less wages — James Leach interrupted an Anti-Corn Law lecture at Oldham in 1841.[3]

Much more numerous than such Chartist protectionists were the qualified free traders. They accepted that corn law repeal was a desirable reform, but contended that all other taxes and impositions which pressed upon the poor ought to be removed at the same time. The corn law should not be repealed by itself, just because it happened to press on masters as well as on operatives:

'Let these men know, that, if it suit them to have a repeal of the corn law, it will also suit you to have with it that of the malt tax, and the excise duties on all the necessaries of life, that we may drink as well as eat cheaply.'

And to this general repeal, the Chartist free traders went on, must be added a Radical political reform:

'Let us teach them, that we will have these things; and to enable us to keep them once gotten, we will have universal suffrage in local as well as general government.'[4]

To such sweeping reform most Anti-Corn Law League supporters

[1] *Ibid.*, 20 Mar. 1841.   [2] *Ibid.*, 5 June 1841.
[3] *Anti-Bread-Tax Circular*, 21 Apr. 1841.
[4] *Manchester Guardian*, 21 Dec. 1839.

were, of course, firmly opposed, and in consequence the hostility between the Chartist free traders and the League was no less than the hostility between the Chartist protectionists and the League.

This hostility expressed itself chiefly in the interruption of League meetings. '[The Leaguers] have not had a meeting', admitted a League supporter in 1842, 'where the public were admitted, which has not been upset by the chartists; the resolutions of the league being negatived, and one in favour of the charter being substituted.'[1] At a meeting of the League in Manchester in March 1841, for example, the Chartists attended in force and seem to have successfully forced one of their own nominees into the chair in place of the mayor of Manchester.[2]

Thus the agitation of the Anti-Corn Law League only added to the atmosphere of class difference in Lancashire. The operatives refused to believe that the employers in agitating for repeal of the corn laws genuinely had the interests of their workpeople at heart.[3]

The burden of the National Debt — 'the debt mis-called "national" '[4] — was a particular theme of Chartist grievance, and it too had its place in the pattern of Chartist class conflict in Lancashire. 'The debt that was originally borrowed has been paid off seven times over', wrote John Campbell, secretary to the National Charter Association, in 1841, 'yet the producers have to pay and repay this debt without ever stopping.'[5] The poor, the Chartists contended, were in the hands of unscrupulous middle-class speculators. It was these speculators who had helped to bring distress upon the people: 'the blood and bones of thousands of our fellow-creatures,' declared the Manchester Universal Suffrage Association, 'the miserable inhabitants of the manufacturing districts, are yearly smeltered (sic) into gold to feed the voracious and never-satisfied appetites of sagacious speculators and money-mongers.'[6]

---

[1] Ibid., 3 Sept. 1842.
[2] Manchester Times, Manchester and Salford Advertiser, Northern Star, 20 Mar. 1841.
[3] See below, pp. 343-9.
[4] Manchester Guardian, 20 Jan. 1840.
[5] J. Campbell, An Examination of the Corn and Provision Laws (?1841), p. 62.
[6] Manchester and Salford Advertiser, 21 July 1838. 'In 1792 there were not more than 30 Lunatic Asylums in England and Wales, now there are above 300, an awful proof of the ravages made upon human reason by the false pride and inflated notions of prosperity entertained by rag-money speculators.' (R. J. Richardson, Exposure of the Banking and Funding Systems (1841), p. 32.)

Thus yet another grievance was added to the many which the operatives of Lancashire felt they had against the middle classes 'They said the national debt arose out of the wars,' remarked Bronterre O'Brien at a Chartist lecture in Manchester; 'it was no such thing. It arose with the middle classes of society.'[1]

The differences between masters and men were political as well as economic in character. To the operatives the great Reform Act of 1832 had come by 1838 to seem like a great betrayal. They had helped the middle classes into power: they had expected that in return the middle classes would help to ease their burdens. But this expectation had not been realised. 'The radical reformers', declared Joseph Fitton, a veteran Lancashire reformer, in 1838 'thought they saw a decided improvement in the reform bill on the old system, and they gave up their abstract principles of radicalism at the time, on the understanding that, if insufficient, they were to have something substantial.' But they had waited six years 'for the blessings of the reform bill without receiving any advantage'. They had been driven therefore to take up the Charter: 'they were driven to the position at which they first started from — he meant universal suffrage, annual parliaments, vote by ballot, and no property qualification.'[2]

These Chartist political demands were as unacceptable to most of the Lancashire merchants and manufacturers as their economic philosophy. Annual parliaments, wrote the *Manchester Guardian*, would only increase 'the expense, the trouble, and the turmoil of electioneering'; payment of members would bring 'the lucre of private gain' into politics; and universal suffrage would give the vote 'to every drunkard and blackguard in the kingdom'. The suffrage was not a right, as the Chartists claimed: 'it is merely an expedient for obtaining good government; *that*, and not the franchise, it is to which the public have a right.'[3]

Instead of seeking the franchise, the cotton masters believed that the poor ought to seek education. Not until they were much better educated could the people reasonably lay claim to a vote. 'If the working classes desire to raise their condition', Sir Benjamin Heywood told the Manchester Mechanics' Institution in 1840, 'they must do it by exerting themselves for their own moral and

---

[1] *Manchester and Salford Advertiser*, 25 May 1839.
[2] *Ibid.*, 10 Nov. 1838.
[3] *Manchester Guardian*, 15 Nov. 1837; 23 April 1832.

ntellectual improvement. Instead of seeking, in the first instance, an extension of their political privileges from the legislature, let them seek a system of rational and liberal education for themselves and their children.'[1] 'Let the people have a good education,' declared J. E. Taylor, editor of the *Manchester Guardian*, 'and, with the habits it would induce, the bribe of the intoxicating draught would be less powerful. Till then the elective franchise could not with safety be extended.'[2]

To most of the operatives the argument that they should be educated before they could act seemed merely a specious sidetrack. The poor were not too ignorant, they felt, to judge of the thing that mattered, their own depressed condition. The poor needed the franchise to protect themselves much more than did the rich, 'for a rich man's riches would protect him, but the poor man wanted the franchise to protect his poverty.'[3] Nor in any case, the Chartist leaders flattered their hearers, were the poor so very ignorant: 'if education means any thing, it means the acquirement of knowledge, and have you not as much knowledge as the present £10 electors of England?'[4]

Such assertions naturally did not convince the middle-class merchants and manufacturers, and they remained firmly convinced throughout the Chartist period that until the poor were better educated there could be no question of a democratic electoral system in England.

They were convinced also of another more practical Chartist danger. The Chartist threat to property seemed an even more urgent issue than the threat of Chartist reform. The prospect of a National Convention, wrote the *Manchester Guardian* in December 1838, was nothing like so serious as the prospect of local violence and destruction of property: 'this is the really dangerous and alarming symptom of the present agitation; because the objects sought by it are present to the view, and palpable to the understandings of those who are incited to mischief.' The Chartist leaders, the *Guardian* believed, hoped 'to bribe the poor to aid their designs, by holding out hopes of wholesale plunder and confiscation'.[5]

How serious the threats of the Chartist leaders really were is

---

[1] Sir B. Heywood, *Addresses delivered at the Manchester Mechanics' Institution* (1843), p. 121.
[2] *Manchester Times*, 29 Sept. 1838.   [3] *Northern Star*, 25 July 1840.
[4] *Manchester Guardian*, 26 Sept. 1838.   [5] *Ibid.*, 19, 22 Dec. 1838.

questionable, as we will see later. But the cotton employers treated them as serious enough, and thus yet another factor of division was created between masters and men in Lancashire.

Closely related to this fear of violence was the police question. The establishment of a borough police force in Manchester in 1839 was strongly opposed by the local Chartists. The 'blue bottles', the 'Bourbon police' were a logical consequence, the Chartists realised, of the incorporation of Manchester in 1838, which they had also opposed. All corporations, R. J. Richardson told a meeting of ley-payers called to oppose the Police Bill in 1839, were 'bad in principle, and worse in practice':

'... If suffered to spread over the land corporations would be the means of centralising that despotic power which was making rapid strides over the land. The means of centralisation were a brutal police force in every large town ... this armed police force would for ever act against the people.'[1]

In opposing incorporation and the new police the Chartists were closely associated with the local Manchester Tories. 'Ultra-tories and ultra-radicals,' wrote the *Guardian*, 'conservatives and chartists, were banded together apparently on the most friendly and familiar terms.'[2] To both Tories and Chartists the reorganisation of local government under the Municipal Corporations Act was a hated innovation, almost as hated as the New Poor Law against which they had also agitated together. To the middle-class manufacturers of Manchester, on the other hand, incorporation seemed a logical piece of rationalisation in local government, not least because it gave to them control of local affairs; while the new police force, which displaced the medieval watch system and the handful of constables controlled by the local Police Commission, seemed a necessary creation to protect their property from expected Chartist violence. The incorporation and police questions were therefore two further issues dividing masters from men in Manchester. 'Sheer hatred of the middle-class men', wrote the *Manchester Times* of the Tory-Chartist alliance against incorporation, '[had] caused the extremes to meet.'[3]

Many factors thus contributed to turn class cleavage in Lancashire into active Chartist class conflict — incorporation, the new

[1] *Ibid.*, 10 Aug. 1839.   *Ibid.*
[3] *Manchester Times*, 8 Dec. 18

police, middle-class fear of violence, the National Debt, the opposition of the cotton masters to the Six Points and their support for
the New Poor Law, their opposition to the trade-union and Ten
Hours movements, and above all, their seeming callousness in the
face of serious economic distress among their operatives. Not all
this pattern of conflict between masters and men was appreciated
by all the operatives; many of them were too ill-educated or too
hungry to make such a coherent analysis. But the *feeling* of class
conflict, if not its rationalisation, was there nonetheless. It under-
lay the whole story of Chartism in Lancashire.

III

It is against this background that we must set the story of Chartism in Lancashire. At every stage in its rise and decline we will find
the class issue paramount, aggravated usually by economic distress.

Chartism in Lancashire had a long history behind it. The Radical
tradition had been strong in the area ever since the 1790's, when
Thomas Walker and a group of middle-class reformers established
the Manchester Constitutional Society. This middle-class agitation
had failed, in part because of working-class opposition: the Manchester operatives of the 1790's were intensely 'loyal'.[1] During the
Napoleonic Wars, however, their loyalty had collapsed under the
pressure of economic distress and they themselves turned to reform. The movement developed which culminated in the celebrated
Peterloo Massacre of 1819, an event the memory of which remained a great political force in Lancashire even after the Chartist
period had ended.[2] After Peterloo local Radical agitation subsided
for some ten years until the Reform Bill crisis. The Manchester
Political Unions were then very active, a working-class Union being
supported mainly by weavers and a lower middle-class Union
mainly by shopkeepers.[3] In the wake of the Reform agitation came
the trade-union, Ten Hours, and Anti-Poor Law agitations of the
early and mid-30's. These three movements were the immediate
predecessors of the Chartist agitation in the area and they merged
into it: they are therefore especially important in the present context. R. J. Richardson, who in the mid-30's was secretary both of

[1] A. Prentice, *Historical Sketches and Personal Recollections of Manchester* (2nd
edn, 1851), Ch. I.
[2] See my book, *Peterloo* (1958).
[3] See A. Briggs, 'The Background of the Parliamentary Reform Movement in
Three English Cities', *loc. cit.*

the Manchester Operative Trades Union and the South Lanca
shire Anti-Poor Law Association, became in 1838 secretary of the
new Manchester Political Union and an active Chartist. He pub
licly repudiated his own Anti-Poor Law Association, declaring that
there could be no hope of effecting repeal until the Charter was
achieved.[1] Lancashire Chartism represented a desperate and des
pairing attempt by the operatives to improve the grim conditions
of industrial life.

The mood of despair prevailed throughout. Despair spurred the
operatives to take up Chartism in the hope of improving their con
ditions, but despair with Chartism itself quickly undermined what
ever prospects of success the movement might have had. This cycle
of despair, hope in Chartism, and then despair again was twice
gone through, in 1838-9 and again in 1841-2. Cooke Taylor des
cribed the atmosphere in Stockport in the early summer of 1842
when for a second time despair with Chartism was setting in. The
operatives of Stockport, he wrote, had become 'a broken-spirited
and broken-hearted population; their despair has assumed the form
of listlessness and apathy; words of hope are received with a
shake of the head and a melancholy smile. "All that remains for
me is to lay down and die" was the expression of a fine though
faded young woman, when I expressed a hope that times would yet
mend.'[2]

The first symptoms of Chartism in the area came early in 1837.
On 22 March 1837 a meeting in favour of all Six Points of the
Charter was held in Stockport, though the Charter was not men
tioned by name.[3] A month later a meeting was held in Manchester
to petition for annual parliaments, universal suffrage, and the bal
lot;[4] and in July after the end of the official proceedings for the
nomination of candidates in the general election, O'Connor and
O'Brien addressed the working-class remnant of the meeting in
favour of 'democratic principles', probably the principles of the
Charter.[5] Russell's 'Finality' declaration at the end of the year
further stimulated democratic feeling. At a meeting of a body call
ing itself the Salford Reform Association on 5 December, a resolu
tion was passed in favour of the ballot, universal suffrage, and short
parliaments even though the Association does not seem to have

[1] Driver, *op. cit.*, pp. 395-6.   [2] Taylor, *op. cit.*, p. 186.
[3] *Manchester and Salford Advertiser*, 25 Mar. 1837.
[4] *Ibid.*, 29 Apr. 1837.   [5] *Ibid.*, 29 July 1837.

been an ultra-Radical society.[1] More certainly Chartist were two bodies founded in 1838, the Manchester Universal Suffrage Association and the Manchester Political Union (the M.P.U. may have been merely a continuation of the Suffrage Association under another name).[2] The M.P.U. was quite a 'respectable' society; its chairman in the autumn of 1838 was J. W. Hodgetts, a manufacturing chemist, and two of its secretaries (who seem to have changed frequently) were R. J. Richardson, a printer already mentioned, and Richard Cobbett, a solicitor and son of the great William: Archibald Prentice, chief proprietor of the *Manchester Times*, was also a member.[3] The Union met every Monday during the autumn of 1838 in the Carpenters' Hall, Manchester, to discuss the progress of reform. 'Peace and goodwill', it has been written, 'fairly saturated its objects and rules.' Members were especially 'to bear in mind that the strength of our Society consists in the *Peace*, *Order*, *Unity* and *Legality* of our proceedings, and to consider all persons as enemies who shall in any way invite or promote violence, discord, or division, or any illegal or doubtful measures'.[4] The influence of the M.P.U. in Lancashire during the second half of 1838 was very great, and it was around this body that Lancashire Chartism first crystallised.

The greatest achievement of the M.P.U. was a monster Chartist meeting held on Kersal Moor, near Manchester, on 24 September 1838. This meeting was the greatest of a series of large-scale Chartist demonstrations held during the summer of 1838. It had a dual purpose, to demonstrate the strength of the new Chartism to the upper and middle classes and the Government, and to elect local delegates to the Chartist National Convention. Richardson and James Wroe, a veteran Radical of the Peterloo period, were chosen by the meeting as the Lancashire delegates to the Convention.

As a demonstration, the meeting was a great success. There was an impressive array of speakers and delegates, representing all parts of the Chartist world — Birmingham, the L.W.M.A., Newcastle, Leeds, and many other places. John Fielden was in the chair, Stephens and O'Connor were the chief speakers. All the

---

[1] *Manchester Guardian*, 6 Dec.; *Manchester and Salford Advertiser*, 9 Dec. 1837.
[2] An Address from the M.U.S.A. appeared in the *Manchester and Salford Advertiser* for 21 July 1838 after which no further mention is made of the society.
[3] Prentice seconded a resolution to 'watch closely' the Anti-Poor Law crisis at Todmorden in November 1838. (*Ibid.*, 1 Dec. 1838.)
[4] J. West, *History of Chartism* (1920), pp. 97–8.

South Lancashire Chartists seem to have flocked to the meeting;
Political Unions came in from Stockport, Royton, Crompton,
Ashton, Dukinfield, Leigh, Rochdale, Middleton, Bury, and Bolton, as well as a host of craft trade unions.[1] The *Manchester Guardian* estimated that about 3,500 trade-unionists marched in procession and about 1,300 members of Political Unions. Just how many
people attended apart from these genuine Chartist enthusiasts is
more doubtful. The *Guardian* thought that about 30,000 people
were present in all, but the *Morning Advertiser* believed the total to
be nearer 300,000. Archibald Prentice reckoned after careful calculation that nearly 50,000 people attended, and this was perhaps the
most accurate estimate. Certainly more people went to the meeting
than to any other in the area since Peterloo. The memory of that
outrage was not forgotten: the banners carried at Peterloo were
carried again to Kersal Moor.[2]

The great support given to the meeting was the consequence of
widespread economic distress. Stephens, in the remarks already
quoted, voiced the feelings of most of his audience when he said
that the Charter was really a knife and fork question. 'It was em-
phatically a meeting of the Trades,' wrote the *Manchester Advertiser*:

'— of the industrious artisans and labourers of Lancashire . . . with a
view to the effecting of those political changes which shall arrest their
rapidly downward progress, and secure to them something like a
reasonable proportion of those benefits which their own skill and industry so abundantly provide for others.'[3]

By 'others' the Chartists of Lancashire meant especially their own
employers: the theme of class conflict was ever-present.

For the rest of 1838 meetings were held regularly throughout the
area, many of them by torchlight. At these torchlight meetings the
restraint reflected in the rules of the M.P.U. began to be cast aside.
'The psychological effects of large crowds and excited speakers

[1] The prominence of the trade unions at this first great Chartist meeting is
worth noting: it emphasises the link between the trade-union agitation of the
early and mid-30's and the Chartist agitation. The following trades were represented: United Trades, Tailors, Smiths and Wheelwrights, Dyers, Joiners, Fustian Shearers, Callenderers, Painters, Men's Boot and Shoemakers, Marble
Masons, Masons, Ladies' Shoemakers, Labourers, Bricklayers, Marble Polishers
and Sawyers, Spinners, Farriers. (*Manchester Guardian*, 26 Sept. 1838).
[2] *Ibid.*, 26 Sept. 1838; *Manchester Times, Manchester and Salford Advertiser*,
29 Sept. 1838.
[3] *Ibid.*

vere emphasised by the eerie surroundings; it was but a short step
rom torchlight meetings to factory burning.'[1] He had preached
peace all his life, O'Connor told a meeting at Rochdale in Nov-
mber, but at the same time he was always prepared for war. 'One
of those torches (pointing at one near at hand) was worth a thousand speeches: it spoke a language so intelligible that no one could
misunderstand.'[2]

Middle-class opinion in Manchester became thoroughly alarmed
by these torchlight demonstrations. The Kersal Moor meeting in
September had not disturbed the editor of the *Guardian* over-
much: he had never seen 'any large assemblage in which there was
less appearance of excitement, or community of feeling with the
speakers'. But the torchlight meetings during the autumn completely changed his attitude. The magistrates and the Government,
he wrote urgently in December, were too lethargic: there was
danger of 'incalculable mischief in the manufacturing districts'.[3]

Certainly the torchlight meetings were noisily impressive. It
seems probable, however, that their violent language, far from encouraging a Chartist revolt, actually led only to a decline in Chartist
strength during the winter of 1838–9. There is evidence that physical force doctrines drove away far more operatives from the
Chartist cause than they attracted to it, and that the Chartists by
the spring of 1839 had begun to lose that large volume of unorganised support which had made the Kersal Moor meeting so successful.

The Chartist leaders themselves soon began to quarrel over the
physical force question. Serious dissension broke out within the
M.P.U. R. J. Richardson, who had been sent as delegate to the
National Convention, was replaced early in May by another delegate. He was denounced as too moderate, as 'middle-class'; several
other leaders were rejected for the same reasons. 'One would certainly have thought', commented the *Guardian*, 'that such politicians as Nightingale, Willis and R. J. Richardson went far enough
to satisfy anybody; but such appears not to be the fact.'[4]

On 6 May 1839 a special meeting of North of England delegates
had to be called to revive a spirit of union within the Chartist

[1] Hovell, *op. cit.*, p. 119.
[2] *Manchester Guardian*, 10 Nov., 12 Dec. 1838.
[3] *Ibid.*, 29 Sept., 12 Dec. 1838.
[4] *Manchester and Salford Advertiser*, 11 May, *Manchester Guardian*, 8 May
1839.

ranks. The meeting became a rally of the physical force party. Edwin Butterworth expressed what he claimed were now the opinions of the Manchester Chartists:

> 'They were satisfied that petitioning would not do . . . . They were for ulterior measures, but had not adopted any specific plan. They were for supporting the national convention, and would be guided by any plan it might point out to them.'[1]

Thus the National Petition was virtually repudiated by the Chartists even before it had been rejected by the Commons, and the threat of 'ulterior measures' was brought forward in its place. To the violent language which had prevailed since the previous autumn was added by the spring of 1839 a threat of definite and probably violent action. 'Every man', declared William Benbow, 'and every boy of twelve years of age, should have a stilletto a cubit long, to run into the guts of any who should attempt to oppose them.'[2]

But if exponents of physical force, or at least exponents of the *threat* of physical force, were now taking control of the M.P.U. and of Lancashire Chartism, there is no evidence that support for physical force was spreading among the majority of Lancashire operatives. On the contrary, for many the trend was now away from the violence which Chartism had come to imply. 'This morning', wrote Sir Charles Napier, the new military commander in the north, on 11 May, 'I hear the Chartists have told off thirty men to fall on each soldier. But I have also heard of a society among the labourers for assisting each other when out of work, where a fine is inflicted on any man who speaks about Chartism.' 'The people', he wrote three days later, 'are tired of the physical-force party, and if magistrates and armed associations would but give them courage they would reject the violent Chartists.'[3] The Chartist extremists, he believed, were few in number; they could easily be overpowered by the local authorities. The tense atmosphere in the area was due not to widespread support for Chartist violence, but to exaggerated middle-class alarm.

The most striking evidence of the decline in Chartist influence was the comparative failure of a second Kersal Moor demonstration held on Whit Saturday, 25 May 1839. The extremists now in control of the M.P.U. had had high hopes of this meeting. At the

---

[1] *Manchester and Salford Advertiser*, 11 May 1839.
[2] *Manchester Guardian*, 24 April 1839; Hovell, *op. cit.*, p. 135.
[3] Sir W. F. P. Napier, *Life and Opinions of General Sir C. J. Napier* (1857) Vol. II, pp. 32–3, 34.

delegate meeting of 6 May, William Tillman, the new secretary of the Union, had declared (with significant emphasis on the class theme) that the Chartists intended 'to show the cotton lords of Manchester that they could get up a grand demonstration; . . . he hoped they should present at the time, not only glittering banners, but a bolder front in "a wall of flesh" that should be a terror to their oppressors'.[1] But in the event, the audience at this second meeting was markedly smaller than that at the first Kersal Moor meeting in September; Napier estimated that not more than 30,000 people were present in all.[2] And of these 30,000 the greater part, remarked *The Times*, seemed to be more interested in the horse races which followed the meeting than in the meeting itself.[3] One Chartist leader had told Wemyss, the local military commander, that the reformers would assemble half a million men on Kersal Moor: 'these things do not alter my opinion', commented Napier, 'that we shall have a quiet week.'[4] He was proved right: some twenty thousand fewer operatives attended the Chartist meeting in May than had attended the Chartist meeting in September.

After the second Kersal Moor meeting the Chartists turned to planning a National Holiday. This prospect spread further panic among the middle classes. 'Alarm! Trumpets! Magistrates in a fuss,' wrote Napier on 30 July, 'Troops! Troops! Troops! North, South, East, West!'[5] Such alarms took no account of the actual weakness of the Chartist position.

This weakness was tacitly admitted at a Chartist delegate meeting held at Rochdale on 25 June. The delegates at the meeting resolved to create 'a better and more efficient organisation', to adopt 'measures to prevent the further arrests of any of the advocates of the people', and 'to consider the position occupied by the convention'.[6] Desire for reorganisation, fear of arrest, doubt about the effectiveness of the National Convention — all were symptoms of the growing Chartist weakness. And despite their resolution to prevent further arrests of Chartist leaders it is instructive to notice that most of the delegates were themselves arrested during the course of the next six weeks. Timothy Higgins, the delegate from the Ashton Radical Association, was arrested on 1 July and '27 stand of arms'

[1] *Manchester and Salford Advertiser*, 11 May 1839.
[2] Napier, *op. cit.*, Vol. II, p. 39.   [3] *The Times*, 28 May 1839.
[4] Napier, *op. cit.*, Vol. II, p. 35.
[5] *Ibid.*, Vol. II, p. 66.
[6] *Manchester and Salford Advertiser*, 29 June 1839.

found in his house.[1] The Rev. W. V. Jackson, G. H. Smith, Christopher Doyle, Tillman, Linney, and Benbow, the leading Manchester extremists, were all arrested at the beginning of August.[2] 'After this only a handful of Chartist leaders were left in the district to prepare for the National Holiday.

The Chartist following was almost as restricted as the Chartist leadership. On 4 August the Chartists attended church at several towns in the area; but they were few in number when compared with the working-class populations of the towns in question — only 150 at Manchester, 1,500 at Stockport, 3,000–4,000 at Bolton, and 4,000 at Blackburn.[3] Eight days later, on 12 August and on the days following, despite the abandonment of the scheme by the National Convention, an attempt was made to start the National Holiday in the area. The Chartists paraded in most of the cotton towns, and forced several factories to close.[4] The very fact, however, that they had to go about attempting to close the factories was significant: it showed how limited the Chartist following had now become. If the Chartists had had general working-class support, the operatives would never have gone to the factories in the first place. Here a distinction can probably be drawn between the factory operatives and the domestic handloom weavers. The latter, the most distressed of all the poor, probably remained attached to Chartism long after the factory operatives had given it up, and they were probably much more ready to be attracted to desperate measures.[5] Certainly the relationship between distress and Chartism was very marked. At Rochdale and Oldham, where trade had recently improved, work continued as usual on 12 August. At Oldham an operative meeting declared that the National Holiday was unnecessary and urged that the Charter should be worked for only by peaceable means.[6] Support for the National Holiday was thus very limited; and without working class unanimity it could have no hope of success. Within a week the movement had collapsed. 'This town and its neighbourhood', reported the *Manchester Guardian* on

---

[1] *Ibid.*, 6 July 1839; Hovell, *op. cit.*, p. 158.

[2] *Manchester Guardian*, 3, 7, 10 Aug. 1839.

[3] *Ibid.*, 10 Aug. 1839; H. U. Faulkner, *Chartism and the Churches* (1916), pp. 35–6.

[4] *Manchester Guardian*, 14, 17 Aug.; *Manchester and Salford Advertiser*, 17 Aug. 1839.

[5] Taylor, *op. cit.*, pp. 68–9.

[6] *Manchester Guardian*, 14 Aug.; *Manchester and Salford Advertiser*, 24 Aug. 1839.

24 August, 'have been during the past week as quiet and peaceable as at any period within the last ten years.'

By September the Chartists themselves were admitting their failure. 'It must be admitted', Dr Fletcher of Bury told a Chartist tea party in Manchester on the 25th, 'that they had been attempting something which they had not either the strength or the wisdom to enable them to effect.' Fletcher still hinted at the use of force, but he now believed that it should be controlled locally, not by a distant National Convention: 'if the working classes would fight, they must begin themselves, and the convention must be not the father of the act, but the child of it.'[1] A month later, on 28 October, a meeting was held in Manchester to choose a council 'to act on behalf of the radicals of Manchester'. It was probably significant that the word 'Radical' was revived: 'Chartist' had lost favour. Edwin Butterworth was forced to deny the existence of 'apathy' among the working classes, blaming the Chartist failure on 'a defection on the part of the leaders'.[2] It seems certain, however, that apathy was widespread among the operatives. Economic distress was as great as ever,[3] but whereas a year before distress had moved the operatives to Chartist enthusiasm, now it left them only in a state of apathetic despair.

Early in November came the Newport rising. Whether the Lancashire extremists intended a simultaneous outbreak or whether they subsequently planned a rising to coincide with Frost's conviction, will probably never be known for certain. Hovell suggests that the Chartist leaders did plan something, but that they were unable to act because of lack of popular support.[4] And this was probably the case. At a Manchester Chartist meeting on 18 November to discuss the Newport rising the chairman regretted the smallness of the numbers attending, and Tillman, secretary of the M.P.U., condemned the apathy of the people.[5] The *Manchester Guardian* declared in January that 'a rather extensive conspiracy' had existed, but that 'the numbers and means of the conspirators' had been 'in most cases as contemptible as their plans were wild and extravagant'.[6]

---

[1] *Manchester and Salford Advertiser*, 28 Sept. 1839.
[2] *Ibid.*, 2 Nov. 1839.
[3] 'We anticipate a dreadful winter', wrote the *Manchester Times* on 23 Nov. 1839.
[4] Hovell, *op. cit.*, pp. 183–5.
[5] *Manchester and Salford Advertiser*, 23 Nov. 1839.
[6] *Manchester Guardian*, 18 Jan. 1840. Two years later Bronterre O'Brien asserted that the 'men of the north' definitely encouraged the Newport rising. 'Frost never intended that there should be an outbreak, but he had been led to

The comparative failure of the second Kersal Moor meeting, the collapse of the National Holiday, the apathetic local response to the Newport rising, all showed how rapidly the Chartist position had declined during 1839. The first phase of the Chartist movement in Lancashire was almost over. The final blow came in the spring of 1840 when most of the Chartist leaders were imprisoned.[1] The Chartist organisation was concentrated in the persons of the leaders; without them it collapsed.[2]

IV

The second phase of Chartist history had to begin therefore, with a reorganisation of the movement, a reorganisation which would lay more emphasis on structure and less on personalities. This took place during the twelve months from July 1840 to June 1841. A national delegate meeting was called at Manchester for 20 July 1840 to discuss the question. James Leach of Manchester (a rising figure in the movement) was in the chair.[3] Eventually, out of a host of rival schemes there emerged the National Charter Association. This Association 'with the same title, but with varying purpose' was to dominate the Chartist movement for the rest of its existence as a significant political force.[4]

The reorganised movement gradually began to find its feet. In August 1841 O'Connor was released from prison and the agitation immediately took on a further impetus. During the autumn he made a triumphal tour through the north, and on 27 September a great demonstration was held in his honour at Manchester. Between 2,500 and 3,000 members of Chartist Associations and trade unions marched in procession to the meeting. Here was a striking indication of the revival of organised Chartist strength.[5]

O'Connor's success was not, however, unqualified. His quarrel with O'Connell which had deep roots[6] was revived over the corn

---

expect that in case he was forced to anything of that kind, he should have the sympathy and support of other parts of the country, and the parties who made him believe this were those who sacrificed him' (*Manchester and Salford Advertiser*, 11 Dec. 1841).

[1] Rosenblatt, *op..cit.*, pp. 205–6.
[2] Hovell, *op. cit.*, p. 188.
[3] *Northern Star*, 25 July 1840.
[4] Hovell, *op. cit.*, p. 197.
[5] *Manchester and Salford Advertiser, Manchester Times, Northern Star*, 2 Oct. 1841.
[6] See above, p. 10. See also E. L. H. Glasgow, 'Feargus O'Connor: Irishman and Chartist' (Unpublished M.A. Thesis, Manchester University ,1950), p. 41.

law question. Whereas O'Connor vigorously opposed the Anti-Corn Law League, O'Connell quite enthusiastically supported it. As a result, rival O'Connorite and O'Connellite factions grew up among the Irish in Manchester. A few days before the demonstration to welcome O'Connor to the town the O'Connellites called a meeting by placard: 'who has been the uniform opponent', it asked, 'of any alteration of the unholy bread tax? Feargus O'Connor .... If the people are to conquer, let them be united; united they never can be while O'Connor leads.'[1] Warned by this placard the O'Connorites took steps to secure the peaceability of their meeting, for the O'Connellites had successfully broken up an earlier meeting in May.[2] They arranged for a body of police to be present at their demonstration, and the curious spectacle ensued of a Chartist meeting assembling under police protection.[3] That they should need such protection showed the strength of the O'Connellite Irish party in the area: an important section of the Manchester working class was left permanently hostile to O'Connor's Chartist campaign during the great events of the next twelve months.[4]

But despite Irish defections, the Chartist cause made rapid progress in Lancashire during the winter of 1841–2. Many cotton operatives turned for a second time to political reform in the hope of relieving their economic distresses. The revival of Chartism can be measured by the increase in the number of 'localities' of the N.C.A. — only about 80 in February 1841, about 300 by December 1841, and about 350 by April 1842.[5] Of the 300 in existence at the end of December some 60 were in Lancashire and Cheshire; Yorkshire also had 60, London about 30, and Nottingham and Derby about 25.[6] The North of England thus dominated the new movement.

---

[1] *Manchester Guardian*, 29 Sept. 1841.
[2] *Manchester and Salford Advertiser*, *Manchester Times*, 22 May 1841.
[3] *Manchester Guardian*, 29 Sept.; *Manchester and Salford Advertiser*, *Manchester Times*, *Northern Star*, 2 Oct. 1841.
[4] Faucher described the O'Connellite Irish in Manchester: 'the Irish are perpetually in a state of agitation. Often they assemble by hundreds at the corner of Oldham and Ancoats streets. One of their number reads in a loud voice the Irish news, the addresses of O'Connell, or the circulars of the Repeal Association; and afterwards, the whole is commented on without end and with great clamour, by the closely pressed crowd. They are so strictly organised, that in the twinkling of an eye, one or two thousand can be collected at any given spot' (Faucher, *op. cit.*, p. 28).
In losing the support of this highly organised section of the working class the local Chartist cause clearly lost a great deal.
[5] *Northern Star*, 24 Dec. 1841; 30 Apr. 1842.
[6] The Lancashire and Cheshire 'localities' were as follows: Redfern St., Miles Platting, Manchester Youths, Brown St., Chorlton, Tailors and Shoemakers

When in June 1841 an Executive Committee of the N.C.A. wa
elected, three of its six members were Lancashire men, McDouall
Leach, and John Campbell (the secretary), as well as Abel Hey
wood, the treasurer.[1] Chartism had become increasingly centred i
the north since 1839, and Manchester was the metropolis of th
north.

The 'localities' of the N.C.A. found important allies in the craf
trade unions. Sixty-four trade-union delegates attended a Chartis
meeting at Manchester in March 1842.[2] The combination o
working-class political and industrial organisations which ha
been so prominent in 1838–9, was thus revived once again.

On 12 April the National Convention met in London. James
Leach, the delegate from South Lancashire, was elected vice-chair
man. 'Chartism', he told the Convention, 'never stood better i
this district than it did at present.' Over 300,000 people, he claimed
had signed the National Petition in his area.[3] This represented a
quarter or more of the total population; clearly, even allowing fo
exaggeration, the Chartist petition had received very extensive
working-class support in Lancashire.

But despite this widespread support the National Petitio
achieved nothing. It was thrown out of Parliament, and once more

---

[all in Manchester]; Lancaster; Preston; Chorley; Liverpool; Prescot; Warrington
Mottram; Hyde; Stalybridge; Ashton; Mossley; Millbottom; Oldham; Shaw;
Newton Heath; Failsworth; Rochdale; Milnrow; Radcliffe; Accrington; Pilking-
ton; Prestwich; Wigan; Eccles; Burnley; Colne; Leigh; Chowbent; Salford
Delph; Stockport; Chester; Nantwich; Davyhulme; Royton; Glossop (Derby).
New Mills (Derby); Bolton; Bury; Bacup; Middleton; Heywood; Lees; Black-
burn; Openshaw; Lower Moor; Birkenhead; Dukinfield (*Northern Star*, 24 Dec.
1841).

[1] *Ibid.*, 5 June 1841.
[2] Delegates attended from the Bricklayers, the Silk Dyers, the Glass-cutters,
the Engravers, the Mechanics, the Joiners, the Calico Printers, the Shoe-makers
and Tailors, the Weavers, the Smallware weavers, the Colliers, the Overlookers,
the Fustian Cutters, the Painters, etc. (*Ibid.*, 19 Mar. 1842.)
[3] *Northern Star*, 23 Apr. 1842. T. S. Duncombe in presenting the National
Petition named the areas which had contributed 10,000 or more signatures. They
included:

Manchester	99,680	Bolton	18,500
Rochdale	19,600	Salford	19,600
Stalybridge and District	10,000	Stockport	14,000
North Lancashire	52,000	Preston and District	24,000
Oldham	15,000	Ashton	14,200
Macclesfield and Suburbs	10,000	Wigan	10,000
		Burnley and District	14,000

These were thus the main centres of Lancashire and Cheshire Chartism. London and its suburbs, according to Duncombe, contributed some 200,000 signatures; the Lancashire and Cheshire contribution, it will be seen, was more than
half as large again. *Parliamentary Debates*, 3rd ser., LXII (1842), 1375.

Chartism was left face to face with its own ineffectiveness. Once more the cotton operatives began to despair and to realise that Chartism could never bring relief for their distress; and once more the movement went into a rapid decline. In June 1842 a new Executive for the N.C.A. was elected; only 205 'localities' voted; their number had fallen by more than a third since the spring.[1]

Yet although by the summer of 1842 despair about the prospects of Chartism was setting in, as it had done in 1839, this time despair did not lead to apathetic acceptance of distress but (after a pause) to direct industrial action.

Economic distress was now at its peak.

'Any man passing through the district', wrote the *Manchester Times* on 9 July, 'and observing the condition of the people, will at once perceive the deep and ravaging distress that prevails, laying industry prostrate, desolating families, and spreading abroad discontent and misery where recently happiness and content were enjoyed. The picture which the manufacturing districts now present is absolutely frightful. Hungry and half-clothed men and women are stalking through the streets begging for bread.'

'Stockport to Let', one wag chalked on the door of an empty house in Stockport: one house in eight was empty in the town.[2] A soup kitchen in Manchester was dispensing a thousand gallons of soup per day to the poor.[3] This was the background to the Plug Plot strikes.

The spark which set off the explosion was a threatened reduction in wages, already much reduced. A meeting of protest was held on Mottram Moor on Sunday, 7 August at which some 8,000–10,000 operatives were present. The meeting passed resolutions calling for the Charter and for 'a fair day's wage for a fair day's work'.[4] Events soon proved that this latter demand was much the more widely supported. All work had ceased in Ashton on the 5th, and on the 9th the strikers there marched into Manchester. Within hours the strike had spread throughout the cotton districts. In nearly every town work stopped and excited meetings of operatives assembled to demand fair wages and fair hours of work. A meeting of about two hundred trade delegates gathered in

---

[1] *Northern Star*, 25 June 1842.
[2] T. E. Ashworth, *An Account of the Todmorden Poor Law Riots . . . and the Plug Plot* (p.p., Todmorden, 1901), p. 19; Census 1841.
[3] *Manchester Guardian*, 21 Jan. 1843.
[4] *Ibid.*, 10 Aug. 1842.

E

Manchester on 11 August and demanded a ten-hour working day and fair rates of wages for both weaving operatives and factory workers; detailed wage rates were drawn up for every branch of the trade.[1]

Thus within a few days a great and spontaneous upsurge of feeling had taken place: extreme suffering had led to sudden action.

'The people in the neighbouring towns were entirely ignorant of what was coming; there was no combination among them to have a general strike; no deputies had travelled to arrange it, and yet there was a bond of union so firm, that by almost universal consent the movement was sanctioned and adopted. This bond was stronger than a written and sealed bond; it was the bond of suffering and of servitude; it was the feeling that life was become a round of helpless drudgery, or the endurance of forced idleness with want and starvation.'[2]

The strike was thus a sudden economic explosion, not the beginning of a planned political revolution. There was no causal connection between Chartism and the outbreak. Many of the strike meetings did indeed pass vague resolutions in favour of the Charter, but the audiences were much more interested in work and wages than in Chartism. The Chartists made no attempt to claim the credit for the outbreak, but merely attempted to exploit it once it had occurred. By a coincidence a national Chartist delegate meeting had been called to meet in Manchester in the third week of August; O'Connor, McDouall, Cooper, and most of the national leaders of the movement were present. The meeting passed a resolution strongly urging the strikers to remain out until the Charter had been won: 'while the Chartist body did not originate the present cessation from labour,' it declared, the Chartist delegates none the less wished to express 'their deep sympathy with their constituents, the working men now on strike; . . . we strongly approve of the extension and continuance of the present struggle till the PEOPLE'S CHARTER becomes a legislative enactment'.[3] This appeal does not seem, however, to have had much effect. Its impact was seriously undermined by differences within the Chartist leadership. O'Connor advocated peaceable action in support of the strikes and the Charter. McDouall, on the other hand, was all for physical force; he urged the people to 'leave the decision to the God

[1] *Manchester Guardian*, 13, 17, 27 Aug.; *The Times*, 23, 26, 27 Aug. 1842.
[2] *Anti-Bread-Tax Circular*, 6 Oct. 1842.   [3] *Northern Star*, 20 Aug. 1842.

of justice and of battle'.[1] The Chartists were thus seriously divided at a vital moment, and their division lost them whatever chance they may have had of gaining control of the strike movement. Nothing was more remarkable, observed the *North of England Magazine* in retrospect, 'than the feebleness and incapacity of the Chartist body' during the Plug Plot crisis.[2] Not that their ineffectiveness saved the Chartist leaders from arrest; by the beginning of October virtually all of them, national and local leaders alike, had been arrested.[3]

To escape arrest McDouall fled the country. His appeal to physical force had met with almost no response: the strike movement in Lancashire was remarkable for its peacefulness. Plugs had been pulled out of factory boilers (hence the name given to the movement), but this was generally the limit of popular violence. 'The object has not been to destroy, but simply to stop,' remarked the *Manchester Times* on 20 August; 'and the simplest and least destructive manner has been chosen . . . . While at a distance Manchester is thought to be in a state of siege, the whole town may be traversed without a single act of violence being witnessed.'

But peacefulness could not in itself make the strike movement a success. Bound by *laissez-faire* economic beliefs and confident in the support of the military,[4] the cotton masters offered no concessions. Reluctantly but steadily the operatives returned to work. Some mills in Manchester were already back in production as early as 17 August. Within a month the great strike had petered out.[5]

v

The fact that the Plug Plot strikes could break out without Chartist assistance and the ineffective part played by the Chartist

[1] *The Times*, 19 Aug. 1842.
[2] *North of England Magazine*, Sept. 1842, p. 499.
[3] *Manchester Guardian*, 1, 5 Oct. 1842; Hovell, *op. cit.*, p. 262.
[4] Over 2,000 soldiers with 6 pieces of artillery in Manchester alone (Hovell, *op. cit.*, p. 262).
[5] *Manchester Guardian*, 20 Aug. 21 Sept. 1842.
The London protectionist press (and also the *Manchester Courier*) claimed that the Plug Plot strikes in Lancashire were the work of the Anti-Corn Law League. *The Times*, for example, carried the headline on 12 Aug.: 'The Anti-Corn Law League Riots'. At a meeting in Manchester on 25 Aug. Cobden, on his honour, 'either as a public man or as a private citizen', entirely denied the charge (*Manchester Guardian*, 27 Aug. 1842). When he saw that he could not gain control of the outbreak O'Connor also began to claim that the strikes were the work of the League: they were, he asserted, a device of the mill-owners to reduce wages and divert men's minds from the Charter (*Northern Star*, 20 Aug. 1842).

leaders during their course, showed how weak the Chartist movement in Lancashire had become by the summer of 1842. It was in fact destined never fully to revive again. Between 1842 and 1846 a great change came over the social atmosphere in Lancashire. The hostile feeling of the operatives towards their employers which had poisoned the social atmosphere for so long and which the Chartists had exploited so assiduously, at last began to lessen. Between 1842 and 1846 both the attitude and the aspirations of the Lancashire working classes underwent a remarkable change.

A key factor underlying this changed attitude was a revival of trade prosperity; during 1843 the severe economic distress which had prevailed since 1837 at last came to an end. 'The year 1843', wrote the *Manchester Guardian* at the beginning of the year, '. . . opens under brighter auspices. Food is much cheaper, and there is more employment.'[1] By August 1844 the paper was able to look back on twelve months during which wages had been higher than at any time 'since the memorable three years ending in 1836'.[2] Even the handloom weavers shared in the revived prosperity; by August 1844 they were earning 'quite as high wages as at any period since 1825'.[3] In Little Bolton in the first quarter of 1842 outdoor poor relief had cost over £700: for the same quarter of 1843 it cost under £300.[4] By the end of 1843, therefore, the all-important economic stimulus to Chartism had been removed. Chartism was the creed of hard times: as those hard times disappeared, so also did much of the appeal of the Charter.

But, in any case, Chartism, as we have seen, had begun to lose its appeal in Lancashire even while the distress was still at its height. In the Plug Plot movement the cotton operatives had repudiated Chartist political action and had turned to direct economic action. After the failure of the Plug Plot those operatives who (in a time of revived prosperity) were still inclined to agitate, did not revert once again to Chartism but continued to look to economic action. They turned once more to the three campaigns of the 30's which had merged into Chartism — the Ten Hours, trade-union, and Anti-Poor Law movements.

The Ten Hours campaign became prominent again early in 1844; the government produced a Factory Bill which Ashley unsuccess-

[1] *Manchester Guardian*, 4 Jan. 1843.
[2] *Ibid.*, 3 Aug. 1844.
[3] *Ibid.*, 17 Aug. 1844.
[4] *Ibid.*, 17 Jan. 1844.

fully attempted to amend into a Ten Hours Bill.[1] Lancashire was
an important centre of the renewed campaign, and significantly we
find many of the former local Chartist leaders active in the new
movement, especially Leach, Schofield, Jackson, and Doyle. These
former Chartist leaders did not expressly give up their Chartism,
but they put it very much in the background. At a meeting in Manchester in March 1844, for example, Leach declared that 'although
he would stand second to no man in the advocacy of the charter, he
did not think this a proper time for its introduction'. Doyle spoke
in much the same terms.[2] Here was a frank enough admission that
Chartism was dead as an important political force in Lancashire:
the former Chartist leaders now saw greater scope for popular agitation within the Ten Hours movement.

Alongside this revival of the Ten Hours agitation came a revival
of trade-union agitation. The craft trade unions, as we have seen,
had played a prominent part in the local Chartist movement from
1838 to 1842; with the decline of Chartism and the recovery in
trade larger-scale operative trade unions began to revive. Most
prominent of these was the Lancashire Colliers' Union, said to
have nearly 10,000 members by the end of 1844.[3] The Associated
Operative Cotton Spinners Union also flourished,[4] as well as a
Building Trades Union.[5] Clearly many Lancashire operatives had
turned from Chartism to trade unionism after 1842.[6]

Just as the trade unionism of the 30's revived, so also did the
opposition to the New Poor Law of 1834. Graham's Poor Law Act
of 1844, which in effect confirmed the provisions of the act of 1834,[7]
revived all the old bitterness in the eastern parts of the cotton district. From the end of 1844 to the end of 1845 a whole series of protest meetings was held in the centres of the new movement, Oldham, Rochdale, Ashton, and Middleton, as the time came for the
introduction of the new system. Many of the old Anti-Poor Law
leaders returned to lead the new campaign, particularly John
Fielden and James Taylor of Rochdale (formerly an active Chartist
and delegate to the National Convention of 1839). In the four

---

[1] J. L. and B. Hammond, *Lord Shaftesbury* (3rd edn, 1925), pp. 94ff.
[2] *Manchester Times*, 16 Mar. 1844.
[3] *Manchester Guardian*, 9 Oct., 27 Nov. 1844, 22 Jan. 1845.
[4] *Ibid.*, 16 Oct. 1844, 29 Jan. 1845.
[5] *Ibid.*, 20 Nov. 1844.
[6] S. and B. Webb, *History of Trade Unionism* (revised edn, 1920), pp. 186ff.
[7] S. and B. Webb, *English Local Government. English Poor Law History: Part II* (1929), I, pp. 177–9.

towns feeling ran quite as high as during the mid-30's; 'it appears
to be the prevailing opinion', wrote the *Manchester Guardian*
of the state of feeling in Rochdale, 'that some terrible calamity
is about to befal (*sic*) the defenceless inhabitants of that devoted
borough.'[1]

Thus after 1842 some of the popular energy which had gone into
support of the Chartist movement was diverted back to the three
movements which had originally merged into Chartism. Here was
part of the reason for the Chartist decline. But this was by no means
the whole story. During the years of Chartist predominance, the
Anti-Corn Law League had gathered strength, and in the 1840's
competed for popular support.

Until 1842 the attempts of the Anti-Corn Law League to win
working-class support had been largely unsuccessful. The Chartists, Cobden admitted at Manchester in August 1842, had succeeded in compelling the League 'to make our agitation a middle-
class agitation'.[2] After 1842, however, we find popular feeling
slowly coming over to support of the middle-class League. This
development helped to close the social gulf in local society. The
coming together of middle and working classes in support of repeal
of the corn laws smoothed away much of that atmosphere of social
tension which the Chartists had exploited for so long, and encouraged in its stead an atmosphere of social union between
masters and men.[3]

The cotton operatives had begun by doubting the sincerity of
their employers' enthusiasm for corn law repeal. They had believed that their masters wanted cheap bread only so that they
could pay low wages. Wages, it was thought, were linked to the
level of bread prices. If (thanks to the corn laws), the protectionists argued, prices were high, then high prices were balanced by
high wages. But between 1843 and 1846 these arguments were
doubly disproved. During the period of prosperity from 1843 to
early in 1845 though prices were low, wages were high; and during
the bad times of 1845-6 though prices were high, wages became
low. The protectionist arguments were proved fallacious: the
level of wages was not rigidly linked to the price of bread. And if
this were not so, then the cotton masters in seeking repeal of the
corn laws could not be accused of seeking only to lower the wages

---

[1] *Manchester Guardian*, 13 Sept. 1845.   [2] *Ibid.*, 27 Aug. 1842.
[3] Yet see below, pp. 366-8.

f their operatives. Perhaps, the more intelligent operatives began o argue, the claim of their masters to be seeking to benefit their workpeople as well as themselves was sincere.

'The rapid advance in the price of wheat during the last four months', wrote the *Guardian* in December 1845, '— accompanied, not as it had been alleged would be the case by an increase, but by a very evident tendency to a decline in wages, — at once convinced the intelligent working men of this district, that the object of their masters, in seeking the repeal of the corn-laws, was not to lower wages; and that employers and employed were equally interested in obtaining a plentiful supply of food.'[1]

This important change of view became apparent during the winter of 1845–6 when a spate of workmen's Anti-Corn Law meetings was held in the cotton towns. A meeting was held, for example, at Stalybridge on 11 December; it was called by a requisition 'signed by large numbers of operatives and shopkeepers' and not containing the name of a single manufacturer, 'thus showing' (commented the *Guardian*) 'the great alteration which has taken place in the minds of the working classes on this important question'.[2] 'He was once a chartist,' declared one operative at a repeal meeting in Stockport, 'but now he had seen the necessity of adopting sounder views . . . . He attributed most of the sufferings of the people to the corn-laws.'[3]

Common feeling against the corn laws thus brought masters and men together. The development of a social conscience among the employers also helped to increase friendly feeling. Manchester was in the forefront of the sanitary reform, parks, and libraries movements of the middle and late 40's. The growth of middle-class enthusiasm for social reform, observed the *Manchester Advertiser* at the end of 1844, had promoted 'the gradual advancement of a more friendly feeling between the two extreme classes'.[4]

Even *laissez-faire* economics was becoming rather less of a barrier between classes. Some masters were growing a little less rigid in their adherence to its dictates and some workmen were beginning to accept a few of its truths. At Bolton in August 1845 a remarkable tea-party was given by the operative cotton spinners to some of

[1] *Manchester Guardian*, 17 Dec. 1845.   [2] *Ibid.*
[3] *Ibid.*, 20 Dec. 1845.   [4] *Manchester and Salford Advertiser*, 28 Dec. 1844.

their employers; its purpose was 'to commemorate the great and important fact of the masters having made two advances of wages, not only without strike, but with the utmost cheerfulness and good-will'. Here was striking evidence of a more conciliatory attitude among the employers. And if conciliation was growing on one side, understanding was also growing on the other. Thanks to the 'march of intellect', declared one operative cotton spinner at the gathering, working men 'were now better able to appreciate their true position. They had begun to look at the markets, to the price of the raw material, to the amount of supply and demand'. In other words, the new political economy was beginning to be openly accepted among some of the men as well as among the masters.[1] Even the new Cotton Spinners Union, founded in 1843, was influenced by the new spirit of cordiality between masters and men. The secretary of the union declared in October 1844, that, although the union was seeking an advance in wages, it was anxious not 'to stir up that bad feeling which formerly existed between us and our employers'.[2] This feeling was reciprocated. Only two years after the Plug Plot strikes the *Manchester Guardian*, the organ of the cotton masters, was able to congratulate its readers on 'the general spirit of cordiality which prevails between the great mass of the working classes and their employers'.[3]

The class tensions on which Chartism had flourished were sinking out of sight. The people had begun to see, wrote the *Guardian*, 'that their interests and those of their employers are identical, and that the doctrines taught by Feargus O'Connor, Richard Oastler, and other firebrands of the same school, were only ministering to their evil passions and prejudices.'[4] In May 1846 the *Guardian* described the decline of Chartism in Mossley. A few years before Mossley had been a Chartist stronghold; now it was a stronghold of corn law repeal. The Chartist assembly room was closed, 'and the boards which comprised the floor, from which the Doyles, the Rosses, etc. held forth, and made known the principles of the *Northern Star*, are now converted into a resting place for swine. Some ill-natured people say, they were never used for a better purpose.'[5]

In the summer of 1846 the corn laws were at last repealed. All

[1] *Manchester Guardian*, 9 Aug. 1845.
[3] *Ibid.*, 5 Oct. 1844.   [2] *Ibid.*, 16 Oct. 1844.
[5] *Ibid.*, 9 May 1846.   [4] *Ibid.*, 9 Aug. 1845.

classes in Lancashire went wild with enthusiasm; flags were hoisted from the mills, church bells were rung. 'We wish you many years of life,' the Manchester Chamber of Commerce told Peel, 'that you may enjoy the proud fame which your patriotism so justly merits.' If Peel had lost office, declared Cobden at the final meeting of the Anti-Corn Law League, he had gained the country.[1] Certainly he had gained Lancashire.

Alongside the Anti-Corn Law agitation the Ten Hours campaign had gone steadily on. Meetings were held regularly throughout 1846 with the former Chartists Leach and Dr Fletcher of Bury very prominent. In the final struggle for the Ten Hours Bill in 1847 the Lancashire operatives played a leading part. Eighty-three memorials from Lancashire and Yorkshire factory districts were presented to Lord John Russell in the spring of that year.[2] When the bill finally passed, there was great jubilation among the factory operatives. The *Ten Hours' Advocate*, the local organ of the movement, printed the text of the bill in gold on a special sheet.[3] The Lancashire Central Short Time Committee celebrated 'the glorious success' of its efforts, and singled out Fletcher for especial congratulation for his work.[4] He had been much more successful here than in his work for the Charter.

By 1847 Fletcher was no longer a prominent Chartist; he had not persisted after the great failure of five years before. But, in fact, at the time of the passing of the Ten Hours Act Chartism was showing some signs of revival. 'An effort is now making in several quarters', noted the *Guardian* in August 1846, 'to infuse fresh life into the defunct body of Chartism.'[5] O'Connor's National Land Company had been floated at the end of 1846, and he endeavoured vigorously to secure widespread support for it in Lancashire. Every Sunday night meetings were held at the Carpenters' Hall in Manchester at which the new truths were expounded.[6]

During the latter part of 1846 and throughout 1847 the trade depression which had returned in the summer of 1845 became increasingly severe. In May 1847 the *Manchester Examiner* calculated that 84,000 operatives were working short-time and that 24,000 were unemployed; only 77,000 were working full-time.[7] The

---

[1] *Ibid.*, 1, 4, 8 July 1846.
[2] *Manchester Guardian*, 6 Mar. 1847.
[3] *Ten Hours' Advocate*, 5 June 1847.
[4] *Ibid.*, 12 June 1847.
[5] *Manchester Guardian*, 15 Aug. 1846.
[6] *Manchester Examiner*, 18 Apr. 1846.
[7] *Ibid.*, 15 May 1847.

Guardian blamed the 'torrent of Irish immigration' for increasing the pressure of distress; the Irish had brought 'their usual rags, and wretchedness, and improvidence'.[1] Cholera too was spreading. Altogether, the year 1847 was a terrible one.

The growth of distress, by the same process as ten years before, seems to have increased the appeal of Chartism. O'Connor claimed that his land scheme would bring cheap and plentiful food: 'if a man wanted cheap bread,' he told an audience at Newton in August 1847, 'he must grow it himself.'[2] To half-starved operatives such an idea necessarily had some appeal. The old theme of class rivalry too was revived. The present economic system, the Chartists told their hearers, favoured only the employers; what was needed was the Land Plan, which would make the operatives 'independent of the caprice and whim of master capitalists'.[3] A local series of lectures repeated these arguments throughout the cotton towns during the second part of 1847.

But though by the end of 1847 the Chartist movement had shown signs of revival in Lancashire, it was far from being the powerful movement of the early 40's. In its retrospect of the year, the *Manchester Guardian* was able to congratulate the operatives on the patience with which they had borne their misfortunes; the working classes, the editor went on, had at last learnt the truths of *laissez-faire* economics. Despite all the distress there had not been 'the slightest tendency to riot or outrage'; this was proof, concluded the *Manchester Examiner* writing in the same vein, that the operatives now not only understood 'the great principles by which trade is governed, but that they can appreciate the difficulties which surround the capitalists, and the efforts which have been made to lighten their pressure upon the workmen'. In short, the new spirit of social union between masters and men was standing the test of hard times.[4]

In March 1848, however, rioting broke out in Manchester. The *Examiner* had to admit that 'the profound tranquillity' had at last been broken. On 8 March an attempt was made to open a workhouse; on the following day several mills were attacked, and on the 10th there was further rioting. This was not, however, a movement

---

[1] *Manchester Guardian*, 15 May, 11 Dec.; *Manchester Examiner*, 22 May 1847.
[2] *Manchester Guardian*, 25 Aug. 1847.   [3] *Manchester Examiner*, 13 Mar. 1847.
[4] *Manchester Guardian*, 27 Oct. 1847, 1 Jan. 1848; *Manchester Examiner*, 4 Sept., 23 Oct. 1847.

in favour of the Charter; the outbreak was almost entirely the work of boys and youths. 'Not a single motive has ever been avowed,' declared the *Examiner*, 'not a single cry for change has been set up.'[1] The Chartists themselves repudiated the movement; Leach, the old Chartist leader, agreed that it was the work of 'mischievous imps and lads'.[2]

Thus, when during the 'Year of Revolutions' the peace was broken in Lancashire it was not by a Chartist revolution. Leach told his followers to assist the authorities in putting down the rioting.[3] Whether he would have countenanced violence if it had looked like being widely supported is another matter. But as it was, the larger part of the working class remained amazingly quiet:

'The working classes, generally,' wrote the *Guardian*, 'have shown the very best spirit on this occasion. Not only is there no political excitement abroad amongst them, but, so far as we can learn, there is little or none of that hostile feeling towards their employers which, on some former occasions, has given rise to disorder. In all cases, that we have heard of, they have shown a disposition to remain quietly at their work, and, generally, a great willingness to defend their own labour and the prosperity of their employers against the attacks which have been made upon both.'[4]

There was thus little danger of revolution in Lancashire. The temptation to violence, Chartist or otherwise, was staunchly resisted by the cotton operatives: the new spirit of social union enjoyed a great triumph.

The Chartists none the less still pressed on with their plans. Though their following was so much smaller, they went through the same motions as in the great days of 1838–9 and 1841–2. Another National Convention was elected, including delegates from Manchester, Stockport, Bolton, Oldham, Ashton, and Bury.[5] In support of the presentation of the National Petition on 10 April a whole spate of meetings was held during the first ten days of the month; on 10 April itself nearly every town had a meeting.[6] But when the presentation of the petition ended in fiasco the bottom

---

[1] *Manchester Guardian, Manchester Examiner*, 11 March 1848. Of fourteen people arrested for their parts in the rioting, only four were aged more than twenty.

[2] *Manchester Examiner*, 14 Mar. 1848.   [3] *Ibid*.

[4] *Manchester Guardian*, 11 Mar. 1848.

[5] *Northern Star*, 8 Apr. 1848. Daniel Donovan and James Leach were the Manchester delegates.

[6] *Manchester Guardian*, 12, 15 Apr.; *Manchester Examiner*, 11, 15 Apr. 1848.

fell out of the movement; its real weakness in Lancashire was revealed and dissolution quickly followed. After 10 April there was some talk among extremists of achieving the Charter by force, but there was limited support for such schemes. What the *Guardian* called 'make-believe demonstrations' continued until the end of the summer, but there was no real danger.[1] The few disturbances there were — chief among them the murder of a policeman at Ashton on 14 August[2] — were symptoms not of strength but of weakness. 'They were the acts of a small minority who preferred open revolt for the very reason that they were too few to effect anything by peaceful agitation.'[3] Even some of those who had remained faithful to the movement during its weakest period from 1842 to 1846 now began to give up. W. P. Roberts had stood as Chartist candidate for Blackburn at the general election of 1847, but in May 1848 he publicly repudiated the Chartist organisation:

> 'Chartists, like others,' he told a Chartist audience at Blackburn, 'ought to live and learn . . . he would live and die a chartist; he would remain in the ranks in which he had always been. At the same time he had learned, from the folly and violence and nonsense which chartists had exhibited, that there was nothing to be hoped for from chartist organisation . . . there were not 10,000 enrolled chartists in the country.'

Roberts recommended his hearers to join the new 'Little Charter' movement which Bright and Hume had started in the spring of 1848.[4] This was a movement for household rather than for universal suffrage, and for triennial rather than annual parliaments.[5] By the end of the year O'Connor himself was lending some support to the new movement and its half-measures.[6] For all practical purposes Chartism in Manchester had dissolved.

[1] *Manchester Guardian*, 3 June 1848.
[2] *Manchester Guardian, Manchester Examiner*, 19 Aug. 1848.
[3] P. W. Slosson, *The Decline of the Chartist Movement* (1916), pp. 103–4.
[4] *Manchester Examiner*, 27 May, 10 June 1848.
[5] *Ibid.*, 22 Apr. 1848; Slosson, *op. cit.*, p. 182.
[6] R. G. Gammage, *History of the Chartist Movement* (1854), p. 372.

Chapter Three

Chartism in Leeds

J. F. C. Harrison

I

The organised Chartist movement in Leeds may fairly be said to date from the early autumn of 1837. It was at a meeting on Woodhouse Moor in late August that the decision was taken to form a Leeds Working Men's Association. Cleave and Vincent, delegates from the London Working Men's Association, had spoken at the meeting, urging the Leeds men to follow the example of the metropolis;[1] and as a result a provisional committee had been elected. Three weeks later the first general meeting of the Leeds Working Men's Association was held, at which an address was given by the treasurer, John Francis Bray.[2]

The ground for the developments of September 1837 had been long prepared. Leeds in the 1830's was second only to Manchester as a centre of Radical and working-class movements in the north, and nowhere was the variety and complexity of the pattern of working-class endeavour more clearly demonstrated. Trade-union activity, Short Time Committees for factory reform, the struggle for the unstamped press, Owenism, co-operative stores, and the extension of the suffrage — all claimed the support of Leeds working men. These movements were not so much rivals competing for support, nor even complementary parts of a greater national movement, as different expressions of a general discontent and a reaching out to a more just and equitable organisation of society. The movements tended to fade into one another; and the new cause with the more urgent dynamic absorbed the energies that had previously gone into an earlier movement, which had either achieved its object, or, more usually, come up against invincible opposition. Thus it was that the Leeds Working Men's Association overshadowed earlier movements, while drawing together diverse elements from several different sources. The personalities of the new Association

---

[1] *Leeds Times*, 2 Sept. 1837.   [2] *Ibid.*, 23 Sept. 1837.

are significant not only as the political leaders of the working classes
at that time, but also as men who had participated in other movements for social betterment. In their aggregate social experience
was summed up the dynamic behind the Chartist movement in
Leeds. Who they were, and what manner of men they were, is thus
directly relevant to the nature of Chartist origins in the town.

Probably the highest common factor among the nine original
members of the committee of the Leeds Working Men's Association was previous participation in radical politics in the town.[1] Already in the years following the end of the Napoleonic Wars men
who were to become leaders of working-class causes in the 1830's
were active in the movement for political reform in Yorkshire. In
February 1819 an Association of the Friends to Radical Reform
was established in Leeds;[2] and radical literature and ideas were
flourishing in the town.[3] This agitation died down somewhat
after 1823, but was revived in the autumn of 1829 with the formation of working-class political unions. The Leeds Radical Reform
Association organised mass meetings on Hunslet Moor, invited
Cobbett to lecture in the town, and carried on a vigorous propaganda for universal suffrage, the ballot and annual parliaments.
Following a visit of Henry Hunt, the veteran hero of Spa Fields
and Peterloo, a new organisation, the Radical Political Union was
formed in November 1831; its secretary was William Rider, later
one of the original members of the committee of the Leeds Working
Men's Association, and a militant Leeds Chartist.

Until 1829 the radicals in Leeds had been on friendly terms with
Edward Baines (editor of the *Leeds Mercury*) and the Whigs
through a common opposition to the Tories. But from this time
onwards working-class suspicion of Whig industrialists, whose
cause Baines espoused, deepened, until hatred of 'Bainesocracy'

---

[1] The nine original members of the provisional committee were Robert Nicoll,
Joshua Hobson, John Francis Bray (treasurer), William Foster, William Rider,
Thomas Tannet, David Green, George White, and Robert Martin (secretary).
The chairman of the Woodhouse Moor meeting was Joshua Hobson, and the
resolution to form the Leeds W.M.A. was moved by George White and seconded
by Bray. *Leeds Times*, 2 Sept. 1837.

[2] *Leeds Mercury*, 20 Feb. 1819.

[3] James Watson, employed at this time as a warehouseman in Leeds, described
how one evening in the autumn of 1818 while passing along Briggate, 'I saw at
the corner of Union Court a bill, which stated that the Radical Reformers held
their meetings in a room in that court. Curiosity prompted me to go and hear
what was going on. I found them reading Wooler's *Black Dwarf*, Carlile's
Republican and Cobbett's *Register*'. W. J. Linton, *James Watson, a memoir* (1880),
p. 17.

made possible a Tory-Radical alliance.[1] The experiences of 1829 to 1832 disillusioned many Radicals as to the nature of the struggle for parliamentary reform, and when the newly-revived Leeds Radical Association put forward its programme in December 1835 it did so in the form of five principles — equal representation, annual parliaments, universal suffrage, vote by ballot, and no property qualifications for Members of Parliament.[2] Among the founders of the Leeds Working Men's Association, two — Joshua Hobson and Robert Nicoll (editor of the radical *Leeds Times*) — were already prominent in this Radical Association. Thus when they adopted the Six Points of the People's Charter as their official programme in the summer of 1838 the Leeds radicals were following a tradition which, in its political aspects, was already perfectly familiar to them.

In the person of Joshua Hobson, however, far more than a West Riding tradition of Radical politics was epitomised. Born at Huddersfield in 1810, Hobson received little formal education, for his mother had been left a widow with four small children to support. He was first apprenticed to a joiner, but later worked as a handloom weaver near Oldham; and while in Lancashire contributed revolutionary effusions to the local papers under the name of 'The Whistler at the Loom'.[3] Upon his return to Huddersfield he was rapidly caught up in the activities of the local Short Time Committee — an organisation which had sprung up spontaneously to support Hobhouse's bill for factory reform[4] — and on a bright Sunday morning in June 1831 he found himself one of a little deputation of Huddersfield operatives who waited upon Richard Oastler at Fixby Hall to solicit his aid in their struggle. From this memorable meeting came the 'Fixby Hall Compact', the union between Oastler and the working people of the West Riding on the great 'Factory Question'. Hobson's *Voice of the West Riding*, though originally intended as the organ of the Short Time Committees, inevitably led him into other forms of working-class

[1] For an example of this virulent anti-Whig feeling, see William Rider's pamphlet, *The Demagogue, containing extracts from the unpublished memoirs of Edward Baines, Esq. M.P.* (Leeds, 1834).

[2] *Leeds Times*, 2 Jan. 1836.

[3] The main source for biographical details of Hobson is the long obituary notice in the *Huddersfield Weekly News*, 13 May 1876. There are also some (rather inaccurate) details in D. F. E. Sykes, *History of Huddersfield and its vicinity* (1898), pp. 301–2.

[4] A similar body had also sprung up in Leeds, of which William Rider was a prominent member.

struggle. The first number of the paper appeared on 1 June 1833
and by 6 August he was already serving a six months sentence of
imprisonment in Wakefield gaol for publishing an unstamped
paper. In 1835 and 1836 he served two more imprisonments in the
same cause.[1] In the autumn of 1834 he moved to Leeds, where he
set up as a printer and publisher,[2] and for the next twelve years he
remained as the chief publisher of Radical material in the West
Riding. He printed and published the Chartist *Northern Star* from
its inception in 1837 until its removal to London in 1844, and was
also for a time editor of the paper. Likewise he printed and published Owen's *New Moral World* from 1839 to 1841 from his
Market Street premises in Leeds. His name as publisher and
printer appeared on nearly all the local Owenite and Chartist pamphlets and books of the time,[3] and he himself wrote pamphlets in
defence of Owenite Socialism.[4] Such was the background experience of one who was soon to play a dominant role in the Chartist
movement in Leeds.

A similar story could be told of the first treasurer of the Leeds
Working Men's Association. The lectures and writings of John
Francis Bray establish him as one of the most remarkable of all the
early working-class Radicals in Yorkshire. He was born at Washington in the United States in 1809.[5] His ancestors were farmers
and clothiers in the Huddersfield district, and his father had lived
in Leeds before emigrating to America as an actor and singer. He
returned to England in 1822, and after his death, young Bray was
adopted by an aunt who was a milliner in Leeds. Later Bray was

[1] C. D. Collet, *History of the Taxes on Knowledge* (1933 edn), p. 22. The case
of his first imprisonment was raised by William Cobbett in the House of Commons. Cf., also, a MS. letter (in the Tolson Memorial Museum, Huddersfield)
from Cobbett to Hobson upon his release from Wakefield gaol, in which Cobbett expresses sympathy with him but warns him not to repeat the offence.

[2] He apparently entered into partnership with Alice Mann, the widow of
James Mann who had been for many years the leader of the Radical movement
in Leeds.

[3] Typical of these was his *Labourers' Library* series, 1841–2, in which he pub-
lished as penny pamphlets works and extracts by Cobbett, O'Connor, John Francis
Bray, and James Napier Bailey; his annual *Social Reformers' Almanac*; and his
Social Reformers' Cabinet Library (1840).

[4] E.g. his *Socialism as it is! Lectures in reply to the Fallacies and Misrepresenta-
tions of the Rev. John Eustace Giles, Baptist Minister, Leeds* (1838). This consisted of a series of four lectures by Hobson.

[5] The main source for details of Bray's life and work is H. J. Carr, 'A critical
exposition of the social and economic ideas of John Francis Bray, and an estimate
of his influence upon Karl Marx.' (Unpublished Ph.D. thesis, London University, 1943.) Biographical details of Bray are also given in the same author's
article, 'John Francis Bray', in *Economica* (1940).

apprenticed to printers in Pontefract and Selby and subsequently
went 'on tramp', looking for work. He experienced great hardship
at this time, having no money and living in low lodging houses;
and he vowed that if he ever obtained work he would discover the
basic causes of 'trampism'. In 1832 he returned to Leeds and obtained employment as a compositor, but in the following year,
when Hobson was imprisoned for publishing his *Voice of the West
Riding*, Bray volunteered to go to Huddersfield to continue the
issue of the paper. He took charge of the office while Hobson was in
prison, and brought out the *Voice*. When Hobson was liberated
Bray got a job in York, with time to turn his attention to the discovery of the causes of 'trampism'. At first he thought it was due to
the inferiority of monarchy to republicanism, but after a time he
came to the conclusion that both systems of government were
equally hostile to the workers' cause. In a letter to his brother
Charles in America in 1835 he stated that he had decided to take
part in the labour movement in England; and in December 1835 to
February 1836 he published a series of letters (signed 'U. S.') in the
Leeds Times, entitled 'Letters for the People', in which he dealt
with natural rights and human equality. Towards the end of 1837
he returned to Leeds, having got a position as compositor on *The
Yorkshireman*; and it was there in the autumn of that year that he
played a leading role in founding the Leeds Working Men's Association.

In an able letter in the *Leeds Times*, addressed to 'Fellow Producers of Wealth', Bray emphasised the need to examine 'first
principles', and urged the need to fight 'the battle of the masses'.[1]
At the first general meeting of the Association he delivered an opening address, and again spoke of the need for an examination of the
whole social system by working men themselves, not relying on
others. He stressed the need to change the social whole as well as
obtain political changes; and called on the working men of Leeds
to make 'a stand for Free Examination and Discussion — a stand
for Principles — a stand for Equal Rights and Equal Laws'. In
November 1837 he gave a series of three public lectures on 'The
Working Class — Their True Wrong and their True Remedy',[2]
which formed the skeleton of his chief book, first published in

---

[1] 2 Sept. 1837. The letter was signed 'An Associate', but there can be little
doubt that the author was Bray, especially in view of the appeal, so typical of
Bray, to 'first principles'.
[2] Advertisement in the *Leeds Times*, 11 Nov. 1837.

F

Leeds in weekly numbers at the end of the following year. Bray
Labour's Wrongs and Labour's Remedy; or, the Age of Might and th
Age of Right was a closely reasoned exposition of the Socialist them
of unequal exchange, and a demand for social justice — that ever
man should possess the whole produce of his labour. His debt t
William Thompson, the co-operative Socialist, and to Owen wa
considerable, although his solution to the immediate problems of
society — joint-stock communities organised on a national basis —
was peculiarly his own. In later years Bray's work received notic
on account of the use made of it by Marx in his *Poverty of Phil*
sophy, but at the time of its publication it did not create the st
which its author had fondly hoped for. Its philosophical and inte
lectual approach precluded its appeal to any but the *élite* of th
Leeds working classes, though Hobson reprinted part of it as
penny pamphlet in his *Labourers' Library* in 1842. Nevertheless
the fact remains that it was the product of a working man living i
Leeds. It affords striking proof of the quality of the best contem
porary working-class thought; and it suggests the importance o
Owenism as one of the constituent elements in the matrix of Leed
working-class thought from which Chartism was to emerge.

One other member of the committee of the Leeds Working Men'
Association was also a noted Owenite. David Green, the publishe
of Bray's *Labour's Wrongs*, was a bookseller in Briggate, and late
the chief instigator of an Owenite community experiment begun i
1845 as the Leeds Redemption Society.[1] But Owenism in the lat
1830's was essentially a movement of ideas, not a mass politica
organisation, and it is perhaps significant that of the three Owen
ites on the first committee of the Leeds Working Men's Associa
tion — Bray, Green, and Hobson — only the last identified him
self actively with the Chartist organisation.

Neither William Rider nor George White (both members of th
Leeds Working Men's Association in 1837, and the chief exponent
of physical force Chartism in Leeds in 1839) was the type of mai
to be much influenced by the complexities of Owenite socia
theory.[2] They belonged to a tougher proletarian tradition, which

---

[1] For an account of this venture see my pamphlet, *Social Reform in Victoria*
Leeds; the work of James Hole, 1820–1895 (Thoresby Society, Leeds, 1954).
[2] White was an Irishman and a woolcomber by trade. Gammage was impresse
by his inflexible perseverance and determination, his frankness and bravery. He
was ready to do anything for the cause, whether collecting subscriptions or bat
tering the head of a policeman. Rider was probably a printer, and, like Whit

ad suddenly found fuel for its fire in the outburst of popular feel-
ng against the New Poor Law.[1] In Leeds this movement did not
ttain anything like the intensity that it did in Huddersfield or
ther parts of the West Riding, and the emergence of the Working
Men's Association as the heir of the older Leeds Radical Associa-
ion created a different type of Chartism from that born of a mass
movement goaded by fear and desperation. Several strands were
voven together into the background pattern of the Leeds Working
Men's Association — political radicalism, Owenism, the Short
Time Committees, and the struggle for a free press. But its original
im was to secure independent working-class political action.

The outer shape of Leeds Chartism was thus determined largely
by its origins in earlier Radical and working-class movements. But
underlying these were distinctive economic and social factors
which also helped to give a somewhat different basis to Chartism in
Leeds from that found elsewhere in the West Riding. Leeds by the
830's was a rapidly expanding centre of the woollen, flax, and
ngineering industries, with a growing commercial as well as manu-
acturing population. By 1839 it was a town with over 10,000 oper-
tives employed in power-driven mills, and a large, strongly Non-
onformist middle class.[2] But it did not have any large numbers of
lepressed handworkers, such as handloom weavers and wool-
ombers, and in this it was markedly different from other West
Riding towns such as Halifax and Bradford. True, there were at
east 10,000 handloom weavers in the clothing district round
Leeds, and also quite considerable numbers in the out-townships
uch as Holbeck, Wortley, Armley and Bramley.[3] But in the 'town'
tself there were in 1839 only 1,289 handloom weavers and 138
voolcombers out of a total employed population of 61,675.[4] The

vas later employed by O'Connor as a reporter-cum-agent for the *Northern Star*.
Ie apparently found little favour with Gammage, who remarked that he was as
plain in speech as in personal appearance. See R. G. Gammage, *History of the
Chartist Movement, 1837–1854* (1894 edn), pp. 64, 154.

[1] See above, p. 11.

[2] It was even customary in the 1830's to elect annually seven Nonconformists
s Churchwardens of Leeds parish church. See James Rusby, *St. Peter's at
Leeds* (1896), pp. 282–3.

[3] Figures quoted in *Reports from the Assistant Handloom Weavers' Commis-
ioners*, Part III (1840), p. 529.

[4] 'Report upon the condition of the town of Leeds and of its inhabitants By a
Statistical Committee of the Town Council, October 1839' printed in the *Journal
f the Statistical Society of London*, II (1839–40), pp. 397–424. Out of a total
population of 82,220 the Committee reported that 61,675 were actively employed,
s follows:

significance of these figures is that in Leeds — unlike other Wes
Riding centres — there was no basis for a continuing mass Chartis
organisation drawing its strength from a large class of desperat
handworkers. Certainly the Leeds working classes suffered from
severe unemployment and sheer destitution in the years betwee
1838 and 1842;[1] but there was always the hope of the return o
prosperity once the trade depression had been weathered. In Leeds
Chartism had to strike roots in a different kind of soil[2] — the soil o
factory operatives, shopkeepers, and small tradesmen — with the
result that the bloom was perhaps less exciting, but nevertheles
not without its own quiet merit.

II

From the start, the Leeds Working Men's Association was fa
from being a homogeneous body. There were at least three separate groups, each with distinctive aims and purposes. Nicoll expressed the views of the first group when, in his editorials in the
Leeds Times,[3] he urged the formation of a Leeds Working Men's
Association along the lines of the earlier Radical political unions
He had been impressed by the efforts of the London Working Men's
Association earlier in the year, and his aim was the establishment o
an independent, working-class organisation to agitate for the five
(political) points of his 'Radical Creed'.[4] The Owenites formed a

Engaged in manufacture by power:	10,663
Handloom Weavers:	1,289
Woolcombers:	138
Select trades:	13,233
Miscellaneous ditto:	17,916
Other children and domestic servants:	18,436

The Assistant Handloom Weavers' Commissioner also observed that such hand
loom weavers as there were in Leeds received higher wages than those in the
villages some way from the town — op. cit., p. 550.

[1] In the autumn of 1841 an Operative Enumeration Committee investigated
the extent of distress through unemployment in the town. The Committee
claimed, on the basis of personal visitation, that out of 4,752 families examined
consisting of 19,936 individuals, only 3,780 persons were in work, while 16,156
were unemployed; and that the average weekly earnings amounted to only 11¼d
per head. Three months later 16,000 persons were on the books of the Leeds
workhouse as receiving parochial relief; while in addition to this 10,000 persons
had received relief from a voluntary subscription fund of £7,000. Samuel Smiles
Autobiography (ed. Thomas Mackay), pp. 114–15.

[2] George White on his release from his second imprisonment in January 1844
did not return to Leeds or Birmingham (where he had previously been active)
but to Bradford, where he found a militant body of Chartist woolcombers, much
more congenial to him than the 'moderate' Radicals of Leeds. Northern Star, 13
Jan. 1844; 9 Nov. 1844.   [3] 19, 26, Aug. 1837.

[4] Elaborated in a series of five editorials in the Leeds Times, 18 Feb. to 18 Mar.
1837.

econd group, and Bray made it quite clear in his addresses to the
Association that what he had in mind was fundamental social
change rather than a political programme.[1] He was anxious that
working-class reformers should not be sidetracked through following either Whig constitutional reforms or Chartist demands for
universal suffrage. The members of the third group, dominated by
Rider and White, were prepared for more extreme methods than
either of the other two groups. With the foundation of the *Northern
Star* in November 1837 they rapidly fell under O'Connor's influence, and before long were distinguished as the leading physical
force men in the town.

Effective action by such a coalition of diverse groups was difficult, and for some months the Association contented itself with
lectures, addresses and occasional protest meetings.[2] But the issues
dividing reformers at this time could not for long be glossed over,
and at a meeting and dinner organised by the Leeds Association in
January 1838 they were clearly exposed to view.[3] The speakers on
this occasion were Augustus Harding Beaumont (editor of the Newcastle *Northern Liberator*), O'Connor, Dr Taylor and Sharman
Crawford, M.P. The remarks of the last speaker annoyed Beaumont, who angrily proclaimed himself a physical force man. He
was received with groans, and replied by denouncing 'the dulcet
tones of the very moderate Radicalism of Leeds'.

The tempo of the times was such as to strengthen the hands of
the militants during the winter of 1837–8. The struggle against the
New Poor Law in the West Riding, the trial of the Glasgow cotton
spinners, and the general depression in trade, all helped to swell a
rising tide of opposition both to the Government and the 'millo-
cracy'. A significant straw in the wind was the phenomenal success
of the *Northern Star*, which within four months of its establishment was selling nearly 10,000 copies a week.[4] The idea of a popular
newspaper for the West Riding originated with a group of

[1] *Ibid.*, 23 Sept. 1837.
[2] E.g. a course of three lectures on 'The theory and construction of the English
language' by the Rev. William Hill, editor of the *Northern Star*, to enable working men to acquire the elements of grammar. *Leeds Times*, 10 Feb. 1838.
[3] *Ibid.*, 13 Jan. 1838.
[4] Estimates of the circulation of the *Star* vary considerably. Alexander Paterson, 'Feargus O'Connor and the *Northern Star*' (article in the *Leeds Mercury*
(Supplement), 24 Feb. 1900) gives its circulation in 1837–8 as 9,822 copies per
week, which was 300 more than the *Leeds Mercury*; in 1838–9 it had risen to
32,692; and a maximum of 'nearly 50,000' was ultimately reached. Mark Hovell,
op. cit., pp. 173, 269 n. 1, gives 48,000 as the maximum (in Feb.–May 1839), and

Leeds radicals, the main promoters of the scheme being Joshu
Hobson and William Hill,[1] pastor of a New Jerusalem Churc
(Swedenborgian) at Hull. But the successful launching of the ven
ture was the work of O'Connor, who was able to secure the neces
sary funds to start it.[2] The importance of the *Northern Star* in th
development of Leeds Chartism was twofold. First, it meant tha
the most powerful of all the organs of the Chartist cause was im
mediately available to the local movement. Produced on the door
step was this great Yorkshire Radical newspaper, whose full title wa
the *Northern Star and Leeds General Advertiser*. It gave detaile
reports of any little meetings of Radicals anywhere in Yorkshire
and wrote them up with as much care as if they had been nationa
concerns. It became an institution in all working-class gatherings
and the numbers who listened to it being read in public houses and
workers' cottages extended its influence beyond the figures indi
cated by the number of copies sold.[3] In comparison with its sociall
educative role in directing attention to burning social issues, it

states that the figure declined rapidly to 18,780 in 1840, 13,580 in 1841, an
9,000 at the end of 1843. Both Frank Peel, *op. cit.*, and Benjamin Wilson, *Th
Struggles of an old Chartist*, p. 3, quote estimates of 60,000 as the maximum
The following statistics from the Tory *Leeds Intelligencer*, 10 Aug. 1839, shov
the comparison between the *Star* and other Yorkshire newspapers in 183
and 1839, (The figures are for a period of 13 weeks, thus showing a rise in th
weekly circulation of the *Star* from 10,400 to 42,000 during the course of the yea
1838–9):

Paper	3 months Apr.–June 1838	3 months Apr.–June 1839
Northern Star	135,320	547,000
Leeds Mercury	117,000	126,000
Leeds Intelligencer	48,000	44,000
Leeds Times	36,000	24,000
York Herald	48,000	47,000
York Courant	32,000	44,000
Yorkshire Gazette	17,500	30,000
York Chronicle	8,000	6,000
Yorkshireman	21,000	30,000

[1] Hill was the son of a Barnsley handloom weaver, and worked at the loom
himself as a youth. After acquiring some education, he kept a school near Huddersfield, and subsequently published two books on English grammar. He then
travelled the country as a lecturer on phrenology, and in the mid–30's settled
at Hull as pastor of a New Jerusalem Church. He combined his pastorate with
activity in the Chartist cause, including editorship of the *Star* from 1837 to 1843.
In 1844 he went to Edinburgh, where he edited a trade journal; but later returned to Hull where he was editor and proprietor of the *Hull Express*, 1863–4.
He died in 1867. (Paterson, *loc. cit.*)

[2] See Eric Glasgow, 'The Establishment of the *Northern Star* Newspaper', in
History (1954), pp. 54–67.

[3] See Wilson, *op. cit.*, p. 10. Also Joseph Lawson, *Progress in Pudsey during the
last sixty years* (1887), p. 64.

rude appeals and pandering to popular tastes were of secondary importance.[1]

Second, it secured for its promoter, O'Connor, a personal predominance in the Chartist movement in the north. Behind those Leeds Chartists who were prepared to support O'Connor there was all the weight of a powerful organ of the press. As O'Connor's star rose rapidly throughout the summer of 1838 so also did the fortunes of his followers in Leeds. Within the Leeds Working Men's Association this ascendancy soon became manifest. Bray and the Owenites dropped out; Nicoll died of consumption in December, and the *Leeds Times* under his successor became critical of O'Connor, who had already repudiated Lovett and the London Working Men's Association.[2] By the time the People's Charter was published in May 1838, the Leeds Working Men's Association no longer seemed an appropriate body to conduct the agitation as the O'Connorites wished. In June it was replaced by the Great Northern Union. At its inaugural meeting on Hunslet Moor the main speakers — O'Connor, White, Rider, and Collins of Birmingham — spoke for outright measures;[3] and O'Connor hoped that the Union would be a means of uniting all reform associations in the area.

From the time of the official adoption of the Charter at the great Birmingham meeting in August 1838, the main efforts of the national Chartist movement were directed towards the election of delegates to the National Convention to be held in the following February. Under the auspices of the Great Northern Union enthusiastic meetings in support of the Charter were organised during the early autumn throughout the West Riding. At Leeds preparations were made for the monster demonstration to be held at Peep Green[4] on 15 October. A week previous to this a preparatory meeting in Walton's Music Saloon, with William Rider in the chair,

---

[1] Cf. Hovell's condemnation of the low level of the *Star*, following Francis Place's opinion that the *Star* had degraded the whole Radical press. Hovell, *op. cit.*, p. 96.

[2] *Leeds Times*, 24 Feb. 1838. By May there were complaints that agents were pressing sales of the *Star* at the expense of the *Times*, and by Sept. the *Star* was threatening a libel action against the *Times*. *Ibid.*, 5 May, 25 Aug., 15 Sept. 1838.

[3] *Ibid.*, 9 June 1838.

[4] Peep Green (now usually known as Hartshead Moor) was the most convenient centre for all the great West Riding Radical demonstrations, being about equidistant from the main towns of the Riding. It is in the form of a large natural amphitheatre, and suitable for very large gatherings of people. At the demonstrations the Moor was like a fair, with huts erected for the sale of food and drink, and wives and families accompanying their menfolk. From Bradford, Huddersfield, Halifax, Dewsbury, and other towns in the West Riding the delegates

was attended by 400–500 people.[1] George White in his speech a
this meeting regretted that in Leeds, where there were so many
Radicals, so few came to meetings; and he hoped there would be
great turn-out to Peep Green in a week's time. But in the event he
was disappointed. For whereas Bradford, Huddersfield and Hali
fax poured out in their thousands to Peep Green, the Leeds delega
tion was not more than two hundred.[2] However, despite the defection of the Leeds men, the meeting was an impressive demonstration of the mass nature of West Riding Chartism; and O'Connor
Rider, and Pitkeithly were elected as West Riding delegates to the
National Convention. The fiery speeches of O'Connor and Peter
Bussey on this occasion were indicative of the temper of the movement in the West Riding throughout the winter of 1838–9. As the
long winter nights drew in, vast torchlight meetings were held on
the moors, and speeches and schemes became increasingly inflammatory. Even in 'moderate' Leeds the 'torchists' organised their
meetings. In February 1839 a crowd of 3,000 assembled on St
Peter's Hill, with banners and lanthorns, to listen to George White
and two comrades (William Thornton and Thomas Cliffe) from
Halifax.[3]

Throughout the spring and summer of 1839 the O'Connorites
attempted to set the pace for Chartism in Leeds, but they did not
receive the support for which they had hoped. At an open-air
meeting in Leeds on Easter Monday, addressed by O'Connor, Hill,
White, Rider, and Dr Taylor, several references were made to the
lukewarmness of the men of Leeds and the need for militant action.
O'Connor, who said that he did not advocate a civil war in England, added that if the people could not get their rights by peaceful
means, then he (O'Connor) would be found at his post fighting
with the people. White called himself 'not so much a *Radical as a
Revolutionist*'. He had been twitted by Neddy Baines and his
friend on the right (the reporter for the *Leeds Times*) for what he
had said at the Peep Green meeting, he declared, but he still held
the same opinions . . . . 'They would never get anything until they
were able to take it by force (renewed cheering); and if those who
heard him thought they could, they were deceiving themselves.'

---

marched in formation — often several thousands strong — with banners flying
and bands playing.
[1] *Leeds Times*, 13 Oct. 1838.   [2] *Ibid.*, 20 Oct. 1838.
[3] *Ibid.*, 2 Mar. 1838.

Rider, just back from the National Convention where he had formed an extreme left-wing junta with Harney and Richard Marsden, said that '. . . the citadel of corruption cannot be taken by paper bullets (hear, hear). There is a crew of some sort — I don't know whether I am one or not — called physical force men, who are for trying something more than argument. It is this that makes the Whigs and Tories tremble . . . .'[1] And he went on to urge the meeting to be armed, and to do more than merely petition: 'I believe this petition will do no good.'

It was this conviction that led to Rider's resignation from the Convention,[2] which was announced at the next West Riding mass demonstration at Peep Green on 21 May. This time the Leeds Chartists, led by Thomas Ellis, formed up in the Union Room for the march. A flag suspended from the window, surmounted by a cap of liberty, and inscribed 'Liberty or Death' gave offence to the Mayor, who ordered them to withdraw it. After some protests they did so, and contented themselves with a less revolutionary banner inscribed 'Leeds Northern Union. We demand our rights, liberty, justice, and humanity'. The Peep Green meeting was a model of peaceable organisation; no liquor was sold, and William Thornton opened the proceedings with prayer.[3] But Bronterre O'Brien

---

[1] *Ibid.*, 6 Apr. 1839.

[2] His behaviour in the National Convention in April had not been such as to enhance either his own or the assembly's reputation. After loudly announcing his resignation on the grounds that he had lost all confidence in the National Convention, he reversed his decision the next day and sought to take his seat again. For this he was strongly condemned by Lovett, Cleave, and Hetherington; whereupon he repeated 'his firm belief that there were only eight men of principle in the Convention'. He was accused of being the tool of a small minority of extremists, led by Harney; and the Convention passed a resolution censuring him as 'a very vacillating and inconsistent member'. A motion to expel him from the Convention was proposed by Hetherington. But O'Connor secured its withdrawal, asserting that while Rider 'was no sunflower', he was a fit and proper person to sit in the Convention, and 'had been returned by a great constituency at a great meeting'. The *Leeds Mercury* gleefully reported these dissensions in the National Convention; and in a leader headed 'National Convention — a rough Rider', Baines commented: 'The best laugh we have had for many a day has been enjoyed whilst reading the exquisite proceedings of that Senate of Solons and Catos, the "National Convention", touching the refractory conduct of the illustrious member for the West Riding — William Rider, Esq., heretofore stuffweaver, afterwards printer's runner, and now stipendiary Senator, and colleague of Feargus O'Connor Esq., and that "decent fellow", Peter Bussey, Esq.' *Leeds Mercury*, 27 Apr. 1839.

[3] Thornton was a Methodist local preacher, and Benjamin Wilson of Salterhebble who was present on the occasion records that at the end of the prayers O'Connor put his hand on Thornton's shoulder and said, 'Well done Thornton, when we get the People's Charter I will see that you are made Archbishop of York'. Wilson, *op. cit.*, p. 3.

expressed the general sentiment when he declared that the people
were 'determined to have the People's Charter, peaceably if they
could, and forcibly if they must'.[1] Earlier in the month the Leeds
magistrates had deemed it prudent to enrol special constables and
the yeomanry cavalry resident in the area were assembled for exercises — even though Leeds was 'proverbially peaceable'.[2] From
various parts of the country came reports of arrests of active Chartists; and during the next few weeks the Leeds members feared arrest at any time. The Chartist organisation in the town (the Leeds
Northern Union) was by now completely dominated by White (the
secretary), Rider, and men such as Joseph Jones and Charles Connor.[3] The talk now was all of 'ulterior measures' to secure the aims
of the Charter; and placards advocating this appeared on the walls
in Leeds.[4] Withdrawals from the banks, abstention from all ex-
cisable articles of luxury, and exclusive dealing were the main
methods proposed. But in the background lurked the attractive
sanction of a 'national holiday'.

It was in this atmosphere of rising tension that White was suddenly arrested.[5] He and Wilson (an unemployed man with a starving wife and child) had been appointed by the Great Northern
Union to collect subscriptions for the 'National Rent' in Leeds.
They had accordingly visited shopkeepers and publicans in the
town to solicit donations, using two books — a subscription book
and a Black Book — for this purpose. On entering a shop White
presented the subscription book to the shopkeeper and demanded
that he should read the declaration written inside the front cover.
If the shopkeeper refused to subscribe he was condemned as an
enemy of the people, dark hints about the recent riots and bloodshed at Birmingham were thrown out, and White solemnly entered
the recalcitrant's name in the Black Book. The defendants stated
that they had merely been concerned to find out who were the
friends of the Convention in Leeds. But the evidence of some thir-
teen shopkeepers and publicans convinced the magistrates that it
was a case of extortion by threats, and they accordingly committed
the prisoners to the next York assizes in eight months' time. In the

---

[1] *Leeds Times*, 25 May 1839.   [2] *Ibid.*, 11, 18 May 1839.
[3] Jones was a shoemaker and chairman of the Leeds Northern Union at this
time. Connor was an Irishman who frequently proclaimed that he was a 'revolutionist' and condemned the 'sham-radicalism' of the *Leeds Times*. *Ibid.*,29 June
1839.
[4] *Ibid.*, 27 July 1839.   [5] *Ibid.*, 27 July, 3, 31 Aug. 1839.

meantime, since bail was refused, they were to be lodged in York gaol. This enraged White beyond measure. 'You call this justice!' he roared from the dock — and proceeded to damn the Whigs and their 'justice' in forthright terms.

But he was liberated on bail later in the month, and was thus left free in Leeds during the troublous times of the winter of 1839–40. What his activities at this time really amounted to it is impossible to determine. Certainly he was fully alive to the possibilities of capturing other meetings, whether on national education,[1] the Corn Laws, or operatives' distress, for the Chartist cause; and in December he was busy among the 10,000 unemployed workers in Leeds.[2] But whether or not he was embroiled in plans for a rising in Yorkshire in the autumn of 1839 is not clear.[3] Had there been any plan for a Yorkshire insurrection to coincide with the Newport Rising, White would almost certainly have been involved. In Leeds, however, as in other centres the secrecy of the movement at this period is by now practically impenetrable; and it remains one of the obscure corners of Chartist history. The grim winter of 1839–40 saw the end of the first period of Chartism in the West Riding, in a series of risings in Sheffield, Bradford, and Dewsbury. The familiar pattern of unemployment and police spies, followed by clashes with the soldiers and arrests, was repeated in these towns during January 1840.[4] With the crushing of these revolts and the arrest of the leaders, Chartism for the time being came to a standstill.

In Leeds there was no rising. But here too the Chartist movement died down in the early months of the new year. In March White was sentenced to six months imprisonment[5], and thereafter disappeared from the Leeds scene. After serving a particularly rigorous sentence[6] he returned to the town for only a few months, before going

---

[1] E.g. at a meeting on national education organised by the British & Foreign Schools Society, with Edward Baines in the chair, the Chartists (led by White) succeeded in unseating Baines, and elected Joshua Hobson in his place. Hobson then conducted the meeting along his own lines, until the police put an end to the proceedings. *Ibid.*, 7 Sept. 1839.

[2] E.g. reports of meetings on Hunslet Moor and in the Court House. *Ibid.*, 14, 21, 28 Dec. 1839.

[3] According to Dr John Taylor, White had been sent round the West Riding towns by O'Connor at the time of the Newport Rising to say that there would be no rising in Yorkshire as it was all a government plot. David Williams, *op. cit.*, p. 202.

[4] *Northern Star*, 18 Jan., 21 Mar. 1840. Cf. also the exposure of the alleged police spy, Robert Peddie, at Bradford, *ibid.*, 1 Feb. 1840.

[5] *Ibid.*, 21 Mar. 1840. Wilson, his accomplice, received 4 months.

[6] The *Leeds Times*, 13 June 1840 reported that White '. . . is now at hard labour in Wakefield House of Correction, under the most rigid prison discipline, no

to Birmingham as an agent-reporter for the *Northern Star*. In March O'Connor too was convicted at York of seditious libel, and in May sentenced to eighteen months' imprisonment. The collapse of the physical force wing was now virtually complete, and the Leeds Northern Union quietly disappeared.

III

The rapidity of the revival of Chartism after the defeats of the winter of 1838–39 has been remarked upon by most historians of the movement. In Leeds, however, it was a revival with a difference. It was not simply that new persons came forward to provide the leadership, or that a new policy and new methods were adopted. More significant was the form of organisation which the Leeds Chartists adopted when compelled to fall back on their own resources. It was as if, when once the pressure of O'Connorism was removed, they reverted to their own indigenous brand of radicalism. The body which they now established was the Leeds Radical Universal Suffrage Association. Neither in its title nor rules was there anything which would have appeared strange to a Radical of the mid–30's.

Its objects were clearly set out in the Rules adopted at the inaugural meeting held in James Illingworth's public house, the White Horse Inn, in Vicar Lane:

> 'The attainment of Universal Suffrage and the other main points of the Charter, by the use of every moral and lawful means, such as petitioning Parliament, procuring the return of Members of Parliament who will vote for Universal Suffrage and the other points of the Charter, publishing tracts, establishing reading rooms, holding public meetings for addresses and discussions, and giving public lectures on subjects connected with the politics of the country.'[1]

Membership was open to all those desiring Universal Suffrage and the other points of the Charter 'by the means set forth in Rule 2' (above). The entrance fee was 2d., and payments were 1d. a week. Every twenty members were to form a class, and to pay their subscriptions to a collector — a method of organisation made familiar

---

friends being allowed to see him, not even his own father. He is said to be in such a bad state of health that he has fallen off the treadmill twice, and on one occasion it was found necessary to carry him to bed. . . .' On his release, White wrote a series of letters to the *Northern Star* (beginning 16 Jan. 1841) on the illtreatment of prisoners in Wakefield gaol.

[1] *Northern Star*, 2 May 1840.

by the Methodists. The officers were to be elected by ballot every
two months.

The new body clearly represented the moderate as opposed to
the physical force wing of Leeds Chartism.[1] It was James Illingworth (now treasurer of the Association) who had moved a resolution at the Easter Monday meeting in 1839 calling for unity among
reformers[2] — a plea which had gone unheeded amidst the exciting
appeals of White and Rider for immediate action. Nevertheless, the
militants from the old Great Northern Union, such as Connor and
Jones, did join the new body, which by July was reported to be in a
flourishing condition.[3] Leeds had got away to an early start in the
revival of its Chartist organisation. But in June meetings of West
Riding delegates were held at Dewsbury to consider plans for the
wider reorganisation of the Chartist movement, to be put before the
forthcoming Manchester conference.[4] From this came the form of
national organisation which was to last, for the remainder of the
history of Chartism; and in the autumn of 1840 the Leeds branch
of the National Charter Association replaced the Radical Universal
Suffrage Association. The change was really in name only, for the
personnel and policy remained unaffected.[5] The physical force men
were still to be heard in Leeds for many months,[6] but their influence was never again as great as it had been in 1839.

The new temper of Chartism was nowhere more clearly illustrated than in the fresh direction into which Chartist energies were
directed during the next eighteen months. A Leeds Total Abstinence Charter Association sprang up;[7] the Hunslet Union Sunday
School was conducted jointly by Teetotallers and Chartists;[8] and

[1] This was reflected in the officers of the new body — Benjamin Knowles
(President), Joseph Wilkinson (Vice President), Andrew Gardner (Secretary),
James Illingworth (Treasurer). The Council contained at least two militants
from the Northern Union, William Roberts and Joseph Jones. *Ibid.*, 2 May 1840.
[2] *Leeds Times*, 6 Apr. 1839.
[3] *Northern Star*, 18 July 1840. Similar Associations were also reported from
villages near Leeds.
[4] *Ibid.*, 6, 27 June 1840.
[5] The meetings continued to be held at Illingworth's inn until February 1841,
when a building formerly used as a chapel, at the corner of Cheapside, Shambles,
was secured. *Ibid.*, 6 Feb. 1841. The Association also began to organise itself on a
ward basis at this time. *Ibid.*, 2 Jan. 1841.
[6] Rider, for instance, remained firm to his physical force convictions as late as
1854 — see his letter printed as Appx. A to Gammage, *op. cit.*, p. 403.
[7] The first annual tea party was held on Friday, 1 Jan. 1841, and was 'numer-
ously attended'. William Rider was among the speakers. *Northern Star*, 9 Jan.
1841.
[8] The leading figure in this venture was T. B. Smith, 'a kind of Chartist local

the Leeds Charter Debating Society was established 'to cultivate that talent which, for want of opportunities, has lain so long dead'.[1] Lectures, addresses, and discussions took the place of torchlight meetings;[2] and the Chartist preacher in Vicar's Croft became a familiar figure.[3] As the Leeds Charter Association satisfiedly reported, the meetings

> '. . . get ever more respectable, are better conducted, less uproarious, and partake more of the reasoning and intellectual qualities . . . .'[4]

Public speaking was practised on Sunday afternoons — usually by 'the more rational and well informed' young men in the Association.

Nevertheless, either despite or because of pursuing this policy, the Leeds Chartists failed to gain any mass following. Whereas at the 1841 summer elections the two Chartist candidates for the West Riding — Lawrence Pitkeithly and Harney — were supported by a majority at the hustings, in Leeds even the show of hands went against the Chartist candidates. At a meeting of 80,000 people on Woodhouse Moor, Leach and Williams could not muster sufficient votes to go to the poll.[5] How was it that in Leeds, which all contemporaries admitted to be a home of radicalism, the Chartist movement apparently made so little impression? Why did the Leeds Chartist movement remain a small group of able, intelligent enthusiasts — almost a general staff without an army?

In part the answer lies in the very fact of a strong Radical tradition in Leeds. Had the local Chartists felt able to ally themselves

---

preacher'. He was also Vice President of the National Anti-Tobacco and Temperance Association. *English Chartist Circular*, Vol. I (1841), p. 145. Cf. also his suggestion for a National Charter Association Sunday School Union, to coordinate Sunday Schools for adults and children. *Ibid.*, Vol. II (1842), p. 46.

[1] *Northern Star*, 27 Mar. 1841.

[2] At an early meeting of the Leeds Radical Universal Suffrage Association it had been resolved that 'a reading room and library is highly necessary for the purpose of giving to the working classes an opportunity of acquiring information as cheaply as possible'. *Ibid.*, 23 May 1840. A single issue of the *Star*, 12 Feb. 1842, contained reports of lectures and addresses delivered at Chartist meetings in Leeds, Holbeck, Hunslet, and Woodhouse.

[3] E.g. the following notice in the *Northern Star*, 10 July 1841 — Mr T. B. Smith will preach tomorrow evening at half past six, in Vicar's Croft, on God's promised reward for the faithful performance of public duty. Text: Romans 37.3. William Hick and 'Mr. Parker' were similar local Chartist preachers.

[4] *Ibid.*, 15 Jan. 1842.   [5] *Ibid.*, 3 July 1841.

with the dominant strain of radicalism their political fortunes might have been different. But it was precisely on this question of an alliance with middle-class radicalism that the important issues in 1841–42 turned. At the time of the formation of the Leeds Working Men's Association it had been possible for the *Leeds Times*[1] — representative of middle-class radicalism in the town — to urge that the new body should seek to gain its object in two ways: a display of moral force, i.e. mobilising public opinion; and a display of physical force, to back the moral force if necessary. But the experiences of 1839 had convinced the middle classes, Radical as well as Whig, that physical force from any quarter was to be avoided like the plague. Thus Dr Samuel Smiles, who had assumed the editorship of the *Leeds Times* from January 1839, roundly condemned the government for using physical force to put down Chartism, while dissociating himself equally from the Chartist physical force men.[2] But it was not only the Chartist extremists who found it impossible to come to any satisfactory agreement with Smiles and the middle-class Radicals. Any Chartist to whom the Charter had any significance at all felt bound to stand aside from such an involvement. It was in vain that Smiles protested that he was a Chartist in principle;[3] that Chartism 'is indeed the IDEA of the age; having its origin and seat in the universal human mind'.[4] Like his discovery that 'above all other agitations, the Chartist agitation is a Knowledge Agitation',[5] it seemed too disingenuous to carry much weight. There were not wanting those among the Leeds Chartists who welcomed the idea of a class alliance. But for most Chartists the terms on which such an alliance could be purchased were too high.

Since 1837 a lot of water had flowed under the radical bridges, and from the middle of 1840 a distinct rightward trend is apparent in the policy of Smiles and the *Leeds Times*. Hitherto the paper had identified itself with Chartism in principle, though not supporting individual Chartists or specific measures. But from the summer of 1840 this was abandoned and a temporising policy on the suffrage question was substituted. Smiles became secretary of the newly formed Leeds Parliamentary Reform Association,[6] which advocated household, not universal suffrage. In addition, the traditional support of the *Leeds Times* for the Short Time Committees was

---

[1] In an editorial by Nicoll, 26 Aug. 1837.
[2] *Leeds Times*, 10 Aug. 1839.
[3] *Ibid.*, 13 July, 16 Nov. 1839.
[4] *Ibid.*, 1 June 1839.
[5] *Ibid.*, 8 June 1839.
[6] See below, p. 357.

dropped, and the Anti-Corn Law League was made the centre of interest and agitation.[1]

The danger that a strong agitation against the corn laws would divert attention from the struggle for the Charter had been realised by the Leeds Chartists in the winter of 1838–39. This, rather than any specific objection to repeal in principle, explained their tactic of capturing or breaking up Anti-Corn Law League meetings;[2] and this was the policy that was pursued with renewed impetus from the beginning of 1841. The common argument was that the anti-corn law agitation was merely a middle-class device to shelve the struggle for the Charter, and this appeared the more plausible in Leeds since the chief Anti-Corn Law Leaguers declared in favour of household, not universal suffrage.

The efforts of the Leaguers to win support among the working classes, and the determination of the more militant Chartists to scotch these efforts provide the material for the more exciting episodes in Leeds Chartism during 1841. Beginning in January with what the *Northern Star* dubbed 'the Fox and Goose Club',[3] the Leeds Chartists fought hard to expose the 'duplicity' of the middle-class Radicals. 'Chartists, beware! — keep your eyes open,' warned William Rider in a letter condemning the cant and humbug of 'the pigmy Doctor' (Smiles).[4] Yet the case for a middle-class/working-class alliance as apparently the only way of carrying through the repeal of the corn laws and effecting financial reforms was strengthened by the defeat of the Whigs in the 1841 summer elections. In the West Riding, as elsewhere, the Chartists had concentrated their venom against the Whigs, thus playing into the hands of the Tories, who were victorious. Militant Chartism in the industrial West Riding was primarily a struggle against the middle classes, and this was true also in Leeds of the minority of class-conscious Chartists. Hence the difficulty of effecting a movement based on an alliance with the middle classes, whether Radical or Whig. The great stumbling block was universal suffrage, and here there was little to choose between the Smilesian Radicals and the Bainesocracy. Without working-class support there seemed little hope of securing those

[1] See a letter from the Leeds Short Time Committee in the *Northern Star*, 5 Feb. 1842, to the effect that 'until 20 months ago' the *Leeds Times* had always supported the Short Timers, but since then had become increasingly hostile. Items of League news began to be very fully reported.
[2] Examples were reported in the *Leeds Times*, 2, 9 Feb. 1839.
[3] *Northern Star*, 23 Jan. 1841.
[4] *Ibid.*, 6 Feb. 1841.

eforms which were necessary to complete the economic and social
egemony of the middle classes. But the price of that support was
othing less than universal suffrage, and that they were not pre-
ared to pay. This was the dilemma which, during 1841–42, bedevil-
:d all attempts in Leeds to promote a middle-working-class fusion.[1]

To have granted support for universal suffrage would have been
antamount to a Chartist victory — and that was too much to ex-
ect of the middle classes. For they saw no less clearly than the
:hartist leaders that, once a mass political democracy had been
stablished, a social democracy could not long be delayed. If co-
peration between Chartist working men and middle-class Radicals
vas to be effected it would have to be in some field other than
ational politics. In some places and at a later date education
fforded such an opportunity. In Leeds the opening was found in
ocal government.

IV

The experiences of the first phases of the Chartist movement in
Leeds were not such as to evoke very sanguine prospects for the
uture. By 1842 the movement appeared to have almost exhausted
he practical possibilities of furthering the cause of the People's
:harter. The educational and rational approach, on the model of
he London Working Men's Association, had been swept aside in
he summer of 1838; the appeal to physical force, with talk even of
nsurrection, had met with a negligible response in Leeds; and the
:omplete Suffrage movement was condemned to impotence
hrough mutual distrust and intransigence. There was always the
ossibility of recourse to a Tory-Radical alliance;[2] but this was never

[1] Thus at the election of Leeds delegates to the (Sturgeite) Complete Suffrage
:onference in Birmingham in December 1842, Smiles withdrew from the con-
est because he was not willing to be bound by the instructions of the meeting,
vhich were to support universal suffrage and the Charter. The delegates elected
vere in fact all Chartists. *Ibid.*, 24 Dec. 1842.

[2] The most spectacular example of this, of course, was the Factory movement
ieaded by Oastler and the Short Time Committees. In Leeds the Tories were
ully aware of the value of securing working-class allies, and William Beckett,
he Rev. W. F. Hook, J. R. Atkinson, and others were prepared to support Oper-
tive Conservative Societies. The Leeds Operative Conservative Society was
ounded in 1835, and by 1836 claimed over 200 members. Its aim was 'to combat
he Whigs and Radicals and to organise the working class for the Tories'. A
ibrary, newspapers, and journals were provided in the meeting-room in Vicar's
:roft. Its main achievements seem to have been in attending to registrations, and
upporting Tory candidates at municipal and parliamentary elections. The
ecretary was William Paul, and the chief centre of support was Holbeck. See W.
'aul, *A history of the origin and progress of Operative Conservative Societies*
Leeds, 1838).

G

very attractive in the long run since the Tories had really very littl
to offer in return for working-class support. In fact, the obvious way
forward had all been tried — and found to be blocked. The turnin
to municipal affairs was an attempt to find a way out of this impass.

The genesis of the idea of municipal Chartism in Leeds date
from January 1840, when George White attempted to get Joshu
Hobson elected as one of the town's Improvement Commis
sioners.[1] Under the Leeds Improvement Act of 1824 the commis
sioners to carry out the provisions of the Act consisted of the J.P.
together with nineteen citizens elected annually at a vestry meetin;
held in the Parish Church vestry on the first Thursday in January
The minimum qualification for a commissioner was occupation o
property to the value of £40 per year.[2] In 1838 and 1839 Tory com
missioners were elected. But in 1840 an alliance of Whigs, Radicals
and Chartists combined to defeat the Tory bloc. Joshua Hobson
was not elected, but John Jackson, a Chartist corn miller of Hol
beck, was included in the successful list. The following year the
crowd at the election was so great that the meeting had to be ad
journed from the vestry to the Free Market, where George White
and Joseph Jones took advantage of the occasion to harangue the
assembly.[3] The Liberals' list was again carried.

But in January 1842 the Chartists won a resounding victory
With William Brook (from now on one of the leading Chartists ir
the town) elected to the chair, the adjourned meeting in Vicar's
Croft carried the Chartist list on a show of hands, after both the
Whig list (of sitting members) and the Tory list (proposed by the
Operative Conservatives) had been defeated. The Chartist list,
which was moved by William Hick (of the *Northern Star* office) included seven of the late commissioners, but the *Star* assured its
readers that all the nineteen were 'staunch friends of the people's
cause'.[4] The victory, however, was not one which could be

[1] *Leeds Times*, 4 Jan. 1840.

[2] The 1824 Act is included as an appendix in William Parsons, *Directory of the Borough of Leeds* (1826).

[3] *Leeds Times*, 9 Jan. 1841.

[4] *Northern Star*, 8 Jan. 1842. The Chartist list was as follows: Horatio Wood (solicitor), Joseph Pickard (machine maker), William Binns (cloth manufacturer), Joshua Hobson (printer), Edward King (wool-stapler), William Hartley (broker), Joseph English (butcher), William Sellers (chandler), John Ardill (clerk), Thomas Otley (innkeeper), Joseph Woodhead (builder), George Wood (gentleman), George Dufton (gentleman), Joshua Barnard (toll bar farmer), Henry Wilks (gentleman), John Oldroyd (innkeeper), Joshua Raper (builder), John Whitehead (machine maker), Thomas Button (cloth manufacturer). *Leeds Times*, 8 Jan. 1842.

epeated; for in July 1842 the old Improvement Act was superseded
by a new one, which did away with the election of commissioners
and empowered the Town Council to implement the Act through
appropriate committees.[1] If the Chartists were to continue their
new line of advance they would now have to elect not Improvement
Commissioners but Town Councillors. And that was what they
proceeded to do.

This idea indeed had been put forward even before the 1842 Improvement Act had made it a compelling condition of further progress. An article in the *Northern Star*[2] the week after the January
victory had concluded:

'Are the Chartists of Leeds generally aware that the qualification for a
Town Councillor is lower than for an Improvement Commissioner?
And have they asked themselves the question whether those who have
power to carry the election of Commissioners may not be able to carry
the election of Councillors if they try? The thing is worth thinking of.'

The next municipal elections were not due until November, but
in April the Chartists gained encouragement from a victory in another field of local endeavour. At the annual meeting of parishioners
the Chartist list of churchwardens for the Parish Church was carried *en bloc*.[3] The custom was that of the eight churchwardens (one
for each ward of the old parish) one was nominated by the Vicar,
and seven were elected at the vestry meeting. For some years previous to 1843 it had been the practice to elect a bloc of seven intact,
chosen from lists put forward by the Nonconformists, Churchmen,
and Chartists. From 1837 to 1841 the Nonconformist list had been
carried *en bloc*. But in 1842 seven Chartists, headed by Benjamin
Knowles (who had been President of the Leeds Radical Universal
Suffrage Association in 1840) were elected.[4] From 1843 the Vicar

---

[1] *Leeds Improvement Act*, 1842. Throughout the summer of 1842 a struggle
was waged between those who wished the new Improvement bill to keep power
in the hands of the ratepayers at large, by means of direct election of the Board
of Commissioners, and those who wished to restrict the right of franchise,
Northern Star, 11 June 1842.

[2] 8 Jan. 1842.

[3] J. Rusby, *op. cit.*, pp. 282–3.

[4] At the end of their year of office the Tory Vicar paid tribute to the conscien-
tious way in which they had performed their duties. An amusing anecdote concerning the refusal of the Chartist wardens to pay Mrs Fothergill (the cleaner)
for sweeping the church is recorded. The Vicar suggested that, since they were
poor men, they should take it in turn to clean the church themselves. If they
refused to agree to this he would employ Mrs Fothergill as usual and then bring
an action against them for the repayment of her wages. See W. R. W. Stephens,
Life and Letters of W. F. Hook (7th edn. 1885), p. 351.

insisted on each name being voted on separately, but the Charti
list was nevertheless carried in that year and again in 1844 ar
1845. Thereafter individual Chartists continued to be elected
churchwardens.

Meanwhile throughout the summer of 1842 preparations we
going forward for the November municipal elections. A Centr
Municipal Election Committee was set up in July to organise th
return of Chartist councillors.[1] The officers appointed at the fir
meeting were Joshua Hobson (chairman), William Barror
(treasurer) and William Brook[3] (secretary). Ward committees we
established as it was hoped to put forward several Chartist cand
dates. The *Northern Star* in an eve-of-poll editorial stressed th
'necessity for the Chartists acquiring local power'; and urge
Chartists to capture 'those outposts to general government, th
local offices', since 'local power is the key to general power'. Thi
power is within the reach of Chartists — 'It rests with themselve
to put forth their hand and clutch it. It offers itself to their grasp —
let them seize it!'[4] However, only two Chartist candidates actuall
stood in 1842 and neither was successful. Hobson, who conteste
the West, Hunslet, and Holbeck wards polled 205 votes in Hunsle
where the main contest was fought, nearly 400 in Holbeck, and i
the West ward a mere 53. William Barron polled only a handful o
votes in the East ward.[5]

This result was not unencouraging, however, for the immediat
background to the elections had been by no means auspicious. I
August the West Riding had been convulsed by the Plug Riots. Be
ginning in Lancashire the movement had spread across to Tod
morden and the towns of the West Riding, where the prevailing
unemployment and distress provided ample basis for spontaneou
sympathetic action.[6] During the third week in August excitemen

---

[1] *Northern Star*, 30 July 1842.
[2] A tailor and draper of George Street. He was treasurer of the Leeds Charter
Association, and was one of the delegates nominated to the general council o
the National Charter Association from Leeds. *Ibid.*, 24 Sept. 1842.
[3] A tobacconist and tea dealer of Kirkgate. He later acquired a small nail-
making business in Swinegate. He was secretary of the Leeds Charter Association and one of the most active Chartists in the town.
[4] 29 Oct. 1842.
[5] *Ibid.*, 5 Nov. 1842; and *Leeds Mercury*, 5 Nov. 1842.
[6] A Memorial from the Mayor, Aldermen, and Burgesses of Leeds to H.M.
Treasury, in July 1842, stated, 'Never at any former period in our recollection
has this manufacturing district experienced distress so universal, so prolonged, so
exhausting, and so ruinous'. After four years of depression it was estimated that
every fifth person in the borough was a pauper — 16,000 individuals out of a

n Leeds ran high.[1] On Saturday came news of the turn-outs in the Vest Riding, to be followed on Sunday by movements of troops hrough the town. William Beckett, M.P. (Colonel of the Yorkshire Hussars), the Earl of Harewood, Prince George of Cambridge, and Lord Cardigan, all arrived to command various units of Hussars nd Lancers; and on Monday 1,500 special constables were sworn n. Reports of riots and clashes in Halifax came in during Tuesday, nd a meeting of 4,000 operatives on Hunslet Moor passed resolu- ions in favour of the Charter. Then on Wednesday the turn-out began in the villages near Leeds. Some 6,000 operatives stopped all mills in Calverley, Stanningley, Bramley, Pudsey, and the immedi- te neighbourhood. Next they drove in the plugs at mills in Armley, Wortley, Farnley, Hunslet and Holbeck. By five o'clock in the evening they were marching down Meadow Lane, Leeds, from Holbeck. All mills in the town were stopped, including Marshall's, where J. G. Marshall attempted to defend the mill gates, but was driven back. There was a clash with the police at one of the mills, nd Prince George and the Lancers were brought up to disperse he strikers. During an attack on the mill of Titley, Tatham, and Walker, in Water Lane, the Riot Act was read, two pieces of artil- ery were paraded, and thirty-eight people were arrested. On Thursday morning the town was quiet, except for a turn-out at the coal pits at Hunslet and Middleton. The pits were again visited on Friday when fourteen prisoners were taken. A meeting on Hunslet Moor was dispersed by police and soldiers. About 1,200 infantry arrived in the town, the White Cloth Hall was used as a temporary barracks, and General Brotherton was sent from London to take command of the district.

Such was the extent of the disturbances in Leeds. Of the thirty- eight prisoners taken during the affray on Wednesday evening, twenty-seven were committed to York for trial on 3 September, and received sentences varying from two to eighteen months' im- prisonment.[2] The fourteen prisoners from Beeston and Churwell, who were mostly colliers, were similarly treated. There is little evidence to show that the local Chartists were responsible for the riots, though they were certainly prepared to make political capital

population of 80,000 were existing solely on workhouse relief. B.M. Add. MSS. 40,612.

[1] The following account is taken from the *Northern Star*, 20 Aug. 1842, and John Mayhall, *Annals of Yorkshire*, Vol. I, pp. 483–6.

[2] *Northern Star*, 27 Aug., 10 Sept. 1842.

for the Charter out of them. None of the leading Chartists in the town were among the prisoners, nor were there many strangers among the rioters. The affair was basically a violent reaction of unemployed operatives, spurred to desperation by hunger and destitution. Nevertheless the Chartist name was almost inevitably connected with the outbreak; and this, coupled with the government's policy of arresting Chartist leaders,[1] did not augur well for the Chartist cause in the autumn of 1842.

Against this background, Hobson's performance in the November municipal elections was very creditable, and the local Chartist cause showed little sign of waning. A highly respectable soirée in the Music Hall, Albion Street, was held in honour of Thomas Slingsby Duncombe in December;[2] and lectures, instruction groups, and Sunday schools flourished throughout the winter. As the time for the next municipal elections drew near, Chartist activity was directed towards the return of two Chartist candidates. Ward committees were revived, and lectures by David Ross on local government were delivered in the West, North-east, Hunslet and Holbeck Wards.[3] John Jackson and Joshua Hobson were both returned for Holbeck, the latter heading the poll with 571 votes.[4]

Two lone Chartists on a council of sixty-four, dominated by a strong majority of middle-class Liberals, were not sufficient to affect policy very decisively. The most they could — and did — do was to make a stand on issues of principle, and insist on asking uncomfortable questions about matters which the majority would have preferred to gloss over. Hobson was by nature an 'awkward' man, one who by temperament would always be in a minority opposition. Hence the Council proceedings were soon enlivened by charges and counter-charges, bickerings and recriminations. In the following year the Chartist caucus was enlarged to four, with

[1] The Rev. William Hill and T. B. Smith were arrested in Leeds and taken to Manchester, on a charge of uttering seditious language at a meeting of Chartist delegates in Manchester on 16 Aug. *Ibid.*, 8 Oct. 1842.

[2] Admission was by ticket only. The blessing at the beginning was pronounced by the Rev. William Hill; and a programme of glees, songs, and recitations was interspersed between the speeches. *Ibid.*, 24 Dec. 1842.

[3] *Ibid.*, 30 Sept. 1843.

[4] The *Leeds Times* which had expressed strong disgust when Hobson's nomination was announced, refused to include Hobson among the 'reformers' (liberals), but classified him as a Tory. It also pilloried certain tradesmen who had supported Hobson, by drawing attention to the way they had voted, and holding them up for public condemnation.

he election of George Robson, a butcher, for the West Ward, and
Villiam Brook for Holbeck.[1]

The elections of 1845 brought four Chartist candidates to the
olls, but only one — Thomas White, the retiring councillor for
North-west Ward — was successful.[2] The election in 1846 was
marked by a lively contest in Holbeck, at which the Chartist candidates were John Jackson (the retiring councillor) and John Ardill,
ormerly employed on the *Northern Star* and now a milk seller of
Bramley. Opposed to them were two Liberal manufacturers, Wil-
iam Ingham and G. B. Pearson. The fight was hotly contested. At
ne time sixteen cabs, of both parties, stood opposite the polling
booth; and over the committee room of Jackson and Ardill '. . . the
reen flag flaunted in the breeze and bid defiance to all crowds'.[3]
But the Chartists were defeated. Jackson was again unsuccessful in
847; but Robson and Brook retained their seats, and in addition a
Chartist painter from Wortley, George Gaunt, was elected.[4] Dur-
ng 1848 and 1849 there were further accessions to the Chartist
roup, notably the redoubtable Joseph Barker of Wortley and his
rother Benjamin[5] so that during 1849–50 the Chartists on the
Council numbered seven. For another three years Chartist candidates continued to be returned; Dr F. R. Lees, the temperance
worker, and Robert Meek Carter (a coal merchant and co-
perative pioneer) in 1850; William Parker, a coffee-house
keeper, in 1851; and Thomas Scholey, a butcher, and John Ard-
ll in 1852. But 1853 was the last time that the Chartist label
was used, when R. M. Carter and John Williamson, a grocer, were
elected.

Thus, after ten years, municipal Chartism in Leeds came to an
end. What had been its character and what had it achieved during
hat decade? Within the Council chamber the Chartist group never
numbered more than seven or eight at any one time, although be-
ween 1843 and 1853 some twenty-five Chartist candidates had
contested elections, eighteen successfully so. These men were for
he most part shopkeepers and small tradesmen, not proletarians.
They had little in the way of a distinctive Chartist municipal programme, but they spoke up volubly on specific issues. On three in
particular they could always be relied upon to make themselves

[1] *Leeds Times*, 2 Nov. 1844.   [2] *Ibid.*, 1, 8 Nov. 1845.
[3] *Ibid.*, 7 Nov. 1846.   [4] *Ibid.*, 6 Nov. 1847.
[5] *Ibid.*, 4 Nov. 1848; 3 Nov. 1849.

heard. First, as an unprivileged minority on the Council they wer implacably opposed to 'arrangements' and jobbery.[1] Second, the were deeply suspicious of the police, and determined to prevent th slightest extension of police powers.[2] Third, they could always b counted on voting in favour of keeping expenditure down — eve though this conflicted with their more positive convictions.[3] Thes three merely negative principles did not amount to a programme At best, they resulted in a more or less consistent policy on a fev particular matters; at worst, they produced personal vendettas an the washing of dirty linen in public.[4]

Outside the Council chamber, municipal Chartism had import ant effects. Almost inevitably the Chartist councillors, because c their prestige and experience, assumed the leadership of the Chart ist organisation in the town. Leeds Chartism thus became eve more markedly than before a movement of Radical small tradesme and artisans, with its influence centred in the newer working-clas areas of the town, especially Holbeck. It was not a proletaria movement based on handworkers, as at Bradford, nor a base fo the power of new national leaders like Ernest Jones at Halifax. Th existence of Chartist councillors gave to the Leeds organisation : certain stability and weight, if not respectability. The movemen

[1] Almost the first thing that Hobson did after his election in 1843 was to ob ject to serving on committees unless elected in open council, since he refused to be party to 'arrangements' whereby committees were selected on a party basi beforehand. *Northern Star*, 18 Nov. 1843. Again, at the Council meeting on Dec. Hobson and Jackson moved that all committees including the Watch Com mittee should be open to the public, but were defeated. *Ibid.*, 9 Dec. 1843.

[2] The charges made against the police led to a libel action between the Super intendent of Police (William James) and Councillors White and Brook in 1844 *Ibid.*, 12 Apr. 1845; also a printed apology from White, dated 14 Feb. 1845 (Copy bound in with the *Leeds Improvement Act, 1842*, in Leeds Referenc Library.) Joseph Barker in 1849 not only voted against an extension of the polic system to Bramley and Wortley, but even opposed the grant of a pension to police constable who had completed twenty years' service with the Leeds Force *The People*, Vol. II (1849–50), p. 3.

[3] Thus Barker voted against beginning the municipal sewerage scheme in 184 because it would entail a 6d. rate, and he considered that rates were already heavy enough in a time of much unemployment. Yet he approved strongly of the scheme in itself. *The People*, Vol. II, p. 9.

[4] E.g. the case of Alderman Bateson, raised by Joshua Hobson in 1843–4. The allegation was that Bateson, a member of the Watch Committee, at the time o the Plug Riots in Leeds, had sent for William Smith, a machine maker employing a number of men, and had told him that he would greatly serve the public cause if he would turn his men out, for they would know how to draw the plugs in masterly way, and could if necessary blow up the boilers. The evidence for this was a letter sent by Smith to William Busfield Ferrand (M.P. for Knaresborough who had sent it to Hobson. The latter demanded a select committee of inquiry be set up to investigate the matter. After many other charges and counter-charges the matter was shelved. *Northern Star*, 6 Jan. 1844.

simply could not be brushed aside as the well-meaning but misguided strivings of unemployed operatives. Municipal activity in-
tegrated the Chartist movement into the tradition of established
radicalism in Leeds.

V

Municipal Chartism, by definition, was not much concerned
with the wider national issues of the movement; and it is hard to
escape the conclusion that Chartism in Leeds during the five years
between 1843 and 1848 was in something of a backwater. The
transference of the *Northern Star* to London in November 1844
removed several top-level Chartists from the town,[1] and was indicative of the general shift of the centre of Chartism away from the
north. Left to their own devices, the Leeds Chartists carried on
with their meetings in the Bazaar, Briggate, listening to addresses
by West Riding Chartist lecturers, and singing the Chartist an-
them, 'Spread the Charter through the land'.[2] New names —
Squire Farrar,[3] James Harris,[4] and John Shaw[5] — appeared in the
reports of meetings, and a good deal of time and energy was devoted to the land question.

The first meetings in connection with O'Connor's land scheme
were held in May and June 1845, and thirty-five members were
enrolled. Councillor Brook took the initiative.[6] Weekly payments
were to be made on Monday nights and in the first ballot for the
allocation of land two Leeds men — James Edwards and George
Hearon — were successful. That the idea of starting a new life
amidst rural surroundings had a strong appeal to workers in industrial Leeds is not difficult to imagine; and the various schemes for

[1] E.g. Hobson and G. J. Harney. Hill had been dismissed from the editorship
by O'Connor in July 1843 and in Oct. 1845 Hobson, who had succeeded him, was
also dismissed.

[2] *Northern Star*, 25 Nov. 1843.

[3] Squire Farrar had come from Bradford to reside in Leeds. He had been a
close friend of John Tester, the leader of the Bradford woolcombers in their
turn-out in 1825, and was a noted radical and 'infidel'. Cf. the reference to him
in G. J. Holyoake, *History of Cooperation* (1875 edn), Vol. I, p. 13.

[4] He was treasurer of the Leeds Chartist Association and a member of the
executive committee of the National Charter Association. *Northern Star*, 17 Feb.
1844.

[5] His name appears in reports of most meetings of Leeds Chartists from 1843
to 1848. He was later (1848) the district missionary lecturer for the Leeds-Brad-
ford area. *Ibid.*, 15 Apr. 1848.

[6] *Ibid.*, 31 May 1845. Brook was the Leeds and District delegate to the Annual
Conference of the Chartist Land Company, where he took an active part in the
discussion, particularly in defending O'Connor. *Ibid.*, 12 Dec. 1846.

land settlement such as the Leeds Redemption Society, home colonisation for relief of the unemployed,[1] and the Radicals' Freehold Land Societies,[2] indicate that reformers of several kinds in the '40's pinned their hopes to it. Yet because of this the Leeds Chartists found the field to some extent already occupied, and they inevitably entered into competition with the Owenites.[3]

From none of this activity, however, did the later phases of Leeds Chartism stem. A combination of severe trade depression, mass unemployment,[4] and high food prices in 1847 reproduced conditions similar to those of 1838 and 1842, and in 1848 unrest in Ireland and revolutions on the Continent provided inspiration for renewed political activity. Chartism sprang suddenly to life. In place of the routine meetings to discuss the business of the Land Company, the Leeds Chartists now flocked to listen to George White again, this time discoursing on the revolution in France.[5] He started with the fundamental rights of man, then cited cases of distress in England and Ireland, and after a lengthy denunciation of 'the rottenness of the whole system' in England, enthusiastically welcomed 'the glorious revolution in Paris'. He proposed a great West Riding demonstration at Peep Green in support of the French revolutionaries;[6] the tyrants and despots were being pulled down from their seats; the time for action — to get the Charter — had come.

The enthusiasm for Chartism in Leeds during March and April 1848 exceeded anything that had been known since the early days

---

[1] E.g. the society formed in Leeds by Hook, Beckett, and J. G. Marshall to promote a scheme of allotments for the relief of distress in the town. *New Moral World*, 1 Apr. 1843. At a meeting of the Leeds Tailors' Society in 1844 it was resolved to raise 'the land question' as a means of solving unemployment at the next general meeting at Manchester. *Northern Star*, 22 Mar. 1845.

[2] See J. E. Ritchie, *Freehold Land Societies; their history, present position, and claims* (1853). See below, p. 337

[3] A series of Saturday evening meetings was held in Leeds to hear discussions on the relative merits of the Leeds Redemption Society and the Chartist Land Plan. No reconciliation of the opposing views was effected. *Northern Star*, 17 Oct. 1846.

[4] The *Leeds Times*, 15 Apr. 1848, gave figures of the number of Leeds operatives and families dependent on poor relief as follows: Nov. 1847–5,635; Dec. 1847–6,558; Apr. 1848–7,420. A typical example was quoted — Peter Fairburn, machine maker, who usually employed between 400 and 500 hands, had only 20 men at work in April.

[5] *Northern Star*, 11 Mar. 1848. The change in tone between mid-February and mid-March is very marked in the reports of meetings in the *Northern Star*.

[6] It was held the following week. Processions from Bradford, Leeds and Halifax were successfully organised. The republican flag was flown, and addresses were delivered by White, Kydd, and Shaw. *Northern Star*, 18 Mar. 1848.

of the movement. Large and successful meetings in Vicar's Croft, with attendances of anything from 10,000 to 15,000 were held weekly, the speakers being local Chartist leaders, notably Brook, Harris, Robson, Jones and Barker.[1] An attempt was made to broaden the mass basis of the movement through an alliance with the Irish Repeal Confederation of Leeds. At a joint meeting in Vicar's Croft, to petition for the return of Frost, Williams, and Jones, the tricolour flag was flown, with the inscription, 'Republic for France, Repeal for Ireland, the People's Charter for England, and no surrender'. The *Leeds Times* saw little to recommend in this alliance, fearing that the 'good sense and moderation' which had hitherto characterised Leeds Chartism would be overwhelmed by the wilder and more extreme Irish elements.[2] But they need not have worried. Brook and Hobson repeatedly condemned all appeal to physical force, and when a speaker in Vicar's Croft advocated such methods he was accused of being a spy and told to sit down.[3] Again, at a meeting on Woodhouse Moor in April, although the Irish members supported Shaw, who had declared himself in favour of physical force, the majority favoured the moral force arguments of Barker and Brook.[4]

In May, however, a new temper of urgency and desperation began to appear in the Chartist movement in the West Riding. Arming and drilling was reported from many places, and beginning on 28 May sporadic violence broke out. At Bradford 2,000 Chartists fought against an equal number of special constables, police, infantry and dragoons,[5] and at Bingley an attack was made to release Chartist prisoners. In Leeds, as on previous occasions, the repercussions of this general trend in the West Riding were felt, but only in a mild form. A deputation of militant Bradford Chartists led by David Lightowler had apparently visited the Leeds men and urged them to establish armed Chartist bodies to seize power. In Bradford such organisations had been formed under the title of 'Life and Property Protective Societies' or 'National Guards'. The Leeds Chartists agreed to do likewise, and on the following Sunday

[1] Reports in *Northern Star*, 4 Mar. to 27 May 1848.
[2] *Leeds Times*, 8 Apr. 1848.
[3] The speaker was a stranger, Charles Newell, who claimed he was an old Chartist. But he was interrupted and made to sit down. *Ibid.*, 15 Apr. 1848.
[4] *Ibid.*, 29 Apr. 1848.
[5] H.O. 41/19, May 1848. An account based largely on these events is contained in the novel, *Looking for the Dawn: a tale of the West Riding* (Bradford, 1874) by the Bradford writer, James Burnley.

morning some 200 of them paraded for drill on Woodhouse Moor. The Leeds magistrates promptly issued a warning against drilling — which then either ceased, or was carried on secretly.[1] Thus of the fifty-eight persons tried at the next Yorkshire assizes for riot and sedition, only one was from Leeds; and he was a young man, A. Tomlinson, who received eighteen months imprisonment for a seditious speech at the Toftshaw meeting in June.[2]

VI

The government's policy of intimidation and arrests,[3] followed by harsh sentences, during the summer of 1848, successfully crushed the immediate threat, but it did not extinguish Chartism. In Leeds the movement still had five more years of life, in which new interpretations and new personalities came forward. Representative of these new trends was Joseph Barker and his journal *The People*, printed and published by him at Wortley.[4] Born at Bramley in 1806, Barker was the son of Wesleyan weavers. After educating himself, he became a Wesleyan Methodist preacher (1828), but subsequently progressed through the New Connexion, Quakerism, 'Barkerism', and Unitarianism, to a secularist position. In 1846, during his Unitarian phase, he was assisted by Unitarian friends to set up a printing establishment at Wortley, and began publishing a series of cheap reprints. In 1848 he founded *The People*, most of which he wrote himself.[5] It declared itself to be Republican and 'ultra-democratic'. Like W. J. Linton's *English Republic* (which at first (1851) was also printed and published in Leeds) it was an attempt to adapt Chartism to new needs and conditions.[6] The

[1] *Leeds Times*, 3 June 1848; *Northern Star*, 3 June 1848.

[2] *Ibid.*, 5 Aug. 1848. The Toftshaw meeting was attended by some 7,000 to 8,000 people; James Harris (Leeds) was in the chair, and the usual delegations with their banners were there. *Ibid.*, 17 June 1848.

[3] George White was arrested in Bradford in Sept., sentenced to one year's imprisonment and imprisoned in Kirkdale gaol; John Shaw was sentenced to two years' imprisonment for sedition. David Lightowler was tried at York on a charge of drilling and sentenced to nine months' imprisonment. Joseph Barker was also brought to trial, but subsequently discharged. See Gammage, *op. cit.*, Ch. XII; and *A full account of the trial . . . of Joseph Barker* (bound as an appdx. to *The People*).

[4] See Joseph Barker, *History and Confessions of a man, as put forth by himself* (Wortley, 1846); and also the later biography, *Life of Joseph Barker written by himself* (ed. J. T. Barker, 1880).

[5] Three vols. in all were issued: I (1848–9), II (1849–50), III (1850–1). The journal came to an end with Barker's emigration to America.

[6] Linton regarded the Republican movement as a development forward from Chartism, and superior to it. See his article, 'Forward from Chartism' in the *English Republic* (1851), pp. 83–5.

stimulus and inspiration for republicanism came from the continental revolutions of 1848, strengthened by distinguished democratic refugees from Poland, Hungary, Italy and France who sought political asylum in this country. But the significance of the idea was that it represented one aspect of the demand for 'the Charter and something more', which could lead in other directions than Ernest Jones's well-known programme of socialism.

Of more importance than its republicanism, which institutionally was almost sterile,[1] was *The People's* emphasis on the need for some general union of all reformers.[2] Chartism in Leeds during its last five years (1848–53) represented a coming together of reformers from several different fields of popular endeavour. The Radical social content of popular Nonconformist thought was well illustrated in Joseph Barker, the Chartist councillor for Holbeck. Robert Meek Carter,[3] Dr F. R. Lees,[4] and John Holmes[5] were all members of the Owenite Leeds Redemption Society and of the Leeds Flour Mill. Lees also had an international reputation as a temperance reformer, and Holmes was an authority on trade unionism and consumers' co-operation. These were the men who by 1850 were known in Leeds as Chartists. The name had come to denote one who favoured a policy of independent working-class radicalism, tied to neither wealthy middle-class Liberals nor Radicals.

The last Chartist candidates in Leeds were R. M. Carter and John Williamson, who were elected in 1853. Thereafter the ex-Chartists fought as Radicals or as Liberals. Chartism as an organised movement had come to an end. But the men and the principles

[1] W. E. Adams, *Memoirs of a Social Atom*, 2 vols. (1903), p. 266, stated that the Republic was 'not so much a form of government as a system of morals, a law of life, a creed, a faith, a new and benign gospel'. Adams was attracted to Republicanism after his disillusionment with Chartism.

[2] See Barker's article, 'The comparative usefulness of different classes of reformers', in *The People*, Vol. II (1850), pp. 378–9. Cf. also Thomas Cooper's similar suggestion at this time for a 'Progress Union' to combine the efforts of different types of reformer, in *Cooper's Journal* (1850), p. 1.

[3] Born in 1814 at Skeffling, East Riding, of humble parentage, and self-educated. He was a co-operative pioneer in Leeds and a supporter of many schemes for social reform. Became an alderman in 1862 and was M.P. for the town, 1868–74.

[4] See Frederic Lees, *Dr F. R. Lees, a biography* (1904). Also *The Truth Seeker* (1846–50) edited by F. R. Lees.

[5] A draper of School Close, Leeds. He was the author of several pamphlets on cooperation, and an advocate of arbitration in industrial disputes. He contributed a paper on the West Yorkshire Coal strike of 1858 to the *Report of the Committee upon Trades Societies*, published by the National Association for the Promotion of Social Science, 1860.

for which they had fought were not dead, and two years later they were revived as the Leeds Advanced Liberal Party. In October 1855 a circular was sent out announcing a meeting to consider the formation of a new political association to unite the more advanced members of the Liberal party in Leeds. Of the fourteen signatories to this circular at least eight were old Chartists, and a further three were ex-Owenites. At the inaugural meeting David Green stated the need for a new organisation since the terms 'Radical' and 'Chartist' had now largely gone out of use. The points of the Charter and the experience gained in municipal affairs were included in the new programme.[1] Thus there was continuity between the Chartist movement and the manhood suffrage associations of the 60's. When the Leeds Working Men's Parliamentary Reform Association was established in 1860, it was led by the men who seven years previously had been the last of the Leeds Chartists.[2] The wheel had come full circle. Leeds Chartism had grown out of earlier Radical movements, and now it had itself given birth to new Radical movements well attuned to the mood of mid-Victorian England.

[1] Adopted at a meeting in November. The main points of 'The Creed' were (1) manhood suffrage, (2) vote by ballot, (3) shortening of the duration of parliament, (4) more equitable adjustment of representatives to population, (5) abolition of the property qualification for M.P.s, (6) promotion by merit in the civil military, and naval services, (7) reform of the existing relations between church and state, (8) purity in the election of municipal representatives, and efficiency and economy in the management of local affairs. Two other points — national secular education under local control, and abolition of the laws of entail and primogeniture — were considered, but rejected. *Leeds Times*, 24 Nov. 1855.

[2] See *Report of the proceedings of the Yorkshire Reform Conference, held in the Town Hall, Leeds, Nov. 18 and 19th, 1861*. . . . (Leeds, 1862).

Chapter Four

Chartism in Leicester

J. F. C. Harrison

I

The story of Chartism in Leicester has long been one of the better-known aspects of the history of the movement — thanks largely to the account in Thomas Cooper's widely read autobiography.[1] Recently a detailed narrative of Leicester Chartism, based on a thorough study of the local newspaper sources, has been published.[2] It will not, therefore, be the object of this study to go over this familiar ground again, but rather to examine what appear to be the most significant characteristics of Leicester Chartism, with a view to either modifying or confirming the established interpretations of the Chartist movement as a whole.

From a preliminary survey of the timing of Chartist events in Leicester and the county the local story would appear to harmonise with the general pattern of the movement. But a closer inspection suggests that some of the traditional generalisations are not entirely adequate to explain the local developments. An interpretation in terms of O'Connor versus Lovett, of 'physical' versus 'moral' force, or of handworkers against machine workers is not wholly substantiated by the local evidence. From the pages of the *Northern Star*, in the pronouncements of Northern leaders, or from sympathisers close to Westminster such impressions may easily be gleaned. But Leicester Chartism needs to be seen first through Midland eyes.

To this end it will be convenient to include developments in the county as well as in the borough. Loughborough, the only town of any size in Leicestershire in the nineteenth century apart from the borough itself, was the centre of vigorous Chartist activity. Ties of friendship and family, and similar conditions of local employment

[1] *The Life of Thomas Cooper. Written by himself.* The first edition in 1872 sold out rapidly, and by 1874 7,000 copies had been printed.
[2] A. Temple Patterson, *Radical Leicester. A History of Leicester 1780–1850* (1954).

drew the Chartists of the two towns together. Geography too con-
spired to further the alliance, for they were separated by only twelve
miles of good turnpike. At the main crises in Chartist history — in
the winter of 1839–40, August 1842, and the early summer of 1848
— Chartist groups in the two places worked in double harness.

Viewed analytically rather than chronologically, there are three
aspects of Leicester Chartism upon which investigation may be
centred — first, the condition of the framework knitters, who provided the main dynamic of Chartism as a mass movement in the
area; second, the quality of the local leadership and the problems
presented by a strong middle-class, Nonconformist-Radical tradition in the town; and third, the curious and meteoric interlude of
Thomas Cooper's two-year dominance of Leicester Chartism. But
first it is necessary to sketch in the main outlines of the local story.

II

In Leicester, as in the northern towns, the genesis of Chartism
was in the coming together of several streams which had been running swiftly during 1836 and 1837. Political disillusionment with
middle-class Radicals and the stimulus of the struggle for an unstamped press had led to the establishment of a Leicester Radical
Working Men's Association in August 1836. Its programme was
universal suffrage, vote by ballot, and triennial parliaments.[1] The
framework knitters, after the collapse of their attempts at union in
1834, felt once more the desperate need to build defences against
the progressive depression of their wages, which by the spring of
1838 had fallen to an average of 7s. for a full week's work. In February of that year they resolved to re-form their union.[2] But it was
the terrible fear of the New Poor Law which in Leicester, as in the
West Riding, introduced a note of urgency into all forms of working-class protest. At first the full rigour of the new law had been
mitigated by the discretion of a Tory Board of Guardians. But in
1837 a great new workhouse, with accommodation for over five
hundred paupers, was begun at the top of Conduit Street; and the
horrors of a true Malthusian Bastille now loomed large before
thousands of framework knitters who lived in a state of intermittent
or complete unemployment. The local movements of protest

---

[1] George R. Searson, *A quarter of a century's Liberalism in Leicester, 1826–1850*
(Leicester, n.d.), p. 66.
[2] *Leicester Chronicle*, 24 Feb. 1838.

emed, however, to have reached an impasse; various roads for-
ard to working-class betterment had been tried and found to be
locked. When therefore in the summer of 1838 the People's
harter was officially launched it provided just that necessary in-
piration for a new organisation — Leicester Chartism.

The initiative in the matter was taken by the Loughborough
adicals. At a meeting of operatives in the late August of 1838 it
as resolved to form 'The Loughborough District Branch of the
Jational Union, centred at Birmingham'.[1] In the chair was John
kevington, and speeches were made (amongst others) by T. R.
mart, J. Culley, and George Turner, all well known in the district
s working-class Radical leaders. The programme of the new asso-
iation was simply stated to be 'the five Radical principles', and to
utsiders it appeared to offer little more than the old familiar
Radical mixture.[2] But of the popular strength of the new movement
here could soon be no doubt, for two months later it mobilised a
nass meeting variously estimated at 3,000 to 7,000 people, com-
lete with banners, bands, and delegates from Nottingham. Skev-
ngton, as usual, was in the chair; and the meeting began — signi-
icantly — with the singing of the Corn Law Hymn to the tune of
he Old Hundredth.[3]

In the meantime, the movement in Leicester had got under way.
At a meeting of 400 operatives in All Saints Open, the decision was
aken to establish the 'Leicester and Leicestershire Political Union'.[4]
The speeches on this occasion reveal clearly the various impulses
ffecting the leaders of working-class thought in Leicester. John
Seal, in the chair, argued that if the working classes could have the
nunicipal franchise they should have the parliamentary franchise
oo; in the very ward in which they were meeting (All Saints) the
nunicipal electors were mainly working men, which was surely
proof that they could be trusted with the parliamentary franchise.[5]
Finn, a leader of the framework knitters, then moved the resolution

---

[1] *Ibid.*, 1 Sept. 1838.
[2] Indeed, the *Leicester Chronicle*, 10 Nov. 1838 continued to refer to it as the
Loughborough Radical Association.
[3] *Ibid.*, 10 Nov. 1838.   [4] *Ibid.*, 13 Oct. 1838.
[5] The parliamentary electorate in Leicester had been almost halved by the
1832 Reform Bill, mainly through the exclusion of the non-resident freemen
voters. There still remained, however, a considerable number of working-class
freemen electors, whose 'ancient right' franchise was protected under the 1832
Act, irrespective of whether or not they were £10 householders. The municipal
franchise after 1835 was extended to all ratepayers. For details of the results of the
1832 Act in Leicester, see Patterson, *op. cit.*, pp. 192–3.

H

establishing the Leicester and Leicestershire Political Union, base
on the principles of the People's Charter, and went on to outlin
the chief grievances of the people. First, he said, the taxes were ur
fair because, being mainly on articles of consumption, they dis
criminated against the poor man. Second, the Corn Laws were in
jurious 'because they prevented a man from taking his labour int
the best market, whilst they protected injuriously the agricultura
interest'. However, he did not wish to pursue this further lest i
should divert attention from the People's Charter. Third, th
Church was an incubus upon the people — though he hastened t
reassure the meeting that he himself was not an infidel. Fourth, th
Poor Laws were based on an entirely wrong foundation, namel
that every man could find employment and earn sufficient to sup
port himself during illness and unemployment. This was not true
He therefore urged the need to unite in support of the Charter, as
remedy for these grievances. He expressed profound mistrust c
the middle classes, who had secured enough reform to suit thei
purposes. He confessed that hitherto he had not been in favour o
universal suffrage, believing that household suffrage would give th
working men all they wanted. But he now saw that nothing les
than universal suffrage would suffice, since the Whigs and middle
class Radicals would swindle them as they had done over the Re
form Bill. He welcomed the introduction of the ballot, as being
means of ending drunkenness at elections. He said he was oppose
to the use of physical force, and advocated petitioning; only thos
who were not working men (such as O'Connor, Oastler, and
Stephens) favoured physical force; Lovett and the working me
were moral force Chartists. Roberts, a book-keeper by trade, and
teetotaller, then made a short speech. He said it was time for the
people to choose leaders from amongst themselves. If they got thei
own representatives into Parliament they would do away with the
Poor Law and remedy all other grievances. Weeks, a woolcomber
then reminded the meeting that the freemen (who had the franchise) did not represent the majority of working men in the town
And finally John Markham, after moving a resolution in favour o
the Charter, called for a great public demonstration to whicl
Thomas Attwood and other members of the Birmingham Politica
Union should be invited.

The Birmingham leaders, however, were not present at the nex
rally; their place was filled by delegates from Loughborough, Nun-

eaton, and Nottingham, and the star speaker was Feargus O'Connor. It was unfortunate that Monday, 19 November, the day fixed for the official adoption of the Charter in Leicester, should have been a very wet day. Nevertheless some 2,000 operatives braved the rain to support the demonstration in the Market Place.[1] On the hustings, erected outside the Corn Exchange, was a square ensign, inscribed 'Peace, Law, and Order', and surmounted by a cap of liberty. The main Chartist supporters came to the Market Place in procession, carrying their banners and flags. 'Labour is the source of all wealth' proclaimed one banner; 'It is better to perish by the sword than by hunger', read another. 'No Poor Law Bill', 'Away with oppression, and justice for Ireland', 'The rights of the People and nothing less', 'Liberty and Prosperity', 'We have beaten the Aristocracy' and 'The restoration of Poland' were other inscriptions, indicative of the medley of popular causes, grievances, and sentiments to which the new movement was heir. The meeting began with the solemn singing of three verses by the Corn Law Rhymer:

> God of the Poor! shall labour eat?
> Or drones alone find labour sweet?
> Lo, they who call the earth their own,
> Take all we have, — and give a stone!

> Yet bring not thou on them the doom
> That scourged the proud of wretched Rome,
> Who stole, for few, the lands of all,
> To make all life a funeral.

> Lord! not for vengeance rave the wrong'd,
> The hopes deferred, the woes prolonged;
> Our cause is just, our Judge divine;
> But judgement, God of all, is thine!

John Markham, in the chair, asked the meeting to stand fast despite the inclement weather, and explained that the Mayor had procrastinated and finally refused them the use of the New Hall (in Wellington Street). The delegates from Nottingham and Nuneaton then moved and seconded the adoption of the People's Charter, Woodhouse (the Nottingham delegate) adding that its object was

---

[1] *Leicester Chronicle*, 24 Nov. 1838.

to secure justice for the productive classes and to implement S
Paul's dictum that if a man would not work neither should he eat
O'Connor's speech was a long and sarcastic attack on John Bigg
and the 'Whigs' of the Town Council, the conclusion being tha
there was little to chose between Whigs and Tories since they botl
defrauded the people. This sentiment was repeated by the nex
speaker, T. R. Smart, from Loughborough. The Seal brothers
John and Richard, then moved thanks to the chairman, and th
meeting was concluded.

This meeting had been held in the morning; in the evening ther
was a dinner in the Town Hall, attended by 250 people. On th
entrance of O'Connor the band played 'See the conquering her
comes'. The chairman was John Skevington from Loughborough
who opened with a short speech, after which three toasts were pro
posed — 'The people, the legitimate source of all power', 'The
Queen — but only as the advocate of the rights and liberties of the
wealth-producing millions of her subjects', and 'The town and
trade of Leicester'. Replying to the last toast, Markham said he
could not say much upon it, and referred to the failure of attempts
at a *rapprochement* between the employers and framework knitters
in March and April. The toast to O'Connor was sandwiched between the singing of 'Millions be free' and 'Hearts of Oak', at the
end of which he rose to reply. His speech was mainly a repetition of
his address in the Market Place that morning. After a general attack
on the Government and the Whigs he went on to deal with Ireland,
the Church, the Poor Law and the corn laws. On the last he was
particularly anxious that the men of Leicester should press for universal suffrage before turning their attention to the corn laws;
'they must not have the soup until they had got the ladle to eat it
with.' The corn laws should be repealed only after universal suffrage had been won; otherwise the working classes would merely be
used to struggle for the manufacturing interest, 'to create a greater
competing power for the manufacturers to speculate upon.'

These proceedings of the Leicester Chartists during the first few
weeks of their organisation displayed nearly all the points which
were to characterise the movement throughout its history in the
town. For the next ten years Chartism was a force to be reckoned
with in Leicester, and for five years after that the name could still
evoke strong partisan feeling. But throughout that time the movement developed very little in new directions; the essentials were all

here by November 1838. The mixture of practical working-class grievances, scraps of Ricardian Socialist argument, and a background of Nonconformist liberal Christianity varied little throughout the period of Leicester Chartism. Similarly the unsolved problem of relations with the middle classes was always there, whether it centred on the question of the corn laws, the suffrage, or the removal of Nonconformist religious disabilities.

The great significance of the events of November 1838 was that they marked a break with the middle classes. This was a stage which had to be reached at some period in all centres before an independent Chartist organisation could be established. Hitherto, as Finn confessed, it had been possible to believe in the efficacy of middle-class radicalism. But the recent industrial and social experiences of the Leicester framework knitters had convinced them that their grievances would meet with little practical sympathy from the middle classes. They had therefore no alternative to breaking with the Liberals; and, since their third force was not politically strong enough to attain its ends by itself, they were soon tempted into temporary flirtation with the Tories.

The breach with the Liberals having once been made, the events of the grim winter of 1838–39 were well calculated to widen it further. Although there is little evidence of insurrectionary groups among the Chartists, either in the borough or county, during 1839, there was certainly an air of desperate determination among working men, and a corresponding plenitude of rumours and fears among the propertied classes. Even Markham, the most statesman-like of the Leicester Chartist leaders, felt goaded into violent language; and said that as the government

'... were prepared to butcher the people on the first provocation, therefore they (i.e. the Chartists) must be prepared to meet aggressive force by force, and do as gentlefolks did, ornament their mantlepiece with arms, arms, arms!'[1]

In the same month the Loughborough magistrates reported that the framework knitters, under the influence of Stephens' speeches in the north, were buying arms, and raising funds to send delegates to the National Convention.[2]

By Whit Monday, however, Markham had recovered his

[1] *Leicestershire Mercury*, 24 Jan. 1839; Searson, *op. cit.*, p. 86.
[2] H. O. 40/44, 30 Jan. 1839.

equilibrium. Leicester and Loughborough had sent Smart and
Skevington as delegates to the National Convention, and a public
meeting at which they were to report back was arranged for Whit
Monday, on a piece of land in Belvoir Street, lent by John Biggs.[1]
The delegate for Stalybridge, J. Deegan, was also billed to speak. In
his opening remarks from the chair Markham advised good conduct at the meeting, and then launched into an attack on the tyrants
and despots. Speeches were made by Swain, Crow, Weeks,
Burden, Smart, Skevington, Seal, and other local leaders. But it was
Deegan who set the cat among the pigeons. In a long speech he
roundly abused the Whigs and Tories, and then declared:

> 'We will obtain our rights, peaceably if we can, forcibly if we must. If
> we cannot obtain them by fair means, by argument and reason, we will
> obtain them by other means, by the pistol, the bullet, the pike, and
> the bayonet.'

For this he was taken to task by Markham, who said that he was
pleased that in Leicester a better understanding existed between
the magistrates and the people than in some other towns. In
Leicester working men could meet without fear. He therefore advised them to keep within the law, and be suspicious of those who
came among them and advocated violence.

The tactful handling of the Chartists (who claimed over 600
members in Leicester) by John Biggs and the Leicester magistrates
was not repeated in some other towns. The Birmingham Bull Ring
riots early in July called forth protests from the Leicester Chartists[2]
and a feeling of nervous apprehension and mounting tension is discernible in reports during July and August. Particularly was this so
in Loughborough, where the magistrates were inclined to be unduly
panicky. In July they forwarded a petition to the Home Office
asking that troops be stationed in the town, a request which was
granted temporarily.[3] At the same time they arrested two Chartist
leaders, George Turner and Charles Jarratt, both framework
knitters, on a charge of using seditious language at a public meeting.[4] The prosecution, however, had to be dropped because of lack
of witnesses. Thereafter the Loughborough Chartists continued
their meetings 'in private',[5] or, as the alarmed magistrates

---

[1] *Leicester Chronicle*, 25 May 1839.   [2] *Ibid.*, 13 July 1839.
[3] H.O. 40/55, July 1839.   [4] *Leicester Chronicle*, 27 July 1839.
[5] *Ibid.*, 10, 17 Aug. 1839.

preferred to put it, 'in secret'.[1] In the neighbouring hosiery villages, particularly in Shepshed and Mountsorrel, enthusiastic Chartist meetings were held; and as the autumn drew on reports of arming and organisation in classes of ten alarmed the magistrates.[2]

Although there was no outbreak either in Leicester or the county parallel to the riots in other parts of the country, the atmosphere remained tense, and in January 1840 the Leicester magistrates thought it necessary to request the Home Office to send arms for the special constables in the town.[3] It was reported that the Chartists in the county believed there would be a rising, beginning in the north. The informant, W. Heyrick of Thurmaston Lodge (Chairman of Quarter Sessions), nevertheless gave it as his opinion that:

'. . . if I were to judge only from what I believe to be the small number of Chartists in this county I should think it very improbable that any movement should be attempted; indeed, considering the quality of part of the lower population, and their propinquity to, and connection with Nottingham, the seat of a kindred manufacture, I am surprised to find them so quiet, and I do really attribute the paucity of information afforded partly, and chiefly, to the small extent of Chartism.'[4]

Of the borough, Samuel Stone (Clerk to the magistrates) reported similarly:

'After the most careful enquiries the magistrates are of opinion that there is no disposition to violence on the part of the inhabitants of Leicester, and they feel that there is little fear of any disturbance of the peace originating in this Borough, although it is possible an outbreak arising in other parts of the county might extend to this place . . . .'[5]

During the early months of 1840 Chartist activity in Leicester was unspectacular. Heyrick commented in February that 'in this town there has been no meeting of Chartists, even for a petition'.[6] Reports of the meetings in the Chartist room in All Saints Open dealt only with routine matters.[7] The fact was, that already the energies of the leading Leicester Chartists had become absorbed in

---

[1] H.O. 40/44, 28 Nov. 1839.
[2] *Ibid.*, and *Leicester Chronicle*, 17 Aug. 1839.
[3] H.O. 40/55.
[4] H.O. 40/55. Heyrick to Duke of Rutland, 11 Jan. 1840.
[5] *Ibid.*, Stone to Lord Normanby, 13 Feb. 1840.
[6] *Ibid.*, Heyrick to H.O., 10 Feb. 1840.
[7] E.g. *Leicester Chronicle*, 1 Feb. 1840; *Northern Star*, 28 Mar. 1840.

wrangling with the middle-class reformers over the issues of house
hold suffrage and the repeal of the Corn Laws.[1] Only in the count
did Chartism appear — perhaps because of reports from industri
ous police spies and alarmist local justices — to be a possible men
ace to law and order.[2]

In July the Leicester Chartists sent delegates to the Mancheste
meeting for the reorganisation of the movement, James Taylo
representing Loughborough and T. R. Smart the borough.[3] Th
new pattern of a National Charter Association was adopted on thei
return, the Leicester, Loughborough, and Nottingham Branche
being grouped together in the Chartist Association of the Midland
Counties.[4] The main purpose of this federation was the support o
a full time lecturer-organiser. In this role Jonathan Bairstow ap
peared in Leicester, first as a temporary appointment, but late
(1841–42) on a more permanent basis. The reorganisation in th
autumn of 1840 did not produce any new types of Chartist activity
nor did it throw up a new local leadership, as was the case, for in
stance, in Leeds. Yet a new phase of Leicester Chartism clearly be
gan in the spring of 1841, stamped with the dominant personality o
a new popular leader.

Thomas Cooper had only arrived in Leicester the previous
November.[5] The offer of a job on the *Leicestershire Mercury* had
brought him up post haste from Greenwich, not to assume the
leadership of local Chartism (of which he had scarcely heard) but to
earn his bread and butter. The plight of the stockingers and the
earnestness of the local Chartists soon shocked and impressed him,
and his passionate nature reacted violently. He rapidly identified
himself with the popular cause, wrote a few articles for a struggling
Chartist weekly, *The Midland Counties Illuminator*, and was given
a month's notice by the manager of the *Mercury*.

' "Never mind, Tom," said my old friend Winks . . . "don't you leave
Leicester. There will be something for you to do soon."

' "Don't leave Leicester!" said a group of Chartists, whom I met in
the street, and who had heard of my dismissal; "stay and conduct our
paper; George Bown wants to give it up." '[6]

---

[1] E.g. participation in the Anti-Corn Law demonstration in February (*Leicester
Chronicle*, 29 Feb. 1840); and discussions with William Biggs and others on
household suffrage in April (*Ibid.*, 18 Apr. 1840).
[2] E.g. H.O. 40/55, Deposition of police spy, 20 Feb. 1840.
[3] Gammage, *op. cit.*, p. 183.   [4] *Leicestershire Mercury*, 26 Sept. 1840.
[5] The account in this paragraph is based on Cooper's *Life*, pp. 132 ff.
[6] *Ibid.*, p. 145.

They offered him thirty shillings a week — which they could not pay. So he took over the paper, debts and all, established himself in a shop in High Street, and threw himself wholeheartedly into the Chartist cause. The accession of strength which the talents of such a man inevitably brought soon became manifest. Elected secretary of the Leicester Chartist Association, he embarked on a full time programme of open-air preaching, indoor lecturing, and Chartist journalism. By October 1841 the membership of the Leicester Chartist Association was 460, and the target was 1,000 by the end of the year. This was not reached, but the figure had been raised to 732 by the end of December.[1]

The increased tempo of Chartist life in Leicester from mid 1841 to August 1842 was very marked. A great deal of activity, considerable publicity, and an impressive increase in membership there undoubtedly were. But when the quality of much of this effort is examined it does not appear in such a favourable light. Great energies were being directed into paths which led nowhere. Leicester Chartism showed only too clearly the gropings, frustrations, and blind alleys which beset the working classes in their attempts to orientate themselves in the new industrial society of the 40's.

Three groups of activities in particular illustrate this. First, there were the continual clashes with the Anti-Corn Law Leaguers. These were by no means new, but under Cooper's leadership a definite technique of attack was worked out. If a Corn Law repeal meeting was held in the open air, as on 1 June 1841, the Chartists organised a counter-demonstration in the same place and tried to disrupt the meeting;[2] if it was held indoors, as in July 1842, they attempted to capture the platform, to install their own chairman, and to convert the meeting into a Chartist rally.[3] But even when they were successful, as they usually were, it is difficult to see what had been achieved, except a demonstration of numerical strength. There was an air of futility, too, about Chartist participation in the parliamentary elections in Nottingham and Leicester, which occupied the Leicester Chartists during the summer of 1841. Since they could not vote, their contribution was limited to a demonstration at the hustings; and the net result was a long series of charges and counter-charges about Tory gold.[4]

---

[1] *Northern Star*, 16 Oct., 24 Dec. 1841.   [2] *Ibid.*, 5 June 1841.
[3] *Ibid.*, 30 July 1842. Cf. also the accounts of the breaking up of meetings in *Ibid.*, 19 Feb., and Searson, *op. cit.*, p. 104.
[4] Cooper, *op. cit.*, pp. 149, 152–3; *Northern Star*, 27 Nov. 1841.

Even more futile was the direction of Chartist energies into quarrels among themselves. Cooper's rise to dominance meant the corresponding eclipse of Markham, and in the autumn of 1841 the split between the two leaders and their followers came into the open. Henceforth there were two rival Chartist organisations in the town — Markham's group which continued to meet in All Saints Open, and Cooper's new Shakespearean Association of Leicester Chartists, meeting in the Shakespearean Room in Humberstone Gate. The Liberal press now revelled in the vituperation which the two groups poured on each other. The *Leicestershire Mercury* printed the charges and counter-charges in a weekly column headed 'The Chartist Division'.[1] In January a meeting was held in the Town Hall to investigate the charges made by Cooper against Markham. Skevington was in the chair, and on Smart's suggestion it was agreed to postpone the hearing of both sides until a member of the National Executive could be present as arbitrator. Cooper, however, refused to attend.[2] The hearing therefore took place without him, and the secretary of the National Charter Association, John Campbell of Manchester, pronounced in favour of Markham. Despite subsequent attempts at reconciliation[3] the division persisted until March 1843 when Cooper disappeared finally from the Leicester scene.

Nevertheless, during the summer of 1842, the Chartist cause in Leicester and the county flourished. The Shakespearean Association, which in May numbered 1,350 members, grew steadily, reaching 2,300 in July, 2,700 in August, and nearly 3,000 by the end of the year.[4] By August seven dozen copies of *Cleave's Chartist Circular* were being sold weekly in the town.[5] In the villages a vigorous propaganda was prosecuted, Cooper and Beedham covering the hosiery centres round Leicester, and Skevington and Jarratt those in the north of the county.[6] Chartist Associations sprang up in these villages, and delegate meetings were held in convenient centres such as Mountsorrel.[7] It was a political propaganda such as was not seen again until the early days of the I.L.P.

The climax of these events was reached in the third week of

---

[1] Dec. 1841–Feb. 1842.   [2] *Leicester Chronicle*, 22 Jan., 5 Feb. 1842.
[3] E.g. in May 1842, *ibid.*, 7 May 1842.
[4] *Northern Star*, 28 May, 9 July 1842; R. J. Conklin, *Thomas Cooper the Chartist* (Manila, 1935), pp. 125, 165.
[5] *Northern Star*, 6 Aug. 1842.   [6] *Ibid.*, 14 May, 18 June, 9 July, 16 July 1842.
[7] By June there were Chartist Associations in the following villages: Thurmaston (80 members), Wigston (80), Anstey (50), Burbage (60), Earl Shilton

August. Beginning with a turn-out of the colliers in West Leicestershire (Whitwick, Pegg's Green, and Snibston), the developments
were at first unconnected with Chartism.[1] Despite belated attempts
by the Loughborough Chartists to organise the miners,[2] their dispute seems to have been from first to last a simple industrial grievance, involving demands for better rates and conditions. Outside
influence was limited to visits from delegates of the Staffordshire
colliers. But the local magistrates were apprehensive and requested
additional protection. A division of police under the Chief Constable of Leicestershire, supported by two troops of the Leicestershire Yeomanry, were therefore moved into the area over the week-
end, 13–14 August. Overawed by this display of force, the striking
miners avoided any breach of the peace.

During the following week the strike spread to the stockingers of
Loughborough and the surrounding villages.[3] Again, the Chartists
were to some extent taken unawares by the swift development of
the strike. At the beginning of the week, far from planning the
National Holiday, they were absorbed in arrangements for sending
Skevington to Manchester as delegate to the National Convention.
Only on Friday did they turn their attention to active support of
the strikers. The turn-out in Loughborough was by then complete,
and the strikers' next task was to call out the workers in the neighbouring villages. It was for their part in furthering this that
Skevington and Jarratt were arrested and charged with using inflammatory language. Brought before the Justices at once, Skevington was bound over, but, since he could not produce the necessary
sureties, he was committed to the county gaol in Leicester. He remained there from Saturday afternoon until the following Tuesday, when satisfactory bonds were produced. The arrest of their
leader and his dramatic whisking away to Leicester with an escort
of Dragoon Guards roused the Loughborough Chartists to renewed
action over the week-end, and on the following Monday came a
clash with the police and pensioners. A party of between 300 and
400 strikers set off to march to Mountsorrel, but were overtaken by

---

(50), Oadby (40) — *ibid.*, 18 June 1842. Chartist Associations were also reported
in Sileby, Shepshed, and Narborough — *ibid.*, 6 Aug. 1842.
[1] *Leicester Chronicle*, 20 Aug. 1842.
[2] The *Leicester Journal*, 26 Aug. 1842, carried a report of 'a notorious Chartist'
named Pepper, who had visited the miners and tried to stir them up.
[3] The details are taken from the *Leicester Chronicle*, 20, 27 Aug. 1842, and the
Leicester Journal, 19, 26 Aug. 1842.

the police at the Royal Oak on Leicester Road. Some resistance was offered by the strikers, and seven arrests were made. The prisoners (framework knitters and a needle maker) were fined and bound over, but as four of them could not find bondsmen they were committed to gaol. On their way to the railway station an attempt was made to release them, and the police were pelted with stones from a bridge. Arrests of strikers continued during the next few days, most of them being committed to prison under the Vagrancy Act.

In Leicester the movement began with a turn-out of the glove hands, which was rapidly extended to all sections of the hosiery trade. Cooper was away from the town, on his way to the Manchester Convention, when he heard of the riots in the north and the instructions for a general strike. He wrote to the Leicester Chartists, whom he had left under Beedham's guidance, telling them to call a meeting in the Market Place and support the strike for the Charter. But in fact they had acted before the receipt of his letter. On Monday, 15 August, mass meetings, estimated at between 5,000 and 6,000, were addressed by the Chartist leaders, and there was talk of a general strike until the Charter was the law of the land. Similar meetings were held on Tuesday and Wednesday, and on Thursday speakers from Staffordshire arrived, and a large procession went round the town forcing all glove and stocking hands to turn out. There were some assaults and violence, and the magistrates called out the yeomanry and swore in a hundred special constables. A clash with the police and the specials occurred at the West Bridge during the day, but the main incidents were in the evening. A mass meeting in the Market Place was ordered to disperse, the Riot Act was read, and the police used force to break up the assembly. The turn-outs then withdrew, but re-formed later on the Recreation Ground on Welford Road. This meeting was broken up by the yeomanry, stones were thrown, and the flag bearers and several others were arrested. At a late hour the meeting was again re-formed on the other side of the town, in Abbey Meadow. The next morning some four or five hundred strikers assembled at the bottom of Humberstone Gate to march to Loughborough. They had only reached Belgrave, however, when they were overtaken by the Chief Constable with a party of county police and a troop of yeomanry. The ensuing 'Battle of Mowmacre Hill' put an end to the plans of the marchers, who fled across the fields, leaving four prisoners.[1] The strike continued until the middle of the following week and then collapsed. Seventeen rioters were brought before the magistrates. All were bound over or fined.[2]

The Chartists were in no sense instigators of the turn-out, but once it had begun the Shakespeareans did all in their power to further it. The local situation was well described in a letter written by William Corah, who carried a Chartist flag at the Welford Road demonstration on the Thursday evening:

Leicester, Aug 18th 1842

'Dear Father,

Spread the Charter through the land. Let Britons bold and brave join hand in hand. I write you these few lines to inform you of my circumstances: my wife is on the point of Death. She has got the Fever, and I am altogether in an unsettled State. I must now inform you of the State of our town, we have had meetings every Night this week consisting of from 3 to 2,000 men, yesterday morning a body of persons came round to our shop and fetched us out, they then commenced to fetch the cut up hands and the wrought hose hands out, they assembled at Night to the tune of 20,000 men or upwards and swore that by the Ghost of many a murdered Englishman and English woman, they would work no more till the People's Charter becomes the charter of the land, they are assembled this moment in the Market Place, and before the day is over they mean to fetch the Bread and Beef where it is to be had, they are going round now. I am just informed while I am writing that they are stopping all the mills and factories and God speed the plow, you will see that I am working Gloves at William Adams, Burleys Lane, Church Gate, Leicester. I remain your Son and Brother Chartist,

William Corah.

N.B. they are all Chartists here,
please to send this directly to Sam Lintwilers, Ashby Road, Loughborough.'[3]

The local Chartist leadership had few ideas as to how political advantage might be taken of the turn out, apart from the vague sentiments reflected in Corah's letter. The magistrates on their side were determined to stand firm. Thus William Jones, a Chartist lecturer from Liverpool, was arrested for making an inflammatory speech

---

[1] When later it became fashionable to laugh the danger of Chartism away, the episode was treated with derisive humour, as in Benjamin Newell's *The Battle of Mowmacre Hill, an heroi-comic poem* (Leicester, 1852). But to contemporaries it did not appear in this light.
[2] *Leicester Chronicle*, 27 Aug. 1842.   [3] *Ibid.*

in the Pasture on Sunday, 28 August. The *Leicester Chronicle* was highly critical of the charge of 'inflammatory' language, and pointed out that the evidence came only from a turnkey at the borough gaol two policemen, and two framework knitters.[1] The strongest sample of his language was calling the police 'blue vampires', 'the unboiled blue', and prophesying 'when the day of boiling comes, Woe to the unboiled'. He also referred to the cavalry as 'scientific cut-throats' and 'hired assassins'. For this he was committed to the next Borough Assizes, when he was sentenced to six months' imprisonment.[2]

The August riots also terminated the vigour of Cooper's leadership in Leicester. On his return from Manchester he found the town 'in a state of terror and discouragement',[3] but before he could rally the Chartist forces he was arrested and taken to Stafford on charges arising out of his speeches in the Potteries. He came back in November, receiving a rapturous reception from his devoted Shakespeareans.[4] But in his absence the organisation had gone to pieces, his wife was seriously ill, and he himself was on bail. He took part in the Christmastide preparations for the Birmingham Complete Suffrage Conference, but thereafter the worry of his impending trial overcame him, and he left Leicester virtually for good in March 1843.

In Leicester, as elsewhere, reports of Chartist activity in the local press declined markedly during the mid-40's. Until the end of 1842 hardly a week passed without some item of Chartist intelligence, but by the middle years of the decade there was often no mention of Chartism for months at a time. To later Liberal historians it seemed natural that Chartism should disappear with the return of good harvests and reviving trade:

'The year 1844, compared with some of its predecessors, was particularly quiet. This was in a large degree owing to the abundant harvest of 1843, with the promise of another equally good. There was an improvement in trade, in the revenue, and a more cheerful tone prevailed.'[5]

But what in fact had disappeared were the turn-outs, the demonstrations of starving stockingers, and the Poor Law riots. The

[1] 3 Sept. 1842.
[2] For an account of his harsh treatment before Baron Gurney, see Gammage *op. cit.*, pp. 230–1.
[3] Cooper, *op. cit.*, p. 211.
[4] *Ibid.*, p. 219; *Northern Star*, 19 Nov. 1842.   [5] Searson, *op. cit.*, p. 114

Chartist organisation remained intact, and many local working men remained faithful to their belief that Chartism was the only means of ending their condition of wage slavery and asserting their full dignity through political democracy. To the public at large their activities were practically unknown; the Chartists had no paper of their own, the local press ignored them, and the *Northern Star* was now a London paper dependent for its provincial news on what local correspondents cared to send it. But inarticulateness does not necessarily denote non-existence. The strength of the Chartists in 1848, when events once more forced them into the news, is inexplicable in terms of an organisation which had been defunct for the previous five years.

The outlines of Chartist history in Leicester during this time can be dimly discerned. Lectures, discussions, and open-air meetings in the Pasture and in neighbouring villages formed the core of local activity.[1] From time to time a public meeting in the Market Place would be called, as in March 1844, when George White, the militant Bradford Chartist, presented a petition calling for the release of Thomas Cooper.[2] In the same year a Chartist Adult Sunday School was opened.[3] A delegate was sent to the 1846 National Convention in Leeds, and was elected its secretary.[4] The Land Scheme found enthusiastic supporters in the town who contributed regularly to its funds and became shareholders in it.[5] None of this was exciting 'news', but it was the normal weekly and monthly routine of a struggling working-class political body. For a small number of earnest, Radical working men the Chartist Room was the centre of their social and political life. The old wounds within the Leicester Chartist body gradually healed after Cooper left the town. The old leaders — Markham, Smart, Beedham and Skevington — did not desert the cause, and a few new men came forward, notably Henry Green, a grocer, and George Buckby, the leader of the framework knitters. Bairstow, the full time lecturer-organiser, remained in the district until 1846.[6]

---

[1] See reports in the *Northern Star*, 17 Feb., 25 May 1844; 8 Feb., 31 May, 28 June 1845.

[2] Conklin, *op. cit.*, p. 208.   [3] *Northern Star*, 30 Nov. 1844.

[4] Thomas Martin Wheeler; *ibid.*, 8 Aug. 1846.

[5] *Ibid.*, 18 July 1846 ('Meet every Monday evening at 7 o'clock at 17 Archdeacon Lane'); 11 Dec. 1847 (Election of officers — Z. Astill, secretary; G. Noon, treasurer; C. Arnold, scrutineer; C. Gibson, treasurer for the local fund). Contributions from the Leicester branch appeared in most of the lists of payments to the Land Company published in the *Northern Star*.

[6] *Ibid.*, 23 May 1846.

At the borough election in July 1847 the Chartists came back into the news for a short time. Buckby made a determined effort to intervene, first by promising to go to the hustings as a Chartist candidate, and later by using his Chartist influence to support the two 'ultra' Liberal candidates, Richard Gardiner and Sir Joshua Walmsley.[1] But in the following year the Leicester Chartists were back in the news with a vengeance when the events of 1848 awakened once more all the old hopes and fears in the town.

The stimulus to this Chartist revival in Leicester as elsewhere was the news of the revolutions in Europe. The 'tyrants and despots' were fleeing, a glorious awakening was at hand. Surely the time had come for all true democrats to strike a blow for the Charter, to get rid of our own tyrants and despots. At a crowded meeting in the Amphitheatre in March, with Henry Green in the chair, such sentiments were enthusiastically received, the petition in favour of the enactment of the Charter was adopted, and a congratulatory address to the French Republic endorsed.[2] For the next four months Chartist activity in the town and county was important 'news'. On the first Monday in April a demonstration in the Market Place was attended by 7,000 to 8,000 people; the Leicester section of the National Petition was carried on a pole, with the inscription, 'National Petition; number of signatures 42,884 — 143 yards in length.' After a speech by Buckby, who was about to go to London as delegate to the National Convention, the crowd formed into a procession and escorted him to the station. In the evening a meeting of 3,000 operatives met in the Amphitheatre and affirmed their confidence in the people's leaders, Duncombe and O'Connor.[3] The main object of the meeting, however, was to effect an alliance with the middle-class reformers, and to this end the platform included Passmore Edwards, who was visiting the town, John Collier, president of the Leicester Complete Suffrage Society, and J. F. Winks. The *Leicester Chronicle* was at this stage in favour of such a policy of collaboration with the Chartists.[4] But the events of the following week were sufficiently alarming to create caution in most middle-class minds. Reports of arming, bullets being cast, and pikes being bought from Birmingham circulated in the town, and an appeal for specials was made.[5] On Sunday a thousand-strong

---

[1] *Leicester Chronicle*, 31 July 1847.
[2] *Leicester Chronicle*, 25 Mar. 1848.
[3] *Ibid.*, 8 Apr. 1848.
[4] *Ibid.*, Editorial Notice.
[5] *Ibid.*, 15 Apr. 1848.

procession marched to Loughborough and back. On Monday, 10 April, the tricolour was flown at a meeting in the Market Place, and it was decided to meet every evening that week to hear reports from the National Convention and the House of Commons.[1]

At Loughborough there was similar enthusiasm. A meeting of 4,000 people to listen to Dr McDouall was held on 4 April, and throughout the week daily meetings in the Market Place drew crowds of up to 3,000.[2] The presence of the Mountsorrel quarrymen, carrying their hammers, on the one side, and the provocative display of police and military force on the other, was a severe test of Skevington's powers of leadership. He presided at all meetings, and was widely admired for his good-humoured handling of the situation.[3] From other parts of the county came reports of Chartist demonstrations; from Hinckley and Earl Shilton in the south-west, as well as from Wigston, Countesthorpe, and the villages nearer Leicester.[4] It is clear that during the week of the presentation of the Charter there was a widespread air of expectancy. Great hopes had been built up, and detailed instructions to the local authorities had been issued by the Home Office.

What then was the effect of the fiasco of the Kennington Common demonstration and the rejection of the National Petition? Certainly not the feeling that all was lost. Indeed, there is more evidence of a rising temper in the Leicester Chartist movement after April than before it. April 10 was not a watershed in the history of Leicester Chartism. During the next three months militant Chartism was probably as strong in Leicester and the county as it had ever been. The degree of police precautions alone suggests something more than men and movements of straw.[5] During April the routine 'precautions' in Loughborough amounted to 500 specials together with yeomanry and dragoons, in addition to the normal police force.[6] When it was announced that O'Connor would visit Loughborough in June the magistrates first tried to pretend

[1] *Ibid.*   [2] *Northern Star*, 8, 22 Apr. 1848.
[3] The report to the Home Office stated that order was maintained by Skevington. H.O. 41/19.
[4] *Ibid.*
[5] To attribute such measures solely to grossly exaggerated fear is not altogether satisfactory. Frederick Goodyer, the Chief Constable of Leicestershire (who had previously been Superintendent of the borough police force), was an efficient and far from panicky man. In any case, the police had by now had ten years experience of Chartism.
[6] *Northern Star*, 22 Apr. 1848.

I

that the meeting would be illegal and then, when Skevington called their bluff, they tried to terrorise Chartist supporters by a display of force. The centre of the town was packed with police, specials, pensioners, a troop of Dragoon Guards, two troops of yeomanry, and a company of the 87th Infantry Regiment. When O'Connor arrived at the station the magistrates talked to him and persuaded him not to proceed with the demonstration. He therefore made a speech at the station, urging his 'children' to behave peaceably, and continued his journey to London. Skevington then conducted the meeting in the Market Place.[1] Elsewhere in the county Chartist meetings were banned or overawed by force. For instance, a hand-bill announcing a meeting near Blaby in June was immediately countered by a ban from the magistrates. Despite a sharp downpour of rain some 200 people attended, 50 police and specials were sent to the meeting, and the speaker, George Hubbard, a stocking maker and Chartist from Countesthorpe, was taken into custody.[2] In Leicester a similar tough attitude on the part of the authorities was manifest, though here it was directed not so much against Chartist activity as Poor Law rioters. The Bastille Riots in May arose out of relief grievances of the unemployed, and for a week there was daily hand-to-hand fighting in the streets between the un-employed and the police and pensioners.[3] So ferocious was the conduct of the police and their auxiliaries that subsequently a com-mittee was set up to investigate cases of police brutality. The lead in this was taken by Markham and the Chartists, but the com-mittee also included a number of middle-class Radicals such as the Rev. J. Bloodsworth and Thomas Cook (later of travel agency fame).[4]

Internal evidence also suggests that the morale of the Chartist body during the summer of 1848 was high, and that there was in fact a fairly widespread feeling of militancy. In the borough the Chartists were divided, Markham and Green favouring a policy of alliance with the middle classes, Buckby and Warner preferring an independent, physical force line. In consequence Buckby split off from the Leicester Charter Association in June, and formed the Working Men's Chartist Association. He claimed a membership of 300 — as compared with 1,200 in the parent body.[5] In the same

[1] *Leicester Chronicle*, 17 June 1848.
[2] *Ibid.*, 24 June 1848. For similar instances see *ibid.*, 22 July 1848.
[3] *Ibid.*, 20 May 1848.   [4] *Ibid.*, 27 May, 10 June 1848.
[5] *Ibid.*, 17 June 1848.

month appeared a pamphlet, *Physical Force*,[1] by George Bown, a veteran of over fifty years standing in the Radical cause in Leicester. He was careful not to urge bloodshed, but his 'sober, earnest, and deliberate advice' was 'GET ARMS'. How much arming in the town and county there really was is now impossible to determine,[2] but unless police action is to be ascribed to needless panic there must have been some such activity.

This is confirmed by scraps of evidence such as that of John Sketchley, who was for ten years the secretary of the South Leicestershire Chartist Society.[3] After describing the banning of open-air meetings in the villages round Hinckley, and the defiance of the ban, he wrote:

'I was a member of the committee for the county which was entrusted with the necessary arrangements for any emergency . . . . But the 10th of April passed without an insurrection in London. Though London had fallen through the fault of some one, in the Midlands at any rate we did not despair. The work of organisation still went on, and drilling, etc., became the order of the day. As Autumn approached this became more general.'

Government spies were known to be at work and one was identified on the local Chartist organisation committee. In September the police made repeated searches for arms, and Sketchley received a private note that he was to be arrested on information laid by an informer. Being forewarned, however, Sketchley was fore-armed; and the police had to retire baffled. A similar attempt to arrest him a few weeks later was also foiled. Nevertheless the Chartist organisation began to disintegrate under this continual police pressure, and there was a noticeable falling away from the movement. As Sketchley put it,

'. . . the end was coming. The arrest of so many of the leaders, the severe measures of the Government, the vigilance and the growing feeling that there was no great leader left able to lead the people to victory, were all tending to demoralise the party . . . .'

[1] *Physical Force. An address to all classes of reformers, but especially to those who are unjustly excluded from the Franchise* (Leicester, 1848.)
[2] Cf. the report of a club to purchase arms, in the *Leicester Chronicle*, 3 June 1848. See also a report of the enrolment of Loughborough Chartists in a National Guard in May — H.O. 41/19.
[3] 'Personal Experiences in the Chartist Movement', *Today*, July 1884, pp. 20–9.

George Wray, who had recently come to the fore among the Chart ists in the borough, in a letter the following March lamented the decay of Chartism when once employment returned.[1]

But Chartism in Leicester and the county did not disappear; fo another five years a remnant struggled hard to keep the movemen alive.[2] They continued to meet and to agitate, and at times they managed to make themselves heard on questions of the day. George Wray was sent as delegate to the National Convention in March 1851,[3] and national Chartist speakers could be sure of an enthusi astic response from the local working men. A camp meeting a Mountsorrel in September 1850 attracted a crowd of 20,000 to listen to Ernest Jones and O'Connor.[4] Two years later similar meetings were still being held at Mountsorrel, and Jones and Gammage could find sympathetic hearers in Leicester when they went on to visit the town.[5] At the 1852 borough elections the Chartists were vociferous in their support of Walmsley and Gardiner, the 'advanced' Liberals.[6] Buckby indeed suggested the old Chartist tactic of exclusive dealing to support them, and the *Leicester Chronicle*, which supported the moderate Liberals, Palmer and Wilde, branded John Biggs and his followers as Red Republicans and Chartists.[7]

The following year, however, saw the last revival of Chartism in Leicester. At a great Whit Monday Radical demonstration, led by John Biggs, the Chartists carried their banners and the Framework Knitters' Committee had a tableau with Buckby and other prominent Chartists.[8] In July Jones and Gammage addressed a large Sunday Chartist demonstration at Mountsorrel.[9] In Leicester they were enthusiastically welcomed to the New Hall, and the

[1] *Northern Star*, 3 Mar. 1849.

[2] Cf. the Liberal version of the end of Chartism, in Searson, *op. cit.*, p. 149 — 'A number of minor reforms remained to be made . . . but all the great battles had been fought and won by the close of 1849. With this consummation political agitations, which had their rise in the poverty of the masses, ceased to be violent. Good trade, higher wages, cheap food, and multiplied comforts led working men to be not less in earnest about their political rights, but to strive for their enfranchisement by making common cause with the great body of reformers throughout the country. Hence, in the year 1850, Chartism had well nigh disappeared, and its old leaders were pointed out as the "extinct volcanoes" of that fiery eruption'.

[3] Gammage, *op. cit.*, p. 370.   [4] *Ibid.*, p. 355; *Leicester Chronicle*, 7 Sept. 1850.

[5] Gammage, *op. cit.*, p. 393.

[6] *Leicester Chronicle*, 20 Mar., 12 June, 3 July 1852.

[7] *Ibid.*, 5 June, 3 July 1852.

[8] *Leicester Journal*, 20 May 1853; *Leicester Chronicle*, 21 May 1853.

[9] *Leicester Chronicle*, 16 July 1853.

Leicester Chronicle was moved to comment editorially on the Chartist revival in Leicester and the neighbouring villages.[1] Nothing came, however, of the revival. The Chartist organisation as such was thereafter heard of no more, and the ex-Chartists turned their energies into other, and potentially more fruitful fields of popular effort. After fifteen years the narrative of Chartism in Leicester and Leicestershire had come to an end.

III

The main dynamic of Leicester Chartism was the condition of the framework knitters. To middle-class contemporaries it seemed axiomatic that there was a direct connection between Chartist activity and the state of the hosiery trade. Leicester, until later in the century, was essentially a one industry town, and consequently depression in the hosiery trade meant widespread unemployment, social unrest and a swelling of the Chartist ranks. With an improvement in trade there was a return of employment and a lessening of interest in Chartism. This view seems substantially correct for Chartism as a mass movement, notably in 1842 and 1848. But the appeal of Chartism to many framework knitters at a deeper and more permanent level needs a somewhat different explanation. The relationship here is not only to the state of the hosiery trade at a particular time, but also to the general working conditions within the industry throughout the 1830's and 1840's.

The close connection between Chartism and framework knitting is shown clearly in two respects. First, there is a high degree of correlation between the main centres of the industry and the places from which there were reports of Chartist activity. Second, many of the local Chartist leaders were framework knitters. It was estimated that in 1844 there were 20,311 knitting frames in Leicestershire, of which 4,140 were in the borough, the remainder being in 86 different places in the county.[2] The frames were not distributed evenly throughout Leicestershire, however, but were concentrated in certain localities. Of these the first was the Soar Valley, dominated by Loughborough, and stretching from Thurmaston through Mountsorrel and Sileby to Barrow-on-Soar. In the north-west a line of hosiery villages stretched from Shepshed to Castle Donnington,

---

[1] *Ibid.*
[2] William Felkin, *History of the Machine-Wrought Hosiery and Lace Manufactures* (1867), pp. 465–6.

including Hathern and Long Whatton. South of Leicester was
another group, including Enderby, Narborough, Whetstone,
Cosby, Blaby, Countesthorpe, Wigston, and Oadby, and stretching as far as Kibworth, Arnesby, and Shearsby. In the south-west
Hinckley had no less than 1,750 frames, and the neighbouring villages of Earl Shilton, Barwell, and Burbage were also important
centres. Now these villages were precisely those from which the
Northern Star, the *Leicester Chronicle*, and the Home Office sources
reported active Chartist organisation. They were the areas to which
Thomas Cooper and John Skevington turned their attention during
the most active period of Chartist evangelism in the summer of
1842. It was to the stockingers of Mountsorrel and Loughborough,
as well as the borough, that Jones addressed his appeal for a Chartist revival in the early 1850's. In the eastern half of the county
there were practically no stocking frames, neither was there any
Chartism.

Among the earlier Chartist leaders Finn was a framework
knitter, and prominent in the 1838 plan for co-operation between
employers and workers to regulate conditions in the industry.
Swain was a small master stockinger, and at Loughborough Skevington's henchmen, Turner and Jarrett, were framework knitters.
After 1846 the most active of the Chartist leaders in Leicester was
Buckby, who was also the leader of the framework knitters.
Sketchley from Hinckley was similarly a stockinger. At a somewhat lower level — in the small hosiery villages for instance —
there is evidence to suggest that the most prominent local Chartist
was often a framework knitter.[1] Even those Chartist leaders who
were not framework knitters were fully aware of, and sympathetic
to the demands of the stockingers. It was the revelation of conditions in the industry that made Thomas Cooper a Chartist.[2] John
Johnson, chairman of the framework knitters' appeal committee in
1844, and a prominent Leicester Chartist, appears to have been a
shoemaker by trade.[3] But indeed it was impossible to live in a town
so dominated by the hosiery trade as was Leicester in the first half
of the nineteenth century and not be aware of the general pattern of
life in the industry.

[1] E.g. George Hubbard, 'an active physical force Chartist from Countesthorpe'.
Leicester Chronicle, 24 June 1848.
[2] *Life*, Ch. 13, 'Leicester: wretchedness of stockingers'.
[3] I am indebted to Dr E. R. Ward, a great–grandson of John Johnson, for this
information.

The general history of hosiery manufacture in Leicester and the county has been dealt with elsewhere and need not be repeated here.[1] It will suffice to outline only such aspects of the industry as are directly relevant to the Chartist movement. By the 1830's the industry had developed various branches in addition to stockings. Shirts, cravats, braces, socks, and gloves were all made in the town. Most, though not all, of this was worsted hosiery, the cotton and silk branches of the trade being concentrated in Nottingham and Derby. In the borough there had also developed a cheap line of stocking manufacture, the cut-ups, or straight down hose; and the traditional wrought (i.e. fully fashioned) hose tended to be made mainly in the county. The basis of all this manufacture was the hand knitting frame, which was worked either in the stockinger's own home or in the small 'shop' belonging to a master stockinger. Steam power was not introduced into the industry until 1845, when Thomas Collins first collected a number of frames together into a 'factory' in Barkby Lane.[2] The domestic basis of framework knitting remained until much later than the period of the Chartist agitation.

From the early nineteenth century two factors had combined to undermine the independence of the stockinger — the system of frame letting and the growth of middlemen. Although in the eighteenth century some stockingers had owned their own frames, by the 1830's this independence had disappeared, and virtually all frames were hired. The owners of the frames were of three different types — hosiers (or manufacturers), middlemen (bagmen), and persons not connected with the trade who let the frames solely for the profits of their rents. Among the varieties of middlemen it was not always possible to categorise exactly. But in addition to the 'putter out' who simply gave out the yarn for the hosier and collected the hose when it had been made, there were two types of genuine contractor. The undertaker, or master stockinger, contracted with the larger hosiers to supply hose, and then put out the work to a number of framework knitters. Similar to, and often

---

[1] Notably by Dr L. A. Parker, in *Victoria County History — Leicestershire*, Vol. III (1955), pp. 2–23; Patterson, *op. cit.*, and W. Felkin, *Account of the Machine Wrought Hosiery Trade* (1845), and *History of the Machine-Wrought Hosiery and Lace Manufactures* (1867). The main contemporary source is the *Report of the Commission on the Condition of the Framework Knitters* (1845). See also the pamphlet by W. G. Jones, *Leicester Stockingers, 1680–1890* (Leicester, 1891).

[2] Jones, *op. cit.*, p. 8.

indistinguishable from this type was the bagman or bag hosier. He flourished particularly in certain country districts, and manu factured on his own account. It was from the twin institutions of frameletting and middlemen that most of the grievances of the framework knitters stemmed.

Frame rents were by no means the only grievance, but the struggle for their abolition became synonymous with and symboli-cal of the general struggle to improve the stockinger's lot. Tradi-tionally the rent for a frame was ninepence per week, but with the introduction of the new wider frames the rent went up. A constant complaint of the stockingers was the uncertainty and variability of frame rents. A full week's rent was paid whether or not there was a full week's work, and it was paid whether the frame was in the stockinger's home or in the employer's shop. In the latter case an additional charge for standing room was also made, together with charges for light, fuel, and needles.[1] Thus it was not uncommon in 1844 for 3s. in charges to be deducted from weekly earnings of 10s.; and there were cases where men who had had work for only two or three days in the week found that they had worked for nothing else than the frame rent.[2]

But, as Thomas Cooper discovered,

'. . . it was by a number of petty and vexatious grindings, in addition to the obnoxious "frame rent", that the poor framework knitter was worn down, till you might have known him by his peculiar air of misery and dejection, if you had met him a hundred miles from Leicester. He had to pay, not only "frame rent", but so much per week for the "standing" of the frame in the shop of the "master", for the frames were grouped together in the shops, generally, though you would often find a single frame in a weaver's cottage. The man had also to pay threepence per dozen to the "master" for "giving out" of the work. He had also to pay so much per dozen to the female "seamer" of the hose. And he had also oil to buy for his machine, and lights to pay for in the darker half of the year. All the deductions brought the aver-age earnings of the stocking-weaver to four and sixpence per week. I found this to be a truth confirmed on every hand.

'And when he was "in work", the man was evermore experiencing some new attempt at grinding him down to a lower sum per dozen for

[1] Robert Bindley, *The history of the struggle for the abolition of Frame Rents and Charges* (Leicester, 1875). Bindley was a framework knitter who gave evidence before the Truck Commission in 1871.
[2] *Northern Star*, 12 Oct. 1844, letter signed by John Johnson and Thomas Winters.

the weaving, or at "docking" him so much per dozen for alleged faults in his work; while sometimes — and even for several weeks together — he experienced the most grievous wrong of all. The "master" not being able to obtain full employment for all the frames he rented of the manufacturer, but perhaps only half employ for them — distributed, or "spread" the work over all the frames . . . . But the foul grievance was this: each man had to pay a whole week's frame rent, although he had only half a week's work! Thus while the poor miserable weaver knew that his half-week's work, after all the deductions, would produce him such a mere pittance that he could only secure a scant share of the meanest food, he remembered that the owner of the frame had the full rent per week, and the middleman or "master" had also his weekly pickings secured to him.

'Again; a kind of hose would be demanded for which the frame needed a deal of troublesome and tedious altering. But the poor weaver was expected to make all the alterations himself. And sometimes he could not begin his week's weaving until a day, or a day and a half, had been spent in making the necessary alterations. Delay was also a custom on Monday mornings. The working man must call again. He was too early. And, finally, all the work was ended. The warehouses were glutted, and the hosiery firms had no orders. This came again and again, in Leicester and Loughborough and Hinckley, and the framework knitting villages of the county, until, when a little prosperity returned, no one expected it to continue.'[1]

Cooper's final hint that the low condition of the framework knitters was due to more than the specific grievances already listed sets the problem in a somewhat wider perspective. The distress of the stockingers, caused by their low earnings and long periods of complete or partial unemployment, was not the result of competition between the economically dying handworker and production by power machinery. The truth was that the trade of framework knitting, like that of handloom weaving, was overstocked with labour. Only in exceptionally prosperous times was there enough work to go round. The system of frame rents directly encouraged employers to spread the work over as many knitters as possible, even though this meant that each would have less than a full week's work, since thereby the maximum number of rents would be obtained. The organisation of the industry was well calculated to encourage over-crowding; there was, in fact, a premium on

---

[1] *Life*, pp. 140–2. Cooper omits another common grievance, that of truck. The stockinger was frequently paid in kind by the bagman, who in many cases also kept a shop.

idleness.[1] The industry was very susceptible to changes in fashion
new lines or new markets, offering higher rates than the average
attracted fresh workers, who remained to swell the numbers in the
industry long after the temporary boom had gone. Entry into the
trade was easy. Apprenticeship had decayed or become meaning-
less by the 1840's, and in any case the work was normally only
semi-skilled. Youths and girls in their teens could easily manage
an ordinary frame. The concentration of the industrial life of the
area upon hosiery restricted alternative job opportunities, and it
was customary for children to follow their fathers at the frame.

The wretched pattern of family and working life which was all
that such conditions permitted appears clearly from several contemporary descriptions.[2] Daniel Merrick,[3] who had been a framework knitter in Leicester in the 40's, drew upon his experience later
in *The Warp of Life*.[4] The pamphlet describes, and points a moral
from the life of William, the son of a Leicester stockinger earning
8s. for 80 hours of labour per week. The petty tyrannies of the bagman reduced the father to a state of fear and trembling each week
The struggle to keep alive absorbed the total energies of the family,
but despite all efforts,

'the following was the general bill of fare. The oldest girl, Mary Ann
was sent to Mrs Kindheart, the landlady of the "Horse and Trumpet"
to ask whether she would give them some tea leaves, and having obtained them, they would be used over again by the family. Some bread
to this would complete the meal. Very little in the shape of meat ever
entered the house, unless it was a pennyworth of "liver" or three-
halfpenny worth of what is known as "back fat". Even this meagre
fare was not always to be obtained. Frequently on Saturdays none of
the family could have any dinner because the funds were exhausted.
For clothing they were greatly dependent upon charitable gifts from
ladies and gentlemen in the neighbourhood.'[5]

[1] Bindley, *op. cit.*, pp. 18–19, accused a Leicester manufacturer later of encouraging his men to borrow money for drink on Mondays ('opening the bank')
so that they would not work and thereby embarrass him by over-production.
[2] E.g. Cooper's account in *Life*, Ch. 13. Felkin, *op. cit.*, p. 459, also describes
the wretched condition of a family of framework knitters whom he visited in
Leicester in 1844.
[3] 1827–88. A leader of the framework knitters in the 1860's and 1870's, Merrick was President of the T.U.C. in 1877 when the annual meeting was held in
Leicester. (Obituary, in *Leicester Daily Post*, 21 Feb. 1888.) Merrick does not
seem to have played an active part in the Chartist movement, but he was a witness of the events of 1842 and 1848, and describes these in his pamphlet.
[4] *The Warp of Life, or Social and Moral Threads* (Leicester, 1876).
[5] *Op. cit.*, p. 7.

William was soon set to work as a winder and, after an interlude in a brickyard, became a framework knitter. Politics played no part in his subsequent career (through drink and an improvident marriage he was led to an early death), but in the shop in which he worked

'. . . politics were the general theme for discussion and conversation. A Chartist newspaper was taken weekly . . . . Sometimes Feargus O'Connor's Land Scheme was discussed, and upheld by some as the only means to raise the poor from their impoverished condition and break the bonds of their oppression. Others agreed it was very well so far as it went, but the cure for the people's ills was in making the six points of the People's Charter the law of the land. The universal feeling of these operatives was that so long as they were kept in a state of political bondage they would be simply the tools of the classes of society above them in social status.'[1]

It was the custom in the shop to have a break for tea at five o'clock, and this was the usual time for discussion:

'Some would seat themselves on the winders' stools, some on bricks, and others, whose frames were in the centre, would sit on their "seat boards". Then they would commence a general discussion upon various matters, political, moral, and religious. After tea a short article would be read from the *Northern Star*, and this would form the subject matter for consideration and chat during the remainder of the day.'[2]

The appeal of Chartism to the framework knitters as a remedy for their depressed condition was made the stronger by the failure of other methods. Luddite violence had long ago been stamped out. Social and economic advance through trade societies had come to naught. Attempts to revive the Rev. Robert Hall's plan for co-operation between employers and workers had been rebuffed by the hosiers.[3] Owenite co-operation had failed to capture the imagination of more than a handful of thoughtful artisans.[4] For a time hope was pinned to Parliament and the courts, but no legislation of significance was forthcoming;[5] and in Chawner's case the Queen's

---

[1] *Ibid.*, pp. 18–19. [2] *Ibid.*, p. 22.
[3] Feb.–Apr. 1838. See Patterson, *op. cit.*, p. 298.
[4] There is some evidence that Buckby favoured producers' co-operation as a remedy for the framework knitters' grievances. *Leicester Chronicle*, 8 Jan., 13 May 1848.
[5] Despite the exhaustive enquiry into the conditions of the industry by Muggeridge in 1845, no legislation affecting frame rents resulted. Sir Henry Halford's bill in 1847 to abolish frame rents was defeated. Felkin, *op. cit.*, pp. 473–8.

Bench held that frame rents and charges were not illegal.[1] These
roads had thus turned out to be blind alleys; the appeal of Chartism
was that it seemed to offer a new way forward.

There was one particularly strong link between Chartists and
framework knitters — the new Poor Law. The high incidence of
unemployment and partial employment forced the framework
knitters into a close acquaintance with the harsh conditions of the
Bastille system in Leicester. The need for leadership in their Poor
Law struggles was a powerful incentive towards Chartism. At all
the crucial points in its history the Leicester Chartist movement was
associated with, though not identical with, agitation on Poor Law
issues. At its launching in 1838 the Chartist movement had been
borne forward on the wave of resentment against the New Poor
Law. In 1842 Thomas Cooper led the unemployed stockingers
singing through the streets, and tried to defend those stockingers
on trial for the April workhouse riots.[2] The Bastille Riots of May
1848, arising out of grievances of the unemployed in the workhouse
stone yard, added a fierce tone in a period of rising Chartist militancy.[3] The rioters and demonstrators on these occasions were not
Chartists, simply unemployed stockingers. But they sang Chartist
hymns, shouted Chartist slogans, and the leading Chartists were
usually in sympathy with their demands. Poor relief had its connections too with the frame rent question, as was skilfully shown in
the appeal for public support to back up Chawner's case.[4] The
stockingers argued that because of frame rents and charges their
wages were reduced to below subsistence level, and they were
therefore, forced to ask for poor relief to make up the deficiency
whereas if they received their full wages (i.e. without deductions
for frame rent) they would not need relief. As they succinctly put
it:

'If we fall on the parish, you have to support us; if we get our right
we can support ourselves; we therefore trust you will assist us.'

[1] Chawner v. Cummings, 1844. This was a test case brought by a framework
knitter, Chawner, against his employer, claiming that the sums deducted for
frame rent had been illegally withheld. A verdict in favour of the plaintiff was
given at the Leicestershire Assizes, but was reversed on appeal to the Queen's
Bench. Felkin, op. cit., p. 456.
[2] Life, pp. 175, 177, 183–5.
[3] Leicester Chronicle, 20 May 1848. Also Merrick, op. cit., pp. 31–2.
[4] 'The Stocking Makers' Address to the Ladies and Gentlemen of the town
and county of Leicester, for the purpose of raising a fund in aid of the action for
putting an end to the illegality of frame rents.' Northern Star, 12 Oct. 1844. The
chairman of this appeal committee was John Johnson, a Chartist.

Thus from its inception the Chartist movement in Leicester was closely linked with the struggles of the framework knitters. After 1846 this characteristic (epitomised in the leadership of Buckby) was especially strong, and it helps to explain the continuance of Chartism after 1848. Frame rents and charges were not laughed out of existence in the spring of 1848, and in consequence neither was Leicester Chartism. In a moment of unusual sympathy the editor of the *Leicester Chronicle* gave an insight into the matter. He castigated the rich for their failure to appreciate the desperate condition of thousands of unemployed stockingers in the town and county; and concluded:

> 'With these things before us . . . we should not be surprised if, to a man, the framework knitters of this town and district were proved to be Chartists. In their ideas CHARTISM has an import of which the unsympathetic can form but a feeble notion. It means a renovation of all things — a regeneration of the social state — a political millennium. It means better wages, limited hours of labour, comfort, independence, happiness — it means, in short, all that the fond heart of suffering man pictures to him of joy and prosperity in his happiest moments.'[1]

IV

Although the condition of the framework knitters provided the dynamic for Leicester Chartism as a mass movement, it was only in its later stages that the leaders were predominantly stockingers. From 1838 to 1846 the composition of the leadership suggests that Chartism had a wider appeal. Two main types of leader appeared — the man from outside the area, usually a full-time lecturer-agent, and more or less ephemeral; and the local man who devoted his spare time to the Chartist cause. The latter provided a degree of stability and usually served the movement continuously throughout the whole decade from 1838 to 1848. Among the leaders of this type there was a fairly high degree of homogeneity, produced by three marked characteristics. In the first place they were all self-educated working men or small tradesmen; there were no influential middle-class supporters. Second, a majority of them had a strong Nonconformist (usually Methodist) allegiance. And third, many of them had had experience in Radical and working-class movements of various kinds before 1838. These factors, together with a strong middle-class Nonconformist Radical tradition and the absence of

[1] 8 Apr. 1848.

an Irish element among the stockingers, produced a distinctive type of Chartist leadership in Leicester.

Foremost among the Chartists in the town was John Markham. He was for many years a shoemaker in Belgrave Gate, but later became an auctioneer and furniture broker. He was a local preacher for the Primitive Methodists until his expulsion from the connexion.[1] From the launching of the Leicester and Leicestershire Political Union in October 1838 until the enquiries following the Bastille Riots of May 1848 his name appeared in every phase of Chartist agitation. Self-educated, he was a fine example of the shrewd, level-headed type of working-class Chartist leader. Of his devotion to the principles of the Charter there could be no doubt, but he had no time for insurrectionists, and only once did he go so far as to use physical force language. As the Chartist organisation gradually disintegrated after 1848 he turned his energies in new directions, and in 1852 was elected to the Town Council for North Saint Margaret's ward.[2]

At Loughborough John Skevington's career (1801–50) showed many similarities.[3] His father, Joseph Skevington, was a leading Primitive Methodist preacher in the district, and at the age of fourteen John acquired local fame as 'the boy preacher' on the Loughborough plan. Shortly afterwards he became a Primitive Methodist travelling preacher, and in 1822, 1823 and 1824 travelled successively at Halifax, Barnsley and Bradwell. His lameness, however, compelled him to give up travelling and he returned to Loughborough where he continued his preaching until 1836, when he left the connexion.[4] By this time he was widely known as a democrat,

---

[1] *Midland Counties Illuminator* (1841), quoted in Conklin, *op. cit.*, p. 91.

[2] He was re-elected in 1855 and 1858. John Storey, *Historical Sketch of . . . the Borough of Leicester* (1895), pp. 211–17. His election in 1852 was as a Liberal and supporter of John Biggs, though the *Leicester Chronicle*, 30 Oct. 1852, continued to refer to him as a Chartist.

[3] The following details are taken from reports in the local press and from H. B. Kendall, *The Origin and History of the Primitive Methodist Church* (2 vols., 1903), Vol. I. I am also indebted to Mr Feargus Stevens and Mrs E. E. Stevens, descendants of John Skevington, for information about him. C. M. Phillips of Garendon Hall, in a report to the Home Secretary dated 30 Jan. 1839 described Skevington as 'the husband of a respectable bonnet maker', and went on to say that he and Smart were 'both reckless men, destitute of character' — H.O., 40/44.

[4] This was over a disagreement on policy concerning Dead Lane Chapel, which had fallen into serious financial difficulties. Skevington was trust treasurer at the time. At the close of his life he attempted to reunite with the Primitive Methodists but they rebuffed him, perhaps because of Hugh Bourne's strong dislike of 'speeching radicals'. Kendall, *op. cit.*, pp. 318, 334–41. Loughborough

and spoke frequently on the hustings at election times. 'From early
life', he wrote, 'I advocated the rights of the many.' When Chartism appeared in 1838 he was regarded as the natural leader of the
movement in Loughborough. His influence among the working
classes there was acknowledged to be very great,[1] and, like Markham, he always appears to have used his power to prevent violence.
He too was no insurrectionist. The springs of his Chartism were
not far to seek; in the knowledge that the end of his life was near he
wrote:

> 'As an advocate of the principles of the People's Charter, I found
> nothing on inspection to condemn in them, nor in my advocacy of the
> same, but a firm conviction that though a man may be a Chartist and
> not a Christian, a man cannot be a Christian and not a Chartist unless
> through ignorance.'[2]

At the National Convention in 1839, where he sat as delegate for
Loughborough, he protested against O'Brien's motion in July calling off the National Holiday, though when it came to the vote he
supported the motion, and in September he voted for the dissolution of the Convention.[3] His arrest and short spell in Leicester gaol
in 1842 did nothing to check his ardour. When the chairman of the
bench expressed the hope that Skevington would now learn to be
peaceable, he jestingly replied, 'Yes — now that I have been to
College.'[4] Until his death in 1850 he inspired and organised the
Loughborough Chartists; and in 1848 his followers presented him
with a testimonial and his portrait in oils, 'for his great services to
the cause of liberty'.[5]

Associated with Skevington and Markham in the early days of the

---

was an early centre of Primitive Methodism and was the head of the 3rd circuit
from 1818. Until 1822 Leicester was in the Loughborough circuit.

[1] E.g. his control over the meetings in Loughborough Market Place in 1848 —
H.O. 41/19. Kendall, *op. cit.*, p. 337, repeates a (legendary?) story that at one
time the Loughborough men came to Skevington and said: 'Skevington only
speak the word, and we will tear up every stone in the Market Place,' but he refused to countenance such violence.

[2] From a MS. by Skevington, quoted in Kendall, *op. cit.*, p. 337.

[3] Gammage, *op. cit.*, pp. 147, 156. He was also elected to the National Convention in Manchester, in 1842, his expenses being met by the Loughborough
Chartists. (*Leicester Journal*, 19 Aug. 1842.)

[4] *Leicester Journal*, 26 Aug. 1842. To continue the story — the magistrate replied that he hoped Skevington had learned something there. 'Yes', said
Skevington, 'shall I give you a specimen?' 'No', replied the magistrate, and as
Skevington left the court he observed, 'Now you have made me a greater Chartist
than ever'.

[5] *Northern Star*, 29 Apr. 1848. The portrait was painted by J. Boden, and was
presented publicly by Thomas Cooper.

movement were several men whose previous activities had been
such as to make them readily identifiable as 'friends of the people'.
In Leicester John Swain, a small master stockinger, had been a
member of the Leicester Radical Working Men's Association
established in August 1836, and was active in the Anti-Poor Law
agitation. It was at his house that Thomas Cooper lodged when he
first became a Chartist. The Seal brothers were similarly established Radicals before the advent of Chartism. John Seal, a newsagent and bookseller, was an Owenite. He had been prominent in
1830 in the Leicester branch of the National Association for the
Protection of Labour, and was later active in the Working Men's
Association, of which his brother, Richard, was secretary.[1] William
Burden, an artisan, also combined his Chartism with a faith in
Owenite socialism[2] — though for the most part the Leicester
Owenites kept aloof from the Chartist movement.[3] There were also
veterans of even earlier Radical movements among the Chartists.
Bown, 'a fine intellectual old man',[4] had been an active Radical in
the town since 1792, and used his pen in support of the Chartist
cause. Thomas Raynor Smart (1772–1847) was Skevington's chief
assistant at Loughborough until 1842 (when he moved to Leicester,
and later to Markfield) and accompanied him as fellow delegate to
the National Convention in 1839. He was born near Loughborough,
of working-class parents, and his thirst for knowledge and consequent efforts at self-education led to his appointment as a super-
visor of excise. He suffered for his Radicalism by losing his job
after holding it for seventeen years, and thereafter maintained a
precarious living as a school-master.[5] His daughter married J.
Culley, a Loughborough Chartist and Primitive Methodist.[6]

Such then was the stuff of which the leadership of Leicester

---

[1] Searson, *op. cit.*, p. 66.

[2] E.g. at a meeting in the All Saints Open room in January 1840 he read passages from the *New Moral World* on the currency question. *Leicester Chronicle*, 1
Feb. 1840.

[3] Cooper, *Life*, p. 174.

[4] *Ibid.*, p. 145. Cooper had not always entertained such high opinions of Bown.
At the time of his (Cooper's) arrest he had accused Bown of deserting his Chartist
principles in order to 'get a place' (Inspector of Nuisances) worth £50 a year.
Leicester Journal, 2 Sept. 1842. Bown was editor of the Leicester Chartist periodical, *The Midland Counties Illuminator*, 1841, before Cooper took it over (*Life*,
p. 145) and also wrote two pamphlets on 'Physical Force'.

[5] *Leicestershire Mercury*, 27 Apr. 1839.

[6] The Culleys were leading members of the Primitive Methodist Church,
Robert Culley being one of the earliest travelling preachers (1818) in Loughborough and Leicester. J. Culley was an active Chartist from 1838 to 1848. and
his wife organised the female Chartists. *Northern Star*, 3 June 1848.

Chartism was made. But to complete the description one further element needs to be added, namely the leaders who came from out-side. They were not very numerous, and, with the exception of Cooper, exerted little distinctive influence on the movement. They were clearly men of a rather different stamp from the local Chart-ists, being perhaps tougher and less disinterested in that they de-pended on the movement for their livelihood. John Mason, the former Tyneside shoemaker, who had so impressed Cooper in 1840, did not stay long in Leicester,[1] and Bairstow, who spent several years of his career as a Chartist lecturer in the Leicester district, did little to enhance the prestige or power of the movement.[2] James Duffy (a militant Irishman who had been sentenced to three years' imprisonment in 1840 along with Holberry, the Sheffield martyr) was left in joint charge of the Shakespeareans when Cooper left Leicester in August 1842. But his stay was too short to make any lasting impact in the town. Indeed, it was characteristic of all the leaders from outside that, although their forceful personalities and powers of oratory were admired, they failed to effect anything which in the local context seemed really constructive.

The difference between local Chartist leaders and those from outside was not simply between moral and physical force men, though the outsiders were perhaps the more inclined to make 'in-flammatory' speeches. Indeed, among all types of Leicester Chart-ists the issues between moral and physical force were not always clearly defined, nor were they always mutually exclusive. Very few Chartists in Leicester, whether locals or outsiders, professed to favour physical force as a principle, and fewer still were prepared to advocate insurrection. But between strictly constitutional petition-ing and revolution was an infinite number of gradations. Ack-nowledged moral force men, such as Markham, could occasionally be driven to urge their followers to be armed, while a leader like Cooper, who was prone to make impassioned and hot-headed

---

[1] Cooper, *Life*, p. 135.

[2] Cf. the unfavourable allegations against him from several quarters. Cooper, *op. cit.*, p. 250, accused him of mismanaging his (Cooper's) business when he left Leicester. The Loughborough Chartists complained that he had made improper use of money for his salary — *Northern Star*, 17 Dec. 1842; and Searson, *op. cit.*, p. 110, attributed his notoriety to breaking open William Jones' carpet bag while he was under arrest and wearing the imprisoned man's new suit. Perhaps it should be added that he was only eighteen when he left his trade of handloom weaving to become a Chartist lecturer. His powerful speech at his trial in 1843 impressed the judge, who commented on it in his summing up. *Trial of Feargus O'Connor and 58 Others* (1843), pp. 273, 382.

K

speeches suggesting or implying the use of violence, calmly assumed that he was still a moral force man because he ended with a
peroration about peace, law, and order.[1] In Leicester, as elsewhere
there were moral force Chartists who were prepared to use physical intimidation, and there were physical force men who were not
prepared to go beyond threats of violence. George Bown, who
openly avowed physical force as a principle of social and political
progress, and urged the people in 1848 to 'GET ARMS', added:

> 'but while I urge the right and duty to possess arms, I by no means
> counsel their use.'[2]

He cautioned against the shedding of blood, and argued that only
the union of moral and physical force methods would achieve results:

> 'If ever the government and aristocracy can be induced to concede the
> full enfranchisement of the enslaved portion of the United Kingdom
> it will be only when Moral and Physical Force are so associated as to
> make their joint power irresistible. Concession will be obtained when
> vengeance is dreaded.'[3]

The convenient fiction that the division between moral and physical force was a division between legal and illegal methods is not
supported by the evidence from Leicester. Most Chartists, and
particularly those inclined towards a belief in the ultimate necessity of insurrection, were impatient of the distinction at all. To
John Sketchley later, it seemed that:

> 'The quarrels on moral or physical force were most lamentable; as
> though the use of physical force could never be moral; or as though the
> moral and the legal were synonymous terms. The fact being that the
> legal and the moral are generally the very opposite of each other,
> while, as a rule, the quickest way to put an end to tyranny and oppres-
> sion is the most moral and the most legitimate.'[4]

---

[1] Cf. the Attorney General's clear exposition of this point in *ibid.*, p. 339. 'I
think Mr O'Connor and the Chartists have made a great mistake in point of law
— I may almost say in point of fact. They seem to think that, provided no bones
are broken, peace, law, and order are preserved. Their notion seems to be that if
5,000 people march to a mill, and present their physical intimidation, bludgeons, etc., and with threats upon their brow; then, provided the parties go out
without being forced out, it seems to be the opinion of these defendants that
there is no violation of the law. They fancy that physical intimidation is moral
force.' See also the reference to Cooper, p. 345.

[2] *Physical Force*, p. 14.   [3] *Sequel to 'Physical Force'* (Leicester, 1848), p. 6.
[4] *Op. cit.*, p. 22.

Even those Chartists who had no serious intention of flouting the law did not take kindly to homilies on the illegality of physical force — especially from those middle classes who had been markedly more tolerant of such methods during the Reform Bill struggles of 1830–31. And it was the contention of O'Connor and many other Chartists that the Plug Riots of August 1842 were in origin an attempt by the Anti-Corn Law Leaguers to use physical force methods to intimidate parliament into repealing the Corn Laws.[1] Physical force — or rather a combination of physical and moral force, it was alleged, was not invented by the Chartists, but was a time-honoured method of securing social and political change, used by all classes (including the middle classes) in all societies since ancient times.[2]

Nevertheless, such arguments, however convincing they seemed to their proponents, were never sufficient to allay the fears of the middle classes. Chartism in Leicester remained from first to last a movement of proletarians and small tradesmen who were sympathetic to and dependent on them. The formation of a genuinely independent Chartist movement in 1838 had come as a severe shock to the middle-class Radicals in Leicester, and they never ceased to regret this (to them) mistaken decision to split the reformers' bloc. Efforts to close this breach henceforth attracted a large part of the energies of many middle-class Radicals and some Chartist leaders. The ideal of an alliance between the middle classes and the working classes was never without an advocate somewhere throughout the whole period of Chartism in Leicester. In part the reasons for this are not far to seek. The tradition that the 'natural' political enemy of both the working and the middle classes was the aristocracy died hard, and in the recent struggles of the middle-class Nonconformist Radical reformers against the Church and Tory bloc entrenched in the Old Corporation, working-class sympathies had been on the side of the Radical interest. But successful as the middle-class Radicals had been in 1832 and 1835 they still felt apprehensive of their ability to maintain and extend their newly-won positions in the face of an organised Tory counter-attack. There was a double need to come to some understanding with the leaders of working-class influence in the town — because

[1] *Trial of Feargus O'Connor . . .* , pp. 415 ff.
[2] Bown's first pamphlet was mainly given over to examples of physical force and revolution in Greek, Roman, French, and British history, written in the best eighteenth-century polemical style.

of the accession of popular strength which such an alliance could bring and to prevent such strength falling into the Tory camp.

That this was no mere hypothesis was clear from the readiness with which the Chartist leaders were prepared to co-operate — at a price — with the Tories during elections. Chartist voting strength in the town was negligible.[1] But popular acclamation at the hustings and an impressive demonstration of physical strength (or even intimidation) were not without their value, and these made up the one type of political goods which the Chartist leaders could deliver. In March 1839 Markham was accused of receiving Tory gold at the borough election,[2] and at the 1841 elections Markham, Swain, and Cooper were all implicated in arrangements with the Tories. Cooper later described one of these transactions in his autobiography, but there were others. The Tory principal was Joseph Phillips, a Leicester banker, and he arranged for payment to be made to the Chartists for their support on the show of hands at the hustings. According to Cooper the Chartists received 5s. and 2s. 6d. each; similarly at the county elections Phillips was enabled to pay 330 men 3s. each, and to recompense the Wigston band for their services.[4] But Cooper was uneasy about supporting the Tories in this way, and argued later that the Chartists were reluctantly forced into it by the Whigs. 'If the middle class will come out for the Chartists,' he urged, 'the Chartists would come out for the middle class.'[5]

But there was the rub. To the middle classes the Chartist price — universal suffrage — was too high; and to the Chartists nothing less could be acceptable as an earnest of middle-class sincerity. Yet from both sides there was no lack of effort to reach a mutually satisfactory rapprochement — spurred on first by the Corn Law issue, and then by the Complete Suffrage movement.

[1] Swain said that the Chartists in Leicester had not twenty votes amongst them. Cooper, *Life*, p. 150. But at the Whit Monday demonstration in 1839 Markham corrected Deegan and said that in one village in the county there were 25 voters of whom 23 were Chartists. *Leicester Chronicle*, 25 May 1839.

[2] *Ibid.*, 23 March 1839.

[3] Cf. *The Comical Jugglers; a new comic drama* (Leicester, 1841). The pamphlet is a satire upon the transactions between the Tories and Chartists. The copy in the Leicester Reference Library is annotated in a contemporary hand as follows: 'Characters: Joseph Smoothtongue, Host (Joseph Phillips); The Jolly Shepherd, Swain (John Swain); Mark'em, John (John Markham); The Great Illuminator, or Immortal Rushlight (Thomas Cooper).'

[4] Letter from Cooper in the *Morning Chronicle*, 23 Feb. 1842, quoted in Conklin, *op. cit.*, p. 83.

[5] *Leicester Chronicle*, 20 Nov. 1841.

On the Corn Law question the local Chartist leaders held differing opinions. Markham and Swain thought the corn laws were a great evil, and were in favour of repeal, but argued that this was not possible without a further reform of Parliament through the enactment of the Charter.[1] Burden could see little benefit to the working classes from repeal, and suggested that machinery was more prejudicial to working men than the corn laws, and that cheap bread would mean low wages.[2] Smart was of a similar opinion. Cooper saw the repeal issue chiefly as a possible means of bargaining for the Charter — 'Give us THE SUFFRAGE, and we *will* help you to abolish the Starvation Laws and all other bad laws.'[3] But the most widespread attitude was probably that expressed by John Mason to the All Saints Open Chartists in 1840:

'Not that Corn Law Repeal is wrong; when we get the Charter we will repeal the Corn Laws and all the other bad laws. But if you give up your agitation for the Charter to help the Free Traders, they will not help you to get the Charter. Don't be deceived by the middle classes again. You helped them to get their votes — you swelled their cry of "The bill, the whole bill, and nothing but the bill!" But where are the fine promises they made you? Gone to the winds! They said when they had gotten their votes, they would help you to get yours. But they and the rotten Whigs have never remembered you. Municipal Reform has been for their benefit — not for yours. All other reforms the Whigs boast to have effected have been for the benefit of the middle classes — not for yours. And now they want to get the Corn Laws repealed — not for your benefit — but for their own. "Cheap Bread!" they cry. But they mean "Low Wages". Do not listen to their cant and humbug. Stick to your Charter. You are veritable slaves without your votes!'[4]

Such suspicions of the middle-class repealers were greatly strengthened by the decision in February 1840 to form a Working Men's Anti-Corn Law Association.[5] The new movement succeeded in attracting Finn, a Chartist and framework knitter, as chairman, and William Jackson, another leader of the framework knitters, as secretary, but it never took shape as a genuinely independent working-class organisation. It was in fact impossible to disguise the middle-class character of the repeal agitation, and Chartist tactics towards

---

[1] *Leicester Chronicle*, 1 Feb., 29 Feb. 1840. [2] Searson, *op. cit.*, p. 90.
[3] *Midland Counties Illuminator*, 29 May 1841, quoted in Conklin, *op. cit.*, p. 78.
[4] Cooper, *Life*, pp. 136–7. [5] Searson, *op. cit.*, p. 90.

it were calculated accordingly. From 1840 to 1842 both parties spent their time in alternately wooing and ignoring, conciliating and threatening the other side. At one time they would sit together on the same platform and make speeches welcoming alliance between the classes;[1] at another Cooper would lead his Shakespearean brigade to break up Anti-Corn Law meetings by force.[2]

It was the realisation that some positive concession by the middle classes offered the only hope of overcoming Chartist suspicion that lay behind the Complete Suffrage Movement. In April 1840 William Biggs made an effort to unite all reformers on a basis of household suffrage, triennial parliaments, and the ballot.[3] But the Chartists refused to be drawn into this, and the *Northern Star*[4] congratulated them for 'not walking into the Whig trap of Household suffrage', but standing firm for nothing less than universal suffrage. No progress was made from this position, and it was not until the end of 1841 that the middle-class reformers were prepared to raise the stakes. The lead now came from John Biggs, who in his Midland Counties Charter, offered universal suffrage (but limited this to males over 25, with 12 months residence) and triennial parliaments.[5] Again the Chartists stood firm for nothing less than their Six Points. It was now clear that the only bid which stood any chance of acceptance by the Chartists was universal suffrage. And so in March 1842 a Leicester Complete Suffrage Association was formed, under the leadership of John Manning, J. F. Winks, and the Rev. J. P. Mursell.[6] The weakness of this local Sturgeite movement was that it represented only the left wing, largely Baptist, element among the middle-class Radicals. Its effectiveness as an instrument of reconciliation of the middle and working classes was therefore seriously limited; and in fact even Mursell and his followers could not manage to agree with the Chartists sufficiently to elect four delegates to the Birmingham Complete Suffrage

---

[1] *Leicester Chronicle*, 19 Feb. 1842.
[2] Cooper later denied that he had disturbed Anti-Corn Law meetings (*Life*, p. 181), but accounts in the *Northern Star*, 19 Feb., 9 July, 23 July 1842 make it clear that he broke up such meetings by force.
[3] *Leicester Chronicle*, 18 Apr. 1840.
[4] 30 May 1840.
[5] *Leeds Times*, 8 Jan. 1842.
[6] *Leicester Chronicle*, 7, 14 May 1842. Mursell was the successor of the great Robert Hall at Harvey Lane Baptist Chapel, and was known to the Chartists as 'Parson Barearm' because of his pledge at a public meeting that 'When the time comes, my arm is bared for Universal Suffrage'. (Cooper, *Life*, p. 181.)

Conference early in 1843.[1] Nevertheless, extension of the suffrage remained for some years the only practical basis on which the middle-class Radicals could hope to enlarge their following among the working classes; and after the repeal of the corn laws in 1846 the advanced middle-class Radicals were prepared to make another effort to gain working-class support. This time John Biggs's adoption of manhood suffrage was not without its effect in attracting some of the moderate elements among the Chartist leadership: as the Chartist organisation disintegrated after 1848, Markham and some others had little difficulty in finding their place within the Biggsite fold.

But for many — perhaps a majority — of Chartists in Leicester such a coming to terms with the middle-class Radicals seemed no more feasible in 1848 than it had done in 1842. If Chartism had been purely a political movement, such a rapprochement might have been possible. But the dynamics of Chartism lay elsewhere — in the system of frame rents and charges, in hatred of the New Poor Law, and in a general desire to escape from the humiliations of a system of wage slavery. For these grievances and aspirations the middle-class Radicals could offer no sympathy whatsoever. Many of them, like the Biggses, were among the leading hosiers in the town; and for all of them adherence to the doctrines of political economy involved a firm belief in the efficiency of the New Poor Law. The gulf between the two classes was by no means un-bridgeable, but even in Leicester, where the middle classes were more than usually sympathetic, and the working-class leaders were far from extreme, a firm alliance between the classes was unattainable in the 40's.

Religion provided the most important common denominator. Many of the Chartists were active Nonconformists. Markham and Skevington were Primitive Methodist preachers; Cooper had been a local preacher for the Wesleyans; and Finn was pastor to a congregation of General Baptists. It was, therefore, to be expected that Chartist activities would sometimes assume a Nonconformist religious guise. The organisation in classes of ten at Loughborough, open-air preaching in Leicester and the nearby villages,[2] camp

---

[1] *Northern Star*, 24 Dec. 1842; and Cooper, *Life*, pp. 220–1.

[2] The following example was typical: 'Last Sunday Thomas Cooper preached three times — Infirmary Square in the morning ("Be ye all of one mind" — St Peter), Russell Square in the afternoon ("Miserable comforters are ye all" — Job), and in the Market Place at night ("My soul is wearied because of murderers"

meetings at Loughborough and Mountsorrel, and a Shakespearean Chartist Hymn Book were devices already familiar in another context to hundreds of working men. But if working men utilised Methodist forms and techniques for the Chartist cause, conversely Methodist thought and attitudes were assimilated into Chartism. Life for the working man was not to be lived in separate compartments; his religion and his social and political strivings had to be harmonised. Nor was this a very difficult task, for religious sanction for most radical opinions could be found in the New Testament, which had the added advantage of being completely invulnerable to all charges of lack of respectability and disloyalty. The desire for a religion free from credal beliefs, conceding the right of private judgement, and unconnected with any ecclesiastical hierarchy, was widespread. There were many who would have agreed with William Lovett that they had come

> '... to look upon practical Christianity as a union for the promotion of brotherly kindness and good deeds to one another, and not a thing of form and profession for the mercenary idlers to profit by ....'[2]

In Leicester this was not a point of division between the Chartists and other social and political reformers. For a liberal type of Christianity, untheological, undoctrinal, and suspicious of all priestcraft, was not confined to working men. It was just as characteristic of the fashionable and influential middle-class congregations at the Great Meeting (Unitarian) in Bond Street or Harvey Lane Baptist Chapel. The prevalent ethos of Leicester was Nonconformist in a broad sense. This did not mean that Nonconformity could provide the much-sought-for bridge between the middle and working classes; the abstention of the Chartists from any prominent part in the Church Rates struggle, for instance, is significant. But at least the Chartists and the middle-class reformers talked the same language; they each had a part of a recognisably common heritage.

— Jeremiah). Mr Beedham preached at Great Glen in the morning, Oadby in the afternoon, and Wigston at night'. *Northern Star*, 28 May 1842.

[1] Kendall, *op. cit.*, Vol. I, p. 336, suggests that there was a fear among Primitive Methodists that Leicester Chartism would draw men away from the connexion, because of the Chartist camp meetings, hymns, singing processions through the streets, and preachings.

[2] *Op. cit.*, p. 37.

V

The only Leicester Chartist who attained anything like a national reputation was Thomas Cooper.[1] Although born in Leicester in 1805, his parents had left the town while he was still a baby, and he was virtually a stranger to Leicester when he reappeared in November 1840. His Chartist career in the town lasted barely two years, yet such was the impact he made that in later years, when memories had begun to fade, his name was invariably the first to be recalled in any discussion of the Chartist days. His colourful, passionate personality, his great energy and drive, and powerful speech left an indelible impression upon his contemporaries. He was also the only one among the Leicester Chartist leaders to suffer imprisonment for the cause.

Yet when he came to Leicester he was quite ignorant of Chartism: 'I had never before either seen or conversed with a Chartist, to my knowledge.'[2] Up to this time Cooper had taken no part in any working-class or political movements. His life in Lincolnshire and brief sojourn in London had given him no first hand experience either of the new industrialism or of the suffrage, Poor Law, and Ten Hours struggles. His close association with Wesleyanism — socially and politically the most conservative of the Methodist connexions — was not calculated to foster such interests; and his complete absorption in the delights and rigours of self-education had for a time encouraged an escapist rather than a practical outlook on life. It was the shock occasioned by his sudden discovery of the extent of misery and starvation among the Leicester stockingers that jolted him out of his former indifference: 'I had been incredulous as to the deep destitution of the working classes in the manufacturing districts, until I became a resident therein.'[3] But when he had been brought face to face with such conditions he reacted violently with all the impulsive energy of his passionate nature. This soon lost him his job on the *Leicestershire Mercury*; and, despite the advice of old friends such as J. F. Winks, he plunged

---

[1] The main source for Cooper's life is of course his autobiography. Conklin's biography follows this closely, with extended references to some aspects of his work. There is also an essay on Cooper by G. D. H. Cole in *Chartist Portraits* (1941).
[2] *Howitt's Journal*, Vol. III (1848), p. 243. This article on Cooper by Samuel Smiles, in the series 'Poets of the People', was based on Cooper's account of his life given during his defence at his first trial.
[3] *Ibid*

wholeheartedly into the Chartist movement, '. . . as the means of redeeming (the people) from the dreadful condition into which they were fallen.'[1]

Cooper was received with friendship into the little group of local Chartist leaders — Swain, Markham, and the Seal brothers. They helped him to establish a small newsagent's business in High Street; they encouraged him to take over George Bown's Chartist paper, the *Midland Counties Illuminator*, and they offered him every facility for preaching and addressing public meetings. Given Cooper's superior abilities and the full-time nature of his position, the result was a foregone conclusion; 'the Chartists soon elected me their secretary.'[2] By the summer of 1841 he was the acknowledged tribune of the Leicester working classes. Whatever dreams of national ascendancy in the Chartist movement he may possibly have had later, it is clear that at this stage Cooper was motivated by a sincere desire to right the wrongs of the people; he flung himself into the movement without regard for his reputation or career. No doubt 'the fiery excitement' of Chartism[3] awakened hitherto dormant strains in his personality; it was the sudden appeal of activism to one who was always a man of great passions and enthusiasms, one who never did things by halves. Nevertheless, he had to have some way of supporting himself and his wife, and this he found within and through the movement itself. Chartism became for him a livelihood as well as a cause in which he believed; he became in effect the full-time (and badly paid) official of a voluntary organisation.[4] His status was different from that of Markham and Swain, who had their respective trades.

Cooper's situation was, of course, by no means unique. His was a problem familiar to many self-educated artisans of the nineteenth century. The education which they acquired at such great cost made them changed men.[5] Some were content to remain at their old trades, famed locally as the weaver-poet or the working-man-philosopher. But others no longer felt able to do this, and they were

---

[1] *Ibid.*   [2] Cooper, *Life*, p. 148.
[3] *Ibid.*, p. 260.
[4] After being turned out of his first shop in High Street, Cooper secured a better one in Church Street. He opened coffee-rooms, sold bread as well as newspapers, and turned the shop into a central office of the local movement. In this way he attained a modest degree of prosperity; during the latter half of 1841 he 'had a really good business'. *Life*, p. 162.
[5] Cooper's prodigious feats of self-education, which resulted finally in a nervous breakdown, are detailed in chapter 6 of his *Life*.

faced with the problem of finding a new niche for themselves in society. This was by no means easy for men with no capital beyond a background of mixed general reading and an independent turn of mind. Almost invariably they gravitated into school teaching, journalism, lecturing, book selling, or a Nonconformist pastorship — all jobs in which they could combine a modest income with opportunities for continued reading and unorthodox opinions. Cooper graduated through all these situations during the thirty years following his self-education, and his Leicester Chartist leadership coincided with his journalist-lecturer-bookseller phase. His position in the Chartist movement is perhaps seen most fruitfully not as a bid for political power[1] (despite some ambitious intentions expressed in 1842), but rather as a stage in the progress of a self-educated shoemaker.

The objective fruits of Cooper's work as a Chartist in Leicester suggest some such interpretation. That tension should arise between the new star and the old leaders was highly probable in the nature of the case; whether or not Cooper was ambitious, no man in Markham's position would relish being supplanted by a stranger whom he had first cherished like a cuckoo in the nest. Their quarrel and the division of the Leicester Chartists into two rival factions, engaged in public bickering, during the winter of 1841–42, was probably the greatest disservice which Cooper rendered the local movement. His view of the role of a local, working-class leader was also at times seriously defective, amounting in effect to demagogy. Thus he explained his adulation of O'Connor (with whom he later quarrelled) on the grounds that

'the immense majority of Chartists in Leicester, as well as in many other towns, regarded him as the only really disinterested and incorruptible leader. I adopted this belief because it was the belief of the people . . . .'[2]

He saw himself as 'the people's instrument, rather than their director'; for it was thus:

'that a popular leader keeps the lead: his temperament, nature, and powers fit him, by quick sympathy, and strong, energetic will, to become the people's mouthpiece, hand, and arm, either for good or evil.'[3]

[1] Cf. Patterson, *op. cit.*, pp. 320–4.   [2] Cooper, *Life*, p. 179.
[3] Letter by Cooper, printed as an Appendix in Gammage, *op. cit.*, p. 408.

But for the rest Leicester Chartism gained much from his activity in the town. A succession of Chartist periodicals — the *Illuminator, Extinguisher, Commonwealthsman, Chartist Pioneer*[1] — even though each was short lived, gave the Leicester movement the inestimable advantage of its own press.

It was indeed symbolic, though coincidental,[2] that Cooper's faction should have styled themselves 'The Shakespearean Association of Leicester Chartists'. As Cooper wrote later, he had not joined the Chartists expecting to spend his time in rough houses at elections, but rather to help the people through more worthy means. To a man with such a passion for learning, adult education appeared as a desirable and possible method of working class social progress. Moreover, his old friend J. F. Winks, now a bookseller in the town, was a pioneer of Adult Schools;[3] and Cooper had already collaborated with him in such efforts in their Gainsborough days. Cooper's Shakespearean Adult Sunday School was attended by 'many scores'[4] of men and boys throughout the winter of 1841–42; the classes were named after past heroes of popular liberty — John Hampden, William Tell, George Washington, William Cobbett; and the Bible, Channing's *Self-Culture*, and contemporary tracts were used as lesson books. On week nights Cooper lectured regularly on poetry, history, geography, and phrenology. It was certainly not his fault that these educational efforts came to an end in the spring of 1842; had he remained another winter in Leicester he would have revived them. But he could not but sympathise with the temper of the starving stockingers who replied to his entreaties to continue the school: 'What the hell do we care about reading, if we can get nought to eat?'[5] To this no satisfactory answer could be given in educational terms; the limits of adult education as a method of social advance had for the time being been reached.

The fruits of educational effort, however, are often not immediately apparent, and a good deal of adult education must amount to little more than the planting of seeds which may or may not germinate later. In Leicester the growth of a little group of Chartist poets, inspired by Cooper and continuing after his departure, was a

---

[1] See letter from Cooper in the *Northern Star*, 9 July 1842.
[2] The name was derived from the room in Humberstone Gate in which they met.
[3] See his *History of Adult Schools* (1821).   [4] Gammage, *op. cit.*, p. 406.
[5] Cooper, *Life*, p. 172.

uccessful example of this process. John Henry Bramwich,[1] a
tockinger, was best known for his hymn, 'Great God, is this the
patriot's doom?'[2] composed for the funeral of Holberry the Sheffield Chartist who died in York gaol; but he also contributed to
Cooper's *Extinguisher* (1841) and the *Shakespearean Chartist Hymn
Book*. William Jones, a glove hand, likewise published his poems in
the *Hymn Book*, and also in the *Northern Star*.[3] His long poem,
The Spirit, or a Dream in the Woodlands[4] was written 'during the
dreadful crisis of '47 and '48', when he was unemployed. Rather
than submit to 'the degrading influences of the stone yard and Bastile
— the tests of pauperism in Leicester', he betook himself to the
woods, to think. The result was an expression, in poetic form of his

'. . . firm conviction that social wrong, and the morally degrading
causes which have pressed so long and so heavily upon working men,
especially in the manufacturing districts, can only have permanent removal in proportion to the growth of the masses in Knowledge, Temperance, and Self-respect.'[5]

His friend William Whitmore, a young house painter, published
poems later in *Cooper's Journal* (1850), and *Firstlings*, a collection
of his verse, appeared in 1852. Through his friendship with John
Roebuck, a member of the London Working Men's College, his
work was brought to the notice of Tom Hughes, who sponsored the
publication of a further selection of his verse in 1859 under the title
Gilbert Marlowe, and other poems.

The best of this verse was often insipid and banal; the worst was
just plain ranting doggerel. In this it was typical of the poetic effusions of the movement as a whole. Even Ernest Jones, perhaps the
best of the Chartist poets, was little more than a competent versifier. Gerald Massey's lyrics suggest the same verdict, and most of
Cooper's *Purgatory of Suicides* is now simply unreadable. It was
perhaps not to be expected that self-educated working men should

---

[1] 1804–46. After sixteen years' service in the army he returned to Leicester and
worked at the frame. Cooper wrote his obituary notice in the *Northern Star*, 4
Apr. 1846, and included a moving letter written by Bramwich as he lay dying
slowly of consumption.

[2] Reprinted in Gammage, *op. cit.*, pp. 214–15.

[3] E.g. 20 Sept. 1845, 'Autumn's Departure'. See also *The Leicestershire Movement; or Voices from the Frame and the Factory, the Field and the Rail, etc.*
(Leicester, 1850), a weekly periodical which printed verse and articles by this
little group of Chartist poets.

[4] London and Leicester, 1849.

[5] Preface to *The Spirit*.

produce great poetry; like Johnson's female preaching, the wonder was not that it was indifferently done, but that it was done at all The Chartists were too much the products of their age to be able to rise beyond the limitations of early Victorian ideas about poetry. But the value of Cooper's inspiration to these Leicester Chartists was not primarily in the verse they produced, but in the intellectual and moral growth of which the verses were a manifestation. Through Cooper's efforts the significance of Chartism for them was not primarily the hope of political or even social emancipation which it unfolded, but an intellectual awakening and spiritual enrichment.

The trial of Cooper for his part in the Plug Riots, his subsequent imprisonment in Stafford gaol, and his later quarrel with O'Connor form no part of the story of Leicester Chartism. It is an interesting speculation as to what would have happened in Leicester had he been in the town during the week of the August (1842) turnouts. There were indeed not wanting those to accuse him of being like Napoleon, who led his armies to Moscow and then deserted them.[1] But the general attitude towards him after his arrest was sympathy or pity, even though he had by this time alienated many potential allies, Radical as well as Chartist, by his egotism.[2] The truth is that he was by nature an 'awkward' man, self-opinionated and prickly, and more difficult to work with than under. To some extent these were the defects inherent in his virtues. But they set definite limits to the effectiveness of his contribution to the Chartist movement in Leicester. On the local organisation he left no permanent mark, and his most lasting influence was as an individual inspiration in the lives of a small group of intelligent working men. After his departure the local movement resumed its former ways. Out of the fifteen years there was a Chartist organisation in Leicester, Cooper was involved in it for barely two. Like a bright meteor he appeared suddenly, streaking high into the night, and then disappearing — leaving behind nothing save the memory of a dazzling progress.

[1] E.g. George Bown, Leicester Journal, 2 Sept. 1842.
[2] E.g. the Leicester Journal, 2 Sept. 1842, expressed sorrow that Cooper should see all his schemes so utterly defeated; since he was such a vain and overbearing man, this would be a sufficient punishment in itself.

Chapter Five

Chartism in Suffolk

Hugh Fearn

I

Conditions in Suffolk in the 1830's and 1840's were such as to foster the emergence of the Chartist movement in the county. They were hardly likely, however, to sustain its growth. There were local grievances galore, but the successful assertion of them depended on the mobilisation of agricultural labourers, a difficult section of the community to organise for any period of time. A core of politically minded men in Ipswich itself worked hard in the Chartist cause, but the results they achieved were disappointing.

Before 1832 Suffolk was represented in the Commons by sixteen members, two elected for the county as a whole, and two for each of seven boroughs — Aldeburgh, Bury St Edmunds, Dunwich, Eye, Ipswich, Orford and Sudbury. The decline in economic importance of at least half of these places, especially the small coastal towns, meant that in relation to the country as a whole Suffolk was over-represented. Nonetheless, the privileged few in these small towns clung to their old privileges with unyielding tenacity, guarding jealously their right to elect members. In some instances the handful of freemen and burgesses treasured their votes because they were able to obtain large sums of money for them. In other instances, the members were elected under the patronage of local magnates with 'influence', men like the Duke of Grafton, the Earl of Bristol, and the Marquess of Hertford.

After the passing of the Reform Act of 1832, county representation was increased to four, by the division of the county into an eastern and a western division, each electing two members. The three coastal boroughs lost their rights to send members; and the Borough of Eye, 'an *exceedingly rotten borough*',[1] managed to avoid complete disfranchisement by extending its boundaries for parliamentary purposes to include ten neighbouring parishes. With one

[1] William Cobbett, *Rural Rides* (1885 edn), Vol. II, p. 291.

member representing Eye, and two members each for Bur
St Edmunds, Ipswich and Sudbury, the total Suffolk representatio
was eleven, as against the former sixteen. Further, in 1841, ex
cessive bribery and corruption at Sudbury reduced the representa
tion to nine, and after that election this borough lost the right t
return members.

Many of the more flagrant abuses which had existed before th
Reform Act of 1832 continued in municipal and local government
This was true of the coastal boroughs and the more populou
towns of Ipswich and Bury St Edmunds which were adversely re
ported upon in the Report of the Municipal Corporations Commis
sion of 1835. John Buckle, a Commissioner, summed up the situ
ation in Ipswich in the following terms:

'The practical working of the system may be summed up in bribery
invasions of political liberty, and destruction of industrious habit
among freemen . . . . Considered with respect to the Corporate Bod
only, it is an ill-regulated republic; considered with reference to th
local community, it is an oligarchy of the worst description.'[1]

The oligarchical nature of the municipal Government was eve
more marked at Bury St Edmunds, where

'a few individuals, uninvested with any representative character, an
uncontrolled by any local responsibility, have become the depository
of all municipal powers and privileges of the borough. This self
elected body appoints the local magistrates, manages without publicity
the property granted to the inhabitants, and exercises all the patronag
of the Corporation . . . .'[2]

Before the Reform Act, 1832, this self-elected body had the exclusive privilege of electing the two Members of the Borough, and
in the exercise of this privilege it generally elected representatives
nominated by the families of two local magnates of opposite politics,
those of the Duke of Grafton and the Earl of Bristol.

It was natural, therefore, that the first election after the passing of
the Reform Act should evince speculation in Bury St Edmunds as
to the outcome of the battle between privilege and patronage on the
one hand and the more extended franchise on the other. Patronage
was successful, although disappointment at the result led to rioting
by the supporters of the Reform candidate. An account published
in 1833 indicates that there was an interest in reform in Bury St

[1] *Report of the Municipal Corporations Commissioner* (1835), p. 2034.
[2] *Ibid.*, p. 2175.

dmunds, though it was not deep enough or lasting enough to help
ae propaganda of Chartism a few years later.[1] Reform groups, such
s the one at Bury, had come into being in support of the agitation for
ae Reform Bill. Avoiding the establishment of permanent organ-
ation the members of such groups tended to set up committees for
ome special purpose at times of political excitement. A typical
roup met at Woodbridge, known as 'The Bull Parliament', its
aders being mostly prominent dissenters.[2] Reformers such as
aese were not inclined to risk their businesses or their personal
afety by any persistent agitation; though some were active later on
a the Complete Suffrage Union.

The 1841 Election necessitated three attempts in Ipswich to
lect two members to Parliament. The findings of bribery in the
riginal contest and the proof of bribery at the second contest neces-
itated a third attempt at which Henry Vincent was a candidate in
ae Complete Suffrage interest. But the outstanding evidence of
olitical abuse was the disfranchisement of the Borough of Sud-
ury as a result of excessive bribery and corruption at the 1841
lection. The investigating Parliamentary committee established
hat about £5,000 had been expended by the candidates in an at-
empt to induce the men of Sudbury to elect them, and that the
reater part of this money could only have been required for pur-
oses of bribery. The extent to which bribery and corruption
xisted is further emphasised by the difficulties which the Com-
aittee had in discovering who had received bribes, though they
aamed seventeen recipients and twelve people who had assisted in
ae distribution of the bribes. Among these named recipients and
gents were handloom weavers; and in 1842 the Select Committee
n Handloom Weavers collected specific evidence on the effects of
lection bribery on the Sudbury weavers. The main recommenda-
ion of this report was the abolition of the Bribery Oath, as this was
aot held in any esteem by those resorting to bribery. Whereas il-
egal expenses had been met, the ordinary legal expenses remained
n part unpaid; and the investigation revealed that in Sudbury it
vas customary to transfer from one election to the next, under the
itle of fixtures, the unpaid bills of the election last held.

The evidence in so far as the county electorate is concerned is

[1] W. B. Frost, *An Account of the Election of the Members for the Borough of Bury
St Edmunds, Dec. 13 and 14, 1832* (1833, Bury St Edmunds).
[2] Glyde Collection (MSS.), *Materials for a History of Woodbridge* (Ipswich
.L.).

L

that the franchise had been but little extended by the provisions
the 1832 Act. The increase in the number of voters was small an
further, the total number of voters was very limited when compar
with the total male population of 71,376 over twenty years of ag
Facts concerning the limited franchise, the existence of bribery a
corruption, and the use of patronage were sufficient to excite sor
Chartist activity. To gain momentum, however, the moveme
needed the direction of a politically conscious core, and this was
be found in Ipswich. This Ipswich group of politically conscio
men had been brought into political activity by one or more
several causes. The several causes were dissatisfaction with the r
forms already achieved (although many of the group possessed t
franchise), a militant Nonconformist attitude towards the privileg
of the establishment, a social consciousness of the iniquity of t
New Poor Law and, to a lesser extent, the influence of trade-unic
organisation. The existence of this politically conscious minority ar
the prevalence of electoral abuses meant that politically the Charti
agitation in Suffolk had a reasonable chance of success whe
strengthened by the prevailing economic and social conditions.

During the first half of the nineteenth century the population
Suffolk grew slowly in comparison with the tendency in Englan
and Wales generally, as the following figures show.

Census Returns; *Percentage increase on previous total*

	England and Wales	Suffolk
1811	14%	9%
1821	18%	16%
1831	16%	9%
1841	14%	6%
1851	13%	7%

The considerable difference between the Suffolk trend and tha
of England and Wales during the same period can be accounte
for by a migration from the county.[1] Migration outwards wa
somewhere in the region of 8,000 for the decade 1831–40, and c
20,000 during the years 1841–50. This tendency to migrate was n
new thing to Suffolk people, and Miss Redstone attributes this mor
modern migration in part to religious persecution.[2]

[1] The calculations which support this conclusion will be found in Appendix
of my unpublished M.A. Thesis, University of Sheffield, 'Chartism in Suffolk'.
[2] L. J. Redstone, *Suffolk* (1930), pp. 85, 86.

It is, however, more reasonable to suppose that the migration at
is time was, in the main, the result of economic causes, for by
361 the movement of Suffolk natives had proceeded to such an ex-
nt that some 105,989 lived elsewhere in England, with some 491
Wales, as against 337,070 remaining in their home county. There
as also migration overseas. In part, the movement overseas and to
her parts of England and Wales was a consequence of the belief
at better conditions prevailed elsewhere, in part the consequence
: an overstocked local labour market.[1]

Leaving agriculture on one side, the industrial structure of Suf-
lk was in a state of transition. Ipswich, as the principal town in the
unty, and a port, reflected in its trade and commerce the needs
nd demands of the neighbouring countryside. Its importance as a
ort was less than in former days, the shipbuilding yards had de-
lined, the whaling industry had had but a short success, and until
844, when the Wet Dock was constructed, shipping was handi-
apped by the necessity of unloading heavy cargoes some three
iles from the town. Nevertheless other industries were develop-
ig and in particular the manufacture of agricultural implements.
his industry was also developing elsewhere, at Leiston and
easenhall in East Suffolk. It is in these two neighbourhoods,
pswich and Saxmundham (a town near to Leiston and Peasenhall)
hat Chartism in the main took root, though none of the active
eaders appear to have been engaged in this industry.

Founded originally to meet a local demand, these three firms,
Ransome of Ipswich, Garrett of Leiston and Smyth of Peasen-
all, had by the middle of the nineteenth century attained a more
han local importance in their manufactures and employed several
iundred factory workers.[2] In the early 1840's Ransome's felt
he pinch. Time and time again unemployed operatives attended
lay-time meetings arranged by the Chartists, and as late as 1848 a
nidday meeting was attended by considerable numbers of unem-
loyed operatives from Ransome's.[3]

The difficulties experienced by these three firms during the
1840's were minimised somewhat by the foreign trade which they
then possessed. At home agriculture was in a state of depression,
and for the vast majority of the Suffolk agricultural labourers

[1] See G. R. Wythen Baxter, *The Book of the Bastilles* (1841), p. 202.
[2] *V.C.H. Suffolk*, Vol. II (1907), p. 285; Ransome, Sims and Jefferies Ltd.,
Royal Records (1939, Ipswich).
[3] *Suffolk Chronicle*, 25 Mar. 1848.

employment and working conditions were far from good. These conditions were not the result of dispossession through enclosure of land, for only 96,104 acres were enclosed between 1729 and 187 mainly consisting of commons and waste-land, approximating to 1 per cent of the whole acreage of the county. The larger part of the county had been enclosed much earlier and, certainly in those part of Suffolk where Chartism was active, enclosed farming with the employment of agricultural labourers had long been the practice.

It was these employment conditions which were now critical Weekly wage rates in 1846 were on the average 10s. per week; and by 1853 they were slightly lower, on the average about 9s.[1] But the majority of agricultural labourers were paid on a task or piece-work basis. The rates paid for task work varied according to the nature of the work performed. For mowing permanent meadow grass for hay in 1846, the rate was between 2s. and 2s. 6d. per acre, according to the bulk of crop. The price for mowing an acre of wheat ranged from 6s. to 8s. per acre, according to whether it was a light or heavy crop.[2] Total earnings depended, however, upon the composite earnings of a family, and upon regularity of employment Dr Kay (Assistant Poor Law Commissioner for Norfolk and Suffolk) classified the earnings of 539 families in these counties in 1838 as follows:[3]

Families	Composition	Average number of children per family	Average annual income £ s. d.
36	Single Men	—	25 1 4½
64	with no children at home	—	30 12 10½
166	with all children under 10	2⅞	32 13 2
120	with one child above 10	3$\frac{7}{10}$	35 9 0¾
92	with two children above 10	4$\frac{9}{10}$	40 10 1
44	with three children above 10	5¾	45 11 9
15	with four children above 10	7	50 18 6
1	with five children above 10	—	42 13 0
1	with six children above 10	—	52 0 0

[1] J. Glyde, *Suffolk in the Nineteenth Century* (1856), p. 348.
[2] H. Raynbird, 'Essay on Measure-Work,' *Journal of the Royal Agricultural Society* (1846), pp. 123–4.
[3] J. P. Kay, 'Earnings of Agricultural Labourers in Norfolk and Suffolk,' *Journal of the Statistical Society of London* (1839), pp. 181ff.

he real wages of these families needed to be measured, but this
Dr Kay did not investigate. One Suffolk labourer with a wife and
ve children, the eldest girl aged 9½ years, and earning 10s. a week,
pent weekly in 1839, 6s. 10½d. for 2½ stones of flour, 3d. on yeast,
s. 7½d. on rent, 10d. on coals, 3½d. on candles, leaving 1½d. balance
vith which to provide for the other necessities of his family.[1]

Insufficiency of income was accompanied by insecurity through
regular employment. In 1844 one cause or one fear of loss of em-
loyment was the use by farmers of threshing machines. Labourers
egarded these machines as hindrances to employment and they
esorted to incendiarism. The local press contained reports of fires
n successive weekly issues, and it was the opinion of a contempor-
ry that:

'The occupiers of land lived in a state of nervous excitement, looking
about their premises every night before retiring to rest, apprehensive
of their crops being destroyed by the match of the incendiary . . . .
Farm produce was as insecure in this district of England, as the life of
a landlord's agent was in some parts of Ireland.'[2]

This bout of incendiarism besides being directed against farmers
vho possessed threshing machines was also directed against the
property of men who sat upon the Boards of Guardians.

By 1849 the condition of the agricultural labourers had improved
omewhat, though much remained to be done. Wages were still
ow. The New Poor Law, it was considered by some farmers, had
nade the Suffolk labourer more independent, and he had lost the
disinclination to work of former years.[3] Conditions did not, however, inspire the agricultural labourers to join the Chartist move-
nent, except in the Saxmundham area. Glyde expressed the
opinion that:

'As a body the agricultural labourers have a much keener appetite for
bread than for the franchise, and those best able to form an opinion
know they are much more anxious to keep out of the Union house,
than to have the privilege of entering the Polling Booth.'[4]

In the main, those in need of assistance had recourse only to the aid
available from poor relief. Before the enforcement of the provisions of the 1834 Act and the injunctions of the Poor Law

[1] *Suffolk Chronicle*, 13 Apr. 1839.   [2] Glyde, *op. cit.*, p. 126.
[3] W. Raynbird and H. Raynbird, *On The Agriculture of Suffolk* (1849), p. 62.
[4] Glyde, *op. cit.*, p. 185.

Commissioners, the Speenhamland system had been in widesprea
operation in Suffolk with demoralising results upon the poor and th
employer class. The rates of allowance drawn up by the magistrat
varied not only from district to district but also in the parish
within a district.

Until the 1834 Act was enforced a certain amount of outdoor re
lief was administered in Suffolk by the Poor Law Incorporation
These Incorporations which consisted of the parishes in one
more Hundreds had been brought into being in the latter half
the eighteenth century by Private Acts of Parliament. These In
corporations, each having its own House at Industry, aimed at re
ducing the cost of maintaining the poor. This reduction of the poo
rates was to be achieved by using the labour of the able-bodied poo
to earn money in the House of Industry to maintain both them
selves and the dependent impotent poor, who would need ai
anyhow. The chief employment provided was spinning of yar
which was sold to Norwich woollen manufacturers, but the de
pressed state of this industry in Norwich in the latter part of th
eighteenth century meant that the Incorporations had stocks o
hand which they were unable to sell. The Incorporations furthe
failed to achieve any economy in poor-rates by reason of the pay
ment of substantial sums in outdoor relief. Inefficiency of manage
ment was a final factor in the failure of the Incorporations t
achieve their intended objective. Sooner or later each House wa
handed over to paid officials to run, who not being adequatel
supervised resorted to embezzlement of stores, materials and cash
The state of affairs thus described did not go uncriticised, but
remained for the more stringent application of the 1834 Act t
effect any remedy.

The remedy so effected was the more severe in the eyes of th
working classes than would perhaps have been the case had the ad
ministration of the Incorporations been more effective. It is note
worthy that in their speeches in the County the Ipswich Chartist
often referred to the evils of the New Poor Law. In 1838 when thei
activity was getting under way they blamed the Poor Law Guar
dians in Ipswich for prohibiting the supply of food or indulgence
to the inmates of the workhouse by friends or relatives of th
paupers. It must be said in defence of the local Board that it wa
forced into some such action by the Assistant Poor Law Commis
sioner who drew its attention to the entries in the Porter's book o

ιe bringing into the House of food and other things for the in-
ιates. The local Guardians therefore decided 'that in future no
rticle should be introduced into the House unless sanctioned by
ιe regulations of the Board of Guardians'.[1] This was not a unani-
ιous decision, for the Minute Book entry records nine in favour
ιd six against the resolution, whilst James White in his speech to
ιe Ipswich Working Men's Association stated that four of the
ιuardians abstained from voting.[2] White, who was a Guardian
ιected by St Margaret's Parish (Ipswich) was one of the Guardians
ho voted against the resolution. He was so much opposed to it
ιat he sought to instigate public opinion against it, and solicited
ιe assistance of the Chartists in Ipswich in the matter.[3] Reflecting
ιe opinion of the labouring classes, the Association was deeply in-
ιgnant, and said so in no uncertain terms. Admittedly the Guard-
ιns did not rescind the offending resolution as a result of the agita-
ιon, but they modified their rules.[4]

Certainly a great reduction in Poor Law costs was achieved by
ιe more stringent administration under the 1834 Act. In 1839 and
840 the amount collected in poor-rates was respectively £141,871
ιnd £141,536 as against £279,489 in 1831/2.[5] The reduction in the
ιosts of maintaining the poor was only secured gradually as more
ιnd more Unions came under the administration of the Commis-
ιoner and the local Boards. In 1835/6 only three Unions compris-
ιg 101 parishes with a population of 58,368 people had been in
ιxistence for a year or more, with a 44 per cent reduction in expendi-
ιre. In eight other Unions which had been in operation for less
ιan twelve months the saving in Poor Law expenditure had been
7 per cent.[6] The provision of the 1834 Act that in future able-
ιodied paupers would only be able to obtain relief by entry into the

[1] Ipswich Board of Guardians, *Minute Book No. 2*, p. 597.
[2] *Suffolk Chronicle*, 1 Dec. 1838.
[3] *Essex and Suffolk Times*, 1 Dec. 1838.
[4] Ipswich Board of Guardians, *Minute Book No. 2*, p. 601. 'It having been pro-
ιosed . . . that every aged Pauper in the Workhouse who has been accustomed to
ιse of Tobacco and Snuff should have a portion of it delivered to him or her every
ιeek at the cost of the Union, It was agreed to, Provided that the Medical
ιfficer in attendance at the Workhouse approved thereof . . .': p. 604, 'That with
ιe desire to keep alive the sympathies of the children of the aged poor towards
ιeir parents, and of relations towards their children, it is resolved, that small
ιupplies of Grocery, Fruit and Confectionery, shall be allowed to be introduced
ιs presents to the aged and to the children in the school-room, the Porter weekly
ιeporting the articles brought into the House.'
[5] L. White, *Directory of Suffolk* (1844), p. 18.
[6] *Second Annual Report of the Poor Law Commissioners*, 1836, London,
ιp. 32, 33.

workhouse caused the greatest concern. Where an out-allowance
was given it was usually insufficient for the needs of the family
whether given in money or in kind.[1] The Book of the Bastille contains many references to the treatment of the poor in Suffolk
which indicate that the Chartist outcry against the operation of the
New Poor Law was not entirely baseless.

The conditions, then, out of which Suffolk Chartism was to
emerge were economic distress, social unrest, hatred of the New
Poor Law, a claim to representation in the Commons, and opposition to the Church Rate. The task of the leaders in Ipswich was
doubly difficult for they had to convince the working classes that
the needed reforms could be achieved by political means such as
they professed. Its spread to the rural areas was assisted by the
grievance and discontents of the agricultural labourers. These conditions were not sufficient, however, to enable the Movement to
capture the interest of the agricultural labourers to any great extent, or for any length of time.

II

The first phase of Suffolk Chartism (1838–40) witnessed the
growth of Working Men's Associations in the county. This phase
began with the founding in December 1837 of the Ipswich association
with aims based upon those of the parent-association in London.
The whole of the Chartist activity in Suffolk may be considered as
an attempt to propagate those aims in the face of opposition from
other classes and of the apathy of the working classes themselves.
The Association recognised this at the start, and aimed therefore at
founding its work upon the 'intelligent and morally influential portion of the working classes'.

The Ipswich association embarked upon its programme with an
enthusiasm which might well have been tempered by a more careful consideration of its objectives. The activity in January 1838 appears to indicate that the members had a none too clear conception

[1] '. . . I met with a poor woman the other day. "What is the matter with you,
you look half-starved?" "Why, Sir, my husband is always afflicted with rheuma-
tism and can never earn more than 14d. per day when in full work; but now he
has nothing to do, nor has he had for five weeks past and we have a sick daughter
at home." "What allowance have you?" "My husband went to the Board when
he was out of work a fortnight . . . and the Board granted us one stone of flour a
week." "And how much money?" "Not one farthing. . . ."' Wythen-Baxter,
op. cit., p. 144.
[2] See pp. 117, 134–6, 142–5, 192, 200, 230, 373, 517, 528, 563, 564 and 566.
[3] Suffolk Chronicle, 30 Dec. 1837.

of the manner in which they were to acquire political and social rights for all. In the first instance they resolved to support 'partial measures' for reform, and when criticised by the London association they rescinded the resolution on the grounds that the agitation

'now carried on for "extended Suffrage" is another attempt to divert us from our rights.'[1]

It was seemingly easier to amend a resolution than to effect a change of heart, for later in January they invited a former Whig member for Ipswich to address a public meeting. The purpose of this meeting was perhaps to ascertain the viewpoint of a prospective parliamentary candidate upon the aims of the Association, in the belief that it might be an advantage to have a sitting member who was sympathetic to the Chartist cause.[2]

Still in its infancy the Association embarked upon a programme of parliamentary reform in earnest. During February and March 1838 three meetings were held. The first was to petition the House of Commons for five reforms, the second was to adopt a resolution expressing dissatisfaction with the Government in power, and the third was to petition the Queen to remove her Ministers. These meetings produced no measurable results, but they indicate the line of action which the Association took in this formative period; and it is possible to discover some of the ideas which the local leaders held and the arguments which they advanced. These views are indicative of the wide composition of the men who joined the Chartist movements, of their several interests and varied backgrounds.

In support of the demand for universal suffrage three arguments were advanced. First, the right to vote should be independent of the property which an individual might possess. This view was expressed by Henry Lovewell, a journeyman tailor who already possessed the franchise, and who some years before had been a foundation-member of the Mechanics Institute. Second, Nathaniel Whimper, a wine-merchant, emphasised the Christian basis of equal political and social rights. Third, Joseph Bird, a bricklayer emphasised universal suffrage as a means of attaining a rational system of government. Universal suffrage, he maintained, should be accompanied by voting by ballot, and the necessity for this was borne out in the testimony of Charles Bird, a master-painter who already possessed the franchise. He said:

[1] *Ibid.*, 6 Jan., 3 Feb. 1838. [2] *Ibid.*, 3 Feb. 1838.

'I stand before you as one of the present constituency — I have a vote, but instead of it being a benefit to me, it is a positive injury. I have ever exercised that vote, to the best of my judgment, and not for my own selfish or pecuniary advantage. The consequences has been that I have sustained an injury — and for Want of the Ballot. I always went fearlessly to the Poll and recorded my vote for the people, and thus I became a marked man, and many individuals who favoured me in business with their favours, withdrew from me.'

The Chairman at this Petition Meeting was Robert Booley, a skilled coachworker at Catt and Quadley's Forge and a Nonconformist lay-preacher. His Nonconformist training and the early optimism of the movement is revealed in his speech:

'Let such Societies as this be formed throughout the country, let our principles be adopted by them, let them act with prudence, and carry forward their principles by argument and moral energy, and a voice will be raised that no Legislature will be able to silence.'[1]

On occasions, when the Ipswich Association intended to attract a wider audience, meetings were held at the Ipswich Arms Inn or at the Town Hall. Generally, however, meetings were usually held at weekly intervals in a room belonging to Joseph Pearce in Tacket Street.[2] In May 1838 the Association had upwards of one hundred and fifty members, of which number sixty already possessed the franchise. For the first few months of its activity, communication with the L.W.M.A. and contact with the neighbouring association in Colchester (Essex) provided the only links with the outside movement. No real effort had been made to spread the agitation to the county of Suffolk, and indeed as the county awaited the initial stimulus of the Ipswich Association, so the Ipswich Chartists needed an outside stimulus to get them on the way.

This stimulus was provided in the launching of the National Petition and the planning of a National Convention. Within a week of the mass meeting at Newhall Hill[3] the working men of Ipswich were urged to follow the example of their brethren of the north and to attend a meeting in the Town Hall in support of the national petition.[4] *The Suffolk Chronicle* gave considerable coverage of the proceedings and enthusiastically concluded that,

'With the exception that the Birmingham gathering far exceeded in numerical strength . . . the identity between the two meetings were

---

[1] *Ibid.*, 10 Feb. 1838.   [2] *Ibid.*, 17 Feb. 1838.
[3] See above, p. 26.
[4] *Essex and Suffolk Times*, 11 Aug. 1838; *Suffolk Chronicle*, 18 Aug. 1838.

(*sic*) equal. There was the same community of interests; the same spirit, and the same determination to work out by every means afforded in the Constitution, the redemption of the people from the political bondage of the Whigs and Tories . . . .'

There was a capacity crowd at the meeting. The large meeting and the fact that the Petition was national news, meant that no longer could the anti-Chartist local press ignore the Association. This meeting was important in that it provided the Ipswich association with its first publicity in the columns of the unsympathetic and hostile local newspapers, the *Bury and Norwich Post* and the *Ipswich Journal*. Now the seeds of opposition were being sown, and, as in later instances, propagandist reporting was preferred to fair report.

'It was evident from the addresses delivered by the majority of the speakers,' reported the *Ipswich Journal*, 'that their covert object is a general confiscation of property, to be effected under the pretext of securing equal political rights, or in other words: to bring all men to the same level. When men like these talk of "rights of equality by nature" and blurt out their venom at those who have amassed property . . . and call them knaves and plunderers of the working classes; their object is too apparent to be concealed by the transparent veil of "patriotism" which they invariably raise to hide their real motives.'[1]

Having decided at this meeting to take part in organising the National Petition, the Ipswich association resolved that the Petition should remain at the Town Hall for three days for signatures to be added, and thereafter for a period at the Ipswich Arms. Within a week 500 signatures had been obtained and a fortnight later the number had risen to eight hundred.[2] This total had been reached in part by the sympathetic response of the rural areas,[3] a fact which encouraged the Association to campaign further by sending copies of the Petition to Woodbridge, Framlingham, Debenham, Hadleigh, Stowmarket and Eye.

The Association, however, proposed to do more than collect signatures.

'It is the intention of the Ipswich Working Men's Association to re-echo the sound — agitate, agitate, until you get your rights — through the county of Suffolk, until every village and town in the

---

[1] *Ipswich Journal*, 18 Aug. 1838.
[2] *Essex and Suffolk Times*, 8 Sept. 1838.
[3] *Suffolk Chronicle*, 8 Sept. 1838.

county ring with Working Men's Associations. We will send missionaries into the county to preach the true and faithful doctrines of radical reform, and there is no doubt that success will attend our efforts.'[1]

There is no evidence to show that the Ipswich association did anything immediately to further these aims. They were preoccupied with the approaching municipal elections which provided an exercise in miniature for the local Chartists. The Ipswich Chartists having decided on 9 October

'not to support any candidate . . . who will not pledge himself to acknowledge the true representative system, and vote in Council as the majority of the electors in Ward meeting assembled, shall request him',[2]

they issued a handbill under the signature of the Chairman urging their fellow-townsmen

'to refrain from voting for any individual who will not be guided by the sentiments and opinions of the majority of his constituency in Ward meeting assembled.'[3]

In the Westgate Ward the Chartists approached one of the Whig candidates at an electors' meeting, but he refused to go to the poll 'pledged'. His chances of success on polling day seemed to be dwindling; and so Donald McPherson and Booley (two leading Chartists) desirous of saving the Whigs at the eleventh hour and, thinking that he might have misunderstood the nature of their demands, approached him again. The Whigs agreed to the demands of the handbill and thus obtained the support of McPherson, Booley and other Chartists who possessed the franchise, but even so the Tories were successful.

The action of McPherson and Booley caused, however, a division in the ranks of the Ipswich Chartists. John Goslin, an operative, (who for some time had remained outside the Association's activities, though active in earlier reform agitation) and William Gartard, a carpenter (the first Secretary of the Ipswich Association) moved a vote of censure. The Association took two weekly meetings in debating the matter, and finally defeated Goslin's vote of censure by 29 votes to 11. Goslin left the Association having found it 'impossible to act with men, the majority of whom could sanction

---

[1] David Stollery, an Ipswich Chartist, speaking at a meeting in Colchester, *Essex and Suffolk Times*, 15 Sept. 1838.
[2] *Ibid.*, 13 Oct. 1838. Letter from 'Scrutator'.
[3] *Ibid.*, 24 Nov. 1838.

such a dereliction of principle'.[1] This was most unfortunate for the Chartists, for Goslin, a fine orator, had in the latter months of 1838 been one of the leading speakers and advocates of Chartism and might have been useful to the Association which now sought to extend its influence in the county.

Working-class people in the county were by this time beginning to take notice of the accounts of Chartist activity in Ipswich. At Sternsfield, near Saxmundham, agricultural labourers meeting to discuss the nature of their distress and likely remedies, finally concluded that, although the repeal of the corn laws might be desirable, the only full remedy was in the success of the Chartist agitation.[2] With increasing frequency groups of men like this were now inviting the Ipswich Association to send deputations to address them.

The Ipswich Association responded to the request of these agricultural labourers but the meeting was held in the neighbouring parish to Sternsfield. The Friston neighbourhood was a stronghold of Toryism, and the squires and Tory farmers used their utmost endeavours to prevent the attendance of their men at the meeting. One farmer gave each of his labourers a bushel of potatoes to stay away. Mr Hammond of Snape Hall gave a treat to his labourers on the same night.[3] None the less upwards of one thousand people were present, which meant that they had assembled from a wide area for the occasion. After the open-air meeting the East Suffolk Working Men's Association was formed during a session at the Chequer's Inn, Friston.[4] It is not quite clear what was the relationship of Chartist bodies in this area around Saxmundham. It seems likely that the small groups in surrounding villages became branches of the one W.M.A. formed at this Friston meeting.

Certainly it was in this part of Suffolk that the greatest activity was to be found, outside of Ipswich, and where the opposition was to try and assert itself most strongly. The occasion which created a concentration of opposition was the calling of a public meeting at Carlton Green, near Saxmundham, on Boxing Day 1838. Lord John Russell received communications from four groups of people over an area of roughly fourteen miles radius.[5] It was the magistrates

[1] *Ibid.*, 22 Dec. 1838. Letter from Goslin.   [2] *Ibid.*, 17 Nov. 1838.
[3] *Suffolk Chronicle*, 1 Dec. 1838.
[4] *Ibid.*
[5] H.O. 40/39.

at Framlingham who expressed the greatest fears and suggested that the Home Secretary should move troops from Ipswich to Saxmundham (a distance of about 21 miles), warn the coast-guards at Aldeburgh to be in readiness and at the disposal of the magistrates in case of necessity, and send a police force to Sax-mundham before 26 December. Lord John Russell does not appear to have shared the anxiety and fears of his correspondents whom he recommended:

> 'to watch the proceedings and to be prepared by swearing in a suffi-cient number of special constables to maintain the Peace.'[1]

The local magistrates were unable to obtain any assistance from the Home Office, and as events worked out none was needed. All passed off peaceably.

The Ipswich Association sent a somewhat larger deputation on this occasion. On their arrival at Bigsby's Corner, on the outskirts of Saxmundham, at 9.30 a.m. on Boxing Day, they were met by a crowd of between five and six hundred people. A procession was formed and led by the deputation they marched through Sax-mundham to Carlton Green, several people carrying home-made banners. On their way their following increased, and the whole ac-tivity inspired the *Essex Mercury* to say:

> 'The day was delightfully fine; the sun shone forth in all its majesty and grandeur, and tipped the hills with gold, while all nature looked serene. The scene was indeed a most exhilarating one, though there was no music to enlighten (*sic*) it, save the hum of thousands of voices.'[2]

Though the fears of the opposition in the Saxmundham district seem to have been exaggerated, it must be admitted that there was a possibility of disorder; and in part the activity of the Chartists in the virile North may have strengthened the magistrates and others in their dread of possible outbreaks. Indeed the Ipswich Associa-tion itself shared doubts about the worthwhileness of 'physical force' and twice within a month debated the question and declared itself overwhelmingly in favour of 'moral force'.[3] This express repu-diation of 'physical force' Chartism had little affect upon the grow-ing opposition which manifested itself in the written and spoken

---

[1] H.O. 41/13. *Disturbances Entry Book*, pp. 271, 277, 279, 286.
[2] *Essex Mercury*, 11 Jan. 1839.
[3] *Essex and Suffolk Times*, 22 Dec. 1838.

word, and by individual and concerted action. Despite opposition, the Ipswich Association continued to agitate. Upwards of 2,500 signatures had been obtained towards the end of January 1839.[1]

In November 1838 the Ipswich association had sent a deputation to Hadleigh where an Association was formed.[1] On 7 December some five or six hundred artisans assembled in the yard of the Crown Inn, Bildeston to listen to the speeches of the Ipswich delegation. Resolutions were passed in favour of the Charter but there is no evidence that an Association was formed.[2] In February 1839 a somewhat precarious Association was founded at Stowmarket.[3] In considering an invitation to address the working classes of Sudbury, the Ipswich Association was more cautious. Its reasons for not sending speakers are set out in a letter addressed to the working men of Sudbury.

> 'A large number of the working men of Sudbury and others interested in the People's Charter, expressed a desire for a deputation from our Association to wait upon them and with the assistance of a delegate from the National Convention, to explain to them the objects of the National Petition, when the corrupt parties of that town, fired with malignant rage, declared their determination to upset any meeting that might be called for that purpose, and eventually drive them from that place. Not wishing to be the cause of creating any riot or disturbance for the minions of the law to fasten their clutches upon, the Association have adopted the plan of addressing them through the medium of the Press . . . .'

Nevertheless the letter concluded,

> 'At a proper season we shall be with you; in the mean time, be vigilant to increase your strength, and persevere in well-doing . . . .'[4]

It was at this particular moment in time that Suffolk was visited by two delegates from the National Convention.[5] The two missionaries sent were William Gill (a delegate to the Convention from Sheffield) and John Deegan (a delegate from Hyde, Stalybridge, Glossop and New Mills). They received their Suffolk baptism amid Tory opposition.[6] They addressed meetings at Ipswich,

---

[1] *Suffolk Chronicle*, 26 Jan. 1839.
[2] *Ibid.*, 15 Dec. 1838; *Essex Mercury*, 11 Dec. 1838; *Bury and Norwich Post*, 19 Dec. 1838.
[3] *Suffolk Chronicle*, 9 Feb. 1839.   [4] *Suffolk Chronicle*, 27 Apr. 1839.
[5] Hovell, *op. cit.*, p. 129.
[6] *Suffolk Chronicle*, 9 Feb. 1839; *Ipswich Journal*, 16 Feb. 1839.

Hadleigh, Debenham, Woodbridge, Stowmarket and agricultural labourers at Benhall Green (for the Saxmundham area).[1] Garrard, the local Secretary in Ipswich, in a letter to the National Convention, expressed the opinion that the visit of the delegation had done great good. He stressed the need for a wider and more concentrated agitation in the rural areas believing,

> '. . . it is the Agricultural labourers we want to enlist to our cause, once that object is affected our cause is sure and it will eventually triumph.'[2]

Writing again to the Convention a few weeks later, Garrard sent the final instalment of signatures to the Petition. The total number of signatures obtained in Suffolk was 7,100. Garrard expressed a wish that there had been even more, and said that he hoped to be able to send National Rent shortly.[3]

With the transference of the National Convention from London to Birmingham a new phase in Suffolk Chartism began under the influence of the Ipswich Association in May 1839. The association was aided in this by the visitation of another delegation from the Convention, and sought to get the 'ulterior measures' approved at meetings at Ipswich and at Eye.[4] The mid-summer of 1839 seems to have been barren of any outstanding activity, and the late summer proved to be a period of great anxiety for the Chartist movement nationally.

The Chartists of East Suffolk evidently did not allow the apparent indifference of the National Convention nor subsequent national events to sap their enthusiasm. In the autumn of 1839 they began to organise themselves much more effectively, at any rate for a time. The improved organisation found expression in the founding of the East Suffolk and Yarmouth Chartist Council, which comprised two delegates from each Association within the area, and was to meet monthly. Constituent Associations were required to subscribe liberally to the organisation and to delegate rent. The inspirer of this activity was John Goodwyn Barmby, Esquire, of Yoxford (near Saxmundham). His life seems to have been devoted to the support of several utopian aims before he finally became a Unitarian minister. In 1845, Frost described him as

---

[1] *The Charter*, 31 Mar., 7 Apr. 1839.
[2] B.M. Add. MSS. 34,245A, Letter from Garrard to the National Convention, 11 Mar. 1839.
[3] Letter of 2 May 1839, *loc. cit.*   [4] *Suffolk Chronicle*, 25 May 1839.

'a young man of gentlemanly manners and soft persuasive voice, wearing his light brown hair parted down the middle, after the fashion of the Concordist brethren, and a collar and neck-tie à la Byron.'[1]

Certainly at this time the Chartist initiative in the county had passed to the Friston area, but Barmby's limited association with the movement meant that the newly-formed Council was virtually ineffective. During his association with the movement, Barmby was nominated by the East Suffolk Chartists 'as a fit and proper person' to represent Suffolk at the National Convention in New-castle[2] and, during the second phase of Chartism in Suffolk, the Ipswich National Charter Association wished him to stand as a parliamentary candidate at the 1841 Election.[3]

As far as they could, the members of the Ipswich Working Men's Association had attempted with some initial success to stir their fellow-townsmen and the working classes in the countryside into some active participation in the Chartist cause. They were less successful than they might have been because they were not all agreed upon the whole of the Chartist programme. In the years 1841-2 two bodies competed for the support of the reform-minded in Suffolk. Some of the Chartists were attracted to the National Charter Association, which eventually ruled supreme, becoming more active in the years after 1842. Others were drawn into the politics of the Complete Suffrage movement, thereby participating with other groups in the agitation for political reform.

The first development in Ipswich was the formation of a Branch of the National Charter Association early in 1841. This body included some of those Chartists who had earlier seceded from the Working Men's Association because of its moderate leanings. The new Chartist group followed the pattern of its predecessor by holding weekly meetings, stressing the necessity of education in Chartist principles and attempting to convince people by moral persuasion. It invited to its meetings the unrepresented classes of Suffolk.[4]

The General Election of 1841 provided an opportunity for the Ipswich Chartists to propose a candidate of their own, and they selected Barmby. But he was out of the country at the time of the election. It was perhaps as well, for the election was declared

[1] T. Frost, *Forty Years' Recollections* (1880), p. 57. See also D.N.B. article.
[2] *Suffolk Chronicle*, 7 Dec. 1839.   [3] *Ibid.*, 19 June 1841.
[4] *Ibid.*, 13 Mar. 1841.

corrupt, and the re-election was also declared void because of bribery and corruption. The third election campaign within twelve months brought Henry Vincent to the town as an independent candidate, but standing, so it was contended, in the colours of the Complete Suffrage Union. His election campaign and subsequent visits to various places in the county gave a great start to the work of the Complete Suffrage Union in Suffolk. His oratory and influence to a large extent ensured that the Union should, for a time at least, make progress at the cost of the National Charter Association which was still in its infancy in Suffolk.

The Vincent candidature in 1842 inspired the *Suffolk Chronicle* to print an Editorial on 'Representation in Ipswich' in the following glowing terms:

'Ipswich has signalised itself by a victory which few who have heard — and who have not — of the corruptness of its constituency could have deemed within the bounds of probability. Yes, we never felt prouder of our "ancient town" than at the present moment. Within its walls, this week, a blow has been struck at Faction — from which Faction can never recover. True, a brace of Conservatives have been legally declared its representatives, but the glory consists in having in future only one faction to contend with instead of two. Henceforth the political battles to be fought in this Borough will be The People against the Tories. The Whig Party is now rapidly undergoing the process of complete annihilation.

This grand triumph of principle has been achieved by the presence of Henry Vincent, whose highly moral and intellectual, and, we may also add, truly religious addresses, kindled so mighty a flame of enthusiastic patriotism in the bosoms of all who heard him ... that without resorting to any of the common electioneering stratagems ... that he polled 473 votes, being within 70 of the number obtained by the Whig candidates at the previous contest .... Henry Vincent leaves the town with the knowledge of the fact that he carries away with him the hearty approbation of the majority of its inhabitants, and comforted by the assurance that he has planted a goodly tree among them which will bring forth fruit in due season.'[1]

Vincent seemed quite happy about the result, and again contested the seat in the 1847 Election, although he was again unsuccessful.

Vincent did not immediately gain the support of the moderate

[1] *Ibid.*, 20 Aug. 1842. Four election ballads used by Vincent are in the Glyde Collection, Ipswich P.L.

pswich Chartists in 1842. They had invited Colonel Thompson and Joseph Sturge to become candidates, but 'in default of these gentlemen appearing, there can be no objection to Mr Vincent'.[1] Vincent, accepting the moral conditions which he imposed upon himself as a candidate, made the most of the channels still open to him for soliciting the votes of the electors. His strongest weapon was his oratory. He also used election leaflets and printed a formal address in the *Suffolk Chronicle*. The programme upon which Vincent sought the votes of the electorate was

   (i) an endeavour to obtain electoral reform, upon the basis of Complete Suffrage;

  (ii) the provision of a more widespread education in order that 'the child of the honest poor man should have its mind trained in everything requisite for the promotion of its spiritual, moral, political and social interests';

 (iii) the separation of the Church from the State, and the abolition of the Church Rate, or any other assessment made for the support of a particular sect;

 (iv) free trade — involving the abolition of the corn laws;

  (v) abolition of unmerited pensions;

 (vi) 'the equating of the National Expenditure to the limits of the People's means of contribution,' and opposition to the Income Tax;

(vii) opposition to the maintenance of a Standing Army.[2]

In this programme there was much to attract a diversity of voting interests, but the very diversity precluded some rigid Chartists from supporting him.

The presence of Vincent in Ipswich and the enthusiastic support which he attracted, formed a good foundation upon which to build the work of the Complete Suffrage Union. He was not himself at the meeting when the Ipswich Branch was founded, but he did not leave Suffolk without sowing the seed elsewhere. The attendance at the meeting called to found the Ipswich Branch was somewhat thin, and most of those attending belonged to the working classes. This gave point to McPherson's unsuccessful attempt to obtain an adjournment 'in order that the middle classes might have an

---

[1] *Suffolk Chronicle*, 13 Aug. 1842. A speech of Donald McPherson, auctioneer, tea-dealer, opponent of Church rates and former chairman of the Ipswich Working Men's Association. See above, p. 160.

[2] *Ibid.*, 13 Aug. 1842.

opportunity of attending and offering an explanation as to their true motives'.[1] The proceedings of this meeting were a portent of things to come. The Complete Suffrage Union in Ipswich was founded upon an uneasy alliance of the middle and working classes, with many of the early Chartists as well as the middle classes remaining aloof.

In Sudbury also a Branch of the Union was formed, and as a result of Vincent's address on 25 August 1842 there was certainly an immediate accession of members.[2] In October of the same year the Complete Suffrage Union managed to take root in Woodbridge, an agricultural town, where there had been little or no Chartist activity at an earlier date, and where the Suffrage appeal was likely to be more acceptable. The enrolment of members appears to have surpassed the most sanguine expectations of the local organisers.[3]

The Complete Suffrage Union activity in the county had barely started when the occasion of the Birmingham Conference at the end of 1842 caused a disturbance which considerably hampered the Union's progress and demonstrated the differences in the local reformers' ranks. The earlier Chartist leaders in Ipswich were not prepared to allow the Union leaders to rig the elections as they had hoped. In particular, William Garrard, the local National Charter Association secretary, urged his associates to rouse themselves out of their apathy and to attend the public meeting to ensure that they were properly represented at Birmingham.[4] Whether or not the working classes did respond to the extent which Garrard and others would have liked is not clear, but at any rate the more radical Chartist element was able to make its opinion felt at the meeting and to secure half of the representation to the Birmingham Conference. Vincent and William Fraser, a local tailor and active Complete Suffrage Unionist, were successful moderate candidates alongside Garrard and Donald McPherson who represented the more militant wing.[5]

From Ipswich, Vincent went to Woodbridge, where a highly respectable and influential audience gathered in the theatre to hear him.[6] It was about a fortnight later that the Woodbridge branch elected two representatives to the Conference. At this meeting an

[1] *Ibid.*, 20 Aug. 1842.   [2] *The Nonconformist*, 31 Aug. 1842.
[3] *Suffolk Chronicle*, 22 Oct. 1842.   [4] *Ibid.*, 19 Nov. 1842.
[5] *Ibid.*, 26 Nov. 1842; *The Nonconformist*, 30 Nov. 1842.
[6] *Ibid.*, 30 Nov. 1842.

attempt was made to secure the election as one of the delegates of Gammage, later the historian of the Chartist movement.[1] The 'Chartists' in Sudbury unsuccessfully attempted to get one of their own members elected to the Chair, opposed the resolution to send four delegates to the conference, and disputed the nominees of the Branch.[2]

At the Birmingham Conference itself one Woodbridge delegate voted in favour of the Bill of Rights, but the Ipswich delegation was divided. Vincent and Fraser voted for the Bill of Rights; McPherson and Garrard supported the Charter.[3] On the return of the delegates to their home town, each party accused the other of misrepresenting the people they had been delegated to represent.[4] None the less the Ipswich Branch remained surprisingly optimistic.

This optimism soon faded. In Woodbridge where expectations were high in the early part of 1843, no further reports of activity have come to light. In Sudbury nothing is reported after Vincent's lecture tour in February 1843.[5] Indeed from the very limited evidence of the local press it seems that with the exception of a single lecture by Vincent at Bury St Edmunds in September 1843, the playing-out of the Complete Suffrage interlude in Suffolk was left to its adherents in Ipswich. Here too the activity was strictly limited. The middle-class element which dominated the Complete Suffrage movement from the start was now its sole survivor. The working-class element seems by this time to have come to the conclusion that the remedy for the economic distress could not be achieved through political channels. Indeed for a few years, attempts to enlist working-class support in Suffolk, even for pure Chartist aims, met with little success.

Before attempting to assess the success and the influence of Chartism in Suffolk it is necessary to trace the third and final phase of the agitation which ended in 1848. After the failures of 1839 and 1842, it seemed to the Suffolk labourers that more desperate methods were necessary to bring relief. The Suffolk newspapers of 1844 have no reference at all to local Chartism, but issue after issue contains reports of incendiarism. It would seem therefore that if Chartism was to regain any hold on the working classes, and really

[1] *Ibid.*, 21 Dec. 1842; *Suffolk Chronicle*, 17 Dec. 1842.
[2] *The Nonconformist*, 21 Dec. 1842; *Ipswich Express*, 20 Dec. 1842.
[3] *Suffolk Chronicle*, 14 Jan. 1843.
[4] *Ibid.*, 14, 21 Jan., 4, 11 Feb. 1843; *The Nonconformist*, 18, 25 Jan. 1843.
[5] *Suffolk Chronicle*, 11 Feb. 1843.

to appeal to the agricultural labourer, its propagandists had to formulate a clear-cut economic and social policy, in addition to a
political programme, which so far had proved ineffective. This the
movement never achieved nationally, and its chances of ever doing
so were remote, because of the variety of needs from district to district, and in particular the diverse demands of industrial and rural
areas. Although the 'Back to the Land' programme of O'Connor
emerging out of the discontent of the industrial north, prepared the
ground for the final Chartist agitation in Suffolk, the economic
benefits promised by the O'Connor scheme appealed exclusively
to the artisans in the Suffolk towns. Branches of the Land Company were established at Sudbury and Ipswich.[1]

In the final phase of political agitation, culminating in the events
of 1848, only Sudbury and Ipswich were concerned, and it is for the
latter town that most of the evidence for this phase is available.
The Sudbury Chartists evidently exercised great care in obtaining
signatures to the last Petition,[2] but the end of the Suffolk Chartist
activity, like its beginnings, was confined to activity in Ipswich,
this time to the Ipswich Chartist Association.

The Ipswich Chartist Association was founded in 1847 during
the course of Vincent's second election campaign in the town. He
was aided by a committee of non-electors, including Garrard, and
the committee decided to remain in existence after the election as
an independent reform body having no connection with the Chartist movement nationally.[3] The opportunity for local participation
in politics having passed, the Association could not long delay the
consideration of its true aims and purpose. If, as its name suggested,
it was to bring into existence the reforms advocated by the People's
Charter, it had to realise, and did realise, that this could not be
achieved in municipal isolation. Accordingly, in October 1847, the
Association resolved to affiliate to the National Charter Association, and thus re-formed a Branch of the N.C.A. which earlier had
failed to maintain itself. The proposal to affiliate was made by
Goslin, and the seconder was McPherson.[4] Thus in 1848 some of
the propagandists of 1838 were still active.

There is not much report of activity in the press, but two public
meetings in February and March 1848 mark the final attempts to

[1] *Northern Star*, 28 Feb., 18 Apr.; *Suffolk Chronicle*, 25 Nov. 1846.
[2] *Ibid.*, 22 Apr. 1848.   [3] *Suffolk Chronicle*, 28 Aug. 1847.
[4] *Ibid.*, 30 Oct. 1847.

stimulate interest in Chartism in the town. So far as is known no attempt was made to extend the appeal to the countryside; indeed failure in Ipswich was a sufficient reason for lack of missionary enterprise. Gradually the amount of newspaper publicity which Chartism received in Suffolk had diminished. The absence of evidence in the press does not necessarily mean that Chartist activity in the county had entirely ceased. It is fitting that the final words of the Suffolk Chartist story should be those of William Garrard, the Ipswich carpenter without the franchise, who had been associated with local Chartism since its infancy. In a letter to the *Suffolk Chronicle* in 1850 he wrote:

'In the absence of political excitement I am happy to inform you that the public is about to be relieved from such a monotony by the organising of the democratic elements in Ipswich, having for its object the political enfranchisement of the masses, such as indicated in the People's Charter. A preliminary meeting has already been held, and an aggregate one is to take place next week, when steps will be taken to commence a vigorous agitation for the winter season by aid of public meetings, lectures by men of popular note, and a distribution of tracts . . . .'[1]

Nothing has been discovered about this attempt. It may be that Ipswich Chartism was not yet dead, though moribund.

III

If the influence of Suffolk Chartism is measured in terms of its contribution to the national movement, its significance was small indeed. Admittedly signatures were obtained for each of the organised petitions and limited sums were contributed to the several appeals of national executives at various times, yet until 1848 no Suffolk man was ever a delegate to a National Convention. In that year it was Samuel George Francies, secretary of the Ipswich Charter Association, a newcomer and a critic of the 'old guard' who was chosen. By that time O'Connorism itself was in danger of collapse.

The same story seems to be true of East Anglia as a whole,[2] although Norwich was a militant centre in the early days of the movement. It welcomed Harney in 1838 (while ignoring Cleave) and

---

[1] *Ibid.*, 5 Oct. 1850.
[2] See W.E.A., Eastern District, *Chartism in East Anglia* (mimeographed, Cambridge, 1952), 24 pp.

chose him as a delegate to the Convention. It also included a prominent group of physical force Chartists.[1] Norfolk as a whole was as quiet as Suffolk, and in Essex bodies like the Colchester W.M.A., founded in January 1838, laid stress on 'political intelligence' rather than on drastic action. There was keen suspicion of the extremism of the industrial north.

Taking Suffolk as a typical East Anglian county, the greatest failure of Chartism was its inability to capture the interest and continued allegiance of the agricultural worker. Certainly in the first phase the movement took root in the countryside and had a vigorous but short life in the neighbourhood of Friston, but this was probably due to the close proximity of the Leiston works of Messrs. Garretts. Generally speaking the spadework in the rural areas was done by the townsmen of Ipswich.

The Chartist cause in the countryside was hindered by the isolation of the agricultural worker in the social and economic dependency which he then experienced. His horizon was a limited one, hence his resort to incendiarism in 1844 when angered by unemployment and the threat of the Poor Law 'Bastille'. Suffolk Chartism cannot then be said to be rural Chartism, despite the initial missionary activity in 1838-9. Even the incentive of O'Connor's 'back to the land' scheme did not inspire the local rural worker. He neither subscribed to the Fund, nor became convinced of the usefulness of the Scheme as a whole.

The periods of Chartist agitation in Suffolk when the opportunity for gaining ground seemed most fruitful were those when the press and the local authorities, as at Ipswich, were sympathetic towards the aims of the movement. Never at any time advocating physical force, Suffolk Chartism seems to have had some sympathetic support from the press and the magistrates in Ipswich. This accounts more than any other factor for its initial success in 1838-9. Later this liberal sympathy was evident in the temporary appeal of the Complete Suffrage movement. In 1848 the changed attitude of the magistrates in Ipswich was probably due more to a fear of a local repetition of events on the continent rather than of Chartism itself.

It is impossible to discover what type of working men consti-

[1] *Ibid.*, R. Young, 'The Norwich Chartists'. Cf. A. F. J. Brown, 'The Chartist Movement in Essex'. For an angry Norwich meeting, see *Northern Star*, 10 Nov. 1838.

tuted the rank and file of the Suffolk Chartists. It is possible, however, to compile a list of those who spoke at Chartist meetings in Suffolk, as reported in the press, and also to attempt to discover their trades. Of the sixty-eight recorded names, about half can be so identified. They comprised eight carpenters, five painters, five tailors, three shoemakers, three coachbuilders, and one each of the following trades, bricklayer, blacksmith, butcher, currier, hatter, auctioneer, wine-merchant, and innkeeper. A majority of these were journeymen, but a minority owned their own businesses.

Suffolk Chartism can be likened to a boomerang, hurled from Ipswich in 1838, and returning to its place of origin in 1848 with no one there having the power or the desire to hurl it once more. In Ipswich, by 1850, improvements in trade and in the economic condition of the worker lessened the immediate need for the reforms which the Charter advocated. As in other parts of the country, the intelligent workers looked elsewhere for their Utopia. Men who had been active in the Chartist agitation in the town found an outlet for their energy in the co-operative movement, although here again three attempts were necessary before the Ipswich Industrial Co-operative Society was firmly launched.[1]

[1] Ipswich Industrial Co-operative Society Ltd., *Through Sixty Years* (1926), p. 15.

Chapter Six

Chartism in Somerset and Wiltshire

R. B. Pugh

I

Apart from greater Bristol and greater Plymouth, Bath in the 1830's was the largest town in the west. It was a town in decay, for its tourist industry had already waned, and it had no other source of wealth.[1] No doubt its half-derelict economy, its mounting population and the beggars, who had infested it since the days of fashion helped to endow it with Radical sentiments, and to make it, as it was said, 'the most vigorous reforming city of the empire.' Roebuck represented it in the parliaments of 1832 and 1841; one of its Aldermen, James Crisp, had been a Radical since the days of Hunt and often chaired Chartist meetings; and two of the Napiers, also Radicals, lived in or near it.

Lying close to Bath on the east and south was a cluster of much smaller towns, all save Frome in Wiltshire,[2] whose economy was being dislocated by technological changes in the manufacture of cloth. In this good ground Chartism could easily take root. Bath, therefore, with its denser population and pool of Radical gentry, furnished the little towns with leadership, and received in return the adherence of a proletariat largely dependent upon the declining cloth trade. Without Bath the Chartists of Wiltshire would have been poorly led; without Wiltshire the Chartists of Bath would have lacked the exhilaration of a mission-field.[3]

A Bath Working Men's Association was in existence in August

[1] See H. Earle, *Guide to Bath Ancient and Modern* (1864), pp. 230–56; C. Spender and E. Thompson, *Bath* (1922), pp. 101–4.
[2] In 1831 the three city parishes of Bath, together with Lyncombe and Widcombe, Bathwick and Walcote, numbered 50,800, in 1841 53,830. The chief Chartist centres in Wiltshire and Somerset were Trowbridge (10,863), Bradford (3,352), Westbury (2,495), Frome (12,240). The figures in brackets are the census figures for the 'ancient' parishes.
[3] W. L. Caldecot told the Home Secretary in April 1840 (H.O. 40/55, 23 Apr. 1840) that 'there never had been any political danger' in Bath, least of all then. The magistrates of W. Wiltshire would have used quite different language. Certainly the proportion of Chartists to total population was much higher in Trowbridge and Bradford than in Bath.

1837, only a little more than a year after the parent society in London had been formed. It was under the direction of three well-known Bath Chartists of later years, the brothers Samuel and George Morse Bartlett, both shoemakers, and Anthony Phillips, a plasterer, and was already advocating in a manifesto two of the Six Points of the Charter — universal suffrage and the ballot.[1] Just before the ensuing Christmas, posters demanding three of the Six Points were displayed in the city, and their appearance was followed by a large public meeting in the Guildhall at which middle-class Radicals mingled with the Association. Sir Charles and Sir William Napier dominated the meeting, which carried resolutions in favour of universal suffrage and shorter parliaments.[2] An even more spectacular meeting took place six months later. Its 'highlight' was the coming of Henry Vincent from London, perhaps his first visit to the city which later was to furnish him with home and pulpit. The occasion deserves a brief description. On Whit Monday 1838 the Working Men's Association supported by many citizens and contingents from Bristol and Trowbridge assembled on the North Parade and, passing through Widcombe and over the old bridge, conducted Vincent to the Corn Market. As the procession filed along the route, the bells of the abbey pealed out and cannon were fired. One of the Bolwells took the chair, and George Bartlett, Richard Mealing and Crisp spoke in condemnation of the state of the poor. Samuel Bartlett then moved a resolution in favour of universal suffrage and in so doing 'introduced' the Charter, which was adopted after Vincent had commended it for an hour and a half. The day ended with a crowded meeting in the banqueting-room of the Guildhall at which Vincent spoke to a 'highly intelligent and respectable body of persons', at least half of whom were women. Democratic songs were sung and supporters from Bristol and Trowbridge made speeches.[3] Thus was the Charter brought to the notice of the citizens, with the clang of triumph and the blessing of the middle classes.

One more spectacular meeting took place in Bath in this year of preparation. On 17 September the working classes and

---

[1] B.M. Place Collection, Newspaper Cuttings, Vol. 56, 1836–June 1838, p. 116. There are 43 volumes of newspaper cuttings collected by Francis Place, and forming sets 47, 48, 56 and 66 of the Place Collection. They have been used as one of the main sources for this study and are referred to below as 'P.C.'.
[2] *Ibid.*, p. 169.
[3] *Ibid.*, p. 214 (first numeration).

trade-unionists living near the city gathered in a field on Combe Down. They had marched thither in procession from Bath, Bradford and elsewhere, flying the customary banners with 'strong' inscriptions. Two loaves were brought to the meeting — a cheap foreign one, and a dear British one — a gesture which was welcomed with loud applause. The main object of the meeting, however, was not to promote free trade in corn but to consider the adoption of the Charter and the National Petition commending it to Parliament, and to appoint a delegate from the Bath district to attend the National Convention. The speakers were a mixture of Chartists and middle-class Radicals. Bartlett and Mealing, speaking for the Chartists, successfully moved resolutions condemning class legislation. Colonel (later Sir William) Napier, the leading Radical present, defending the resolutions, commended annual parliaments, universal suffrage, and the ballot, provided that they could be achieved without violence, but repudiated Attwood's plan and any form of republicanism.[1] Samuel Bartlett, Phillips and W. P. Roberts, 'the People's Attorney-General',[2] then moved with like success in favour of five of the Six Points (equal electoral districts were not mentioned) and one of the Bolwells and Joseph Twite persuaded the meeting that the National Petition adequately embodied its views. Vincent spoke extravagantly against the workhouses, the 'three devil kings' who governed them, the 'two things' who now represented Bath, M.P.s in general, and the four 'knaves' (Russell, Brougham, Peel and Wellington) who kept the people down. Napier protested against the attribution of knavery to the Duke, but Vincent was unabashed. Mealing was then elected as the city's delegate to the Convention, and a committee appointed to raise and manage a Convention fund.[3]

The scene now shifts eastwards into Wiltshire. The first Chartist meeting in that county, a large but orderly one, seems to have occurred in Trowbridge Market Place on 12 June. Cox, a Trowbridge working man, presided, and William Carrier, a humbly-born

---

[1] H. A. Bruce, *Life of Sir William Napier* (1864), Vol. I, pp. 524–8, prints part of his speech.

[2] Born in Chelmsford, the son of a clergyman; cousin of Sir N. Tindal, L.C.J. See D.N.B.; *The Times*, 28 Mar. 1840; P.C., 56, Jan.–Apr. 1844, pp. 259–60.

[3] P.C., 56, July–Dec. 1838, p. 118. In the end Mealing also represented Trowbridge, Bradford, Frome and Holt for a while (P.C., 66, *The Charter*, 17 Feb. 1839), although Carrier had been elected for the first two (see below, p. 185). In early March he seems also to have represented Westbury; P.C., 56, Jan.–Mar. 1839, p. 164. He died before Dec. 1842; P.C., 56, Nov. 1842–Jan. 1843, p. 156.

Trowbridge Chartist,[1] and 'the best of all the local speakers',[2] condemned the 'traitorous conduct' of the government, and demonstrated the efficacy of universal suffrage. Vincent, who had been brought to the town by Roberts and others from Bath, supported him in a speech in which he compared the present state of England with the state of France in 1789. By a second resolution moved by Mealing the Charter was adopted.[3] Next month there was a meeting at Holt, then a chapelry in Bradford, at which six or seven hundred people listened to a fiery speech from Carrier,[4] who seems to have been supported by Charles Bolwell, of Bath. This meeting, which Carrier claimed had followed his sowing of 'the first seeds of Radicalism' in Holt 'a few weeks before', was followed by one on Trowle Common, between Bradford and Trowbridge, on 21 September, at which Carrier was chosen to represent the two towns in the National Convention. Some 2,000 people, armed with sticks and clubs and carrying banners, gathered for the election.[5]

The Chartist movement in Somerset and Wiltshire, as we now see it developing, was kept going by a group of local Working Men's Associations in constant mutual correspondence. The Bath Association was the earliest, but we know little about it until 1839. The Trowbridge Association was in being by June 1838, and in November numbered over 550 members, mostly cloth-workers. They rented a large room in the former barracks and met once weekly in the autumn of 1838 and twice weekly in the following February. The Association was financed by the sale of 1d. tickets, and, it was said, by donations extorted from tradesmen by intimidation. There was a corresponding society for women.[6] The Westbury Association also dated from 1838, and likewise issued 1d. tickets. In April 1839 it had about 200 members.[7] Two Bradford Associations, one for each sex, existed in January 1839 — the former in 'large rooms' of its own. In May the two bodies numbered 517 and 324

---

[1] In 1839 Carrier is called both a gig-man and a hatter; H.O. 40/48, Crown brief in the Queen v. Carrier and others (hereinafter cited as Q. v. Carrier) and 24 July 1839. His father was said to be receiving outdoor relief from the Melksham Union: *Wiltshire Times*, 9 Sept. 1922. The son could read; P.C., 56, May–Sept. 1840, p. 410.

[2] R. G. Gammage, *op. cit.* p. 79.

[3] P.C., 56, 1836–June 1838, p. 214 (first numeration).

[4] H.O. 40/48, Q. v. Carrier.

[5] *Ibid.*; P.C. 56, Jan.–Mar. 1839, p. 205.

[6] These facts are taken from P.C., 56, 1836–June 1838, p. 214 (first numeration); H.O. 40/48, 18 Feb. 1839; H.O. 40/40, 24 Nov. 1838; H.O. 40/48, Q. v. Carrier.

[7] B.M. Add. MSS. 34245B, f. 300; H.O. 40/48, Q. v. Carrier.

respectively.[1] There were also associations at this time in Salisbury, Holt, and Frome. The first began early in 1839 in consequence of the missionary zeal of Roberts and Carrier, but it had great initial difficulties, and had held no public meeting by the end of April.[2] The Holt Association numbered about 100 in April 1839.[3] By March 1839 there was a Devizes Association, which met in the Curriers' Arms, Bridewell Street.[4] A small and timid Association had been established in Frome by August.[5]

On 19 November a Chartist meeting was held in Trowbridge and was on so grand a scale that it is worth describing in some detail.[6] Posters announced that visits were to be expected from Vincent, Roberts, and from Hartwell, a foundation member of the L.W.M.A. On the appointed day a crowd of perhaps three thousand assembled at the barracks in the evening. By the light of torches the Chartists marched round the town and halted for speeches in Timbrell Street. There was a discharge of firearms and much shouting, and many wore green scarves or ribbons, green being a Republican colour. One party carried a box supported on two poles, lit with a 'transparency' and bearing the word 'Liberty'. Others carried banners bearing Chartist battle cries.

On reaching Timbrell Street, Carrier denounced the 'higher classes' and urged his hearers to gather at the barracks in a few days and choose a committee, like the one set up in Bath, to collect a Convention Fund. He shouted defiance at the troops and abused the magistrates. Roberts said that his hearers had power to 'cut off fifty crowned heads' and Vincent declared that bonfires could be lit on hill-tops.

A similar torchlight meeting was held in Bradford[7] two days later and in Hilperton on 8 December.[8] In between the two Carrier had tried to carry his message to the villagers of Tinhead. In a metaphor designed no doubt to appeal to a bucolic audience he

[1] P.C., 66, *The Charter*, 27 Jan. 1839; B.M. Add. MSS. 34,245B, f. 280. The women's society was called the Bradford Female Patriotic Association.

[2] B.M. Add. MSS. 34,245A, f. 267; 34,245B, f. 317.

[3] B.M. Add. MSS. 34,245B, ff. 286–7.

[4] H.O. 40/48, 28 Mar. 1839 (Trowbridge Magistrates).

[5] B.M. Add. MSS. 34,245B, ff. 88–90. For a general survey of the associations as they appeared to the Wiltshire magistrates, see H.O. 40/48, undated memorial received 23 Apr. 1839.

[6] This account is based on H.O. 40/40, 24 Nov. and 20 Dec. 1838, and Q. v. Carrier.

[7] H.O. 40/40, 7 Dec. 1838 (Bradford Magistrates); Q. v. Carrier.

[8] H.O. 40/40, 13 Dec. 1838.

announced that he had come to speak about 'that animal called a Government'. He denounced the Queen, the Duke of Wellington and the Archbishop of Canterbury, said that paupers were being starved or poisoned in the workhouses, and promised his auditors 'plenty of roast beef, plum pudding, and strong beer by working three hours a day'.[1]

The large crowds which such meetings attracted, the seditious utterances of the speakers and the display and discharge of firearms and other weapons had for some time been alarming the magistrates. Until 1839 there was no police force in Wiltshire, and only four constables and tithingmen in Trowbridge and Bradford. Though the magistrates, of course, had the power to enrol special constables, they could not always exercise it, and had, therefore, to rely upon military aid. There were, however, no proper arrangements for quartering regular troops. The Trowbridge cavalry barracks had been abandoned after Waterloo and when troops were again stationed in the town in 1826, they had to be billeted in taverns. The innkeepers had grown tired of their lodgers by 1837 and it was accordingly decided that the burden should be shared in rotation with the innkeepers of Bradford and Frome.[2] The Frome innkeepers complained in their turn, and this led the Home Secretary to suggest in May 1838 that the troops might be dispensed with. The Lord Lieutenant of Somerset, however, withheld consent and 37 horsemen accordingly stayed in the area,[3] though in unsatisfactory conditions; as a local magistrate complained in December 1838, the carabineers in Trowbridge, then reduced to 28, were scattered over the town in 'deep and narrow yards' and might easily be prevented from mustering.[4] Moreover, thanks to the rotatory system, the men were shortly afterwards moved on, so that in the critical months of 1839, Trowbridge, the main centre of disturbance, was without military protection. The posting of an additional troop of cavalry at Frome for six weeks from mid-April did not wholly allay the anxiety of the Trowbridge magistrates.[5]

Meetings like those at Trowbridge and Bradford occurred

[1] H.O. 40/48, Q. v. Carrier.
[2] H.O. 40/40, 24 Nov. 1838; H.O. 40/48; Q. v. Carrier, where a chief constable of Bradford refers to 'the other chief constable'. V.C.H. Wiltshire, Vol. VII, pp. 147–8.
[3] H.O. 40/40, 19 May 1838.   [4] H.O. 40/40, 12 Dec. 1838.
[5] H.O. 41/13, f. 390; H.O. 40/48, 4 May 1839.

throughout the towns of England in the autumn of 1838. They began to alarm the Government, which on 12 December forbade by proclamation torchlight gatherings of the working classes.[1] The Trowbridge magistrates tried to promulgate the proclamation, but the townspeople were so overawed by the Chartists that hardly a man dared to display it. Their fears moreover disinclined them from serving as special constables or offering information to the magistrates.[2]

After Christmas meetings began again. Three were held in Bradford in January.[3] Large crowds came to listen to Vincent, whose remarks on 'infant education' were loudly applauded by the women. Though carriage-lamps had replaced torches, and bludgeons firearms, speeches continued inflammatory. On 12 January two meetings, one for men and the other for women, were held in Trowbridge, Vincent being again the speaker.[4] But the opening day of the National Convention was drawing near and thoughts began to turn increasingly to that event rather than to general propaganda. Were the men of the west prepared for 'the coming struggle'? A meeting of delegates from the Associations and the Radical Unions in 'the Western District' took place in Bath on 28 January to answer this question as affirmatively as possible. Phillips presided and speeches were delivered by delegates from Winsley, Bradford, Trowbridge, Frome and Combe Down as well as from Blandford and places in Wales. The meeting, inspired by one of the Bartletts and Vincent, pledged itself to foster the efforts of the Convention and to promote co-operation with working men in other areas. At an evening meeting conviviality mingled with mutual congratulations on 'the glorious result of the day'. Mealing, Crisp and Vincent spoke, and there was a special tribute to G. M. Bartlett, who described the 'real misery' prevailing in every type of district and extolled the merits of American democracy.[5] A few days later Vincent was seen off by an enthusiastic crowd on his way to the Convention.[6]

By February Chartism in Wiltshire was becoming even more alarming to the authorities. It was learned that a Trowbridge blacksmith had received an order to manufacture pike-heads,[7] and some-

[1] H.O. 41/13, f. 249, 261.   [2] H.O. 40/40, 13 Dec., 20 Dec. 1838.
[3] The Charter, 27 Jan. 1839; H.O. 40/48, 15 Jan. 1839.
[4] The Charter, 27 Jan. 1839.   [5] P.C., 56, Jan.–May 1839, pp. 103–4.
[6] Ibid., p. 125.   [7] H.O. 40/48, 18 Feb. 1839.

what later that muskets were being assembled in Bath and sent to Trowbridge.[1] Moreover the movement began to spread in new directions. On 25 February a meeting of from 1,000 to 1,500 persons was held on Crockerton Green in Longbridge Deverill parish. A Warminster justice, reporting this event to the Home Office, remarked that it was the first time that agricultural labourers in the neighbourhood had joined forces with the manufacturing population. He estimated that by March there were some 8,000 Chartists in Warminster and neighbouring parishes.[2] The Warminster area however did not prove markedly disaffected, thanks perhaps to a local decision that the movement should be ignored rather than combated.[3]

On 9 March efforts were made to start a Working Men's Association in the Somerset mining village of Radstock. One of the Bartletts, Phillips and a man called Hayward came from Bath for the purpose and gathered seven or eight hundred without prior advertisement. Bartlett introduced the Charter, condemned the Poor Law and warned the crowd of the sinister implications of the new rural police force; Hayward expounded the economic effects of the Corn Laws, which a narrow franchise perpetuated; Phillips commended sobriety, industry and the pursuit of the rights of the people.[4] The meeting resulted in a partial strike in the Tining Coal Works, and, though the magistrates dealt severely with the leaders, they could not stop another 'tumult' from occurring a few days later.[5] On 10 March Phillips and Roberts visited Melksham,[6] and on 13 March parties from Trowbridge, Bradford, and Hilperton converged on Holt and listened to Vincent, Roberts and a Bolwell. The Holt meeting was in two ways noteworthy, first, because Roberts advocated the use of arms and showed his audience 'an elegant specimen of physical force workmanship', secondly, because both he and Vincent tried to depict the economic condition of the working class. Roberts spoke about the sufferings of agricultural labourers and of the shirt-makers of Portsmouth. Vincent condemned the Government for failing to enquire into poverty or to provide industrious labourers with enough clothes, shelter and food; and he described what he had seen while travelling through

---

[1] H.O. 40/47, 25 Mar. 1839.   [2] H.O. 40/48, 1 Mar. 1839.
[3] H.O. 40/48, 19 Mar. 1839.   [4] P.C., 56, Jan.–May 1839, p. 184.
[5] H.O. 40/47, 22 Mar. 1839.
[6] P.C., 66, *The Charter*, 10 Mar. 1839.

N

rural districts.[1] Too seldom in the west did the Chartists treat their audiences to so much fact. It seems clear that such speeches were having their effect upon industrial Wiltshire. Walter Long, a magistrate, told the Government on 9 March that 'the Association' had enrolled some thousands of members in the Trowbridge neighbourhood, including, he believed, even his own gardeners and farm hands. There was no doubt that the Chartists were armed: they possessed a weapon to repel cavalry and bullets were being sold in the villages.[2] The Home Secretary, however, did not take alarm at these reports, but contented himself with telling Long that he had recommended the repurchase of Trowbridge barracks and with promising to send another troop of cavalry to Bradford.[3]

Apart from propaganda the local Chartists were busy gathering Wiltshire signatures to the National Petition and raising money. By 17 March the Bradford Working Men's Association had sub-scribed £10 towards the 'National Rent'; they had collected 2,680 signatures, the 'females' 1,794. In Holt 184 signed the Petition and in Westbury some 750.[4] The Convention, however, sitting in Lon-don, were dissatisfied with the support that the Petition had re-ceived. They wanted still more signatures and dispatched mission-aries to get them. Vincent was sent on such a quest, and in the course of it arrived at Devizes on 22 March. The public meeting that he convened, however, was broken up by a crowd of 'drunken farmers, lawyers, clerks [and] parsons' led by the Under-Sheriff. Vin-cent adjourned it to the Curriers' Arms, where, supported by two other Chartists, he spoke in private. Their opponents thereupon tried to force an entry into the inn, but the magistrates and con-stables prevented them and dispersed the crowds.[5]

This was the precursor of a still larger meeting in Devizes on Easter Monday (1 April), at which, after speeches by Vincent and Roberts, the Charter and National Petition were to be adopted.[6] The preliminary advertisements caused general alarm. The Trow-bridge and Bradford magistrates warned their Devizes colleagues

---

[1] P.C., 56, Jan.–May 1839, p. 205.   [2] H.O. 40/48, 9 Mar. 1839.
[3] H.O. 40/48, 11 Mar. 1839.
[4] These figures are taken from B.M. Add. MSS. 34,245A, f. 134, B. ff. 286, 300
[5] B.M. Add. MSS. 34,245A, f. 154; P.C., 56, Jan.–May 1839, p. 209 H.O 40/48, 28 Mar. 1839 (Mayor of Devizes).
[6] H.O. 40/48, 28 Mar. 1831 (Trowbridge Magistrates).

that Carrier might be expected to bring large numbers of supporters into the borough, and urged the Government to take precautions.[1] Four troops of yeomanry were called out[2] and at four places — Bradford, Devizes, Melksham and Trowbridge — special constables were sworn in.[3]

Events proved that the bench had some cause for alarm. The Trowbridge Chartists, or some at least of them, were armed with bludgeons, and so was Carrier, who, before he left Trowbridge, told the crowd that he would repel with force any opposition that he might meet.[4] Nor was Trowbridge the only source of danger; there was a convergence of contingents from other towns. Bradford, Chippenham and Bromham were all represented,[5] and the Trowbridge Chartists were expecting parties from Bath, North Bradley, and Southwick and from the workmen building the railway at Box.[6] Vincent estimated that half a mile from Devizes there were as many as 4,000 persons on the march, with their flags and band.[7] If this is a wild exaggeration, the High Sheriff's estimate of 500 is probably too low.[8]

On entering the town, five or six abreast, the Chartists dragged a waggon into the market place. Vincent, Roberts and Carrier mounted it, and their supporters clustered round them. Roberts had hardly started to speak when a hostile crowd set upon the Chartists with stones and bludgeons, knocked Vincent senseless, and captured the Chartist banners. The Chartists barely escaped alive to the Curriers' Arms, and while they were there trying to address their followers, the battle was renewed and grew menacing again. The High Sheriff and magistrates then arrived, and managed to disperse the crowd. This made it possible for the Chartist leaders to be escorted to their gig, but on the way Vincent was struck repeatedly and Roberts had to escape secretly by back ways.

There seems little doubt that the Devizes Tories (as the anti-Chartists were indiscriminately called) were more willing to break

---

[1] H.O. 40/48, 27 Mar. 1839.
[2] They were the Chippenham, Devizes, Melksham and Warminster troops; H.O. 40/48, 29 Mar. (Sheriff), 3 Apr. (Warminster), 1 Apr. (Melksham Magistrates), and 3 Apr. 1839 (Trowbridge Magistrates).
[3] H.O. 40/48, 3 Apr. 1839 (Trowbridge and Bradford Magistrates). 9 Apr. 1839 (Melksham).
[4] H.O. 40/48, 1 Apr. 1839, and H.O. 40/48, Q. v. Carrier.
[5] P.C., 66, The Charter, 7 May 1839.
[6] H.O. 40/48, 29 Mar. 1839 (John Clark to Sheriff).
[7] B.M. Add. MSS. 34,245A, f. 228; H.O. 40/48, Q. v. Carrier.
[8] H.O. 40/48, 1 Apr. 1839.

the peace than their opponents. Their violence, however, if cul-
pable, was effective. A public meeting of Chartists never again
occurred in the borough. Indeed the success of the opposition became legendary, for at a Bristol Chartist meeting about a
month later a 'Tory' tried to rally his followers with the cry of
'Devizes'.[1]

The whole of April was characterised by public Chartist demonstrations in this part of Wiltshire and Somerset. Meetings took
place at Westbury on 2 April,[2] and Radstock on 9 April,[3] but,
thanks perhaps to events in Devizes, they were unexpectedly tranquil. On 11 April Carrier tried to proselytise Steeple Ashton.[4] The
peace was kept, but next day a local farmer dismissed some of his
workpeople who had attended the meeting. One of them resumed
work, no doubt by invitation, and his dismissed fellows assembled
riotously and began to pull his cottage down. Carrier, exploiting
the situation, returned on 15 April, and urged each hearer to save
14s. and buy a musket. Towards the end of the month he spoke at
Freshford and Atworth. On the 29th an itinerant tea-dealer from
Stroud spoke at Westbury of revolution and called upon the crowd
to arm.[5]

In Trowbridge the situation remained tense. The Devizes meeting had not crushed but exhilarated the townspeople, who insulted
the magistrates in the streets and so intimidated the non-Chartist
population that only 100 could be mustered as special constables.[6]
So matters stood on 8 April and on 30 April were no better. The
magistrates at Trowbridge and Bradford were cowed and 'completely in the hands of the operatives'. A Trowbridge magistrate
declared that large quantities of arms were being imported into the
town. Rioters were smashing the church windows; children bearing Chartist mottoes were parading the streets; well-dressed people
were hooted; benefit society funds were raided to buy pistols; and
William Potts, a druggist, displayed in his shop window bullets
labelled 'Pills for the Tories'. On 30 April and 1 May public

---

[1] H.O. 40/47, 4 May 1839, enclosing the *Western Vindicator* of 4 May. For
the Devizes meeting, see *Weekly True Sun*, 4 Apr. 1839; P.C., 66; *The Charter*
7 Apr. 1839; B.M. Add. MSS. 34,245A, ff. 228–9 (Vincent's report to Lovett).
[2] H.O. 40/48, 4 Apr. 1839.
[3] H.O. 40/47, 5 Apr., 9 Apr. 1839.
[4] H.O. 40/48, 16 Apr. and 25 May 1839.
[5] For these details, see H.O. 40/48, (Stillman), 30 Apr. (Badcock and Phipps),
25 May (Hale, Stillman), 29 May (Kendall) 1839; and Q. *v.* Carrier.
[6] H.O. 40/48, 8 Apr. 1839.

Chartist meetings took place in the town, the second to speed Carrier on his way to the Convention.[1]

On the day of Carrier's departure things began to mend. An officer of the Engineers who had reached the town had managed to clear the Chartists out of the barracks which on 5 May were occupied by a force of 19 Metropolitan policemen under an inspector.[2] Their presence strengthened the hands of the magistrates immediately. On the evening of 6 May Potts, accompanied by John Andrews, a Trowbridge sweetmaker, William Tucker, a cobbler, called 'the leader of Westbury'[3] and Samuel Harding, a Trowbridge cobbler, went to conduct a meeting at Chalford, in which Andrews seems to have taken the most active part. The Westbury magistrates gave orders that they were to be arrested. A cordon was accordingly thrown across the Westbury-Chalford road, and Tucker, Harding and Andrews were taken on their return journey. Potts escaped.[4] Haywood, of Bath, who had tried to join his Wiltshire associates, turned back before reaching Westbury.[5]

Another large meeting was planned to take place in Trowbridge next day.[6] The Trowbridge magistrates, fortified by Home Office instructions,[7] called upon the Hussars at Frome and Bradford and two troops of Yeomanry. They then arrested Potts.[8] Roberts who was present at the arrest tried to rally the crowd but was himself arrested.[9] Both were committed to gaol[10] but later bailed. The police searched Potts' house and found some arms and ammunition.[11]

The arrests neither brought the disorder to an end nor assuaged the fears of the magistrates. On Sunday, 12 May, 'a person representing himself to come from Wales' collected many hundred

[1] H.O. 40/48, 1 May 1839; *The Times*, 4 May 1839. It is not clear why he did not attend the Convention from the start, for he had been chosen to represent Bradford and Trowbridge in the previous September (see above p. 176). Probably for the sake of economy, concentration had become essential, see M. Hovell, *op. cit.*, p. 122.

[2] H.O. 40/48, 6 May 1839.

[3] He was then or later treasurer of the Westbury W.M.A.; H.O. 40/48, 7 Apr. 1839.

[4] H.O. 40/48, 8 May (Potts and Neale), 7 May 1839 (Smith, Reeves, Phipps, Orchard and Clifford), Q. *v.* Carrier, Indictments; *The Times*, 11 May 1839.

[5] P.C., 56, May–July, p. 323.

[6] H.O. 40/48, 8 May 1839 (Webb).

[7] H.O. 41/13, ff. 423–6, 462–2.

[8] H.O. 40/48, 8 May 1839 (Trowbridge Magistrates).

[9] H.O. 40/48, Q. *v.* Carrier; H. Graham, *Annals of the Yeomanry Cavalry of Wiltshire . . . 1794 . . . 1884* (1886), p. 108.

[10] *The Times*, 12 June 1839.

[11] H.O. 40/48, 8 May 1839 (Partridge).

auditors and under pretence of preaching 'violently abused' the
powers that be.[1] The old leaders were in fact being replaced by
others from outside the district. In such villages as Keevil, Eding-
ton, North Bradley and Hilperton the 'bad characters' were uniting
'and communicating with each other to the terror of the small
farmers and tradesmen', who, with the constables, were afraid to
oppose them. Though it seemed that the 'better-disposed'
labourers were renouncing their Chartist principles, the district
was still in a ferment, and only the continued presence of the police
and military prevented further outbreaks.[2]

The police, however, could not stay indefinitely and their impending departure kept the Trowbridge magistrates anxious. After
much argument it was arranged that they might stay a little beyond
their time,[3] but on 5 June the 'respectable' inhabitants of Trowbridge met to consider how order should be kept when they were
gone.[4] Such deliberations were indeed necessary for on the same
day five men and two women attacked the barracks at about midnight and fired at a policeman.[5] The police were replaced on 20
June by a troop of cavalry, though they did not occupy the barracks until November.[6] The pacification of the neighbourhood was
further promoted by the formation of a peace association[7] in Warminster in response to a Government circular,[8] and the enrolment
of special constables there two days later.[9]

The arrest of so many of the Wiltshire leaders did not abash the
Chartists of Bath. They went on, calmly if cautiously, with their
preparations[10] for a mass meeting in their own city on Whit Monday, 20 May. Whit Monday seems to have been a day on which the
Bath trade unions were wont to assemble, and it was thought locally
that the Chartists wanted to take advantage of the occasion.[11] While

---

[1] H.O. 40/48, 14 May 1839.
[2] H.O. 40/48, 12 May and 14 May 1839.
[3] H.O. 40/48, 7 May (Long), 9 May (Trowbridge Magistrates), 10 May 1839
(Smyth), 29 May (Magistrates' Petition) and undated Memorial of Inhabitants
of Trowbridge; H.O. 41/14, ff. 44, 108.
[4] *The Times*, 12 June 1839.
[5] H.O. 40/48, 6 June 1839.
[6] H.O. 40/48, 19 June 1839; *V. C. H. Wiltshire*, Vol. VII, p. 148.
[7] H.O. 40/48, 9 May 1839.   [8] H.O. 41/13, ff. 475–6.
[9] H.O. 40/48, printed notice of meeting on 13 May.
[10] B.M. Add. MSS. 34245A, f. 399, a letter from S. Bartlett to Lovett, appealing for Convention delegates to attend and setting out the writer's hopes for a
'numerous and splendid' meeting.
[11] H.O. 40/47, 20 May 1839 (Postmaster).

this may have been the truth, it was also a day designed for demonstrations by the Chartists in other districts.

It was believed that the Chartists intended to arm themselves not only with pikes but with muskets,[1] and certainly some armed Chartists had met at Weston just west of Bath in early May.[2] The civic authorities did not like the sound of this and about 9 May the Mayor convened the borough and county magistrates to consider counter-measures.[3] An appeal to the Home Office resulted in the despatch of some pistols and cutlasses and an authorisation to call out all Chelsea pensioners in Bath as special constables.[4] Eventually 130 police, 600 special constables, 80 tithingmen, a troop of Hussars and six troops of Yeomanry were mustered, and warning handbills widely distributed.[5] The mayor, approached by Phillips, would not let the Chartists assemble in North Parade, even after he had been assured that they would be unarmed and would not speak.[6] In the end the Chartists, unable to find a site nearer the city, met in a field at Midford three miles to the south.[7] The meeting which had been expected to draw 15,000–20,000 turned out to be a very mild affair. According to the best estimates only about a tenth of that number, including women and boys, actually assembled.[8] The largest contingents were from Trowbridge and Bradford, but there were about 250 from Bristol, about 100 from Bath itself, and other parties from Combe Down, Frome and Westbury. They came, in local companies, carrying the usual inscribed banners, and were seen by scouts, 'winding along the sides of several adjoining hills.' William Young, a Bath jeweller and pawnbroker, and a 'very active and zealous partisan' of Vincent and Roberts,[9] took the chair, and in a written address, 'rather violent and intemperate', declared that the meeting intended to petition the Queen to dismiss her present ministers; he appealed alike for

---

[1] H.O. 40/47, 4 May 1839.   [2] H.O. 40/47, 18 May 1839.

[3] H.O. 40/47, 9 May 1839.

[4] H.O. 41/14, ff. 25, 44. The pensioners, who cannot have been of much use, were said to have been shut up all day in the vegetable market, where they were fed through the railings (P.C., 56, May–June 1839, p. 356).

[5] H.O. 40/47, 20 May 1839 (Mayor and Postmaster).

[6] H.O. 40/47, 21 May 1839 (Mayor).

[7] The Chartists said the field was hired (P.C., 56, May–July 1839, p. 356), the Postmaster of Bath that it was lent by Mr Allen, its owner (H.O. 40/47, 20 May 1839).

[8] The mayor estimated the number at 1,500 (H.O. 40/47, 21 May 1839), the county magistrates at 1,500–2,000 (H.O. 40/47, 22 May 1839). The Chartists themselves claimed, 5,000–6,000 (P.C., 56, May–July 1839, p. 356).

[9] H.O. 40/47, 8 July 1839.

unity and for good order. The two Bartletts, supported by Neesom from Bristol, a Convention delegate, called upon the Government to hear the prayer of the National Petitioners. Bolwell, supported by Mealing and by Richard Metcalf of Bristol,[1] moved in favour of the attainment of the Charter. The seven recommendations in the National Convention's manifesto were approved and sympathy expressed for the incarcerated Vincent. The Bath contingent then marched back into the city where the Hussars waved them good-bye. The only disorder reported was the burning of a cornrick. Whether in their speeches the Chartists had confined themselves to peaceful persuasion is uncertain; the *Northern Star* reported that Bolwell had expressly condemned physical force, but the mayor claimed that both he and Neesom had advocated it if moral force should fail.

The Midford meeting in which Bristol[2] and Wiltshire played as full a part as Bath was a Chartist set-back. Indeed the county magistrates declared it to be a total failure and predicted that no similar gathering would recur.[3] No doubt the outcome emboldened the civic authorities to take the repressive measures of the ensuing autumn.

By the end of May disorder was subsiding throughout the area, but Chartists continued to gather. At Bradford early in June a defence fund for Potts, Vincent and their associates was opened at a meeting representative of Bath as well as of the Wiltshire towns.[4] Moreover Vincent himself returned. He had been arrested in London on 8 May and committed for trial, but meanwhile was released on bail. He spoke in a field near Trowbridge on 7 July.[5] He was then living in Bath where he had taken the oaths required of a dissenting minister, and, so protected, continued to preach his political creed. On 15 July the walls of the city were placarded with notices charging the Government with trying to suppress lawful meetings, denouncing the police, recommending a boycott of non-Chartist shopkeepers, and advocating every means 'to beat down all aristocratic principles and powers'. Next day a meeting of the women of Bath was convened in Larkhill Gardens and to this some 250 women and 50 men came. The sentiments in the poster were there

---

[1] By Jan. 1840 he seems to have turned Queen's evidence and to have been in correspondence with the government.
[2] For the state of Chartism in Bristol at this time, see H.O. 40/47, 4 May 1839.
[3] H.O. 40/47, 22 May 1839.   [4] P.C., 56, May–July 1839, p. 415.
[5] H.O. 40/48, 8 July 1839.

embodied in a resolution and carried. Vincent then said that his aim was to unite his audience with the people of the north and 'get the Charter'. If their demands were not granted all should arm themselves under his leadership. The workhouses were denounced, a boycott of taxed goods and a run on the savings-banks recommended, and the late mayor abused amidst laughter and applause. The speech was enthusiastically received and collectors went about the crowd raising money for the Chartist victims.[1] Did Vincent and his hearers then know that three days before the National Petition had been rejected by the House of Commons?

At the end of July a group of residents brought indignantly to the Mayor of Bath a printed handbill, issued by the Northern Political Union, which sought to win the support of the middle classes by driving a wedge between them and the aristocracy. The local version of this document had been printed for the Bath Working Men's Association by John Crawley of Orange Grove, and the Mayor forwarded it to the Home Office suggesting a prosecution.[2] The Home Secretary found the document, which then and afterwards circulated both in Bradford and Trowbridge, to be 'of a very mischievous tendency',[3] and advised the Bath magistrates to prosecute both the printer and its publisher and exclusive vendor, William Young. Both were convicted next year of printing and publishing a seditious libel, fined, and bound over, and Young was also imprisoned for three months.[4]

When the Council of the Convention, shrinking from the consequences of its own initial boldness, sought to test local reactions to the project of the 'Sacred Month', planned to start on 12 August they found the Somerset Chartists singularly forward. At a well-attended meeting on 3 August the Bath W.M.A. promised their unqualified support of a general strike as the best means of obtaining the Charter. The men of Twerton and the Radstock colliers were said to be like-minded.[5] This firm rejoinder was paralleled only in a few places. More typical of the feeling throughout England was the tepid response from Frome; unless the strike should become truly general Frome could only 'follow in the wake'.[6] Yet the Bath Chartists could have pointed to some other places not far

[1] H.O. 40/47, 17 July 1839.
[2] H.O. 40/47, 29 July 1839, with a copy of hand-bill.
[3] H.O. 40/48, 3 Aug., 28 Oct. 1839.
[4] H.O. 40/55, 16 Apr. 1840; H.O. 41/14, ff. 396, 422.
[5] B.M. Add. MSS. 34,245B, ff. 116–17. [6] B.M. Add. MSS. 34,245 B, ff. 88–90.

away, besides Twerton and Radstock, where sympathy for the strike was displayed. People in Bradford were urging it on 1 August, and posters then distributed in the Warminster neighbourhood caused a run upon the savings banks.[1] On 12 August itself a meeting, preluded by handbills widely distributed in Bradford and Trowbridge, was arranged to take place on Trowle Common, but the magistrates took strong counter-measures and though some crowds converged upon the common they did not congregate.[2]

Neither arrests in Wiltshire nor the decision of the Council of the Convention to call off the 'Sacred Month' damped the zeal of the Chartists of Bath, who on 19 August held a most 'spirited' open-air meeting on Beacon Hill Common. Between 5,000 and 6,000 are said to have gathered to move for the formation of a government committed to the enactment of the Charter and the repeal of the Union with Ireland. At an evening meeting on the same day G. M. Bartlett proposed that the Convention should form a National Tract Society for the dissemination of Chartist principles, a more useful vehicle, he thought, than physical force or 'useless excitement'.[3] A few days later Samuel Bartlett tried to enlist the interest of the Convention in tracts.[4] The colliers at Radstock, Timsbury and Newton St Loe were said to be joining the Chartist ranks at this time, and no doubt needed such literature.[5]

Early in November the local magistrates resolved to strike at the Bath Chartists in their very citadel. The Bath W.M.A. had had premises of its own since February at least,[6] and in April they were meeting at a house in Galloway Buildings.[7] By 21 May they had rooms, with tricolour decorations,[8] in Monmouth Street, Upper Bristol Road, over the door of which they proudly flaunted their name.[9] Seven to eight hundred could meet on the ground floor and about the same above. The number of members was said to range from 1,800 to 2,200, and meetings were held weekly.[10] There was

[1] H.O. 40/48, 1 Aug., 13 Aug. 1839.
[2] *The Times*, 17 Aug. 1839; H.O. 40/48, 12 Aug. 1839.
[3] P.C., 56, Aug. 1839, p. 192.   [4] B.M. Add. MSS. 34,345B, f. 192.
[5] P.C., 56, Aug. 1839, p. 192.
[6] Not large enough to accommodate 60 at dinner; P.C., 56, Jan.–May 1839, p. 103.
[7] H.O. 40/47, 5 Apr. 1839. Perhaps the home of Francis Hill, printer and publisher, where the *Western Vindicator* was being edited in November; H.O. 40/47, 16 Nov. 1839.
[8] P.C., 56, Jan.–Apr. 1841, p. 40.
[9] H.O. 40/47, 21 May 1839 (Mayor).
[10] H.O. 40/47, 4 May, 21 May 1839 (Mayor); B.M. Add. MSS. 34,245B, ff. 116–17; P.C., 56, Aug. 1839, p. 192.

also a Female Radical Association,[1] which met in February 1840 at
5 Galloway Buildings,[2] presumably the former home of the men's
association.[3] Phillips was treasurer of the men's association from
August 1837 to February 1839, and Twite in October 1839.[4] The
treasurership seems to have been the senior office. Samuel Jacobs,
cabinet-maker, was secretary in August 1837, and Thomas Bolwell
in June and December 1838.[5] G. M. Bartlett was so acting in the
following August, but his brother Samuel seems to have replaced
him in September.[6] At that time the association was said to be too
poor to send a delegate to the Convention; its funds were engaged in
paying off the debt upon its 'very spacious' rooms.

Into these rooms two police spies intruded themselves on the
evening of 7 November, and mixing with the crowd of 400 listened
to speeches by Phillips, Mealing, Charles Bolwell and G. M.
Bartlett. The Chartists, who, throughout the west, had been rein-
vigorated by John Frost's arrest,[7] were waiting for news of him,
which the elder Bartlett was to bring from Bristol. Phillips made a
pedestrian speech about the poor diet in workhouses, the atrocities
of the police, the need to abolish Queen, Council, peerage, and
royal stables, and the increase of robbery. Bolwell spoke of the imprisonment of Vincent, Frost and their associates, and hoped for
the levelling of Monmouth gaol. Both called upon the people to
arm. Bartlett made an altogether better speech. The time had
come, he said, to set aside all minor and local questions, such as the
workhouses and the activities of the Town Council, and to concentrate upon determining the proper centre of authority. Was it to be
the parties or 'the principle of the constitution'? Want, springing
from oppressive taxes, had caused all past revolutions. Public discontent, ignored by Parliament, might lead to 'a most fearful con-
vulsion'. 'Recollect', he went on, 'if anything should take place and
you should be unsuccessful the deed will be criminal; if successful,
according to the statement of Mr Roebuck and the Benthamites
generally, the deed would be glorious.' But he did not favour physical

[1] P.C., 56, May–July 1839, p. 436; B.M. Add. MSS. 34,245B, f. 201.
[2] P.C., 56, Feb.–Apr. 1840, p. 243.
[3] Last heard of in Dec. 1841, when it was called the 'Females' Society' and
Miss Twite and Mrs Whitaker were the leading lights; ibid., Sept.–Dec. 1841, p.
410.
[4] Ibid., 1836–June 1838, p. 116; Jan.–May 1839, p. 104; Sept.–Nov. 1839, p.
85.
[5] Ibid., 1836–June 1838, pp. 116, 214; H. A. Bruce, op. cit., Vol. I, p. 474.
[6] B.M. Add. MSS. 34245B, ff. 116–17.
[7] See below, p. 238.

revolutions. 'If you are the majority the desire for reform will become general,' and Parliament will concede the reform. Not force but propaganda was the hope of the people. Such at least are the more significant passages according to Bartlett's own sworn testimony. The police, however, declared that he also called upon his audience to arm.[1] His words were taken down, and he, Phillips and Bolwell were tried for sedition on 28 December.[2] Bartlett was convicted and sentenced to nine months' imprisonment. The trials of the other two were postponed.[3]

These arrests and prosecutions made little immediate difference to the resolve of the Chartists of the west. On 5 December delegates from Bristol, Trowbridge, Bradford, Frome and places in Gloucestershire met in Bath, appointed a Bristol man, Lewis, to represent the western district at the next convention, and appealed to other western Chartists to unite. The 'forward state of organisation' in Trowbridge was particularly commended.[4] The Chartists there, after losing possession of the barracks, had hired a room, subsequently described as a public house, in Middle Rank, which they had licensed for 'religious worship' as a 'democratic chapel'.[5] By the end of November, however, they were meeting in greater secrecy.[6] There was excitement at the beginning of November in expectation of events in Newport, special constables had to be sworn in,[7] and a little later three soldiers stationed in the town were assaulted.[8] In December the class collectors in the town tried to devise a means of establishing Frost funds in adjacent towns and villages.[9] Rumours of risings began to circulate again among the magistrates,[10] arms were found in a weaver's house at Studley,[11] and Chartist literature was reaching the remove village of Wingfield.[12]

In the early months of 1840 Chartist enterprise was concentrated on demanding an amnesty for Frost, Williams and Jones, whose

[1] H.O. 40/47, 8 Nov. 1839.
[2] The Treasury Solicitor met the costs of prosecution: H.O. 40/55, 1 May 1840; H.O. 41/15, ff. 464, 497.
[3] H.O. 40/47, 31 Dec. 1839; P.C., 56, Dec. 1839–Jan. 1840, p. 56 (second numeration).
[4] P.C., 56, Dec. 1839 and supplement, p. 78.
[5] The Times, 13 Aug. 1839.
[6] H.O. 40/48, 30 Nov. 1839.
[7] H.O. 40/48, 7 Nov., 30 Nov. 1839.   [8] The Times, 23 Nov. 1839.
[9] P.C., 56, Dec. 1839 and supplement, p. 25.
[10] H.O. 40/56, 21 Jan. 1840.
[11] H.O. 40/48, 10 Dec. 1839.   [12] H.O. 40/48, 14 Dec. 1839.

sentences had been commuted from death to transportation on 1 February. Simultaneous meetings were held in Bath, Trowbridge, Bradford, Frome, and Chippenham on 10 February, the day of the Queen's marriage, to voice this demand. Several thousands are said to have attended the Bath meeting on Beacon Hill, the Bolwells, Samuel Bartlett, R. K. Philp and Francis Hill being the chief speakers. The plea was extended from a pardon for the three convicts to an amnesty for all political offenders.[1] The Trowbridge Chartists were thwarted in their design to hold a public meeting, owing to the forceful measures of the magistrates. Instead two meetings were held in the Democratic Chapel and memorials adopted for despatch to Brougham. Carrier was the leader in this demonstration.[2] The Bradford meeting, at which Potts was to have spoken, seems to have dispersed quickly,[3] but those at Frome and Chippenham achieved their object.[4] Enthusiasm, however, was hard to maintain. Late in February the women's association in Bath backed the *Northern Star*'s plan for enabling the womenfolk of Frost and his fellows to appear before the Queen and plead for mercy,[5] but the response in Wiltshire and indeed throughout the country was disappointing although the Bath females renewed their appeal in April.[6]

For this apathy resumed prosecutions were no doubt in part responsible. In March the leaders of the Wiltshire insurrection in the previous summer stood their trial. They were now charged, at the instance of the Crown,[7] with conspiracy to cause riotous and seditious meetings. Carrier, Potts and Roberts were found guilty and sentenced to two years' imprisonment, the first with, the others without hard labour. The charges against Harding, Tucker and Andrews were not prosecuted, as they were not held to be ringleaders.[8] Vincent, though originally indicted in Wiltshire,[9] seems to have been awaiting trial in Monmouthshire, where he had already been convicted and sentenced to a year's imprisonment. Some Wiltshire magistrates tried to secure his removal from Monmouth to Salisbury to stand his trial with Carrier and the others, as they thought that an example should be made of him in their own

---

[1] P.C., 56, Feb.–Apr. 1840, p. 183.   [2] *Ibid.*, p. 202; H.O. 40/56, 11 Nov. 1840.
[3] H.O. 40/56, 11 and 25 Feb. 1840.   [4] P.C., 56, Feb.–Apr. 1840, pp. 182, 204.
[5] *Ibid.*, p. 243.   [6] *Ibid.*, pp. 243, 267, 401.
[7] The Crown met the costs of the prosecution: H.O. 40/56, 18 May 1840.
[8] H.O. 40/56, 11 Mar. 1840; *The Times*, 13 Mar. 1840.
[9] P.R.O., Assizes, 25/27.

county.[1] The Home Office does not seem to have been averse to
this,[2] but in the end he was tried at Monmouth on other charges
and sentenced for a further year. On 18 April, Phillips and
Charles Bolwell were convicted. Bolwell was sentenced to six
months' imprisonment, but Phillips was merely bound over for
two years, which had been an additional sentence in Bolwell's
case.[3]

Vincent was feared by the magistrates not only as a speaker but
as the editor of the *Western Vindicator*.[4] This allegedly seditious
weekly, so popular with the western and Welsh Chartists,[5] started
about December 1838 and continued to come out even after Vincent's detention.[6] It voluntarily ceased publication, however, on 14
December 1839.[7] In the following April proceedings were started
in Bath against Thomas Bolwell and Philp for selling it,[8] but were
withdrawn in June, to the gratification of the 'lower part of the community' who thought that the Government had secured enough
convictions.[9]

II

The disciplinary measures of the Government were thus completed in the Bath region by April. In July 1840 when the Manchester convention gathered to reconstitute the vestige of Chartism, Philp represented Wiltshire,[10] and propounded a new scheme
of organisation which, if we may trust his own account, was adopted
with very little alteration.[11] Thus was brought to birth the National

[1] H.O. 40/56, 25 Feb. 1840.   [2] H.O. 41/15, f. 397.
[3] The charges against Bolwell and Phillips are uncertain. They were first
charged with sedition, as was Bartlett; H.O. 40/47, 31 Dec. 1839. The Mayor of
Bath said that they were eventually convicted of uttering seditious language;
H.O. 40/55, 20 Apr. 1840. When the prosecuting solicitors' costs were paid, the
Home Office stated that Bartlett had been prosecuted for sedition, Bartlett, Bolwell and Phillips for conspiracy, Phillips for sedition, and Bolwell for sedition;
H.O. 41/15, f. 497. On the other hand the solicitors told the H.O. some weeks
earlier that the separate indictment against Bolwell for sedition had not been
tried but stood over against him *in terrorem*.
[4] E.g. H.O. 40/56, 25 Feb. 1840.
[5] W. Dorling, *Henry Vincent* (1879), p. 20.
[6] In November it was printed and published by Francis Hill, 5 Galloway
Buildings, Bath.
[7] H.O. 40/55, 26 June 1840.
[8] H.O. 40/55, 23 Apr. 1840. It is not clear who initiated the proceedings; the
H.O. (H.O. 41/15, f. 451), the Mayor (H.O. 40/55, 29 Apr. 1840), and the magistrates collectively (H.O. 40/55, 5 May 1840) all repudiated responsibility.
[9] H.O. 40/55, 26 June 1840.
[10] B.M. Add. MSS. 27821, f. 312.
[11] R. K. Philp's *Vindication of His Political Conduct*, pp. 17, 18.

Charter Association, which for many years to come embodied
Chartist orthodoxy. Local W.M.A.'s began to transform themselves into branches of the N.C.A. The Frome group was to be
reorganised on 19 August,[1] the Bath and Westbury groups
in October and November respectively, and N.C.A. membership cards were flourished at a Trowbridge meeting on 26
October.[2]

These activities apart, the Bath region occupied itself in the
latter part of 1840 in lionising the released convicts and lamenting
the fate of those who were still detained.[3] Roberts was the first to be
set at liberty. He reached Trowbridge from Fisherton gaol on 7
July and was received by a band, and a crowd of 2,000.[4] G. M.
Bartlett came out next. He left Ilchester on 26 September, and,
after addressing the Chartists of Yeovil,[5] reached Bath on 12
October, where he was joined by Charles Bolwell. They were
greeted with ceremony. Guns were fired, and the 'noble-minded
men of Trowbridge', with deputations from other western centres,
entered the city, and formed a procession carrying inscribed silken
banners. Bartlett spoke twice. His imprisonment had by no means
crushed him, for he at once condemned any flirtation with the
orthodox parties and demanded universal suffrage and nothing less.
A few days later, accompanied by Charles Bolwell, he paid a fraternal visit to Trowbridge, where he announced his conversion to
total abstinence and attacked the Owenite Socialists for their failure to recognise that social reform must await a change in the
balance of political power. The expedition was not confined to
speech-making and tea-drinking, but included visits to a cloth
factory.[6]

The fate of political prisoners continued to be a topic of interest
throughout the first half of the next year. Meetings to demand the
release of Frost, Williams and Jones were held in Bath on 4 January, and Yeovil on 25 January. On 22 February the Bath Chartists
resolved to memorialise the Commons on behalf of Robert
Peddie, a Yorkshire Chartist charged with riot and conspiracy.[7]
A National Petition for the liberation of all 'victims', preceded

[1] P.C., 56, May–Sept. 1840, p. 350.
[2] P.C., 56, Oct. 1840–Feb. 1841, pp. 106, 156, 182.
[3] P.C., 56, May–Sept. 1840, pp. 410, 412.   [4] H.O. 40/56, 8, 12 July 1840.
[5] P.C. 56, Oct. 1840–Feb. 1841, p. 54; H. Solly, *These Eighty Years* (1893),
Vol. I, p. 349.
[6] P.C., 56, Oct. 1840–Feb. 1841, pp. 75, 106.
[7] P.C., 56, Jan.–Apr. 1841, pp. 40, 196, 253; Gammage, *op. cit.*, pp. 176–7.

by a Convention, was resolved upon by the Chartist body, an
meetings in support of it were held at Yeovil, Westbury and Bat
in March.[1]

Naturally enough great interest was taken in Vincent's case. Th
Bath Chartists petitioned for his release in December 1840 and h
was set free on 31 January. He reached Bath on 16 February an
promptly delivered two stirring lectures on democratic goverr
ment, sobriety, and unity.[2] His imprisonment had convinced hi
of the need for the mental and moral improvement of the workin
classes, and on arriving in Bath he resolved to found a mutual in
struction society and start a stamped Chartist newspaper.[3] Th
second aim at least was realised, for he joined forces with Philp, an
from their printing house at 1 Chandos Buildings they edited an
issued *The National Vindicator*. Of the other persecuted leade
Potts was liberated on 11 August several months before the expira
tion of his sentence,[4] and Carrier the same month after his har
labour had been remitted.[5]

Agitation for the release of 'victims' and their reception on re
lease, if an exciting, was not the most important activity of the loc
Chartists. Throughout 1841 meetings of more sober purpose –
for business, discussions or lectures — were occurring. Hov
frequent and regular such meetings were cannot reliably be judged
but early in 1841 the Bath Chartists seem to have met at least onc
a week, and in May and August there were 'weekly' meetings i
Salisbury.[6] The growing earnestness of Chartism is marked especi
ally by an increase in lecturing, but outside Bath there was little in
digenous eloquence. Charles Bolwell toured south Wiltshire i
April, reported upon the experience in Trowbridge, and als
spoke in Bradford.[7] McDouall, a national figure, visited Trow
bridge in June.[8] Clewer, apparently a professional Chartist 'tee
totaller', spoke in Bradford and Melksham, and, supported b
Bath Chartists, in Trowbridge.[9] Ruffy Ridley, from Chelsea

[1] P.C., 56, Jan.–Apr. 1841, pp. 223, 313, 326.
[2] *Ibid.*, pp. 28, 253; P.C., 56, Oct. 1840–Feb. 1841, M.S., annex f. 67.
[3] *Ibid.*, f. 71; P.C., 56, Jan.–Apr. 1841, p. 253; Oct. 1840–Feb. 1841, M.S
annex, f. 71.
[4] *The Times*, 4 Aug. 1841.
[5] *Ibid.*, 3 Apr. 1841; P.C., Sept.–Dec. 1841, p. 18.
[6] Reports survive of meetings in Bath on 25 Jan., 14, 16, 21 and 25 Feb. P.C.
56, Jan.–Apr. 1841, pp. 196, 237, 253. For Salisbury meetings, see *Ibid*, May–
Aug. 1841, pp. 36, 430.
[7] *Ibid.*, 56, Jan.–Apr. 1841, pp. 415, 417.   [8] *Ibid.*, May–Aug. 1841, p. 284.
[9] *Ibid.*, p. 445; Sept.–Dec. 1841, pp. 118, 128–9.

another professional, spoke in Salisbury,[1] and Vincent in Bradford.[2]

Chartism in the West, having passed through successive phases of violence and depression, was now becoming more stable and more highly organised. The more flourishing associations now met in premises of their own, the Trowbridge and Bradford Chartists in 'Democratic Chapels',[3] the Frome Chartists in 'Rooms',[4] those of Salisbury and Westbury in their secretaries' homes.[5] Eventually Salisbury Chartists acquired a lecture-room and those in Melksham a meeting-room.[6]

The 'Democratic Chapel' in Trowbridge has a particular interest. Towards the end of the year the landlord tried to turn the Chartists out, but by June 1840 they had managed, by gifts and loans, to purchase the building from him. By the following June the premises had been divided, part being used as a 'chapel' for meetings, and other parts as dwellings and shops for grocers and drapers. Lenders could become shareholders.[7] The Bath Chartists had for long occupied their own room or 'rooms', but by October 1841 these were no longer sited in Monmouth Street but at 3 Galloway Buildings.[8] On special occasions they hired Mr Salisbury's rooms in Kingsmead Square, not having the means to acquire, as Philp put it, a 'glorious hall' of their own.[9]

The Manchester Convention of July 1840 contemplated the establishment of 'classes' in each village and 'councils' in each town and county. This system, which Philp had sponsored on behalf of several Wiltshire Chartist groups, seems to have owed something to Trowbridge, where 'class-collectors' were already in existence at the end of 1839.[10] Philp himself in his *Vindication* attributed the prevalence of Chartism in Trowbridge entirely to the 'class' system. Although the federation of the 'classes' into regional

[1] *Ibid.*, May–Aug. 1841, pp. 310, 429–30.
[2] *Ibid.*, Sept.–Dec. 1841, p. 118.
[3] The Whitehill or (*perperam*) Whitehall Chapel in Bradford is first mentioned in Apr. 1841; P.C., 56, Jan.–Apr. 1841, p. 417.
[4] First mentioned 7 Nov.; *ibid.*, Sept.–Dec. 1841, p. 257.
[5] The Charter Coffee House in Salisbury is first mentioned 28 Apr. *Ibid.*, May–Aug. 1841, p. 36. William Tucker's house in Melksham is first mentioned 7 Mar. *Ibid.*, Jan.–Apr. 1841, p. 286.
[6] *Ibid.*, May–Aug. 1841, p. 474; Sept.–Dec. 1841, p. 118.
[7] P.C., 56, May–Sept. 1840, p. 174; May–Aug. 1841, p. 199; *Philp's Vindication*, p. 17.
[8] P.C., 56, Sept.–Dec. 1841, p. 157.
[9] *Ibid.*, May–Aug. 1841, p. 46.
[10] *Ibid.*, Dec. 1839 and supplement, p. 25 (first numeration).

groups was apparently illegal, a so-called Wiltshire 'county council' was formed in west Wiltshire and from March 1841 until January 1842, if not later, met each month. Monthly meetings were held at Westbury, Bradford and Bromham (and probably in other places) and stray meetings at Frome and Cockerton in the autumn of 1842. Delegates from Trowbridge, Bradford, Warminster, Westbury, Mere and Monkton Deverill attended fairly regularly, and from Holt, Devizes, the Lavingtons, North Bradley, Melksham, Frome and Shaftesbury rather less often. Absent delegates sent letters.[1] There was a county secretary of the Council, found by Trowbridge,[2] and sub-secretaries for all the settled associations.[3] In August all associations and village classes were asked to contribute one farthing weekly to the Executive Council in Manchester, passing the money through the county treasurer.[4]

The delegates at the Wiltshire conferences listened to reports upon the state of the faith in the constituent districts, considered local propaganda, collected money, and debated national policy. If the reports may be trusted, the faith flourished, though it was generally insisted that more lectures would bring more converts. A Bradford delegate even admitted that before October his town had been 'very dead in the cause', though lectures had revived its zeal.[5] There was also a complaint from Frome in November that people were too poor to pay their subscriptions, and Warminster and Westbury lacked premises.[6] The May conference proposed Philp as the West of England representative on the National Executive.[7]

While the Bath Chartists stood apart from these deliberations, they always acted as a stimulus to their Wiltshire brethren and once drew them to their own city. The occasion was the West of England and South Wales Delegate Meeting on 18 October 1841 held to give effect to the plans of the Executive and to extend Chartism in that region. Delegates, to whom a kind of agenda paper had already been circulated, attended from Bath, Frome, Bradford and Trowbridge, and from some Gloucestershire places, and letters

---

[1] *Ibid.*, Jan.–Apr. 1841, p. 286; May–Aug. 1841, pp. 199, 408; Sept.–Dec. 1841, pp. 118, 157; Jan.–Mar. 1842, p. 122; Sept.–Oct. 1842, p. 364; Nov. 1842–Jan. 1843, p. 162.

[2] John Moore, a Trowbridge man, was secretary until Aug. 1841. He was succeeded by James Haswell.

[3] A list is to be found in P.C., 56, Sept.–Dec. 1841, p. 408.

[4] *Ibid.*, May–Aug. 1841, p. 408.   [5] *Ibid.*, Sept.–Dec. 1841, p. 118.

[6] *Ibid.*, p. 257.   [7] *Ibid.*, May–Aug. 1841, p. 34.

from Yeovil, Mere, Salisbury, Warminster, Monkton Deverill and
Melksham were read as well as from more distant places. The prevailing distress, which four delegates described, was thought to be
fostering Chartism, and in Bath, Bradford and Frome at least, to be
favourably disposing the middle classes towards it. A written report
on conditions in Trowbridge where there was local dissension
spoke gloomily of the diverting effects of Socialism, but Haswell,
the chief Trowbridge delegate, contradicted it. The truth was, he
said, that no one could hold a meeting there without the Chartists'
consent, though a party of professed Christians was trying to make
trouble. Though the delegates were optimistic on the whole, there
was a widespread demand for more lecturers, Mere clamour-
ing for Clewer and Salisbury for Vincent. Bartlett, with characteristic insight, called for more propaganda in the villages, and thought
that 'men of more humble abilities' were better suited than Vincent
'to address the ignorant agricultural labourers'. The outcome
of the conference was three resolutions. The first attributed
the depression to high taxation, the mismanagement of the
national debt, sinecures, and the inflated size of the armed
forces and the police. The second proposed a scheme for
multiplying lectures in Bristol, Gloucestershire, Somerset and
Wiltshire, with the aid of a financial levy. By the third plans
were laid for attracting signatures to the second National
Petition.[1]

From the end of 1840 until well into 1842 various forms of devi-
ationism occupied attention. There is some evidence that at first
the Trowbridge Chartists as a whole favoured Lovett's 'new move',
but by 10 April the official body had repented, retracted their
criticism of the *Northern Star*, and were advocating unity through
the N.C.A. A pro-Lovett section did, indeed, remain — 'the Cal-
vinistic party' as its opponents termed it — but it had been worsted
by August and had seceded by October. It was probably this community that was meeting in the 'Hope Chapel' in the following
August and by the following September had been reunited with the
rest of the Trowbridge Chartist body.[2] A group of Chartists meeting in Salisbury on 28 April, and a delegate conference of the
N.C.A. for west Wiltshire held on 2 May adopted the same point of

[1] P.C., 56, Sept.–Dec. 1841, pp. 156, 200 (first numeration).
[2] *Ibid.*, p. 118; May–Aug. 1841, pp. 18–19, 408; July–Aug. 1842, p. 295,
Sept.–Oct. 1842, p. 162.

view towards Lovett as the O'Connorite Chartists of Trowbridge
had done, though they accepted Collins as a fit person to sit on
the National Petition Convention.[1] Vincent and Philp claimed
membership of both Associations.[2] Philp was plainly drawn towards Lovett's ideas. In May 1841 he advocated schools and
libraries, and in December was pleading for class unity.[3] But
neither his influence nor Vincent's swung Bath into Lovett's camp,
for the Chartists there included vocal opponents of the 'new plan'.
At a Chartist meeting early in January one of the Bolwells
and G. M. Bartlett emphasised that education was not essential to statesmanship,[4] and at the Bath conference of October 1841 Bartlett openly criticised Lovett, without apparent
opposition.[5]

Other forms of dissent were also combated. At an Anti-Corn
Law League meeting in Bath on 23 December 1840 Philp spoke
against the League, arguing the prior necessity of achieving political liberties.[6] On 11 January a public meeting in Bath to consider
how to relieve the poor in winter was attended by many Chartists
who pointed to the Charter as the means.[7] Somewhat later Philp
and Crisp tried to give a meeting of the Protestant Operative Association a Chartist bias by moving Thomas Bolwell, 'an operative',
into the chair, vacant by the non-arrival of a London barrister.[8] In
the same year a Yeovil Chartist moved a Chartist amendment
against the same Anti-Corn Law lecturer who had spoken in Bath
in December.[9] On 20 December the Liberals of Bath, of all per-
suasions, sponsored a large Anti-Corn Law meeting in the Guildhall at which 'many respectably dressed females occupied the bal-
cony'. The Chartists and the committee of the Liberal Society had
arranged beforehand that the Liberals should propose the repeal of
the corn laws and the Chartists 'full, fair and entire' representation of the people. Accordingly several leading Chartists took platform seats, and Vincent, Philp, Roberts and one of the Bolwells
spoke. Resolutions in favour both of repeal and Chartism were proposed by Edridge, the Liberal City sheriff, and seconded by Bolwell, and it was agreed that these should be embodied in petitions
to Parliament. Prominent citizens expressed delight at this union of

[1] *Ibid.*, May–Aug. 1841, pp. 34, 36.   [2] Hovell, *op. cit.*, p. 236.
[3] P.C., 56, May–Aug. 1841, p. 46; Sept.–Dec. 1841, p. 410.
[4] *Ibid.*, Jan.–Apr. 1841, p. 107.   [5] *Ibid.*, Sept.–Dec. 1841, p. 157.
[6] *Ibid.*, Jan.–Apr. 1841, p. 28.   [7] *Ibid.*, p. 107.
[8] *Ibid.*, p. 356.   [9] H. Solly, *op. cit.*, Vol. I, p. 370.

.he classes, though the effect of the meeting was a little spoiled
when O'Connor arrived later in the day and at a private Chartist
gathering confessed that he saw no difference between Whig and
Tory.[1]

The lecturing programme which the delegate meeting of October
had advocated took shape in November. Philp and Charles Clarke,
the Bath sub-secretary, went to Trowbridge early in the month and
spoke of the sufficiency of the Charter as a means of removing distress.[2] Later in the month Clarke went on tour alone, visiting
Bradford, Frome, Kingston Deverill, Mere, Shaftesbury, Melksham and Yeovil, and ending up at Trowbridge, where he reported
on his experiences. The Frome and Mere meetings were not successful, but there was much enthusiasm at Kingston Deverill.[3] The
Yeovil meeting was also well attended, but resulted in the dismissal
from their employment of the two leading Chartists in the town.[4]
Clarke was a young ironmonger's apprentice, 'tall, slim and dark-
haired with a pleasant smile'. He was a religious man, and used to
hold short services during his lecture tours through Somerset and
Gloucestershire. He is found lecturing again in Bath in December
and January.[5]

Local Chartists at this time not infrequently mixed piety with
politics. In Bath a Christian Chartist church had been set up,
where Vincent is said to have preached regularly, but only one of
his sermons is on record.[6] Philp, speaking in December in Bath and
in Yeovil, contrasted the precepts and practice of Christianity with
the 'exactions' of the Church,[7] and in February Thomas Bolwell
defined 'true religion' as 'the love of our fellow creatures'.[8] Vincent,
Charles Bolwell and G. M. Bartlett also lectured in Bath between
January and April, but on current secular topics.[9] Outside speakers
were rare, but E. P. Mead of Birmingham preached twice at

[1] P.C., 56, Sept.–Dec. 1841, pp. 396, 409–10.
[2] Ibid., pp. 200, 265.
[3] Ibid., pp. 311, 344–5, 365.
[4] Ibid., p. 367. Their offence seems to have been that they joined in preparing a
handbill, advertising the meeting, which bore the words 'Thou shalt love thy
neighbour as thyself', Solly, op. cit., Vol. I, p. 394.
[5] Ibid., p. 384; P.C., 56, Sept.–Dec. 1841, p. 384; Jan.–Mar. 1842,
p. 123.
[6] Hovell, op. cit., p. 202. See also P.C., 56, Sept.–Dec. 1841, p. 384; Jan.–Mar.
1842, p. 315. G. J. Holyoake, Sixty Years of an Agitator's Life (1892), Vol. I,
p. 104.
[7] P.C., 56, Sept.–Dec. 1841, pp. 367, 384.
[8] Ibid., Jan.–Mar. 1842, p. 175.
[9] Ibid., pp. 18, 123, 406; Apr.–June 1842, pp. 70, 152.

Trowbridge in January,[1] and Marriott of Bristol spoke on 'the right of labour' in April.[2]

Three rather unusual meetings were held in Bath during February 1842. At the first the local Chartists were visited by some leaders of the National Executive. From the chair Crisp predicted that 'the middle classes were about to join us' and Leach, speaking for the Executive, agreed. Campbell, also speaking for the Executive, gave a warning of the danger of departing from the Charter, and Philp tried to canvass members for the N.C.A.[3] A few days later there was a great public meeting by moonlight on Beacon Hill Common quite in the old style, with band, banners and a procession. The object was to induce the middle and working classes to unite in memorialising the Queen to dismiss the ministry. The memorial was adopted, after G. M. Bartlett, Philp and a Bolwell had spoken for Chartism, and another man for the repeal of the corn laws. Bartlett refused to associate himself with any denunciation of Peel who, he thought, was cutting his own throat by his protectionism and forcing the middle classes into the Chartist camp.[4] A week later another public meeting, though a less splendid one, was held at which Philp, Roberts and Vincent followed Bartlett's line. Vincent improved the occasion by a little homily upon the Christian virtues, the need for unity and the harm done in the world by 'the priesthood'. He also told his listeners how he had been at an Anti-Corn Law League gathering in Devizes a few days before and had there preached Chartism.[5] These three meetings suggest that in Bath at all events the Chartists were turning the tables on the Corn Law repealers. Only a few months back the Whigs had convened the meetings and the Chartists had tried to convert them to their own purposes. It was now the Chartists who convened the meetings and took the lead in creating a united front.

No sooner had these demonstrations ended than the Sturge Declaration was brought to Bath. A joint meeting of some 100 Chartists and Liberals was held at the Liberal Association's rooms on 7 March. Admiral Gordon, a Liberal, who had attended the meeting of December 1837, took the chair, and other leading figures of that party — Thomas Spencer, Herbert Spencer's uncle and Curate of Hinton Charterhouse, Crisp, and Edridge — were in

[1] *Ibid.*, Jan.–Mar. 1842, p. 139.   [2] *Ibid.*, Apr.–June 1842, p. 149.
[3] *Ibid.*, Jan.–Mar. 1842, p. 173.   [4] *Ibid.*, p. 198.
[5] *Ibid.*, p. 315.

tendance. The Chartists included Roberts, Vincent, Philp, Twite, Clarke, a Bolwell, and the Bartletts. Philp, Vincent, and Clarke all aligned themselves with Sturge, although Philp qualified his position by saying that he would not slacken until all the Six Points were won. G. M. Bartlett took an opposite line and moved an amendment which was lost. The Chartists then adjourned to their own rooms, where a Bolwell took the chair, and, with perhaps improper partiality, sided with Sturge. In a powerful speech Bartlett denounced the Declaration as a trap and was supported by John Hopkins, who asked whether the forthcoming Sturge Conference would not defeat the National Convention's ends. Philp, backed by Clarke and Roberts, moved that the Declaration be greeted with satisfaction', and, after this had been amended to 'much pleasure' their motion was carried. Bartlett then moved that all should struggle for the whole principles of the Charter, and was seconded by Twite. Vincent, diverging a little from his previous attitude, spoke in favour of this and it was carried. Both he and Roberts made heated, though covert, allusions to the dictatorship of O'Connor. Crisp closed with the recommendation that the petition should be signed but with the reflection, sagacious though inconsistent with his views of February, that all the talk about the middle classes coming over to the Charter was 'moonshine'.[1]

Such at least is the story as it appeared in the *Star*. But G. M. Bartlett reported the meetings himself, and Vincent, Roberts, Philp and Clarke declared afterwards that he had misrepresented the facts. They claimed that while they had welcomed the Declaration they had also repeatedly contended that the Charter, whole and entire, was needed to give it effect. At a subsequent public meeting they condemned Bartlett for the falsity of his reports after Bartlett, supported by Marriott of Bristol, had rather lamely defended his work. Thomas Bolwell, although he retained his fidelity to O'Connor, seems to have been one of those who impugned Bartlett's accuracy.[2] But whatever the precise facts, some of the leading Bath Chartists were plainly diverging from strict orthodoxy into Sturgeism, partly from conviction, partly through irritation with O'Connor. In conformity with this change of outlook Vincent and Clarke allowed themselves to be elected, together with Spencer, as delegates to the Complete Suffrage Conference in Birmingham, and

[1] *Ibid.*, p. 339.
[2] *Ibid.*, pp. 382–3. For Philp's case, see his *Vindication*.

Philp and O'Connor began slanging matches in the pages of the
Vindicator and *Star*.[1]

It was exasperating to the O'Connorite Chartists to have to face
this distraction just when a Convention was assembling to prepare
the presentation of the second National Petition in the Commons. Plans for the petition had long been laid. It had been
adopted in Bath at a large meeting in August, and at Trowbridge and Westbury in October. At the Bath delegate conference on 18 October it was resolved to declaim the text at all
Chartist meetings and to expose the document in streets and
markets, so as to attract all possible signatures. By January three
Chartists were distributing blank sheets in Salisbury, and there
had been much success in collecting signatures in surrounding
villages.[2] The Convention, after a postponement, met in London
in April, Roberts and Philp, and perhaps Samuel Bartlett, representing the region.[3]

The rejection was accepted in Bath rather as a challenge to renewed effort than as a shattering calamity. At a Whit Monday tea
meeting, attended by the O'Connorite faction in the city, an encouraging report of Chartist prospects was given, and Bartlett (presumably George) suggested that in order to make their society
more interesting and attractive to the youth of all classes 'a sort of
"Benefit Cricket Club" ' should be formed. In June the establishment of a discussion class was contemplated.[4] When on 10 July
Bartlett delivered a funeral oration upon the Sheffield Chartist
Holberry, who had died in York gaol, an optimistic spirit prevailed,
and next day it was resolved to draw up a remonstrance to the Commons and to petition the Queen, thus showing, it was said, that the
Chartists of Bath were alive. Nothing seems to have come of this
intention. Roberts, whose indignation against O'Connor had evidently cooled, attended the meeting, at which there was some denunciation of 'middle-men' who were 'moving under the guise of
being Chartists'.[5] Next month there was a rush of lectures. Charles
Bolwell spoke twice in Bath before leaving for London,[6] and that

---

[1] P.C., 56, Jan.–Mar. 1842, pp. 394–5, 412.
[2] *Ibid.*, p. 97; Sept.–Dec. 1841, pp. 17, 157, 158, 244; Jan.–Mar. 1842, p. 97.
[3] Gammage, *op. cit.*, p. 208. Roberts and Philp seem to have been elected at
Trowbridge in March, while earlier in the year Roberts, Philp, G. M. Bartlett,
F. W. Simeon and J. Coop had been nominated for Gloucestershire, Somerset
and Wiltshire, P.C., 56, Apr.–June 1842, p. 7; Jan.–Mar. 1842, p. 29.
[4] *Ibid.*, Apr.–June 1842, pp. 274, 395.
[5] P.C., 56, July–Aug. 1842, pp. 69–70.   [6] *Ibid.*, p. 207.

flamboyant orator, Jonathan Bairstow, addressed meetings at Trowbridge and Bath.[1] Ruffy Ridley arrived in Trowbridge on 5 August, and went thence to Bromham, Bradford, and Westbury, and Roberts spoke in Trowbridge.[2]

The Complete Suffrage Movement did not catch on immediately in the West. Apart from Bath, only Yeovil can be said to have welcomed it on arrival. Among the glove-cutters and furniture manufacturers of that town Chartism seems to have started rather late, under the direction of John Bainbridge, a journeyman upholsterer from Yorkshire, and a house-decorator called Stevens. They were eventually joined by Henry Solly, a Unitarian Minister, who became a convinced Chartist though he never joined the N.C.A. The group were opponents of physical force and at least as much interested in 'uplift' as politics.[3] Too remote and isolated to profit much from the attentions of itinerant lecturers, the Yeovil Association was thrown back on its own resources and conducted a succession of debates and discussions, sometimes lasting from week to week. While upholding the principles of the Charter, combating the Corn Law repealers, demonstrating their loyalty to the National Executive,[4] and championing 'victims', Yeovil had nevertheless expressed a sneaking fondness for Lovett in May 1841[5] and at once manifested an interest in the Sturge Declaration when it was issued. With the aid of the Dorset Chartists, Solly was sent as a delegate to the Birmingham Conference of 1842, and he brought back a report that gave rise to confidence that the Charter would soon be obtained.[6] He himself became increasingly associated with the Complete Suffrage movement,[7] and in July went westwards on a missionary tour. His lectures in Taunton were received enthusiastically and there and in Bridgwater Unions were formed.[8] At the same time his associates in Yeovil turned themselves into a mutual improvement society and while continuing to debate great general issues[9] seem to

---

[1] *Ibid.*, pp. 205, 207.
[2] *Ibid.*, pp. 207, 295.
[3] H. Solly, *op. cit.*, Vol. I, pp. 334–5, 346–7, 396.
[4] P.C., 56, Jan.–Mar. 1842, p. 33.
[5] *Ibid.*, May–Aug. 1841, p. 34.
[6] Solly, *op. cit.*, Vol. I, pp. 376, 381, 383.
[7] See his letter of encouragement to Sturge when standing for election to Parliament, P.C., 56, Apr.–June 1842, p. 324.
[8] *Ibid.*, July–Aug. 1842, p. 147.
[9] E.g. 'Ought the people to be educated?', 'Is Improvement in machinery beneficial to the working classes?'; P.C., 56, July–Aug. 1842, pp. 12, 147, 180, 192; Nov. 1842–Jan. 1843, p. 38; Solly, *op. cit.*, Vol. I, pp. 396–8.

have dropped specifically political aims. The departure of Bainbridge and Stevens and later of Solly himself greatly weakened the group, which eventually became a boot and shoe club.[1]

The persistence of O'Connorite Chartism in Bath is the more remarkable because the Bath Chartists had now lost several of their best men. O'Connor had continued his attacks on Philp, printing letters of denunciation from the orthodox O'Connorites of Bath and other towns. On 4 June Philp denied the charge that he had 'formed another society' in the city, and declared that the division there, 'little though it be', was not due to him and Vincent, but to misreporting in the *Star*. Philp's repudiation seems to have been disingenuous, for before 13 June Vincent had publicly proclaimed, with Philp's support, that the time for separation had come and that he could not co-operate with the 'quarrellers'. The schismatics moved on 27 June to 2 Church Street, where, under Thomas Spencer's chairmanship, they remodelled themselves as the Bath Complete Suffrage Association, announced weekly meetings, and issued addresses on poverty and the Corn Laws.[2] At Trowbridge, where there had been a little initial support for Sturge,[3] Philp spoke in July, advocating class unity, but also pleading for continued support of the N.C.A.[4] Neither he nor Vincent, however, played any further part in Chartism in this region, though Vincent continued to practise the faith outside it.

III

Vincent, short of build though graceful, was only twenty-five when he first visited Bath.[5] The intemperateness of youth no doubt reinforced the pugnacity that usually characterises small men and endowed his early speeches and articles with a terrifying violence and irresponsibility.[6] Millbank and Oakham cooled him down and he came out of prison an abstainer, a democrat, and a lover of enlightenment.[7] While a prisoner he spent eight hours a day on his

---

[1] *Ibid.*, Vol. I, p. 400.

[2] This account is based on P.C., Apr.–June 1842, pp. 4, 306, 351; July–Aug. 1842, pp. 6, 90, 177.

[3] *Philp's Vindication*, p. 28.

[4] P.C., 56, July–Aug. 1842, p. 12.

[5] This sketch of Vincent rests mainly on P.C., 56, Oct.–Dec. 1840, M.S. annex, ff. 7, 16, 17, 21, 25, 29, 31, 39.

[6] He freely used phrases like 'the Devizes Murders' and 'the Tory ruffians'.

[7] He recommended his fellow prisoner, Charles Bolwell, to spend a part of each day in study; P.C., 56, May–Sept. 1840, p. 412.

own education, reading seriously, under the tuition of Francis Place, history, geography, economics and English literature, and improving his knowledge of French and arithmetic. He found Godwin's 'plan of progressively improving the minds of the people' well calculated 'to calm my impetuous mind', for it taught him that political progress cannot outdistance public opinion. He learnt from history that modern material improvements had created conditions where the extremes of luxury and misery confronted one another. On returning to society he became a practising Christian, of liberal tendencies, no longer lost, as Holyoake put it, in 'the dark valley of unseeing faith', but dwelling 'on the hills of orthodoxy, where some light of reason falls'.[1] He ceased to advocate violence and was renowned for his high principles and independence of conduct.[2] His gifts as a speaker have been appraised by Gammage, his fellow-Chartist, who said that he had been known as the 'Demosthenes of the West'. His fluency, facility, enthusiasm, versatility and powers of mimicry made him a most valuable exponent of his faith, particularly among women, who admired not only his attractive voice and features but his plea for the elevation of their status. But while he could rouse the passions, he could not form and mature the judgement, and this perhaps explains in part why he remained a lecturer, with a 'cultivated style of oratory', and was never a politician.

The Bath Chartists soon lost another prominent leader, though from the opposing camp. In September G. M. Bartlett, a strong O'Connorite, died, mourned by a thousand.[3] Standard works on Chartism ignore this interesting character. Born near Somerton but domiciled in Bath, he understood the divergent outlooks of town and country, and was as keen to evangelise the one as the other. An abstainer and a believer in self-improvement, he taught himself to read French and Latin 'with propriety'[4] and his speeches show that he had some knowledge of the history of revolutions.[5] No doubt his

[1] Holyoake, *op. cit.*, Vol. I, p. 104.
[2] P.C., 56, May–Dec. 1844, p. 69. The last phrase is a quotation from *The Times*.
[3] P.C., 56, Sept.–Oct. 1842, pp. 122, 162.
[4] *Ibid.*, Oct. 1840–Feb. 1841, pp. 54, 106; Sept.–Oct. 1842, p. 122.
[5] H.O. 40/47, 11 Nov. 1839; 'I refer you to the causes of all past revolutions and will prove to you that the causes have been poverty, want and oppression'. 'You find that all revolutions have been occasioned by rashness and intemperateness on the part of the ruling powers'. In 1842 he referred to the revolutions in Spain and Portugal and the establishment of democracy in Yucatan; P.C., 56, Jan.–Mar. 1842, p. 338.

education raised him from a shoemaker to a reporter.[1] He seems to have been a convinced democrat, a Republican,[2] and in the main an opponent of physical force.[3] Though he opposed any movement which he felt might undermine the simple gospel of the Charter,[4] there is a freshness and originality in his speeches which contrast favourably with the dogma and denunciation that were the core of most Chartist oratory. With him a light went out in Radical Bath.

One or two places in the region felt the ripples of the Plug Plot in the late summer of 1842. Chard was the chief centre, where the workpeople in several of the lace factories went on strike on 22 August. A Radical Association, of Chartist sympathies, had been formed in the town in 1840, but the movement appears to have gained little ground.[5] As soon as the strike started the magistrates summoned a troop of Yeomanry, who on arrival were pelted by the strikers. On 24 August the 'turn-outs' induced other classes of workmen to join them, and two to three thousand gathered in the streets armed with 'destructive weapons' and after an address by suspected Chartists from the Town Hall, marched round the town. The borough authorities appear to have parleyed with them through a group of local notables headed by an alderman. They agreed to ask the Yeomanry to leave if the strikers would undertake not to molest them. The Yeomanry thereupon withdrew, but the strikers against the advice of their leaders broke their side of the compact, pursuing the Yeomanry with stones and pointed bludgeons, and stirring up disorder in the country round about.[6] There the matter seems to have ended. The ultimate causes of the disturbance were no doubt economic, but the temper of the people had evidently been inflamed by Ruffy Ridley, who was providentially in the neighbourhood in the course of his tour. He visited the town on 19 August, and spoke for two hours in the market place to a crowd of a

---

[1] He became a *Star* reporter in Mar. 1842. *Philp's Vindication*, p. 4.

[2] See Sir William Napier's rebuttal of his arguments in a letter to the *Bath Guardian*, H. A. Bruce, *op. cit.*, Vol. I, p. 517.

[3] His remarks at the meeting of 19 Aug. 1839 and his account of his speech on 7 Nov. 1839 show him as a 'moral force' Chartist. The police, however, alleged that on the second occasion he advocated armed revolution.

[4] He attacked Owenite Socialism at Trowbridge in Oct. 1840 for its efforts to achieve social improvement before the balance of political power had been changed, but later said that Chartists and Socialists were only divided upon method; P.C., 56, Oct. 1840–Feb. 1841, pp. 106, 109.

[5] P.C., 56, Feb.–Apr. 1840, p. 173.

[6] H.O. 45/259, 26 Aug. and 27 Aug. 1842; P.C., 56, July–Aug. 1842, p. 305.

thousand. He was followed by a local workman called J. B. Woodward, who preached the Six Points, and won some members for the Association.[1]

From Chard Ridley went on to Trowbridge where the Plot had caused great excitement, as indeed it had in Bath. He spoke twice on 21 August in the 'Democratic Hall' and next day there was a public meeting in Charter Square to test the state of public sympathy with the Northern strikers.[2] The police estimated that about 2,000 gathered to hear Ridley's remarks, which included conventional denunciations of the civil list, references to Frost and the other 'patriots', and warnings against police spies and provocative agents. The speaker advocated a strike as the means to achieve the Charter. William Dyer, a local shoemaker, moved a resolution of sympathy with the people of the north, and a workman from the Potteries also spoke. Though the meeting was noisy and mud was thrown, there was no breach of the peace.[3] Trowbridge did not go on strike and never again harboured a Chartist meeting that verged upon the disorderly.

None of the West of England Chartists was snared by the prosecutions that followed upon the Plug Plot, but those prosecutions had a deeply depressing effect. The Bath Chartists, indeed, continued to meet weekly,[4] and in new premises,[5] but, as always in times of despondency, their thoughts began to turn to pointless lamentation over 'victims'. A meeting of sympathy was held on 28 November, at which Twite appealed for more young recruits, and spoke affectionately of the deceased Chartists of the city. One of the Bolwells tried to show that Chartism had grown stronger in the past five years, but his words can have carried little conviction.[6] Gammage who conducted a lecture tour through Bath, Trowbridge and Salisbury early in November inevitably chose the uselessness of persecution as one of his themes.[7]

News of the Complete Suffrage Association is rather more abundant. To the alarm of the mayor the Bridgwater Association

[1] P.C., 56, July–Aug. 1842, pp. 284, 305. This is a report in the *Northern Star*, of 27 Aug. which says that Ridley went to Chard on 'Friday last'. This should mean 26 Aug., but the other evidence shows that the preceding Friday is meant.
[2] P.C., 56, July–Aug. 1842, p. 287.
[3] H.O. 45/262, 23 Aug. 1842; P.C., 56, July–Aug. 1842, p. 284.
[4] *Ibid.*, Sept.–Oct. 1842, p. 65.
[5] Before 29 Oct. they had moved from 3 to 5 Galloway Buildings, described as 'commodious rooms'. *Ibid.*, p. 364.
[6] *Ibid.*, Nov. 1842–Jan. 1843, p. 156.
[7] *Ibid.*, Sept.–Oct. 1842, p. 364; Nov. 1842–Jan. 1843, p. 13.

placarded the town in August and announced weekly meetings.¹
William Leash, Independent Minister of Chapmanslade, lectured in
Westbury on 5 September and stimulated the formation of a local
union,² which even went so far as to advertise for members in the
Wiltshire Independent, and eventually acquired rooms. In October
efforts were made to start a union in Melksham, with the help of
Charles Clarke, who next month lectured for the cause in Bath to
an audience that was 'highly delighted' with his 'honest and manly
eloquence'.³ When Thomas Spencer spoke in Trowbridge later in
November he was listened to by many of the middle classes.⁴ The
year closed with elections to the second Birmingham Complete
Suffrage Conference to which were sent delegates from Bath,
Bridgwater, Bradford, Devizes, Frome, Melksham, Trowbridge
and Westbury. Salisbury, where the sub-secretary seems to have
been a tolerably firm supporter of O'Connor,⁵ was significantly absent. Collins represented Westbury, otherwise all the delegates
appear to have had a local connexion. At the Conference most of
the delegates from Wiltshire and Somerset voted for Sturge's Bill
of Rights in preference to the Charter, but they were greatly out-
numbered, and the Complete Suffrage movement faded away. With
it went Clarke.

Very little occurred during the next two years, for Chartism
throughout the kingdom was in the doldrums. Only the Bath and
Trowbridge Chartists seem to have been really alive, though there
was fitful activity in one or two other places. In January 1843 Bath
celebrated the birthday of Tom Paine at a supper which became
almost an annual event.⁶ Gammage lectured at Salisbury and
Monkton Deverill in February.⁷ In April Trowbridge listened to
Roberts speaking on the 'victims' and in June passed some resolutions for their relief.⁸ In July O'Connor paid his second visit to
Bath and went on to Frome and Trowbridge.⁹ Neither the Bath
nor the Trowbridge meeting was well attended, though large

¹ H.O. 45/259, 26 Aug. 1842 (Mayor).
² P.C., 56, Sept.–Oct. 1842, p. 83.
³ *Ibid.*, Sept.–Oct. 1842, p. 344; Nov. 1842–Jan. 1843, pp. 16, 38, 142.
⁴ *Ibid.*, p. 97.
⁵ During the crisis of Mar. 1842, however, he seems to have declared for
Vincent, Roberts and Philp; *Philp's Vindication*, p. 28.
⁶ P.C., 56, Jan.–Apr. 1843, p. 57; Jan.–Apr. 1844, p. 166; Jan.–Apr. 1846, p.
33; P.C., 47, Jan.–Apr. 1848, pp. 58, 79, 91.
⁷ P.C., 56, Jan.–Apr. 1843, p. 140.
⁸ *Ibid.*, p. 330; May–Aug. 1843, pp. 123, 201–3.
⁹ *Ibid.*, pp. 201–3, 203, 218–19.

crowds are said to have gathered to escort him into Trowbridge.
The late summer and autumn were devoted to improving the
Chartist organisation. Meetings on this subject, addressed by J. W.
Clark, of Ledbury, took place at Bath and Trowbridge,[1] and
Roberts attended the September Convention at Birmingham as
delegate for Bath.[2] Later in the month the Bath Chartists decided
to revive the West of England delegate meetings for Somerset,
Bristol and Gloucestershire, as the best means of rejuvenating the
movement.[3] The first of these took place in Bath on 15 October, but
Bristol was the only town to send a representative, or at any rate a
vocal one. The value of such meetings was, however, reiterated and
a November meeting was called in Bath.[4] Another, to which Bath
sent representatives, took place at Wotton-under-Edge next
April.[5]

At the delegate meeting in October there was dismayed comment
upon the fall in numbers in both Bristol and Bath, though it was
consolingly suggested that quality had replaced quantity and that
the principles of Chartism were 'farther and deeper spread'.[6] The
delegates also tried to contrive lecture exchanges between neighbouring towns, but only two seem to have occurred.[7] During the
winter, however, Bath itself had quite a spate of lectures,[8] and
Sunday evening meetings were revived after a two years' lapse.[9]
The two Bolwells played a leading part in this resuscitation:
Charles, who had been for a while a professional lecturer with a
base in London,[10] must have been particularly useful. The state of
Ireland, which had already engaged the sympathies of the Trowbridge Chartists in June, was twice chosen as the theme for lecture
or discussion.[11] In April the Bath Chartists tried to canvass the
'trades societies' in the city to join them in a public agitation
against the Masters and Servants Bill.[12] Whether they succeeded is

[1] *Ibid.*, p. 309.
[2] *Ibid.*, Sept.–Dec. 1843, p. 14.
[3] *Ibid.*, p. 82.
[4] *Ibid.*, pp. 148–9.
[5] *Ibid.*, Jan.–Apr. 1844, p. 388.
[6] *Ibid.*, Sept.–Dec. 1843, pp. 148–9.
[7] *Ibid.*, pp. 169, 259.
[8] At least eight occurred between 9 Oct. and 12 Feb.: P.C., 56, Sept.–Dec. 1843, Jan.–Apr. 1844.
[9] P.C., 56, Sept.–Dec. 1843, p. 169.
[10] He delivered his farewell lecture in Bath on 8 Aug.; P.C., 56, July–Aug. 1842, p. 207. He was lecturing in London in Dec. 1842; *ibid.*, Nov. 1842–Jan. 1843, p. 123. He was described as 'late of London' in Sept. 1843; P.C., 56, Sept.–Dec. 1843, p. 82.
[11] *Ibid.*, May–Aug. 1843, p. 108; Sept.–Dec. 1843, pp. 259, 377.
[12] *Ibid.*, Jan.–Apr. 1844, p. 388.

unknown, but when the Bill was shelved the Chartists celebrated
'the people's victory' at a tea meeting.[1] The summer was enlivened
by lectures from McGrath, who descended upon Bath and Trowbridge, speaking once on the condition of Ireland.[2] At the well-
attended Trowbridge meeting conventional resolutions were
carried in support of the Charter and in condemnation of class
legislation. The *Star* reporter may have claimed with justice that
'Trowbridge is itself again'.[3]

Here as elsewhere the last three years of effective Chartism were
dominated by O'Connor's land schemes. Interest in the land had
manifested itself in Bath as early as May 1843 when Marriott of
Bristol lectured upon it,[4] and a year later a public Chartist meeting
in the city considered land nationalisation in the light of American
experience.[5] In July 1845 a Bath branch of the Chartist Co-operative Land Society was formed, with a committee and secretary,[6]
and shares purchased in both Bath and Devizes. Swindon, Bradford and Yeovil were subscribing by September, and Trowbridge
by December.[7] Thomas Clark, who later founded the National
Charter League, visited Bath and Trowbridge in October and
spoke about the Land Plan. His reception in Trowbridge seems
to have been particularly good; many of the middle classes listened,
and there were several enrolments.[8] Otherwise the year was un-
eventful. The Bath Chartists seem by 1845 to have given up their
old premises and to have met in a private house or at a Walcot inn,
where, besides debating, they supped and danced.[9]

There is little further to relate about the Bath Chartists. Early in
1846 interest in Frost, Williams, and Jones, now called 'the Chartist
exiles', was renewed. A local committee was formed to organise a
public meeting at which their repatriation would be demanded, but,
though the meeting took place, enthusiasm was not sustained.[10] By
October there were two branches of the Land Society in the city,[11]
but upon what principles they were divided from one another is
not apparent. In the same month a large audience heard Clark and
McGrath speak about the Land Society's objects and seek support

---

[1] *Ibid.*, May–Dec. 1844, p. 50.   [2] *Ibid.*, p. 114.
[3] *Ibid.*, p. 143.   [4] *Ibid.*, May–Aug. 1843, p. 51.
[5] *Ibid.*, May–Dec. 1844, pp. 10, 33.   [6] *Ibid.*, 1845, p. 234.
[7] *Ibid.*, pp. 230, 262, 309–10, 367. The little village of Stratford-sub-Castle,
near Salisbury, was also contributing at this time.
[8] *Ibid.*, p. 335.   [9] *Ibid.*, pp. 177, 234, 365.
[10] *Ibid.*, Jan.–Aug. 1846, pp. 14, 41.   [11] *Ibid.*, Aug.–Dec. 1846, p. 111.

or a new parliamentary petition.[1] Meetings continued to be held mainly in houses and taverns, until, very early in 1847, more permanent quarters were found at 1 St Margaret's Hill, Walcot Parade.[2] Plans were then laid for regular weekly meetings, and for a reading-room and classes, but whether these arrangements lasted is uncertain. By February 1848 ordinary meetings were again occurring at 5 Galloway Buildings, public ones usually at the Bazaar Rooms in Quiet Street, or the Theatre Tavern in Monmouth Street.[3]

By October 1847 it had once more become necessary to reorganise 'the association',[4] and on 2 November a public meeting was held at which the Charter received as much attention as the land plan.[5] A few days before a delegate conference at Southampton considered how to 'agitate' Wiltshire and other counties.[6] Schemes for the formation of a second land company were supported in February 1848,[7] and in early March at a public meeting to resist increases in taxation, the Bolwells succeeded in carrying a Chartist resolution.[8]

In some other places in Wiltshire and Somerset activity continued. In June 1846 the Yeovil and Devizes branches had enough vigour in them to send in resolutions supporting O'Connor in his quarrel with Cooper.[9] The Yeovil branch was still holding meetings in March 1848,[10] the Devizes branch was buying land shares as late as March 1849.[11] If we may judge from such subscriptions, groups were also alive in Market Lavington, Trowbridge, Bradford, Bridgwater, and from March 1847 at Salisbury, as well as at such tiny places as Littleton Pannel (in West Lavington), Mells, and Monkton Deverill.[12] In the autumn of 1847 Bridgwater listened to lectures, two by McDouall on the Land and the Charter,[13] and Salisbury to a local Chartist called Sidaway.[14] The branch at

---

[1] *Ibid.*, pp. 121, 137.
[2] *Ibid.*, Jan.–Aug. 1846, pp. 33, 244, 265; Aug.–Dec. 1846, pp. 77, 111, 121; Jan.–July 1847, p. 23.
[3] *Ibid.*, Jan.–Aug. 1846, p. 41; July–Dec. 1847, p. 257; P.C., 47, Jan.–Apr. 1848, pp. 100, 216; Apr.–Aug., p. 309. In the Theatre Tavern, Vincent and Philp had separated themselves from the O'Connorites.
[4] P.C., 56, July–Dec. 1847, p. 256.   [5] *Ibid.*, p. 286.
[6] *Ibid.*   [7] P.C., 47, Jan.–Apr. 1848, pp. 100, 187.
[8] *Ibid.*, p. 196.   [9] P.C., 56, Jan.–Aug. 1846, pp. 219, 221.
[10] P.C., 47, Jan.–Apr. 1848, p. 217.   [11] P.C., 48, Jan.–Apr. 1849, p. 264.
[12] Based on the weekly lists of share subscriptions in P.C., 56, 1846, 1847.
[13] *Ibid.*, July–Dec. 1847, pp. 168, 253.
[14] *Ibid.*, p. 212. He was the Salisbury district delegate to a conference in Aug. 1847; *ibid.*, p. 105.

Market Lavington claims to have met weekly in October 1847 an
January 1848.[1] At the land conferences in the summer of 1847 Bat
and the Salisbury and Swindon 'districts' were represented.[2]

The agrarian twist given to the movement doubtless aroused o
fostered interest in Chartism in places where there was little en
thusiasm for its political aims, or which had previously been re
pelled by a movement with conspicuously industrial affiliations
Hence the prominence of Devizes, Lavington and the villages. Bu
since the early days of Chartism a new industrial recruiting centr
had emerged in Wiltshire, which, had the faith itself survived
would perhaps have eclipsed Trowbridge and rivalled Bath. I
1840 the Great Western Railway resolved to build an 'engin
establishment' and locomotive repairing shops at Swindon, and i
January 1843 the shops were opened. The railway station was al
ready in use.[3] These developments led to a rapid influx of new ele
ments into the local population, some of them drawn from fa
away.[4] Among the immigrants was David Morrison, the leader o
Swindon Chartism, who claimed that when he first went to the
town in 1842 Chartism was unknown.[5] Through him land share
were transmitted. Moreover he and his associates began to conduc
propaganda in the neighbourhood. Thus Wroughton, Wanborough
Broad Town and Cricklade were visited in 1846 and 1847, and
members enrolled, and it may be inferred that the Malmesbury
group owed its origin to the same inspiration. At a meeting of the
Swindon branch of the Land Company at Eastcott in Septembe
1847 a Broad Town man, who had successfully balloted for a
three-acre plot, was proudly exhibited.[6] Later in the year, Thomas
Clark delivered a 'most splendid' public lecture in Swindon itself,
after which, it seems, a branch of the National Charter Association
was formed, though the original motive had been to advertise the
Land Company.[7] By January 1848 a 'council' of management had
been constituted,[8] but the branch had no rooms of its own and met
in inns.

---

[1] *Ibid.*, p. 244; P.C., 47, Jan.–Apr. 1848, p. 78.
[2] *Ibid.*, July–Dec. 1847, pp. 14, 52, 105.
[3] E. T. Macdermot, *History of the Great Western Railway* (1927), Vol. I, pp.
119–21, 152–6.
[4] L. V. Ginsel, *et al.*, *Studies in the History of Swindon* (1950), pp. 143–6.
[5] P.C., 47, Aug.–Dec. 1848, p. 289.
[6] P.C., 56, 1845, p. 262; Aug.–Dec. 1846, pp. 61, 111, 172; Jan.–July 1847,
pp. 46, 266. July–Dec. 1847, p. 169.
[7] *Ibid.*, pp. 339, 351–2.   [8] P.C., 47, Jan.–Apr. 1848, p. 90.

The spring of 1848 passed off very quietly throughout the region. On 4 March a meeting was convened in Swindon market place to congratulate the French people on their 'glorious triumph'. The Chief Constable of Wiltshire thought that it had been timed to attract the mechanics coming off duty at the railway station, but few seem to have attended and no disorder occurred.[1] Between 18 March and 9 April other meetings followed in the same neighbourhood: at Lyneham, Wotton Bassett, Stratton St Margaret, Highworth, Cricklade, Wanborough and Blunsdon. The police attended all of them, but no 'outrage' came to their notice. The local speakers included J. Arkell, of Stratton St Margaret, Morrison, and one Spackman, whose name suggests a connexion with Bradford.[2] The 'most exciting and insidious language', however, was used by people from outside the district, of whom William Dixon was one.[3] The Trowbridge magistrates, who duly published a warning about the Kennington Common meeting, assured the Home Secretary that no trouble was to be expected in their town.[4] At Bath on 13 March a well-attended meeting at the Bazaar Rooms adopted both an address to the Parisians and the National Petition. Charles Bolwell moved the Petition in a speech of 'thrilling eloquence', and Phillips seconded him 'in one of his humorous speeches'. The address to the people of Paris was proposed by G. Cox, a master hatter, and middle-class reformer.[5] No disorders followed the meeting, and when 10 April dawned Bath, like Swindon and Trowbridge, was tranquil.

Bath had been represented at the Convention on 4 April by Charles Baldwin, a person not otherwise known. It was not represented at the National Assembly on 1 May, but Arkell represented Swindon. Later in the month resolutions in support of O'Connor were carried at Swindon and Monkton Deverill.[6] In June the Bath branch of the National Land Company held its annual meeting at what was called the meeting-room of the Land and Charter Association, at the familiar address of 5 Galloway Buildings.[7] In November a meeting was held in London to consider the reorganisation of Chartism, at which Morrison reported that Chartism had declined in Swindon itself owing to the dismissal of many men by

[1] H.O. 45/2410⁰ (3), 4 Mar. 1848.   [2] V.C.H. Wiltshire, Vol. VII, p. 45.
[3] H.O. 45/2410⁰ (3), 12 Apr. 1848.   [4] Ibid., 8 Apr. 1848.
[5] P.C., 47, Jan.–Apr. 1848, p. 224.
[6] Ibid., Apr.–Aug. 1848, pp. 105, 166, 167.
[7] Ibid., p. 309.

the Railway Company, but was growing in Cricklade.[1] On report
ing back to his principals, the news was spread that 'levies' ha
been received from Salisbury and Trowbridge.[2] And so with shar
subscriptions still coming in from Devizes and Bath, the story end
abruptly in March 1849.

IV

During its ten years of activity Chartism gained hardly any hol
in the rural areas of Somerset and Wiltshire.[3] It is true that ther
were some groups in Wiltshire villages, but it can usually be prove
or inferred that, as at Bromham or Hilperton, industrial worker
were settled in them. There was, of course, no lack of poverty in th
villages, nor, as the events of 1830 showed,[4] were villagers as a clas
reluctant to revolt against authority. The failure of the rural population hereabouts to adhere to Chartism lay rather in the cleavage
between town and country, and the deep suspicion of the urban
mob felt by countrymen. Not, of course, that every town in the two
counties was addicted to Chartism. In Somerset no Chartist groups
have been traced, for instance, in Shepton Mallet, Wellington,
Crewkerne, or Wells, and there was little Chartist activity in
Bridgwater and Taunton. In Wiltshire there was no Chartist
organisation in Marlborough, and little activity in Calne and Chippenham.

Where Chartism was present in these counties, cloth was usually
being manufactured.[5] A technological revolution was in progress in
the cloth trade, and, partly in consequence of it, the manufacture of
cloth in the West of England was being concentrated into fewer
centres and within those centres into fewer business units. These
developments cannot have failed to cause economic distress to
some workers, and, since Chartism was a protest against distress, it

---

[1] *Ibid.*, p. 289. [2] *Ibid.*, p. 311.
[3] The distribution of Chartism in this region is very largely measured by
newspaper evidence. This usually takes the form of reports sent in by local correspondents, with the result that those groups with articulate leaders may make a
better showing than they deserve, while the importance of others, whose leaders
were illiterate, may be minimized.
[4] J. L. and Barbara Hammond, *The Village Labourer* (Guild Books, 1948),
Vol. I, Ch. X.
[5] There is no published history of the West of England textile industry in the
age of Chartism. The present writer is indebted for his knowledge of it to Dr
R. P. Beckinsale's unpublished *The West of England Woollen Industry* and
Miss J. de L. Mann's article on the industry in Wiltshire in *V.C.H. Wiltshire*,
Vol. IV, p. 148.

may be concluded that the movement penetrated the two Avon valleys in consequence of these economic upheavals. Its presence or absence, strength or weakness, in particular centres is, however, much harder to explain. Certainly its strength in a given place is not attributable to any single economic factor. Thus both Trowbridge and Frome favoured the concentration of handlooms in small workshops and both were slow to adopt power-looms. Yet in Trowbridge Chartism was active, indeed militant, and in Frome inconspicuous. In fact all that it seems safe to say at present is that, in the main, extreme destitution was less favourable to Chartism in this region than a moderate degree of it. Of all the cloth towns Bradford suffered the greatest disasters, but Chartism, which had at first been strong there, declined *pari passu* with the staple industry.

Apart from economic causes personal influence must have counted for a great deal in maintaining Chartism in particular places. The extraordinary persistence of the movement in the remote and diminutive village of Monkton Deverill can hardly be dissociated from Stephen Tudgey, its vocal sub-secretary in 1841 and local agent for the *Star*,[1] although the relative proximity of the declining flax industry of Mere may have been a contributory cause. Another 'newsvendor', John Wilkinson of Salisbury, and 'a very intelligent and respectable man',[2] seems to have long administered the group formed in that city in April 1839, and to have proselytised the environs, where cloth (as distinct from carpet) factories were closing. In Trowbridge, where the movement was so vigorous, there was a succession of leaders. John Moore, 'as determined a Chartist as any in the west,'[3] bridged the gulf between the 'physical force' and 'moral force' phases of the movement, for he had been treasurer of the local W.M.A. in 1838 and had become the sub-treasurer of the N.C.A. by April 1841. He therefore helped to fill a void created by the disappearance of Potts and Carrier, who played no part after their release from prison.[4] Moore is last heard of in December 1841,[5] but in 1840 a new generation had arisen,

---

[1] P.C., 56, Jan.–Apr. 1841, p. 286; Sept.–Dec. 1841, p. 408.
[2] B.M. Add. MSS. 34,245A, f. 317.
[3] P.C., 56, Oct. 1840–Feb. 1841, p. 106.
[4] *Ibid.*, Feb.–Aug. 1840, p. 30; May–Aug. 1841, p. 2. Carrier seems to have spoken for the last time at a meeting held in Trowbridge in 1841 to signalise his release: *ibid.*, Sept.–Dec. 1841, p. 57.
[5] *Ibid.*, p. 365.

which included Job Rawlings, a pamphleteer, versifier, and pilla of the Zion Strict Baptist Chapel.[1] Among later arrivals was tha 'highly intelligent young man' John Stevens, who had come int view by August 1841, was local sub-secretary in 1844 and was off t Philadelphia by 1847.[2] Thus, though no individual lasted indefin itely, one generation fertilised the next.

The course of Chartism in Bath was likewise interrupted by several deaths and apostasies. After 1842 there are no further sign of Vincent, Philp, and Clarke, and G. M. Bartlett was dead. Janu ary 1844 saw the last of Samuel Bartlett and Twite; and Young disappeared in June.[3] New men, however, of whom little is known took their places. That 'sterling Chartist' Hopkins, who made hi debut in October 1841, chaired a meeting in November 1847 and was still collecting money in November 1848.[4] James Chappell, sub secretary of the local N.C.A. in June 1842, was secretary of the National Land Company branch five years later.[5] Charles Cottle, first emerging in March 1844, harboured that branch in his house, and Franklin, who made a contemporaneous appearance, became its treasurer.[6] In Bath, indeed, a few Chartists actually stayed the whole course. Thomas Bolwell, a member of the W.M.A. in 1837, presided at the last recorded public meeting in the city more than ten years later.[7] To Gammage he was already a leading Bath Radical in 1838,[8] and was known as the 'veteran patriot' in 1845.[9] Anthony Phillips, who was also prominent in 1838, had become by November 1842 'the father of Chartism in Bath',[10] and under the name of 'our old Chartist victim, Father Phillips' played his part in the meeting of March 1848.[11] At that meeting there also spoke the master-hatter Cox, 'our veteran general of the Bath division'.[12] He had been associated with Chartism in 1841, and though little in the public eye may have been active enough behind the scenes to have deserved the title with which

[1] *Ibid.*, Feb.–Apr. 1840, p. 202. There are two of his pamphlets in the B.M.
[2] *Ibid.*, May–Aug. 1841, p. 408; Jan.–Apr. 1844, p. 238; 1845, p. 335; Jan.–July 1847, p. 245.
[3] *Ibid.*, Jan.–Apr. 1844, p. 166; May–Dec. 1844, p. 114.
[4] *Ibid.*, Sept.–Dec. 1841, p. 200; Jan.–Mar. 1842, p. 339; July–Dec. 1847, p. 286; P.C., 47, Aug.–Dec. 1848, p. 351.
[5] P.C., 56, Apr.–June 1842, p. 351; July–Dec. 1847, p. 14.
[6] *Ibid.*, Jan.–Apr. 1844, p. 351; Jan.–July 1847, p. 46.
[7] P.C., 47, Jan.–Apr. 1848, p. 224.   [8] Gammage, *op. cit.*, p. 78.
[9] P.C., 56, 1845, p. 335.   [10] *Ibid.*, Nov. 1842–Jan. 1843, p. 156.
[11] P.C., 47, Jan.–Apr. 1848, p. 224.   [12] *Ibid.*

he *Northern Star* decorated him. At any rate his presence at the
closing demonstration symbolises the benefit that the middle
classes conferred upon the Chartists of the city and through them
upon the Chartists of the west.

Chapter Seven

Chartism in Wales

David Williams

I

T he Swansea *Cambrian*, which had the largest circulation of any weekly newspaper in Wales in the early nineteenth century, claimed that Chartism was but an extension of the agitation against the New Poor Law.[1] This agitation was as pronounced in rural Wales as it was in the industrial areas, and among the most active participants in it were the leaders of Welsh Dissent, many of them of middle-class origin. On this account, features which were apparent in Chartism elsewhere, namely religious Nonconformity and agrarian discontent, acquired an added prominence which gave to the movement in Wales its special nature.

Its central figure was a Carmarthen solicitor named Hugh Williams. Williams's father was a timber merchant who became actively engaged in lead-mining near his home in Montgomeryshire. In 1840 Williams's sister became the wife of Richard Cobden, who eventually formed a partnership with Bright and others to take over the lead-mines. Hugh Williams and Cobden were associated in other business ventures. There is no doubt, therefore, of Williams's middle-class affiliation. His father was a member of the Independent denomination, and Williams thereby inherited the radicalism of Welsh Nonconformity, its impatience with religious disabilities and its insistent demand for equality in Church and State. He was admitted a solicitor in 1822. He practised in Carmarthen and married a woman, twenty-five years his senior, who was possessed of considerable property at St Clears, in that neighbourhood. His private life was unsavoury (Cobden's daughters were accustomed to refer to him as 'our bad uncle'[2]), and when his wife at length died in 1861 at the age of ninety he married, within two months, a woman thirty-nine years younger than himself. One brother practised as a solicitor in London and had chambers in Gray's Inn

[1] *Cambrian*, 15 Nov. 1839. [2] W. J. Linton, *Memories* (1895), p. 91.

Road; another was an ironmonger in Holborn. Williams himself was frequently in London on business. In some way he came into contact with the London Radicals at the time when they were hammering into shape a working-class programme; in particular, he became the intimate friend of Henry Hetherington,[1] who, with William Lovett and others, formed the London Working Men's Association in 1836. He brought their ideas back with him to Carmarthen, and, in the autumn of that year, organised what he claimed to be 'the first Radical meeting in South Wales'.[2] When a branch of the W.M.A. was formed in Carmarthen early in 1837, he became its secretary.[3]

These decades saw a remarkable growth in Welsh Nonconformity; from being a small minority in the early years of the century, the Nonconformists, in 1851, accounted for three-quarters of the population of Wales. Numerous periodicals appeared in Welsh to cater for them, the most notable being *Y Diwygiwr* (The Reformer), the magazine of the Independents, started in 1835. It was published in Llanelly, which was now rapidly becoming industrialised, thereby displacing the neighbouring town of Carmarthen as a centre of population. Its editor, an Independent minister, David Rees, took as his motto O'Connell's slogan: 'Agitate, agitate, agitate.' He argued that Chartism was consistent with Christianity, and urged workers elsewhere to follow the example set them in Carmarthen by setting up branches of the W.M.A.[4] The periodical circulated in both rural and industrial Wales; Nonconformity, in fact, proved to be the chief, if not the sole, emotional link between the rural and the industrial workers. Thereby the discontent generated by living and working conditions in the towns overflowed into the countryside and reinforced the older radicalism of rural Nonconformity. Besides, there were significant changes within Nonconformity itself in these years, notably a tendency within the denominations towards Unitarianism. This, for example, led to the formation of a Unitarian body at St Clears. One of its members, David John, a blacksmith by trade, became pastor of the Unitarian church in Merthyr Tydfil in 1826. He and his two sons, David John and

[1] Linton, who was closely associated with Hetherington, believed that he was Welsh (*ibid.*, p. 87). Hetherington was a Londoner, but he may have had Welsh connections.
[2] Lovett Collection, Vol. I, p. 250.
[3] The Carmarthen W.M.A. sent a congratulatory address to J. A. Roebuck on 11 Feb. 1837. Lovett Collection, Vol. I, p. 22.
[4] *Diwygiwr*, 1838, p. 372.

Matthew John, were to become the leaders of radicalism in that town. Associated with them was another Unitarian, Morgan Williams, a weaver and proprietor of a small flannel factory. He was the most gifted writer among the Merthyr Radicals, and, in 1834, he produced a short-lived periodical, *Y Gweithiwr* (The Worker), much of which he wrote himself.[1] He became the secretary of the Merthyr W.M.A. when it was founded in October 1838.[2]

A third centre of Welsh radicalism was to be found in the flannel towns of mid-Wales, namely Welshpool, Newtown (the birthplace of Robert Owen) and Llanidloes. The Welsh textile industry was, in the late thirties, experiencing intense economic depression, and there was much poverty. Dissent was also strong in the three towns, and so bitter was the opposition to the Poor Law that in April 1837 a troop of cavalry had to be called out to protect the Assistant Poor Law Commissioner from violence.[3] Here, again, the leader was of middle-class origin, although, unlike the other Radicals, he came from an Anglican family. He was Thomas Powell, a native of Newtown. He had been apprenticed to an ironmonger in Shrewsbury and had worked at this trade in London before buying an ironmongery business for himself at Welshpool in 1832. Whether he was a childhood acquaintance of Hugh Williams is not known (they were born within thirty miles of one another); nor is it known if he came into contact with Hetherington in London. He certainly became intimately associated with both men later on, and it was Hetherington who was sent from London to the three towns as a Chartist missionary and who founded branches of the W.M.A. there in November 1837.[4] But mid-Wales was within the orbit of the Birmingham Political Union, and it was a native of Welshpool, Charles Jones, who played a large part in 1831 in organising the Union as a disciplined force. After its revival in 1837[5] it was mainly from Birmingham that Radical ideas were introduced into mid-Wales in the summer of 1838, and Political Unions on the Birmingham model were formed at Llanidloes and Newtown. These ideas were expounded in the locality by Richard Jarman, a native of

[1] Copy of No. 4, 1 May 1834, in H.O. 52/25. J. B. Bruce, in an accompanying letter to the Home Office, wrote that Williams was the author of the English part, and John Thomas, a Carmarthenshire man who kept a school in Merthyr, the author of the Welsh part.

[2] Lovett Collection, Vol. I, p. 296; H.O. 40/40.

[3] This occurred at Llanfair Caereinion, eight miles from Welshpool and ten miles from Newtown; H.O. 52/35; *Seren Gomer*, 1837, p. 218.

[4] Lovett Collection, Vol. I, p. 140.   [5] See above, p. 21.

Llanidloes. Whatever rivalry there was between the two organisations ceased when the P.U.'s and the W.M.A.'s coalesced throughout the country, the Birmingham men accepting the Charter and the Londoners agreeing to their Petition. There followed the first Chartist demonstration in Wales, properly so called, held at Newtown on 10 October 1838. The number present was variously estimated as between 3,000 and 5,000, and the crowd was drawn both from the towns and from the surrounding countryside. A Birmingham Radical named Pierce was present, but the principal speaker was Charles Jones. According to Gammage, he was a tall, distinguished-looking man who had originally intended to take Holy orders. It was he who was chosen as delegate to the Convention.[1]

Two months later a further meeting was called for Christmas Day at Caersws (six miles from Newton) where a workhouse was being built. In view of the hostility to the New Poor Law, the authorities feared that an attempt would be made to destroy the building. They therefore swore in special constables and called out the yeomanry. Despite the assembly of several thousand men, the meeting was peaceful, for Powell and Jones urged them to avoid physical force until all constitutional means had failed.[2]

II

Strange to say, the agitations of the South Wales coalfield were not harnessed to the movement until a late date. There was much discontent among the industrial workers, on account of truck and low wages in particular, but it remained singularly unorganised. There had been rioting in Merthyr in 1800, followed by the execution of two men. A strike in 1816, which began at the Tredegar iron works in Monmouthshire against a proposal to reduce wages, spread rapidly and soldiers were sent into the area, but the employers gave in on this occasion and withdrew the reduction. Another strike for the same reason in 1822, beginning at Nantyglo, spread even more widely until it involved most of the Monmouthshire industrial valleys but then suddenly collapsed.[3] In June 1831 occurred the Merthyr riots. Their cause is still obscure, but in all probability they were due to truck and to a threat to reduce wages. They began with an attack on the house of the clerk to the Court of

---

[1] Lovett Collection, Vol. I, p. 270; Gammage, *op. cit.*, p. 47.
[2] H.O. 40/40, 73/54.
[3] For this strike, see numerous letters in H.O. 40/17 and 52/3; also Llangibby MSS. in N.L.W.

Requests, led by Lewis Lewis, a haulier by occupation. A troop of Highlanders was immediately summoned, and Lewis Lewis was active in urging the crowd to disarm them. In the firing that ensued several were killed and others (among them some of the soldiers) were wounded. Cavalry was then brought into Merthyr; yet the following day a mob outside the town turned back troops which were bringing supplies of ammunition, and disarmed a company of the Swansea yeomanry. Lewis Lewis was condemned to death for his share in the riot, but his sentence was changed to one of transportation. A young collier, Richard Lewis ('Dic Penderyn'), was accused, on the evidence of two Merthyr tradesmen, of being the man who had wounded one of the Highlanders. He was sentenced to death and executed in Cardiff gaol. There is considerable reason to doubt his guilt, and he is not known to have taken any other part in the rioting, while his family claimed that he was not in the crowd at all.[1]

It was not until immediately after the Merthyr riots that there was any evidence of unionism in South Wales.[2] The Friendly Associated Coalminers' Union Society obtained a foothold in Merthyr, but the coal owners refused to employ union men and after a lock-out of eight weeks the Union collapsed. The Monmouthshire valleys then witnessed the outrages of the Scotch Cattle who 'scotched' unpopular workmen.[3] Robert Owen's Grand National Consolidated Trades Union was greeted with much enthusiasm, but it collapsed just as suddenly as it had spread. There followed still further outrages of the Scotch Cattle. Yet, during all these years, there was very little evidence of any working-class movement in Monmouthshire.

The Monmouthshire industrial valleys radiated from a focus at Newport, and the town witnessed great expansion in the early nineteenth century on that account. It had a long tradition of agitation for municipal reform and of opposition to the boroughmongers, the Morgans of Tredegar (whose mansion was just outside the town). It was this which brought John Frost into prominence. When he led the Chartist march on Newport on the night of the 3–4 November 1839, Frost was a middle-aged man, fifty-five

[1] In addition to full accounts in the weekly press, see H.O. 52/16. *Tarian y Gweithiwr*, 14 Aug. 1884, has the reminiscences of a nephew of the man who married Dic's widow. (I owe this reference to Dr Eric Wyn Evans.)

[2] For unionism in Glamorgan, see H.O. 45/54, 52/16, 52/25.

[3] For Scotch Cattle, see H.O. 52/21, 52/23, 52/25.

years of age, and was a prosperous draper, a most unlikely combination for the leader of a working-class insurrection. His radicalism stemmed from a doctrinaire position which he held with the rigidity of a self-educated man, and from disagreeable personal experiences. He was brought up as a Nonconformist (of the Independent denomination). In the few years in which he served as shopman to a merchant-tailor in London he came under the influence of the London Radicals, and when he acquired a business of his own in his native town, in the first decade of the century, he immediately threw himself into municipal politics. A family quarrel about a will brought him into conflict with a local attorney, Thomas Prothero,[1] who was both the all-powerful town clerk of Newport and the agent of the Tredegar estate. This led the impetuous Frost to publish a dozen pamphlets in 1821 and 1822 which expounded the rights of the burgesses of Newport as well as the need for both municipal and parliamentary reform. Significantly, they did not refer to the unrest of those years in the neighbouring coalfield. But they also libelled Thomas Prothero, and Frost found himself obliged to pay £1,000 in damages in a civil action, and sentenced to six months' imprisonment in Cold Bath Fields in a criminal action for libel. This personal experience was to add bitterness to his advocacy of reform.

For some years after his release Frost devoted himself to his business. Characteristically, it was not the distress of the industrial workers which brought a renewal of his pamphleteering, but a passionate sympathy with the peasants' revolt in south-eastern England in the winter of 1830, of which there was an echo in Monmouthshire. For Frost was a reformer of the Cobbett type; indeed, he acknowledged Cobbett as his 'master' and attributed his political education to Cobbett's *English Grammar*. Most of the Radicals of his day looked to the progress of industry to further the welfare of the working class; like Cobbett, Frost looked back to the relative prosperity of the countryside in his youth, and drew an idealised picture of it. It was oppression by the squirearchy which roused him to a white heat of anger; at no time did he show any real understanding of the grievances of the industrial workers. Like Cobbett, also, his favourite instrument of reform was a manipulation of the currency.

Frost threw himself into the agitation for the Reform Bill, and

[1] Grandfather of the historians Lord Ernle and Sir George Prothero.

found himself co-operating for a time with Thomas Prothero and his junior partner, Thomas Phillips. That these two men, the foremost Whig reformers in Newport, were his personal enemies no doubt helped Frost to realise that the workers could hope for as little from the Whigs as from the Tories, 'two plundering factions who have robbed the people without mercy.' Certainly the disillusionment which Chartists are reputed to have felt after the Reform Act of 1832 was not necessary in the case of Frost; he had not had any such illusions. Yet his star was now in the ascendant: he was elected a councillor under the new Municipal Corporations Act; he became a justice of the peace, an improvement commissioner and a guardian of the poor; in November 1836 he became the second mayor of Newport and a harbour commissioner in virtue of this office. All these duties he performed with great thoroughness and competence, and his experience made him stand out among the Chartists later on, for they had few 'respectable' leaders (as contemporaries used the term). He took advantage of his position to expose jobbery and corruption in the municipal affairs of Newport and to mitigate the severity of the New Poor Law. But his vendetta with Thomas Prothero continued, and was exacerbated in 1837 and in 1838. He seems to have withdrawn a little from public life at this time, and when a branch of the W.M.A. was founded at Newport in the summer of 1838,[1] it was the work not of Frost but of a baker named William Edwards. It was at the request of this branch that Frost, as a magistrate, convened a meeting on 30 October to explain the principles of the Charter and thereby began his association with the Chartist movement.

In the meantime Hugh Williams had sent an emissary named William Jenkins[2] from Carmarthen to address meetings at Pontypool, Merthyr, Newport, Swansea and Llanelly. Williams, himself, attended as a delegate at the assembly in Palace Yard, Westminster, on 17 September 1838, called as a preliminary to the summoning of the Convention. He assured the other delegates that 'the Radicals of South Wales were prepared to assert their rights at any time and in any manner they might be called upon by the London committee'.[3] It was after Jenkins's visit that a W.M.A. was formed at Merthyr, with Morgan Williams as its secretary. Like the Chartists of

[1] In July 1838 according to *The Charter*, 10 March 1839.
[2] He had been arrested in Dec. 1835 for selling copies of Hetherington's publications; *Carmarthen Journal*, 26 Dec. 1835.
[3] *Ibid.*, 21 Sept. 1838 (admittedly a hostile source of evidence).

Montgomeryshire, the Merthyr branch organised a mass demonstration for Christmas Day, to be held at Penrheolgerrig, a mile or so out of the town on Aberdare Mountain. The principal speaker was Hugh Williams, and he was, with acclamation, elected delegate to the Convention.[1] He met with opposition from the borough authorities in arranging a meeting in his own town, Carmarthen, and it did not take place until the night of 9 January. It took the form of a torchlight procession in the principal square of the town, attended, it is said, by about four thousand people who milled around in the narrow streets.[2] Both William Jenkins and Hugh Williams addressed them, and Williams was again elected to the Convention. Precisely a week later an attempt was made at Narberth, twenty miles away, to give practical effect to the opposition to the New Poor Law by burning down the workhouse which was then being built. Despite the offer of considerable rewards, no information could be obtained of the identity of the incendiaries.[3] William Jenkins deplored this outrage when he sought to hold a Chartist meeting at Narberth three weeks later. He was now going around the towns and villages of west Wales, but met with very limited success. Yet it was in this neighbourhood that the destruction of two tollgates in May marked the beginning of the Rebecca Riots.[4] Hugh Williams was not able to take his seat in the Convention until 10 May. He brought with him 27,147 signatures to the petition from the four shires of Glamorgan, Carmarthenshire, Pembrokeshire and Cardiganshire.[5] He also presented tricolour banners, in green, white and blue (to symbolise earth, sun and sky) to W.M.A.'s in London, Merthyr, Carmarthen and Pontypool, and composed a song 'Freedom's Tricoloured Banner' for these occasions. This, and a number of other poems, several of them written by himself, he published as *National Songs and Poetical Pieces*, printed by

[1] H.O. 40/40, 41/13.

[2] The government on 12 Dec. 1838 had forbidden torchlight processions.

[3] *Carmarthen Journal*, 1, 8 Feb. 1839; H.O. 43/56, 73/55.

[4] Chartist meetings were held at Narberth, Haverford West, Pembroke, Fishguard, Llanfihangel Abercowin and Adpar as well, no doubt, as at other places. Aberaeron was said to be a 'restless, radical town' and there were said to be numerous Chartists in Llandysul. 'Two Birmingham Chartists' were reported to be in the neighbourhood of Efail-wen, where the first Rebecca riot took place; *The Charter*, 24 Feb. 1839; H.O. 40/46, 40/51, 41/13. For the Rebecca Riots see my *The Rebecca Riots. A Study in Agrarian Discontent*, 1955.

[5] Glamorgan: Merthyr 14,710, Swansea 3,368, Ynyscedwyn 806; Carmarthenshire: Carmarthen Borough 1,043, 'sundry parishes' 5,091; Pembrokeshire, comprising Narberth, Saundersfoot and Templeton 1,103; Cardiganshire, including Llandysul and Cribyn 1,026. B.M. Add. MSS. 34,245A, f. 332.

Hetherington and facetiously dedicated 'to the Queen and her
countrywomen'. Their literary merit is small, but, when the Rebecca
Riots were at their height, Sir James Graham thought it necessary
to bring them to the attention of Sir Robert Peel as they were 'very
mischievous and exciting'.[1]

The London W.M.A. made a fateful decision in choosing, as
their missionary to Monmouthshire, the young orator, Henry Vincent, for he was destined to become the hero of the Monmouthshire
colliers and iron workers. The coalfield at the time was relatively
prosperous and wages were high.[2] Vincent's impassioned oratory
nevertheless carried away the more thoughtful workers, while his
diablerie and his facetiousness appealed to the less responsible. He
thus united, in an uneasy alliance, the solid Nonconformist element
with the adherents of the Scotch Cattle, and the alliance had serious consequences later on. The Monmouthshire Chartists held
their first mass-meeting on New Year's Day, and chose for its
location the village of Pontnewynydd above Pontypool. Thither
came Vincent and Frost, both making their first appearances in the
Monmouthshire valleys, and Frost was elected a delegate to the
Convention. Both men used what the authorities called 'violent and
inflammatory language'. This involved Frost in a controversy with
the Home Secretary, Lord John Russell, to whom he wrote a resounding letter which was published in the press and brought him
nation-wide notoriety. But it led eventually to his removal from the
commission of the peace, thereby adding another grievance to those
from which he already suffered.[3]

Thus Wales was represented in the Convention by three delegates, Charles Jones for Montgomeryshire, Hugh Williams for
Carmarthen and Merthyr,[4] and also for Swansea, and John Frost
for Monmouthshire. Strangely enough, Chartism had found no
echo on the North Wales coalfield. None of the three delegates took
a prominent part in the Convention; nor would they have attracted
much notice but for the incidents which took place later in the
year.

[1] B.M. Add. MSS. 40,448, f. 363.
[2] Report of Sir Edmund Head, Assistant Poor Law Commissioner, 10 July
1839, gives a detailed list of wages in various occupations, H.O. 73/25.
[3] In addition to the authorities cited in my *John Frost*, pp. 124–7, there are
several letters referring to this episode in H.O. 41/13, 52/41, 52/42. The original
letter to Lord John Russell is in H.O. 52/40.
[4] Through some misunderstanding he did not take his seat as a delegate from
Merthyr. B.M. Add. MSS. 34,245A, f. 444.

The first of these incidents occurred with dramatic suddenness in mid-Wales. The Chartists of Montgomeryshire sent a request to the Convention for a 'missionary', and, once more, Hetherington was chosen.[1] On his return he submitted a lengthy report to the assembly. He had reached Welshpool in the first week in April, and had proceeded to Newtown, Llanidloes and Rhayader, accompanied by Charles Jones and Thomas Powell, returning via Newtown and Welshpool.[2] He had had an enthusiastic welcome, and reported that the men were arming and drilling. He had even heard that an order for three hundred muskets had been sent from Newtown to Birmingham. He thought that the 'physical force men' in the district could turn out six hundred armed men. Hetherington was a 'moral force man', and he had conveyed to them the instructions of the Convention that they should avoid 'everything illegal'. If he believed these reports to be true, it is strange that he should have made a gift of the information to the authorities by discussing them openly in the Convention.

The local magistrates certainly took the reports seriously, and sent a request for troops to the Home Secretary.[3] He contented himself with sending down three metropolitan policemen to help in the work of preserving order and of arresting those responsible for drilling and training the Chartists. They arrived at Llanidloes on Monday evening, 29 April, accompanied by the police officers of Newtown and Welshpool, both of whom were already unpopular with the Chartists because of their interference with Chartist meetings.[4] They were lodged in the Trewythen Arms. Meanwhile special constables were being sworn in.

To understand the riot which took place next day it is essential to bear in mind that it was entirely unpremeditated. Neither Charles Jones nor Thomas Powell was in the town, nor does any responsible Chartist seem to have taken part in it; nor, indeed, do the flannel mills seem to have stopped work until it was all over.[5] News of the presence of the policemen in the Trewythen Arms got abroad early in the morning, and a meeting was summoned by bugle to the

---

[1] His expenses amounted to £12 19s. 6d.; *Western Vindicator*, 22 July 1839.
[2] *Shrewsbury Chronicle*, 12 Apr., 2 May 1839; Lovett Collection, Vol. II, p. 2.
[3] H.O. 40/46.
[4] These two men were Blinkhorn and Armishaw. Blinkhorn was paid by subscriptions from private individuals, as the Newtown vestry would not pay him; H.O. 52/38.
[5] E. Hamer, *A Brief Account of the Chartist Outbreak at Llanidloes* (Llanidloes, 1867, reprinted 1939), p. 34, shows that they did not stop till midday.

Q

Severn bridge, a quarter of a mile away.[1] While this was in progress the police arrested three men as they were passing the inn, and took them inside. The by-standers (many of whom were women) showed hostility to the police, and the Chartists were hastily brought from the Severn bridge. The mayor of the town, an inoffensive surgeon, was inside the inn; the ex-mayor (a man aged thirty-five), also a magistrate, either by accident or design found himself outside. According to his own version he thought it wise, in the interests of safety, to shout with the mob; there is no doubt that it was he who smashed the first pane.[2] He then slipped away and rode to Shrewsbury to give a highly exaggerated account of the riot to the Lord-Lieutenant. The crowd proceeded to rush the hotel and rescued the prisoners. They dragged the mayor and the two local policemen from underneath a bed and severely manhandled them. By this time, Thomas Powell had arrived in the town. He succeeded in calming the crowd, rescued the two policemen and took the Welshpool man away in his chaise.

The authorities were strangely slow in reacting to the situation. From Tuesday to Saturday they ceased to function, and the more responsible Chartists made their own arrangements to patrol the town. There were, in fact, no further disturbances whatsoever; the economic life of the town went on as before. But, on Saturday, infantry arrived from Brecon, followed by the Montgomeryshire Yeomanry Cavalry, who were pelted on their way through Newtown. The South Shropshire Yeomanry Cavalry were also brought into the Severn valley, and on 9 May the 12th Regiment arrived, travelling by sea from Cork to Aberystwyth and thence on foot over Plynlymon. There was an immediate search for the released prisoners and for those who had taken part in the rioting, and substantial rewards were offered for information. The number of weapons found was negligible, but thirty-two persons were arrested. Hugh Williams was hastily summoned to prepare their defence. At the Montgomeryshire Summer Assizes several were given various periods of imprisonment; one Llanidloes man, accused of stabbing a constable, was sentenced to fifteen years' transportation, and two

[1] The bugle was celebrated by Hugh Williams as 'The Horn of Liberty'; *National Songs and Poetical Pieces*, 1839 (1840), p. 59. It was published as a broadside, and a copy was found on the person of William Jones, one of the leaders in the march on Newport. The name of the bugler was Baxter; he was not Lewis Humphreys (one of the prisoners) as stated in my *John Frost*, p. 156.

[2] Even Hamer, who is antipathetic to the Chartists, makes this perfectly clear.

men from Llanidloes and one from Newtown to seven years' transportation for training and drilling.[1]

Of far greater significance than the riot itself was the attempt to
use it to get at the leaders. Warrants were issued for the arrest of
both Powell and Jones, and instructions were given to the Post
Office to open all letters addressed to Hetherington.[2] A sheriff's
officer was sent to Birmingham, and on to Manchester, in search of
Jones, but did not succeed in taking him.[3] Powell, on the other
hand, was arrested at his home in Welshpool on Sunday, 5 May.
The authorities went to remarkable lengths to resist his bail. To
formulate a charge against him, they had to fall back on words said
to have been used by him at Newtown, on 9 April, during Hetherington's visit. It is strange that even the most hostile weekly newspaper, which reported the meeting at length and gave much prominence to Charles Jones's remarks on that occasion, had not attributed any seditious utterances to Powell. He was tried with the
rioters at the Welshpool Assizes, his defence, like theirs, being prepared by Hugh Williams. Witnesses were contradictory, the one
person who claimed to have heard the precise words attributed to
Powell being the under-sheriff's clerk who had been active in resisting his bail. The jury hesitated, but eventually returned a
verdict of guilty with a recommendation to mercy on account of the
protection he had given to the policemen. But the judge, Sir John
Patteson, maliciously used this to illustrate Powell's 'power over
the mob'. He attributed the rioting entirely to the inflammatory

[1] Information concerning the Llanidloes riot is to be found in the weekly press;
in H.O. 40/40, 40/46, 40/51, 40/57, 41/13, 41/14, 41/15, 41/16, 52/41, 52/46;
Cardiff Public Library MS. 371; B.M. Add. MSS. 34,245B 35 and 49; N.L.W.,
St Asaph Miscellaneous 481. The following N.L.W. Calendars are of documents
in the possession of the Earl of Powis: *Calendar of Letters and Documents relating
to the Chartist Riots in Montgomeryshire*, 1935 (281 items); *Calendar of Letters
and Documents relating to Chartism in Shropshire*, 1941 (55 items, covering
August 1842); *Calendar of Letters and Documents rleating to Chartism in Shropshire, 1842*, 1949 (38 items covering July–Nov. 1842); *Calendar of Correspondence relating to the Montgomeryshire Yeomanry Cavalry, 1809–41*, 1949 (39
items).

N.L.W. MS. 12888E is a rough draft entitled 'Chartism in Montgomeryshire'
by E. R. Horsfall Turner, a local historian of repute. It was written in the last
year of his life (he died 9 March 1936) and was not completed. Part of what he
wrote seems also to be missing. The author had studied the riot in great detail,
but does not indicate his sources very clearly. That he was unable to write up his
work in completed form is a serious loss to Chartist literature. He was a warm
partisan of the Chartists, and is bitterly critical of the ex-mayor, T. E. Marsh,
whom he regarded as the 'villain of the piece'.

[2] H.O. 79/4.

[3] Cardiff MS. 371; Powis Calendar (1935), 203.

speeches of Powell and others. Moreover he declared the Convention itself to be an illegal assembly. He sentenced Powell to twelve months' imprisonment, and demanded crippling sureties for his good behaviour for five years (£400 from himself and two others of £200 each), before he should be released. In this the judge seems to have overreached himself, for when Powell came out of gaol twelve months later no such sureties were demanded.[1]

Two days after Powell's arrest, Henry Vincent was seized and placed in Monmouth gaol, thereby starting a train of consequences of the utmost importance, for Vincent had become immensely popular with the industrial workers of Monmouthshire, and his arrest inflamed their feelings to a remarkable degree.

Vincent does not seem to have visited Glamorgan in 1839, although the coalfield extended without interruption across the boundary of the two shires. Yet Chartism continued to spread in Merthyr Tydfil, which provided nearly three times as many signatures to the Petition as did Newport.[2] The Merthyr Chartists were all reputed to be 'moral force' men, in contrast with those of Dowlais and of north Monmouthshire.[3] Morgan Williams had, indeed, succeeded in combining a little profitable business with his politics, by inducing them to wear blue flannel waistcoats as distinguishing garments (while their ladies wore blue flannel aprons), and, dressed in this uniform, they attended church in a body later in the summer.[4] In Aberdare, the movement centred around the Unitarian chapel, and so abjured physical force.[5] Even Swansea and its hinterland provided almost as many signatures as did Newport. There, it was Hugh Williams who was responsible for the spread of Chartism, for the area was not far from his home in Carmarthen.[6] But the centre in Glamorgan which came next in importance to Merthyr Tydfil was in the lower reaches of the Rhondda, from Dinas, whose mines foreshadowed the great industrial development

[1] Shrewsbury Chronicle, 24 July 1840.
[2] Merthyr, 14,710, ut supra; Newport, 5,500; B.M. Add. MSS. 27821, f. 143.
[3] C. Wilkins, The History of Merthyr Tydfil (Merthyr Tydfil, 1908), p. 423.
[4] Ibid., p. 424; Earl of Bessborough (ed.) Lady Charlotte Guest: Extracts from her Journals, 1833–52 (1950), p. 94; Bute MSS. (C.P.L.), XX, 20. The Bute MSS. in C.P.L. comprise letters addressed to the Marquis of Bute, the Lord-Lieutenant for Glamorgan. Upwards to a hundred outgoing letters from the Marquis are in Bute Letter Books, Nos. 13 and 14, in N.L.W. These, however, are nearly all requests for information, and supply very little themselves.
[5] Bute MSS., XX, 72, 78.
[6] Ibid., XX, 6.

of the two Rhondda valleys later in the century, down to Pontypridd (then generally called Newbridge)[1] where the river joins the
Taff. The leader at Dinas was a shopkeeper, William David, whose
father had founded the Baptist chapel in that neighbourhood and
who was, himself, one of its trustees.[2] But far more spectacular was
the leader at Pontypridd, an eccentric surgeon named William
Price.[3] He was thirty-nine years of age, the son of an Anglican
clergyman. He had strongly supported Sir Josiah John Guest in the
recent parliamentary contest in Merthyr; and he succeeded in convincing Lady Charlotte Guest that he deplored physical force,[4] but
the judgment of a contemporary that he was 'a fit subject for a
lunatic asylum'[5] has been generally accepted by subsequent opinion. When Vincent, on 22 April, addressed a meeting at Blackwood
(a mining village in the Sirhowy valley which was precisely half-way
between Merthyr and Newport), the chair was taken for him by Dr
William Price.

Vincent's arrest, on 22 April, led to a demand for a great demonstration at some central spot,[6] and Blackwood was again chosen.
This took place on Whit Monday, 20 May, when some 30,000
people are said to have been present. It was one of the 'simultaneous
meetings' being held throughout the country, and the chief speaker
was Frost. By this time Frost was being driven, step by step, into
more dubious agitation. In his famous letter to Lord John Russell
he had held that the Convention had for its sole object the presentation of the Petition to Parliament; now it fell to him to explain the
'ulterior measures' to gain the Charter, namely a run on the banks,
a general strike (the 'sacred month') and exclusive dealing. Besides,
the authorities were seeking to get him into prison, as they had succeeded in doing with Lovett, Vincent, Thomas Powell and others.
It is significant that, to bring a charge against him, they had to go
back to New Year's Day, to the 'violent and inflammatory language' he had used at Pontnewynydd. Some days later they indicted him also with criminal libel on Thomas Phillips, the mayor

---

[1] Not to be confused with Newbridge, Monmouthshire, also a Chartist centre.
Dinas contributed £4 5s. to the National Rent, Newbridge £5 15s. 6d. and
Upper Boat £3 7s. 6d.; *Western Vindicator*, 10 Aug. 1839.
[2] J. R. Williams, *Ystradiana* (1886), pp. 33–4; John Thomas, *Soariana* (n.d.),
p. 6; 'Morien', *History of Pontypridd and the Rhondda Valleys* (1903), pp. 202–5.
[3] He is best known because his trial for burning the corpse of his child legalised
cremation.
[4] Bessborough, *op. cit.*, pp. 90–1.   [5] Bute MSS., XX, 5, 20.
[6] Newport Museum MSS., 'Letter from Morgan Williams', 25 Apr. 1839.

of Newport, in a placard in which, as a rhetorical flourish, he had urged the taking of hostages as security for the safety of the Chartist leaders in prison. Perhaps it was unfortunate for Frost that he was not arrested on these charges; be that as it may, to understand his leadership of the march on Newport on the night of 3–4 November it is important to realise that there were already charges against him which would bring him a long term of imprisonment. In a sense he had burnt his boats.

The riot at Newport was of small proportions; its importance lies entirely in the question whether it was part of a general plan of insurrection, and as such it merits close attention. The rejection of the Petition in July and the rioting in Birmingham, the sentence on Vincent and the abandonment of the national strike in August, and the petering out of the Convention in September, all exasperated the industrial workers of Monmouthshire. Frost continued his speechifying, at Glasgow, at Merthyr, at Cardiff and elsewhere. He seems to have convinced himself that 'a great part of the army' were Chartists, and would not fire on Chartist demonstrators,[1] without considering what would happen if they did. There is evidence that firearms were being distributed, both in Glamorgan[2] and in Monmouthshire.[3] Frost had probably mentioned to two or three members of the Convention his fear that the miners might attempt to release Vincent by force, and it is natural to believe that they discussed, in secret amongst themselves, the possibilities and consequences of such a rising.[4] It was no doubt on this account that Peter Bussey of Bradford, an advocate of physical force, on his return home from the Convention, called a meeting of delegates to Heckmondwike, near Bradford, which met on 30 September, (two weeks after the Convention had disbanded).[5] According to Lovett's account,[6] the delegates were informed of the intention of the Welsh to rise, and, although some thought it premature, decided on a simultaneous rising in the north. It was after this meeting, if we are to believe Lovett, that the northerners approached O'Connor and were misled by him into believing that he was prepared to take

[1] *Western Vindicator*, 11 May 1839.   [2] Bute MSS., XX, 21, 23.
[3] Newport Museum MSS., evidence of several persons.
[4] William Ashton stated that he was present at such a discussion before the Convention dissolved. *Northern Star*, 3 May 1845. (I owe this reference to Dr Albert Schoyen.)
[5] I was unable to date this meeting when I wrote my *John Frost*, which therefore requires correction. I owe the date to Dr Schoyen.
[6] W. Lovett, *The Life and Struggles of William Lovett* (1876), pp. 238–41.

command. Dr John Taylor states further that O'Connor immediately sent George White (a *Northern Star* reporter) around various towns to say that there was to be no rising, that it was all a Government plot. What is certain is that two days later he wrote to the *Northern Star* to cancel a speaking tour in Lancashire,[1] and that, on 4 October, he left for Ireland.

Frost, on his return from the Convention, continued to counsel moderation. He even wrote to the authorities to urge that Vincent's treatment should be more lenient as 'the agitation had now subsided'.[2] Yet, on 3 October, he hastened up the Monmouthshire valleys to a meeting at Nantyglo because of a report that the workers were about to rise in arms to liberate Vincent from Monmouth gaol. The meeting was held at the beerhouse of Zephaniah Williams, soon to distinguish himself as one of the leaders of the march on Newport. Williams had progressed from Nonconformity to agnosticism, and had been much abused on that account. He was a very able man, earning his living as 'a master collier'. Frost tried to convince his listeners that a rising was premature, but his reception was cool. On the other hand, the meeting loudly cheered the rigmarole of William Jones, 'the watchmaker', who was to be the third leader in the march on Newport. Jones was an entirely irresponsible person, an unsuccessful actor who kept a beerhouse as well as practising his trade. Besides, this meeting was followed by another in secret, at a beerhouse a mile or two away, of which our only information comes from the reminiscences of Dr William Price.[3] Here a stormy discussion continued into the early hours of the morning, Frost arguing in favour of a monster demonstration while the others wanted an armed rising. No agreement seems to have been reached, and the meeting ended uproariously. Evidently the more extreme elements among the workers, inflamed by months of talk of physical force, were determined on violence.

In the weeks which followed, Frost's movements are difficult to ascertain. It was announced that he would attend a dinner at Bury on Monday, 14 October,[4] but he was unable to do so because he

---

[1] I owe the reference to Dr Schoyen. For White, see above, pp. 70–1.

[2] Letters dated 28 Sept. 1839 in J. and T. Gurney, *The Trial of John Frost* (1840), pp. 515–16; (the shorthand account of the trial).

[3] *Cardiff Times and South Wales Weekly News*, May–June 1888, reprinted as a pamphlet: *The late Dr Price, the famous Archdruid* (Cardiff, 1896).

[4] *Northern Star*, 28 Sept. 1839. (Fielden, J. P. Cobbett, Dr Taylor and Oastler were expected to attend.)

was detained in Manchester.[1] This proves that he visited the north within these critical weeks, but what contacts he had with other leaders on that occasion is not known. His last letter to the *Western Vindicator*, dated 22 October, was addressed from Newport,[2] and he may have been at home at that date, but the evidence is not conclusive. A report of possible risings in Wales and the North reached Hetherington in London on Tuesday, 29 October.[3] He evidently had no previous knowledge of them, for he took his informant to see Dr John Taylor after midnight, presumably at the first possible moment. This informant was none other than Charles Jones, who was still in hiding since the riots at Llanidloes.[4] Taylor immediately proceeded to the North to see Peter Bussey, evidently taking Jones with him, and in Bradford he learned that the rising was to take place on the Saturday night.[5] Bussey and Taylor decided to send Jones to Wales to ask the Welsh to put off the rising for ten days, while Taylor himself went on to Newcastle.

The Chartist lodges in Monmouthshire were now meeting almost nightly, both in public and in private. They were addressed by Williams and Jones, but not, apparently, by Frost, and there was much bitter dispute between the advocates of moral and of physical force. It was on Sunday, 27 October, that Frost informed Dr Price that the rising was to take place on the following Sunday night. Frost was deeply agitated, according to Price; he wept like a child and talked of heaven and hell. But it was now too late to turn back. The crucial meeting was the one held in secret at the Coach and Horses in Blackwood on Friday afternoon, 1 November. Knowledge of what transpired there is available from the depositions of a youth, William Davies, who subsequently married one of Frost's daughters.[6] There were some thirty delegates present, including Frost, Williams and Jones. Price was seen at the door of the inn, but does not seem to have attended the meeting.[7] Each

[1] *Northern Star*, 19 Oct. 1839. [2] *Western Vindicator*, 26 Oct. 1839.
[3] Lovett Collection, Vol. II, p. 211.
[4] Letter of Robert Edwards, one of Hetherington's employees, 6 Nov. 1839. H.O. 40/44. (I owe this reference to Dr Schoyen.)
[5] Lovett Collection, *loc. cit.*
[6] Newport Museum MSS. Davies absconded twice in the weeks which followed. On the first occasion he was arrested at Canterbury, at the house of his uncle, a Baptist minister, as he was making his way to the Continent (*John Frost*, p. 253). On the second occasion he went to Hetherington in London, and was placed in hiding at Woodford, in the house of W. J. Linton; (W. J. Linton, *Memories* (1895), p. 43).
[7] Newport Museum MSS. Bute MSS., XX, 105, says that both Price and William David attended the meeting.

delegate indicated the number of men in his lodge who were armed and could be relied on, and it was estimated that they could muster 5,000 armed men. Final agreement was then reached on a plan to march on Newport on Sunday night in three contingents, one from Blackwood under the leadership of Frost, the second from Nantyglo and Ebbw Vale led by Zephaniah Williams, and the third from Pontypool under William Jones, all three to meet at Risca, above Newport.

On the Saturday William Davies went to Newport to buy arms. There a stranger was brought to him by Frost's young son, and Davies brought him back to Blackwood to see Frost. Davies knew that he came from Bradford, thus confirming the accounts of both Lovett and Dr John Taylor, for the stranger was undoubtedly Charles Jones.[1] Jones argued that a rising was premature, but Frost replied that it could not now be put off, as the time had been agreed upon the previous day. Jones left about nine o'clock in the evening, making apparently for Birmingham.

The miserable fiasco of the march on Newport need not be described at length. Sunday proved to be a wet day, and by the evening a violent storm had arisen. Frost's contingent set off about seven o'clock, trudging along badly made roads in the pouring rain in complete darkness. Williams's men were particularly riotous. They made contact with Frost below Risca, and were joined by some of Jones's men, but Jones himself had returned to Pontypool, ostensibly to fetch another contingent. When dawn broke Frost and Williams decided to move on without him. The intention to occupy Newport before daybreak had miscarried. The authorities had been taken completely by surprise, but the delay had alerted them. They swore in special constables, arrested a few of the Newport Chartists and held them in the Westgate Hotel. When the demonstrators arrived they made for the hotel shouting 'surrender our prisoners'. Only a few minutes previously the mayor had moved a detachment of thirty soldiers into the Westgate; it is out of the question that the Chartists could have known that they were there. A scuffle began at the door of the hotel; shots were fired and the soldiers replied with a volley right into the crowd. Staggered by this unexpected development, the Chartists dropped their arms and fled in wild

---

[1] Dr Taylor does not name the messenger sent to Wales; Lovett does name him, but errs in thinking he was sent by O'Connor. Davies said that the stranger appeared to be a young working man under thirty-five years of age and that he was intelligent. Possibly Jones was disguised.

confusion. Within a few days Frost, Williams and Jones were under arrest.[1]

The conduct of the Glamorgan Chartists in respect of the riot is difficult to understand. One of those killed at Newport carried a membership card of the Merthyr W.M.A.,[2] and some Merthyr Chartists undoubtedly took part.[3] Morgan Williams and his associates were moral force men, and he, himself, was, on the day of the riot, on his way home from London where he had gone to buy a printing press. There was a Dowlais delegate at the Coach and Horses on Friday, and Dowlais men were seen on Sunday morning making their way towards Monmouthshire,[4] where they joined Zephaniah Williams's contingent. But there had clearly been inadequate notice, for it was after news of the fiasco at Newport had reached Dowlais on Monday that a meeting was called to take place early on Tuesday morning. By seven o'clock on that day, some five to six hundred men had assembled above the Dowlais works, and some proceeded to Rhymney where they put out the blast furnaces. The others, after being addressed by the ironmaster, Sir Josiah John Guest, adjourned until six o'clock in the evening when they assembled at their usual meeting-place on Aberdare Mountain. There they passed resolutions deploring the events at Newport and agreeing to return to work the following day.[5] Further south, at Gelligaer (across the Glamorgan border from Blackwood), some three hundred of the four hundred men employed in the collieries in the district are said to have been at Newport, no doubt as part of Frost's contingent. Of these, one was detained at Newport, and three others thought it wise not to return home.[6] Even the moral force men of Aberdare took fright when the news reached them, and three went into hiding, including the Unitarian minister, but they returned on finding that there was no charge against them.[7]

---

[1] In addition to the sources for the riot cited in my *John Frost*, see outgoing letters in H.O. 41/15 and 41/16 (some 223 items) which, however, add little that is new.

[2] *Monmouthshire Merlin*, 9 Nov. 1839.

[3] H.O. 40/45 says that very few Merthyr men took part and that those who did were probably 'tramps'.

[4] H.O. 40/45; Bute MSS., XX, 35; Bessborough, *op. cit.*, p. 99.

[5] Bute MSS., XX, 31, 42, 43; *Cambrian*, 9 Nov. 1839; Bessborough, *op. cit.*, pp. 101–3.

[6] For the Chartists of Gelligaer and Llanfabon, see Bute MSS., XX, 93, 121, 122, 127, 130, 133. *Bute Letter Book*, No. 13, p. 245, gives the two leaders in this district as Thomas Giles of Llanfabon and William Owen of Llancaiach.

[7] For the Aberdare Chartists, see Bute MSS., XX, 69, 72, 77, 78. *Bute Letter Book, No.* 13, p. 225, gives the leaders at Aberdare as John Williams, a weaver, and Thomas Evans, a shoemaker.

Most mysterious of all were the activities of Dr William Price and his associates in the Rhondda Valley. Dr John Taylor had understood that it was Price who would take command in Wales,[1] and William Jones had encouraged his men by assuring them that he expected Price to join them with seven pieces of cannon.[2] William David was greatly agitated at the turn of events. He told an associate that 'serious work' was expected in Newport on Monday, and that 'it was better to join with the Monmouthshire men than be a lout or a coward'.[3] According to tradition the Chartists assembled at Dinas and marched down the valley as far as Hafod (in the direction of Pontypridd) but then went home.[4] Possibly this was because of a poor turn-out, for a local coalowner states that the miners had deserted their houses and taken to the woods to avoid being pressed into joining.[5] A warrant was issued for David's arrest, but he absconded to America.[6] The authorities were very anxious to know the whereabouts of Dr Price. They were not sure whether he had left the district or not. They could not establish a case against him, and it was not until 30 November that they issued a warrant for his arrest. Even so, this was only on a charge of riot and breach of the peace, and they thought it best to withdraw the warrant in the hope of being able to establish a more serious charge.[7] According to his own graphic account, Price had meanwhile made his way to Paris.

Strange to say, it was on the day after the riot, that is, on the Tuesday, that the greatest alarm was felt at Cardiff. A rumour reached the town of an imminent attack by large bodies of Chartists from the direction of both Pontypridd and Caerphilly, with the intention of destroying the new union workhouse.[8] Constables were sworn in; military defence was entrusted to a naval officer whose ship was in the harbour; an American naval captain brought his men to the aid of the authorities; buglers were stationed on all roads

[1] Lovett Collection, Vol. II, p. 211.　　[2] Newport MSS., several entries.
[3] Bute MSS., XX, 1.
[4] 'Morien', op. cit., pp. 202–5, says they assembled at Hafod and were to march up to Dinas, and then on to Cardiff, but that they thought better of it and went home. See also Cardiff MS. 6.5.
[5] Bute MSS., XX, 85. This was Walter Coffin, later M.P. for Cardiff, said to be the first Nonconformist to sit in Parliament.
[6] Bute MSS., XX, 61, 74, 78, 85, 94, 98. 'Morien', loc. cit., says he returned home in 1845.
[7] Bute MSS., XX, 41, 73, 74, 78, 93, 94, 95, 98, 102, 103, 105, 133. Bute Letter Book, No. 13, p. 346 (10 July 1840) greatly regrets the return of Price to his home near Pontypridd. See also pp. 368, 394, 416.
[8] Bute MSS., XX, 46, 50, 57; H.O. 40/46.

entering the town, and scouts were sent out in the direction of the hills.[1] It was believed that Price[2] and either William David[3] or his son[4] were at the bottom of this new attempt. But the observers returned at two o'clock in the morning with the report that all was quiet, and there seems to have been no basis for the rumour at all.

In the trial which followed, Frost, Williams and Jones were condemned to death, but, through the intervention of Chief Justice Tindal, their sentence was commuted to transportation for life. Several other Chartists received lesser sentences.

The importance both of the prolonged examination of witnesses after the riot and of the trial itself rests not so much in their outcome as in the light they throw on the motives of the Chartists. Frost's public utterances until the end indicate that he favoured a mass demonstration, preferably on polling day. His weeping during the interview with Price shows the predicament which he found himself in, since he must either abandon the Chartists and be called a traitor or take the lead in a hopeless venture. It was easy for the prosecution to select items from the evidence given by witnesses and bring a charge of treason based upon them. The nature of the secret discussions in the lodges can be surmised from Zephaniah Williams's 'confession', which purports to outline a 'plan to overthrow the present government of England and establish a republic.'[5] Five thousand men, he says, were to march from Merthyr to occupy Brecon; a similar number from north Monmouthshire were to seize Abergavenny; the Chartists from the Pontypridd area (also numbering five thousand, apparently) were to advance on Cardiff; an equal number were to take Newport. Wales was fixed upon for the outbreak as there were so few soldiers stationed in the area; the English Chartists were not to move until they found that the Welsh mails did not arrive at the usual time. Messengers were despatched to various centres in England to give intelligence of the preparations being made in Wales, and Zephaniah Williams claimed to have spoken to one of them after he had returned — possibly an echo of Charles Jones's visit.

All this wild talk bears little relation to what actually happened, for Zephaniah Williams himself led the men of north Monmouth-

---

[1] Bute MSS., XX, 31.   [2] Ibid., XX, 103.
[3] Ibid., loc. cit.   [4] Ibid., XX, 94, 137.
[5] Letter to A. McKechnie, 25 May 1840, in Lord Tredegar's Library, now in Tredegar MSS. in N.L.W.

shire not to Abergavenny but to Newport. Even the most hostile witnesses against him at his trial asserted that he had repeatedly as-sured his followers that there would be no bloodshed. It is known that the stopping of the mail had been discussed in the secret meet-ing at Blackwood on the Friday before the riot. The prosecution seized upon it as evidence of a general conspiracy. But Frost's eloquent counsel, Sir J. F. Pollock, was able to destroy this 'mail theory', with devastating effect on the jury, for he showed that the Welsh mail did not go direct to the Midlands; it was taken to the Severn Ferry and on to Bristol by a separate coach, and the Bristol coach for Birmingham did not wait for it if it had not arrived on time. The Chartists elsewhere were, no doubt, threatening to rise, but there is no evidence that the Newport riot was to be the signal for a general rising. Nor is there much sense in believing that the Chartists even intended to 'seize' Newport. The three contingents could so easily have entered the town from three directions, and, if necessary, destroy the bridge to stop the mail, but they were at pains to join forces outside the town, at the expense of bringing the Pontypool men considerably out of their way, and they entered the town from the other side. This would confirm the belief that their purpose was a mass demonstration; as a plan to capture the town it is patently absurd. Equally absurd is the theory that their purpose was to liberate Vincent. There had been much talk of doing this, and Pollock seized on it as an explanation which might seem reason-able to the jury. But Vincent was imprisoned in Monmouth; if the Chartists thought to liberate him they would not have brought the Pontypool men down to Newport, then making them almost retrace their steps to Usk before proceeding an equal distance in the oppo-site direction to Monmouth. The only reasonable explanation of the Newport riot is that it was intended as a monster demonstra-tion.

But if contemporaries were mystified about the intentions of the Chartists, they were in no doubt as to the cause of the trouble; it was Nonconformity. The chaplain at Monmouth gaol enquired into the religious affiliation of the prisoners, 'to discover in what congregations sedition throve best.' He found that of forty-nine prisoners, forty-one were sectarians, and he suspected that the few who claimed to be Anglicans were deceiving him. 'I think', he said, 'that it would be difficult to find more than one or two whose religious instruction was not derived from the minister of the

Meeting House as well as from the clergyman of the Parish Church.' Strange to say, some of the prisoners had once been choir boys, 'their lapse into dissent and their progress in Chartism keeping pace one with the other.'[1]

The authorities showed great energy in tracking down those who had taken part in the riot, and all Chartists in South Wales fell under suspicion. Rumours were circulating that there might even be an attempt to release the prisoners. When sentence was passed a flood of petitions for their reprieve reached the Queen, and these continued after Frost, Williams and Jones had departed for Tasmania. Two of these petitions came from Merthyr Tydfil. The attitude of the Monmouthshire workers towards the men of Merthyr was said to be threatening. Frost, however, does not seem to have felt that he had been betrayed by them, for Morgan Williams was the recipient of one of the few letters which he wrote on board the convict ship,[2] and both men, for that matter, continued to be firm admirers of Feargus O'Connor. The *débâcle* at Newport did not prevent Morgan Williams from proceeding with his periodical, for *Udgorn Cymru* (The Trumpet of Wales) appeared in March 1840, a threepenny monthly, printed and published by David John, junior, and Morgan Williams in Glebeland, Merthyr Tydfil. In the early numbers there was considerable material in English, and it was the demands of their English readers which led the two editors to issue a twopenny English monthly, *The Advocate and Merthyr Free Press*, of which the first number appeared in July 1840. The Lord-Lieutenant of Glamorgan sent copies of both periodicals (with translations of the *Udgorn*) to the Home Office. After the tenth issue, in April 1841, the *Advocate* disappeared; the *Udgorn* survived until October 1842.[3]

The *Udgorn* lavished much praise on O'Connor, and when Chartism was revived by the O'Connorites, in the National Charter Association, at a meeting of delegates at Manchester on 20 July 1840, David John attended to represent Merthyr Tydfil, Aberdare, Pontypridd, Newport and Pontypool.[4] Meetings were then held at

---

[1] Usk MSS., Prison Report; (in full in my *John Frost*, p. 324).
[2] Dated 8 May 1840, Tredegar MSS.
[3] In addition to the references in my *John Frost*, p. 333, see H.O. 41/15 and 45/54 (for copies of the *Udgorn* and the *Advocate*). *The Times Tercentenary Handlist*, p. 232, gives 22 Oct. 1842 for the last issue of the *Udgorn*. *Bute Letter Book No.* 13, has numerous letters concerning these Chartist periodicals.
[4] *Udgorn*, Aug. 1840; *Advocate*, Aug. 1840; H.O. 40/57; Lovett Collection, Vol. II, p. 196.

Dukestown, Abersychan, Dowlais, Merthyr Tydfil, Pontypridd, Dinas and Maesteg, attended by delegates from the north, and the authorities became much concerned at this sudden revival.[1] Morgan Williams was elected to the executive of this new body, and attended its Convention in London in May 1841.[2] Meanwhile a more sinister aspect had appeared in the activities of a Chartist missionary named Black.[3] He addressed a meeting in Merthyr on Christmas Day, 1840,[4] and in Newport early in the New Year.[5] In June 1841 a package addressed to a man named Moore, which was to be called for at Pontypool, was opened by the authorities and was found to contain two muskets, two bayonets, a fowling piece and five bullet moulds, in addition to a quantity of Chartist literature, and when it was claimed by Black he was promptly arrested. Nevertheless he was sentenced only to a month's imprisonment as a rogue and vagabond.[6]

The summer of 1841 witnessed a general election. Morgan Williams allowed his name to go forward for Merthyr and used the hustings to expound Chartism but did not choose to go to the poll.[7] The Newport Chartists nominated Dr William Price,[8] and, when he did not appear, put forward William Edwards, the original founder of the Newport W.M.A. Like Morgan Williams, Edwards used his opportunity to address the meeting, but when he wished to withdraw before the poll his followers insisted that his name should go forward, and he received no votes at all, a result probably unique in parliamentary annals.[9] There ensued a bitter quarrel among the Chartists which did great harm to their cause in Monmouthshire.

[1] Bute MSS., XX, 157.
[2] *Udgorn*, June 1841.
[3] He was apparently a Notts. man; *Udgorn*, Aug. 1840, gives his name as George Black.
[4] *Merthyr Guardian*, 26 Dec. 1840.
[5] *Silurian*, 16 Jan. 1841, says that Charles Jones of Llanidloes was present at Newport with Black. *Bute Letter Book, No.* 14, p. 157 (12 May 1841), speaks of Black, 'a paid Chartist agent', collecting signatures in Cardiff for a petition to release Frost, Williams and Jones.
[6] In addition to the references in my *John Frost*, pp. 328–9, see H.O. 40/57, 41/16, 45/49.
[7] Bessborough, *op. cit.*, pp. 123–4.
[8] Price had returned home as early as March 1840; *Bute Letter Book, No.* 13, p. 308.
[9] R. J. Blewitt 330, William Edwards 0; *Silurian*, 3 July 1841.

III

Chartism revived in the early months of 1842 when the National Charter Association submitted another petition to Parliament. Morgan Williams took up 36,000 signatures from Merthyr Tydfil, Aberdare, Pontypridd and Tredegar to the Convention in London on 12 April.[1] He assured the assembly that the Glamorgan men were all staunch supporters of O'Connor, with no Sturgeites to be found among them, and his return to Merthyr was the occasion of a mass-meeting addressed by himself, by David John and by William Gould, a grocer, now coming to the fore as a Chartist leader.[2] In the succeeding weeks several meetings were held in the neighbourhood. The Merthyr Chartists now seemed to be more Radical than those of Monmouthshire, for, on 18 April, during Morgan Williams's absence a large gathering between Rhymney and Tredegar had passed resolutions in favour of forming a branch of Sturge's Complete Suffrage Union.[3] The summer of 1842 was one of intense industrial depression, leading to strikes at Cyfarthfa and Dowlais in August. There were several meetings at the common above the Dowlais works,[4] and the Monmouthshire men were invited to join, but the response from Ebbw Vale is said to have been: 'You left us in the lurch at Newport, and now you may go to the devil your own way.'[5] Other meetings were held on Aberdare Mountain. Morgan Williams appears to have taken little part in them, although, as late as August 1842, the Lord-Lieutenant of Glamorgan was considering the desirability of arresting him.[6] Leadership had now passed to William Miles, a more extreme Chartist. The ironmasters of Cyfarthfa and Dowlais took strong action and sacked those of their workmen who were known to be Chartists.[7] Distress

---

[1] *Udgorn*, 11, 23 Apr. 1842. For Chartism in 1842 see Walter Morgan, 'Chartism and Industrial Unrest in South Wales in 1842', *National Library of Wales Journal*, X (1957), 8–16, an analysis of letters to Octavius Morgan, M.P., February to September 1842, in Tredegar Collection (N.L.W.).

[2] *Merthyr Guardian*, 14 May 1842.

[3] Walter Morgan, *op. cit.*, p. 11. A Sturgeite meeting was held at Merthyr on 22 Dec. 1842, *Silurian*, 31 Dec. 1842; another at Pontypool on 25 Oct. 1843, addressed by the Rev. Thomas Spencer, when the chair was taken by the Rev. Micah Thomas, president of the Baptist Academy at Pontypool, H.O. 45/453; another at Newport, 28 Feb. 1844, H.O. 45/642.

[4] *Merthyr Guardian*, 20 Aug. 1842.

[5] Bute MSS., XXII, 20 (letter dated 6 Sept. from Captain Napier of the Glamorgan police to Home Secretary).

[6] *Bute Letter Book*, *No.* 14, pp. 125–6 (23 Aug. 1842) and pp. 128–30 (27 Aug. 1842).

[7] *Cambrian*, 26 Aug. 1842; *Merthyr Guardian*, 10 Sept. 1842.

had brought with it a revival of extremism. The workmen's benefit clubs were again said to be buying muskets, and the authorities were keeping a watchful eye on William Miles and the dismissed Chartists at their rendezvous, the Three Horse Shoes Inn in Georgetown, Merthyr Tydfil.[1]

The depression in the iron industry led many workers to return to their homes in west Wales. There, the Rebecca Riots had broken out in the summer of 1839, as we have seen, with the destruction of two turnpike tollgates, but had then subsided. The revival of rioting in the winter of 1842 coincided with the depression in industry, and it continued to spread like a contagion throughout west Wales in the following year. That it took the form mainly of an attack on the tollgates was almost accidental; they were tangible objects which could be destroyed. The most spectacular incident in the rioting was, in fact, the ransacking of Carmarthen workhouse on 19 June 1843. The fundamental cause of the rioting was poverty, owing to the pressure of a greatly increased population on a backward economy, intensified by the industrial depression which had lowered the demand for agricultural produce.

The Times correspondent (Thomas Campbell Foster), who was sent to investigate, was convinced that there were no 'Chartist crotchets', no 'political disaffection' behind the rioting.[2] Yet the connection between Chartism and the Rebecca movement is close for both sprang from the same underlying causes. The main connecting link between them is Hugh Williams. He was still closely associated with Hetherington, for it was Hetherington who had published his *National Songs and Poetical Pieces* in 1840. Furthermore, when Hetherington was prosecuted for blasphemy in 1841, Williams lent money to Thomas Powell, who had become one of Hetherington's shopmen on being released from prison, to buy Hetherington's business, so that his property could not be distrained upon for any fine that might be imposed.[3] There is no evidence to show that Williams took part in a single Rebecca riot, but he prepared the legal defence of the rioters, as he had done for the Llanidloes Chartists. Moreover, when the rioting died down in the autumn of 1843 it was replaced by a series of mass-meetings at

---

[1] *Merthyr Guardian, loc. cit.*, says that the dismissed men met at the Three Horse Shoes Inn. For the participation of Wales in the 'plug plot', see Walter Morgan, *loc. cit.*

[2] *The Times*, 30 June 1843.

[3] W. J. Linton, *James Watson, A Memoir* (1879), p. 51; *Memories* (1895), p. 96.

R

which Williams was the principal speaker. It was he who drew up several of the petitions submitted to the Queen. Naturally, toll-gates, high rents and insecurity of tenure figured in them, but otherwise the grievances listed were those of the Chartists, notably the poor law. The petitions even demanded the dissolution of parliament and an extension of the franchise, illustrating thereby both the affinity between the two movements and the use made by Hugh Williams of the rioting to propagate Chartist ideas.

Rebecca proved to be a great mystery to the Chartists, even to Bronterre O'Brien's *Poor Man's Guardian*, although this was printed by Hetherington. It devoted three articles to the rioting and it concluded that it had best be left alone, for the grievances of tenant farmers were of little concern either to their own labourers or to industrial workers.[1] The approach between the two movements was, in fact, made by the Rebeccaites. Emissaries were sent to Merthyr Tydfil, and their requests for information and assistance were discussed at the Three Horse Shoes Inn.[2] When three Rebecca leaders were tried by a Special Commission at Cardiff in October 1843, several of the jury were from Merthyr Tydfil. Their names were read out at the Three Horse Shoes together with a letter from Hugh Williams hoping that the Chartists would 'do their best' for these jurymen. They responded by threatening to 'scotch' anyone who had dealings with them, and left letters lying about the levels at Cyfarthfa naming them and urging the miners to boycott their businesses. Two jurymen did receive threatening letters, but no reprisals appear to have been taken.

The meetings at the Three Horse Shoes were highly subversive, and it is strange that, from the start, there should have been in the Chartists' inner councils an informer who supplied detailed reports to the authorities.[3] Morgan Williams and David John do not seem to have attended, but the latter's brother, Matthew, was present occasionally, and so also was William Gould. The leaders were more obscure men, William Miles (whom we have already noticed), and David Ellis, a violent speaker who addressed meetings in other places as well. The chief interest in the informer's reports is the light they throw on the workings of the arms clubs. These were

[1] 2, 9, 16 Sept. 1843. My attention was kindly drawn to these articles by Dr Caradoc Morris. The Manchester Chartists, also, 'did not know what Rebecca meant to do'; H.O. 45/454.

[2] For detailed references see my *Rebecca Riots, ut supra.*

[3] H.O. 45/453.

disguised as benefit clubs, and there were several in Merthyr.[1]
When enough money was collected, lots were drawn and the successful member would then visit a gunsmith, of whom there was
one in Merthyr and another in Pontypridd. Yet even within
the assembly at the Three Horse Shoes there was dissension,
the extremists, for example, reproaching William Gould with
having mismanaged things at the time of the Newport riot, and
there was talk of dividing into two associations. By February 1844,
Colonel Love, the officer commanding troops in South Wales, was
able to report that the arms clubs had ceased to exist through lack
of funds.[2]

For a brief period, interest in Chartism was displaced in Merthyr
Tydfil by trade-unionism. The Miners' Association had been
founded in November 1842, and two delegates from Newcastle
arrived in Merthyr in February 1844, staying at the Three Horse
Shoes Inn. Their gatherings were thinly attended to begin with,
but later they had some success.[3] There was an immediate threat of
dismissal by the ironmasters, and this, together with full employment, led once more to the collapse of unionism.[4] In the following
years, occasional meetings to petition for the release of Frost, Williams and Jones, served to keep Chartism alive.[5] It flared up with
the intense depression of 1848 and the outbreak of revolution in
France. There was a revival in Newport, where Frost's cousin and
namesake took a prominent part,[6] but the chief centre again was
Merthyr Tydfil. At a meeting held in the Market Square on 20
March, Matthew John and Gould were the chief speakers, and the
delegate chosen to attend the London convention was David
Thomas, a cooper, a *habitué* of the Three Horse Shoes. The fiasco
of the convention led to an angry meeting in the Market Square on
18 April, and, when a counter demonstration was held three weeks
later to present a loyal address to the Queen, Gould and Matthew
John sought to convert it into a Chartist meeting and it broke up in
great confusion. The earlier leaders of Chartism were notably

---

[1] E.g. at the Travellers, the old Angel, and opposite the turnpike gate at
Cefn.
[2] H.O. 45/642.
[3] Col. Love reported, 22 March 1844, that 10 Dowlais, 15 Penydarren, 20
Plymouth and 200 Cyfarthfa miners had joined; H.O. 45/642.
[4] H.O. 41/18, 45/642.
[5] H.O. 45/1431.
[6] To the confusion of several writers on Chartism, who have thought that the
more celebrated Frost had returned to Newport.

absent, while those now prominent were themselves the moderates among those who frequented the Three Horse Shoes. This complete lack of unity in the ranks of the Chartists accounts, to a great extent, for the apparent failure of the movement in Merthyr Tydfil if not, also, in the country as a whole.

Chapter Eight

Chartism in Glasgow

Alex Wilson

I

It was no mere accident of history that the Chartist movement was inaugurated in Scotland. It spread widely among the working classes of Scotland and took deep root in local organisation in many parts of the country. In Scotland, organisation on a national, if somewhat rudimentary, basis was instituted a year earlier than in England. For almost the entire Chartist period, the agitation was more strongly organised in Glasgow than in Leeds, Manchester or any other large Chartist centre. In Scotland, the movement was characterised by its relatively well disciplined pursuit of long-term ends by means of education and social reform. This social reformist character of Scottish Chartism was to be seen in Chartist schools, Chartist co-operative stores, and Chartist temperance societies. Above all it was to be seen in the Christian Chartist movement, which became so powerful in 1840 and 1841 that it alarmed both the Established and the Dissenting Churches.

The general course of the movement in Scotland can be seen from the following table which analyses the activities of Chartist organisations throughout Scotland. The analysis is based on reports published in Chartist and other newspapers of the 1830's and 1840's. Most of these reports were concerned with public meetings and demonstrations arranged by Chartist groups and with the weekly or monthly discussions of Chartist committees. In addition there survive reports of individual and group contributions to Chartist funds for other purposes than the maintenance of local agitation. These purposes included the sending of local representatives to regional and national conferences, the building or renting of Chartist Halls, the conducting of 'dramatic performances' and 'social evenings', the running of Chartist churches, Chartist schools, Chartist co-operative societies, and Chartist temperance societies, as well as the publication of pamphlets, circulars, and weekly and monthly newspapers.

The table indicates a rapid growth of local Chartist branches in 1838 and 1839, the maintenance of a fairly strong agitation until 1842, and the stagnation and virtual decay of Chartist organisation thereafter.

Year	Scottish local Chartist organisations in existence	(of which) fairly active	Important (Scottish) Chartist Publications	Scottish Chartist Churches	Affiliation to the National Charter Association
1838	76	30	3	—	—
1839	169	57	4	4	—
1840	124	33	4	20	—
1841	61	10	5	23	—
1842	94	12	3	14	—
1843	36	7	2	10	4
1844	13	—	—	8	6
1845	15	1	—	6	6
1846	19	4	(1)	4	5
1847	5	—	(1)	4	1
1848	20	6	1	2	2
1849	9	—	(1)	2	4
1850	7	—	—	2	—
1851	10	—	—	2	10

It should be noted, however, that, in the early years of the agitation, organisation lapsed in many (and sometimes formerly flourishing) districts, while in other areas decayed organisations took on a new lease of life, often after a year's quiescence. At the Scottish Chartist Conventions of August 1839, September 1840, and January 1842, representatives attended from 63, 50 and 62 districts, respectively, but only about 45 districts maintained a reasonably continuous form of organisation throughout the period 1838 to 1842. Of these only nine or ten could be said to maintain a very active agitation throughout these years, and outside Glasgow and its suburbs, only Aberdeen, Dundee, Hawick, Vale of Leven and, possibly, Edinburgh and Paisley might be included in that category.

Especially in the early stages, attempts were made to co-ordinate local activities and missionary expeditions were despatched to try to set up regional associations. County associations existed, for varying periods of time, in Ayrshire, the Borders, Midlothian,

Fifeshire and Kinross, Forfarshire, Lanarkshire, Perthshire, Renfrewshire and Stirlingshire. Within the large towns, Glasgow, Edinburgh, Dundee, Paisley and Aberdeen there were often several Chartist organisations, usually in alliance but sometimes in competition with one another.

After 1842, a handful of associations maintained a tenuous link with the National Charter Association, showing some interest in the plans of their English brethren, and contributing to the funds sponsored by them. Apart, however, from some enthusiasm shown for the National Land Society, especially in 1846, there was more slumber than agitation in the movement. Apart from Land Society branches and a few Chartist Churches, less than a dozen districts could be said to maintain organised life. Of these Aberdeen, Dundee, and Edinburgh developed sporadic though occasionally substantial activity, but only Glasgow could claim to be very energetic throughout the years 1843 to 1851, and even there Chartist activity was on a sadly reduced scale compared with the years 1839, 1840 and 1841.

II

When the Birmingham Radicals launched their Reform campaign in Glasgow on 21 May 1838, the place had been chosen carefully after much deliberation of the Birmingham Political Union in the winter and spring of 1837–8.[1] Of all the great cities of the kingdom, Glasgow offered the greatest certainty of providing a 'monster demonstration' in support of their demands for universal suffrage, vote by ballot and annual parliaments. In Glasgow they could count on the support of Radicals who had organised mass meetings and processions in the 1831–2 Reform agitation, and of trade-union leaders who were disturbed and angry at the alleged persecution of the Glasgow cotton spinners' leaders after their long strike in 1837, and apprehensive of the intentions of the Government concerning its promotion of a Parliamentary Inquiry into the activities of trade unions. Throughout April 1838, John Collins had paraded Glasgow and the West of Scotland as the missionary of the men of Birmingham, making sure of the ground, and enlisting promises of support which were almost embarrassingly numerous.

On 10 April, many of the middle-class reformers of Glasgow had

[1] *Birmingham Journal*, 11 Nov. 1837, 13, 24 Jan., 3, 24 Feb., 3 Mar., 14, 21, 28 Apr., 12 May 1838. See also above, p. 23.

met in the Town Hall to approve the Birmingham plan of campaign and to appoint a committee to organise a demonstration to which Attwood and the Birmingham leaders would be invited. James Turner of Thrushgrove thought that the former 12,000 members of the Glasgow Political Union could be enrolled in the new cause. Robert Wallace of Kelly, Mr Ure of Croy, Alexander Hedderwick, Mr Birkmyre, Dr Walker and most of the former leaders of the Political Union promised their support. James Moir and Bailie William Craig believed that the working classes could play a most important rôle in the new cause. The working men of Glasgow would assert their rights in a peaceable and quiet spirit. They only required to be made aware that they were trusted and that there was a desire to do them justice, in order to call forth their best feelings.[1]

A fortnight later, more than 200 delegates of trade unions, workshops, factories, and districts around Glasgow attended a meeting of the Glasgow Central Committee, and unanimously resolved to come forward with their flags, banners and music. They planned a demonstration at which 3,000 powerloom weavers and 3,000 colliers would march with many thousands of other workmen from all towns within twenty miles of Glasgow. The 'Grand Demonstration' would be held on Glasgow Green on 21 May and would be followed by a soirée in the evening.[2]

Monday, 21 May 1838 was a dismal rainy day, but despite the unfavourable weather all public works were at a standstill and seventy trade unions marched in a procession stretching for more than two miles. Forty-three 'bands of music' all in uniform met Thomas Attwood at Parkhead, and large bodies of reformers from Lanarkshire and Renfrewshire villages marched into Glasgow. About 300 banners were carried, including many Anti-Corn Law banners, and a Covenanters' flag. On Glasgow Green, a great multitude, estimated at between 30,000 and 100,000 by Liberal and Conservative newspapers and at between 100,000 and 200,000 by the Radical Press, assembled to hear their new political redeemers, Messrs Attwood, Douglas, Salt, Edwards, Muntz and Collins of Birmingham, and Dr Wade and Mr Murphy of the London Working Men's Association.[3]

[1] *Birmingham Journal*, 21 Apr. 1838; *Scotch Reformers' Gazette*, 14 Apr. 1838.
[2] *Birmingham Journal*, 28 Apr. 1838.
[3] *Scots Times*, 23 May 1838; *Birmingham Journal*, 26 May 1838; *Northern Star*, 2 June 1838.

The chairman of the meeting was James Turner, the most highly esteemed of the Glasgow reformers, who reminded the assembly of the Thrushgrove reform meeting of 1816, which had provided the correct mode of peaceful behaviour for all reform meetings in Glasgow since that time.[1] Attwood declared that he for his part was no revolutionist, and that he was doing all in his power to prevent revolution. Against the reformers, he declared, there were arrayed all the aristocracy, nine-tenths of the gentry, all placemen and pensioners. On their own side they had no strength save the justice of their cause. Now that the men of Glasgow had met, 48 other towns would follow suit. Once the 49 delegates of these towns had met in London, he would like to see the House of Commons that would reject their petition! But if God made them mad, then another and yet another petition would be sent. Then they would make a general strike, such as the ancient Romans had made on the Aventine Hill until their wrongs were removed. 'The men of Birmingham were willing either to assist or to lead them on . . . . In the cause of peace, loyalty and order, the men of Birmingham would not shrink from assisting them even to the death.'

During the next ten days, Scotland, especially the western and midland counties, was in a ferment of political excitement. After a pilgrimage to Elderslie, with its memories of Wallace, and a demonstration in Paisley, Attwood, the Messiah, returned home on 23 May. His apostles, however, made triumphant visits to Kilmarnock, Stirling, Perth, Dundee, Cupar, Dunfermline and Edinburgh, and before the Birmingham deputation had left Scotland, a great mass of the working classes had been introduced to the National Petition. However imperfectly they might have understood its political content, they warmly acclaimed it as their political creed and their hope of social salvation.[2]

By the beginning of June, the National Petition had been adopted in Glasgow, Edinburgh, Perth, Dundee, Dunfermline and at county meetings in Renfrewshire, Ayrshire and Fifeshire. Several of the Working Men's Associations and a few of the surviving Political Unions espoused the new cause with the familiar programme. Some of the Radical Associations, formed under the spell

[1] James Turner of Thrushgrove (1768–1858) was a Glasgow tobacco merchant who had provided a field on his property, near St Rollox in October 1816, for the largest Radical meeting in the West of Scotland during the 1816–19 agitation. See *Glasgow Examiner*, 6, 13, 27 May 1854.
[2] *Birmingham Journal*, 2, 9 June 1838; *Northern Star*, 2 June 1838.

of Dr John Taylor and Feargus O'Connor in 1836, re-named themselves Universal Suffrage Associations. Those which regarded such a technicality as unnecessary were no less ardent in the cause.

The success of the appeal of the men of Birmingham to the Radicals of Scotland had exceeded most expectations. Their intervention in Scottish political life had been well timed, despite cold and wet weather. The effects of the 1837 depression were still severely felt. The undercurrent of discontent with the existing social system, and with many aspects of the new industrial system had never been stronger. The large class of handloom weavers felt their increasing degradation with great bitterness. Class legislation, especially in the form of corn laws, seemed a powerful cause of their distress.

Many trade-unionists were afraid that Daniel O'Connell would push the Government into legislation restricting the rights of trade unions, and were convinced of the need for greater influence over the actions of the legislature and administration. Furthermore the scriptural teaching of Collins and his messianic faith readily endeared him to Scottish audiences, with their Covenanter traditions, while Attwood's position as a middle-class leader attracted considerable support from the Scots middle classes. It was the middle-class political leaders — printers, merchants, brewers, editors and shopkeepers — who had figured most prominently at the Glasgow meetings.

What was less certain, however, was whether the campaign would outlast the visit of the Birmingham Radicals. Several of the most popular national political leaders, including Lord Durham, O'Connell and (to a lesser extent) O'Connor had received in earlier years a resounding welcome from the Scottish reformers, but within a few weeks little had been left behind except the memory of their visits. Nor had any of the political agitations under working-class leadership lasted for more than a few months. Invariably their strength had melted with industrial recovery.

Throughout the summer of 1838, such a melting away of Radical strength seemed to be taking place in Glasgow. Apart from further visits by Dr Taylor and Feargus O'Connor in July, there was little political activity.

Yet below the surface there were several factors which augured well for the Glasgow agitation. There was emerging a small but increasingly vocal newspaper-reading section of the working classes. Many intelligent artisans had begun to take an active interest in schemes of social reform, in trade-unionism, in co-operation, in temperance, and, more recently, many of these group leaders had begun to assert themselves in politics. Many of them regarded the extension of the suffrage as the only practicable road to the abolition of the Corn Laws. In addition, there was a growing group of local politicians who were sufficiently impatient with the Whigs to seek a share in the reflected glory of Attwood and his movement. They had enjoyed the feeling of responsibility derived from their minor rôles in the Political Unions, and middle-class and working-class men alike, they felt they could win still greater glory as the office-bearers of new political organisations. They enjoyed the arguments, disagreements and compromises of regular committee meetings, and were secretly delighted in leading little factions against each other. They were fascinated by their game of politics and contrived always to play their game within reasonable and legal limits. Then when the agitation slumbered, and their regular meetings lapsed, the old adversaries found pleasure in meeting together again at any excuse for honouring one of the old comrades, or in manoeuvring themselves into positions of leadership in the new movements for suffrage extension, for continental liberty, for humanitarian causes which later and gradually took over the public platforms from Chartism.

Until the spring of 1839, there had been little inclination amongst the Scottish Chartist associations to look to Glasgow for leadership. The Radical movements in Scotland had always tended to be focused on Glasgow and the West of Scotland, but after May 1838 what leadership had been forthcoming had been chiefly from Edinburgh, and had been concentrated in the efforts of John Fraser[1]

---

[1] *John Fraser* (1794–1879) was a Johnstone school-master who had been imprisoned, but later exonerated, for his part in the Radical agitation of 1819. In 1836 he went to Edinburgh, where he helped to found the Edinburgh Radical Association and the Edinburgh Teetotal Association. He was an advocate of Hygeism and an agent for Morison's (Vegetable) Pills. In January 1838 he reported the trial of the Glasgow cotton spinners for the *Northern Star*; and in the initial stages of the Chartist movement he did more than any other person to create a strong agitation in Scotland. His position as spokesman of the Scottish Chartists, however, was destroyed by the reaction to the Calton Hill meeting in Edinburgh on 5 Dec. 1838, when he and the Rev. Patrick Brewster denounced the insurrectionary methods of J. R. Stephens and Feargus O'Connor. (See below, p. 256.) With a handful of supporters in Edinburgh, Fraser carried on an unending controversy against O'Connor and all those who tolerated O'Connor. After 1841, he increasingly devoted himself to making a fortune from musical

and Abram Duncan.[1] The organisation of the east and south had been greatly advanced by them in the summer and autumn of 1838, and no one in the west could rival them. Around Paisley, a group of satellite associations had grown up, which for a time accepted the leadership of the Rev. Patrick Brewster. At the conference in Edinburgh on 5 December 1838, to which delegates of Scottish Radical Associations had been called by Fraser and Duncan to discover the use of physical force, and at the demonstration on Calton Hill when the resulting moral force resolutions were given an authoritative send-off, Brewster was encouraged to play a leading part. When several associations repudiated these Calton Hill resolutions, Brewster's momentary leadership faded. As a result of the intervention of Dr John Taylor, he failed to secure election to the National Convention as the representative of Renfrewshire. Thereafter his genius consisted chiefly of playing the rôle of a solitary rebel and of displaying the profoundest disrespect for other men's opinions, and in Glasgow he was regarded more as a troublemaker than as a genuine Chartist leader.[2] The only really outstanding personality in the west had been Dr John Taylor, who had many followers in Ayrshire and Renfrewshire. After the failure of his newspaper the *New Liberator* in the spring of 1838, however, Taylor ceased to play any significant rôle in Glasgow. Taylor was in many respects well suited to be the

---

lectures, given by himself and his daughters, in tours of Britain and the United States. In his old age, he returned as a wealthy and respected citizen to Johnstone. Still a Radical Reformer, he received a presentation for his public services in 1872.

[1] Abram Duncan was a Glasgow woodturner, who was probably the best known operative in political circles in Glasgow throughout the 1830's. At most important political functions in the West of Scotland, he acted as the spokesman of the Glasgow trade unions. He coined the mottoes: 'the grey goose quill will be more efficacious than the popgun, bayonet or musket'; and 'we must shake our oppressors well over the mouth of Hell, but we must not let them drop in'. For several years he earned a living as a peregrinating lecturer on temperance, Chartism, and political economy, and as the Chartist pastor in Arbroath. Later he emigrated to the United States.

[2] Patrick Brewster (1788–1859) was the younger brother of Sir David Brewster, Principal of Edinburgh University. He aspired to the Chair of Church History at Glasgow University but never rose beyond the second charge of Paisley Abbey. For his 'Seven Chartist and Military Sermons' he was suspended from his ministerial functions. Although he has often been regarded as the central figure of the Scottish movement, this humourless and unromantic figure merely hovered on the fringe of the movement, highly critical of the main trends. Of much greater importance was his long advocacy of reform of the Scottish Poor Law. He was also well known as a campaigner for Total Abstinence, and Negro Emancipation.

counterpart in Scotland of his colleague and friend O'Connor. He was certainly the only man who could have become a great demagogue, but he left the building up of the Glasgow movement to men with many of whom he had little sympathy and few of whom had the slightest aspirations for power outside their own city.

With the election of delegates to the London Convention, each from a fairly well-defined locality, the local associations began to look to their delegates for leadership. This allegiance was quickly transferred to the Convention as a whole, but weeks passed and the Convention was still not leading in any one definite direction. The interest and faith of the local associations remained largely unabated, but they wanted to know what were the best ways in which they could help the General Convention. The recently formed associations were always busy enough building up their organisation, and allowing their members to go through the process of declaiming the principles of the Charter to each other. The older associations, however, were beginning to be bored with the same old voices. They wanted to undertake fresh practical tasks.

There was certainly no intention to look to Glasgow rather than to the Convention for leadership, but there was a growing tendency to consider that Glasgow should be the prime mover in all Chartist plans for Scotland. Glasgow was increasingly attending to missionary work in its region. Its Chartist Committee was becoming more self-conscious and ready to accept further responsibilities. Its members had been drawn largely from the trades organisations and a handful of men who had played some part in the Glasgow Political Union. Several men were emerging from amongst these non-commissioned officers of the trade-union and political world who had qualities of leadership and imagination. While the influence of Edinburgh was steadily declining throughout the first half of 1839,[1] the prestige of Glasgow was slowly rising.

Impetus was given to this transfer of power to Glasgow with the publication in July 1839 of the *Scottish Patriot* which was to be the press organ of the Glasgow Chartists. While meetings in Glasgow were declaring their 'full confidence' in the General Convention and their full support for it 'in all constitutional measures',

[1] The sharp reaction to the Calton Hill 'moral force' resolutions, carried in Edinburgh in December 1838 was a factor of importance in the national shift.

Thomas Gillespie, the secretary of the Glasgow Universal Suffrage Association, was busy sending out circulars to the principal Scottish associations. Did they favour the holding of a delegate conference to consider the best means of furthering the organisation of Scotland? If so, where should it be held? By the end of July, Gillespie had received 50 replies. Of these, 49 associations approved of the proposal, and 40 thought the conference should take place in Glasgow.

At the Delegate Conference which was held in Glasgow from 14–16 August 1839, there was widespread agreement that the agitation must be kept alive until 'some favourable accident' brought about universal suffrage. Agreement on the form that this agitation should take was not, however, unanimous. Aberdeen strongly repudiated any countenancing of a separate Scottish Convention, and anything which might bring about a divorce from the English movement. Aberdeen also wanted to stop petitioning, but Stonehouse wished to keep the table of the House of Commons 'groaning' under thousands of petitions. Most associations felt that however little redress of their grievances might be expected from petitions to the House of Commons, petitioning was the only plan which provided a safe and legal, as well as a popular, basis for the movement.

Efficient organisation, at local, county and national levels, for the 'creation, mobilisation and direction of Public Opinion', was regarded as the vital key to the success of the Charter, and the most important decision of the Conference was the establishment in August 1839 of a Central Committee for Scotland. This body and its permanent secretariat were to be supplied with funds from the district associations in proportion to the number of their members. These funds were to be 'appropriated to the purposes of engaging lecturers, printing and circulating political tracts and doing all in their power to disseminate knowledge among the people with the view to organising Scotland'.

Of the fifteen members appointed to this committee, only John Duncan of Edinburgh lived more than six or seven miles from the centre of Glasgow. Six of its members were directors of the Glasgow Universal Suffrage Association. Six of the others were officials of associations in the suburbs or in neighbouring burghs, but both they and the two remaining members were often prominent in the meetings of the Glasgow U.S.A. Aberdeen and Edinburgh, rivals of Glasgow, might justifiably refer to the Universal Suffrage Committee for Scotland as 'the Glasgow Committee'.

III

The story of Scottish Chartism in the following two and a half years is primarily concerned with the efforts of the Glasgow Chartist leaders to translate into reality the aims of the Glasgow Conference. They strove to provide an air of respectability, non-violence and moral idealism to the whole Chartist movement. Aided by the facts of geography, particularly remoteness from English leaders and, to a lesser extent, English newspapers, the Glasgow Chartists sought to rescue Chartism from O'Connor and Harney, and to swing it towards alliance with middle-class Radicals under the leadership of men like Hume, Roebuck, and Sturge.

When they failed to recruit more than a handful of the middle-class Radicals who had been members of the Glasgow Political Union into the Glasgow Universal Suffrage Association, they established a Universal Suffrage Electors' Association, and recruited more than 275 electors in its first month. When they failed to enlist the continuing support of more than one-third of the local trade unions, and realised that within 15 or 20 miles radius of Glasgow there were many villages which had never heard of Chartism, they reorganised the Glasgow and neighbouring Chartist organisations into the Lanarkshire Universal Suffrage Association with professional missionaries. When they found it difficult to raise organisational funds by subscriptions, they organised Saturday evening concerts, 'social evenings', dances, and even dancing classes. When the local clergymen would not espouse the movement, and especially if they decried it, they would encourage the establishment of Sabbath services conducted by Chartist preachers. When they had exhausted the surplus energy of their followers (and their fury against the harsh sentences passed on English and Welsh Chartists) in the organisation of Defence Funds for Frost and other 'victims' and their wives and families, they promoted a 'Petition Campaign' to inundate members of Parliament with countless petitions from individuals and small groups. When Corn Law repealers refused to give equal importance to universal suffrage in their free-trade campaign, they organised the packing of middle-class public meetings and carried Chartist resolutions giving universal suffrage priority over all other demands.[1] When such tactics were resisted by the Lord Provost and other chairmen, the Chartists would filibuster or otherwise disrupt the meetings, so that few meetings could be peaceably held which did not pay lip-service at least to the principles of the Charter. When 'martyrs' to the Chartist cause were released from prison cells, 'Liberation Demonstrations', tours and soirées were arranged in their honour.

During most of 1840 and 1841, Scottish Chartism seemed to be passing through a period of assertive and over-confident adolescence. Through efficient party organisation, especially in the Glasgow region, it could overawe any of its rivals. In the West and South-east, Chartist temperance associations were growing up, and were even holding their own delegate conferences. Considerable attention and enthusiasm was shown in Chartist co-operative stores of which there were at least sixteen, besides those which were reported to exist 'in almost every village' in Fife. Several Chartist associations now rented halls for periods of six to twelve months, and a few claimed to possess their own halls. In the newspaper press there was weekly advocacy of Chartism through the *Scottish Patriot*, the *True Scotsman*, the *Perthshire Chronicle* and several provincial newspapers including the *John O'Groats Journal*, which carried the cause of Chartism within a few miles of Duncansby Head, in addition to the still widely circulated *Northern Star*. 'We may not be producing great effects upon the government', concluded the *Scottish Patriot* at the end of 1840, 'but we are forming a character for the people which they have never before possessed — making them intelligent by instruction, and moral by inculcating the principles of total abstinence . . . . At the present moment the Chartists hold the most prominent position of all parties in the kingdom . . . . Universal Suffrage has now been carried from the public arena into the domestic hearth of the working classes. It has become a part of the social character of the people. It is associated with their amusements. It has become identified with their religion.'[2]

It was perhaps this identification of Chartism with religion, and the growth of the Chartist Church movement that were the outstanding features of Scottish Chartist organisation in 1840. There

---

[1] These tactics were followed at meetings of the Emancipation Society, the Emigration Society and several other societies, as well as at Anti-Corn Law and Household Suffrage meetings.

[2] *Scottish Patriot*, 26 Dec. 1840.

were at least 20 Christian Chartist Churches in existence in Scotland by the beginning of 1841, when a delegate conference of Chartist Churches was held in Glasgow. In more than 30 localities, Chartist services of worship were regularly conducted, and 'a Chartist place of worship is now to be found on the Lord's Day in almost every town of note from Aberdeen to Ayr'.[1]

Yet even in the most flourishing years, the seeds of disintegration of the movement were always visible. The Glasgow leaders of the Universal Suffrage Central Committee never succeeded in obtaining adequate financial backing for their projects. While faithfully supported with funds and encouragement by a handful of associations, their best ideas never managed to arouse as much interest in Scotland as schemes connected with the name of O'Connor.

One of the best indices of the real strength of Chartist organisation in Scotland was to be found in the fluctuating fortune of the Chartist newspaper press. In the early days of the movement, organisational strength lagged far behind the superficial strength of the movement, and again, in the latter phases of the agitation, considerably more importance was generally credited to the movement than could be justified by its comparatively weak internal organisation. In the latter period, it was often claimed that elaborate organisation was no longer required to convert the working classes of Scotland to the principles of the Charter. Nevertheless, it seems clear that the heyday of the Scottish movement coincided with the period in which the Chartist publications enjoyed a wide circulation — a period which was heralded by the publication of the *Scottish Patriot* in July 1839, and which was ended exactly three years later by the demise of the *Chartist Circular*.

By then the major sections of the Chartist press had disappeared. The *True Scotsman* had ceased publication in March 1841, the *Scottish Patriot* in December 1841 and the *Perthshire Chronicle* in April 1842. The *Chartist Circular* itself had been meeting with increasing difficulties, through declining circulation and agents' debts, for at least nine months before it ended.

The year 1842 was an unhappy one for the Scottish movement. Industrial depression ruined its finances, and O'Connor gained an ascendancy which destroyed the influence of the most capable of the Glasgow leaders. The plans of the third Scottish Convention for a further reorganisation of the Scottish movement were destroyed

[1] *Northern Star*, 16 Jan. 1841.

by O'Connor's private war on the 'Saints' of the 'Glasgow Chartist Synod', and their despair of uniting an O'Connorite movement with a Sturgeite middle-class movement. These internal disputes over questions of leadership and policy and fruitless declarations of war against all other popular movements brought inevitable disruption to a movement within whose ranks were numbered 'repealers and anti-repealers, Anti-Poor Law men and Malthusians, O'Connorites, O'Brienites, Cobbettites, Churchmen, Dissenters and no-Church-at-all men, and others . . . differing in their views of political economy, morals and religion wide as the poles asunder'.[1]

During the early years of this heterogeneous Scottish movement, its strength had lain in the tolerance allowed to its members on all questions apart from the fundamental principles of the Charter. To it, the Glasgow leaders had imparted an enthusiasm for organisation, for the development of educational and propagandist services, for the teaching of self-reform and self-improvement as the source of social and political improvement — and their almost complete confidence in the efficacy of non-violent means of agitation. Demonstrations of physical strength, such as had been employed by the Whigs and Radicals of 1831–2, were considered both permissible and desirable. But even if the carrying of demonstration of physical power to the brink of civil war might be a justifiable method of preventing revolution, there was never any intention among the Glasgow Chartists to approach anywhere near that limit. For them wisdom, vigour, perseverance and the employment of constitutional and peaceful means were the essential basis of a successful agitation; and it was probably in the ability of the Glasgow Chartists to regard the movement as a long-term affair, and to build a tradition of loyalty to the basic principles of radicalism that their chief contribution lay.

Even after 1842, Glasgow remained one of the strongholds of the Chartist movement, but it could hardly claim to be the centre of a national agitation, for the Scottish movement had virtually disappeared. The older leaders faded into the background but others always emerged to fill their places, often to spend most of their energy fighting their former colleagues who had transferred their allegiance to the Complete Suffrage movement. Anxious committee meetings were still held, but membership and the scale of activities

[1] *Northern Star*, 26 Feb. 1842.

were sadly reduced. The older members were increasingly found
to be reminiscing about the early period — the 'Golden Years of
Chartism'.

The years 1839–42 had been ones of remarkable achievement on
the part of the Glasgow Chartists. They had suffered many disappointments and failures in these years, but several of their projects
for the expansion and strengthening of the Chartist cause had succeeded far beyond their initial expectations. Perhaps the main
reason for the continuing strength of the Chartist party in Glasgow
lay in the nature of the local leadership, for into the Glasgow agitation was drawn a remarkable number of capable, intelligent and
relatively unambitious men. Few, if any of them, were inspiring or
outstanding leaders. Each had his own constructive individual idea
to contribute to their assortment of projects but none was capable
of attracting to himself a large band of devoted followers. Rather
they were a group of reliable lieutenants, shrewd and self-reliant,
yet patient, co-operative and zealous, who were capable of mobilising the rank and file of the movement in sustained support of broad
decisions taken at a national level.

IV

Amongst this band of Glasgow lieutenants, none had more
stamina and less imagination than James Moir, a prosperous tea-
merchant, who, throughout almost the entire period of the Chartist
agitation, stood out stolidly as the figurehead of Glasgow Chartism.[1]
Despite his lack of constructive ideas and a strong tendency towards pomposity, the esteem in which this Glasgow 'shopocrat' was
long held was not altogether misplaced, for Moir had a keen sense
for the feeling of the majority, and a political conscience which invariably instructed him to support that feeling. Not less important
were his considerable fund of common-sense and his widely
respected kindliness and sincerity.

Moir's political career falls into three fairly well-defined sections. In the first period 1831–8, he made his appearance on the
political stage as a zealous and self-effacing member of a clique of

---

[1] *James Moir* (1806–80) served an apprenticeship in the Glasgow Political
Union during the Reform Agitation in 1831 and remained prominent in Glasgow
politics for the rest of his life. [He was elected to the City Council in 1848, and,
except for 1865–8, he always held a seat on the council. In 1867 he was president
of the Scottish National Reform League. In later years he became a baillie and a
J.P.]

Liberal Reformers who decided to take in hand the reformation and direction of the municipal affairs of Glasgow. After a partially successful search for respectability and prestige in local politics, James Moir was drawn gradually into the camp of the advanced Radicals in 1838 — partly under the influence of a few esteemed colleagues, but largely in pursuit of a more widespread popular acclaim than he had yet tasted.

Then, in 1839, in the absence of any outstanding personality in the Glasgow movement, and largely due to his middle-class status and respectability, the mediocre Moir blossomed forth as the leader of the Chartists. At the 1839 General Convention, and at several later national conferences Moir was the delegate from Glasgow. A mild O'Connorite, he acted as the censor of the Glasgow movement and denounced all deviations unless sanctioned by O'Connor. Eventually he quarrelled with O'Connor on the question of Chartist participation in local government and opposed the National Charter Association.

The final stage in his career began at the end of 1848 when he achieved a fourteen-year-old ambition by defeating the ex-Lord Provost and M.P. for the city, Alexander Hastie, in the City Council elections. This heralded a period in which Moir became known as a somewhat eccentric councillor and baillie.

While the Glasgow Chartists looked to Moir as the figure-head of their party, it was to William Pattison that they looked for constructive ideas. At the time of the inquiry into the activities of trade unions and combinations of workmen in 1838, Pattison was secretary of the Glasgow United Trades. He was a steam-engine maker — a highly paid operative who could maintain his family in comfort, and a holder of the franchise since 1832. This trade-union secretary, with his strong belief in the value of organisation, became the main force behind the moves for strengthening Chartist organisation in Glasgow, Lanarkshire and Scotland in 1839 and 1840, and he was one of the strongest influences against the subservience of the Scottish movement to O'Connor's wishes.

Pattison was well imbued with those qualities which were supposed to characterise the Scottish working-classes of the nineteenth century. He was prudent and zealous, reliable, self-reliant and self-assured. He lacked neither determination nor energy, and he was of a sufficiently independent nature to wish to make decisions on what he regarded as the merits of each question — even if such decisions were unpopular and against the tide of Chartist opinion. A powerful speaker with a strong sense of humour, he prided himself on always being frank and outspoken and believed that nothing was to be gained by abuse of opponents. Violent language and violent measures could never do any good to their cause. No sacred month, nor any bloody insurrection was necessary, but merely a rigorous dissemination of Chartist principles. This could best be done by frequent orderly public meetings, and by the distribution and sale of political tracts. 'That mighty engine, the press' must be put into full operation in the work of instructing the people and convincing the middle classes of the justice of the people's claims. The success of Chartism would depend largely on middle-class aid, but even by themselves the working classes could do much to increase their power and influence in the community. Education, by means of published propaganda, well-organised associations, and the employment of talented lecturers, was the basis of a sound agitation. The model Chartist was William Lovett.

In pursuit of his object of winning over public opinion to the Chartist cause, Pattison was a fruitful source of constructive advice. Various projects, including a weekly Chartist circular, a Chartist Joint-Stock Printing Press, a Chartist and Tradesman's Hall, and Universal Suffrage Trades Union Associations to be combined within a Universal Suffrage Association were produced by him. The plan for the contemplated trades associations was approved in September 1839, but was eventually abandoned in December 1839 in favour of a further plan of Pattison for organising Lanarkshire on a uniform basis of district associations.[1]

Much of the work of the new organisation overlapped with that of the Universal Suffrage Central Committee for Scotland and the two bodies were hardly distinguishable. Both committees drew nearly all their members from Glasgow and its immediate vicinity, and though only four of the twenty directors of the Lanarkshire Association were members of the Central Committee, they were always in close liaison and their discussions were always coloured with a Glasgow outlook. The old district associations retained their previous identity, and the Glasgow trades participated no more actively than before. The U.S.A. was successful, however, in providing the Chartists of Glasgow and its surrounding villages with a centralised system of information so that any decision reached in

[1] *Scottish Patriot*, 21 Sept., 7, 21 Dec. 1839, 18 Jan. 1840.

the centre could be known in virtually every workshop and factory throughout the city and the surrounding region within two or three hours. This proved to be a most efficient weapon in the hands of the Chartists in their dealings with other organisations, compelling them to concur in Chartist demands, or at least to treat these demands with respect at their public meetings.

Another creation of Pattison, although this time an indirect one, was the Glasgow Democratic Club. This was formed in December 1839 as the rallying ground of disquieted Republicans and O'Connorites who were impatient with the tactics of the Universal Suffrage Central Committee, and it was a direct consequence of a squabble between Pattison and Thomas Gillespie, a former secretary of the Glasgow Universal Suffrage Association. Ostensibly the quarrel was fought out on the issue of petitioning, but for some time Gillespie had opposed most of Pattison's projects. Circumstances, including the difficulty of finding employment which would enable him to attend committee meetings, were forcing him to play a much less active part in the movement after the summer of 1839 than he had been accustomed to play, and he appeared to be rather resentful of the dominant rôle which Pattison had assumed in Glasgow.

For Pattison it was imperative that the Scottish Chartists should retain the character of a petitioning body. Only in such a way could they legally keep alive their agitation. When Pattison invited the Central Committee, on 7 November 1839, to declare its intention to petition again, he was supported by Moir, Matthew Cullen and James Proudfoot.[1] Gillespie, however, argued that the Central Committee was recommending measures before consulting the rest of the country on whether or not these were acceptable. Many Chartists were sick of petitioning and there was danger of causing schisms over such a recommendation.[2]

This wrangle over petitioning continued throughout November, December and January. Gillespie's services to the movement had

---

[1] Matthew Cullen was a power-loom dresser, and served as joint chairman of the Universal Suffrage Central Committee, 1839–40, and vice-president, 1840–2. He was a lay Chartist preacher and advocate of Total Abstinence. From 1843 to 1866 he was regarded as the spokesman of the working classes at public meetings for political reform, trade-union matters, co-operation, Poor Law reforms, public baths and slave emancipation. James Proudfoot was a grain dealer who emigrated to America in 1844. He was president of the Glasgow Universal Suffrage Association 1838–40, and a member of the Universal Suffrage Central Committee for Scotland 1839–42, being its president from 1840–2.

[2] Scottish Patriot, 9 Nov. 1839.

been considerable and he had many sympathisers both inside and outside Glasgow.[1] The outcome of the quarrel was the formation of the Glasgow Democratic Club by Gillespie's associates, led by Allan Pinkerton, who withdrew from the Glasgow Universal Suffrage Association, complaining of the failure of the Central Committee to consult England.[2] This provoked Pattison to demand why they should consult England. After all, England had never consulted Scotland before deciding important moves. In any case, whom could they consult in England? Was there any Central Committee, or Convention, or any large properly organised district with which they could communicate?

The new Democratic Club began its activities by inviting Harney to lecture in Glasgow — an invitation which was hardly calculated to quell the bickering of the two factions. Rumours were aired that Harney was a spy in the pay of Lord John Russell and the Glasgow Universal Suffrage Association promptly advertised in the Glasgow newspapers disclaiming any connexion with him. Pattison told Harney that he would have had to wait fifty years in Northumberland before he (Pattison) would have consented to invite him to Glasgow, but both Pattison and his colleagues were surprised by the mild tone of Harney's speeches, and there was no further abuse of him after this date.[3] Pattison and the Glasgow leaders continued to show considerable reserve both towards Harney and most of the English Chartist tourists who began to find a market for their lectures in Scotland; but Harney himself went cheerfully on his way through the West of Scotland praising the work of the Central Committee.[4]

The *Chartist Circular* which maintained a circulation of 22,500 per week during its first year, and which ran for almost three years was perhaps the most spectacular success of Pattison's schemes.

[1] *Scottish Patriot*, 23 Nov. 1839. Outside Glasgow Gillespie was strongly supported by the Renfrewshire Political Union and the Aberdeen W.M.A. (*Scottish Patriot*, 21 Dec. 1839; 4 Jan. 1840.)

[2] *Scottish Patriot*, 7 Dec. 1839. Allan Pinkerton (1819–84) emigrated to the United States in 1842, where he founded the famous Pinkerton detective and strike-breaking agency. During the Civil War he was Abraham Lincoln's bodyguard.

[3] *Scottish Patriot*, 1 Feb. 1840.

[4] In June, the Lanarkshire Universal Suffrage Association advertised that they had no connection with the Democratic Club and its President, Harney. They further intimated to Branch Associations that they in no wise countenanced itinerant lecturers agitating the country upon their own account, the services of all lecturers sent by them being either gratuitous or paid by a regular salary out of the funds of the association. (*Scottish Patriot*, 20 June 1840.)

Based on the Anti-Corn Law Circular it provided a four-page folio paper selling at a halfpenny. It not only spread the gospel of Chartism, but produced confidence in the central organisation which enabled that predominantly Glaswegian body to maintain a degree of unity in the Scottish movement.

The success of the *Chartist Circular* was primarily due to the abilities of William Thomson of Westmuir, the most modest and self-effacing of the Scottish leaders. Shepherd, handloom weaver, trade-unionist, co-operator and editor, Thomson was a fine example of the talent to be found amongst the working classes of Scotland.[1] Although he normally remained inconspicuously in the background, Thomson was one of the most important of the Chartist leaders. From the inception of the Universal Suffrage Central Committee for Scotland, in August 1839, until six months after its demise in January 1842, Thomson remained General Secretary of the Scottish Chartists. From September 1839 to July 1842, he was also editor of the *Chartist Circular*.

Little space is required to record Thomson's Chartist activities. Except for a number of meetings in Lanarkshire in the first half of 1840, Thomson undertook few engagements outside his regular duties. He declined to be sent to conferences or demonstrations in England; and even in debates within the Central Committee he took little part. Unless directly referred to, he seldom expressed his own opinions. His routine duties as editor and secretary were quietly and efficiently performed, and at no time was there any question of replacing him in these offices.

The policy of the *Chartist Circular* towards the internal politics of the movement reflected the character of its chief progenitor, W. C. Pattison, and of its almost anonymous editor. The *Chartist Circular* was never allowed to become a vehicle for sectarian dogmas and it constantly emphasised the importance of tolerating differences on minor issues in order to preserve the unity of the movement on the major issue of universal suffrage. 'If any man will

[1] Thomson had been the Secretary of the General Protecting Union of the Handloom Weavers of Scotland, and editor of the *Weavers' Journal* from October 1835 to April 1837. Later he was connected with Dr Taylor's *New Liberator*. In earlier years he had been known in the West of Scotland as the advocate of co-operation, and the founder of economical societies. In this field he had been responsible for the establishment of about 70 victualling societies operating on co-operative principles. He argued strongly against the principle of dividend on purchases; *Glasgow Argus*, 24 July 1834; *Weavers' Journal*, 2 May 1836; *Scottish Patriot*, 1 Aug., 21 Nov. 1840.

join us for the one great point (Universal Suffrage) we will gladly receive his help, nor will we frighten him away by insisting that he shall agree with us on all other points.'[1]

Foremost among the features which characterised the *Chartist Circular* were the constant exposition of the basic principles of Chartism and the extolling of such historic advocates of universal suffrage and annual parliaments as the Duke of Richmond, Major Cartwright and the 'political martyrs' of 1793–4. There were essays on the ballot (by Dr John Taylor), on the middle classes, on Household Suffrage and the relationship between the Chartist and corn law repeal movements. From December 1841 to June 1842 there was a constant series of leading articles on Complete Suffrage, copied from the *Nonconformist*. The views of Bronterre O'Brien on such questions as 'Can Reform be obtained without Revolution?', were given considerable space; and the 'Means of effecting a Bloodless Revolution' was a frequent topic. There were also articles expounding the plans of Lovett and Collins for educational and moral reform, and considerable attention was paid throughout to questions of Chartist churches and schools, a 'National System of Education', the need for the 'Emancipation of Women' and Temperance Reform. Comparisons of British institutions with those of the Republican United States of America and even of France were favourite items. Such articles were supplemented by tales of George Washington, Kosciusko, William Tell and other heroes of liberty among whom were included William Wallace, Robert Bruce, John Knox and even Kings James I and V.

Of the other Glasgow Chartist publications, by far the most important was the *Scottish Patriot*. This weekly paper was founded in July 1839 'to fill the need for a national journal advocating sound radical principles'. It reflected the desire of the Glasgow leaders to bind the Scottish Chartists into a more coherent and organised movement, but it was chiefly the consequence of the dissatisfaction of the Glasgow Chartists with the reporting of their activities and plans in the *Northern Star* and the *True Scotsman*. To some extent it was also a protest against what it considered the tendency of the *True Scotsman* to incite division within the ranks of the Scottish Chartists.[2]

[1] *Chartist Circular*, 6 Nov. 1841.
[2] The *True Scotsman* was published in Edinburgh from 20 Oct. 1838 to 27 Mar. 1841. In its first year it maintained a substantial circulation, but after December 1839 it was constantly struggling to arrest a steady decline in

The *Scottish Patriot* was owned, printed and edited by Robert Malcolm, editor of the half-Chartist *Scots Times*, who was guaranteed against financial loss in the *Patriot's* first year by the sponsors, the delegates of the Trades (Unions) and the directors of the Glasgow Universal Suffrage Association.[1] It was designed to appeal not merely to Chartists but also to a wide range of middle-class reformers. Its first declaration of policy on 6 July 1839 comprehended a vast field of political, social and economic reform. A fifteen-point programme included not merely the enactment of the Charter and reform of the House of Lords, but also free trade and the abolition of the Corn Laws, currency changes, reduction of military and naval expenditures, reform of the Post Office and of corporations, and a long list of educational and legal reforms including the abolition of capital punishment and reform of the Poor Laws.

In May 1838, Malcolm had espoused the cause of the Birmingham Radicals, but his *Scots Times* had never been considered as a Chartist paper by the local Chartists. He himself was regarded rather as 'an honest reformer, a liberal shrewd politician . . . a scholar and a gentleman'.[2]

His editorial columns in the *Scottish Patriot* epitomised many of the best features of the Glasgow movement, its patient determination to convert public opinion to its cause, its zeal for social reform, and its passion for truth and justice. Malcolm's language was sober, and his outlook displayed a remarkable equanimity and a perennial optimism. 'Nothing stands the test of abuse and ridicule better than sound principle,' declared Malcolm, who like Thomson of the *Chartist Circular* and unlike John Fraser of the *True Scotsman* appeared desirous of remaining in the background of the movement. His policy seemed to be to reflect the opinions of the majority of the Glasgow leaders, but to ignore as far as possible all internal Chartist squabbles.

This approach to local politics resulted in the *Glasgow Patriot* being rudely assailed in the columns of the *True Scotsman* for the 'lack of independence' of its editor, for his 'equivocal' position

---

circulation, and to overcome financial difficulties. Its circulation fell from 2,500 copies per week in the first quarter of 1839 to about 500 per week in the first quarter of 1841. It came back to life in March or April 1842, and continued to exist for about 15 months with a circulation averaging 350 to 400 copies per week.

[1] *Robert Malcolm* (1781–1850) was a bookseller and printer who had a love of literature and a taste for denunciation of local government corruption.

[2] *Chartist Circular*, 11 Dec. 1841.

between Whigs and Chartists, for his 'neglect' of teetotalism, and above all for his 'toleration' of 'physical force Chartists' within the movement. On occasion, the *Scottish Patriot* was enlivened by spirited rejoinders to such attacks, and fresh wrath was kindled when it called its rival an 'anomalous paper' and Fraser a 'Political and Medical Quack'. Normally, however, the *Scottish Patriot* forbore from following the example of the *True Scotsman*.[1]

The accusations of the *True Scotsman* that the *Scottish Patriot* was over-indulgent of physical force were hardly fair. Dr John Taylor, O'Connor, Dr McDouall and even Harney were all treated with scrupulous respect, but the tone of the paper was always one of peaceful social revolution and gradual reform. It encouraged the Glasgow Chartists in their work of organising the movement on a petitioning basis, and in their promotion of Chartist Churches and schools. Despite its desire to see the Corn Laws abolished, it maintained a critical attitude towards the Anti-Corn Law League and the supporters of Household Suffrage, but it persisted in its hopes of an eventual alliance between the Chartists and repealers on the basis of both universal suffrage and repeal.

On 11 November 1840, the Universal Suffrage Central Committee for Scotland decided to form a joint-stock company to purchase the *Scottish Patriot*. A capital of £1,000 was to be subscribed in £1 shares, payable in monthly instalments of 2s.[2] The scheme was backed by Moir, Proudfoot, W. S. Currie, J. D. Rodger and Thomson,[3] but its chief promoter once again appears to have been William Pattison who campaigned for its support in Glasgow and neighbourhood. Despite only slight evidence of Chartist support, the scheme seems to have had some degree of success, for out of it grew the National Printing and Publishing Company of Scotland, which survived for several years.[4]

---

[1] *Scottish Patriot*, 17 Oct. 1840; *True Scotsman*, 21 Sept. 1839 and throughout October, November and December of that year.

[2] *Scottish Patriot*, 2 Jan. 1841.

[3] Walter Smith Currie was secretary of the Gorbals Universal Suffrage Association. He was a middle-aged bookseller and stationer in Nelson Street, and one of the most humorous of the Chartist speakers and poets. John P. Rodger was a well-paid operative who had been a member of a Glasgow Anti-Corn Law Committee in 1836. He was president of the Bridgton Radical Association from 1838 to 1839; a director of the Glasgow U.S.A. 1838–9; and a member of the Universal Suffrage Central Committee for Scotland from 1839 to 1842. In 1842, he became secretary of the Glasgow Complete Suffrage Association, and in February 1843 he sued Moir for £500 damages for alleged defamation of character.

[4] Among its publications was the *Practical Mechanic and Engineers' Magazine* edited by W. C. Pattison. (*Glasgow Saturday Post*, 19 Dec. 1846.)

Until April 1841, at least, Robert Malcolm's direction of the *Scottish Patriot* seems to have been maintained, for the tone and style of the paper remained the same as before. In January it had announced that it was being run at a 'heavy loss', but by February its circulation was maintained at what should have been a satisfactory figure, about 1,200 copies per week.[1] When O'Connor toured Scotland in October 1841, he paid a 'high eulogium' to the *Scottish Patriot* which he advised Scotsmen to read in preference to his own *Northern Star*, but when he returned to Glasgow two months later, to pay another 'high eulogium' to the paper, it was defunct, and suggestions were being made that it should be replaced by a *Scottish Star* edited by Bronterre O'Brien.[2]

Robert Malcolm employed as a reporter for his papers his nephew Robert Malcolm jnr. who had been educated as a medical student but who soon developed a taste for politics and literature. In the *Scots Times* he wrote clerical sketches, caricaturing fanatical clergymen and describing Glasgow Churches and churchyards. But his heart was in Chartist meetings which he reported for the *Scottish Patriot*, and in which he participated in a hot-headed and impulsive fashion.

He shared little of his uncle's tact and caution and none of his aversion for the public platform. He became well known as a member of the committees of the Glasgow Universal Suffrage Association and the Universal Suffrage Central Committee for Scotland. In the Lanarkshire Universal Suffrage Association, he became one of the leading platform speakers, and despite his hot-headedness, one of the moderates who deprecated extremists of all kinds. With Pattison and Arthur O'Neill,[3] he had a strong sympathy with the Corn Law repeal movement, and with Joseph Hume and the Parliamentary Radicals. His desire to avoid all language offensive to the middle classes meant that he lost popularity and suffered abuse at the hands of the increasingly aggressive O'Connorites.[4]

---

[1] The sale of newspaper stamps to the *Scottish Patriot* fell from 8,000 (which was exceptionally high) in November 1840, to 3,000 in January 1841. Its circulation had been good throughout 1840 and it is difficult to see how it could have been running at a 'heavy loss' — unless its agents were heavily in debt to it. Its half-brother, the *Scots Times* was then in the last stages of its decline, and Malcolm may have been losing money on the two papers taken together.

[2] *Northern Star*, 16 Oct. 1841, 29 Jan. 1842; *Scotsman*, 12 Jan. 1842.

[3] See below pp. 273-7.

[4] *Scottish Patriot*, 27 Mar. 1841; *Northern Star* 27 Mar., 25 May, 12 June 1841.

By January 1842 Malcolm was sufficiently back in favour to be appointed secretary to the third Scottish Convention; but within a month he was being hissed down at public meetings by the O'Connorite Chartists for moving amendments for 'full, free and fair representation' instead of the more familiar Chartist formula.[1] Along with Pattison, Malcolm McFarlane, James Hoey and John Rodger[2] he was one of the leading Chartists who joined the Sturgeite movement, and for several years he was a leading member of the Glasgow Complete Suffrage Association, strongly opposing any reconciliation with the O'Connorites so long as they persisted in their 'folly' of interfering with 'public meetings for similar causes'.[3]

Besides Robert Malcolm jnr. other capable young men among the Glasgow Chartists were Arthur O'Neill and Samuel Kydd. Kydd was a young shoemaker, whose exuberance and energy quickly established him as one of the most ardent O'Connorites, and one of the most effective lecturers of the Glasgow Charter Association in 1842. He emerged, however, when Glasgow Chartism was already in decline, and apart from a few weeks in 1845, when the Glasgow Chartists appointed him as their Scottish missionary, he was soon lost to the Glasgow movement.[4]

Arthur George O'Neill appeared on the Chartist stage about the

---

[1] *Northern Star*, 29 Jan., 26 Feb. 1842; *Chartist Circular*, 29 Jan. 1842.

[2] Malcolm McFarlane was a skilled cabinetmaker, a prosperous trade-unionist with a Benthamite zeal for the 'moral and physical elevation of the working classes'. In 1839, he was vice-president of the Glasgow Universal Suffrage Association, and in 1842 vice-president of the Glasgow Complete Suffrage Association. He was one of the most level-headed of the Glasgow Chartists and one of the most popular of the Chartist preachers. James Hoey was president of the Gorbals Universal Suffrage Association from 1838 to 1840, and was one of the strongest advocates of Total Abstinence.

[3] *The Nonconformist*, 30 Aug. 1842; *Northern Star*, 29 Aug. 1842, 15 Apr. 1843; *Glasgow Saturday Post*, 2 Sept., 29 Nov. 1843. After the demise of the *Scottish Patriot* Malcolm was employed by the Liberal *Glasgow Chronicle* and the Radical *Glasgow Saturday Post*. In 1844 he emerged as one of the champions of Repeal of the Union with Ireland. Amongst the Repealers he gave lectures on 'Teetotal Principles' and on questions of education and morals. He became a valued adviser of the Glasgow Repealers, who made him a presentation for his services in 1845. See *Glasgow Saturday Post*, 26, 30 Oct., 28 Dec. 1844, 18 Jan. 1845; *Glasgow Examiner*, 15 June 1844.

[4] *Northern Star*, 23 Oct., 17 Dec. 1842, 31 May 1845. Kydd soon forsook his shoemaking trade for law studies, and for the Chartist and factory movement agitations. In 1848 and 1849 he was the mainstay of the National Charter Association and the National Land Company. Later he became private secretary to Richard Oastler, and under the pseudonym 'Alfred' he published in 1857, a *History of the Factory Movement*. (See above, p. 11.) Several years later he realised his ambition to be called to the bar. *Northern Star*, 6 Jan., 19 May, 27 Oct. 1849; *Newcastle Weekly Chronicle*, 23 Aug. 1879.

time of the first Scottish Convention in Glasgow, and it was h
more than any of his colleagues who was responsible for the sprea
of the Christian Chartist movement in Scotland and, after 1840, i
England. Half-Scots and half-Irish, O'Neill was becoming know
at the age of twenty-one as a perambulating encyclopaedia used b
Working Men's Associations and scientific institutions. He ha
been a university student with a wide range of interests including
theology, physics and physiology, and, in 1839, his scientific ap
proach was spilling over into politics with lectures on 'Civi
Government, scientifically considered'. It was apparently by suck
adult educational engagements that O'Neill earned a living.[1]

At the Scottish Convention of 1839 O'Neill played little part in
the proceedings, but he was sufficiently well known to be elected a
member of the Universal Suffrage Central Committee for Scotland. On that Committee, O'Neill took little part in policy debates, but concerned himself most actively in the propagandist
work of the organisation. He was another strong believer in the
need for educating and organising public opinion in support
of the principles of the Charter, and he evinced great zeal in
missionary work in central and western Scotland during the autumn
of 1839.

The introduction, at that time, of Chartist Sabbath services
brought a great demand for the services of O'Neill, who quickly
became the most energetic and popular of the Chartist lay preachers.
When he preached in Glasgow on 13 October 1839, the Universal
Suffrage Hall was 'packed to suffocation', and hundreds were
refused admission. At Campsie, a fortnight later, he preached the
first Chartist sermon to be heard there. The hall was crowded to
excess; 'a large proportion of the fair sex' was present and 'the
neighbouring village of Milton was almost completely forsaken'.
'Chartist congregations, to become general in every corner of the
land,' declared O'Neill, required only 'Chartist preachers, men
who would tell the truth and the whole truth, and who would not
scruple to raise their voices against any vice, whether in Church or
State — rejoicing that such a spirit of inquiry and discontent
should be spreading through the masses.'[2]

When the Lanarkshire Universal Suffrage Association was
formed in January 1840, Arthur O'Neill was appointed as its first
full-time paid missionary. During the week, he would be engaged

[1] *Scottish Patriot*, 6 July 1839.   [2] *Ibid.*, 9 Nov. 1839.

in forming branch associations throughout the country, and, on Sundays, he would preach to Chartist congregations. For several weeks he held meetings almost every day, but he soon found that outside the larger towns and villages Chartism was not so flourishing as was generally believed. In some places, he found that the Chartist agitation had never been heard of, while in others his hosts were often unable to arrange meetings for him, because they could not obtain the use of the local schoolhouse or the Church Hall, or because they could not overcome the influence and opposition of the ironmasters and mill-owners.

At Shotts Iron works, which he visited several times, the masters threatened to take drastic action against the Chartists. At Blantyre a mill proprietor intervened at O'Neill's meeting to intimidate the weavers. In Carmunnock there was not a single Chartist when O'Neill arrived in the village, and in Lanark and Cambuslang he had several disappointments before meetings and committees were successfully organised. In one or two places which had been organised in 1838 or 1839, O'Neill found deadly apathy. His perseverance, however, enabled him to raise a crop of small branches — often with the help of the village shoemaker, often as the result of crowded meetings in buts-an'-bens, sometimes held at breakfast hour.[1]

Always optimistic about the prospects of Chartism, O'Neill was never complacently blind to the weaknesses of the Chartist organisation and the mistakes of its leaders. From his tour of central Scotland in November 1839, he reported that the cause was 'not making a great noise', though it was progressing 'much more surely than at any past period of its existence'. The *Chartist Circular* was doing 'immense good', and the resolutions of the Central Committee were 'cordially approved of'. On one subject, however, he had been invariably opposed, and had been forced to change his opinions, 'being completely converted to the side of those who consider that the Corn Law Agitation is doing our cause much good, and that . . . it has already done much injury to our cause . . . to oppose them publicly.'[2]

O'Neill's aim was to make earth 'as like heaven as possible'. For this end, he strongly advocated, at his meetings, various kinds of self-help activities by working men, such as the promotion of temperance and co-operative retail societies. Sobriety, respectability

[1] *Ibid.*, 29 Feb. 1840.　　　　　　[2] *Ibid.*, 9 Nov. 1839.

and intelligence, he preached to his fellow non-electors, were qualities 'absolutely necessary to the recovery of Universal Suffrage'. Above all he wished to secure unity amongst the Chartists. The question of the hypothetical use of physical force ought not to be constantly raised by the moral force men. They should always remember how much they held in common, and should avoid discussion on matters which inevitably caused disunity. O'Neill's zeal in agitation of Christian Chartism and temperance, and his undoubted sincerity, earned him the respect of all factions of the Scottish movement — a respect enjoyed by few other Chartist leaders.[1]

O'Neill seldom intervened in any of the more important meetings in Glasgow, but his services to the Lanarkshire Universal Suffrage Association were recognised in June 1840, when in preference to Moir and other Glasgow leaders he was appointed as a delegate to the Birmingham demonstration to celebrate the release from prison of Collins and Lovett; O'Neill regarded this demonstration as an opportunity to reunite the Chartists of England and Scotland. 'No other time', he wrote to the *Northern Star*, 'would be more favourable to the achievement of a fellow feeling between the two countries.'[2]

At the Birmingham demonstration on 27 July 1840, O'Neill was regarded as the chief spokesman of the Scottish delegates. In his speeches, he chose to emphasise the necessity of effecting a union between the middle and working-class supporters of reform. His fellow countrymen, he declared, would not despair of winning over the middle classes. He was then appointed secretary of the Delegate Conference held to discuss the plan of national organisation submitted from the Chartist conference in Manchester earlier in the month. About this plan he waxed enthusiastic and seconded the resolution which proposed the establishment of a National Association; but on his return to Glasgow O'Neill found that warm approbation of his conduct at Birmingham was qualified by caution over the promotion of a national Chartist organisation of dubious legality. Nor could O'Neill find any support for his proposal to organise another great National Petition; and throughout the autumn of 1840 his main activities lay in missionary work in the

[1] *Ibid.*, 12 Sept., 28 Nov. 1840; *True Scotsman*, 21 Nov., 12 Dec. 1840.
[2] *True Scotsman*, 11 July 1840; *Northern Star*, 11 July 1840; *Scottish Patriot*, 25 July 1840.

West of Scotland, lecturing on metaphysics as well as on the progress of Chartism and temperance.[1]

Thereafter O'Neill disappeared from the Scottish scene. A
friendship which had developed between him and Collins, who had
been deeply impressed by O'Neill's manner, opinions and ability at
the Birmingham conference, resulted in O'Neill being invited to
deliver a series of lectures and sermons at the opening of the
Christian Chartist Church in Newhall Street, Birmingham.[2] On his
arrival in Birmingham a deputation of Midland Chartist delegates
invited him to become their district lecturer. This offer was declined, but O'Neill remained as a pastor of the Christian Chartist
Church and quickly became one of the leading Chartist figures in
the Midlands.[3]

Since Glasgow Chartism remained on a highly organised basis
for a period of over three years, it might be supposed that financial
stability had been achieved. This, however, would be no more
than superficially true. Certainly, money was forthcoming to cover
the expenditure on those projects which were undertaken by
the Central Committee, but this simply meant that they seldom
attempted anything which was obviously beyond their financial
capabilities, and what strength they did enjoy could last only as
long as the prosperity of their shoemaking treasurer, George
Ross.

Throughout the lifetime of the Glasgow U.S.A. (1838–40), the
Lanarkshire U.S.A. (1840–2), the Central Committee for Scotland
(1839–42) and the Glasgow Charter Association (1842–5), Ross
remained the financial backer and benefactor of these organisations.[4]
He was one of the pillars of respectability of the movement, and
while he held responsibility for the finances, no question of mis-
handling funds ever arose. Scrupulous attention was paid to en-
suring not merely that all financial dealings were honest, but also
that they always appeared so. His single-mindedness and sincerity
more than balanced his dullness and lack of imagination, and

[1] *Scottish Patriot*, 1, 22 Aug. 1840.
[2] *Northern Star*, 2 Jan. 1841. In September 1840, Collins had tried to persuade
the second Scottish Convention to send O'Neill to Birmingham to help him
revive the cause there. *Scottish Patriot*, 26 Sept. 1840.
[3] H.O. 40/56, 9, 24, 27, 31 Dec.
[4] George Ross had a well-established boot and shoe business in the Trongate
which he had developed since 1821. He claimed to have been connected with
Radical politics since 1817. In 1837 he was elected a Commissioner on the Police
Board, and in 1846 he was elected a member of the newly-established Parochial
Board. See *Glasgow Saturday Post*, 12 Dec. 1846.

T

earned him the respect of middle-class Radicals as well as o
Chartists.[1]

The only criticism that could be made against Ross was that his
willingness to dip into his own pocket to meet commitments prevented him from ever harshly demanding appropriate contributions from each organised district. Although from time to time
Ross issued warnings of impending financial collapse they were
usually lacking in urgency, and even in favourable conditions few
district associations faced up to their financial obligations.[2] Economic distress may well have been the culminating blow which
ended the work of the Central Committee for Scotland and killed
the *Chartist Circular*, but several large and populous districts never
pulled their weight with financial assistance for the centre, at any
period.[3] Ross was prepared to play the rôle of a paternal statesman
rather than an exacting taskmaster. Had his methods of financing
the movement stimulated zeal in others to emulate his example,
they might have been beneficial. But they did not, and in the virtual
collapse of the movement in 1842, some of the seeds had been sown
by Ross himself.

v

Feargus O'Connor had never lacked enthusiastic supporters in
Scotland. Ever since his visit to Scotland in December 1836,
O'Connor exercised a strong influence over the working-class
Radicals. During the early months of the Chartist agitation in 1838,
O'Connor was eclipsed by the leaders of Birmingham and remained
a secondary figure, but he had endeared himself to large sections of
the working classes by his militancy, his panegyrics on behalf of the
Glasgow Cotton Spinners and his defence of the Rev. J. R.
Stephens.

[1] In 1848 and later years he was often called to the chair at public meetings for
the encouragement of the Parliamentary Radicals and for the expression of sympathy with the oppressed Liberals of Hungary and other Continental countries.
Glasgow Saturday Post, 25 Mar. 1848; *Glasgow Examiner*, 10 June 1848, 22 Apr.
1852; *Northern Star*, 1 Sept. 1849.

[2] *Scottish Patriot*, 4 Nov. 1840. *Chartist Circular*, 18 Sept. 1841, 29 Jan. 1842.
In November 1840 indebtedness to Ross, which had been £126 in May 1840, had
been reduced to £22. By June 1842, however, he was owed £180. In November
1843, this had been reduced to about £60 as a result of dramatic representations
of the 'Trial of Robert Emmett' produced by the Chartists of Greenock and
Glasgow. (*Chartist Circular*, 18 June, 9 July 1842; *Northern Star*, 1, 29 Apr., 13
May, 2 Dec. 1843.

[3] For various extra-local purposes, at least £1,275 was raised by the Scottish
Chartists in the twenty months ending September 1840. During the next fifteen

His position seemed to be strengthened after several Scottish Chartist organisations rescinded 'moral force' resolutions which were carried at a central meeting of Scottish Radical Associations at Calton Hill, Edinburgh on 5 December 1838.[1] The Chartists of Edinburgh were themselves divided on the issue, and in the wave of opposition which mounted O'Connor clearly regarded himself as the presiding genius of the Scottish movement. In his Scottish tours he flattered the Scottish leaders and eulogised their organisational efforts. But apart from John Taylor, there were few Scotsmen whom O'Connor seemed genuinely to trust and respect. He could rely on Moir, Proudfoot and Ross, on all of whom he showered constant praise, but there was never any mutual love between many of the local leaders and O'Connor. Towards men with ideas of their own, he always showed considerable reserve. In particular he seemed distinctly uneasy over their social reformist tendencies, which he found he could not control. Such men were occasionally stigmatised in general terms as 'leaders', but O'Connor found himself forced to withdraw his ban on certain types of agitation such as Christian (or 'Bible') Chartism, because of the appeal which they exercised over the rank and file of the Scottish movement.[2]

Even the most important of the leaders of the Scottish movement were soon made to realise that estrangement from O'Connor might mean leadership without followers. Yet it was not merely fear of suppression which bound local leaders to O'Connor. Probably more important was the element of mutual usefulness, and O'Connor displayed remarkable tact and patience in his dealings with these men. Not only did many of them enjoy adulation in the columns of the *Northern Star*, but the more practical amongst them realised the value which his blessing could confer on their projects, for there was little hope of success for any scheme which required mass support unless it could obtain the approval of the Chief Censor of

---

months, only about £115 was raised. The latter sum was primarily for organisational purposes, while the earlier sum was for a much wider variety of purposes.

[1] W. G. Burns of Dundee clearly stated the case for the 'moderates' at Calton Hill. 'It is very easy to talk of physical force when warming our toes before the fire. Even if we succeeded in wresting our rights from the ruling powers by its means, the demoralising influence of the struggle would disqualify us from enjoying their beneficial influence. . . . Physical force never succeeded in establishing the people's claim for justice. It has only removed one despot to put another in his place,' (Add. MSS. 27,820, f. 345). O'Connor replied that by 'moral force, he did not mean the moral power of the Scotch Philosophers nor their chippings of the Excise and their attacks upon the Teapot,' (*ibid.*, f. 357).

[2] *Northern Star*, 16 Jan., 8 May 1841.

Chartism. Only those who were reckless of the unity of their movement, as well as of their own status within it, could think of flouting O'Connor's authority.

The ascendancy which O'Connor had established over the Chartists of Scotland was well demonstrated in April 1841 by the complete shattering of the 'New Move' of Lovett and Collins, and by the second thoughts of those leaders who had given initial support to the 'New Move'. In Glasgow, Robert Malcolm jnr., and William C. Pattison were the chief victims. On 6 April, Pattison resigned his office of vice-president of the Lanarkshire Universal Suffrage Association, of which he had been the chief architect. On the same day, James Jack resigned from the office of secretary of the association, and his successor, William Brown, was soon able to write to O'Connor that 'such is the testimony of public opinion towards your patriotism that on all public occasions you have been brought forward as the lion of our cause — no meeting concludes here without the name of Feargus O'Connor, coupled with the Charter, receiving three cheers'.[1]

O'Connor was delighted with his Scottish tour in October and November 1841, and with the Scottish people whom he declared he would uphold in all his speeches as 'the stronghold of democracy'. There were many large meetings on Glasgow Green and elsewhere, and several splendid soirées.[2] Only two more months had elapsed before he returned to Scotland; and when the third Scottish Convention assembled in Glasgow on 3 January 1842, he presented his credentials as the representative of Rutherglen and Elderslie. Although O'Connor took little part in the proceedings, he appeared to be as benevolent as usual towards his Scottish colleagues, but from his report on the conference several weeks later, it emerged that he had found little at the Convention with which to be delighted. He had been a most unhappy man at Glasgow, where he had had to contend, 'almost single-handedly', against 'the saints' of the Glasgow Chartist Synod. 'There were ten Glasgow preachers, all Whigs — not a drop of Chartist blood in their veins.'[3]

[1] *Scottish Patriot*, 10 Apr. 1841; *Northern Star*, 22 May 1841. In June 1841 Pattison felt sufficiently strongly about the O'Connorite policy of supporting Tories at the impending General Election, that he caused a minor disruption of the Lanarkshire Universal Suffrage Association on the issue.

[2] *Northern Star*, 16, 23 Oct., 20 Nov. 1841; *Glasgow Chronicle*, 25 Oct., 3, 5 Nov. 1841.

[3] *Chartist Circular*, 29 Jan. 1842; *Northern Star*, 29 Jan. 1842. The Glasgow

Not only had the Convention expressed its disapproval of the National Petition 'proposed by the English Executive Council' on the grounds that it embraced questions of detail, such as the repeal of the Poor Law Amendment Act and of the Act of Union with Ireland, but Pattison, the most heinous sinner of the Synod, had even moved a resolution 'deprecating interference with meetings which had for their object the removal of what he termed "infamous monopolies" — a most rascally resolution — one calculated to hand us over bound neck and heels to the League.'[1]

'Scotchmen,' declared O'Connor, 'should disunion be sown amongst you and should you require my aid, send for me and you shall have a third visit this winter.' A third visit did not prove necessary 'to clip the wings of the rotten leaders of Glasgow'. The seeds of disunion had been effectively sown and within a few weeks there was a fairly clean division between the supporters and opponents of O'Connor. For the latter, the emergence of the Complete Suffrage movement was a most welcome promise that Chartism might yet be able to throw off the tutelage of O'Connor.[2]

Pattison, Thomson, Rodger, McFarlane, Robert Malcolm jnr. and Cullen were amongst those who joined the Complete Suffrage movement. Since the inception of the Glasgow Universal Suffrage Association, they had been active members of almost every important committee and their defection or excommunication led to the demise of the Lanarkshire Universal Suffrage Association.

When Moir, Proudfoot, Ross and Brown[3] attempted to continue the tradition of Glasgow Chartism with the formation of the Glasgow

'saints' to whom O'Connor took objection included Pattison, McEwan, Jack, McFarlane, Rodger, Walker, Hoey, Currie and Chisholm.

[1] *Northern Star*, 29 Jan. 1842.

[2] *Northern Star*, 5, 26 Feb. 1842. O'Connor's Scottish followers required little prompting from the *Northern Star* on the attitude which they should adopt towards Complete Suffragism. This was promptly named 'The Plague', and the 'Complete Suffrage Humbugs' were regarded as being identical in all respects with corn law repealers.

[3] William S. Brown, a compositor, was the secretary of the Lanarkshire U.S.A. in 1841–2. He became secretary of the Glasgow Charter Association, and was well known as a Chartist preacher in Glasgow and the surrounding districts. He and David Harrower established a printing business which did most of the printing work required by the Chartists. In April 1848, they were arrested for printing a placard headed 'Threatened Revolution in London'. Brown emigrated to Boston U.S.A. at the end of 1850, where he was disappointed to find that Universal Suffrage was 'not producing many of the fruits predicted of it in the old country'. (*Northern Star*, 23 July 1841, 24 Sept. 1842, 22 Apr., 1 July, 9 Sept. 1843, 25 May 1844; *Glasgow Saturday Post*, 8, 11 Apr. 1848; *Glasgow Herald*, 14 Apr. 1848; *Glasgow Examiner*, 19 Apr. 1848.

Charter Association in May 1842, the response was disappointing, and despite O'Connor's blessing the lack of executive talent was a serious handicap. The continued adherence to orthodox Chartism of such established figureheads as Moir, Ross and Proudfoot offered little promise of vitality in the new association, but a small group of men emerged whose determination to further the cause of Chartism made up for much of their somewhat colourless and erratic personalities. During the next ebb-tide of Chartism, in the period 1842–5, they still maintained the Glasgow association as one of the strongest in the country.

The most prominent of them was John Colquhoun — 'honest John Colquhoun' as he was always called by O'Connor. For several years he had been well established in the Glasgow movement without achieving notoriety other than as one of the most ponderous of the Chartist speakers. The *Scottish Patriot* reporter knew him well as 'that stubborn speaker against time'.[1]

Colquhoun was one of the most orthodox admirers of O'Connor and had always been in favour of the closest possible association with English Chartist organisation. He was one of the most fervent advocates of systematic Chartist disruption of Anti-Corn Law meetings, and in July 1841 he was one of the Chartist electors who voted Tory. In January 1842, at the Scottish Convention he supported the National Charter Association protest against the Scottish petition, which excluded references to Irish Legislative Union Repeal and to the abolition of the Poor Law Amendment Act.[2]

In 1843, he was the chief organiser of banquets in honour of the Rev. William Hill, Duncombe and O'Connor; and he led the faction which urged union with the National Charter Association. As a member of the Glasgow executive of the N.C.A., he opposed any reconciliation between his group and the Sturgeites which would involve the cessation of Chartist hostility to Anti-Corn Law League meetings. In October 1846, however, he became a member of the local Registration and Election Committee, formed at Moir's instigation against O'Connor's wishes, and thereafter this 'old and tried friend' who had stood by the Chartists 'in the hour of trial' faded from the Chartist platforms.[3]

---

[1] *Scottish Patriot*, 21 Sept. 1839, 10 Oct., 21 Nov. 1840.
[2] *Glasgow Chronicle*, 27 Oct. 1841; *Northern Star*, 16 July, 4 Sept. 1841, 12 Feb., 3 Sept. 1842.
[3] *Northern Star*, 24 Feb., 25 Mar., 15 Apr., 15 July, 9 Sept., 16 Sept. 1843, 17 Oct. 1846.

The President of the Glasgow Charter Association from 1842 to 1844 was Thomas Aucott. Like Moir, Proudfoot, Ross and Colquhoun, Aucott was one of those staunch middle-class Scotsmen for whom O'Connor frequently professed an admiration. Apart from a dogged reluctance to admit defeat, however, Aucott had little to offer the Glasgow movement. If only the people would be true to themselves, ran his constant plea, they would find many of his class ready to struggle with them. Nevertheless, even Aucott was bound to be discouraged by the gradual Chartist decline, and after the failure of the incipient revival in the autumn of 1846, he seems to have abandoned all hope of Chartist success.[1]

His successor as chairman of the Glasgow Charter Association in 1844 was James Smith, who was notable only for provoking a squabble between Dr McDouall and the National Charter Association in January 1845. Seven months earlier, Smith had deplored the continued existence of the Glasgow Charter Association, and sought its dissolution in order to make possible fuller association with the N.C.A. Smith's efforts to link the Chartists of England and Scotland more closely together were then countered by Dr McDouall, who advocated the establishment of separate Charter Unions for England and Scotland. As secretary to the Glasgow branch of the N.C.A., Smith complained to the Executive Committee of the N.C.A., under whose auspices McDouall was supposed to be lecturing. The disclaimer of all responsibility for McDouall's conduct by the N.C.A., its support of Smith's allegations, and its publication of the 'private' correspondence of Smith and McDouall in the *Northern Star* led to all-round recriminations.[2]

Along with Smith, the staunchest supporter of O'Connor and his land scheme, was the venerable Duncan Sherrington. One of the directors of the Glasgow Charter Association, and treasurer of the Glasgow branch of the N.C.A., Sherrington moved the dissolution of the former body, in June 1844, to secure closer co-operation with the English body. In Glasgow, Sherrington was the chief enthusiast for the Chartist Co-operative Land Society, which rekindled something of the old faith in the Chartist cause from 1845 to 1847. In December 1845, Sherrington was sent to the Land

[1] *Northern Star*, 24 Sept., 28 Oct. 1842, 22 Apr. 1843, 24 Oct. 1846; *Glasgow Saturday Post*, 12 Dec. 1846.
[2] *Northern Star*, 25 May, 15 June, 22 Oct., 28 Dec. 1844; 4, 11, 25 Jan., 1 Feb., 10 May 1845.

Conference at Manchester as the delegate from almost all the Scottish branches.[1]

This was the first occasion since 1842 on which a Scottish Chartist delegate had been sent to a conference in England, and it was marked by the election of Sherrington as chairman of the conference. Thereafter for the next five years Sherrington retained his faith in O'Connor and the Land Plan, and was quick to refute all allegations against the feasibility and administration of the scheme.[2]

By far the most colourful personality amongst the later Glasgow Chartists was that of James Adams, who became well known at public meetings in Glasgow as 'Parson' Adams, the Chartist preacher of the Nelson Street Chapel. He became an implacable opponent of O'Connor in 1848, and still led a Chartist rump in 1858.

Adams first became prominent late in 1842, when he was one of the Glasgow Chartist delegates to the Complete Suffrage conference in Birmingham. By 1843, he had established himself at the top of the Chartist hierarchy, where he strongly opposed the efforts of Colquhoun to secure union with the N.C.A. In the same year, Adams chaired meetings of unemployed, proposed resolutions in honour of Hill, Duncombe and O'Connor, and toasted 'Feargus O'Connor, the man of the People'. By January 1845, however, his attitude towards O'Connor had changed, and he was risking his popularity by defending O'Brien and Dr McDouall against O'Connor and the *Northern Star*, which he believed was being used 'to destroy talented Chartists of independent views'.[3]

In the Chartist revival of 1848 Adams emerged as the leading figure in Glasgow. At the Chartist meeting in the City Hall on 24 March, he was elected delegate to the National Convention. Three days later he was cheered by the Irish Repealers for his advocacy of union between the Chartists and Repealers. Petitions, he declared, were of no use, unless there was 'something behind them' which would show the House of Commons that the petition was 'the reflex of something which was not of a praying or petitioning character'. From his earliest days he had been 'a democrat and a

[1] *Northern Star*, 25 May 1844, 10 May, 6, 13 Dec. 1845; *Glasgow Examiner*, 15 June 1844.
[2] *Northern Star*, 16 Feb., 2 Mar. 1850; 30 Aug. 1851.
[3] *Northern Star*, 10, 31 Dec. 1842; 6 Aug., 23 Sept., 2 Dec. 1843; 26 Apr. 1845 *Glasgow Saturday Post*, 18 Jan. 1843; *Glasgow Chronicle*, 24 Feb. 1843.

Repealer', and he was 'now convinced that the period of Ireland's redemption' was at hand.[1]

At the National Convention in London in April, Adams used rather more moderate language, although he carried with him a petition bearing over 100,000 signatures from Glasgow and Lanarkshire. He had not come to compromise their cause, he exclaimed, nor to commit suicide. In Glasgow, he maintained, the middle classes were beginning to co-operate with the Chartists, and there was fraternisation between the Irish and the Chartists.[2]

When the Chartist National Assembly met a month later to discuss the formation of a new national organisation, its members were startled to find Adams leading several of the Scottish delegates in strong objections to the title and financing of the National Charter Association. Adams, who had recently paraded Scotland in company with Ernest Jones and Dr Hunter of Edinburgh as missionaries of the National Convention, quickly turned his objections over the handling of the funds of the N.C.A. into a full-blooded attack on the absent O'Connor. So long as they called themselves the 'Chartist Association', he argued, it would be dubbed 'O'Connor's Association'.

In this, Adams was supported by Alexander Henry and James Shirron of Aberdeen, Henry Rankine of Edinburgh and his Glasgow colleague, Andrew Harley, who all considered O'Connor to be 'a barrier to the power of the democratic party'. Harley declared that in Scotland they had tried to get up a national movement, but they had failed because of the belief that it would be under the control of 'a certain individual who had done all the damage he could to the movement'.[3]

Harley's heresy brought swift retribution from his Glasgow constituents, who disclaimed his authority to 'sow the seeds of dissension by attacking the character of individuals connected with the public cause', and recalled him. Adams, however, was apparently popular enough to escape the 'public indignation' called forth by the attack on O'Connor. He was nominated for election to the National Executive, but had to be content with an appointment as a commissioner for six weeks.[4]

Glasgow was hardly affected by the fit of excitement which seized many parts of the country in June 1848. A demonstration by

[1] *Glasgow Saturday Post*, 25 Mar., 1 Apr. 1848. [2] *Northern Star*, 8 Apr. 1848.
[3] *Northern Star*, 22, 29 Apr., 6 May 1848. [4] *Ibid.*, 13 May 1848.

Chartists and Repealers on Glasgow Green, on 10 June, was described as the 'most signal failure which has occurred in Glasgow
for the last twenty years'. On an exceedingly beautiful day, not
more than 6,000 to 7,000 were reported to have been present —
only as many as would have been called forth on any occasion by a
boat-race or a cricket match. 'There was a good deal of speechifi-
cation,' and 'the same old story' was told once again, but 'the only
thing approaching to strong language . . . was emitted by . . .
Parson Adams who stated that for his own personal convenience,
recreation and amusement, he had joined a society recently instituted in Glasgow for the practice of target shooting, and that the
club intended to purchase their muskets at the wholesale price'.[1]

When O'Connor toured Scotland in October 1848 he was as
usual wildly applauded by his supporters. Yet even O'Connor failed
to rekindle much Chartist enthusiasm. In Aberdeen and Glasgow,
his meetings were notable chiefly for the interventions of Shirron
and Adams, who attempted to expose 'the vile impostor whose un-
principled hypocrisy' had destroyed the National Convention. In
Glasgow, Adams was hissed and groaned at, and denied a hearing.[2]

The same scene was re-enacted on 6 June 1850 when O'Connor
arrived in the City Hall, Glasgow to lecture on the affairs of the
French Republic. 'James (Parson) Adams began to attack O'Connor, and created uproar and confusion.' The chairman withdrew
hoarse, but Adams refused to stand down. 'Poor Feargus sat on the
right side of the chairman, the impersonation of patience and
patriotism.' George Ross was called to the chair, as was usual in
cases of emergency, but even Ross could not persuade Adams to
submit, nor could he persuade the crowd to hear Adams. The meeting was dissolved, and the audience was ushered out by the police,
while O'Connor mounted the table and addressed the tail of the
meeting on the suppression of free speech in France.[3]

By that time little remained of the once formidable network of
Chartist associations. The few organisations which struggled on
to preserve their identity were poorly supported, and often lacked
the assistance of the most influential of their former leaders. By
the criterion of reported membership, the Glasgow 'locality' of the
National Charter Association still remained the strongest in the

[1] *Glasgow Examiner*, 13 June 1848; *Glasgow Herald*, 13 June 1848.
[2] *Scotsman*, 25 Oct. 1848; *Glasgow Examiner*, 28 Oct. 1848.
[3] *Ibid.*, 8 June 1850.

country.[1] But for many years, the Glasgow leaders had been dis-satisfied with their strength, and were constantly thinking up fresh schemes for increasing membership. The last of these took place in the spring of 1851. In March, the N.C.A. branch was reformed with Adams as secretary, and two months later it merged with a rival group under Charles Don. 'Union is Strength,' declared their joint address to the Glasgow Chartists. Henceforward their policy would be 'Measures not Men'.[2]

The Chartist revival of 1851, however, was of the feeblest kind and thereafter Chartist organisation faded away. By 1852, the Glasgow movement had been superseded by, or absorbed into the Parliamentary Reform Association; and in September 1852, James Turner of Thrushgrove was again to be found presiding over a meeting of the Glasgow Reform Association which adopted a programme of household suffrage, triennial parliaments and vote by ballot. The only differences between this and similar meetings in 1833–6 were an accompanying demand for Equal Electoral Dis-tricts and the fact that the 'overflowing meeting' was composed mainly of working classes.[3] The wheel had come full circle, al-though the energies of old Chartists were still applied to social reformist movements of all types. Throughout the 1850's and 1860's Cullen, McFarlane, Adams, McFadyen, McAdam, Hoey, Ross, Moir and many other former Chartist leaders were to be found playing parts in the co-operative and trade-union move-ments, the campaigns for the abolition of capital punishment, the protection of the Sabbath, assisted emigration, temperance, negro emancipation and Scottish Poor Law Reform, and in the organisa-tions to support Italian and Polish independence. The same veterans were always ready to mount the platform whenever there was any whisper of manhood suffrage and parliamentary reform, and several of them played prominent parts in the John Bright reform campaigns of 1858 and 1866.

[1] *English Republic*, October 1851.
[2] *Northern Star*, 15 Mar. 1851; *Glasgow Sentinel*, 29 Apr., 21 Aug., 29 Nov. 1851.
[3] *Glasgow Examiner*, 24 Apr., 2 Oct. 1852. The Glasgow Reform Association included in its membership more than 1,000 working-class men. Its secretary was William C. Pattison.

Chapter Nine

National Bearings

Asa Briggs

I

The previous studies in this volume have described the local Chartist background and the local Chartist chronicle in a group of different places: the last three studies are concerned with more general themes — O'Connor's Land Plan; relations between the Chartists and the formidable and powerfully organised Anti-Corn Law League; and the attitude of successive governments to the movement. Local factors cannot be omitted, however, even in this second survey. The appeal of the Land Plan varied from one part of the country to another. It was strong in the industrial north and weak in the purely agricultural areas, but it seems to have been persistently powerful in small towns, particularly those with declining industries. Places like Newton Abbot and Tewkesbury in the West, Coggeshall and Braintree in the East, and Belper and Newark in the Midlands figure in the accounts.[1] Relations between the Anti-Corn Law League and the Chartists followed a fairly regular pattern, but the League itself had its own geography, and the relative strength of the two organisations was the key to the unfolding of local Radical politics.[2] Finally, Government was not in a position to maintain law and order on a uniform basis in different parts of the country. There was intense local fear not only of centralised police but of centralised bureaucracy. The widespread opposition to the New Poor Law of 1834 before the Chartist movement began and to the Public Health Act of 1848 after it had reached its climax depended on an exploitation of these fears. On the ladder of public authority the Privy Council, the Cabinet and the Home Secretary were at the top, but the local magistrates were on the rungs. They were chosen by the Crown on the recommendation of the Lord Lieutenants, and though they varied in quality — in some parts of the country there was a shortage of eligible candidates — they were almost always deficient in

[1] See below, pp. 319–22.   [2] See below, pp. 353–4.

self-reliance. 'The magistrates of every town and village', Napier wrote, 'will tell . . . the same story, that their town or village is the "focus of Chartism" whereas it is only the focus of their own fears.'[1] The most important national force was the Army, by 1848 'seated like a spider in the centre of its web, on the diverging lines of iron road'.[2]

Attitudes of non-Chartists towards the Chartists depended much on local circumstances. At Leicester, for instance, it was claimed that 'the wiser part of the Chartists consists here of more reflective men than elsewhere':[3] it was only outside influences which caused trouble. At Leeds, Dean Hook found it just as easy to get on with the Chartists as with his regular Churchwardens. In South Wales, Lady Charlotte Guest, the highly intelligent and versatile wife of Guest, the great ironmaster, was at pains to distinguish between *her* Chartists and the rest. Her first reference to the subject in her Diary concerned a meeting of local magistrates called together in December 1838 to examine the implications of the spread of 'the opinions of a discontented set of idlers, who wish to stir up dissension . . . and sign petitions for the cession of certain privileges, which they dignify by the name of "The People's Charter" '. A few months later, however, she was more discriminating. 'In this population of thirty thousand people and upwards there are only two thousand Chartists and they appear perfectly orderly and say they intend nothing but to petition the Queen, in which, as far as this district is concerned, I really believe them. They seem quite different in tenets, etc., from the rabble of Birmingham.'[4] Clearly she knew more of Merthyr Tydfil than of Birmingham, for it was in Birmingham that middle-class Radicals, who began by sympathising with the Chartists, blamed the changed atmosphere of protest after 1839 on the existence of the rabble in the North.

II

In turning from local factors in the history of Chartism to its national bearings and significance, a new set of perspectives is necessary.

[1] H.O. 40/53. Napier to the Home Secretary, 22 Aug. 1839.
[2] *Democratic Review*, Oct. 1849. See F. C. Mather, 'The Railways, the Electric Telegraph and Public Order during the Chartist Period' in *History*, Vol. XXXVIII (1953).
[3] *Leicester Chronicle*, 17 Aug. 1839. 'They may be equally sincere in their views regarding the desirability of the Charter', the writer went on, 'but their eyes are too open to allow them to use pikes and torches'.
[4] Lady Charlotte Guest, *Extracts from her Journal, 1833–52* (ed. by the Earl of Bessborough, 1950), pp. 85, 91. There were many 'good quiet, intelligent Chartists' in Birmingham. *Birmingham Post*, 24 Nov. 1885.

Historians in the past have tended to study it exclusively as a
dramatic episode in the history of the labour movement — 'the
first independent movement of the workers' or in Lenin's words
'the first broad and politically organized proletarian-revolutionary
movement of the masses' — and to relate it not only to what came
before but to what came afterwards as the labour movement
'matured'. This familiar approach is useful and fruitful, for there
were many interesting Chartist pointers to the future even in
the early years of the agitation — the emphasis on mutual help
and the refusal to lean on other sections of the community; the
attempt to establish friendly relations with other working-class
organisations overseas;[1] and the sense that though there might be
many defeats in the short run, in the long run history was 'on their
side'. During the last years of the agitation there was an unmistak-
able shift in emphasis from the demand for political reform within
the framework of a parliamentary ideal, a demand which grew
naturally out of eighteenth-century radicalism, to the search for
social democracy, a search which led some Chartists — notably
Jones and Harney — into socialism. 'Chartism in 1850', wrote
'Howard Morton' in the first issue of Harney's *Red Republican*, 'is
a different thing from Chartism in 1840. The leaders of the English
Proletarians have proved that they are true Democrats, and no
shams, by going ahead so rapidly within the last few years. They
have progressed from the idea of a simple *political reform* to the
idea of a *Social Revolution*.'[2] The progression was associated with a
further shift in emphasis from local parochialism to international
commitment and action. Both Jones and Harney looked beyond the
Channel and across the Atlantic to social movements abroad: they
were prepared not only to analyse foreign social situations, but to
propound a foreign policy of their own.

The changing outlook of Chartist leaders after 1848 was not
necessarily shared, however, by the old Chartist rank-and-file.
There was a growing popular interest in foreign issues, which led
up naturally to the popular excitement just before and during the
Crimean War, and there was a limited interest in further reform of

[1] 'What care we in what language our cherished principles are expressed; —
they are still our principles, whether uttered in Canadian, French, or Belgian,
Dutch, or Polish, or modern Greek.' *London Dispatch*, 9 Apr. 1837. Cf. the
Manifesto of the L.W.M.A. (13 Nov. 1836), 'Fellow producers of wealth have in
reality but *one great interest*. . . . The interests of working men in all countries of
the world are identified.'
[2] 22 June 1850.

the franchise, but the vision of a new society lost much of its appeal. The shift of emphasis, therefore, was a portent of things to come rather than an effective adaptation to new circumstances. The more eclectic Chartism had been, the more it retained its vigour as a mass movement. The more it had drawn on material discontents and local grievances as well as on ideological inspirations, the more it prospered. The more it had attracted those people who looked back to the past as well as those who looked forward to the future, the more it spread.[1] There was, of course, a heavy price to pay, the heaviest price of all, for the kind of challenge Chartists made when they were part of a nation-wide movement — failure. The price of eclecticism was disunity — local differences, faction fights and quarrels about tactics. The price of dependence on 'hunger politics' was the corroding influence even of limited 'prosperity'. The price of a double, or rather a multiple, appeal was inconsistency and inadequate leadership.[2] The Chartist failure was inevitable, but it robs the movement neither of its interest nor of its importance. The Radical demand for the Six Points survived the failure of the Chartist attempt to secure them: the dream of social democracy lost much of its appeal, but it did not disappear. Taken by itself simply as an episode in working-class history, the story of Chartism has many parallels in more recent periods of history in other parts of the world. Most of the differences in outlook, tactics and even principles, which it reflected, and the basic problem it posed, that of 'independent' action (free from the 'contaminating' influence of well-wishers as much as the 'machinations' of opponents), continue to be relevant in colonial nationalist movements. Even the name 'Charter' has been employed by protest movements in South Africa. Both the psychology and the sociology of Chartism are of abiding interest.

In every Chartist centre there seem to have been at least four

[1] Cf. a speech of Vincent at Watford (Lovett Collection, Vol. I, B.R.L.) with an article of Harney (*Northern Star*, 14 Feb. 1845). 'Would it be for your advantage', Vincent asked his audience, 'that your fields of waving corn, in which the happiest years of your life have been spent, should be superseded by the smoke of chimneys, the clash of machinery, all the squalid filth and poverty of manufacturing hells?' 'It is equality, not feudalism', Harney wrote, 'which is the hope of the many . . . the "golden age" is before, not behind us.'

[2] The Anti-Corn Law League made the most of its single appeal. Some supporters of repeal, who were just as eclectic as the Chartists, notably Perronet Thompson, were unhappy about Cobden's exclusive preoccupation. A Manchester supporter of Thompson called Cobden 'sharp and shallow'. Quoted L. G. Johnson, *General T. Perronet Thompson* (1957), p. 232.

groups of Chartists — a hard core of Radical reformers, whose association with Chartism was one phase, sometimes a formative
phase, in a career devoted to political protest movements of one
kind and another; a group of new recruits to working-class politics,
often consisting of young men; a body of 'loyal supporters', eager
not only to sign petitions and to attend meetings but to participate
in the social activities which provided the 'fellowship' of Chartism
— the procession, the Institute, the Chartist Church or the education class; and a fluctuating rank-and-file, capable of being stirred
to enthusiastic activity, but just as capable of remaining silent and
apathetic.

The first and second groups did not disappear from local or
national politics after 1848. Many of them, like the Leeds Chartists,
took up local government.[1] James Sweet, for example, a Nottingham bookseller, gave good service as a Nottingham councillor, and
as late as 1872 still proclaimed his Chartist beliefs and rejoiced that
so many of the Chartist demands had been granted.[2] Others turned
to co-operation, trade-unionism, temperance and education. In
Colchester, for example, John Howe, who had been an active
Chartist at Thetford and Braintree, founded a branch of the
Amalgamated Society of Carpenters and Joiners in 1861 and for
over thirty years acted as its secretary, while at Halstead James
Hunt and Thomas Ready helped to start the local co-operative
society, took an active part in the life of the working men's club and
became officials of Joseph Arch's Agricultural Labourers' Union.[3]
Other Chartists had more colourful experiences, joining Garibaldi's
army,[4] for example, or battling for reform in Australia. At Ballarat
in 1854 a Reform League was founded which put forward most of
the main Chartist demands and was clearly inspired by ex-Chartists. In the United States many ex-Chartists were completely
assimilated, but a few continued to urge Radical causes in a new
setting. Most important of all, many ex-Chartists continued to
press for parliamentary reform at home.

During the quiet late 1850's, when it was difficult to summon

[1] See above, p. 87. There were municipal Chartists in Sheffield also.
[2] I owe this reference to Mr H. R. Exelby who has been working on the history
of Chartism in Nottingham. Many of the Chartists changed their name, of course,
but as D. W. Heath put it in 1858: 'we, the Chartists of Nottingham, are not the
only parties who have had to alter their names. Perhaps it was the folly of some
that made it policy to do so.'
[3] A. F. J. Brown, 'The Chartist Movement in Essex', cited above, p. 172.
[4] C. H. McCarthy, *Chartist Recollections* (Bradford, 1883).

enthusiasm for further parliamentary reform, some 'veterans of former times' were still prominent,[1] as they still were ten years later in the agitation that led up to the passing of the Reform Bill of 1867, which gave the vote to the working classes of the towns. In Halifax in 1885 Benjamin Wilson, an old Chartist, called together a group of Chartist veterans to a dinner at which those present voted thanks to Gladstone for the further extension of the parliamentary franchise.[2] The full story of the 'Chartist aftermath' will never be written, for it depends on the accumulation of a large mass of local material. Chartist organisation disappeared in the 1850's, but 'the old Chartist spirit' often lingered on. It was still being talked about in the North of England when the Independent Labour Party was founded in 1893.

The history of the third and fourth groups is even more difficult to write, for they consisted of men with 'no names, no individuality . . . anonymous fractions of the multitude'.[3] It is quite misleading, however, to view them as objects rather than as subjects of history, to describe their movements as if they were akin to movements in natural history, or to speak only of 'symbols' and 'myths'. The tendency of some historians to discuss them in these terms produces a parody of social history. Behind the demand for the Charter was a demand for human dignity as well as for material objectives. 'The Chartists were called ugly names, the swinish multitude, unwashed and levellers . . . What they wanted was a voice in making the laws which they were called upon to obey.'[4] Some of the Chartist rank-and-file, it was claimed, had 'more political knowledge than was possessed by any class of men' forty or fifty years before:[5] it could be argued also that the lack of knowledge in the rest was the result of the lack of an educational system, long hours of work, and a social system which rested on an incomplete conception of citizenship.

The ability of the first and second groups of Chartists to appeal to the third and fourth depended not only on the choice of the right language and the requisite degree of understanding but on social

---

[1] *Glasgow Examiner*, 13 Nov. 1858. It described a meeting in the Lower Trades Hall at Glasgow which 'was largely composed of the old Chartist elements, and to some degree pervaded with the old Chartist spirit'.

[2] B. Wilson, *The Struggles of an old Chartist* (Halifax, 1887); *Halifax Guardian*, 11 Sept. 1885.

[3] Letter to the *Spectator*, 1 Mar. 1837. [4] B. Wilson, *op. cit.*

[5] The phrase was applied to the members of the Birmingham Political Union, *Political Union Register*, March 1832.

and economic conditions, the strength and persuasiveness of other voices (including the voices of Church and Chapel) and the responsiveness of government and employers to their needs. 'It is a terrible fact', wrote Harney in 1849, 'that after so many years of "Reform" and "Chartist" agitation, multitudes of men whose every interest would benefit by the triumph of Chartism are yet ignorant of or indifferent to the Charter. This is true not only of agricultural workers, but of a considerable portion of the local population.'[1] After the collapse of Chartism as a mass movement there was much retrospective stock-taking of this kind. 'Even in 1848,' one writer remarked three years after the event, 'when European endeavours lent us a sort of shamed impulse, what were our numbers? Some three or four hundreds . . . paid their tolerably regular pence for a few months . . . . Some four or five thousands, appreciating the eloquence of Ernest Jones, etc., thought it tyranny to be called upon for any regular payment. I cannot count the thousands, or say millions, who made noises at monster meetings. Indeed they were never counted. Why should they have been? They were no part of our party.'[2] But they were a part while the 'party' was a genuine national organisation. They gave it its colour, its force, its power of threat to the established order. 'They felt great disappointment at being abandoned by those whom they said they had supported to the utmost of their power. . . . The consequence of this was the total abandonment of all reliance upon the middle class.'[3] They looked eagerly and hopefully to the Chartist leaders, and the most important of the Chartist leaders, O'Connor, looked to them.

All the groups talked the language of 'class' in a frank and un-inhibited manner. 'If they whose interests are (so) identified', the L.W.M.A. had stated, 'do not investigate the causes of the evils that oppress them, how can they expect others to do it for them?' This conception of mutual self help was associated with the view that 'union of sentiment is essential to the prosecution of any great object'.[4] The 'division of classes', treated by the *Northern Star* as a law of nature and of history, made it essential, it was claimed, for the working classes to preserve and develop an intense feeling of emotional identification. In the North there was no need to dwell on

---

[1] *Northern Star*, 6 Jan. 1849.   [2] *The English Republic* (1851), p. 175.
[3] P.P., Add. MSS. 27,819, f. 24.
[4] Lovett, *op. cit.*, *Address and Rules of the L.W.M.A.*, p. 6.

the reasons for 'union of sentiment'. Engels, who compared the outlook of the Chartists and the 'Socialists', remarked that while 'the Chartists are theoretically the more backward, the less developed . . . they are genuine proletarians all over, the representatives of their class.'[1]

Any full investigation of the Chartist approach to 'class' must take account not only of the demand for 'union of sentiment' but of the impact of recent working-class history and the diffusion of a number of basic economic propositions on different sections of the labour force. The history may be disposed of briefly. It went back to the rise of steam power, the Luddite disturbances, Peterloo and the agitation for Reform. The interests of 'middle classes' and 'working classes' were held to have diverged, and the Reform Bill of 1832 was treated, as the N.U.W.C. had treated it at the time, as a sham.[2] In terms of old-fashioned Radical objectives alone, it had accomplished nothing. 'Not only in the old, but in the Whig mock-Reform-created boroughs as well, were those disgusting practices going on which the Reform Bill was supposed to have abolished'.[3] In terms of social objectives, the Reform Parliaments were worse than the old. 'They had united all *property* against all *poverty*.'[4] They had introduced the New Poor Law, widely regarded as 'a murderer's death-blow to the operative classes'.[5] 'One sole recipe', thundered Carlyle, 'seems to have been needful for the woes of England, refusal of outdoor relief. England lay in sick discontent, writhing powerless on its fever-bed, dark, nigh desperate in wastefulness, want, improvidence and eating care, till like Hyperion down the eastern steeps, the Poor Law Commissioners arose and said, "Let there be workhouses and bread of affliction and water of affliction there".'[6] How the demand for the Charter was linked with the attack on the Poor Law has been fully described in previous chapters.[7]

---

[1] *The Condition of the Working Class in England* (1892 tr. by Wischnewetzky) p. 238. 'Socialists' of the Owenite variety often had no more sympathy with Chartism than Owen himself. For Owen's views, see *New Moral World*, 11 Aug., 1838: for a sample of Owenite views (in Leicester) in 1842, see *ibid.*, 16 July 1842.

[2] See above, p. 20. 'The only difference between Whigs and Tories is this — the Whigs would give the shadow to preserve the substance; the Tories would not give the shadow because, stupid as they are, they know that, the principle of reform once admitted, the millions will not stop at shadows, but proceed onward to realities.' (*Poor Man's Guardian*, 27 Oct. 1832.)

[3] *Chartist Circular*, Vol. I (1840), p. 101.

[4] This was a phrase of O'Brien who argued that the Reform Bill was designed to 'consolidate our institutions in Church and State'.

[5] *Poor Man's Guardian*, 2 Aug. 1834.   [6] *Chartism* (1839).

[7] See, especially pp. 11–13.

The economic propositions used to support the case for separate class action were three in number, and they were being stated, apparently often quite independently, in several parts of the country — first, that labour was the source of all value, and its rights could only be defended by the workers themselves; second, that manufacturers were forcing labour to work over-long hours and robbing it of a portion of its proper reward; and third, that exploitation was being assisted by the existence of a 'reserve army' of labour which forced down wages and worsened working conditions. These three propositions were part of the regular oratorical equipment of many platform speakers and working-class journalists as well as of social theorists like J. F. Bray and Bronterre O'Brien who stated the propositions in analytical form. The *Poor Man's Guardian* and the *Northern Star* often went further in directly associating economic exploitation and governmental authority. 'The middle classes', remarked the former, 'are the real tyrants of the country. Disguise it as they may, they are the authors of our slavery for without their connivance and secret support no tyranny could exist. Government is but a tool in their hands to execute their nefarious purposes.'[1]

Although Chartist grievances were by no means always couched in such sophisticated language, Chartists almost everywhere were suspicious of alliances with the middle classes. Many of the detailed local studies have qualified this general statement and the study of the relations between Chartists and Leaguers which follows[2] examines it more closely.[3] It was only after 1848, when corn law repeal had been achieved and working-class objectives had still not been secured, that some of the leading members of the Chartist rump came round to the view that a broader Radical front could be created once more. O'Connor, twisting and turning, talked of an alliance between 'mental labour on the one hand and manual labour on the other': Harney, who by that time was attacking O'Connor, was himself working with middle-class reformers in 1851 and 1852: five years later, Jones who had written earlier that

---

[1] *Poor Man's Guardian*, 2 Nov. 1833.   [2] See below, Ch. 11.

[3] Manchester's would-be Sturge, Archibald Prentice (see above, p. 43) failed completely in his local plan to harmonise the political activities of the two classes. He believed not only in an extension of the suffrage but that 'the way to "slay enmity" is to show love'. (*Manchester Times*, 4 Dec. 1841). For his pains he was condemned as 'the traitor and renegade Prentice (*Manchester Guardian*, 7 Sept. 1839) and 'one of the hired tools of the Bazaarites' (*Northern Star*, 19 Mar. 1842).

'an amalgamation of classes is impossible where an amalgamation of interests is impossible also',[1] had come round to the view that 'there can be no doubt as to the wisdom of allying with the middle classes and their leaders if they offer such a measure of reform as we can be justified in accepting'.[2] This declaration was in a very real sense a Chartist epitaph.

It is impossible to understand Chartist arguments about class without fitting Chartism into British history as a whole. In concentrating on Chartism as an episode in working-class history — with international as well as national implications — too little attention has been paid by social and political historians to class relations in the Britain of the 1830's and 40's. Chartism can only be understood, however, if it is related to social history as well as to socialism.

During the late 1830's and 40's two forms of class consciousness were being forged in Britain, not one — middle-class consciousness and working-class consciousness. Each manifestation of class consciousness assisted the articulation of the other. It was fear of working-class numbers as well as hatred of the handful of landlords which buttressed middle-class consciousness. It was irritation with and frustration engendered by the Anti-Corn Law League, itself a child of the business depression, which was set up after the Chartist movement had been inaugurated,[3] that provoked the Chartists to their most violent class declarations. The *Annual Register* described Chartism in 1839 as 'an insurrection which is expressly directed against the middle classes'.

The League prided itself on being a *middle-class* body, and on the wealth, organisation and moral power which were associated with the adjective. On more than one occasion Cobden acknowledged that its manoeuvres and its artifices, its fervour and its efficiency depended upon middle-class opinions and methods. 'We have carried

---

[1] *Notes to the People* (1851), Vol. I, p. 342. Quoted Saville, *op. cit.*, p. 41. 'CLASS AGAINST CLASS,' Jones went on, 'all other mode of proceeding is mere moonshine.'

[2] Quoted *ibid.*, p. 63. It is important to note that at this time Jones was equally insistent, as Harney had been in 1851 and 1852, on the need to 'keep our own organisation intact and concentrate and strengthen it to the utmost of our power'.

[3] The Manchester Corn Law Association, the progenitor of the League, was founded in October 1838. On 10 January 1839 a small but historically important meeting was held in Manchester 'to consider the proper mode of carrying forward the proceedings of the Anti-Corn Law Association in a manner commensurate with the magnitude of the obstacles to be surmounted'. The *Anti-Corn Law Circular* was first published on 16 April 1839.

it on by those means by which the middle class usually carries on its movements. We have had our meetings of Dissenting Ministers: we have obtained the co-operation of the ladies; we have resorted to tea parties and have taken those specific means for carrying out our views which mark us as rather a middle-class set of agitators.'[1] When the League secured its objective Cobden was even more precise. In a famous letter to Peel he wrote, 'Do you shrink from governing through the bona fide representatives of the middle class? Look at the facts and can the country be otherwise ruled at all? There must be an end of the juggle of parties, the mere representatives of traditions, and some man must of necessity rule the state through its governing class. The Reform Bill decreed it: the passing of the Corn Bill has realised it.'[2] This, as much else in Cobden's writings, was a kind of middle-class Marxism, and Peel put it completely on one side.[3] The Chartists could not ignore it, however, nor the attempts which the leaders of the League made to 'use' the operatives in their agitation. They had no desire merely to serve as 'something in our rear to frighten the aristocracy'.[4] At the same time, it is not surprising, considering differences not only of economic interest but of education, outlook and behaviour, that a large section of the middle classes disliked the thought of working men taking on any more active role.[5] The strength of class feelings is well brought out in a casual remark by Sturge's mid-nineteenth-century biographer. After describing the breakdown in 1842 of the negotiations between the Complete Suffrage Union and the Chartists, he adds, 'Mr Sturge's friends felt thankful that this result left him at liberty honourably to withdraw from much uncongenial fellowship.'[6]

[1] J. Morley, *The Life of Richard Cobden* (1903 edn), Vol. I, p. 249. Cf. an earlier remark of Cobden. 'Let us fraternise with the sensible portion of the mercantile middle-class, and appeal to their money-bags, and our political opponents will be sure to read all we have to say'. Quoted H. Ashworth, *Recollections of Richard Cobden* (1876), p. 25.

[2] Morley, *op. cit.*, pp. 390–7.

[3] See my article on Peel in *British Prime Ministers* (ed. Duff Cooper, 1953).

[4] Cobden to J. B. Smith, 4 Dec. 1841, Smith MSS., M.R.L. See below, p. 348.

[5] Perronet Thompson refused to join Sturge's movement on the following grounds (see L. G. Johnson, *op. cit.*, pp. 243–4) — 'On the coast of Africa we dealt in wood, which was floated by sea. Some kinds of it were so heavy, that the pieces would not swim; and then we tied each piece to a piece of lighter. Now the "Complete Suffragists", because they say the Anti-Corn Law question will not swim, tie it to a heavier. I defy them to prove that out of the actual possessors of political power and influence, where there are ten against the removal of the Corn Laws, there are not twenty against their "Complete Suffrage".'

[6] H. Richard, *Memoirs of Joseph Sturge* (1864), p. 318.

The class attitudes of the Chartists and their unwillingness to draw on any outside support doomed them, if did nothing else, to political failure from the start. If problems relating to the development of labour history are put on one side, it can be plausibly argued that the most important historical feature of the Chartist movement in its contemporary British setting was that it demonstrated not the weaknesses of the working classes, which were obvious, but the strength of the middle classes. It may in fact be regarded as one episode in the development of middle-class consciousness.[1] The Kennington Common incident of 1848 certainly reveals more about middle-class than about working-class attitudes, for the real strength of Chartism in 1848 lay not in London but in the industrial provinces, and if there was a fiasco it lay as much in the exaggerated fears of the middle classes of the metropolis as in the ignominious failure of the Chartists.[2] Perhaps as H. M. Hyndman, the late nineteenth-century socialist put it, 'the worst mistake the Chartist leaders made was that they neglected London until too late'.[3] There was more militant middle-class consciousness than militant working-class consciousness in London in 1848. When Russell made it known that he was willing to allow the Chartists to march to the House of Commons with their petition, the London shopkeepers protested against the 'apathy and inaction' of the Government.[4] When the whole incident was closed and the sandbags had been removed from the Bank of England, Lady Palmerston wrote to Mrs Huskisson about what had occurred. 'Your letter reminded me', she explained, 'that I ought to give you private details of our "revolution" as the papers, though very full, could only give the public ones. Our terrace was divided into districts and all the servants made special constables. . . . I am sure that it is very fortunate that the whole thing has occurred, as it has shown the good spirit of our middle classes.'[5] An American visitor to England shared this assessment of relative power but drew a very different conclusion. 'The middle classes in England, who took up

---

[1] See my article 'Middle-Class Consciousness in English Politics, 1780–1846' in *Past and Present* (1946).

[2] G. W. M. Reynolds claimed (*The Political Instructor*, 26 Jan. 1850) that 'the government converted a movement merely intended to demonstrate the power of an idea into one of physical force and display . . . in reality to combat with a shadow'. For a different view, based on official evidence, see below, pp. 395–8.

[3] *Justice*, 3 July 1886.

[4] See below, p. 396.

[5] For the full letter, see C. R. Fay, *Huskisson and his Age* (1951), pp. 137–8.

arms against the humbler classes (who, much as we may disapprove the manner in which they seek it, have certainly in view altogether, and only, the benefit of the middle classes, the mitigation of national burdens, and the general cause of liberty), have now, with their hands tied behind them, thrown themselves into the power of the government, and all hopes of reform are extinguished, for at least the next quarter of a century.'[1]

III

The middle classes were not yet the Government, however, and it was not repression (as had been the case in 1839 and 1840) but prosperity which extinguished hopes of large-scale reform during the mid-Victorian years. If there was no revolution in Britain in 1848, there was no counter-revolution in 1849. The mid-Victorian years were years of social equipoise, and the militant class language withered on both sides of the class barrier. It became the fashion — particularly in 1851, the year of the Great Exhibition, to sing the praises of all classes. Even before that, in January 1850, the Earl of Essex congratulated the whole nation on the 'state of peace'. 'The high minded feeling of the upper classes' had led them, he remarked, 'to abandon their long rooted prejudices, and to sacrifice their self interest whenever they were called upon to do so for the public good.' The 'sound good sense of the middle classes which led them to avoid extremes' had been parallelled by 'the forebearance of the artisan and operative classes, which though more subject at all times to privations and distresses than other, bore them with patience'.[2]

This was a very English lesson to draw and it contrasted sharply with some of the lessons which members of the governing classes were drawing only a few years earlier.[3] Then there had been debate among the Chartists themselves about the respective claims of 'moral' and physical force. Differences of age, experience and temperament were as important as differences of economic and social status in determining attitudes on this question.[4] In 1838 Lovett

---

[1] Colman, *op. cit.*, Vol. II, p. 371.   [2] *Hansard*, 3rd series, Vol. CX, p. 400.
[3] See below, pp. 390–4, for the Tory view of 'conspiracy' in 1842, a view which had much in common with the views of the troubled years 1815–19.
[4] It was only true in the broadest sense that 'those men (who) were well-fed . . . therefore . . . relied on moral force; but let them labour for one week, and be ill-fed and clothed, and it would soon convert their moral force to physical force'. (*Northern Liberator*, 28 Dec. 1838).

was 38 years old, Hetherington 46, Cleave 46; Harney was 21, Vincent 25, McDouall 24. Both Vincent and Harney became more 'realistic' — though not necessarily less 'romantic' — as the years went by, and in 1848 it was younger men than they who were echoing the most violent language of ten years before. O'Brien learned even sooner. During the course of the Convention of 1839 he came to the conclusion that the Chartists could not match their deeds and their rhetoric, and he was the prime mover of the proposal that the Convention should dissolve itself. During his imprisonment in 1840 and 1841 he came to the conclusion that revolution by force was quite impracticable in Britain. Some of the 'new men' of 1848 had to learn that lesson from new facts, the facts of apathy as much as of disorganisation.[1] By the early 1850's there was no need to learn the lesson at all: the facts spoke for themselves.

The two extreme points of view about 'moral' and physical force were stated clearly in the years of crisis, 1838 and 1839. 'We want the glory and the blessedness of a peaceful triumph,' argued the seasoned Radicals of the Birmingham Political Union. 'We want to strike terror to the foe, and yet not touch a hair of their heads.'[2] 'The men of the North are armed,' exclaimed the young romantic Harney, 'I invite you to follow their example . . . . There is no argument like the sword — and the musket is unanswerable.'[3] Between these two extreme points of view concerning force there was room for a whole spectrum of opinions, and one single Chartist could, and often did, express a whole spectrum of opinions at different times. It is impossible to separate out with any confidence 'moral' force sheep and physical force goats. All the Chartists shared the conviction 'we are many, they are few' and the belief that in struggling for the Charter they were not rebels but honest Britons fighting for their birthright.

> Then rise, my boys, and fight the foe,
> Your arms are truth and reason:
> We'll let the Whigs and Tories know
> That Union is not treason.

They looked back to the struggles for the Reform Bill in 1831 and 1832 when middle-class reformers had not hesitated to threaten the

---

[1] Jones called moral and physical force 'twin cherries on one stalk' (Saville, *op. cit.*, p. 27), but acceptance of physical force as a right was a different matter from recommending its use.
[2] *Birmingham Journal*, 12 May 1838.   [3] *Northern Star*, 9 Feb. 1839.

opponents of the Bill in forceful language.[1] They viewed with alarm the consolidation of force in the hands of the Government — the use of a 'bloodthirsty and unconstitutional' force of police from London, the arming of special constables, the movement of troops, and the employment of spies. They knew that there was nothing illegal about the holding of arms,[2] and most of them accepted at least as a compromise the formula 'peaceably if we may, forcibly if we must'.[3] Where the Chartists differed was in degrees of 'moderation'. Some were prepared to threaten force, others were anxious to regard it as a last defence. Some dabbled in the rhetoric of revolution: others, a tiny minority, thought seriously but not very effectively how a revolution might be accomplished. By 1850 this episode in British history was finished. O'Brien, as on so many other occasions, tried to fit his analysis to the facts of British history. 'The amazing revolution which has lately taken place in the arts and sciences, as applicable to the purposes of human economy, ought naturally to give birth to another revolution of a kindred quality in the political and social mechanism of society. This second social revolution — the transition from proletarianism and wages-slavery to real and universal emancipation — may be effected without the loss of a single life, or the sacrifice of a shilling's worth of his possessions by any man of any class.'[4]

The last two studies in this volume touch on many of these themes. The one that precedes them, however, is unmistakably bound up with the history of the 1840's. O'Connor's Land Plan is strangely characteristic of that speculative decade. O'Connor, like any independent company promoter, travelled about buying and

[1] George Edmonds, who was Clerk to the Birmingham magistrates in 1839 at the time of the Bull Ring Riots, had declared in front of a vast crowd in 1831: 'When he saw the thousands before him, all animated with the same sentiments, he could not help connecting with the moral force they possessed, the physical power which in any emergency or crisis in the country's need might be called into instantaneous action. For sorry as he would be to see weapons in the hands of Englishmen . . . there were times when moral influence was not worth a straw unless backed by physical power.' (*Report of the Proceedings*, 3 Oct. 1831). For the mood of the Bull Ring, see *Report of the Committee . . . to investigate the Causes of the Late Riots* (Birmingham, 1840).

[2] For the legal position, see below.

[3] In Francis Place's view 'the whole of the movement was calculated to alarm every man who did not . . . earn his living by the work of his hands and receive wages'. (P.P. Add. MSS. 27,820, Preface to *Historical Narratives*.) Some Chartists, notably Rev. Patrick Brewster, argued in favour of the complete renunciation of force and the talk of force — (see his *Seven Chartist and Military Discourses* (1843)) — but they were probably a minority.

[4] *The Rise, Progress and Phases of Human Slavery* (published posthumously. 1885)—quoted by G. D. H. Cole, *Chartist Portraits*, p. 262.

elling land without reference to his directors and with an apparent belief in inexhaustible credit. Indeed the *Gloucester Journal* compared O'Connor and George Hudson, arguing that the former had brought ruin to the lower classes and the latter had ravaged the middle classes.[1] An understanding of Chartism is incomplete unless it draws on comparisons of this kind. Chartists and their opponents belonged to two nations, but they were creatures of the same age. Within ten years of the failure of the third Petition, Britain as a whole had moved on to a new course.[2]

[1] *Gloucester Journal*, 8 Dec. 1850.
[2] One of the important subjects treated briefly in this volume is Ireland. A monograph on Ireland and the Chartists is urgently needed. On the platforms of 1848 the grievances of Ireland were discussed as keenly as the Six Points of the Charter themselves, and the Irish element played a big part in the disturbances in the North of England. So long as O'Connell had lived, however, many of the Irish emigrants to England were suspicious of Chartism and joined other agitations. See above, p. 51. Napier, indeed, asked for more Irish soldiers in 1839, for 'the difference of religion and of country form additional barriers around the fidelity of the soldier'. (H.O. 40/53, 29 July 1839). Mrs Rachel O'Higgins of Trinity College, Dublin is working on this subject. Research on Chartism is necessarily laborious, and the monographs already in existence do not always relate to the people or places which the historian considers most important.

Chapter Ten

The Chartist Land Plan

Joy MacAskill

I

It is at first sight a paradox that the 1840's, the time of conscious attempts to grapple with the implications of industrialisation, should be the decade when questions of land ownership and use were thrust into the foreground. The Land Scheme was regarded by many Chartists at the time as a diversion from the main issue of political reform: it has been treated by most historians as a bizarre gesture, a last nostalgic glance at a doomed order. These views may be justified if the Plan is considered as a panacea: yet it was not always so regarded even by O'Connor.[1] In retrospect that aspect seems less important than the discontents and inspirations which political talk of the Plan released. The vision of a new society was less significant than the anxious discussion of the old. For in raising the political and social problems connected with landholding both O'Connor and his critics were asking questions which mattered in general to English society, but with particular urgency to the working classes.

The Chartists shared with many Tories a powerful sense of the recent past. For them, as for the later generation of social historians who rediscovered the village community, industrial England had been created by tearing a section of her people from their roots. The town workers' sufferings were, if not caused by enclosures, at least the next link to them in the chain of events. This approach to recent history did not necessarily lead to a total condemnation of industrialism, but it created a framework in which to examine its problems — the imposition of factory discipline, the health of towns and, above all, the insecurity of employment. If the people were oppressed, was it not because of the concentration of power in the hands of a few landowners? If factory workers were unemployed and land uncultivated should the two not be put

---

[1] See below, pp. 313–14.

together? The Chartist writings on land owed something to the Radical tradition of the Levellers and the eighteenth-century agrarians, for they too had strong feelings about man's natural right to the soil. But they owed more to the pressure and experience of more recent history and of current problems.

Most of the Chartist leaders touched at some time on the land question — O'Brien consistently, Jones and Harney frequently, Lovett and Cooper occasionally. But it was O'Connor, coming to England after the agricultural labourers' revolt of 1830–1, but well acquainted with Irish landlordism, who made it the centre of his thought and action. What were the ideas which led to the Land Plan and how far do O'Connor's writings fit into the background of social unrest in the 1840's?

O'Connor had that awareness, typical of the 40's, that two types of society were facing one another. When he wrote that 'man, in the rampancy of irresponsible power, has driven his brother from those fields where the rewards of his toil would be peace, abundance and independence', he was not referring to that Radical symbol, the seizure of the land from the people at the Norman Conquest,[1] but to the events of his own generation; he followed the 'victims' into the 'manufacturing towns where their lives are embittered and shortened by excessive and ill-requited toil'. Nor was this mere denunciation. He believed passionately that 'such a deplorable state of things as this demands imperatively the labour of every good man to put a period to its existence'.[2]

'The labour of every good man' was demanded for the work of getting back the land for the townspeople and facilitating its cultivation in smallholdings. Pages of calculation, especially in *The Labourer*,[3] were devoted to proving that a livelihood could be made from two, three or four acres. Unlike Cobbett, O'Connor did not dwell persistently on a golden age in the past. Instead he spoke of England 'being on the verge of a transition from the present state of society to a better', and used such phrases as 'faith in progress, in the perfectibility of every human mind'.[4] In an imaginary future

[1] See C. Hill, 'The Norman Yoke' in *Democracy and the Labour Movement*, ed. by J. Saville (1954), Ch. I.
[2] Select Committee on the National Land Company. *Parliamentary Papers* (Reports from Committees) Session 1847–8. Vol. XIX. 1st Report, Appendix (Rules of the National Land Company).
[3] *The Labourer*, a monthly magazine edited by O'Connor and Ernest Jones, London 1848.
[4] *Ibid.*, Vol. I, pp. 70–3.

history of England he declared that history only became 'interest
ing to the reader since the period by common consent called th
Golden Age, which dates from the year 1848' when the people de
manded 'the restoration of the land to its natural and legitimat
and original purpose'.[1]

In this same passage he went on to enumerate the reasons fo
land reform. First, more cultivated land was required as 'the onl
means of arresting famine'. In all his propaganda and finally be
fore the House of Commons Committee, O'Connor stood by thi
view that smallholdings cultivated by spade husbandry would pro
duce more for the country than the existing agricultural structure
He linked this contention with his desire for the country to be in
dependent of foreign resources, a desire which influenced his oppo
sition to the Anti-Corn Law League.

His second reason was social and moral rather than economic
The restoration of land was 'the only means of promoting industry
and independence, by affording to each a labour field and en
couraging the grand principle of self-reliance'. This theme recurred
many times in O'Connor's writings and speeches. The indepen
dence of the cultivator was contrasted with the subservice of th
wage-slave: 'the principle of self-employment' was held to be 'the
surest protection against unequal suffering and man's dispensation'.

The vagueness of the third reason — that the Land Plan was 'the
only means of making machinery man's holiday instead of man's
curse' — prompts one to ask whether O'Connor was entirely negative about industrialism. He compared the effect of machinery on
the workers with the supersession of horses by railways:

'. . . as the railways came into operation the horses were stripped of
one feed after another, until at last they were sold to the knackers for
their flesh. This is precisely the effect machinery has on you.'[2]

On the other hand, some of his comments suggest that instead of
seriously expecting all workers to become smallholders, he was
looking instead to land settlement to have an indirect effect on industrial conditions. The prospect of machinery becoming 'man's
holiday' was perhaps based on his reiterated hope that the living
standard of the comfortable smallholder would be used as a measurement for industrial wages, as 'the only possible means by
which the fair standard of the price of labour can be established in

[1] *Ibid.*, Vol. I, pp. 82–3.   [2] *Land and Its Capabilities* (Manchester, 1842).

the artificial market'.[1] This social measurement was apparently to be achieved individually:

'. . . I was determined to establish a settlement where the poor man could estimate the value of his own labour, below which he would not sell it in the market.'[2]

A more direct effect could be expected by the withdrawal of some of the unemployed from the industrial areas, 'thus securing to the labouring class a competitive market'.[3] O'Connor dealt less than other writers, especially O'Brien, with this problem of 'surplus labour'. Such passages nevertheless show him thinking to some extent in industrial terms, and he certainly opened the columns of the *Northern Star* to proposals for land experiments which had a more limited objective than his own.[4]

One further passage from the 1842 lecture completes this impression of O'Connor's sense of industrial problems. The attack on land monopolists and capitalists was followed by condemnation of the 'middlemen' who, he argued, were especially active in the corn market: one object of land settlement was to relieve the working classes from their dependence on these distributive 'middle classes' — 'Let every man be, to a great extent, his own producer and consumer'. While this demand did not get as close to a solution of the problem of consumption as Bronterre O'Brien did, it illumines the working-class difficulty in accepting industrialism. Working-class support for the Land Plan probably derived less from a sentimental desire to return to rural life than from an inability to obtain as consumers the full benefits of an industrial system. The attractions of the Land Plan must be related, therefore, to the Truck question and the Co-operative Societies' campaign against adulterated food.

In turning to the way in which O'Connor connected the agrarian and political aspects of his Land Plan, one can find no consistent doctrine, merely a rather muddled feeling that there was a connection between landholding and political power. He railed against the 'dangerous political power' which 'the monopoly of land has conferred', yet his denunciation of English, as distinct from Irish, landlords, was always modified by his fear of industrial middle-class

---

[1] *Northern Star*, 2 Jan. 1847.   [2] *S.C.*, 3rd Report, 2439.
[3] *The Labourer*, Vol. II, p. 163.
[4] E.g. 16 Aug. 1845 — 'Field Gardening Operation'; 24 July 1847 — 'Address of Rev. Scholefield'.

power. Those who had attacked the land monopoly in 1832 'vainly hoped to monopolise power themselves for even a worse and more dangerous purpose — for the purpose of constituting England the great Slave-Labour Mart of the world'.[1] At one point he claimed that he 'intended to make the plan a stepping stone to the achievement of political as well as social rights',[2] but he paid no attention to this in practice. McGrath, the financial secretary of the Company, said in evidence about the allottees on Land Company Estates — 'We did not think it was possible to convert them into electors.'[3] It will be seen below that far from using freehold as a means of enfranchisement, as did the Anti-Corn Law League, O'Connor left in confusion the question of whether the allotment holders were freeholders or tenants of the company.[4]

O'Connor was clearly neither an economist nor a political philosopher. His *forte* was action, and it is action in the form of the creation of the Land Plan which will be discussed in this study. Yet his ideas were of great importance. Whatever their inconsistencies, they roused great enthusiasm among many of the readers of the *Northern Star* and were always imaginative enough to fire the discontent of the illiterate and inarticulate. In a sense O'Connor expressed the confusion of ordinary beings in the face of mounting social complexity, but as a propagandist he shared, rather than exploited, this confusion. One is uncertain, however, after reading the evidence to the House of Commons Committee, whether O'Connor with all his muddle, vainglory and fantasy, was farther from the truth than Revans, the Assistant Poor Law Commissioner, who lacking Chadwick's genius echoed his doctrines. It is not so much that Revans was wrong in asserting that the attempt of smallholdings to compete with large-scale farming '. . . is as hopeless as the attempt of the handloom-weaver to compete with the power-loom or the knitting needles to cope with the stocking frame',[5] as that he accepted with unimaginative complacency what he conceived to be natural forces. His dogmatism about general principle blinded him to the need for particular observation. So strong was the suspicion that 'his mind was somewhat prejudiced against the Land Scheme'[6] that several members of the Committee by hostile

---

[1] *Land and Its Capabilities.* [2] *The Labourer*, Vol. II, p. 181.
[3] S.C., 2nd Report, 1158. [4] See below, pp. 332–3.
[5] S.C., 4th Report, 3357. (Revans's Reply to the Poor Law Board.) See above, p. 8.
[6] *Gloucester Journal*, 5 Aug. 1848.

questioning were able to reveal the very cursory nature of his examination of the Land Plan Estates.[1]

His was the mentality which assumes that after one half-truth has been uttered there is nothing more to be said, and thereby stifles protest and initiative. For O'Connor there was always something more to be said, and if it was not all worth hearing, at least it aroused many to their own reflections about the place of individuals in the new society. It seems unlikely that all seventy thousand subscribers to the Land Plan dropped into a state of disillusioned apathy after 1848: many of them undoubtedly went on to carry their feeling for social control and emancipation into other spheres.

II

Feargus O'Connor had extolled the economic possibilities of smallholdings and the virtues of a peasant life from as early as 1841.[2] He continued to revert to the topic in the *Northern Star* and spoke on the question of land reform at the Chartist conventions in Birmingham in 1843 and Manchester in 1844. But it was not until April 1845 that the scheme which was later to gain fame and notoriety as the Chartist Land Plan was finally launched. The National Convention which opened in London on 21 April gave a favourable reception five days later to proposals for a 'Chartist Land Co-operative Society'.[3] A committee was set up which a few weeks later produced the 'Rules of the Chartist Co-operative Land Society, established 19th May 1845, under the sanction of a National Convention, assembled in London April 1845'.[4]

Before this date, despite O'Connor's dominant position in organised Chartism, the land scheme had been only considered as one element in what McGrath called 'the political and social welfare of the working classes of this country'.[5] But in December 1845 a convention at Manchester was called, according to the same witness, 'exclusively for consideration of the land scheme'. Progress was reported, the rules amended, a list of directors drawn up and the decision made to apply for registration under the Friendly Societies Acts. Apparently without further discussion and as a result of the issue of a certificate of refusal (31 July 1846) by Tidd Pratt, the Registrar for Friendly Societies, the name was altered to

[1] S.C., 4th Report, 3426–7, 3781–5.
[2] See *The Remedy for National Poverty* (Leeds, 1841).
[3] *Northern Star*, 3 May 1845. [4] S.C., 2nd Report, Appendix.
[5] S.C., 2nd Report, 955.

the 'Chartist Co-operative Land Company'.[1] Under this title a document describing the company was presented to Whitmarsh, the Registrar for Joint Stock Companies, on 24 October 1846.[2]

Before any reply had been received, the second conference devoted to the land plan was held at Birmingham in December 1846 and was reported in the *Northern Star* of 12 December as the 'Annual Conference of the Chartist Land Company'. There it was decided to establish 'The National Land and Labour Bank' and a new set of rules was drawn up. A few days later a fresh document calling the scheme 'The National Co-operative Land Company' was presented to Whitmarsh on 17 December 1846. The rules approved at Birmingham which were handed in on 25 March 1847, gave the final name as 'The National Land Company'.[3] Yet a fourth set of rules was drafted before the Company took its final shape. At the Lowbands Conference of August 1847, it was decided that since the Bank could not legally be conducted by the Land Company, it should be separated and run by O'Connor as an individual proprietor holding in trust for the company.[4] New rules omitting the Bank were, therefore, circulated under the heading 'National Land Company (Provisionally Registered)'. This last set of rules was handed in during the Parliamentary enquiry,[5] but the Act to dissolve the Company stated in the preamble that the final deed of registration was dated 1 June 1847 and it seems, therefore, that this last set of rules was never sent to the Registrar.[6]

Thus the Company remained 'provisionally', although incompletely, registered until the question of its status was raised in Parliament during the first half of 1848. Finding that registration under the Joint Stock Companies Act was expensive, O'Connor had not completed the final deed, but had decided instead to try by special legislation to get the benefits of the Friendly Societies Acts for the Land Company.[7] Petitions were presented to the House of Commons to this end, during February and March, from Salisbury, Northampton, Horncastle, Bolton-le-Moors and Worksop.[8] These were followed in May by a bill to amend the Friendly Societies Acts. In this short bill, O'Connor attempted to bring

---

[1] S.C., 1st Report, 200; 4th Report, 3256–70. [2] S.C., 1st Report, p. 54.
[3] S.C., 2nd Report. See Appendix for the first three sets of rules.
[4] S.C., 2nd Report, 991–3; 3rd Report, 2176–8. [5] S.C., 2nd Report, 991.
[6] Local and Personal Acts 14 and 15 Vict. 1851, Cap. CXXXIX.
[7] S.C., 1st Report, 185.
[8] *Journal of the House of Commons*, Vol. 103, pp. 277, 280, 283, 333.

within the scope of the Acts societies formed 'for the purpose of purchasing land ... and of erecting on such land dwellings to be allotted to members of the Society, together with certain portions of such land for agricultural purpose....'[1] The bill, however, was never given a second reading. Instead it was decided at the end of May to appoint the Select Committee which gave publicity to the Company's doubtful status.[2]

The Committee reached the conclusion that 'the National Land Company is not consistent with the general principles upon which Friendly Societies are founded' and that it 'as at present constituted is an illegal scheme'.[3] Yet the Committee was not unsympathetic to O'Connor's rather vague idea of special legislation, for the final paragraph of the report reads:

'In submitting these Resolutions to the consideration of the House, it is the opinion of Your Committee that it should be left entirely open to the parties concerned to propose to Parliament any new measures for the purpose of carrying out the expectations and objects of the promoters of the Company.'[4]

Nevertheless nothing was done. Just after the Committee's Report was presented to the House, an article in the *Northern Star* revealed that O'Connor was assuming that the Company would continue and was proposing methods for future purchase and allocation of estates which would avoid one of the main legal objections to the original scheme, the ballot for allotments.[5] Apparently these methods were never worked out, for the *Northern Star* throughout 1849 and 1850 simply reported receipts to the fund for winding up the Company: on 23 August 1851, for instance, two weeks after the passing of the bill to dissolve the Company, the paper carried a report of a 'National Loan Society' which hoped to compete in the market for any company property which might be sold. Until early in 1850, O'Connor seemed to have hoped that the registration of the original company might still be allowed.[6] After a judgment in the Queen's Court Bench in April, this was impossible,[7] but there was still nearly another year's delay before the bill to dissolve the Company was brought in (13 February 1851). The last event in the

---

[1] *Parliamentary Papers*, 1847–8. Bills, Public. Vol. II.
[2] *Journal of the House of Commons*, Vol. 103, pp. 555, 580.
[3] S.C., 6th Report, Resolutions 2 and 3.   [4] S.C., 6th Report, (Conclusion).
[5] *Northern Star*, 12 Aug. 1848.   [6] *Hansard*, 3rd series, Vol. CX, p. 552.
[7] *Journal of the House of Commons*, Vol. 105, p. 508.

institutional history of the Company was its final dissolution by an act passed in August 1851.

This chronology of the central machinery of the Land Plan gives a picture of confusion in the early stages and dilatoriness in the later. During the first eighteen months after the 1845 Convention some delay was inevitable: funds were being collected, branches formed and propaganda meetings held. The proposed company could only materialise if it proved to have membership and financial strength. But from 24 October 1846 there seems to have been a definite intention to register as a Joint Stock Company, and from then until the Lowbands Conference of August 1847 inefficiency was implied in the profusion of rules and titles issued from the Company headquarters in Dean Street, Soho. After the Conference, despite intermittent assurances in the *Northern Star* and *The Labourer*, O'Connor seems to have done nothing until the introduction of the badly drafted bill in February 1848. After the publication of the Reports in August 1848, he was again inactive until pressure in the House of Commons finally led to the Winding-Up Act of 1851. This inattention to important detail remains puzzling, for O'Connor himself was a barrister and so was Ernest Jones, one of the Trustees of the Company and co-editor with O'Connor of *The Labourer*. Nor was O'Connor merely a wild visionary unable to grasp prosaic detail. As a member of the Committee he frequently interpolated questions, and when McGrath, the financial secretary of the Company, gave evidence, O'Connor examined him fully, trying to establish that his financial procedure had been correct, as in the production at conferences of vouchers for money expended, and in the printing of balance sheets in the *Northern Star*.[1] Perhaps as a flourish, he even displayed acquaintance with the exact state of the Company's accounts, referring to 'the £4,000 there for expenses since the society was established', which included 'several bills paid to tradesmen, which they could more conveniently receive at the Land Office than come to me for at Lowbands'.[2]

Neither does O'Connor's delay seem to be due to any forecast of failure to get legal status in some form. In 1848 registration of both Friendly Societies and of Joint Stock Companies was only a few years old, while Co-operative Societies had another four years to wait before they acquired a regular system of registration. On the

[1] S.C., 1st Report, 853–8; 2nd Report, 1171–212.
[2] S.C., 1st Report, 859–60.

other hand economic and administrative ventures were frequently launched by private act of Parliament — from Enclosure Acts and Improvement Acts to the Railway Company Acts which had occupied so much of the time of Parliament in the 1840's. Thus it was natural to assume that the Chartists' own venture would be treated individually. As has been pointed out above, the Committee made a similar assumption in its last recommendation. It may even be that O'Connor felt that there would be no difficulty about formalities and gave his main energies to propaganda in the country. The aspect of the affair which defeats rational explanation and throws one back on the problem of O'Connor's temperament, is O'Connor's failure to take any action after the Committee had reported. There is no evidence of immediate panic after the Report was presented to the House on 1 August 1848: the Land Company petered out rather than burst like the vast speculative bubble which many of its critics declared it to be.[1] Although there were bound to be many financial difficulties, something could have been saved had O'Connor behaved more wisely. Indeed the *Gloucester Journal*, interested in the two estates near Gloucester, hoped that Parliament would not 'permit technical difficulties to defeat the benevolent project' and declared that the defects were not 'inherent or incurable' for 'Mr O'Connor may easily improve his bookkeeping'.[2]

The explanation for this failure probably lay in the emotionalism and instability which were evident in most of O'Connor's writings and which became more marked in the years between the failure of organised Chartism in 1848 and his entry into a lunatic asylum in 1852. In Parliament, O'Connor, who was returned at the elections of 1847, seems not merely to have subordinated the Land Plan to Ireland, but to have forgotten much of its business. For example, on 29 May 1851, when the Report of the Select Committee on the National Land Company was brought up in the House, he declared, thereby contradicting both the *Northern Star* and his own evidence to the Committee, that 'the Land Bank was established subsequently to the land company and entirely against his will'.[3] He seems moreover to have developed a persecution complex and, perhaps through financial difficulties, to have become more concerned with his own fate than with that of his subscribers. In reply to Sir Benjamin Hall, on 1 March 1850, he made a long and wild

---

[1] For an account of the later years of the Land Company see below, pp. 335–6.
[2] *Gloucester Journal*, 29 July 1848.   [3] *Hansard*, 3rd series, Vol. CXVII, p. 128.

defence of his conduct, based on his own expenditure of time and money in the affairs of the Land Company,[1] while in the speech of May 1851 quoted above, he complained that after the matter had been placed before a Master in Chancery 'they refused to send up a clause by which he (Mr O'Connor) might receive compensation under the Winding-Up Act. It seemed as if the object of everyone was to ruin him with expenses'.[2]

This egocentric element in O'Connor's character had obviously dogged the organisation of the Company throughout. Despite promises made during the hearing, the company officials failed more than eighteen months after the provisional registration to produce minutes of more than three Directors' Meetings.[3] To some extent the haphazard nature of company proceedings was doubtless due to O'Connor's behaviour. Whatever his qualities as a leader, they were not those of a committee man. The familiar charges against the 'Dictator of Chartism' in the political sphere can be paralleled in his conduct of the Land Company. For example, the report of the Conference held at Lowbands in August 1847 includes a discussion about the appointment of school-teachers at the estates, which reveals O'Connor's concern to keep appointments in his own hands rather than leave them to the allottees.[4] Even more striking at the same conference was the discussion about allotment rents. It was thought that there might have to be differential rents for different qualities of land and the Conference decided to appoint a 'Jury of arbitration' consisting of O'Connor and 'two practical farmers and two practical labourers'. Only a week later O'Connor referred to the rent question as one 'which the Conference has very wisely devolved upon me'.[5]

It is easy in the light of these facts to ascribe the weaknesses of the central organisation of the Company to two aspects of O'Connor's character, his instability and what William Lovett called his 'anti-democratic conduct'.[6] Nevertheless there are considerations which O'Connor's critics, writing from a liberal standpoint, have ignored. The passionate belief in democracy which informed the work of William Lovett and his wing of the Chartist movement had something of the pristine quality of Tom Paine's *Rights of Man*: it was supported, too, by a confident trust in education and intel-

---

[1] *Ibid.*, Vol. CIX, p. 233.
[2] *Ibid.*, Vol. CXVII, p. 128.
[3] S.C., 2nd Report, 1425–39.
[4] *Northern Star*, 21 Aug. 1847.
[5] *Ibid.*, 28 Aug. 1847.
[6] *Op. cit.*, Vol. 2, p. 315

lectual advancement. But it was still not the democracy of the second half of the nineteenth century. This, as one sees it in the skilled trade unions as well as in working-class politics, was a compound of ideals and experience of practical organisation. With little experience to go by in the 1840's, it is hardly surprising that the affairs of the Land Company were run without detailed attention to the views of directors, shareholders, and annual conferences. O'Connor himself, as Thomas Cooper tells us, 'had had the education of a gentleman'[1] and even to-day such an education is not calculated to secure co-operative working-class action or the acceptance of collective decision.

Moreover O'Connor's Chartist critics such as Lovett, Cooper, and O'Brien were concerned only with opinion-making organisations, not with any which were attempting to run practical schemes. That O'Connor's behaviour was influenced by the nature of his enterprise as well as overriding ambition is suggested by the genuine though intermittent attention he gave both to central detail and to local instructions to ordinary members distant from the London headquarters, about such matters as office procedure and the checking and transmission of money.[2] O'Connor saw himself as the trustee of the Land Company. It was his erratic practice not his theory of leadership which was at the root of the difficulties of the Company.

III

The characteristics which were so fatal to the organisation of a co-operative business were assets when O'Connor tried to rouse enthusiasm, generate local activity and raise money. To turn from Pratt and Whitmarsh — with their exposure of O'Connor's legal incompetence — and from the impatient House of Commons — to the seventy thousand scattered members of the scheme all over the country, is to see a different and more significant figure. Here is energy, imagination and a fanaticism less totally misguided and reactionary than has often been stated. O'Connor maintained a flow of articles to the *Northern Star* and *The Labourer*, commenting pungently on a variety of social problems and driving home the importance of the Land as cause and solution. The work of the company in buying estates and preparing them for settlement was undertaken entirely by O'Connor. In the midst of this activity, he could still be found lecturing on and defending the Plan to

[1] *Life*, p. 100. [2] E.g., *Northern Star*, 2 Jan. 1847.

audiences all over the country. The history of the Land Plan on this level is more exciting and purposeful than the institutional aspects described above.

According both to the various sets of rules and to evidence given to the Committee, O'Connor set about raising £130,000 in 100,000 shares of £1 6s. each. These shares could be paid up in instalments, apparently of any amount: some of the subscriptions sent individually to the *Northern Star* and acknowledged in the weekly lists are as low as one shilling. Two shares entitled the holder to enter the ballot for a two-acre holding, three for a three-acre and four for the largest holding of four acres. When an estate was bought, it was divided into holdings in proportion to the paid-up membership of each class: then the ballot for each was taken separately. Each successful shareholder would receive, in addition to the land, a cottage and an advance of money to help him with seed, stock and initial capital. The amounts in relation to the size of the allotment were to be £15, £22 10s. and £30 respectively.

What progress was made in recruitment for the scheme and collection of this money during the period from the inception of the plan in April 1845 to the parliamentary investigation of June–August 1848? How far had the Company succeeded in 'the realisation of its purpose by the location of its members upon the land . . .'?[1]

By the time of the first Conference devoted to Land Company affairs in December 1845, of the thirty-two districts in England and Wales which were eventually organised[2] all but two, Sunderland and Tower Hamlets, had produced subscriptions. In Scotland, two out of the later four districts had contributed (Glasgow and Greenock). But it is clear that the Company (or Society as it was at this date) was very weak in some of these areas. Both Northampton and Nottingham (and their surrounding districts) were only just beginning to contribute trifling amounts by December. In several cases there were contributions only from the towns which later became the centre of districts containing a number of branches. These were Brighton, Rochester, Norwich, Leicester and Hanley; other towns with branches were Oxford, later in the Banbury district, Scarborough, later in the Hull district, and Kidderminster, later in the Worcester district.

---

[1] S.C., 1st Report, Appendix.
[2] In this context 'eventually' means the Lowbands Conference of August 1847 The *Northern Star* (31 July 1847) published a list of districts and branches.

The Lancashire industrial districts were clearly the earliest source of strength. Manchester itself and the ring of towns south-east of Manchester — Stockport, Hyde, Dukinfield and Staly-bridge, further north Oldham, Rochdale, and Bacup, and to the west Salford, Bolton, Wigan and Warrington, all appear frequently in the returns. The Yorkshire industrial areas, though less strong, reveal Land Company members in Sheffield, Dodworth and Barnsley, Bradford, Hebden Bridge and Leeds. On Tyneside, only Newcastle had contributed a small amount, although there was later to be a strong district covering the Sunderland and South Shields area.

Recruitment in the centres of Midland industry was definitely slower than in Lancashire. The weakness of the movement in Nottingham and Northampton has been mentioned. In North Staffordshire only Hanley had contributed, whereas later there were to be branches in the other Pottery towns and in Stafford and Newcastle-under-Lyme. Derbyshire eighteen months later was to have seven branches, but at this stage members seem to have been confined to Derby and Mottram. Of the six Black Country towns with branches in 1847, only Bilston and Darlaston had contributed during the first year. Birmingham contributions are acknowledged in most weekly receipts, but they are usually small for a town which by 1847 had five branches. Where Manchester sends £10, £15, or £20, Birmingham sends £2, £4, or £5.

This last comparison is perhaps the key to the situation. The first response came from the factory and especially the cotton districts, not from the coal or iron areas, or from the districts of craftsmen and skilled artisans. It has been argued from this that the 'back to the land' movement appealed most to the victims of the factory system, of unemployment and of the new insanitary towns. While there is clearly much truth in this assessment, an interesting feature of the Land Scheme as it developed was the variety of support it commanded. To put the quick response of Lancashire into per-spective, there are two factors to be considered in the situation at the end of 1845.

First, although the great centres of population sent the biggest sums of money, the weekly receipts show that the Land Company had members, branches and secretaries in agricultural areas and southern towns, such as Yeovil, Exeter, Swindon, Devizes, Oxford and Brighton.

Second, it must be remembered that the Land Plan in its first year was an aspect of the Chartist revival after the setback of 1842. O'Connor was calling on the support of Chartists for whom the Land Plan was placed in a reassuring Chartist framework. An experiment was to be made by placing some members on land 'in order to demonstrate to the working classes of the kingdom, firstly, the value of the land, as a means of making them independent of the grinding capitalist; and secondly to show them the necessity of securing the speedy enactment of the "People's Charter", which would do for them nationally what this society proposed to do sectionally.' The conclusion left the land question in the background — 'the accomplishment of the political and social emancipation of the enslaved and degraded working classes being the prominent object of the society.'[1]

It was apparently on the basis of this vague appeal that the progress described above was made during the first few months. Hovell argues that, because at the end of 1845 the net subscriptions available for the purchase of land amounted to less than £2,700, therefore it seemed that 'however much O'Connor might flog the twin steeds of the Charter and the Land their pace remained terribly slow'.[2] Perhaps it was rather a proof of the lingering of Chartist loyalties and hopes that so much should have been achieved. Most of the money was collected from areas which had suffered extensive unemployment only a few years earlier.

At the Manchester Conference of December 1845 the Land Society acquired a more independent status in relation to Chartism as a whole. Its 'Objects' became simply 'to purchase land, erect dwellings, and allot them to its members upon such terms as shall enable them to become small freeholders and to live in comparative comfort and independence'. This was the main theme of the *Northern Star* during the following year, when far more money was collected, new branches were founded, and above all the purchase of land encouraged the belief that 'comfort and independence' were within reach:

> Courage, poor slave! deliverance is near.
> Oh! she has breathed a summons sweeter still:
> Come! take your guerdon at O'Connorville![3]

From the evidence of the weekly receipts collected during the

---

[1] S.C., 2nd Report, Appendix.   [2] M. Hovell, *op. cit.*, pp. 273–4.
[3] *Northern Star*, 22 Aug. 1846.

first few months of 1846 growth was chiefly concentrated in the north and south Midlands. Nottingham, Northampton and Leicester appeared more steadily on the lists. Birmingham contributed regularly, but still only about a third of the amount coming from Manchester. For example, on 14 February 1846 £33 was acknowledged from Manchester and £10 from Birmingham: the comparable figures for 4 April were £25 and £6 respectively. Apart from Bilston, the Black Country hardly figured in the 1846 receipts. On the other hand, there was evidence of growing strength in the smaller towns of the north Midlands, places like Belper and Newark. All the northern industrial areas remained strong supporters and their higher contributions were evidence of expanding membership. Some districts, like Sunderland, began to make up for their late start. The most interesting and least expected element in the accounts of 1846 was the extension of membership in the southern districts. Oxford, Coventry and Brighton, which had branches in 1845, were joined in 1846 by Banbury, Reading, Worcester, Shrewsbury, Winchester, Southampton and Chipping Norton. In the south-west Exeter continued to send small amounts fairly regularly, while in the accounts published in the middle of February, amounts of £3 3s. and £5 were acknowledged from Plymouth, Tiverton and Bath.[1] A branch was founded in Newton Abbot on 6 April, and by September and October Totnes, Torquay and Tavistock figured in the receipt lists. In Somerset and Wiltshire there were small branches at Frome, Bridgwater, Trowbridge and Bradford as well as the older branches at Swindon and Devizes. In East Anglia branches were started at Ipswich and Norwich late in 1846, and there was a new branch at Maidstone.

Thus by the end of 1846 all the regions represented at the Lowbands Conference of August 1847 had a number of branches. During 1847 there was expansion in all areas, but one new element visible in the accounts was the growing interest in the eastern counties: by June 1847 there were branches in Peterborough, Ely, Horncastle and Sleaford. Perhaps more revealing was the evidence of new members being recruited in the neighbourhood of some of the newly founded estates. Herringsgate was bought in March 1846 and contributions appeared from there in August. The Lowbands estate in Red Marley (near Gloucester) was purchased in October 1846 and the Snig's End and Minster Lovell estates in June 1847.

[1] *Ibid.*, 14 Feb. 1846.

In the receipt lists of 3 July a contribution of over £12 was acknowledged from Red Marley. On 10 July subscriptions from Gloucester and Witney were received. In January 1848, two months before the first allotment of land at Minster Lovell, there was a contribution from the small village of Minster Lovell, which was quite separate from the Witney branch. The appearance of a branch at Cirencester, situated between the Oxford and Gloucester estates, in the list of 10 July 1847, was probably a result of this tangible progress of the Land Company.

During the first six months of 1848, there was little change in the general pattern of membership and contribution. The only point of interest in the receipts is the large amounts which occasionally appear from centres which were either of recent origin or which had hitherto sent in small amounts. For example, Swindon which through 1845, 1846 and 1847 missed many weeks and never sent more than £5 at a time, suddenly in one week in January 1848 contributed £33. Leicester and Atherton, which usually sent only a few pounds at a time, were listed in the same accounts for £15 and £13 respectively. In April 1848, Derby sent over £26 in one week: Burslem and Bilston also sent larger amounts in 1848, and to a less marked degree Wolverhampton. The most probable explanation for these fluctuations was the anxiety of existing members to become paid up, in order to be eligible for the ballot, at a time when land allotments were becoming a reality.

This examination of samples of the weekly receipts throws some light on the chief centres of Land Company activity and on the chronology of its growth in various regions. There still remains the question of its relative strength in different areas, of what the branch organisation and subscriptions meant in terms of membership. It is not possible from evidence in the *Northern Star* to estimate accurately the number of shareholders in each district. The acknowledgments in the weekly lists were of totals sent by branch secretaries and give no clue to the number of individual contributions, for it is clear from an examination of the individual instalments sent direct to the centre that their size varied from one shilling to an occasional fully paid-up four shares (i.e. £5 4s.). Then, too, the reports carried in the paper of branch activities were concerned either with the founding of new branches or with reports of successes, the number of new members only being given. Nor is any such calculation as dividing the total membership by the number of branches, likely to yield useful results, for the original evidence is manifestly unreliable. McGrath's statement that 'there are about six hundred branches'[1] seems greatly exaggerated,[2] while there is conflicting evidence concerning the total membership. In the Committee hearings, the accountants Grey and Finlaison accepted the totals of seventy-five thousand and seventy thousand respectively,[3] while making it clear that the office lists had not been properly kept. Elsewhere O'Connor claimed one hundred thousand,[4] but Whitmarsh, the Registrar for Joint Stock Companies, received lists of under forty-four thousand names.[5]

Although it is impossible to arrive at exact figures, there is enough evidence to make some comparison between different areas at the time of the Lowbands Conference. There are probably one or two errors in this list (such as the omission of the Preston branch), and a few new branches may have been formed later. Nevertheless the picture given in August 1847 is not much altered by examination of the later receipt lists, and is probably substantially correct. In interpreting the Lowbands figures England may be divided into the North (i.e. Lancashire and Yorkshire northwards with the addition of the 'Stockport District', which included branches in Cheshire), the Midlands, the South, and London. The 'Norwich' and 'Worcester' Districts for this calculation are included in 'the South' since they belonged socially and historically to those districts which had been important before the industrial revolution. (The 'Worcester District' of the Land Company did not include the Black Country and extended through mainly agricultural districts, as far as Stow-on-the-Wold.) London districts included a few Surrey branches such as Croydon and Dorking. Taking the areas as thus defined, the Company had eighty-six branches in the North, forty-eight in the Midlands, eighty-nine in the South and twenty-four in London. Obviously the branches must have varied in size and one would expect a bigger membership in the large town branches. Nevertheless the branches in small places cannot be dismissed. For instance, a report from Newton Abbot (a town with a population of under twelve hundred in the 1841 census) stated in the summer of 1846 that 'The branch of the

[1] S.C., 1st Report, 1027.
[2] By comparison with the Lowbands Conference list which showed under three hundred.
[3] S.C., 5th Report, 4392, 4541.　　　　[4] *The Labourer*, Vol. III, p. 56.
[5] S.C., 1st Report, 55–8.

Chartist Co-operative Land Society established April 6th 1846 goes on prosperously in spite of opposition. To show the anxiety of the labouring classes to possess land, seventy-six joined in the first eight weeks the branch was open'.[1] Stony Stratford branch reported one week's recruitment as twenty-two while Long Buckby, a small Northamptonshire town, frequently reported such progress as 'several new members' or 'six new members' at weekly meetings.[2]

Another method of comparison is to take the numbers of delegates at the Lowbands conference. McGrath explained to the Committee that 'the country was divided into districts . . . so that each district should have as nearly as possible an equal number of members'.[3] This was unlikely to have been done with greater accuracy than other Company business, and in fact there was a dispute about the number of delegates to which Manchester was entitled.[4] Nevertheless the 'Districts' clearly bore some rough relation to numbers of members, for while 'Ashton', for example, covered only Ashton-under-Lyne, Stalybridge, Hyde and Dukinfield, 'Newton Abbot' had twenty branches and extended as far as Swindon, while 'Rochester' took in Royston and Ipswich. A comparison of the delegates apportioned to the same broad divisions adopted above, gives the following result: the North had sixteen, the Midlands nine, the South nine, and London four.

Even with allowance for errors and uncertainties, it thus becomes clear that the recruits to the Land Plan in the northern industrial districts did not outnumber those in the rest of the country taken as a whole. O'Connor directed his Land Plan primarily to what he called 'the landless, helpless multitude now thronging the filthy lanes, courts and alleys of our cities and manufacturing towns'.[5] That he appealed successfully is certain, but it is also clear from this examination of the geography of popular support for the Land Plan that he was heard by artisans of older and smaller towns, and that many of his supporters could be defined more accurately as craftsmen than as factory hands.

IV

This discussion of the progress of the Land Company has been so far concerned with the recruitment of members. There remains

---

[1] *Northern Star*, 13 June 1846.   [2] *Ibid.*, 3, 24 July 1847.
[3] S.C., 2nd Report, 1686.   [4] *Northern Star*, 21 Aug. 1847.
[5] *Ibid.*, 8 May 1847.

the question of tangible achievement — the purchase of estates and
the history of the minority of members who gained allotments. It
was after all the purchase of the estates which seemed to be turning
dreams into realities, and O'Connor appropriately headed his
letters from the first of his estates 'From Paradise'.

One of the obstacles to practical achievement was the difficulty
of collecting adequate capital from small subscriptions. O'Connor
attempted to overcome this by the foundation of 'the Land and
Labour Bank' at the end of 1846. 'If those with money to lend
would lend it,' he told the readers of the *Northern Star* in the spring
of 1847, 'I would change the whole face of society in TWELVE
MONTHS from this day. I would make a paradise of England in less
than FIVE YEARS.'[1] It was on 2 and 9 January 1847 that the *Northern
Star* carried a large front-page central panel announcing the Bank,
as an integral part of the Land Plan: it was, like most of O'Connor's
ideas, no mere mechanism or means to an end but a path to social
emancipation:

> 'We have been reminded to surfeit that the glory of England consists
> in the equal opportunity afforded to all in the market of speculation.
> We admit the fact, while we assert that the sun of England's glory
> would speedily set if all men were mere agents for the transfer of pro-
> perty, and none were producers of property. And it is in order that the
> latter class which will ever be the large majority may be armed with
> the power of co-operation as a means of placing them upon equality in
> point of protection with the former class that we advocate the principle
> of co-operation, and propose to establish the only medium by which it
> can be efficiently carried out — THE NATIONAL LAND AND LABOUR BANK.'

The bank was to be divided into three departments — deposit,
redemption and sinking fund. The bank apparently never became
firmly enough established to open the sinking fund, but the first
two departments described in this announcement were duly
founded. The deposit department was designed to work as an
ordinary deposit bank, but the redemption department was to be
open to members of the Land Company. Their savings at a rate of
interest of four per cent were to be applied to the reduction of their
rent-charge when they became occupants. They were not allowed
to 'withdraw more than one-half the amount deposited' and were
'obliged to give a month's notice' before they could withdraw any
portion of their deposit at all.[2]

[1] *Ibid.*, 1 Jan. 1847.   [2] S.C., 3rd Report, 2022.

When Price, the Manager of the National Land Company, was examined by the Committee, he claimed about seventeen hundred depositors and a total in the Redemption Department of £683.[1] In the Deposit Department, over £10,000 had been received, much of this coming from working-class societies rather than from individuals. One Manchester branch of the 'Journeymen Steam Engine Makers' and Mill-wrights' Friendly Society', for example, withdrew over £600 from their bank to deposit it in the Land and Labour Bank.[2]

If these totals are correct (and Price apparently produced account books at the hearings), they represent a considerable amount. Nevertheless the difficulties of collecting sufficient funds to build up reserves from working-class sources are obvious. Apart from the basic fact of poverty, a large proportion of working-class savings were short-term in character, easily used up in periods of unemployment. Price himself declared that 'we have suffered immensely from stagnation in trade'[3] and estimated withdrawals at over £4,000 in the period from January to June 1848.[4] In reply to O'Connor at the Committee hearings, Price affirmed that there had been frequent requests for withdrawals without the usual notice, generally on the grounds that depositors were in distress from want of work.[5]

More important than these difficulties, however, was the fundamental unsoundness of the scheme, brought out by Sir Benjamin Hall's relentless questioning of McGrath, the financial secretary of the Land Company.[6] The only security for the depositors' money was the land owned by the Company, but to this land the shareholders also had some claim. The depositors were in the hands of O'Connor and the other directors of the Land Company in that they had 'the power of mortgaging the rentcharge of the property, and disposing of it in any way they pleased for the benefit of the company'.[7] A further element of risk for those using the Bank was that after the decision had been taken in August 1847 to separate the Bank from the Company,[8] the Bank was in the name of O'Connor as sole proprietor. Out of the £16,000 total liabilities of the Bank at the time of the enquiry,[9] the advances to the Land

[1] *Northern Star*, 21 Aug. 1847.   [2] S.C., 3rd Report, 2042.
[3] *Ibid.*, 2036.
[4] *Ibid.*, 1st Report, Appendix (Rules of the National Land Company).
[5] *Ibid.*, 3rd Report, 2083.   [6] *Ibid.*, 2nd Report, 1510–19.
[7] S.C., 2nd Report, 1517.   [8] See above, p. 310.
[9] S.C., 3rd Report, 2068.

Company amounted to £6,391,[1] so that the Company had to play the roles of chief customer and chief backer.

This was certainly the wild speculative element in the Land Plan. The Committee recommendations made no reference to it, and it seems to have given O'Connor more trouble subsequently than the Land Company itself, since he received personal demands for money after the Bank had collapsed. As late as May 1851, O'Connor was fobbing off a demand from an iron-maker in Sheffield for his £67 deposited in the Land Bank. He tried to use the unsettled state of the Land Company affairs as an excuse, but as Roebuck pointed out in the House of Commons, the Committee had considered only the fate of the Company, not that of the Bank.[2] A day or two earlier, O'Connor had made the outburst, quoted above, against the Bank, and the expenses in which it had involved him.[3]

Despite its final disastrous character, the Land Bank probably gave some assistance in the purchase of estates. But since the £6,000 advanced was rather less than one-seventh of the total cost of the five estates the purchase of which was complete by the time of the inquiry, the Bank scarcely justified the extravagant claims made at that for this 'reproductive machinery'. When questions were asked about the allottees who could not be settled with the proposed original capital, the Committee was told by McGrath that 'their hope is that the banking department of the Company will so work as to produce the original sum, and thus enable the directors to locate as many more, and so on until all are located'.[4] Nevertheless the Bank must have had good propaganda value. It certainly enhanced the air of general prosperity, of the translation of ideals into practical achievement, which characterised the Land Plan, at least for the readers of the *Northern Star* during 1847. The ordinary members would not have bothered to make a calculation like that of Mr Finlaison, the actuary witness to the Committee, that even if the original capital had been reproduced in two years, it would have taken one hundred and fifty years to settle all the allottees.[5] They saw only that land was being bought, and that people like themselves were beginning a new life on small-holdings.

The first two Land Plan estates were bought in 1846,

[1] *Ibid.*, 2038.
[2] *Hansard*, 3rd Series, Vol. CXVII, p. 259.
[3] See above, p. 314.
[4] S.C., 2nd Report, 1507.
[5] S.C., 5th Report, 4541.

Herringsgate near Watford in March (later called O'Connorville) and Lowbands near Gloucester in October. Turning the pages of the *Northern Star*, it is even today a strange sensation to leave the columns of fervent preaching to stare at a plan of the Lowbands estate. A drawing in the issue of 14 November 1846 enhances the sudden impression of concreteness, by including round the boundaries of the estate the names of the neighbouring landowners. The effect on those who were basing their personal lives on the hope of a future on the land must have been very deep.

Through the early months of 1847, the paper carried reports of preparation of the land and building of cottages; and O'Connor addressed letters to the *Northern Star* from 'Herringsgate' or 'Lowbands'. He seemed to be supervising the construction of the millennium, rather than writing about it in London. This point was driven home by O'Connor in his speech on May Day 1847 when those successful in the first ballot arrived at Herringsgate to settle on their allotments. At this first estate — O'Connorville — a new period of history was beginning, which would eventually end 'female and child labour in the factories'. Practical accomplishment was a novelty for most working men, because

'. . . many warm-hearted philanthropists have charmed you with the assurance that the land is man's rightful inheritance; but not one has ever attempted to put you in possession of it . . . . A foolish reliance upon those fascinating principles has diverted your mind from the reality — THE ACTUAL POSSESSION OF THE THING ITSELF.'[1]

Even more publicity was given to the settlement of the Lowbands estate in August of the same year. It was made the occasion of the Land Company conference (to which there have been frequent references above). Instructions were given and preparations made in the *Northern Star* from the end of July; on 14 August, they became more precise — a friendly neighbouring landowner, Richard Aston, was willing to accommodate horses and carriages on his land. His interest was not the only example of sympathy in the Gloucester area. For while the *Hertford Mercury and Reformer* had ignored O'Connorville three months earlier, the *Gloucester Journal* not only made sympathetic comments on the scheme of 'our neighbour Mr O'Connor'[2] but sent a reporter

[1] F. O'Connor, *Speech at the opening of O'Connorville*, (Pamphlet).
[2] *Gloucester Journal*, 14 Aug. 1847.

who investigated the background of the delegates,[1] and carried a commentary regretting the general public ignorance of the scheme.[2]

This interest was maintained until the settlement of the third estate, Snig's End, which was only a few miles from Lowbands. The purchase had been made two months before the Lowbands Conference, but the allottees did not arrive until June 1848. The *Gloucester Journal* of 10 June noted that there was to be a demonstration at the opening ceremonies, which would include

'. . . what is eccentrically termed in the bill "a *treat* on the light fantastic toe" ,' in fact 'a select Democratic ball'.

Despite the ironical note and the concluding comment that 'It is not always that the Chartist mania leads to assemblages for such pleasant purposes',[3] the following week's issue carried a sympathetic account of the opening ceremony: just as at Lowbands in the previous year the demonstrators in their best clothes spent several hours in the pouring rain, while it was the lieutenants, McGrath and Clark instead of O'Connor himself, who risked the elements to make speeches. Nevertheless there was hope for the future in that the land appeared to be 'on the whole of better quality than at Lowbands'.[4]

Two more estates were planned in this part of England — Dodford, near Bromsgrove, and Mathon, near Worcester. The most ambitious purchase, that of an estate of five hundred acres at Mathon, was never completed. In fact nearly a year after the Committee of Inquiry, O'Connor forfeited his deposit on it.[5] The Great Dodford estate had been bought before the settlement of Snig's End, but no allotments were made. It was only used in July 1848 for a meeting of Land Company sympathisers from the Black Country, arranged as a gesture of defiance to the 'slanders' contained in the Committee Reports.[6] O'Connor was reported as selling this estate in April 1850[7] but it is probable that he made some profit, or recouped some of the losses of his own contributions to the Company, by selling it piecemeal. For the Winding-Up Act listed various messuages and allotments which had been sold from

[1] *Ibid.*, 21 Aug. 1847.
[3] *Ibid.*, 10 June 1848.
[5] *Ibid.*, 16 June 1849.
[7] *Gloucester Journal*, 20 Apr. 1850.

[2] *Ibid.*
[4] *Ibid.*, 17 June 1848.
[6] *Northern Star*, 22 July 1848.

the Great Dodford estate, and confirmed the sale. The share-holders were to have no claim against that property.[1]

The purchase of four estates in Worcestershire (Lowbands and Snig's End were then in Worcestershire, though now in Gloucester-shire) suggests that O'Connor may have had some policy about settlement in this area, after the initial apparently haphazard choice of Hertfordshire. But beyond the fact that it was an agricultural part of England, with little urban development to force up land prices, there seems to have been no strong reason for the choice. The same considerations would have applied to many other parts of Southern and Eastern England. O'Connor did not deign to discuss this aspect of policy. A letter in the *Northern Star* suggesting that estates should be scattered about the country, both to enable al-lottees to settle nearer their homes and to give advertisement to the Land Plan,[2] was published without any comment. Doubts about O'Connor's boasted acumen were expressed during the Committee hearings, for example by the Poor Law witness, Revans,[3] and the *Gloucester Journal* was later of the opinion that he had been very careless about his estate policy — he had neither examined the quality of the land nor considered its proximity to markets.[4]

These strictures seem applicable to the choice of the remaining estate at Minster Lovell. This is outside the area of the group just considered, but had more connection with it than had Herrings-gate. It adjoins the main Witney–Gloucester road and is only about thirty-five miles from Gloucester. After buying this estate of nearly three hundred acres at an auction in Witney[5] O'Connor wrote a letter in the *Northern Star* of 3 July 1847, describing its advantages. There were two roads already made, the main one to Cheltenham and the road to Brize Norton, on either side of which most of the cottages still stand. This would make the transport of building materials easier, while a freestone and limestone quarry on the estate was a ready source of supply. It seems typical of O'Connor's mentality that he could make separate intelligent observations — not merely the clouds of visionary words which issued out at other times — yet he never weighed one factor against another. The soil was clearly of poor quality: the allotments are on top of a hill,

[1] Local and Personal Acts 14 and 15 Vict. 1851, Cap. CXXXIX, Second Schedule.
[2] *Northern Star*, 24 July 1847.   [3] S.C., 4th Report, 3356.
[4] *Gloucester Journal*, 8 Dec. 1850.
[5] *Oxford Chronicle and Bucks, Berks, and Oxon. Gazette*, 26 June 1847.

across which there is a high wind at most times of the year. The wind probably removed the top soil, and in addition dispirited the allottees who arrived in March 1848[1] and were later adjudged by local people to have 'gone through the most trying hardships and privations'.[2] Much was made by critics of the Plan of the difficulties encountered by the townspeople in facing the weather, when they had spent their life 'shaded alike from the winter's wind and the summer's sun'.[3] This probably applied far more to the Minster Lovell settlement than to the more sheltered estates of Lowbands and Snig's End. Their exposure in the former case must have been psychologically intensified by their isolation. At Snig's End for example, one still passes some of the cottages on the way from Staunton village to the Church, and the whole parish is in any case a scattered one. The allottees were more likely to become a part of the community. At Minster Lovell, Charterville is cut off from the medieval settlement in the Windrush valley. A wife of one of the present allotment holders who was born in Minster Lovell itself had in effect to emigrate to Charterville. It was regarded 'as a terrible place to bring anyone to'. One can imagine the desolation of settlers who, though they came with enthusiasm for the land, were not dedicated to the ideal of an ascetic community life. The cottages, however, separate, neatly constructed, and detached appear today much like the bungalows of the 1930's. They are a reminder that O'Connor, far from being an Owenite, wrote articles against Communism and approved of the gospel of self-help.

The number of members who succeeded in getting allotments before the collapse of the Company was about two hundred and fifty. The total number of allottees named in the Committee reports is two hundred and twenty-six. But this cannot be complete because at Minster Lovell only sixty-five are shown,[4] whereas Christopher Doyle, who managed Charterville in O'Connor's absence, mentions the figure of eighty of whom 'all but two or three' have moved in.[5] There must in addition have been a few extra at Lowbands as the total holdings of the forty-four allottees listed are about thirty acres short of the size of the estate.[6]

The National Land Company therefore took three years to settle a very small proportion of its seventy thousand membership. It was

[1] S.C., 4th Report, 3393.
[2] Oxford Chronicle and Bucks, Berks, and Oxon. Gazette, December 1849.
[3] S.C., 4th Report, 3356.   [4] Ibid., 5th Report, Appendix.
[5] Ibid., 3rd Report, 2680.   [6] S.C., 5th Report, Appendix.

patently insufficient to 'pioneer the way in the glorious work of social emancipation' let alone to modify the 'ruthless monopoly' to which the land had 'fallen a prey'.[1] Yet before dismissing the whole scheme in terms of the failure of its grandiose aspects, it is worth considering more fully the character of the allottees. The history of the Land Company, at least from the time of the inquiry in June 1848, must move to the few individuals who were located.

V

Reference was made above to the probable composition of the membership of the Company. There is more direct evidence about the occupations of at least some of those who were successful in the ballot. The predominance of people 'from the manufacturing districts' was affirmed by McGrath who also speaks of 'the few farm labourers which we have succeeded in locating'.[2] This statement was confirmed by Michael Sullivan, M.P., after his visit to the Gloucester estates,[3] and by a reporter from the *Gloucester Journal*, who, spending 'A Day at Lowbands' six months earlier, had found the majority used to 'a manufacturing life'.[4] What is more interesting however is the question posed above[5] as to the trades of these aspiring farmers. Were they the oppressed victims of the Manchester factories?

Sullivan gave a list of some of the trades he found at Lowbands. They included a cotton overseer, a cotton spinner, a frame-work knitter, a shoemaker, a stocking maker, a tallow chandler and a cabinetmaker. The *Gloucester Journal* also made reference to the 'factory over-looker' who came from Yorkshire and was a widower, with a son of eighteen.[6] It referred too to a cabinetmaker, but mentioned his coming from London. There was also a cabinetmaker, Henry Lee, from Exeter, whom Revans called the most successful farmer at Lowbands.[7]

Although this evidence is confined to Lowbands, more light can be thrown on the settlers on all four estates by an examination of the Population Schedules of the 1851 census.[8] Some of the names of residents returned correspond to those listed as allottees in the 1848 enquiry: in many cases they were entered simply as 'small-

---

[1] *Ibid.*, 1st Report, Appendix, 'Rules of the National Land Company'.
[2] *Ibid.*, 2nd Report, 1147.
[3] S.C., 4th Report.
[4] *Gloucester Journal*, 4 Dec. 1847.
[5] See above, pp. 317–18.
[6] *Gloucester Journal*, 4 Dec. 1847.
[7] S.C., 4th Report, 3356.
[8] H.O. 107/1714, 1731 and 1960.

holder' or 'farmer', but some gave another trade as well. Thus at Charterville we find a 'smith and farrier', and 'a basket-maker'. Living on the Lowbands allotments there were two brothers (Parker) who were brass-founders from Birmingham, a lace weaver (James Goodward) from Nottingham and a tailor (Cornelius Ashton) from Manchester. In addition there was a furrier, Prussian by birth. At Snig's End, there was a blacksmith from Wells, and also Henry Cullingham, a London carpenter.

These examples from different sources show that many supporters of the Company were craftsmen rather than factory hands. Admittedly the evidence of the 1851 census is selective, as these would be the people who tended to survive. On the other hand it is not contradicted by Sullivan's testimony, and it harmonises with the variegated pattern which emerged from the examination of branches and subscriptions.

Before considering the significance of this conclusion for any judgment on the Land Plan, it is worth following the problems of the smallholders after official interest ended with the printing of the Committee reports in August 1848. The tragedy which occurred in the lives of a number of them was not a result of what Sir Harry Verney called 'the delusion which had been practised on those unhappy individuals who had wrecked their hard earnings in so delusive a speculation'.[1] These victims were the vast majority who had no chance of acquiring a farm. For those already allocated, the Committee had left the way open for action which would protect them. There was nothing inevitable about the failure of many of the allottees: on the contrary much of the blame must be laid to Feargus O'Connor's irresponsibility or perhaps approaching madness.

The Committee found that O'Connor had subsidised the Company to the extent of over three thousand pounds.[2] Yet an absurd feature of the finance of the Company was the confusion over the question of rents, which had they been paid would at least have countered some of this debt. The discussion of rents at the Lowbands conference has been mentioned above.[3] When the committee reported, no rent had been collected or even fixed. It was uncertain whether the rate was to be four or five per cent of expenditure and whether all estates were to pay the same.[4] A much deeper confusion

---

[1] *Hansard*, 3rd series, Vol. CXVII, p. 128.
[2] S.C., 6th Report, 4th Resolution.
[3] See above, p. 314.
[4] S.C., 2nd Report, 1489–1501; also 4th Report, Revans.

was evident about the principle of whether the allottees were to be freeholders or tenants of the Company. A casual alteration occurred in the new rules adopted for the National Land Company at the Lowbands Conference.[1] Whereas the rules of the Birmingham Conference (December 1846) had stated that the objects were

'To purchase land, erect dwellings, and allot them to its members upon such terms as shall enable them to become small freeholders and to live in comparative comfort and independence',

the later set dropped all reference to 'freeholders', and with that emphasis on rapid creation of capital which was evident in the enthusiasm about the Land Bank, even declared that this 'continually progressing fund' could be assisted

'by selling, mortgaging, or otherwise disposing of the estates themselves at their increased value, from time to time for the benefit of the company.'[2]

This second clause seems quite incompatible not only with O'Connor's ideals[3] but with the moderate aim of creating a secure tenantry paying ground-rent, which seems to emerge from evidence given to the committee.[4]

This particular example of O'Connor's inconsistencies had practical import for his tenants. The odd element of speculative enterprise allowed to the directors was paralleled in the freedom of those successful in the ballot to sell their right of occupancy.[5] In the list of allottees drawn up by the Committee[6] there were twenty-three 'transfers', i.e. those who had paid money (in one case as much as £90) to the successful balloter for the right to take up the allotment. Payment to the company they would still have to make on the same terms as the original drawers. The few who sold their rights undoubtedly benefited more than any other members of the Land Company, for many of the allotment holders were to discover their real insecurity in the shape of O'Connor's inconsistency.

In October 1849 a small item from Witney appeared in the *Oxford Chronicle* under the heading 'Mr O'Connor and his tenantry at Charterville':

[1] See above, p. 312.
[2] S.C., 1st Report, Appendix, Rules of the National Land Company.
[3] See above, p. 309.   [4] S.C., 2nd Report, 1157, 1164, 1489–1501.
[5] S.C., 2nd Report, 1156.   [6] S.C., 5th Report, Appendix.

... Several of the less fortunate allottees in the estate at Minster Lovell, have lately had distraints levied on their effects at the instance of the proprietor Mr Feargus O'Connor.'[1]

Apparently they resisted and brought an action for assault against the bailiff who, after producing a pistol, had been 'expelled by beat of drum into the adjoining turnpike road'. Although they lost this action the magistrates expressed 'an opinion as to the illegality of distraining at all for rents at this place'. The *Chronicle* report added sympathetically that 'it cannot be surprising that the holders of those allotments, having paid a portion of the purchase in the first instance, then gained possession in preference to a very large number of disappointed subscribers by a toss up, then entered upon the land without any idea of the rent to be paid, never entered into any agreement but considered the property their own, it is not to be wondered at that the parties should resist a demand for which they are, from circumstances totally unprovided for.'[2]

However, a fact unknown both to the *Chronicle* and to the allottees was that £5,000 of the purchase price had been mortgaged. O'Connor made an agreement with the mortgagees, Pinnock and Weaving, on 4 January 1850 which gave them the right to 'make sale and dispose of all and singular profits of all or any part ... of the ... premises'.[3] Until then they had apparently received their interest, but brought a suit of ejectment against the allottees at the instance of O'Connor who presumably wanted to be released from debt.[4] Judgment went against the defendants and in November 1850 the *Chronicle* reported the pathetic departure of the allottees when the sheriff's officer executed the warrants:

'It was anticipated that these proceedings would be resisted in a formidable manner by the occupiers. Nothing of the kind, however, was attempted: each party left in a peaceable manner: many were in a very destitute condition, and exclaimed loudly against the scheme, which in the first instance, told such a plausible tale of the lasting benefits it would confer on the shareholders, but which now had reduced them to the necessity of returning from whence they came, with little or no means, and entirely ruined in their prospects.'[5]

After two years of struggle on unyielding soil, many of them

[1] 13 Oct. 1849.   [2] *Ibid.*, 1 Dec. 1849.
[3] Title Deeds in the possession of Mr H. Holloway, Minster Lovell. Indenture of Release 13 Feb. 1851.
[4] *Gloucester Journal*, 20 July 1850.   [5] *Oxford Chronicle*, 23 Nov. 1850.

must have found it difficult to manage even 'returning from whence they came'. Some probably became the victims of the Poor Law, whose human waste agrarian radicalism hoped to abolish. A few may have stayed to find labouring work in Minster Lovell or Witney. There is for example a James Price on the list of four-acre allottees, and a James Price shown as a father in the baptism register at Minster Lovell, in June 1851. In the 'occupation' column, 'market gardener' has been crossed through and 'labourer' substituted.[1]

The Minster Lovell group were the most unfortunate, but O'Connor attempted the same move on the Gloucester estates. At Snig's End, there was a successful resistance to the bailiffs in August 1850[2] while the Lowbands allottees protested against the demands for exorbitant rents in December of that year.[3] But there was apparently no mortgage on these estates. In the schedules of land given in the Winding-Up Act, only one allotment at Lowbands is shown as sold and this may well be the one which O'Connor had taken for himself on 'transfer'.[4] Herringsgate, perhaps because it was the smallest and least valuable, he seems to have left alone.[5] In fact, the protests from Minster Lovell and Snig's End drew forth a declaration of confidence from the O'Connorville allottees, who commenting on 'some of the allottees on the other estates' go on to assure O'Connor

> 'that the allottees at O'Connorville have no sympathy with such conduct but are aware of the difficulties which the government have thrown in the way of the legalisation of the Land Plan, as well as the opposition you have encountered from the people's enemies.... We most cheerfully acknowledge you as our landlord in trust for our brother shareholders'.[6]

How many allottees managed to survive both the difficulties of their task and their desertion by O'Connor? The census of 1851 was taken before the Winding-Up Act, so that its evidence can be used to test the ability of settlers to survive on their smallholdings, quite apart from the complications of legal entitlement. Minster Lovell was a special case: there only two survived — perhaps through paying the rent demanded. At O'Connorville, six can be

---

[1] Parish Register, Baptisms, Minster Lovell.
[2] *Gloucester Journal*, 31 Aug. 1850.
[3] *Ibid.*, 1, 8 Dec. 1850.
[4] 14 and 15 Vict. 1851, Cap. CXXXIX.
[5] S.C., 5th Report, Appendix.
[6] *Northern Star*, 31 Aug. 1850.

traced, at Lowbands and Snig's End sixteen and twenty-two respectively.[1] Their subsequent history is difficult to follow, but some entries in the Staunton Parish Registers prove that, at least for a few, the Land Company represented a changed mode of life rather than a blurred and disastrous vision. James Brande, a four-acre allottee, and Robert Wilson, a holder of two acres who came from Walsoken in Cambridgeshire, both appear in the register of baptisms in 1855. Their occupation in both cases is 'allottee'. Thomas Halsale from Chorley who originally balloted for two acres is shown in the 1851 census returns as 'Labourer'. Whether or not he retained his own land as well, he did at least spend the rest of his life in rural work, for his death at the age of seventy-five is recorded in the Staunton Burial Register for 1873.

One interesting entry in the Marriage Register for 1873 is that of William Alder How, aged 27. His father whose occupation is shown as 'farmer' is clearly the William Alder How who held four acres on the Lowbands estate. He was born in York but had apparently worked in Alnwick, then Durham before taking up his allotment.[2] The letters protesting against the rent proposals in the *Gloucester Journal*, December 1850,[3] had been signed by him 'On the Part of the Occupants at Lowbands', so that he seems to have been a man of some character. The fact that his son was a mason, that he was marrying the daughter of the innkeeper at Staunton, and that they both signed the register in a good hand suggests that the father had climbed very firmly into the upper ranks of the Victorian working class, either through, or despite of, his connection with the National Land Company.

It must in fact have taken a good deal of tenacity to retain the holdings after 1851. The Winding-Up Act had provided that the allottees paid a sum for past rent.[4] But patience with the Gilbertian pace of Chancery proceedings was then needed. The petition for appointment of a master was filed on 15 August 1851, and a pencilled note on it appointed a master in attendance at Court during the vacation, to supervise the winding-up.[5] By November, an official manager had been appointed but he was merely asking for

---

[1] It is only at Minster Lovell that the estate is clearly defined within the census district. A few may therefore have been missed on the other estates.

[2] See birthplaces of his children. Population Schedules 1851, H.O. 107/1960 (335).

[3] See above, p. 334n.

[4] 14 and 15 Vict., Cap. CXXXIX.

[5] C36/574.

the matter to be moved from one court to another.[1] Although the Chancery Order 'granted the prayer', proceedings did not seem to be expedited, as a Chancery Order of 10 June 1852 appointed a new Master of the Court on the grounds that the original 'Master of Court Humphrey' had been taken ill and had 'ever since continued unable to proceed with any of the business'.[2] Slight progress had apparently been made by the Official Manager in working out a form of conveyance, for in the same year a dispute between William Alder How and Goodchap was brought before the new Master. The declaration of the Court was that the form of conveyance ought to give the Manager an 'absolute right of re-entry' if the rent-charge was more than a year in arrears.[3] This sounds reasonably generous to the allottees, and since there was no further reference to the Land Company in the lists of Chancery Orders, it appears that the rent charges were fixed by the Manager and accepted by the remaining allottees.

VI

What conclusions can be drawn from this survey of the allottees? The existence of a variety of trades, many of them skilled, on the estates, confirms the impression that the entire support for the land company did not come from what J. E. Cussans, speaking of Herringsgate, called 'the most ignorant and poorest part of the community'.[4] If we dismiss the cotton spinner as making a blind protest, as suffering from atavistic land-hunger, what of the Nottingham lace weaver, the Exeter cabinetmaker, or the allottees from rural areas like Walsoken? Why should they want smallholdings?

The recollection of the enclosure movement, the dislike in many cases of town life no doubt play their part. But there are two aspects of industrialism which probably weighed more with such people, insecurity and specialisation. They may well have felt that there was increased security in property ownership. Were their motives similar to those which led during the same period to investment in co-operative societies, building societies and freehold land societies?

A few points of comparison with these contemporary social

[1] C33/1006.   [2] C33/1007.   [3] C33/1016.
[4] MS. note in his own copy of his *History of Hertfordshire*, (1870–81) (Herts. County Record Office).

institutions is interesting. It is worth remembering that the co-operative societies had not yet freed themselves from the Owenite Community idea. The Rochdale Society included in its objects the purchase of estates and assumed that ownership of land would give security to members in time of unemployment. The building society schemes aimed at members of the working class acquiring their own plots: in fact Joshua Hobson (O'Connor's northern antagonist)[1] pointed out that the scheme he worked out for the employment of members on the land, for the National Association of United Trades, could have been registered under the Building Societies Act.[2]

There were a number of freehold land societies founded during the later years of the National Land Company, not all of them connected with Cobden's scheme for enfranchisement: the originator of these plans was supposed to be Taylor of Birmingham. When he attended the inauguration of the Hertfordshire and Bedfordshire Freehold Land Society, the opening speech (made by a Mr Lattimore) was careful to distinguish its appeal from that of O'Connor's to the working-class:

> 'the object was not to induce them to leave their occupations . . . but simply to sweeten their toil with the heritage of freedom.'

Land was to be bought near the towns for gardening, but they were not 'to be induced to go and live on two, three or four acres of land'.[3] *Reynolds Political Instructor* did not accept the distinction, for a few weeks later it commented on a speech by Cobden at Leeds, where he had praised James Taylor, suggesting that he should give 'Honour to whom honour is due', since 'Mr Taylor's scheme is a miniature picture of Mr O'Connor's Land Association'.[4]

This disagreement may throw some light on the second point made above in discussing motives for joining the Land Company, the question of specialisation. It was of course true that O'Connor expected people to leave their occupations and live by agriculture. But pre-industrial village and small-town life was often based on a combination of agriculture and domestic industry. Perhaps this was part of the appeal for people from towns like Devizes, Newton

[1] See above, p. 67.
[2] J. Hobson, *Land Scheme of Feargus O'Connor. 1847–8* (Manchester. 1848).
[3] *Hertford Mercury and Reformer*, 15 Dec. 1849.
[4] *Reynolds Political Instructor*, 5 Jan. 1850.

Abbot, Exeter. The evidence examined of those who stayed on the estates, at least until the time of the 1851 census, confirms the fact that many of them were practising their old crafts. In one or two cases it is clear that they were by no means destitute when they turned to the Land Company. Wolf Moss, the Prussian furrier still at Lowbands in 1851, had paid his £5 4s. for the four acre share in a lump sum,[1] while James Beattie who led the resistance at Minster Lovell was a pensioner getting £18 a year.[2] For them the move must have been as calculated as that of the artisans who were beginning to buy their own houses. Perhaps it was an attempt to get a more varied as well as secure life, rather than a desperate attempt to escape from the grip of industrialism.

Two other considerations arise from this evidence about the background of a few allottees. The first is the question of their suitability for agriculture. Scepticism about the capacity of towns-people to become farm workers, was evident right through the Committee hearings and in numerous contemporary comments. It has remained the basis for retrospective condemnation. But was it so impracticable to expect craftsmen, not all of whom would by any means have been cut off from all knowledge of the country, to be able to cultivate a smallholding? It has been shown that a number of them survived three or four years; the approaching period was to be a prosperous one for agriculture and no doubt some of them would have modified O'Connor's insistence on growing some wheat and would have become market gardeners. It was not this which was the fantastic element in the plan, but rather the numbers involved in relation to the capital, and above all from the allottees' point of view, the carelessness which led to so much loss and difficulty. More capital was of course needed and far more careful direction. It is interesting to notice that Finlaison who examined the accounts for the committee was of the opinion that the impracticable element was the attempt to raise money from individuals:

'It may seem visionary in me to say so but I cannot help thinking the scheme would be practicable by degrees.'

He is thinking in terms of a public company and when asked whether one would be found to advance the money, replied:

'It is a mere opinion but many companies have lately been formed for more visionary purposes.'[3]

[1] *Northern Star*, 21 Nov. 1846 (Receipt lists).
[2] *Gloucester Journal*, 8 Dec. 1850.   [3] S.C., 5th Report, 4400, 4418.

The second question concerns the political outlook of the allot-ees. Reference has been made to O'Connor's lack of interest in the franchise for them.[1] His approach at times was nearer to the Tory view that the working classes should have a stake in the country than to the broad programme of social and political emancipation supported in the *Northern Star*. 'My plan has no more to do with Socialism than it has with the Comet,' O'Connor exclaimed with pride.[2] One of the advantages of having 'a small proprietary class', he argued, was that it would provide 'the only means that can secure a national militia, who will fly to the cry of "My cottage and my country are in danger" '.[3]

Such passages seem to justify Bronterre O'Brien's condemnation that the Land Scheme would extend 'the hellish principle of Landlordism', and by benefiting a small section of the working class, would detach them from the rest 'and destroy the principle of United Action'.[4] On the other hand there seems no reason to suppose that the allottees would have shared O'Connor's views. In fact the tone of letters to their local papers from James Beattie and William Alder How suggests a type of independence which was much nearer to the Lovett school than to O'Connor's haphazard democratic sentiments. Each of these continued with his campaign, Beattie lecturing against O'Connor in Scotland[5] and How, as has been seen, taking an action to Chancery.

These two men were probably exceptional. On the other hand, the *Gloucester Journal* visitor to the Lowbands Conference re-marked:

'the residents at Lowbands are a remarkably intelligent set of men having had their intellects sharpened by a manufacturing life and by political and other discussions amongst their fellow workmen in the large towns of the north'.[6]

While there is no direct evidence of political activity on the estates, it is noticeable that according to items in the *Northern Star* every week, the Land Company branches held frequent meetings. It seems unlikely that they merely collected subscriptions: they were probably as good centres of the sort of political discussion to which the *Gloucester Journal* referred, as ordinary Chartist as-semblies. It would be interesting to know from local evidence how

[1] See above, p. 308.
[2] *Northern Star*, 15 Apr. 1843.
[3] *Ibid.*, 2 Jan. 1847.
[4] *The National Reformer*, 9 Jan. 1847.
[5] *Northern Star*, 30 Aug. 1851.
[6] *Gloucester Journal*, 4 Dec. 1847.

far the membership overlapped. For O'Connor, despite the political confusion to which reference has been made, never dropped the campaign for the Charter from the *Northern Star*, and readers of Land Company news were constantly reminded of wider political questions. Nor is it altogether true, as O'Brien implied, that the discontented believe in only one nostrum. When there is social disturbance and a critical atmosphere, everything is called into question and many remedies are propounded. Their mutual consistency seems unimportant and it is doubtful whether the ordinary Land Company members, including those intelligent men at Lowbands, would have appreciated the *Gloucester Journal's* objection to the scheme as a solution for town problems on the grounds of the 'social retrogression which it involves'.[1]

If the full O'Connorite dream was beyond achievement, was the *Gloucester Journal* right in this judgment? Had the scheme grown with the inflationary power of O'Connor's rhetoric it would of course have been so. A general back-to-the-land movement clearly could have provided no solution for the British working class. But together with other Chartist activities the Plan helped to draw attention to the failure of the social and political system to adapt itself to economic change. Nor did this concern disappear with the Land Company. After 1848 Harney, Reynolds and Jones continued to discuss the land question in relation both to ownership and to the relief of unemployment,[2] Minton Morgan advocated his 'Self-Supporting Industrial Villages'[3] while the economists and the quarterlies debated the right of property in land and the merits and de-merits of smallholdings.[4]

This is not merely a retrospective judgment. The same *Gloucester Journal* critic declared that O'Connor had done 'immense public good by turning public attention to the position of the humbler classes' and, even after the failure of the Company, felt that 'the rural gentry and agriculturists' could profit from the Plan as an example 'to teach them how much many of them had neglected as

[1] *Gloucester Journal*, 28 Aug. 1847.
[2] Harney had stated in 1845 that the land is 'the people's farm' (*Northern Star*, 30 Aug. 1845): Jones put forward the full case for land nationalisation. (See his editorial in the *People's Paper*, 5 June 1852, reprinted in J. Saville, *op. cit.*, pp. 152–7.) See also a series of articles in the *Democratic Review* (1849) on 'The Land, the Common Property of the People'.
[3] *The Christian Commonwealth* (1850).
[4] See, for example, W. T. Thornton, *A Plea for Peasant Proprietors* (1848): *The Westminster Review* (April 1848), 'Primogeniture and Peasant Proprietors.'

landlords to provide for their cottage tenantry the comforts and decencies of a humble home'.[1] In its hope that such a plan would 'teach the legislature, country gentlemen and boards of guardians' to devise a similar scheme 'as a substitute for the Union workhouse',[2] the *Gloucester Journal* had placed the Chartist Land Company in the wider context of that 'condition of England question' to whose formulation the Chartist movement as a whole had contributed much.

[1] *Ibid.*, 29 July 1848.   [2] *Ibid.*, 21 Aug. 1847.

Chapter Eleven

The Chartists and the Anti-Corn Law League

Lucy Brown

I

Between 1838 and 1846 Chartism had a rival in the Anti-Corn Law League: each was a movement which hoped to organise itself on a national scale, and each was at least threatened by competition from the other. During these years, in spite of a variety of attempts at reconciliation, the two movements were for most of the time antagonistic to one another. It is proposed in this study to concentrate on two questions: the first, whether there was in fact common ground between their programmes, which would make joint action possible and desirable, and the second, whether it can be said that either movement noticeably affected the course of development of the other.

It is obvious that there was no organic connection between the expressed aims of the two movements, between repeal of the corn laws on one side and the constitutional reforms of the Six Points of the Charter on the other. Nevertheless, there was no reason why these two demands should be incompatible, and, in fact, in Radical politics since 1815 they had been frequently associated. In 1815 there had been popular riots in London when the Corn Law was being discussed in Parliament; and in 1819 the Peterloo meeting had called both for parliamentary reform and for repeal of the corn laws. Similarly in 1830–2 the two demands had been associated in some places.

The change in attitude came with the passing of the Reform Act, which enfranchised the middle classes, but not the working class. Parliament after 1832 could be accused of legislating in the interests of the middle classes. An editorial in the *Northern Star* in 1846 described the grievances of the working classes after 1832 in the following way:[1]

'As early as 1838 before the Corn Law League was in existence we shewed ... that machinery had pounced upon us with such an unex-

[1] *Northern Star*, 21 Feb. 1846.

pected hop, step, and jump that society was compelled to submit to such laws and regulations as its owners thought proper to impose; that the laws of the country were enacted for an agricultural state of society, and although exhibiting strong symptoms of lordly influence, that nevertheless there was, up to the enactment of the Poor Law Amendment Bill, a strong recognition of the rights of the poor.'

The opposition to the New Poor Law, and the Ten Hours movement, were both important influences in the development of Chartism, and both agitations assumed that the economic interests of employers and workers were hostile to one another. The Anti-Corn Law League, which tried to prove that all classes stood to gain from repeal, encountered a suspicion which each of these earlier movements had already made articulate.

But suspicion of the Anti-Corn Law movement among working-class politicians developed slowly after 1832. Different towns possessed widely different political traditions, and social or economic structures: at no time in this period can generalisations about 'working-class opinion' or 'middle-class opinion' be made without substantial local qualifications, and in the period before the establishment of the League and the *Northern Star*, this is particularly true. In the middle 30's the Corn Laws could not become an issue between economic classes, for interest in them had languished. In Manchester, the Chamber of Commerce only 'aroused itself from its seven years' sleep' in December 1838, under pressure from Cobden and J. B. Smith.[1] In Sheffield the Anti-Corn Law movement received more support from the working classes than the middle classes: a Mechanics' Anti-Bread Tax Association was in existence there before 1832 and survived until the 1840's, whereas it seems that a middle-class association founded in 1834 lapsed. In 1833, Ebenezer Elliott, 'the Corn Law Rhymer', complained: 'The people will soon enough discover the frightful extent of the chasm which separates them from every man who has a decent coat on his back. If a meeting take place on the vital question of the corn laws, and no person above the rank of a small tradesman attend it, what will the ten thousand say?' As late as November 1838, he was still talking in the same way.[2]

---

[1] *Report of the proceedings of the Manchester Chamber of Commerce, 1838–9* (Manchester, 1839); A. Prentice, *History of the Anti-Corn Law League* (1853), Vol. I, p. 88.

[2] M.R.L., J. B. Smith MSS., Elliott to Smith, 18 Oct. 1833 and 7 Nov. 1838.

z*

Elliott himself, and the local Liberal paper, the *Sheffield Iris*,[1] were at first firm supporters of Chartism. In September 1838, Elliott was sent as Sheffield delegate to the meeting of the London Working Men's Association held at Westminster.[2] In the same month he presided at a public meeting in Sheffield, at which the Charter was first publicly brought forward, and for which he composed a hymn:[3]

> For leave to toil, and not in vain
> For honest labour's needful gain,
> A little rest, a little corn,
> For weary man to trouble born.
>
> For labour, food; for all, their own:
> Our right to trade from zone to zone,
> To make all laws for us and ours
> And curb the will of evil powers.

The break came in January 1839. At a meeting addressed by the League's lecturer, A. W. Paulton, the Chartists supported a motion calling for the Charter before repeal of the Corn Laws, and Elliott voted on the other side. Shortly afterwards he abandoned the Sheffield Chartists completely, sharply criticising their advocacy of 'physical force'. The same meeting of January 1839 was followed by the re-establishment of the local Anti-Corn Law association of the middle classes.

The same general course of events, in which an early sympathy between political Radicals and free-traders was lost in 1839–40, can be seen at Leeds and Leicester. At Leeds, Samuel Smiles, the editor of the *Leeds Times*, had originally been sympathetic to the Charter, but in 1840, frightened by the threat of violence in Leeds Chartism, he withdrew his support, and thereafter gave his support to the Anti-Corn Law Association in Leeds.[4] At Leicester, where

---

On Radical politics in Sheffield in the 30's, there are two unpublished B.A. theses in the S.R.L., which summarise the local sources: 'A reinvestigation into the sources of biographical material of Ebenezer Elliott,' by E. R. Seary (1929), and 'Radical activity in Sheffield, 1830–1848', by B. Thickett (1950). See also A. Briggs, 'Ebenezer Elliott, the Corn Law Rhymer' in the *Cambridge Journal* (1950).

[1] See *Sheffield Iris*, 13 July 1838.
[2] See Gammage, *op. cit*, pp. 47–8.
[3] *Hymn, written especially to be sung at the meeting of the working classes, to be held at Sheffield, September 25th, 1838*, (broadsheet in the S.C.L.). It was to be sung to the tune of the Old Hundredth.
[4] See above, p. 83.

protests against the corn làws had in the 30's come from both workers and employers, the Chartists were not at first hostile to repeal: the first open hostility between the Chartists and the League was shown at a meeting of February 1840, and the two groups did not become irreconcilable until about 1842, when the Leicester Chartists were dominated by Thomas Cooper.[1]

With the organisation of the League on a national scale, and the ascendancy of the *Northern Star*, the antagonism became open and general. In this development the initiative lay with the *Northern Star*. Of greater importance than any economic arguments which it put forward was the aggressive proletarianism of its tone. In July 1841, for example, in urging Chartists to abstain from voting in the coming general election, it was stated:[2]

'Monday next is to be the greatest day that ever Yorkshire saw. Fustian against broadcloth! The dignity of nature against the distinction of wealth! . . . Not one kid-skin glove for either [honest Harney or honest Pitkeithly]. Therefore let not a blister appear as a willing brand by being held up for Whig or Tory.'

With its jeers at the 'respectables', the 'millocrats' and the 'shopocrats', and with its constant appeals to the 'fustian jackets, blistered hands, and unshorn chins', it fostered a general contempt for the middle classes. This frame of mind, which made membership of the working class a matter of pride rather than of self-pity, was by no means peculiar to the *Northern Star*. It was shown in the processions organised to celebrate Feargus O'Connor's release from York Gaol in the autumn of 1841; or in the Chartist pride in education, 'I have sometimes come across workers, with their fustian jackets coming apart', wrote Engels, 'who are better informed on geology, astronomy and other matters, than many an educated member of the middle classes in Germany.'[3] Or again it can be seen in the conduct of the Chartists at Nottingham and Sheffield, who, with a verve and resource which recall John Wilkes, attended their parish churches *en masse*, and in Sheffield demanded to hear sermons on texts chosen by themselves.[4] They were certainly unlikely to listen favourably to economic arguments put

---

[1] See above, p. 138.
[2] *Northern Star*, 3 July 1841. For the elections of 1841 cf. p. 373, below.
[3] Engels, *op. cit.*, p. 272. For the processions in honour of O'Connor, see *Northern Star*, 11 Dec. 1841 (reprinted in Hovell, *op. cit.*, pp. 226–7.)
[4] Thickett, *op. cit.*; A. C. Wood, 'Nottingham, 1835–65' in *Transactions of the Thoroton Society of Nottinghamshire* (1955), p. 53.

forward by an organisation of a class to which they were bitterly opposed.

The lecturers and publications of the League cannot be accused of a similar hatred of the working class, but they tended to belittle and perhaps misrepresent the opposition which they met, 'physical force Chartism' being to them often no more than hooliganism. Prentice equated physical force Chartism with a 'rude and violent rabble'; Henry Warburton, the Radical politician, spoke of the 'intended irruption of the Vandals' at a League meeting.[1] The leaders of the League were as class-conscious as the Chartists, but they directed their opposition to the landlords, whose real faults were that they lived on rents rather than on earned incomes, and that they wielded a disproportionate share of political power. The corn laws were attacked as a symbol of this power as much as for any economic effects which they had.

It is necessary to examine more closely the way in which each movement impinged on the other. The League had one single expressed objective, the repeal of the corn and provision laws, and it was careful to prevent any enlargement of its aims, which might at the same time narrow the range of interests which supported it. It took care that it should not, officially, support a general programme of free trade: League pamphlets and periodicals might say in passing that duties protecting British manufactures were harmful, or that the export of all machinery should be freed from restriction, but League petitions did not include these among their official demands. In a letter of March 1841, when the tariff question was becoming for the first time generally canvassed, Cobden strongly attacked those members of the League who wished to launch a general attack on protectionism.[2] If the League's aims were narrowed in this way, it is easy to see that it would have little sympathy with suggestions that it should interest itself as a body in the widening of the franchise.[3]

It would appear at first sight that the League had little need to show direct interest in Chartism, or to attract the support of the working classes. To repeal the corn laws it was necessary either to convert a majority of the House of Commons, or failing that, to rouse the members of the electorate to such a pitch that they would

[1] Prentice, *op. cit.*, Vol. I, p. 214.
[2] J. B. Smith MSS., Cobden to Smith, 28 Mar. 1841.
[3] The relations of the League with the Complete Suffrage movement are discussed on p. 363, below.

in future accept none but candidates pledged to repeal. The political support of the working classes, who were not generally voters, could not be of direct help in forwarding either of these aims.

Indirectly, however, there was much to be gained from their support. The conversion of the Commons to repeal was likely in any circumstances to be a formidable undertaking, as the leading organisers of the League fully realised. Even if the electorate in manufacturing constituencies was solidly and uncompromisingly demanding repeal, there were many more constituencies where the leaders of the League believed that opinion was likely to support the agricultural interest, and more again where public opinion would have relatively little influence. The League's periodicals often reminded readers that pocket boroughs had survived the Reform Act, and that many of them were likely to be in the pockets of landowners: it was difficult to see how anything short of a violent popular explosion could make a breach in the ranks of the protectionists. In the early years of their agitation the leaders of the League hoped that substantial working-class support, if they could get it, would prove a powerful argument to a House composed predominantly of landowners. They were anxious always to show that they were agitating in the national interest, and that all stood to gain from the general prosperity which would follow repeal: the cause must never be considered, as it was from time to time, a 'mere Manchester question'.[1] They believed, correctly as it turned out, that Parliament was more likely to be persuaded by a reasoned national demand than by one which appeared to come from a sectional interest. Hence in organising town meetings and petitions, they attached great importance to those which had been attended, or signed, by large numbers of people in all walks of life: this was equally true both at the beginning and in 1845 when, in entirely different political and economic circumstances, meetings were held all over the country praying that Parliament would open the ports immediately to foreign corn.[2] Wherever the League could claim that it had the support of the working classes, it certainly did so. And, as a later section of this study will show, it was at great pains to disprove suggestions that its members were merely concerned with the reduction of wages.[3]

---

[1] See Letter-book of the Anti-Corn Law League, M.R.L., Sidney Smith (a League lecturer) to the secretary of the League, 17 Apr. 1840.
[2] See below, p. 370.   [3] See below, p. 350.

Beyond this, there was a further reason, not openly acknowledged, why the League should look for working-class support. This was the appeal to the fears of the aristocracy. It was perhaps best expressed by C. P. Villiers in a letter of August 1840 to J. B. Smith, President in that year of the Manchester Chamber of Commerce, and a leading member of the League:

'We had a meeting of the London association on the night of the Chartist meeting, & I thought it not inappropriate to state as strongly as I could my thorough conviction that the working classes are really those most interested in the repeal of the corn laws . . . . My great object in getting them [i.e. the working classes] to speak *out* is that I am convinced that until they do the Aristocracy will never yield — I grieve to say that the *brickbat argument* is the only one that our nobles heed.'[1] Cobden made a similar point when in December 1841 he described the Complete Suffrage movement as 'something in our *rear* to frighten the Aristocracy'.[2] The 'brickbat argument' had been a potent one during the Reform Bill agitation, and could become so again.

Finally there was the important section of the League's promoters who became interested, as individuals, in the Complete Suffrage movement of 1841–2. They supported a drastic widening of the franchise for different reasons: in some cases they rested it on grounds of political justice; in others they argued that it would be necessary in order to push legislation such as the repeal of the corn laws through Parliament.[3] But, of course, the extension of the suffrage would not be of any value unless those enfranchised would support the economic policies of the middle classes.

The attitude of the Chartists to the League was more complex. Unlike the members of the League, with their centralised organisation and their remarkable consistency of propaganda, Chartists had not even the appearance of unanimity. The basis of their hostility to the League was the class antagonism which has been described above. It had been strengthened by the course of events since 1832, and was particularly directed against the Whigs, as was clearly shown when in 1841 O'Connor advised his followers to vote Tory.[4] In supporting the Tories they automatically ranged themselves

---

[1] Smith MSS., Villiers to Smith, undated (August 1840?).
[2] *Ibid.*, Cobden to Smith, 4 Dec. 1841.
[3] See below, p. 355.
[4] Betty Kemp, 'The General Election of 1841' in *History*, Vol. XXXVII (1952).

against the free-trade measures put forward by the Whigs in the Budget of 1841.

Beyond these attitudes three main types of argument may be distinguished. In the first place there were free-traders who stipulated that a fight for the Charter should have priority. This was a view which was commonly expressed by the rank and file of Chartists in different localities, but which was not so much found among national leaders, other than Lovett and his companions.[1]

Other Chartists were modified free-traders: repeal might be desirable, but it would only benefit the working classes if it were accompanied by other measures (which in turn would only be obtained from a House elected by universal suffrage). What these other measures were to be was a matter of opinion, but they were closely related to the different Radical agitations of the 1830's. Some held that the burden of indirect taxation must be reduced, others spoke of the reduction of the National Debt; these two traditional political watchwords could easily be associated. This, the policy of 'equitable adjustment', was put forward editorially in 1840 by the *Northern Liberator* of Newcastle.[2] It was also the point of view repeatedly advocated by Bronterre O'Brien;[3] 'Now he was an Anti-Corn Law Man; he was for the repeal of the Corn Laws; he was for reducing taxation — but they must pardon his saying, for he must speak the truth . . . that the repeal of the Corn Laws, the repeal of the soap tax, the repeal of the malt tax, or the repeal of any other tax was sheer humbug.'

Others, probably influenced by the Ten Hours movement, spoke of legislation restricting factory hours, or regulating wages. These policies varied, but they were concerned with the same basic question — how could wage-earners be sure of getting a share of the prosperity which repeal would bring? If repeal of the corn laws were unaccompanied by other measures, the price of bread would be reduced but wages would be reduced also: if increased imports of corn were paid for by increased exports of manufactures, as the League's lecturers were arguing, then these exports would be produced by greater mechanisation of industry, and not by fuller employment. This was a thesis developed in discussion with the League's lecturers by the Chartist lecturers James Leach, of

---

[1] G. D. H. Cole, *Chartist Portraits* (1941), pp. 55-6.
[2] *Northern Liberator*, 14 Feb., 11 Apr., 23 May 1840.
[3] *Northern Star*, 23 Oct., 1831. See also reports of his speeches in the *Northern Liberator*, 14 Mar. 1840, and in the *British Statesman*, 26 Nov. 1842.

Manchester, and Bairstow, of the West Riding, and it was clearly related to local industrial conditions. Bairstow elaborated the point by saying that 'Ireland was the largest exporting country under heaven, in proportion to its size, and no population was so miserable.'[1]

The thesis that repeal of the corn laws must be accompanied by legislative control of wages and factory conditions gained considerable support from the Chartist rank and file, for underneath it lay the constant fear that manufacturers had adopted the corn law agitation in order to reduce wages: its seriousness was fully recognised by Cobden and the League.[2] The Chartist preoccupation with falling wages deserves attention, since it provides a reason for suggesting a definite association between Chartism and the depressed class of handloom weavers. They were the people whose earnings, in the cotton and silk industries at least, had suffered severely since 1815, and who might be persuaded into a belief that the falling cost of living was partly responsible. It is noticeable that all the doubts about free trade shown by the Chartists had already been expressed by witnesses appearing before the Select Committee on Handloom Weavers' Petitions of 1834–5.[3] Experience was teaching them that cheap bread and falling wages did in fact go together.

A third considerable stream of thought was hostile to the anti-corn law campaign in all circumstances. If repeal were to have the effects claimed for it, it must inevitably reduce the acreage in England under wheat, must reduce employment in agriculture, and swell the ranks of those dependent on the New Poor Law. This fear, and the fear of machinery, were added to the standard arguments of the protectionists — the need for independence in time of war,

[1] The clearest exposition of these views is provided in the reports of two lectures given by Bairstow at Leeds, on 'Labour and Capital, Machinery and Corn Law Repeal', in the *Northern Star* of 15 Aug. 1840. Leach's ideas are set forth in the report of a debate with Finnegan of the League at Manchester, (*ibid.*, 3 Nov. 1840).

[2] See below, p. 367.

[3] See above, p. 8. Note the evidence of Richard Needham, a Bolton weaver, who, when asked if repeal would benefit weavers, replied: 'Not one farthing, excepting a law was to take place that was to secure the present wages we have . . . if we could live upon a shilling a day, the system would take care we did not get 9d. to live upon; that is my idea, and all those I associate with.' Cf. the reply of William Buchanan of Glasgow, to the question whether repeal would stimulate exports: 'We have seen many demands for labour, but the wages of weaving has not increased.' (*Parliamentary Papers*, 1834, Vol. X, questions 5570, 2028.) Cf. John Scott, of Manchester, who argued that free trade would merely stimulate the demand for cheap factory-produced goods, (*Parliamentary Papers, 1835*, Vol. XIII, question 2614). These were the lines on which Bairstow and Leach argued.

and the wholesomeness of work on the land. They argued sometimes for industrial protectionism as well: repeal of the corn laws
must logically be accompanied by repeal of protective duties on
manufactures, and English industries would then be threatened by
competition from foreign countries where the working classes possessed a lower standard of living than they did in England.

This thorough-going protectionism was of importance, as it
represented a point of view stated many times by Feargus O'Connor. His pamphlet of 1841, *The remedy for national poverty and impending national ruin, or the only safe way of repealing the corn laws*,[1]
suggested a combination of agricultural protectionism and the
division of land into smallholdings. The case was fully developed,
along the lines described above, in a pamphlet of 1841 by John
Campbell, *An examination of the corn and provision laws*, which appeared with a strong recommendation from the *Northern Star*.[2]
The editorial comment of the *Northern Star* inclined also towards
protectionism, though it did not do so consistently. Thus, in March
1840 it argued 'that under no circumstances could any benefit arise
to the whole people from a repeal of those laws', both agricultural
and industrial protection being necessary to safeguard the working
man's standard of living. A month later it argued that if the middle
classes joined the campaign for universal suffrage, and it was successful, they would then be able to carry repeal of the corn laws
without difficulty. The article clearly implied that in those circumstances the working classes would consider repeal a benefit to
themselves.[3] In 1838 it had produced yet another argument: the
corn laws 'must be considered as the only means of setting tithelord,
fundlord, landlord, and labour lord fighting, and when they fall out
honest men may come by their own'.[4]

The Chartist attitude to the League was, then, neither consistent
nor clearly thought out. Chartist speakers tended to flounder in
discussion with the well-drilled lecturers of the League, and may at
times have expressed themselves in the heat of a meeting in a way
which did not do justice to their thought. This was most conspicuously true of the famous debate between O'Connor and Cobden in August 1844[5] but it was also true of theses put forward on
other occasions. For instance, it was argued that free trade was bad

[1] Leeds, 1841.
[2] Manchester, 1841; *Northern Star*, 16 Oct. 1841.
[3] *Ibid.*, 28 Mar., 25 Apr. 1841.   *Ibid.*, 24 Mar. 1838.
[5] See below, p. 369.

because it encouraged the export of goods of which the British working classes stood in need;[1] or again, in reply to a familiar argument of the League, 'The inability of the foreigner to deal with us has always been ascribed to the operation of our corn laws, but what, we would ask, must be his position when the price of his food is raised at home? Must it not follow as naturally as night follows day, that if the price of corn is raised abroad, that the foreign labourer will have more to pay for his bread and less to spend upon our manufactures?'[2] A still more unorthodox attack on free trade was made by a Chartist speaker at a meeting at Keighley, who said that 'if the prospects of the Corn Law gentry were realised, he was at a loss to know how people would get through the work, or where the necessary supply of children and females were to come from'.[3]

The response of the Chartists to the corn law question, whether it was in its most or its least lucid form, showed certain general characteristics. The dispute was usually carried on in terms of the economic and political theories to which the League adhered. Chartist speakers at League meetings did not usually put forward Socialist theories of the right to the whole produce of labour. Nor did they, in discussions of employment, make reference to the currency theory of Attwood. In their demands for the legislation to accompany repeal, the Chartists were asking for nothing revolutionary or Utopian, but kept, on the whole, within the range of practical politics.[4] They were trying to give theoretical form to two suspicions, both of which were well-founded, the first that the protestations of the League could not be trusted, and the second that the introduction of free trade was a leap in the dark, which might, in some way which they could not predict, bring damage to themselves. Chartist audiences were looking for a system which would ensure them full and steady employment, and it was not clear to them how free trade would do this.

II

Two phases in the relationship between Chartism and the League may be distinguished. In the first period, down to the summer of

---

[1] *Northern Star*, 20 June 1840. The same argument can be found in leading articles of 3 Feb. 1838, and in the *Northern Liberator* of 4 Apr. 1840.

[2] *Northern Star*, 13 Dec. 1845.   [3] *Ibid.*, 9 May 1840.

[4] The legislative control of wages could not be considered to be practical politics, but to some extent it may perhaps be seen as an alternative to the regulation of factory hours.

1842, there were a number of attempts, both in particular localities, and on a national scale, to find common ground between them; organisations were formed which were pledged both to the extension of the suffrage and to free-trade legislation. In discussing these attempts, precise definition is necessary: all attempts by middle-class Radicals to come to terms with working-class Radicals were not necessarily sponsored by the League, nor were they always attempting to come to terms with local Chartists. In the League's reports of meetings, the word 'Chartist' was often used very loosely. Furthermore, in discussing these attempts, the writer is forced back on to the use of newspaper accounts of public meetings; even given impartial reporting, it is difficult to assess precisely the significance of such occasions.

The strategy of the League can be clearly described, particularly at the beginning of its campaign. It set out first to win the support of the manufacturing towns, and addressed itself to both masters and men. (At the same time it was employing lecturers in agricultural districts.) It would be a great mistake to regard the anti-corn law agitation as a spontaneous political explosion of the bourgeoisie in all manufacturing towns: rather, the first enemy of the League was often the apathy of middle-class opinion. In 1839 and 1840 the League was finding it difficult to pay its team of lecturers.[1] The lecturers themselves complained of the apathy which they encountered in important centres. In Birmingham, J. H. Shearman complained that in the main streets ninety out of a hundred shopkeepers stated that they neither knew nor cared about the corn laws.[2] In Sheffield, the apathy of the middle classes, of which Elliott had complained, still persisted: James Acland, another lecturer, wrote in October 1840 that he was attempting to rouse the 'broadcloth influence': 'I hope the League has better friends than the gentlemen of Sheffield — although I by no means despair of bringing them out, but they are very backward in coming forward.'[3] In Liverpool, a local anti-monopoly association was not reported by the League until December 1841.[4] In June

---

[1] See the Letter-book of the League.
[2] Letter-book, letters dated 28 Oct. and 2 Nov. 1839.
[3] *Ibid.*, letters dated 12–15 Oct. 1840.
[4] *Anti-Bread Tax Circular*, 16 Dec. 1841. But an operative Anti-Corn Law association was formed there in September 1840. Of. the position in Sheffield, above, p. 343. (*Anti-Corn Law Circular*, 14 Aug., 27 Sept. and 31 Dec. 1840.)

1840 Cobden complained that 'so long as Liverpool, Stockport, Warrington, etc. are wholly or partly in favour of the corn laws, the landlords may laugh at us'.[1] Similar accounts of apathy, or of unwillingness to subscribe to League funds, came from Nottingham, from Scotland, from towns dominated by the shipping interest, and finally from London, where J. B. Smith described the change in atmosphere after Manchester as 'descending into a cold bath'.

The explanation of this situation is not difficult: the general case for free trade was too theoretical to have much political impact, and the two concrete arguments which were particularly effective did not apply with equal force everywhere. These were the beliefs that cheaper bread would make a reduction of wages possible, a belief which, however much it may have been disclaimed by the League's organisation, may yet have operated on the minds of manufacturers, and the assertion that greater and more regular imports of wheat from Eastern Europe would enlarge the market for British exports there. Both these arguments were particularly relevant to the problems of textile and hosiery manufacturers in the years 1839 and 1840, since they were complaining in the hosiery industry of German competition, and in the cotton and woollen industries of the threat to their export markets provided by the emergence of the Zollverein. Elsewhere, and particularly in towns where there was a tradition of political Toryism, such as Liverpool, or where the protectionist shipping interest was dominant, such as Hull, the process of conversion to repeal took place more slowly. Like Chartism, the League had its 'geography', even when discussion is confined to the towns.[2]

The League was anxious to collect support wherever it could. It did not often approach Chartist groups or leaders as such, but it paid attention to working-class needs and interests. The clearest evidence of this is given in the choice of lecturers, for public lectures were, at this stage of the campaign, the form of propaganda

[1] Smith MSS., Cobden to Smith, 1 June 1840. He wrote to Smith again in April 1844 in almost identical terms, '. . . it would be well to distribute a few hundred *Struggles* [a League periodical] every week in Blackburn, Wigan, Clitheroe, Warrington, and Macclesfield. — It is quite impossible to overrate the importance of securing these manufacturing boroughs. If they are lost to us at another dissolution we must for decency's sake give up our interference with other boroughs in the agricultural districts. . . . Liverpool is quite beyond our reach. Its bastard aristocracy will choose another Tory Lord in spite of all we can do.'

[2] For the League's rural campaign, see below, p. 368.

on which it most relied.[1] Many lecturers had qualities which could be expected to give them a popular appeal. James Acland, a lecturer and for some time editor of the *Circular*, had been a turbulent agitator in favour of parliamentary and municipal reform, first at Bristol, and then, from 1831 to 1833, at Hull. He was still an inflammatory speaker, 'He talked', complained Bowring, 'of the *right* of the people to *eat*, — as the same as the right to *breathe* — and held language which might easily be construed into a recommendation to *help themselves.*'[2] A. W. Paulton, one of the most diligent and successful of the lecturers, ran into the same kind of trouble: another lecturer, J. H. Shearman, complained that 'he constantly says *"my own individual opinion is that we never can carry this question without an extensive enlargement of the suffrage"* . . . . It may get him a momentary cheer from the Chartists — but it hinders me from getting money.' Yet it was Shearman who went, and Paulton who continued active in the League to the end.[3]

As well as these political Radicals, the League had other lower-paid lecturers of more particularly working-class stamp.[4] One of the most prominent of these was Heyworth Hargreaves, an operative from Halifax, who was an object of especial hostility to the *Northern Star*. His appointment was described as 'an ingenious *move*, the League having in vain despatched the more aristocratic lecturers, Messrs Paulton, Smith, etc. and had now struck upon a new device, that of hiring an operative, in the hope that he could more persuasively appeal to the working people'.[5] Another such lecturer was T. J. Finnegan, who, it is clear from his letters, was barely literate; and a still more striking example was John Murray of Liverpool, who was known as a 'Chartist of the moral influence class' and was invited to become a lecturer in April 1840.[6]

[1] By far the greater number of League pamphlets which survive were published after 1841. Probably pamphlet campaigns were more expensive to run.

[2] Smith MSS., Bowring to Smith, 3 Jan. 1840. In Hull, Acland led a campaign against the powers of the city corporation during the Reform Bill crisis. Its progress was recorded in his weekly newspaper, the *Hull Portfolio* (of which there is a copy in the H.R.L.).

[3] Letter-book: letters dated 28 June and 2 Nov. 1839. Paulton had been lecturing against the corn laws from July 1838, before the foundation of the League. (Prentice, *op. cit.*, Ch. V.)

[4] Sidney Smith was paid £270 a year, and asked for more: Paulton and Greig (another lecturer) were paid similar sums. Murray was offered £80, which suggests a marked difference in their status and functions. (Letter-book, letters of 9 Apr. and 2 May 1840.)

[5] *Northern Star*, 4 July 1840. For Chartist hostility to Hargreaves see also the issue of 9 May 1840 (account of a meeting at Keighley).

[6] Letter-book, Lawrence Heyworth to George Wilson, 9 Apr. 1840.

A second field in which the League tried to cultivate working-class support was in the Operative Anti-Corn Law Associations, which existed, or were founded, in a great many places.[1] The exact status of these associations is difficult to determine; in some towns, such, perhaps, as Liverpool, they may have existed independently of middle-class support.[2] The two most notable and flourishing, however, were clearly subsidised in some form. In Sheffield, Acland reported that 'there is a gang of lazy operative repealers who seem to consider they have a property in any subscriptions raised or to be raised from the broadcloth'. They claimed that Cobden and Smith had told them that the League was glad to bribe them.[3] The second example of a subsidised association was the Operative Anti-Corn Law Association of Manchester, whose meetings were graced by leading Manchester free-traders. Their relationship was shown when in January 1840 a great dinner of League members was followed the next evening by a rather simpler one for five thousand of the operatives at the same place.[4] It is probable that wherever there was an active association of the middle classes their relations with the operatives' associations were much the same.[5]

In the drive to obtain working-class support there were also other movements, not directly connected with the League, but usually sponsored by leading local citizens who were also League members. These appear to have begun, roughly simultaneously, at a number of places in 1840, and to have had a number of features in common. They can be interpreted partly as a reaction to the Whigs' refusal to interest themselves, as a party, in the corn law question: if Parliament would not listen, then there was a case for a platform agitation to secure reform of the franchise.[6] Secondly, the year 1840 was an appropriate time to organise a movement of this kind, for

[1] Operative Anti-Corn Law Associations in existence between 1839 and 1841 have been noted at Bolton, Carlisle, Halifax, Huddersfield, Lancaster, Leicester, Liverpool, London, Manchester, Sheffield, and Wolverhampton. No doubt there were many more.
[2] Cf. above, p. 137.   [3] Letter-book, Acland to Wilson, 14 Oct. 1840.
[4] Both dinners are described in Prentice, *op. cit.*, Ch. X. The operatives' association was organized at Cobden's behest by Edward Watkins, as a means of countering Chartist disturbances at League meetings in Manchester (McCord, *op. cit.*). See also above, p. 59.
[5] At Carlisle, for example, the League claimed that the operatives' association had arisen spontaneously and was very widely supported, while the Chartists complained that the employees of one dominant employer, Peter Dixon, had been forced to form it. *Anti-Corn Law* circular, 20 Feb. 1840; *Northern Liberator*, 10 Jan. 1840.
[6] Villiers' motion of April 1840 was lost by 129 votes to 245.

Chartism had been severely weakened by the failure of the risings of 1839 and the imprisonment, during 1840, of many of their leaders. There seemed a chance of capturing the support of at least a section of the Chartist rank and file. A meeting was held in April at Leicester of what the Chartists described as the 'Moderados', under the chairmanship of the Mayor. The meeting called for household suffrage, triennial parliaments, and the repeal of the corn laws, and William Biggs, the Radical, made a special plea to the working classes to join them in this agitation.[1] This movement seems to have been kept alive to the end of the year.[2] In May 1840, the Chartists of Sunderland were approached by the members of the local Anti-Corn Law Association, who proposed that the two bodies should unite, and make repeal the first object of their joint programme. They were repulsed by a letter stating openly that the Chartist attitude to the middle classes was one of 'violent opposition'.[3] Further episodes of the same kind are recorded as having occurred in the autumn. At Bolton, the *Northern Star* reported at the end of November, 'The sham of agitating for Household Suffrage by this party[4] appears to be abandoned and a desire to "go the whole hog" with the people has been hinted at if the Chartists will only change — not their principles, but their name. It is said they wish coalition and a committee of individuals selected from both parties has been appointed to confer together. The middle classes feel that the landed aristocracy is too powerful for them when unaided by the working men . . . . The Chartists are quite alive to the move and determined not to be jockied.'[5]

The largest and most impressive of these moves, until the national Complete Suffrage Union two years later, was the foundation in the autumn of 1840 of the Leeds Parliamentary Reform Association, of which the leading members were keen supporters of the League, Marshall, the flax spinner, Smiles, Hamer Stansfield, Joshua Bower and Alderman Goodman.[6] The Association, like that projected at Bolton, was to be run by a committee composed both of the middle and the working classes, a form of organisation which inspired the *Northern Star* habitually to refer to it as the Fox and

---

[1] *Northern Liberator*, 2 and 23 May 1840. See above, p. 138.
[2] See *Northern Star*, November 1840.   [3] *Northern Liberator*, 23 May 1840.
[4] *I.e.* the repealers.   [5] *Northern Star*, 21 Nov. 1840.
[6] See Hamer Stansfield, *Compensation not emigration the one thing needful: justice, not charity, what we want*, (lectures delivered before the Leeds Association in January 1842). (Leeds, 1842.)

Geese Club.[1] In January 1841 it held a large meeting at Marshall's mill in Leeds; the Chartists were invited to it and attended it in numbers. They were addressed by Joseph Hume, who recommended a franchise of all taxpayers and by Sir George Strickland, who spoke of household suffrage; on the Chartist side John Collins called for universal suffrage and the points of the Charter. According to the *Leeds Mercury*, in order to avoid Chartist disturbance it was arranged 'to propose only one resolution, in which both [Radicals and Chartists] could alike concur . . . but of course at the expense of removing all distinction between Household and Universal Suffrage'.[2] Justifiably, the Chartists claimed an overwhelming victory.

None of these attempts at co-operation between the classes can be said to have succeeded. In December 1840 the *Northern Star* congratulated its readers that, in spite of the imprisonment of leading Chartists and a favourable political opportunity, the Whigs and Radicals had not bridged the gap between the classes.[3] Nevertheless, while the Chartist bodies in these towns were not won over, it is perfectly possible that some sections of the working class may have been drawn into these movements: the Leeds Parliamentary Reform Association was organising lectures for working-class audiences a year later, and it must presumably have had support of some kind.

It remains to ask how far these various, but persistent, attempts to enlist the interest of the working class in the Corn Law question were successful. It would have been curious if they had achieved nothing: here and there the League claimed successes, but it is noticeable that it did not claim very many, and that those which it did claim were mostly achieved in conditions unusually favourable to its activities. For instance, in Derby a successful meeting was held which was attended by a working-class audience, and this was considered to be a 'snub to the Cavendish interest': a petition from the distressed operative hosiers and glovers against the corn laws was prepared.[4] Here the League may have profited indirectly from hostility to the principal local landowner.

At both Wolverhampton and Sheffield the League also claimed successes, and in both towns political and economic circumstances

---

[1] See above, p. 83.
[2] *Leeds Mercury*, 28 Jan. 1841; *Northern Star*, 30 Jan. 1841.
[3] *Northern Star*, 5 Dec. 1840.   [4] *Anti-Corn Law Circular*, 26 Mar. 1840.

may have been unusually favourable to their propaganda. Wolverhampton was represented in the Parliament of 1837–41 by two strong free-traders, Thomas Thornely and C. P. Villiers, both of whom worked hard to organise local meetings and petitions;[1] while in Sheffield, in spite of Acland's remarks about 'lazy repealers', the work of Ebenezer Elliott must have had some effect. Furthermore, both towns were centres of industries which tended to be organised on a small scale, where the antagonism between employers and employed could be expected to be at a minimum. At Wolverhampton a petition against the corn laws was organised by operatives in the spring of 1840. That their initiative was genuine is suggested by the fact that the account in the *Circular* is fully borne out in the *Staffordshire Advertiser*, a paper unfriendly to the League.[2]

In Sheffield, the tradition of working-class hostility to the corn laws had survived in the town's trades unions. They had first organised a petition against the corn laws in 1833, and in the autumn of 1839 they held two important meetings. At the first, in September, they agreed that the unions should be non-political, and dissociated themselves from Chartism: at the second, in November, they agreed to support the repeal campaign.[3] W. Harrison of the edge tool trade expressed a general point of view when he said, 'If the corn laws were abolished it would give the working men greater strength to resist other evils . . . . Considering these things, though there were many Chartists among them, they were of opinion that if they could overcome the corn laws first, other evils would fall before the persevering stroke of those who struggled for liberty.'[4] This meeting was given great prominence by the League. But after this single episode, nothing more was recorded in

[1] Both were members of the Select Committee on Import Duties of 1840, and Villiers was of course the most notable opponent of the corn laws in the Commons before 1841.

[2] *Anti-Corn Law Circular*, 2 Feb. and 6 Mar. 1840; *Staffordshire Advertiser*, 22 Feb. 1840. The organisers of the petition were employed on short time in a firm making locks. How many signatures they obtained is unknown.

[3] A petition against the corn laws was sent to the Board of Trade by employers in Dec. 1839 (B.T.1/357). They argued that unemployment in the town could be traced to the stopping of exports to the United States, and that it would be reduced if it were possible to import wheat and flour from the United States. It is therefore arguable that the actions of the Sheffield unions can be ascribed to a temporary situation peculiar to Sheffield.

[4] *Sheffield Iris*, 12 Nov. 1839; *Anti-Corn Law Circular*, 26 Nov. 1839, and 1 Jan. 1840. None of the speakers at this meeting is listed in Robson's *Trades' Directory* of Sheffield of 1839, which suggests that the meeting was not in any way managed by employers.

the *Circular* of trade-union activity against the corn laws in Sheffield,[1] and the lead taken there was not followed elsewhere. It is, however, known that some other trade unions in this period, the Iron-founders, Compositors, and Cotton Spinners, passed resolutions in favour of free trade.[2]

There remains the difficult task of trying to assess the value, as evidence of working-class support, of the petitions organised by the League. The Chartists frequently claimed that signatures were obtained by their employers under duress, and they were in a position to know: at Huddersfield 'it was in the counting house and we had to sign'.[3] But while the League was often unscrupulous in the means it adopted to obtain signatures, it could hardly have obtained them from the majority of the population in towns where there was really determined opposition. There were a number of places where the League made sweeping claims. At Rochdale almost every adult male in the town was said to have signed, and the majority of the adult population had also signed at Manchester, Kirkcaldy, Barnsley, and Rossendale (where local Chartists were said to have 'signed to a man').[4]

Much the same difficulty is presented by the League's claims of support from Operative Anti-Corn Law Associations: it is obvious that they depended greatly on support, or pressure, from middle-class organisations, but where they had enrolled very large numbers of members, it would hardly be fair to argue that they had no working-class support at all.

These, then, are examples of the League's relations with working men in general, rather than with organised Chartist bodies. As far as 'formal' Chartism is concerned, the picture becomes more confusing. Some 'moral force' Chartists supported repeal, and where these were relatively strong, harmonious relations between the two bodies were established, as at a meeting of December 1841 in

---

[1] When Harney went to Sheffield as correspondent of the *Northern Star* in August 1841, he described the 'speakers of the trades' as corn law repealers, not Chartists. (*The Trial of Feargus O'Connor and Fifty Eight Others at Lancaster* (1843), pp. 236–7.)

[2] S. and B. Webb, *History of Trade Unionism*, (1920 edn), p. 176.

[3] *Northern Star*, 25 Jan. 1840. Similar complaints came from Bradford, Keighley, and Macclesfield, where it was said that Sunday school children were forced to sign petitions, their teachers writing down their names for them. (*Ibid.*, 23 May and 27 Mar. 1840.) A graphic picture of the League's methods of collecting signatures is given in the evidence on the Epworth Petitions (*Parliamentary papers*, 1843, XI).

[4] *Anti-Corn Law Circular*, 6 Feb. 19 and 26 Mar. 1840.

Bath.[1] Similarly the former secretary of the Chartists wrote, from Exeter in March 1840, offering to work for the League in future.[2] But these instances of co-operation are hardly enough to modify the impression of hostility between the two movements.

In the main Chartist centres opposition to the League, in some form, was general. Meetings were interrupted, in some places broken up. In others, the League itself feared that it would be impossible to hold a public meeting because of the disturbance it would create.[3] The League may have attracted support from individual working men in such places, but neither it, nor such organisations as the Leeds Parliamentary Reform Association, came to terms with Chartist bodies. The most which could be achieved was amicable discussion of the questions which divided them. In Sheffield where it has been shown that there was more working-class support for repeal than in many places, the local Chartists, as a body, echoed the general hostility to the League.[4]

But it may be suggested that there was greater opposition to the League than to free trade itself. At Anti-Corn Law meetings, it was usual to end the proceedings with a resolution condemning the corn laws. At this point a Chartist would rise and propose an amendment, usually that the introduction of universal suffrage was the first thing necessary, and a vote was taken. About the conduct of the voting, and its results, there could be endless recriminations, and it does not seem possible at the present day to judge between rival reports of which side gained a victory. But it is possible, and significant of the real effect which the League was having, to notice the exact form taken by these amendments, and the reasons given for supporting them. Most speeches by Chartist interrupters argued that the corn laws were an obvious evil, but that the Charter should have priority. In Lancashire and the West Riding, the 'orthodox Chartism' of Leach and Bairstow was also expressed by the rank and file; repeal must be accompanied by regulation of the use of machinery.[5] In other places, notably in Sheffield, the corn law agitation was attacked solely as a political deviation. But

---

[1] *Northern Star*, 24 Dec. 1841.
[2] *Anti-Corn Law Circular*, 19 Mar. 1840.
[3] Smith MSS., J. Sturge to J. B. Smith, 1 Oct. 1838, about Birmingham; Letter-book, letters of 14 Feb. 1840 about Forfar, of 19 Mar. about Kirkcaldy, and 31 May about Newcastle.
[4] See *Chartism v. Whigism* (*sic*), and a journal, the *Sheffield Working Man's Advocate*, nos. 1–5, published between 6 Jan. and 3 Apr. 1841 (in S.R.L.).
[5] This argument was put forward at Halifax, (*Northern Star*, 25 Apr. 1840),

AA

the kind of agricultural protectionism put forward by O'Connor and Campbell found noticeably few supporters: between 1839 and 1842 there is one example only recorded in the *Northern Star*, in which an important meeting of the League was captured by a Chartist, West, who spoke at length on the dangerous effects of free trade on the agricultural labourer. This was at Macclesfield, in June, 1841, a town which was a centre of the silk industry, and in which there was a protectionist tradition which dated back to the time of Huskisson. There, a resolution in favour of free trade was entirely defeated.[1]

A number of conclusions are suggested by this account. Both movements were driven to take account of each other. The League believed in its early years that it could not do without a show of support from the working classes, and went to some length to obtain it; Chartist leaders feared this campaign as a dangerous diversion, and organised their campaign against it. When the variations in Chartism from district to district, and the difficulties experienced by Chartists in handling the adroitness of League propaganda are remembered, the political solidarity shown by the rank and file is remarkable.

About opinion on free trade and protection two conclusions may be suggested. Both among the working and middle classes, the opinions expressed varied considerably from place to place, but were relevant to strictly local, and usually contemporary, economic circumstances: while their intellectual formulations might be muddled, neither middle-class nor working-class audiences were content with slogans and generalisations, but required a solid array of facts and figures appropriate to their particular problems. Second, neither agricultural nor industrial protectionism found much support in the towns, in spite of the backing which they had received initially from the *Northern Star*. Had the League been able to offer a simple and convincing reply to the fear that cheaper bread would merely mean lower wages, and had Cobden and Bright not been known as opponents of factory legislation, Chartist opposition might have been much less solid. As it was, there was

---

Keighley (9 May 1840), Bolton, (13 June 1840, 23 Jan. 1841), Huddersfield, (16 Jan. 1841). The same view was also expressed in other parts of the country.

[1] *Northern Star*, 12 June 1841. The account was taken from a local newspaper, the *Macclesfield Courier*. It is interesting to notice that Cobden complained, as late as 1844, of the weakness of the League in Macclesfield.

evidence that the League was beginning to make converts among working men: it was perfectly possible for League speakers to meet organised Chartist opposition in a town, and yet to be supported by other sections of the working class. The political strength of the League, however, depended on its success in rural as well as urban districts: and there, in spite of lecture tours in 1840 and 1841, there was very little evidence of success.

III

The situation thus described came to an end after 1842. Neither the Complete Suffrage movement, nor the disorders of the summer of 1842, comes properly within the scope of this essay, but both radically affected the relations of Chartism and the League. The Complete Suffrage movement, under the leadership of Joseph Sturge, like the earlier movements at Leeds, Bolton, and elsewhere, was an attempt to bridge the gulf between Chartism and middle-class radicalism.[1] But it differed from its predecessors in its scale of operation; it was a national movement, which at the peak of its popularity claimed between fifty and sixty branches in different towns.[2] It also differed from them in that it succeeded, though for a short time only, in winning support from those Chartists who opposed O'Connor.

If it could be shown to have been organised or directly inspired by the League, it would be an event of central importance in this narrative. But the links between the League and the new movement are obscure. The movement began with the publication of a well-known series of articles in the *Nonconformist* on the 'Reconciliation of the middle and labouring classes' which appeared in the autumn of 1841. The *Nonconformist* was a weekly journal, founded in 1841, and edited by Edward Miall. There were particular reasons for the expression of the 'dissidence of dissent' in the autumn of 1841, for the Tory victory at the elections might strengthen the political influence of the Church of England, particularly in education, as well as the influence of the landed interest. The education question touched the deepest anxieties of the Nonconformists as a body, and probably does more to explain the violent tone of the *Nonconformist* than the threat to the Anti-Corn Law agitation. But there were

[1] Sturge's part in the Complete Suffrage movement is shortly described in Henry Richard, *Memoirs of Joseph Sturge* (1864).
[2] Stephen Hobhouse, *Joseph Sturge, his life and work* (1919), p. 73.

many links between Nonconformity and the League: most of the leaders of the League, Cobden, Bright, Sturge, Bowring, were Nonconformists of one kind or another. The League was anxious to present the campaign against the corn laws as a religious one, and in August 1841 had organised a conference of dissenting ministers who agreed in their condemnation of the corn laws. On the other hand, this condemnation was not as unanimous as the League, in its report of the proceedings, had implied.[1]

It was natural to blame the inadequacy of the electoral reform of 1832 for the Tory victory: the articles in the *Nonconformist* on reconciliation were dictated by hostility to Toryism as much as by the desire to curb revolutionary activity among Chartists. They expressed the need for the extension of the suffrage in traditional but uncompromising terms: 'We venture to remind the middle classes that what we withhold from the unrepresented is not our own. We are not in the position of men who deny a favour which it may be inexpedient to grant — but of those who refuse a right to which there exists an equitable title .... Not a single legitimate ground can we assign for our possession of the right to a voice in public matters, which is not available to an equal extent for them.'[2]

On 17 November 1841 the first attempt to found a movement for the extension of the suffrage was taken by Sturge at a meeting of the League, and it met with a mixed response. Some, like Sturge himself, or Bright, regarded both campaigns as morally compelling; there is no reason to doubt the sincerity of their motives. Others like Archibald Prentice, or the lecturers A. W. Paulton and Sidney Smith, held that it was useless to hope for a wise economic policy from a parliament of landowners.[3] Others, including Cobden, were more cynical in their motives. In writing to J. B. Smith after this meeting, he revived C. P. Villiers' 'brickbat argument':

'All present ... including Sturge and Colonel Thompson, were of opinion that it would be desirable to keep the League distinct from

[1] Dr. McCord has assembled a number of letters from ministers who attended the conference and protested against the published account of its findings, *Report of the Conference of Ministers of all Denominations on the Corn Laws* etc. (London and Manchester, 1841).

[2] The *Nonconformist*, 27 Oct. 1841.

[3] See Archibald Prentice, *The Pitt-Peel income tax and the necessity of complete suffrage*, (Manchester and London, 1842). Other examples of this line of reasoning are Richard Gardner, *Address to the middle and working classes engaged in trade and manufactures throughout the Empire on the necessity of union at the present crisis*, (Manchester, 1841), and Rev. Henry Edwards, '*Union!*' the patriot's watchword at the present crisis, etc. (Manchester, 1842).

the question — At the same time there was an impression that it would be desirable to get as many individuals prominently engaged in Corn Law agitation as possible to sign in order to conciliate the people . . . I am not sorry to see Sturge taking up this question. It will be something in our *rear* to frighten the Aristocracy — And it will take the masses out of the hands of their present rascally leaders.'[1]

The leaders of the League were therefore still unwilling to allow their campaign to become involved in general political radicalism: in December 1841 and January 1842 the *Anti-Bread Tax Circular* appeared with editorials sharply critical of the *Nonconformist*.[2] On the other hand, the Complete Suffrage movement succeeded in gaining initial support from those sections of the Chartists who were opposed to O'Connor. A conference was held at Birmingham on 5 April 1842 which was attended by, among others, Vincent, O'Brien, Lovett and Collins. At this meeting, to the surprise of Sturge and his friends, the Six Points of the Charter were carried, and the area of dispute between Chartists and Complete Suffragists was narrowed to the question whether the conference should commit itself to support of the Charter in name. The middle-class delegates objected to a name which had so many associations of violence, while the Chartists regarded these scruples, understandably, as a hint that the middle classes were not wholehearted in their support. It was agreed that a further conference should be held. This took place in December 1842. It was attended by O'Connor himself with many followers; once again the meeting was deeply divided on the adoption of the name of the Charter, but on this second occasion Sturge's party was overwhelmingly defeated, and the effective influence of his movement came to an end.

The disorders of the summer of 1842 had however already destroyed hopes of class reconciliation, and they were followed by recriminations between Chartists and the League. In a series of pamphlets the Chartists claimed that the League had spoken and acted in an inflammatory way, in suggesting that under the corn laws the people's distresses were such that they would be driven into acts of violence.[3] A speech by Cobden along these lines in July

---

[1] Smith MSS., Cobden to Smith, 4 Dec. 1841.
[2] *Anti-Bread Tax Circular*, 2 Dec. 1841, and 27 Jan. 1842.
[3] *The League and the aristocracy; The League threshed and winnowed; League hypocrisy*, etc.; *Treachery of the League; Take care of your pockets;* 'Do as we bid you,' (Manchester, 1842–3).

1842, was particularly keenly attacked by the Chartists.[1] The Plug Plot in Lancashire, it was said, had been deliberately provoked by manufacturers who were members of the League; they had reduced wages knowing that their action would meet with violent resistance. The *Anti-Bread Tax Circular* replied with indignant denials of complicity.[2] While the evidence suggests that the Chartists' accusations were at least much exaggerated, it remains true that the League's propaganda had often been inflammatory. The *Anti-Bread Tax Circular* had maintained a responsible tone, but lecturers such as Acland and pamphlets addressed to working-class readers, had often gone very much further. One example perhaps deserves quotation, a pamphlet published in 1841 by James Hill of the League, entitled *Daily Bread*. This had proposed that the people should form co-operative societies and import corn, and in time of crisis help themselves to it without payment of duty: 'Landowners and legislators should not flatter themselves with the idea, that all who are not comprehended under the class of physical force Chartists are subscribers to the doctrine of passive obedience and non-resistance. There is a point when resistance becomes the highest virtue and the greatest of duties.' The pamphlet was attacked in the *Northern Star* as a 'rascally insidious plot to take advantage of the present extensive unpopularity of the corn laws for bringing the people into collision with the law'.[3] The League had at least a moral responsibility for fomenting unrest.

The failure of Complete Suffrage showed the weakness of those more moderate Chartist elements who, it was hoped, would be led out of the influence of 'their present rascally leaders'. The turn-outs of August 1842 were a further proof of the same weakness. Taken together they served to convince the League that the support of the working classes could not be won, and that even if it could be augmented, there was a limit to its political value. From the autumn of 1842 onwards a clear change in the character of League propaganda may be noticed.

The change did not develop immediately. In September 1842 a meeting of the League was held in Manchester to take stock of the situation. It was addressed by Cobden who made one of his best-known declarations:

---

[1] *Hansard*, 8 July 1842; Hovell, *op. cit.*, p. 260.
[2] See issue of 25 Aug. 1842. See also above, p. 55.
[3] *Northern Star*, 23 Oct. and 6 Nov. 1842.

'I don't deny that the working classes generally have attended our lectures and signed our petitions; but I will admit, that so far as the fervour and efficiency of our agitation has gone, it has eminently been a middle-class agitation. We have carried it on by those means by which the middle class usually carries on its movements . . . .

'But, gentlemen, the present occasion is a very seasonable one for drawing closer the bonds of union between the employers and the employed in this district. The present disastrous commotion arises clearly out of a dispute about wages . . . .

'Now our business is, first to show the working men that the question of wages is a question depending altogether on principles apart from party politics . . . that if we had the Charter tomorrow the principles which govern the relations between masters and men would be precisely the same as they are now . . . .'[1]

He advised the League to undertake a pamphlet campaign to explain the laws governing wages. A series of simple leaflets on wages and prices, written at this time, show that his advice was taken: the League, that is, made one more attempt to remove the causes of disagreement between the classes.[2] But it was nevertheless the last. After 1842, the *Anti-Bread Tax Circular* and its successor, *The League*, published in London, contain very few references to Chartism, and show little interest in working-class needs in general. The movement became, far more than previously, a middle-class agitation. In manufacturing towns there were fewer lectures open to the general public at which the Chartists could make their interruptions, and more tea-meetings, confined to members and to those invited. The *Northern Star*, on the other side, in no way abandoned its hostility to the League, but after 1842 it contains noticeably fewer reports of successful interruptions of League meetings.

For this situation two things were responsible; the decline in Chartism, and an alteration in the strategy of the League. The leaders of the League no longer felt it necessary to campaign for the support of industrial and commercial leaders, and they had lost interest in working-class politics. Instead their campaign was switched from the towns to the rural districts, and from the

---

[1] Speech of Richard Cobden to the Anti-Corn Law League in reference to the disturbances in the manufacturing districts, reported in the *Anti-Bread Tax Circular*, 8 Sept. 1842.

[2] *Anti-Bread Tax Tracts for the People*, nos. 1–3, (Manchester, 1842) Lawrence Heyworth, *How does cheap bread produce high wages and promote general prosperity?* (Manchester, 1842).

population as a whole to the electors. In October 1842 the League launched a great appeal for £50,000 — 'There must be more lectures, more tracts, more conferences, more agitation. Every county and borough elector in the kingdom must be personally visited and a condensed library of evidence and reasoning against the corn laws be placed in his hands. Monopoly will not yield without such efforts . . . .'[1] It is obvious that this immensely ambitious enterprise, which was in fact put in hand at once and carried forward with great vigour in the next six months, would absorb most of the £50,000, and the best part of the energies of the League's paid officials. When it is related to the League's 'register, register', campaign, it demonstrates unequivocally that henceforth the League intended to concentrate its attention on those within the pale of the constitution.

The change in the tactics of the League was dictated by the change in economic circumstances. In the cotton industry there was some recovery in employment in 1843, though distress persisted in the woollen, iron, and coal industries. By 1844 the recovery could be said to be general.[2] The harvests of 1842–4 were good, and the price of wheat fell from the abnormally high levels of the years 1838–41.[3] Thus, at a time when class hostility had been made more bitter by the events of 1842, working-class audiences would be increasingly unlikely to listen to arguments about dear bread. But the fall in wheat prices offered an opportunity of appealing to the discontents of tenant farmers: the League 'likened the manufacturers and the tenant farmers to two buckets in a draw-well — as one goes up the other goes down'.[4]

In 1843 and 1844 the League set to work to exploit divisions of interest within the agricultural community. It told the arable farmer that wheat prices had fallen since 1815, but that the landowner's rent had not fallen in the same proportion: it told the dairy

---

[1] *The Great League Fund. The Council of the National Anti-Corn Law League to the People of Great Britain and Ireland* (leaflet issued at Manchester, 20 Oct. 1842).
The 'condensed library' in question was a substantial and elegantly produced volume, which sold by retail at 1s. a copy. It contained among other things, three pamphlets directed to farmers, selections from Perronet Thompson's *Corn law Catechism*, from Deacon Hume's *H.B.T. letters*, from the evidence given before the Select Committee on Import Duties, and from Baptist Noel's *Plea for the Poor*. (There is a copy in M.P.L., P. 3676.)
[2] Gayer, Rostow and Schwartz, *Growth and Fluctuation of the British Economy, 1790–1850* (Oxford, 1953), Vol. I, p. 338.
[3] *Ibid.*, p. 327. Annual average prices of wheat per quarter were as follows: 1839, 70·6s., 1840, 66·2s., 1841, 64·3s., 1842, 57·2s., 1843, 50·2s., 1844, 51·1s.
[4] *The League*, 7 Oct. 1843.

farmer that the high price of wheat reduced the amount of money which the working classes could afford to spend on meat or dairy products. It pointed out the economic and political insecurity of tenancies-at-will, and urged farmers to fight for leases and for compensation for agricultural improvement, and aptly reminded the public that the Devon Commission was at this time investigating similar problems in Ireland.[1] It also paid attention, though in a more desultory way, to the condition of the agricultural labourer: Bright secured the appointment of a Select Committee of the Commons in 1844 on the game laws,[2] and the *League* carried in 1843 a series of articles on the derelict condition of labourers' cottages in the southern counties.[3]

Such complaints as these were more of a *cahier* of grievances against the aristocracy than an attack on protection, but they suggest once again the social basis of the whole agitation. The rural campaign was directed primarily to tenant farmers who were voters, and it is therefore not strictly relevant to the history of Chartism. In organising meetings in agricultural towns, the League was rarely able to claim much success; and on one occasion at Huntingdon in June 1843 it suffered a resounding defeat.[4] The most striking episode in the whole campaign was the well-known debate between Cobden and O'Connor at Northampton on 5 August 1844. There is, in general, no record of Chartist activity at such meetings, but on this occasion there was careful organisation of supporters both by Chartists and the League. In reply to Cobden's thesis that repeal would benefit all classes, O'Connor could produce no effective reply, but was reduced to a general lament at the progress of machinery in industry.[5]

With the exception of the Northampton meeting, there is little record of clashes between Chartists and the League after 1843. The increasing prosperity of the years 1843–5, and the general association of Peel's tariff reforms of 1842 with it, may have helped to soothe fears of repeal of the corn laws. When in the autumn of 1845 the

---

[1] *Ibid.*, issues of 30 Sept. and 9, 16 and 30 Dec. 1843, 23 Mar. 1844.
[2] *Parliamentary Papers*, 1845, Vol. XII, and 1846, Vol. IX.
[3] See, e.g. *The League* of 9 and 16 Dec. 1843.
[4] This meeting is described in detail in D. G. Barnes, *History of the English Corn Laws* (1930), pp. 254 ff. See G. G. Day, *Defeat of the Anti-Corn Law League* (1844), and J. Hill, *The Defeater Defeated* (Manchester, 1844).
[5] *The League*, and the *Northern Star*, issues of 10 Aug. 1844. There is much detailed information on the League's preparations for this meeting in the Wilson papers. (M.R.L.)

corn law question was approaching its final crisis, Chartist opposition was not heard. In November and December 1845 a great many public meetings were held in provincial towns to petition the Government to open the ports to foreign corn free of duty: there is no evidence that Chartists disturbed them, and some evidence that working-class organisations supported them. This was shown in many parts of the country; there were reports from the cotton towns of meetings organised by cotton spinners to memorialise Sir Robert Peel.[1] In Leicester, a public meeting was held partly as the result of a requisition from the operatives of the town.[2] At a meeting of the West Riding, held at Wakefield, the working classes turned out in force.[3] Such demonstrations, it is true, might have been merely the result of pressure of the employers on their workpeople, but nobody said this. On the contrary speakers and writers referred without fear of contradiction to a marked change in atmosphere. A speaker at Newcastle summed up the situation uncharitably but accurately,[4] 'by contrasting his present reception with that which he had experienced some three or four years ago.' Then 'not one word would the Chartists hear on the subject of the Corn Laws. The insolent fiat had gone forth, that no meeting should be held, unless for the discussion of the Charter; and the meeting was put down by noise and uproar. The patriots of the Charter drove the repealers into holes and corners. What was the contrast exhibited now?' he asked, 'Where was Chartism? Where, he demanded? In response to his demand, Echo answered, where?'

IV

After the repeal of the corn laws, the League was dissolved, so that there could be no further formal conflict between the two organisations. But, as far as the problem was one of reconciliation of the middle and working classes, it was not one to be solved overnight by any piece of legislation. It re-emerged in the Chartist revival and the events of 1847–8, and in the disputes among the leaders of the Chartist rump in the early 1850's.

In the subsequent relations between middle-class and working-

[1] *The League*, 22 Nov. 1845; *Manchester Guardian*, 10 Dec. 1845. See also issues of 3 and 17 Dec. for accounts of speeches at such meetings by repentant ex-Chartists.
[2] *Leicestershire Mercury*, 29 Nov. 1845.
[3] *Manchester Guardian*, 17 Dec. 1845. (Accounts of meetings at Birmingham and on Tyneside say nothing about working-class participation in them.)
[4] *Gateshead Observer*, 20 Dec. 1845.

class radicalism two processes were at work. The first was a mitigation of the economic grievances which had provoked the original Chartist outburst, whether in such measures as the Ten Hours Act of 1847 or in the narrower fluctuations of wheat prices after 1846. The second was the fragmentation of both political movements. The preceding narrative has suggested that there was a wide variety of motives and objectives both among the Chartists and among the League's members. Since neither was a parliamentary party in a position to impose some kind of discipline, political solidarity could only be preserved by a rigid adherence to particular slogans.[1] Without these unifying influences both movements disintegrated, and here and there it was possible for middle-class and working-class groups to find common ground. Among the leaders of the League, Cobden feared the extension of the franchise, and concentrated his interests on financial reform. Bright, on the other hand, recognised in the Chartist revival of 1847–8 a legitimate demand for political power, and continued to devote himself to the cause of franchise reform. 'The case for Parliamentary Reform', he believed, 'is more glaring and undeniable if possible than our Free Trade cause was.'[2] Within the working classes similar divisions of purpose emerged. The trade unions, which had contributed so little to the strength of Chartism, remained non-political, and there were arguments between Harney and Jones in 1851 and 1852 about how to deal with them. Both Harney and Jones came round to the view, however, that there was no hope of political advance without middle-class co-operation. By 1851 Harney was looking to an alliance of Chartists and Radicals. Six years later, with Chartism in complete eclipse Jones himself wrote that 'there can be no doubt as to the wisdom of allying with the middle class and their leaders if they offer such a measure of reform as we can be justified in accepting'.[3]

[1] See above, p. 291.
[2] Quoted in G. M. Trevelyan, *Life of John Bright* (London, 1913), p. 185.
[3] Quoted by J. Saville, *Ernest Jones*, p. 63.

Chapter Twelve

The Government and the Chartists

F. C. Mather

I

Throughout the life of the Chartist movement the relations between the Government and the Chartists were those of mutual hostility. The Chartists denounced the two great parties which governed England in turn, as 'robber factions', 'tyrannical plundering Whigs' and 'tyrannical plundering Tories', upholders of a system of class legislation which deprived the labourer of the fruits of his toil. The politicians, Whig and Tory alike, regarded the Chartists as enemies of property and public order. When the Duke of Wellington wrote of the Chartists in 1842, 'Plunder is the object. Plunder is likewise the means,'[1] he was expressing in rather immoderate language what most men of affairs felt about Chartism.

It must be recognised, however, that the Chartists were much more conscious of the Government than the Government of the Chartists. The *raison d'être* of Chartism was to compel a change in the system by which England was governed. Government, on the other hand, was involved in a multiplicity of problems, foreign and domestic, and, except for comparatively short periods, was not mainly occupied with Chartism. The private papers of statesmen, especially Whig statesmen, are not a fruitful source of information about the movement. Although Lord John Russell was Home Secretary during one period of intense Chartist pressure and Prime Minister during another, the Russell Papers contain only occasional references to Chartism.

It was as a threat to public order that Chartism principally concerned the Government. The movement also commanded a limited amount of electoral influence which did not escape the notice of Lord Melbourne's precariously-based second ministry, for when John Walter of *The Times*, standing as a Conservative candidate,

[1] Wellington to Graham dated 22 Aug. 1842. Graham Papers, Bundle 52B.

wrested the Nottingham constituency from the Whigs by means of Chartist support in April 1841, Lord Melbourne commented gravely to Queen Victoria: 'This combination, or rather this accession of one party to the Tories ... is very likely ... to take place in many other parts of the country in the case of a general election, and forms very serious matter for consideration as to the prudence of taking such a step as a dissolution of the Parliament.'[1] Usually, however, ministers considered this aspect of Chartist strength secondary in importance to the danger of riot and subversion.

Given that much disorder prevailed in England in the late 30's and the 40's of the nineteenth century and that many Chartists were involved in it, the Government was inescapably driven to protect its authority and the persons and property of its subjects by force. The first three sections of this study are devoted to explaining how the three administrations which were confronted by the three main crises of Chartism, in 1838–9, 1842 and 1848, approached the problem of enforcing law and order. But widespread unrest usually indicates the presence of serious defects in society, and the conduct of governments in relation to disturbances cannot be judged properly unless account is taken of willingness to undertake redress of grievances. Thus the last section will be concerned with the part played by remedial measures in the handling of Chartism.

II

When Chartism first became a problem to the authorities, the reins of government were held by Lord Melbourne's second Whig ministry, which took office in April 1835. England in the 1830's and 1840's was far from possessing a clear-cut, two-party system based on sharp divisions of principle.[2] Nevertheless the Whigs were traditionally the party of liberty just as the Tories were traditionally the party of authority, and their heritage affected their attitude towards questions of public order. Lord Melbourne recognised this when he remarked to Lord John Russell in February 1839, à propos 'a united move in favour of tranquillity and order', that 'the Whigs are never forward in that sort of thing'.[3] He did not of

---

[1] *The Letters of Queen Victoria, 1837–61*, ed. by A. C. Benson and Viscount Esher, 1907, London, Vol. I, pp. 332–3.
[2] See N. Gash, 'Peel and the Party System, 1830–50,' *Transactions of the Royal Historical Society* (1951).
[3] Melbourne to Russell, 22 Feb. 1839: Lord Melbourne's Letters (Panshanger Papers, Windsor Castle), Box 15.

course mean that Whigs were indifferent to the security of property. That was hardly to be expected of a party which included some of the largest landowners in the country. He did mean, however, that they were not anxious to embark upon repressive courses against popular movements until the necessity for doing so had been abundantly proved.

The libertarian strain in Whiggery was characteristically represented in the Cabinet by Lord John Russell, who, as Home Secretary, was more than any of his colleagues responsible for dealing with Chartism. By conviction and by family tradition Russell was a doctrinaire Whig, devoted to the ideal of liberty, and anxious to avoid encroaching upon freedom of discussion of political questions. He was also very self-consciously a reformer, and although at this stage of his career his views on reform were by no means advanced, and brought him into sharp conflict, not only with the Chartists, but with the parliamentary Radicals, he cherished the reputation of a great popular leader which he had acquired during the Reform Bill struggle, and brooded immoderately when attacks were launched against him from a Liberal quarter.[1] Thus he was anxious, not only that the measures which he took to combat Chartism should be enlightened, but that they should be generally regarded as enlightened by men of liberal opinion in Parliament and by the middle classes outside.

Russell's temperament did not dispose him to repressive courses. It is fear that usually engenders repression, and Russell, contrary to the impression given by Hovell and West,[2] was no alarmist. He was, in fact, inclined towards optimism, for his second wife, who was surely in a position to know, paid tribute to his 'usual calm and hopeful spirit'.[3] If anything he was too optimistic, and insufficiently aware of the depth of the discontent of the working classes.

With Russell at the Home Office, the Government treated the Anti-Poor Law agitation in the north (from which Chartism as a mass movement grew) with the utmost toleration. Violent resistance to the Boards of Guardians and the Assistant Poor Law Commissioner, Alfred Power,[4] was met by drafting Metropolitan policemen and troops into the area, but no interference was made

[1] Spencer Walpole, *The Life of Lord John Russell* (1889), Vol. I, p. 317.
[2] Hovell, *op. cit.*, p. 140; West, *op. cit.*, pp. 128–9.
[3] *Lady John Russell: A Memoir*, ed. by Desmond McCarthy and Agatha Russell (1910), p. 96.
[4] See above, p. 10.

with the campaign of speeches, pamphlets and newspaper articles by which such violence was encouraged. In December 1837 the Poor Law Commissioners tried to induce the Home Secretary to prosecute Oastler and Stephens for their speeches or, failing that, to prosecute the newly-founded *Northern Star* newspaper, which was giving publicity to those speeches, and publishing inflammatory articles in the form of letters written by Richard Oastler and others. The material in question was certainly calculated to induce the excited populace of the West Riding to attack or otherwise molest Power and the officers of the Unions, a course of action which the mob had already begun to pursue.[1] Nevertheless it seems unlikely that Russell would have taken any notice of the Commissioners' complaint if his attention had not again been drawn to the *Northern Star* through the medium of one of his colleagues, Charles Wood.[2] Thereupon he submitted an open letter appearing in the issue for 2 December, for the opinion of the Law Officers of the Crown, making it clear that he wished them to consider the criminality of the paper, 'not as containing libellous matter against the Government, but as to its tendency to excite resistance to the Laws, or to expose to assassination or personal violence the Assistant Commissioner and others employed in the Poor Law business.'[3] The Law Officers were as averse to prosecution as Russell, and advised against it 'unless any real practical evil has been found to result from the circulation of that paper'. And there, to the exasperation of the Commissioners, the matter was allowed to rest.[4]

So determined was the Whig Home Secretary to avoid the charge of interfering with freedom of discussion that he was quite prepared to tolerate violent speeches and writings. In September 1838 he wrote to the Earl of Harewood, who had sent him some published letters of Richard Oastler advising the working classes to procure arms: 'As far as I can perceive this gentleman's exhortation to the people to arm is not likely to induce them to lay out their money on muskets or pistols. So long as mere violence of language is employed without effect, it is better, I believe, not to add to the importance of these mob leaders by prosecutions.'[5] It was

[1] Poor Law Commissioners to Russell, 9 Dec. 1837, Ministry of Health Papers. P.R.O., 19/63. See also H.O. 73/52 for particulars of enclosures in the Commissioners' letter.
[2] Memorandum, 12 Dec. 1837, H.O. 73/54.
[3] Phillipps to Maule, 18 Dec. 1837, H.O. 49/8.
[4] Frankland Lewis, Lefèvre and Nicholls to Russell, 4 Jan. 1838, H.O. 73/54.
[5] Draft of letter from Russell to Harewood, 18 Sept. 1838, H.O. 52/38.

about this time that the Anti-Poor Law movement was giving place
to Chartism, and Russell made clear his intention of acting towards
the new movement as he had acted towards the old. Thus he forbade interference with the great Chartist meetings which were held
up and down the country in the early autumn to elect delegates to
the Convention.[1] It seems probable that the Home Secretary was
deliberately courting a reputation for liberality, for on 3 October he
seized the opportunity of a dinner in Liverpool, attended by mill-
owners and merchants, to boast of his refusal to put down Chartist
meetings and of his reluctance to sanction secret service expenditure.[2]

As the winter of 1838–9 drew on, the situation in the manufacturing districts changed for the worse.[3] The Chartists began to hold
meetings by torchlight in circumstances which raised fears of incendiarism. Sections of the working class embarked upon a course
of equipping themselves with pikes and pistols, and at Todmorden
on the Lancashire-Yorkshire border fierce destructive rioting occurred. By the end of the third week in November, the Government was taking the agitation in the country more seriously, and
the cabinet was consulted about it. The approach, however, was
rather vacillating. Lord John Russell had been temporarily removed
from the helm by personal catastrophe, the death of his wife, and
Lord Melbourne, the Prime Minister, was compelled to assume a
direct responsibility for internal order. Melbourne was much more
nervous than Russell, and his reputation, derived from the suppression of the Labourers' Revolt in 1830, when he was himself
Home Secretary, is hardly one of leniency. Nevertheless, he approached the conflict with Chartism cautiously and apprehensively.
His scruples were mainly of a legal character. He was afraid of involving the Government in an unsuccessful prosecution like that of
Cobbett in 1831. For a whole week at the end of November 1838,
he wavered on the question of prosecuting Oastler and Stephens.
His long political memory did not furnish an instance of conviction
for words only, and the difficulty was enhanced by the fact that
hitherto Lord John Russell, keen to avoid the slightest suspicion of
espionage, had not procured any accurate reports of speeches or
evidence of their having been delivered.[4] Melbourne also hesitated
before ordering a Royal Proclamation against the torchlight meet-

---

[1] *Ibid.*   [2] *The Times,* 9 Oct. 1838.   [3] See above, p. 44.
[4] Melbourne to Russell, 23, 27 Nov., 1 Dec. 1838, Panshanger Papers, Box 15.

ings. He thought that the meetings 'ought to be illegal', but doubted whether they were so, and 'still more whether my Lord Chief Justice (Lord Denman), a very popular lawyer and much inclined to act the part of Coke and [Holt?] would declare them to be so'.[1] But the Attorney General overcame the Prime Minister's scruples, and the Proclamation was issued on 12 December. A fortnight later, after much diligent searching for evidence, the arrest of Stephens was effected, and a regiment of cavalry was transferred to Manchester from the Irish command to strengthen the hands of the authorities.[2]

These repressive measures produced only a partial return to tranquillity, for soon after the Chartist Convention assembled in London early in February 1839, reports that the working classes were providing themselves with offensive weapons reached the Home Office in greater numbers than before. Nottinghamshire, Monmouthshire and the Newcastle-on-Tyne area were the principal trouble centres. Lord John Russell, who returned to his office early in the new year, was obliged to be more vigilant than he had previously been, and his vaunted dislike of espionage did not prevent him from issuing his warrant to the Postmaster-General ordering him to intercept the correspondence of Wade, Richardson, Vincent and Hartwell, four delegates to the Convention, and to transmit it to the Home Office for scrutiny.[3] But the information derived from this and other sources led Russell to conclude that there was not much danger of insurrection.[4] The belief which he sought to inculcate was that Chartism and the associated sale of arms to the people were simply means by which a few unscrupulous persons extracted money from the working classes, and that the danger would subside of its own accord as the fraud was detected.[5] Thus minded, he resisted the demands of the magistrates for extreme measures against the Chartists. He would not bring in a disarming bill or sanction the formation of armed associations of civilian volunteers.[6] He would not encourage the magistrates to

---

[1] Melbourne to Russell, 9 Dec. 1838, *ibid.*
[2] Jackson to H.O., 19 Dec. 1838, H.O. 40/39.
[3] Warrant signed by Russell, 8 Feb. 1839, H.O. 79/4.
[4] 'It does not appear to me', he wrote to the Duke of Newcastle, 'that those who have encouraged their followers to provide themselves with arms are ready to encounter so fearful a risk.' Russell to Newcastle, 16 Mar. 1839, H.O. 41/13.
[5] *Ibid.* See W. Napier, *Life and Opinions*, Vol. II, p. 6 and *Hansard*, 3rd series, Vol. XLIX, pp. 245–6.
[6] Russell to Newcastle, 23 Feb., 16 Mar. 1839, H.O. 41/13.

break up Chartist meetings, Peterloo fashion, but told them instead to send reports to the Home Office, which would consider whether the speakers should be prosecuted.[1] In practice the Chartist orators were left unmolested for about four months after the arrest of Stephens, partly because the Whigs did not wish to play an oppressive role and partly because they were still very nervous of a rebuff in the Law Courts.[2] Yet playing for safety did not exempt them from criticism, for it was already being suggested, in Parliament[3] and in the columns of *The Times*,[4] that the ministers were behaving towards Chartism with excessive indulgence. These attacks were not powerful enough to compel a reversal of policy, but there is at least a strong presumption that they influenced the Government in its decision to proceed with the removal of Frost's name from the Newport magistracy.[5] A weak minority administration, dependent on the goodwill of Tories and Radicals, had to choose its path with the utmost caution. Excess of zeal in the maintenance of public order would alienate the latter; a deficiency of it would arouse storms of protest from the former. To attempt a repressive policy and to fail in it would be to court opposition from both.

During April the Chartist unrest intensified sharply. There was an alarming extension of the practices of arming and illegal drilling among the working classes, and the disaffected prepared to use barricades in street fighting. Towards the end of the month the attitude of the Government stiffened. The Home Office ordered the arrest of Vincent and McDouall, called up three regiments of regular troops from Ireland and, during the first week in May, issued a Royal Proclamation against training and drilling and circular letters to the magistrates and Lord-Lieutenants encouraging the formation of armed associations and offering to arm the special constables. The restraint which had previously been imposed on

[1] *The Times*, 26 Mar. 1839; H.O. to mayor and magistrates of Stockport, 18 Dec. 1838, H.O. 41/13.

[2] This is evident from the opinions of the Law Officers of the Crown on cases submitted to them in March 1839. Some speeches delivered by Oastler and Feargus O'Connor at the Crown and Anchor tavern in the Strand were judged technically illegal, but the Law Officers advised against prosecution on the grounds that there would be an appearance of harshness in the proceedings, and that it would thus be difficult to obtain a conviction. About the same time the Attorney General refused to sanction a prosecution of the *Western Vindicator* for being published without a stamp, as the infraction of the law was as yet too doubtful. H.O. 48/33.

[3] *Hansard*, 3rd series, Vol. XLV, 106–9; 219–20.

[4] 12 Feb. 1839.   [5] See Williams, *op. cit.*, p. 130.

the magistrates from interfering with Chartist meetings while they were in progress was thrown overboard, and encouragement was freely given by the Home Office to arrest the offending parties at illegal meetings 'at the time of committing the offence'[1] and to seize the weapons of those who attended armed.[2] This was unwise, for a rash and overheated magistracy was hardly the best judge of whether intervention in a meeting was either justified or expedient.

The official attitude towards Chartist meetings, as defined in Whig Proclamations and instructions to the magistrates, was not unreasonable. It was based on the Common Law principle that public assemblages were illegal when they were 'attended by great numbers of people, with such circumstances of terror as are calculated to excite alarm and to endanger the public peace'.[3] This did not rule out large meetings, for the Home Secretary was at pains to make it clear to the Sheffield magistrates in August 1839 that as many as 4,000 or 5,000 people might assemble freely so long as the speeches and the demeanour of the meeting were peaceable.[4] But the Home Office could only indicate in very general terms the circumstances which would render a meeting illegal, and if there was to be interference with the gathering while it was actually on the ground, the responsibility for deciding upon such a course of action would have to rest with the magistrates present on the spot, and they might easily be led on by their fears to magnify the danger, and intervene unnecessarily.

In a chapter entitled 'The Government Prepares for Action', Mark Hovell's study of Chartism conveys the misleading impression that the Government was thoroughly and systematically preparing for a general insurrection of the Chartists on 6 May, the day on which, as originally arranged, their Petition was to have been presented to Parliament.[5] The fact that most of the measures described above were not adopted until a few days before the 6 May, far too late to be of much effect, discredits this view. Hovell supported his contention by affirming that, by 1 May, Napier, the

[1] Circular letter to Mayors and Magistrates of boroughs and Magistrates of counties, 7 May 1839, H.O. 41/13.
[2] H.O. to J. F. Foster, 6 May 1839, H.O. 41/13.
[3] *Copy of letter from Her Majesty's Principal Secretary of State for the Home Department to Colonel Rolleston, M.P., dated 3rd June 1839, on the subject of unlawful meetings* (448), XXXVIII.
[4] Walker to H.O., 24 July 1839, H.O. 40/51; H.O. to Walker, 14 Aug. 1839, H.O. 41/14.
[5] *Op. cit.*, pp. 141–2.

General commanding the Northern District, had completed a concentration of his troops at four or five strategic points.[1] But this is contradicted by an entry in Napier's journal on 9 May: 'I have not called in any detachment.'[2] Had the Chartists risen on 6 May they would in fact have found the Government's defences in a parlous state of disorganisation — the troops scattered in small detachments; the reinforcements from Ireland not yet arrived; the magistrates inert either from fear or indifference and the propertied inhabitants afraid to come forward as special constables to defend themselves.[3] But it seems probable that neither the Home Secretary nor General Napier, whose ear was closer to the ground, took very seriously the threat of a general insurrection on 6 May. The latter was much more concerned about the prospect of an outbreak in the Manchester area at Whitsuntide (c. 25 May) and about the idea of a march on London from the provinces, which Harney was popularising at Chartist meetings.

Napier, who had taken over his command at the beginning of April, and had spent the first month or so getting to know his district, now emerged as the controller of operations against the Chartists. Unlike the Home Secretary, he had given great thought to questions of strategy. He worked out a plan for defending the streets of Manchester against a mob of 100,000,[4] and arranged to use artillery from Nottingham to intercept a Chartist army bound for the metropolis in the hill country of Derbyshire, where his force could be employed most effectively.[5] He took upon himself the duty of bestirring the magistrates of the Manchester area to take measures for the protection of the locality,[6] and as Whitsuntide approached, the forces of authority, strengthened by the arrival of the troops from Ireland, became quite formidable. But Napier was a humane man, and while he laid his plans for putting down an outbreak should one occur, he laboured unstintingly to prevent bloodshed by making great display of his troops to overawe the district and by sending personal messages to the Chartist leaders at Manchester, warning them firmly but tactfully of the impossibility of staging a successful outbreak.[7] He knew, however, that it was not solely from Chartist intentions that the danger of a breach of the

---

[1] *Ibid.*, p. 141.   [2] Napier, *op. cit.*, Vol. II, p. 26.
[3] *Ibid.*, pp. 26–33; Cooke to H.O., 8 May 1839, H.O. 40/51; H.O. to C. H. Leigh, 23 Apr. 1839, H.O. 40/45.
[4] Napier, *op. cit.*, Vol. II, pp. 28–9.   [5] *Ibid.*, p. 33.
[6] *Ibid.*, pp. 33–4.   [7] *Ibid.*, pp. 39–45.

peace proceeded, for he used all his influence with the magistrates to dissuade them from breaking up the great Chartist meeting on Kersal Moor on 25 May, telling them that he would arrest seditious speakers after the meeting had dispersed, when there was little chance of provoking serious riot by doing so.[1] That the Whitsuntide crisis passed peaceably in Manchester and elsewhere was largely to the personal credit of Napier. Of the Home Office little more can be said than that it allowed the sagacious General to have his way.

Hitherto the Government had succeeded in maintaining public order without the assistance of Parliament, but in the weeks of excitement before Whitsuntide it was by no means certain that an appeal to the legislature for additional powers could be delayed much longer. The existing law placed obstacles in the way of checking the accumulation of arms by the Chartists. There was nothing illegal in the mere possession of arms, for the Bill of Rights had declared that 'all the subjects which are Protestants may have arms for their defence, according to their condition and as allowed by law'. As yet there was not even such restriction as was involved in the licensing of fire-arms, and before the magistrates could order the search for, and seizure of, arms kept in private houses, they had to procure positive information that rioting or other violence was imminent, and that weapons were collected together for the use of disturbers of the public peace.[2] Such information was not easy to come by, and there are indications that in the middle of May 1839 the Whig Government was contemplating legislation to facilitate the suppression by the magistrates of what Lord John Russell regarded as 'an abuse of the rights secured by the Bill of Rights'.[3]

Yet Russell was anxious to avoid committing the Government to such a step until absolutely obliged to do so, for he knew that some at least of the Radicals in the House of Commons would denounce

[1] *Ibid.*, pp. 42–3. See above, p. 46. Cf. the position at Peterloo, described in D. Read, *Peterloo* (1958).

[2] When, in August 1839, the magistrates acting for Sutton-in-Ashfield near Nottingham issued a warrant for searching for arms in the house of Joseph Broyan, a local Chartist leader, without specifying the illegal purpose for which they believed the arms were kept, Broyan brought an action against them for illegal search and obtained a verdict with $\frac{1}{4}$d. damages. Memorial of Duke of Portland and three Notts. magistrates, 7 Nov. 1840, H.O. 40/55.

[3] See memorandum of 12 May 1839, signed by Melbourne, which appears to relate to a measure to check the collection of arms for the purpose of plunder and insurrection. Lord Melbourne's Letters, Box 15. Speaking in Parliament on the 15th, Lord John Russell kept open the possibility that the Government might introduce a disarming bill. *Hansard*, 3rd series, Vol. XLVII, p. 1027.

the measure as unconstitutional[1] — a development which would wound still further his declining popularity and would prove embarrassing to the Government, as it depended on Radical support. Thus he procrastinated and, to his intense relief, the calm which descended on industrial England in June made it unnecessary to proceed further. In the improved condition Russell's optimism quickly reasserted itself. By the end of the month the Government, convinced that the storm had blown over, began to withdraw troops from the Northern District.[2]

The move was premature, for the rejection of the National Petition by the House of Commons on 12 July raised the political temperature once more to fever pitch. Incendiary riots in Birmingham, intimidation of shopkeepers, and attacks on factories by mobs bent on turning out the work-people re-energised the Government, and drove the local authorities to behave with greater spirit than before. The middle-class magistrates of the corporate towns, some of whom had been oblivious of danger earlier in the year,[3] acted vigorously against the Chartists, and mass arrests followed. When it was impossible to delay further, the Government approached Parliament a week or so before the session was expected to end, to ask for a Rural Police Bill, a loan in aid of the police in Birmingham and an addition of 5,000 men to the regular army.[4]

Reform of the police arrangements for the English counties was long overdue. The unpaid constables of the parishes and townships were useless to prevent or put down riot, and their deficiencies threw the burden of maintaining order on the yeomanry and regular troops, which could not be conveniently divided to afford adequate protection to all the localities threatened with disturbances. The opportunity to remodel this unsatisfactory system presented itself in March 1839, when a Royal Commission, which had been investigating the English rural constabulary for the past three years, reported in favour of establishing a centralised police force in all the counties of England and Wales. But a weak administration was

[1] In the debate mentioned in n. 2 Russell stated with reference to the question of a disarming bill that 'when extra-ordinary measures were taken in Parliament ... a sympathy was created, and a jealousy excited with regard to the constitution.' *Ibid.*, p. 1026.

[2] Napier, *op. cit.*, Vol. II, p. 50.

[3] When Lord John Russell's Circular to Magistrates was received in Bolton early in May the Town Council decided that no precautionary measures were necessary, *Bolton Free Press*, 11 May 1839. Cf. Patterson, *op. cit.*, p. 308.

[4] *Hansard*, 3rd series, Vol. XLIX, pp. 620–1.

in no position to undertake so radical a measure, which would have encountered the bitter opposition of county magistrates and borough corporations alike. So the project of reforming the county constabulary was put aside for the present session, and only revived when the Chartist pressure of the summer months made further delay inadvisable. The Government then brought forward very hastily a weak permissive measure, so full of flaws that it had to be amended in the following session.[1]

With the return of more peaceful conditions in the second half of August, the Home Office again fell back upon the view that Chartism was at a discount, and showed moderation in the treatment of prisoners. The Home Office papers contain the draft of a letter to the Mayor of Stockport, expressing the Home Secretary's wish that no proceedings should be taken against Chartists who came forward voluntarily and surrendered their arms,[2] and in one instance the Grand Jury remonstrated against the Government's decision to prosecute for conspiracy, a mere misdemeanour punishable by fine and imprisonment, instead of for High Treason.[3] As in October 1838, when Lord John Russell had made his Liverpool speech, the Whigs again showed a disposition to take credit for liberality in dealing with Chartism. At a public breakfast in Edinburgh the Attorney-General, Sir John Campbell, boasted that the Government had put down Chartism 'without one drop of blood being spilled'.[4] His words must have given considerable embarrassment to his colleagues, when, several days later, twenty-two Chartists were shot dead in a riot at Newport, Monmouthshire.[5] This so-called Newport rising provoked a stronger reaction from the Government than the whole of the preceding agitation. When it occurred Lord John Russell was no longer Home Secretary, and his replacement by Normanby, an amiable nonentity, weakened the hold of liberalism on the ministry, for the influence of Lord Melbourne became more marked in home affairs. Moreover, Melbourne believed that the co-ordination and secrecy attaching to the

[1] Announcing the police bill, together with the proposed Birmingham police loan and the army increase, to Queen Victoria, Lord John Russell commented: 'These measures ... will somewhat prolong the session', thus indicating that the bill was brought forward without much premeditation. Russell to Queen Victoria, 23 July 1839. Royal Archives: Correspondence of the Queen with Russell, 1838–9.
[2] Draft minute on letter from Mayor of Stockport to H.O., 22 Aug. 1839, H.O. 40/41.
[3] *The Times*, 17 Aug. 1839.   [4] *Quarterly Review*, Vol. LXV, p. 294.
[5] See above, pp. 234–43.

Newport *émeute* gave it a more serious character than the campaign of unions and great meetings which had preceded it.[1] For these reasons leniency was thrust aside, and, had it not been for the intervention of the Lord Chief Justice, the lives of the Welsh Chartist leaders would probably have been forfeited on the scaffold.[2]

Verdicts of a widely differing character have been passed upon the handling of Chartism by Lord Melbourne's ministry. Hovell believed that the Government dealt with the situation 'in an excellent fashion', but some historians, following the view commonly held by the Chartists themselves, have denounced its behaviour as oppressive and unconstitutional. Neither assessment can be accepted unreservedly.

The charges of unconstitutional conduct levelled against the Government in the columns of the *Northern Star* were usually based on a misunderstanding of the state of the law. Many Chartists questioned the legality of a professional police force;[3] others declined to acknowledge the Common Law prohibition of tumultuous meetings, claiming that to make any meeting legal they had only to procure a requisition signed by seven householders.[4] In reality the Government showed a scrupulous anxiety to keep within the Law in dealing with Chartism, and its policy was in no sense systematically repressive. The reader will search the Home Office Papers and the letters of Whig statesmen in vain for evidence of any systematic plan to crush the popular movement, as by arresting its leaders. It may be argued that, had the Government entertained any such design, it would have struck directly at the National Convention which was pronounced illegal from the bench at the trial of Henry Vincent.[5] Everything, in fact, seems to point to the conclusion that the Whigs were merely concerned to lop off the disorderly excrescences of Chartism, and that they only acted against the movement when they were convinced that the peace was seriously threatened. They held back until the very last

[1] Melbourne to Russell, 6 Nov. 1839. Lord Melbourne's Letters, Box 15.
[2] Williams, *op. cit.*, pp. 190–4.
[3] See report of speech made by Whittle, a delegate to the Convention of 1839. *The Northern Star*, 23 Mar. 1839. In July 1839 William Lovett carried through the Convention a resolution condemning the Metropolitan police detachment operating in Birmingham as 'a bloodthirsty and unconstitutional force from London.' Hovell, *op. cit.*, p. 157.
[4] *The Northern Star*, 11 May 1839.
[5] Report of proceedings at the Monmouth Summer Assize, 2 Aug. 1839, H.O. 40/45.

moment before striking a blow, and seized the earliest opportunity
to proclaim the emergency at an end.

If there is a case against the ministers, it is that they were weak
rather than that they were tyrannical. Their very restraint may be
partly accounted for by their fear of failure and their desire to avoid
being attacked by those whose opposition would be politically
dangerous, and similar considerations held them back from attempting such a thoroughgoing reform of the provincial police
services as was rendered necessary by the prevalence of unrest.
These were natural faults in a minority government lacking the
authority to deal boldly with a crisis, but they furnish reasons for
dissenting from the unqualified praise which Hovell accorded to
the Whigs for their handling of the situation.

III

When Chartism again reached a head, England had a different
government — a Conservative ministry, with Peel at its head, and
Sir James Graham at the Home Office. The movement had been
reviving since the spring of 1840, and gathered strength during the
distressful winter of 1841–2 and the ensuing spring, when the depression of trade and industry reached its trough. On 4 May 1842,
the Chartists presented to Parliament the second great National
Petition, which was rejected by a large majority. But the crisis of
Chartism was ushered in by a strike initially for non-political objects such as higher wages and better working conditions. It began
in the Midland coalfield, and spread during the first half of August to
Scotland and the textile districts of Lancashire and Yorkshire, being
transmitted from place to place by large bands of operatives, visiting
mines and factories, and compelling their inmates to cease work.

As the turnout spread, it became more violent. Fierce clashes
with the military occurred in the West Riding, and in the Potteries
magistrates' houses were attacked and burnt. Step by step Chartism
entered the movement in many centres of discontent. In the second
week of August resolutions in favour of remaining out of employment until the People's Charter became the law of the land were
passed by the strikers in public meetings,[1] and a similar resolution
was adopted by the conference of trade delegates which met in
Manchester on 12 August, to direct the strike.[2] The official leaders

---

[1] J. S. R. Evans to H.O. 13 Aug. 1842, H.O. 45/249.
[2] Gammage, *op. cit.*, p. 218.

of the Chartist movement at first held aloof, O'Connor denouncing the strike in the *Star* as a device of the hated Anti-Corn Law League,[1] but, when they assembled in Manchester on 16 August for the National Charter Association conference, they could hardly avoid assuming the lead of a movement which had become unmistakably Chartist. They, therefore, adopted an address recommending the continuance of the strike until the Charter was conceded, and accompanied it with a Manifesto appealing to 'the God of justice and of battle'.

Graham, as Home Secretary, was disposed to take a much more serious view of the threat of disorder than Lord John Russell had taken in 1839. He believed that England was suffering from a disease endemic in industrial societies, that of over-production, and held that even the good harvest which was in prospect in the summer of 1842 would have only a limited effect in relieving the distress of the people.[2] For this reason, and also because 'these Anti-Corn Law agitators have done their utmost to produce confusion', he anticipated disturbances, expecting them to occur in the winter of 1842–3, for in July 1842 he expressed anxiety to have an extra Brigade of Guards in England before the commencement of winter.[3] When the rioting began five months earlier than he had prophesied, he wrote of it in language which indicated the depth of his alarm. He described it as this 'mad insurrection of the working classes',[4] and affirmed gravely that 'treason is stalking abroad'.[5]

Notwithstanding his fears, the Conservative Home Secretary showed discretion and a sense of constitutional propriety in dealing with the disturbances. 'My own judgement would lead me to be slow to apprehend for words spoken unless a breach of the peace was imminent, as the immediate consequence of the inflammatory language addressed to the multitude,' he wrote to the Lord-Lieutenant of Worcestershire; 'and in all cases,' he added, 'it is desirable that there should be an information on oath and a warrant, and that the apprehension of the party accused should take place after the dispersion of the crowd, and not in their presence at a moment of general excitement.'[6] He also believed firmly that the main responsi-

---

[1] *Northern Star*, 13 Aug. 1842.
[2] Graham to Joseph Sandars, 30 July 1842, Graham Papers, Bundle 52.
[3] Graham to Peel, 24 July 1842. B.M. Add. MSS. 40, 447.
[4] C. S. Parker, *Life and Letters of Sir James Graham* (1907), Vol. I, p. 323.
[5] Graham to Lord Chancellor, 21 Aug. 1842, Graham Papers, Bundle 52B.
[6] Graham to Lyttelton, 8 Aug. 1842, *ibid.*, 52A.

bility for preserving public order rested with the local magistrates, who should use for the purpose a civil force of rural policemen or parochial and township constables, assisted by men of property acting as special constables or as members of volunteer horse patrols.[1] Thus he endeavoured to restrain the use of regular troops until their services could no longer be safely dispensed with.[2]

But the magistrates on whom Graham relied were at first remarkably supine, and offered little or no resistance to the vast turnout processions as they roved from mill to mill, and from town to town.[3] To members of the Government, notably the Duke of Wellington, this inertia appeared to stem from political disaffection,[4] and the project of filing criminal informations against some of the magistrates was seriously entertained.[5] The suspicion was not unwarranted, as many of the magistrates of the corporate towns, and some members of the Lancashire county bench, belonged to the Anti-Corn Law League, which had been fiercely agitating against the Government in the months preceding the outbreak. In the course of that campaign threats had actually been uttered that if, by continuing the bread tax, the Tory Government drove the people to insurrection, the magistrates would not be responsible for putting it down.[6] On the other hand the local authorities could justifiably plead a want of supporting power in extenuation of their inertia. Many of them applied to Manchester for troops, but the military force stationed in that town was so small that their applications were summarily rejected. Moreover, the General Commanding the Northern District, Sir William Warre, took it upon himself to advise the applicants 'to temporise with the people where they feel themselves quite unequal to enforce the law'.[7] Coming from such a distinguished quarter, the advice must have carried weight, and much of the responsibility for the inaction of the magistrates of Lancashire probably rested with Sir William Warre. But, as the Home Secretary realised, the trouble also arose from the magistrates' fears of being criticised for their exertions in

[1] Parker, op. cit., Vol. I, pp. 323-4.   [2] Ibid., p. 323.
[3] See statements of J. and W. Bradshaw and others relative to riots in Stockport, H.O. 45/242; Sir Charles Shaw to H.O. dated 26 Aug. 1842, H.O. 45/249C; See also H.O. 45/347 and 350.
[4] Wellington to Graham, 19 Aug. 1842, Graham Papers, 52A.
[5] Graham to Wharncliffe, 2 Sept. 1842, ibid., 53A.
[6] A. Prentice, History of the Anti-Corn Law League (1853), Vol. I, p. 348. See also above, pp. 365-6.
[7] Warre to H.O. 11 Aug. 1842, H.O. 45/268.

the House of Commons and in the press, as the Manchester magistrates had been criticised after Peterloo.[1]

When it became clear that law and order were breaking down in many parts of the manufacturing districts, the Central Government plunged into action. In the thorough and assiduous attention which he gave to this arduous and unwelcome task Graham exemplified the administrative efficiency which was so important a feature of the new conservatism associated with the name of Peel. 'I have not had a spare moment since the close of the session,' he wrote to Brougham on 21 August. 'My time has been occupied with odious business arising from the mad insurrection of the working classes . . . .'[2] His approach to the problem of disorder was determined and vigorous, for he was convinced that 'force alone can subdue this rebellious spirit',[3] and his own inclinations to severity were reinforced by the promptings of the Duke of Wellington, with whom he kept up a continuous correspondence about the riots, and by those of Queen Victoria. Once the decision had been taken to use troops, large military reinforcements were poured by rail into Manchester, into the West Riding and into the Staffordshire Potteries, and these were instructed to act vigorously against the mobs.[4] The magistrates were bestirred by a circular letter to the Lord-Lieutenants to prevent the forcible entry of a mob into mines, mills and factories, and were advised to do so by stopping the rioters at some convenient point outside the town which was about to be attacked.[5] To tranquillise the country, the Home Secretary endeavoured to prevent the Chartists from meeting in large numbers. His scruples against interference with freedom of speech broke down under the stress of the emergency, and, as his correspondence with the Lord-Lieutenant of Worcestershire shows, he encouraged the suppression of strike meetings as a purely preventive measure, when there was no immediate threat of disturbance. He gave it as his opinion that 'all meetings in large numbers in present circumstances have a manifest tendency to

[1] Graham to Peel, 2 Sept. 1842, Graham Papers, 53A.
[2] Parker, *op. cit.*, Vol. I, p. 323.
[3] Graham to Hardinge, 1 Sept. 1842, Graham Papers, 53A.
[4] In a letter to Colonel Beckett at Leeds the Home Secretary wrote with reference to the rioters: 'You must whop these fellows without loss of time; if once they get ahead we shall find the mtroublesome.' Graham to Beckett, 17 Aug. 1842, Graham Papers, 52A. See also H.O. to Huddersfield magistrates. 17 Aug. 1842, H.O. 41/17.
[5] Dated 15 and 16 Aug., H.O. 41/16.

create terror and to endanger the public peace, that as such they are illegal, and upon notice given that they will not be allowed to be held, they ought to be dispersed.'[1]

The Conservative Government was not content to arrest individual acts of outrage, but adopted bold and carefully thought-out offensive measures designed to bring the entire outbreak to an end. Among these featured a plan to demoralise the insurgents by sowing mutual distrust among them. This idea originated with the Duke of Wellington, who wanted the more trustworthy magistrates to spend money on obtaining information as to the names of the leaders of the outrages, so that these might be placarded as a sign to the rioters that 'some among them gave information to the magistrates'.[2] Graham saw the point of the Duke's proposal, and wrote privately to Sir William Warre at Manchester suggesting that valuable information as to the directors of the outbreak might be wormed out of the prisoners already taken. 'If once these rioters were aware that their plans were discovered, their secrets known, and their evil advisers watched,' he added, 'distrust would be sown amongst them, and the efficacy of your repressive force would be greatly augmented.'[3] It seems probable that the Royal Proclamation issued on 13 August, offering a reward of £50 for the apprehension and conviction of the 'authors, abettors, or perpetrators' of any act of turn-out violence committed during the strike, was designed to destroy the self-confidence of the rioters.[4]

But the counterstroke on which Graham relied most was the arrest of the members of the Manchester Trades Conference. It is now generally agreed that the disturbances of 1842 arose spontaneously from acute distress. But Graham saw them as a closely laid plot. 'It is quite clear', he wrote, 'that these Delegates (i.e. the trade delegates) are the Directing Body; they form the link between the Trade Unions and the Chartists, and a blow struck at this Confederacy goes to the heart of the evil, and cuts off its ramifications.' No sooner, then, did he hear of their resolution in favour of the Charter strike than he sent instructions to Manchester to apprehend them, if not for High Treason, then upon some lesser

---

[1] Lyttelton to H.O., 16 and 18 Aug. 1842, H.O. 45/263; H.O. to Lyttelton, 19 Aug. 1842, H.O. 41/17.
[2] Wellington to Graham, 12 Aug. 1842, Graham Papers, 52A.
[3] Graham to Warre, 12 Aug. 1842, *ibid.*
[4] The head of the Manchester police claimed that in Manchester at any rate it had that effect. Shaw to H.O., 15 Aug. 1842, H.O. 45/249C.

charge, and to convey them with all speed by rail to Lancaster Castle.[1] The Manchester Stipendiary Magistrates, to whom the order was addressed, hesitated at first, thinking the evidence insufficient, but Graham, not to be outdone, sent a Metropolitan Police Magistrate down to Manchester to give them legal advice,[2] and by 19 August he was able to report to the Queen that five of the principal delegates had been arrested and that warrants were out against four others.[3]

These repressive measures soon produced a partial return to tranquillity. By 23 August open rioting was at an end. The woollen and worsted workers of the West Riding and the hatters, bleachers, dyeworkers and iron founders of Lancashire were returning to their work. The cotton operatives of south-east Lancashire and the Midland miners held out for another month, and kept the authorities on their toes by 'hit and run' raids on factories and mines which dared to resume work, but the political element had passed out of the strike. It was once again a dispute over wages and miners' grievances.

The Government was not satisfied with a simple restoration of order. It was determined to probe to the depths of what it regarded as a very dangerous conspiracy, and to discredit the instigators of the outbreak by exposing the enormity of their transactions. Its suspicions fell on both the Chartists and the Anti-Corn Law League. Against the latter it could do no more than commission Croker to write an article in the *Quarterly Review* to prove that the League was mainly responsible for the rising, in the hope that such a publication, based largely on official archives, would discourage subscriptions to the League's campaigning fund.[4] But the Chartists, by adopting the strike which they did not originate, had rendered themselves liable to a heavier punishment. It was not enough that the hundreds of working men who had been rounded up by the authorities should be brought before the Special Commissions at Stafford, Chester and Liverpool on charges of riot, obstruction of labour and demolition of dwelling houses, and mercilessly sentenced to seven or ten or twenty-one years'

[1] Graham to Warre, 15 Aug. 1842, Graham Papers, 52A.
[2] Graham to Warre, 17 Aug. 1842; Graham to Wellington, 19 Aug. Graham Papers, 52A.
[3] *Queen Victoria's Letters, 1837–61*, Vol. I, p. 534.
[4] See G. Kitson Clark, 'Hunger and Politics in 1842,' *Journal of Modern History* (1953), for particulars of this undertaking.

transportation. The whole episode of the strikes must be presented to the nation, through the law courts, as a cold-blooded act of treason, in which the Chartist leaders were deeply involved.

The month following the restoration of order was one of diligent searching for evidence to substantiate the case. The opening of private correspondence at the Post Office was never more widely practised. Letters addressed to O'Connor, McDouall and Dr Scholefield were detained and copied for inspection by the Home Office, as were those of Richard Cobden and T. S. Duncombe, for the Home Secretary suspected collusion between the Chartists and the leaders of middle-class radicalism.[1] An experienced solicitor, Mr Gregory, was sent north by the Government to ferret out and piece together evidence of Chartist conspiracy.[2] The Home Secretary was working for an indictment of High Treason, which he hoped to be able to bring against William Ellis, a Chartist leader in the Potteries (against whom the only evidence was that he had uttered violent and inflammatory speeches to the multitude)[3] and against O'Connor and other participants in the late Chartist conference in Manchester. But the Lord Chancellor and the Law Officers of the Crown thought the proof insufficient to sustain so weighty a charge, and when the warrants against the leading Chartists were issued at the beginning of October, they were made out for conspiracy.[4]

But this small setback did not prevent the Government from pursuing its purpose of representing the events of August as a well planned, organised insurrection, for which the Chartists were largely responsible. Indeed Pollock, the Attorney-General, who less than three years before had put up a magnificent defence of Frost and the Newport rebels, clubbed together in one monster indictment O'Connor, some of the trade delegates, all the Chartist delegates and the leaders of the turn-out mobs. 'I propose to charge O'Connor as a general conspirator with the others,' he wrote, 'and not to proceed against him for Libel merely, or for acting as a Delegate, or taking part at the meeting of Delegates — I propose to try him in the same indictment with the worst of the defendants who headed mobs, made seditious speeches, and stopped mills and factories. I shall blend in one accusation the head and the hands —

[1] Warrants dated 18, 19 and 24 Aug., H.O. 79/4.   [2] *The Times*, 3 Oct. 1842.
[3] Graham to Peel, 30 Sept. 1842, B.M. Add. MSS. 40447. Cf. *The Times*, 4 Oct. 1842.
[4] Graham to Peel, 26 and 30 Sept. 1842, B.M. Add. MSS. 40447.

the bludgeon and the pen, and let the jury and the public see in one case the whole crime, its commencement and its consequences . . . .'[1] A true bill against Sixty Defendants was found by the Grand Jury of the Liverpool Assize on 11 October, and Graham rejoiced that they had 'brought the Chartists into a strait'.[2]

But the advantage could not be quickly pressed home, for all the sixty defendants traversed, which meant that their trials would have to stand over until the spring assizes.[3] For the Government delay was loss, since the alarm which pervaded the propertied classes on the morrow of the disturbances would probably not last for a further six months, and if the prosecution was held up until the spring public opinion would undoubtedly be less favourable towards it. There was also the consideration that it would be desirable to have the proceedings completed before Parliament assembled and provided a forum in which the Government might be criticised.[4] At this point the Attorney-General brought forward a proposal that the prosecution should be transferred to Westminster for a trial at Bar before the full Court of Queen's Bench. This procedure would not only hasten the trial of the prisoners. It would involve the use of a Special Jury, which would not be drawn, as a Liverpool Assize jury might well be, from an area strong in Chartist support. Finally, by its solemnity, and the fact of its being held in London, such a trial would give national importance to what Pollock regarded as 'the most formidable conspiracy that ever existed'. For a trial at Bar was an exalted proceeding reserved for cases of the greatest moment. The last had taken place in 1832, when the mayor and magistrates of Bristol had stood trial for neglect of duty during the Reform Bill riots, and the one before that in 1817.[5] The use which might be made of this publicity may perhaps be inferred from Pollock's remarks. The trial, he wrote, 'will unfold a little of the spirit in which the Anti-Corn Law League have acted . . . also the extent and danger of the Trades Union . . . and the alarming combination called "The Chartist Association".'[6]

Pollock's suggestion was at first favourably received by Peel, and

---

[1] Pollock to Graham, 9 Oct. 1842, Graham Papers, 54A.
[2] Graham to Peel, 12 Oct. 1842, B.M. Add. MSS. 40447.
[3] Pollock to Graham, 12 Oct. 1842, Graham Papers, 54A.
[4] Graham to Pollock, 17 Oct. 1842, ibid.
[5] Pollock to Graham, 12 Oct. 1842, ibid.; 21 Oct. 1842, ibid., 54B.
[6] Pollock to Graham, 19 Oct. 1842, ibid., 54B.

the Government gave it serious consideration. Ultimately, however, it was abandoned on the grounds that the proposal for a Trial at Bar would probably be contested in Court, and that this would cause delay, and thereby defeat one of the main objects of having such a trial.[1]

The defendants were thus left to take their turn at the 1843 spring assizes in Lancaster. By that time the tide of public opinion had already swung in their favour, and the jury behaved with remarkable leniency. In these circumstances the Government, making no doubt a virtue of necessity, did not attempt to press the case for heavy punishments, but the antecedents of the trial, which have just been described, show how wide of the mark were Gammage's suspicions that 'the Government never intended to imprison the defendants', and that they 'purposely left a loop-hole in the indictment out of which their supposed victims might easily escape'.[2]

Sir Robert Peel's government also sought to take advantage of the alarm created by the disturbances to launch an attack upon the Radical press. 'Are we not now able to pounce with effect upon some of the vile trash of which the enclosed is a specimen,' wrote Peel to Graham on 15 October 1842, ' . . . I think public opinion would support us just now, after the experience of recent events, in worrying by prosecution the Editors and publishers of some of the worst papers. I would select political articles and provocations to tumult.'[3] The nature of the publications which were to be attacked emerges clearly from the letter which Graham wrote to the Attorney-General, in pursuance of Peel's wishes. It alluded to '*the Weekly Dispatch, the Anti-Corn Law Circular*' and 'any of the worst Republican Papers', and desired Pollock to consider a prosecution for passages 'exciting the renewal of the attempt to carry the Charter, or any other public measure, by physical force', and to watch the general character of the leading articles in the weekly press.[4] Two months later Peel wrote again to Graham, urging him to 'go to the extreme verge of the Law' in suppressing 'revolting infidel publications and placards'.[5] Shortly afterwards it was reported in the *Illustrated London News* that the Metropolitan Police

[1] Pollock to Graham, 7 Nov. 1842, *ibid.*, 55A.   [2] Gammage, *op. cit.*, p. 239.
[3] Peel to Graham, 15 Oct. 1842, Graham Papers, 54A.
[4] Graham to Pollock, 17 Oct. 1842, *ibid.*
[5] Peel to Graham, 17 Dec. 1842, *ibid.*, 56A.

were not only to open a campaign against booksellers, but were also to examine the libraries of the Socialist institutions.[1]

IV

When Chartism revived in 1848, the Whigs were in office again, with Lord John Russell at the head of the ministry. As an English working-class movement Chartism was much weaker than it had been nine years earlier, but from the Government's point of view it was, in one respect, of greater importance, in that it had acquired international significance. The internal situation in England was being carefully watched from abroad, and the anticipation of a Chartist outbreak on 10 April encouraged revolutionists through-out the continent,[2] and weakened the diplomatic bargaining power of Great Britain.[3] The Government was well aware of this when it made its celebrated preparations to deal with the Kennington Common demonstration, for on the day of the great meeting Lord John Russell wrote to the Queen: 'A quiet termination of the pre-sent ferment will greatly raise us in foreign countries.'[4]

Chartism in 1848 was also closely linked with Irish discontents. Ireland was on the verge of revolt, driven thither by famine, by the example of France, and by the exhortations of the Confederate leaders. It is clear that the Irish situation constituted the Whig Government's major headache, even when English Chartism as-sumed its most menacing appearance. 'There', wrote Lady Russell on 13 April 1848, 'is the weight that almost crushes John, who opens Lord Clarendon's daily letters with an uneasiness not to be told.'[5] But Chartism was inseparable from the Irish agitation. The Irish leaders looked to a military diversion in England as an essential part of their plan of campaign,[6] and their followers in London and the English provincial towns were quick to see the value of co-opera-tion with the Chartists to keep up a state of unrest over here. The London Irish marched to Kennington Common on 10 April with their green banners flying, and were addressed by Harney when they arrived.[7] The outcome of the day was awaited with much

[1] Maccoby, op. cit., p. 248, n. 4.
[2] M. Chevalier à M. G. R. Porter, 16 Avril 1848, P.R.O., 30/22/7.
[3] Palmerston to Russell, 21 Apr. 1848, P.R.O., 30/22/7.
[4] Queen Victoria's Letters, 1837–61, Vol. II, p. 200.
[5] Lady John Russell: A Memoir, p. 99. Lord Clarendon was Lord-Lieutenant of Ireland.
[6] D. Gwynn, Young Ireland and 1848 (Cork, 1949), pp. 167–8, 200.
[7] The Times, 11 Apr. 1848.

interest in the Irish capital,[1] and the Whigs were fully conscious of the Hibernian significance of events in London. 'I trust', wrote Sir George Grey, the Whig Home Secretary, to Prince Albert at 6.45 p.m. on 10 April, 'that the manner in which this day has, up to the present time, proceeded here will have a good effect in Dublin.'[2] Four days later Lord Lansdowne, Lord President of the Council, looking back on the happenings of the 10th, wrote to the Prime Minister: 'It is not our business to magnify the extent of the danger — besides if there has been the commencement of a deliverance — is that deliverance over here or in Ireland?'[3]

Despite these larger considerations, which lent additional urgency to measures taken for the preservation of public order at home, Whig treatment of Chartism was not basically different from what it had been in 1839. The behaviour of the Government was again characterised by forbearance and restraint. It is true that when the Chartists proposed to march with their petition from Kennington Common to the House of Commons on 10 April, some very elaborate preparations were made for keeping the peace, but this does not necessarily signify, as has sometimes been assumed, that the Government had panicked. It may well be that the abundance of precautionary measures resulted not so much from a conviction that these were necessary to prevent revolution as from a desire to forestall violence and bloodshed, by overawing the wilder spirits among the Chartists.[4] Moreover, it has not been sufficiently recognised that the Whig ministers were relatively slow in adopting counter-measures. We have it on Lord John Russell's authority that as Prime Minister he at first thought so lightly of the danger that he was prepared to take the risk of allowing the Chartist procession to cross the river from the South Bank, and deliver its petition to the doors of Parliament, but that he was dissuaded from this course by a friend 'of great experience and acknowledged sagacity'.[5] The reminiscences of an elder statesman written long after the event are not to be accepted as fully reliable evidence, but in this case they receive some corroboration from contemporary correspondence in the Russell Papers. On 4 April,

[1] Jones to Trevelyan, 10 Apr. 1848, P.R.O., 30/22/7.
[2] Grey to Prince Albert, 10 Apr. 1848, Royal Archives, C. 56.
[3] Lansdowne to Russell, 14 Apr. 1848, P.R.O., 30/22/7.
[4] See letter from Russell to Prince Albert, 9 Apr. 1848, *Queen Victoria's Letters, 1837–61*, Vol. II, p. 198.
[5] Earl Russell, *Recollections and Suggestions, 1813–73* (1875), pp. 252–3.

C. E. Trevelyan of the Treasury, who regarded English Chartism in the context of Irish disaffection, and was thus disposed to take a most serious view of it, thought it necessary to advise Russell that the Chartist procession should be turned off at some distance from the Houses of Parliament. He added that the 'shopkeeping and other middle classes in London' were 'calling out against the apathy and inaction of the Government', and that they were desirous of being 'organised and associated' to meet the threat from below.[1] It is also evident from other sources that Sir James Graham,[2] the Duke of Wellington[3] and The Times[4] all deemed it advisable to use what influence they had to ensure that the Government left nothing to chance, and in view of the political weakness of the Whigs, and their dependence on Peelite support, there is at least a strong presumption that this pressure was not without effect.

Even so the Whigs turned a deaf ear to the more extreme counsels which were being urged upon them, such as the Duke of Wellington's suggestion that meetings should be limited by law to such numbers as could properly discuss the question at issue.[5] The Chartists were allowed not merely to meet on Kennington Common, but to march thither in procession from all parts of London. It was only the procession to the doors of the House that was forbidden, and that ban was capable of being justified on grounds of a need to prevent the overawing of Parliament. The prohibition of meetings within a mile of Parliament during the parliamentary session, imposed by the Seditious Meetings and Assemblies Act of 1817, was strictly enforced, for similar reasons, against assemblages in Trafalgar Square, but the Government was slow to put down

---

[1] Trevelyan to Russell, 4 Apr. 1848, P.R.O., 30/22/7.

[2] C. C. F. Greville, A Journal of the Reign of Queen Victoria from 1837–52 (1885), Vol. III, p. 160.

[3] There is a memorandum in the War Office Papers composed by the Duke on 5 Apr. which shows that the Duke was putting forward suggestions for the defence of London even before he was called in to advise the Cabinet, W.O. 30/81. Greville testifies to the Duke's great excitement and anxiety that the Government should be firm, op. cit., III, p. 162. It may well be that his influence on the Cabinet, when he was consulted, did a great deal to stiffen the Government's attitude. But the Duke's responsibility for the governmental preparations has been much exaggerated in the traditional version of the story. Wellington war not put in sole charge of the arrangements, for Russell's account makes it cleas that the programme of proceedings was drawn up by the Commissioners of the Metropolitan Police, and only approved by Wellington along with the rest of the Cabinet. Russell, op. cit., p. 253. The Duke, as Commander-in-Chief, had a particular responsibility for the military arrangements, but these by his own desire were ancillary to the civil plans.

[4] 6 Apr. 1848.

[5] Hansard, 3rd series, Vol. XCVIII, p. 72.

Chartist meetings in Eastern and Central London, contenting itself at first with issuing orders to the police to watch them, and only to prevent them if they were held at unseasonable hours.[1] Only as a last resort, when several meetings had broken up in disorder, and when the matter had been twice raised in Parliament, did it forbid the Bonners Fields demonstration on 12 June.

The Government also hung back from prosecuting the Chartist leaders. When McDouall went down to Bradford at the behest of the Chartist Executive late in May, he delivered himself of a speech designed to induce his hearers to continue arming themselves with pikes, but to discountenance any 'premature' outbreak.[2] The Home Office judged his speech illegal and seditious, but decided against prosecuting him.[3] This seems to indicate that the Government's main concern was for the immediate security of the public peace, and that the threat of an ultimate general resort to arms was not taken very seriously. This impression is confirmed by subsequent events. It would appear that the arrest of Ernest Jones and other Chartist leaders, which was ordered on 6 June, was determined upon in consequence of the disquiet produced by the numerous Chartist meetings and processions held in the metropolis on and after 29 May rather than from any desire to remove the prospective leaders of a rebellion.[4] During the summer months Chartism went underground, clubs, classes and National Guards were formed, and there was communication by means of delegates between widely separated districts. But the Government still displayed no apprehension of an impending revolt. Further arrests were made in August, but these appear to have resulted from the unco-ordinated investigations carried out by the Metropolitan Police Commissioners and the provincial magistrates through their spies. Some of the prisoners received heavy sentences of transportation under the new Treason-Felony Act, but the Government showed no interest in getting to the bottom of the affair. When in the middle of August Mr Frederick Goodyer, Chief Constable of Leicestershire, came to London to interview a batch of Chartist prisoners recently arrested for plotting an outbreak in the metropolis, his object was to trace a connection between them and the Chartist leaders in the country. It is significant of the Government's attitude

[1] *Ibid.*, Vol. XCIX, pp. 337–8. [2] Gammage, *op. cit.*, p. 332.
[3] H.O. to Mayor and Magistrates of Bradford, 25 May 1848, H.O. 41/19.
[4] Russell to Queen Victoria, 1 June 1848, Royal Archives, C. 56.

that the Under Secretary at the Home Office merely sent him to
Scotland Yard with a note.[1] If Graham had been Home Secretary,
the official reaction would almost certainly have been more spirited.

V

Having dealt with the measures adopted by the governments of
the period to enforce the law against the Chartists we must consider finally whether the Chartist movement exercised any influence on the positive social, economic and political policies of
statesmen.

To the main immediate objective of the Chartists, the programme
of universal suffrage, vote by ballot, equal electoral districts, payment of M.P.s, annual parliaments and abolition of the property
qualification for a seat in the House of Commons, there was no
concession whilst the Chartist movement lasted. Members of the
Government were aware that nothing less than the whole Charter
would have satisfied the Chartists,[2] and the aristocratic politicians
of early Victorian England feared the consequences of granting
that more than they feared the risks involved in resisting it. Lord
John Russell believed that a Parliament elected by universal suffrage
would refuse to 'fulfil the engagements entered into between the
people and the public creditor'.[3] Macaulay held that 'universal
suffrage would be fatal to all purposes for which government
exists', and that it was 'utterly incompatible with the very existence
of civilisation', which rested on 'the security of property'.[4] The
Conservative leaders, Peel and Graham, affirmed that the establishment of a franchise based on numbers rather than on property
would bring about the destruction of the 'mixed constitution', with
its balance of Queen, Lords and Commons.[5] The effect produced
by the Chartist movement on men who thought like that was merely
to strengthen their determination to resist its demands, for Chartist
methods of agitation and the fierce antagonism towards the wealthy
displayed so markedly in the language of the second National
Petition confirmed the politicians in their belief that 'spoliation' in
one form or another could not fail to accrue from the granting of

[1] Packe to H.O. 21 Aug. 1848, H.O. 45/2410R.
[2] Speaking in a debate in Parliament in January 1840 Lord Howick rebutted
the suggestion that discontent could be allayed by 'anything short of the entire
subversion of the existing constitution'. Hansard, 3rd series, Vol. LI, p. 778.
[3] Hansard, 3rd series, Vol. XLVI, p. 1089.
[4] Ibid., 3rd series, Vol. LXIII, p. 46.
[5] Ibid., 3rd series, Vol. LXII, p. 936 and Vol. LXIII, p. 81.

universal suffrage. It is not without significance that, when Lord John Russell took up the cause of franchise reform once more, he explained to the House of Commons that the repudiation of revolutionary violence by the English people in 1848 had greatly influenced his decision.[1]

But Chartism was not merely a political programme. It was an expression of intense dissatisfaction with social evils and with the 'unjust laws' which were held to have created them. There is no doubt that during the period spanned by the Chartist agitation the Government directed its attention increasingly to the improvement of working-class conditions. The removal of the taxes on essential foodstuffs, the Factory Act of 1844, the administrative mitigation of some of the harshness of the New Poor Law, the Public Health Act of 1848 and the support given by some politicians at least to the Ten Hours movement furnish examples of this tendency. It is within the scope of this investigation to enquire how far the social policy of governments was directly influenced by the Chartist agitation.

If the Anti-Poor Law agitation of 1837-8 can be regarded as part of Chartism, then it may be said that Chartism compelled the Government to slow down the process of applying the New Poor Law to the northern manufacturing districts. After the Poor Law Commissioners had struggled in vain for some months against the resistance of a violent mob to set in operation a Poor Law union in Huddersfield, they received a letter from the Home Secretary, Lord John Russell, written on 26 June 1837, advising them to wait twelve months before ordering the Huddersfield guardians (whose activities had hitherto been confined to an attempt to elect a clerk) to implement the New Poor Law.[2] About six months later Russell followed this up by instructing the Commissioners not to bring any more of the large manufacturing unions into operation until the whole question of applying the law to the industrial districts had been investigated by Parliament.[3] Here was an instance in which the Government had chosen to make a concession to its opponents in preference to breaking down resistance by force. It must be remembered, however, that the opposition to the New Poor Law cannot be completely identified with Chartism.[4] The

[1] *Ibid.*, 3rd series, Vol. CXXXI, p. 307.
[2] Draft of Russell to Poor Law Commissioners, 26 June 1837, H.O. 73/52.
[3] Frankland Lewis, Lefèvre and Nicholls to Russell, 4 Jan. 1838, H.O. 73/54.
[4] See above, p. 11.

working-class components of the former movement certainly merged imperceptibly into Chartism, but resistance to the Act of 1834 commanded a good deal of middle and upper-class support both inside and outside Parliament which was denied to Chartism. It is important to note that when Lord John Russell wrote to the Commissioners on 26 June 1837 advising delaying tactics, he mentioned among the factors which influenced him, not only the excitement of the community, but the unwillingness of the Guardians to assume the administration of relief and the delicacy of the situation in Parliament, where a committee was considering 'whether the Law could be beneficially introduced in the manufacturing towns of the North'.

The working-class Chartism of 1839 does not appear to have influenced significantly the social thinking of the Whig government. Lord John Russell's speech on the first National Petition in July shows that he attributed the Chartist unrest primarily to the activities of demagogues, and that he saw nothing outstandingly disturbing in the condition of the working classes. 'There are at this time, as I am afraid there will be at most times, a number of working men . . . whose means are exceedingly scanty,'[1] was the most that he was prepared to concede. It is sometimes argued that fear of Chartist discontent was a very strong motive influencing the Whigs to take up educational reform in 1839, the year in which they established the Committee of the Privy Council on Education, purporting also to set up under state management a normal school or training college for teachers intended for the schools for the poorer classes.[2] To a government which viewed disturbances as the work of agitators playing upon a deluded populace educational reform was of all social reforms the one most likely to appeal as a remedy, and Lord John Russell certainly used the prevailing Chartist unrest as an argument for education in June 1839.[3] Chartism cannot, however, have been more than a subsidiary factor strengthening the Government's determination to proceed, for the decision to deal with the educational question was taken towards the end of October 1838, before the Government had become seriously concerned about Chartism. It would appear from the Home Secretary's correspondence with his colleagues that, at that time,

[1] *Hansard*, 3rd series, Vol. XLIX, pp. 240–1.
[2] See for example J. W. Adamson, *English Education, 1789–1902* (1930), p. 131.
[3] *Hansard*, 3rd series, Vol. XLVIII, p. 665.

genuine interest in education and the fear that, if the Government did not act quickly, the educational question would itself be made the subject of a new agitation weighed more heavily with the Queen's ministers than did Chartism.[1]

There is a hint that the wish to combat Chartism may have entered into the calculations of the Whigs, when, in the spring of 1841, they brought forward their ill-fated proposals for reducing the preferential duties on commodities in general demand by and for the working classes — sugar, timber and corn—for Lord John Russell wrote to the Queen in May that 'one consequence of the propositions of the Ministry is the weakening of the power of the Chartists, who have relied on the misrepresentation that neither Whigs nor Tories would ever do anything for the condition of the working classes'.[2] Probably the Government's sudden concern for Chartism at this stage arose from the fact that the Chartists had just demonstrated at Nottingham that, in certain constituencies, they could swing the electoral balance in favour of the Tories and against the Whigs.[3] Lord Melbourne's ministry, with an uncertain majority in the House of Commons, was particularly vulnerable to this kind of attack. It seems probable, however, that the Whig proposals reflected a desire to win middle-class support,[4] and that they were not merely, probably not primarily, influenced by Chartism.

The Conservative Government which took office in August 1841 approached the subject of working-class improvement far less from the angle of party advantage than the Whigs had done. Peel and Graham were much concerned about the distress experienced by the British working classes in the years 1841 and 1842, and appreciated the threat to the security of property arising therefrom.[5] Graham, as we have seen, fully expected serious disturbances. Nevertheless, when the outbreak occurred in August 1842, in the form of a strike for the People's Charter, the Conservative leaders attributed it primarily to a closely laid plot, in which the Chartists, the trade unions and the trade delegates at Manchester were

---

[1] Cottenham to Russell, 25 Oct. 1838; Spring Rice to Russell, 29 Oct. 1838; Russell Papers, P.R.O., 30/22/3.
[2] *The Letters of Queen Victoria, 1837–61*, Vol. I, p. 350.
[3] *Ibid.*, pp. 332–3.
[4] Lucy Brown, 'The Board of Trade and the Tariff Problem, 1840–2', *English Historical Review*, Vol. LXVIII, 1953.
[5] C. S. Parker, *The Life and Letters of Sir James Graham*, Vol. I, p. 328; and *Sir Robert Peel From His Private Papers* (1899), Vol. II, p. 527.

involved. The Prime Minister informed the Queen that the movement was 'not one caused by distress'.[1] Not until the political element had passed out of the strike and the turn-out had reverted to
the position of a trade dispute did the Government see the necessity
for any action other than repression. It then occurred to Graham
that he and his colleagues might be accused of using military force
to compel the operatives and coalminers to submit to the demands
of their masters.[2] Accordingly he wrote letters to Sir Thomas
Arbuthnot, the General commanding the disturbed districts, and to
Lord Talbot, asking them to arbitrate between the masters and the
men and to endeavour to secure redress of the legitimate grievances
of the latter. To Lord Talbot he expressed himself thus: 'I am by
no means prepared to use military force to compel a reduction of
wages or to uphold a grinding system of Truck: to preserve the
peace, to put down plunder and to prevent the forced cessation of
labour by intimidation, these are the sole objects of Government
. . . You cannot render a greater service than by bringing this dispute as to wages to a close; and you will faithfully represent the
Government by marking a kind sympathy with the feelings and just
claims of the workmen.'[3]

Both Peel and Graham entertained rather doctrinaire beliefs in
favour of maintaining the freedom of the labour market and were
averse to redressing the grievances of the workmen by legislation,
but the Conservative Prime Minister was certainly anxious to do
something to reform the abuses which the strikes had brought to
light. He wrote to Graham on 1 September: 'I wish we could with
perfect safety — and without adding to the excitement which prevails — appoint a Commission for the purpose of ascertaining the
real truth as to the state of the relations between the employers and
employed in collieries. I think it would be found that there are
practical grievances — possibly not to be redressed by law — of
which the employed have full reason to complain. What law cannot
effect exposure might. I strongly suspect the profits in many of the
collieries would enable the receivers of them to deal with much
more liberality towards their workmen than they do at present. I
fear there are two galling Regulations — with respect to weight of
coal got and deductions from wages and to dealing with particular

[1] *The Letters of Queen Victoria, 1837–61*, Vol. I, p. 531.
[2] C. S. Parker, *Sir Robert Peel From His Private Papers*, Vol. II, pp. 540–1.
[3] Graham to Talbot, 25 Aug. 1842, H.O. 79/4. See also Graham to Arbuthnot, 25 Aug. 1842, H.O. 79/4.

shops — which justify complaint.'[1] When the disturbances died down, the Government appointed Thomas Tancred as commissioner to investigate mining abuses in the Midland coalfield.[2]

The riots also impressed upon the Government the need for churches and schools, which would re-model the outlook of the turbulent masses.[3] Thus, in 1843, an act to increase the supply of clergy in crowded parishes was passed, and the Home Secretary introduced in a Factory Bill proposals for the Scriptural education of the people. But Graham was far-sighted enough to perceive that the roots of discontent were more economic than moral. By the experiences of August 1842, and by his subsequent observations of the tranquillity which ensued when prosperity returned to the country, he was gradually convinced that the Chartist unrest 'mainly arose from the want of adequate sustenance, in consequence of the high price of food and low wages'.[4] The support which he gave to Peel in the matter of corn law repeal, and his advocacy of a reduction in the import duties levied on other foodstuffs, sprang largely from this realisation.

In the prosperous years of the middle 40's, whilst the numbers of Chartists declined, interest in the condition of the working classes grew, and when the Whigs resumed office in 1846, they were carried forward by a strong current of public opinion to make social reform one of their main objects. The Public Health Act of 1848 was their work. It seems unlikely, however, that the Government's social policy owed much to the revival of Chartism, which once again impinged on the Government's attention in the latter year. Lord John Russell's reaction to the crisis was mainly negative. Prince Albert suggested on the day of the Kennington Common demonstration that, in order to create employment for the working classes of the metropolis, the Government might rescind some recent reductions in building operations at Westminster Palace, Buckingham Palace and Battersea Park, which had been forced upon it by a clamour for economy raised by its own Radical supporters in the House of Commons.[5] Russell replied in a tone which showed appreciation neither of the urgency of such a step, nor of the sufferings of the working man. 'I entirely concur in the general line of

---

[1] Peel to Graham, 2 Sept. 1842, Graham Papers, 53A.
[2] Peel to Graham, 18 Nov. 1842, *ibid.*, 55B.
[3] C. S. Parker, *Sir Robert Peel From His Private Papers*, Vol. II, pp. 546–9.
[4] *Hansard*, 3rd series, Vol. LXXXIII, p. 719.
[5] *The Letters of Queen Victoria, 1837–61*, Vol. II, pp. 198–9.

policy pointed out by Your Royal Highness,' he wrote, 'but as to the employment of workmen, our revenue is deficient, our expenditure great. I should be sorry to diminish ships or regiments. The public departments can in time be reduced, but the only immediate reduction can be in works carrying on for the public.' The sting of the letter was in the tail: 'The masons especially the hodmen are generally infected with repeal or Chartism, and employment has not prevented many of them from having refused to be sworn in as special constables, because the oath contained the Queen's name.'[1] The last four words were underlined.

A fortnight later Russell endeavoured to prevent the Prince from demonstrating his own interest in the welfare of the working class by presiding at a meeting of Lord Ashley's Society for Improving the Condition of the Labouring Classes.[2] The Prime Minister's objection was that the Chartists might interrupt the meeting and, in order to diminish the Prince's enthusiasm, he sent him a copy of a scurrilous Radical publication attacking the Royal Family. It is to Prince Albert's credit that he saw in this only a stronger reason for exhibiting the sympathy of the Crown, and insisted on fulfilling his engagement.[3]

VI

Thus it may be seen that there was a marked difference between the Whig and the Tory reactions to Chartism. The latter was decidedly stronger than the former. There was enough of the old Tory spirit in the new conservatism of Sir Robert Peel to drive its front-bench representatives to deal vigorously (though without resorting to the methods of Pitt and Sidmouth) with the Chartist unrest with which they were confronted as a government in 1842. Graham, the Home Secretary, and Pollock, the Attorney-General, two key figures in the ministry, appear from their correspondence to have been seriously alarmed, and were prone to find a formal conspiracy lurking behind disturbances which historians have since adjudged spontaneous. The Whigs, on the other hand, were less nervous of Chartism, though Lord Melbourne was more so than many of his colleagues. They were sceptical of the prospect of an organised revolt, and dealt with symptoms of excitement and

---

[1] Russell to Prince Albert, 11 Apr. 1848, Royal Archives, C.56.
[2] Russell to Prince Albert, 25 Apr. 1848, *ibid.*
[3] Prince Albert to Russell, 29 Apr. 1848, *ibid.*

disorder rather than with underlying causes, waiting as long as they could before they struck. But it was not only upon the repressive side that the Tory reaction was stronger than the Whig. A study of the correspondence passing between Sir Robert Peel and Sir James Graham in the closing stages of the great upheaval of August 1842 reveals a stirring of the social consciences of the two statesmen which was quite unparalleled by anything to be found in the letters of Melbourne and Russell in 1839 or in those of Russell in 1848. It cannot be claimed that Chartism (if the term can be used to signify the discontent of the masses in 1841 and 1842) produced a revolution in the outlook of the Conservative ministers, for they remained obdurately hostile to Lord Ashley's proposed ten-hour day for factory workers, and the 'Jack Cade system of legislation', of which, to Graham, it seemed the commencement. What can be said is that Chartism, in this wide sense, strengthened their determination to better the condition of the working class by methods which their consciences approved, or were well on the way to approving. For a movement as ambitious as Chartism this was a modest achievement, but it was clearly better than nothing.

Chartist Chronology:

A Select Table of Events

1829	May	The British Association for Promoting Co-operative Knowledge founded in London
	Dec.	The Birmingham Political Union founded
1830	Sept.	Richard Oastler took up the Factory Question in the West Riding of Yorkshire
1831	March	The Metropolitan Trades Union founded
	May	The National Union of the Working Classes founded. Meetings at the Rotunda in London
1832	June	Passing of the Reform Bill
	Dec.	First General Election under the new system
1833	Aug.	Althorp's Factory Act passed
1834	Feb.	The Grand National Consolidated Trades Union founded. (The Builders, Potters, Spinners and Clothiers already had their large unions, and there had been earlier attempts at 'general union')
	March	Prosecution of the 'Tolpuddle Martyrs'
	July	Passing of the New Poor Law
	Aug.	The Grand National Consolidated Trades Union dissolved
1835	Sept.	Municipal Corporations Act passed
1836	April	Beginnings of financial crisis
		Association of Working Men to Procure a Cheap and Honest Press founded in London
	May	Newspaper duty reduced
	June	London Working Men's Association founded
1837	Jan.	East London Democratic Association founded
		The Poor Law Commissioners turned their attention to the North of England and the industrial districts
	Feb.	London Working Men's Association held its first public meeting
	March	Birmingham Petitions on 'industrial distress'
		Widespread complaints of distress from places like Manchester, Nottingham, the West Riding and Scotland
	April	Strike of the Glasgow Cotton Spinners
	May	The Birmingham Political Union revived

	May–June	Conferences between M.P.s and the L.W.M.A. about parliamentary reform
	July	General Election: Defeat of many Radical M.P.s
	Nov.	First number of the *Northern Star*
1838	May	East London Democratic Association changed its name to the London Democratic Association
		The People's Charter published in London
		The National Petition published in Birmingham
		Great Glasgow rally
	June	The Great Northern Union founded at Leeds
		Northern Political Union founded at Newcastle
	Aug.	Great Birmingham rally
	late Summer and Autumn.	Election of Members of the General Convention
	Sept.	Manchester Anti-Corn Law Association founded
	Dec.	Calton Hill 'moral force' resolutions carried in Edinburgh
1839	Feb.	The General Convention of the Industrious Classes met in London
	March	The Anti-Corn Law League set up as a national organisation
	May	The Convention moved to Birmingham
		Beginning of the Rebecca Riots in Wales
	July	The Bull Ring Riots in Birmingham. Chartist arrests
		The Convention returned to London
		The House of Commons rejected the first National Petition (235 votes to 46). Chartist discussions of 'ulterior measures'
		The *Scottish Patriot* launched
	Aug.	Universal Suffrage Central Committee for Scotland founded
		The Bank Rate raised to 5%
	Summer	Many Chartist arrests
	Sept.	The Convention disbanded
		The *Chartist Circular* founded in Glasgow
	Nov.	The Newport Rising
1840	Jan.	Abortive Sheffield rising. Imprisonment of Samuel Holberry
	April	Northern Political Union reorganised in Newcastle
	Winter and Spring.	Large-scale Chartist arrests
	July	Chartist Conference in Manchester. The National Charter Association founded
	Autumn	Attempts to create Chartist-Radical alliance in Leeds

1841 April	Lovett founded the National Association of the United Kingdom for Promoting the Political and Social Improvement of the People
	O'Connor took up the land question as a 'remedy for national poverty'
Aug.	General Election. Tory victory. Sir Robert Peel became Prime Minister
Nov.	Joseph Sturge took up the Suffrage question
1842 April	Complete Suffrage Union Conference at Birmingham
	Chartist Convention in London
May	The House of Commons rejected the second National Petition (287 votes to 49)
July	Trough of the trade cycle. Wage cuts. Unemployment
Aug.–Sept.	The Plug Riots
Dec.	Conference of Chartist and Complete Suffrage representatives in Birmingham. Collapse of the Complete Suffrage Union
1843 March	Trial of O'Connor and other Chartists. Acquittal on main points
Sept.	Chartist Convention in Birmingham. Land Reform accepted. The Chartist Executive moved to London
1844 April	Chartist Convention in Manchester
Aug.	Debate between O'Connor and Cobdon at Northampton
Nov.	Title of the *Northern Star* changed to the *Northern Star and National Trades Journal*. Headquarters moved to London
Dec.	The Rochdale Pioneers opened their Toad Lane store
1845 April	Chartist Convention in London. The Chartist Land Co-operative Society launched
May	Rules of the Land Society published
Sept.	Society of Fraternal Democrats founded
Dec.	Manchester Conference on the Land Plan
1846 June	Repeal of the Corn Laws
Dec.	Birmingham Conference on the Land Plan
1847 April	Financial Crisis
May	Ten Hours Factory Act passed
	O'Connorville opened
July	General Election. Whig victory. Lord John Russell became Prime Minister. O'Connor elected at Nottingham. Harney opposed Palmerston at Tiverton, Ernest Jones contested Halifax

DD

| | Aug. | Lowbands Conference on the Land Plan |
| | Autumn and Winter. | Mounting unemployment |

1848 Feb. Revolution in France

Publication of the *Communist Manifesto*

April Chartist Convention summoned in London

Kennington Common

Third National Petition laughed out by the House of Commons

Joseph Hume's 'Little Charter' movement took shape

May Chartist National Assembly summoned

Select Committee of the House of Commons appointed to investigate the Land Plan

May, June, July. Provincial Chartist disturbances. Large-scale arrests. Imprisonment of Jones and others

Aug. Publication of the Select Committee's Reports

1849 March The National Parliamentary and Financial Reform Association founded

June Parliamentary reform motion, supported by O'Connor and Hume defeated in the House of Commons (286 votes to 82)

Harney launched the *Democratic Review*

Dec. Chartist Delegate Conference in London

1850 Jan. O'Brien launched the National Reform League

Open battle between Harney and O'Connor, culminating in a majority for Harney and the Fraternal Democrats on the Chartist Executive

March The defeated O'Connorites launched the National Charter League

June The *Red Republican* started by Harney. Open propaganda for socialist objectives

July The release of Ernest Jones

Nov. Resignation of the Chartist Executive in protest against O'Connor's tactics

1851 Jan. O'Connorite Chartist Convention in Manchester a failure

Feb. Bill to dissolve the National Land Company

March London Chartist Conference adopted social programme

May Jones started his *Notes to the People*

The Great Exhibition

1852 Jan. The *Northern Star* changed hands and discarded the label 'Chartist'

	April	Harney bought the *Northern Star* and changed its name to the *Star of Freedom*
	May	Jones launched the *People's Paper*. Open quarrel between Harney and Jones
	May	Chartist Convention in Manchester
	June	O'Connor involved in a scene in the House of Commons. Removed by the Sergeant at Arms and pronounced insane
1854	March	Jones summoned the 'Labour Parliament' at Manchester
1855	Aug.	O'Connor died
1858	Feb.	The last national Chartist Convention

Index

413